Edith Wharton

A to Z

EDITH WHARTON

A TO Z

The Essential Guide to the Life and Work

SARAH BIRD WRIGHT

Facts On File, Inc.

Edith Wharton A to Z: The Essential Guide to the Life and Work

Copyright ©1998 by Sarah Bird Wright

All rights reserved. No part of this book may be reproduced or utilized in any form or by any means, electronic or mechanical, including photocopying, recording, or by any information storage or retrieval systems, without permission in writing from the publisher. For information contact:

Facts On File, Inc.
11 Penn Plaza
New York NY 10001

Wright, Sarah Bird.
Edith Wharton A to Z : the essential guide to the life and work /
Sarah Bird Wright.
p. cm.
Includes bibliographical references and index.
ISBN 0-8160-3481-8
1. Wharton, Edith, 1862–1937–Encyclopedias. 2. Women novelists,
American–20th century–Biography–Encyclopedias. 3. Women and
literature–United States–History–20th century–Encyclopedias.
I. Title.
PS3545.H16Z98 1998
813'.52–dc21 97-45574

Facts On File books are available at special discounts when purchased in bulk quantities for businesses, associations, institutions or sales promotions. Please call our Special Sales Department in New York at 212/967-8800 or 800/322-8755.

You can find Facts On File on the World Wide Web at http://www.factsonfile.com

Cover design by Nora Wertz
Illustrations on pages 301 and 302 by Jeremy Eagle

Printed in the United States of America

VB BVC 10 9 8 7 6 5 4 3 2 1

This book is printed on acid-free paper.

With much love to my son,

Alexander Grant Wright,

and to my nephews and nieces,

Richard Oscar Grant III, Ashley Martin Grant,

Charlie D'Arcy Grant, Louise Harrell Grant

and Kathleen Trewhella Grant,

who are following their ancestors in writing,

teaching and studying,

and who well know the joys of the life of the mind.

CONTENTS

LIST OF ILLUSTRATIONS

ix

FOREWORD

Edith Wharton's joy in symmetry and order explains why she cherished poet Thomas Traherne's pronouncement, "Order the beauty even of Beauty is." To scan the more than 450 entries in *Edith Wharton A to Z: The Essential Reference to the Life and Work* is to appreciate the formidable challenge that Sarah Bird Wright confronted in bringing order to the encyclopedic data of a remarkable life. Generalists and specialists alike are indebted to Wright for completing this labor of love. Here Wright documents the myriad persons, places, interests and influences–literary, philosophical, aesthetic–that contributed to Wharton's midlife transformation from a socially prominent heiress to an internationally renowned author. With impressive thoroughness, Wright charts both the lesser-known and the best-known plots and characters for which we remember Wharton. Entries on the travel writing, essays and studies of architecture and landscape design establish that Wharton deserves recognition for her nonfiction as well.

Born into the "hieroglyphic world" of "old New York," Edith Wharton was raised in a conservative social milieu in which class and gender roles were strictly defined, and "new money" was regarded askance. As one of Wharton's most famous characters ruefully reflects, in the moneyed "tribe" to which Newland Archer and his creator belonged, "The real thing was never said or done or even thought, but only represented by a set of arbitrary signs" (*The Age of Innocence*). In late Victorian America, members of the leisured class ordered their lives according to predictable rhythms of the social calendar. As the pendulum swung from one "season" to the next, the rich moved from lavish city homes to "modest" country "cottages," or sailed to Europe for costly shopping and sightseeing expeditions. Intellectual pursuits and professional and artistic ambition were discouraged in men and frowned upon in women. To adorn oneself–and one's homes–was feminine ambition enough.

Yet Wharton always aspired to create beauty of a more enduring kind. Her childhood delight in "making up" stories while she paced the corridors of the Jones family homes sprang from a creative fount that nurtured what she later described as the "secret garden" of her art. Wharton's careful cultivation of that garden bore fruit in nearly forty books in as many years. Her publications ranged from novels, tales, poetry, translations, critical essays and reviews to war reportage, travel writing, and scholarly treatises on interior decoration and home and garden design. Like Margaret Aubyn, the celebrated author from the early novella *The Touchstone*, Wharton was esteemed as "one of the most brilliant women of her day."

Taken together, the entries, photographs and detailed appendices Wright provides–including a timeline of Wharton's life, Jones and Wharton family trees, and primary and secondary bibliographies–make *Edith Wharton A to Z* not only a reference guide but a "life" as well. The story Wright tells is that of a woman who at age 74 still professed herself "an incorrigible life-lover & life-wonderer & adventurer." Even as she neared her death, Wharton could exclaim to a friend about "this wonderful adventure of living."

The "life-wonderer" bridged continents and times–"the age of innocence" and our own post–world war time. Indeed, Wharton lived the first half of her life in the 19th century and the latter half in the next, and spent as many years in Europe as in her native land. An expatriate writer who adopted France as her home, she chronicled the manifold expressions of human nature during a period in which the customs of the country were in flux, the "West" was in decline, and a generation was "lost" among the ruins of the "Great War." By the time World War I ended, Wharton observed, the "old New York" of her youth was "as much a vanished city as Atlantis or the lowest layer of Schliemann's Troy" (*A Backward Glance*).

Wharton's life is in some sense framed by war. Born in 1862 during the Civil War, she lived in Paris during the First World War and was to die in 1937 on the eve of World War II. Through her visits to the trenches outside Paris and to outlying cities and villages obliterated by the war, Wharton witnessed firsthand the devastation of trench warfare and aerial bombings. For the better part of the war, she abandoned the writing of fiction and devoted her energies to charity relief and to essays on "fighting France" (the title of a wartime collection) that were intended to sway her American readership to open their checkbooks and to disavow neutrality. So prodigious were her labors on behalf of France and the war refugees—the orphaned, the homeless, the unemployed—that she was made a chevalier of the Legion of Honor by the French government, an unprecedented distinction for a non-French citizen.

To some extent, after the war Wharton herself was a displaced person. In her Jazz Age novels (e.g., *The Glimpses of the Moon*, *Twilight Sleep* and *The Children*), she portrays the post-war period as "a welter of change": fads replace traditions, cults supplant religions, and multiple marriages and divorces produce "blended" families composed of "steps" and "halves." The drug-induced state of "twilight sleep" (childbirth with no pain) becomes her metaphor for what Wharton judged a tendency to dull physical and psychic pain with drugs, alcohol and sex.

The nearly 100 illustrations accompanying this book, many from Wright's personal collection, tell a story of their own. Readers may better envision the contours of Wharton's personal life by perusing the photographs Wright includes of Wharton, her family and friends and, not least, her much-indulged Pekingese. Snapshots of crucial sites from Wharton's life—from her girlhood home in New York City to the churches of her christening and marriage to the elegant homes and gardens she designed, both before and after her painful divorce from Edward ("Teddy") Wharton, to her grave at Versailles near the tomb of Walter Berry ("the love of all my life," she privately confessed)—complement Wright's efforts to situate Wharton according to place.

The places Wharton visited were many, as entries on Wharton's travels in Europe and Morocco make plain. Importantly, Wright contends that Wharton's extensive readings in history, literature, religion, science and philosophy, and her expertise in the visual and dramatic arts, allowed her to describe for her readers the old and "new countries" she saw with the eyes of a connoisseur. As her travel writing and her studies on architecture, interior decoration and landscape design attest, Wharton looked to the past to glean how we might more happily reconfigure our lives. In this regard, Wharton's first (coauthored) book on design, *The Decoration of Houses* (1897), broke ground. Only now are scholars beginning to credit Wharton for the part she played in creating a new field. In Wharton's view, the subject of that field was ideally conceived as "interior architecture," not decoration.

Her most enduring novels, stories and poems reveal Wharton as an interior architect of a different kind. Novels such as *The House of Mirth* (1905), *Ethan Frome* (1911), *The Custom of the Country* (1913), *Summer* (1916) and *The Age of Innocence* (1920), which earned her a Pulitzer Prize for fiction (the first awarded a woman), disclose Wharton's expertise as an architect of the heart. Such poignant tales transcend the particulars of place and time: even if her characters seem to come from "vanished" worlds like Atlantis, Troy or old New York, the "crucial moments" defining their lives speak to our own understanding of the subtle architecture of the heart.

The resonance between the "interior" plots of Wharton's fiction and those we know from our own lives may elucidate why filmmakers, too, from early in this century to the present, have repeatedly turned to Wharton. Yet as Scott Marshall observes in the comprehensive filmography he contributed to the book, film and television adaptations have yet to do justice to Edith Wharton.

A "life-lover" and "adventurer," Wharton could nonetheless end her memoir, *A Backward Glance*, by stating, "Life is the saddest thing there is, next to death; yet there are always new countries to see, new books to read (and, I hope, to write), a thousand little daily wonders to marvel at and rejoice in. . . ." In glancing backward at her subject, Sarah Bird Wright pays tribute to the fullness of Wharton's life—from the books she wrote and read, to the countries she visited, to her "incorrigible" interest in the "daily miracle" of the "visible world."

—Clare Colquitt
San Diego State University

ACKNOWLEDGMENTS

I am very grateful to many people who have helped, directly and indirectly, with this project over the past few years. The manuscript was immeasurably improved by Clare Colquitt's meticulous reading and analysis. Scott Marshall generously contributed photographs and memorabilia from his own collection as well as his invaluable compilation of film, television and musical adaptations of Edith Wharton's work; he also reviewed portions of the manuscript and rescued me from various misconceptions. His walking tour of Edith Wharton's Lenox at the Edith Wharton at The Mount conference (1997) offered an unforgettable montage of her life there. Meredith Goldsmith read the entire manuscript and offered a number of excellent suggestions. Stephanie Copeland, director of the Edith Wharton Restoration, has been unfailingly encouraging and helpful.

I appealed for assistance and received it in generous measure from Louis Auchincloss, Pauline Metcalf, Kay Fanning, Shari Benstock, Suzanne Jones, Mary Suzanne Schriber and Theresa Craig. I have profited greatly from the advice of Richard S. Lowry of the College of William and Mary, who saw me through my earlier study of Edith Wharton's travel writing and offered incisive analyses of her life and work. I have appreciated the ideas offered by Welford Taylor, Alan Price, Julie Olin-Ammentorp, Carole Shaffer-Koros, Barbara White, Eleanor Dwight and Abby Werlock. Elsa Nettels, Professor Emerita, College of William and Mary, and Jean Blackall, Professor Emerita, Cornell University, have shared perceptive insights and offered welcome camaraderie at Wharton conferences.

Without the advice, encouragement and assistance of Martha Edmonds, Elizabeth S. Scott, Nancy Parrish, Beverly Peterson, Shirley Uber, Margaret Hatcher and Jennifer Hall over the past several years, this project would never have seen completion. I owe an extraordinary debt to Mary Ann Caws for her forbearance in the midst of our

joint Bloomsbury and France project and to Janet Schwarz, who offered steady counsel and assisted with several emergency WorldCat searches.

I am particularly obligated to the authors of three biographies of Edith Wharton: R. W. B. Lewis, *Edith Wharton: A Biography*; Shari Benstock, *No Gifts from Chance*; and Eleanor Dwight, *Edith Wharton: An Extraordinary Life*. I am also most grateful for the meticulous scholarship of Frederick Wegener in *Edith Wharton: The Uncollected Critical Writings* and of Stephen Garrison in *Edith Wharton: A Descriptive Bibliography*. Wegener has facilitated access to many of Edith Wharton's little-known essays, reviews, tributes and other writings. Garrison has provided invaluable bibliographical data about the first and subsequent publication of Wharton's fiction, nonfiction and poetry.

The illustrations could not have been assembled and the research conducted without the expert and prompt assistance I received from many libraries and institutions. I am extremely grateful to Alfred Mueller, Patricia Willis and other staff members at the Beinecke Rare Book Room and Manuscript Library at Yale University for giving me access to the Edith Wharton Collection (YCal 42) and providing many illustrations. I would like to thank Margaret Sherry, William Joyce and AnnaLee Pauls of the Firestone Library, Princeton University, for allowing me to quote from the correspondence between Edith Wharton and Charles Scribner's Sons and for providing the photograph of Charles Scribner II. I am particularly grateful to Saundra Taylor and Julie Simic of the Lilly Library for their assistance with photographs of Walter Berry and of Edith Wharton.

Audrey Johnson of the Library of Virginia, Richmond, made it possible to use a number of illustrations from their collection. Michael Plunkett, Heather Moore and Pauline Page of the Alderman Library, University of Virginia, went out of their way to facilitate use of illustrations from the Clifton Waller Barrett Collection and the periodical archives. Kathleen Kienholz, at the National Academy of Design, was most helpful in obtaining a photograph of a painting of Ogden Codman.

I am particularly indebted to Dr. Fiorelli Superbi, archivist of the Villa I Tatti, Settignano, Italy, who gave prompt assistance with information and supplied the photograph of Gaillard Lapsley. Amanda Smith of the Harvard University Center for the Study of Renaissance Art was also very helpful. I am grateful to the reference librarians in the Earl Gregg Swem Library, College of William and Mary, for their aid on countless occasions. Liza Daum of the Département des Photographies, Bibliothèque Historique de la Ville de Paris, generously secured photographs of the city during World War I and of Edith Wharton.

It is a special pleasure to acknowledge the continuing help of my agent, Jeanne Fredericks, who has carried on the agency founded by the late Susan Urstadt and has been unfailingly accessible and helpful. Michael G. Laraque of Facts On File has been a superb organizer, penetrating reader and sustaining presence during the editing and proofreading stages of the book. I am grateful also to my former editor at Facts On File, Drew Silver, for valuable suggestions in shaping the volume, and to Doris Eder for careful copy editing, and to Anne Savarese for her work during the final stages of preparation. I would like especially to thank Laurie Likoff for her understanding and enthusiasm for the book.

I owe special gratitude to the Edith Wharton Estate and the Watkins/Loomis Agency for granting me permission to use unpublished Edith Wharton material.

My Montana cousins, Rose and Wally King, offered hospitality, books from their remarkable library and leisure for writing. I am most grateful to my brother, Oscar Grant, and his wife, Jane, for allowing me to work aboard their ketch as well as on their porch at Wrightsville Beach, N.C. My son, Alex Wright, has encouraged me throughout my work and guided me through cyberspace and into foreign libraries. Very special gratitude goes to my husband, Lewis Wright, who put up with my presence and absence alike, tolerantly permitted Edith Wharton to be a part of our home and our travels for several years, and made it all possible. It was he who realized that Edith Wharton's account of Mount Athos was the first by an American.

INTRODUCTION

Edith Wharton dedicated her autobiography, *A Backward Glance*, to "the friends who every year on All Souls' Night come and sit with me by the fire." Edith Wharton has, in a sense, been sitting by my hearth for several years now, a friendly presence, yet a formidable one in many ways. She was brilliant, witty, multilingual, a connoisseur of art and artifacts, yet also sensitive, compassionate and, as she once described herself, "housekeeperish." It is not only Edith Wharton who has materialized. She has been accompanied by a battalion of her characters. Among them are Lily Bart in *The House of Mirth*, whose violations of the social code lead to her ostracism and death; Ethan Frome, in the novella of the same name, stoically enduring his grim existence; Charity Royall, in *Summer*, jolting up the Mountain to her mother's gruesome death bed; Mirandolina of Chioggia in *The Valley of Decision*, improvising her performance in a commedia dell'arte production; modest Grace Ansley, in "Roman Fever," masterfully putting the condescending Alida Slade in her place as they gaze at the Roman Colosseum from their restaurant terrace; Evelina Jaspar, in "After Holbein," presiding at her spectral senile banquet; the Bunner sisters, in the story "Bunner Sisters," victimized by a duplicitous suitor as they struggle with their mean little millinery shop; John Ruskin and Walt Whitman, reinvented as pivotal figures in *False Dawn* and *The Spark*, respectively.

It is not often that knowledge of a writer's life illuminates his or her work, but in the case of Edith Wharton, it does so. In several of her novels and short stories she measures the "vintage" society of old New York by European standards, which she knew well. Having lived for eight of her first twenty years in Europe, and having traveled widely in Italy, France, England and Germany, she came close to being James's "passionate pilgrim." She yearned for the intellectual and aesthetic stimulation of the Old World, but never became spiritually detached from the country of her birth. When Henry James observed in 1902 that Edith Wharton "must be tethered in native pastures, even if it reduces her to a backyard in New York," he could not have foreseen that within a decade she would have settled in France, where she lived the remainder of her life. After her divorce from Teddy Wharton in 1913, she built a fulfilling life based on her writing, travels and entertaining. The onset of World War I put an end to the Belle Époque and to the rewarding and productive life she had established. Horrified by the devastation inflicted on her adopted country, she diverted her prodigious energies away from social life and travel and into organizing massive war relief efforts. After the war she only returned to America once, in 1923, to receive an honorary doctorate from Yale University. For the remainder of her life, when not traveling, she divided her time between the Pavillon Colombe, a large French-style villa just outside Paris in St.-Brice-sous-Forêt, where she lived during the summer and fall, and Ste.-Claire Château near Hyères, on the French Riviera, where she spent the winter and spring.

Edith Wharton A to Z has been written with a general audience in mind. I have made use of much secondary material and offered suggestions for further reading for those who find a particular entry to be of interest. Wharton's reputation as a writer has risen considerably since 1921, when Vernon Parrington called her "our literary aristocrat" and complained that although she had done "notable things" she had remained aloof from America. She never gave up her citizenship, however. Her innate powers of discrimination always responded to the heritage of her native country, and she never stopped writing about Americans, who were the subject of her final novel, published posthumously, *The Buccaneers*.

Edith Wharton's fiction and travel writing transcend nationality to become universal. Her work has been reprinted in many editions, has attracted the interest of critics in many countries and has been translated into French, Italian, German, Russian, Chinese, Japanese and other languages. Her work has received structuralist, feminist, Marxist, psychological and sociological readings, among others, but no secondary sources are necessary for the reader to appreciate her novels and short stories. In *The Writing of Fiction* (1925), Wharton makes it clear that her artistic credo was similar to that of Henry James, who believed that "every great novel must first of all be based on a profound sense of moral values, and then constructed with a classical unity and economy of means." The author must not ask what the situation would make of the characters, but what the characters would be likely to make of a given situation. Wharton's characters engage us from our first acquaintance, provoking us to reflection and rereading. Wharton has also been praised for her works of travel, which Blake Nevius has termed "brilliantly written and permanently interesting." They are the embodiment of her connoisseurship, a reflection of her visual sensibility, retentive memory and imaginative powers. Wharton's critical writings, including tributes and eulogies to friends and other writers, are less well known, but are incisive, illuminating and extremely rewarding. Similarly, her poetry has received, with some exceptions, little attention from critics, but was frequently praised in her day.

The layout of *Edith Wharton A to Z* is alphabetical. Cross-references to other relevant headwords, or entries, are given in small capitals. References to articles and books for further reading follow many entries; full bibliographical details are given in the bibliography at the back of the volume. I have provided a list of abbreviations used for the most frequently cited of Wharton's works and for the principal biographical and critical sources on which I have relied.

The entries fall into the categories of acquaintances, friends and family; biographical periods, topics and events; fictional characters; artistic, historical and literary periods, terms and events; places; organizations and institutions; publishing (editors, publishers, periodicals, libraries); special interests and pursuits; works by Wharton; works by other writers; writers and other artists; and honors, awards and prizes.

The first of these might seem to be the most straightforward, but in fact was surprisingly complicated. When Percy Lubbock wrote the first biographical study of Wharton, *Portrait of Edith Wharton* (1944), he deplored the fact that he knew far too little of the "friends on both sides of the ocean who peopled her world . . . and how should a portrait of Edith Wharton give a true likeness if it failed to show her encompassed by the troops of her friends?" In presenting this composite picture of her life, I confess to sharing his lament. I have attempted to include as many of her friends as possible, both in America and Europe, relying on her autobiography, *A Backward Glance*, letters, the work of her biographers and other sources. Her

friends, many of whom began as professional acquaintances, were indeed legion; I apologize in advance for omissions and, for some of those included, the lack of birth and death dates.

In developing entries for the biographical periods and events of Wharton's life, I have been guided principally by *A Backward Glance* and by information discovered by biographers. Wharton's fictional characters are treated within the relevant entries for the works in which they appear, with alphabetical cross-references. Lily Bart, for example, is listed as "BART, LILY," with a cross-reference to *The House of Mirth*. I have focused on the major characters in her fiction.

The third category, artistic, historical and literary periods, terms and events, includes discussions of the Gilded Age, the Belle Époque and World War I as well as the salon, Wharton's feminism and her connoisseurship. The "places" grouping has necessitated some difficult choices, as it would have been impossible to write about every town and region of France, Italy, Germany, Spain, Morocco and England known to Wharton. I have compromised by selecting those that figure most prominently in her works of travel, her autobiography and her letters. The next divisions, for organizations and institutions and for publishing and libraries, presented fewer problems of selection, although it was necessary to condense the discussion of Wharton's prolonged association with her principal publishers, Scribner's and Appleton.

Perhaps no category of entries is more revealing of Wharton's disparate preoccupations and pastimes than the eighth one, "special interests and pursuits." Wharton never met Virginia Woolf, but, when a mutual friend, Lady Aberconway, observed that Woolf had an avid curiosity, Wharton was skeptical. Woolf might be said to have a "poetic mind" but did she have "*true* curiosity"? Lady Aberconway conceded that Wharton's curiosity exceeded that of Woolf and she hoped to have her for a friend. Wharton had a tremendous zest for travel, and was baffled that her friends Paul and Minnie Bourget journeyed twice each year between the French Riviera and Paris without making detours to explore sights they had never seen. Wharton was not only an avid gardener, traveler and writer but was also knowledgeable about architecture, painting, sculpture and interior design. The commedia dell'arte and baroque water theaters fascinated her, as did ghosts, harems, ruins, islands and ship travel. She was in a state of euphoria on her two Mediterranean cruises. The 1926 trip aboard the *Osprey* had all the ingredients for a felicitous voyage: "a congenial party, with lots of books, a full set of admiralty charts, a stock of good provisions and *vins du pays* in the hold, and happiness in our hearts."

Another category of entries deals with the works of Edith Wharton. She is best known, of course, for her fiction, but I have also included her works of travel and criticism. The latter fall into several subsections. There are reviews of travel books, novels, plays and poetry as well as prefaces, introductions and forewords to her own works and to those of other authors. Wharton composed tributes and eulogies commemorating her friend and editor William C. Brownell and also Jean du Breuil de Saint-Germain, Paul Bourget, George Cabot Lodge and Bayard Cutting Jr. In addition, there is a discussion of her poetry and a separate entry on foreign translations of her works.

The tenth grouping of entries pertains to fiction, nonfiction, poetry and dramatizations she reviewed. These were sometimes by friends; examples are Howard Sturgis's *Belchamber*, Paul Bourget's *Outre-Mer*, Geoffrey Scott's *The Architecture of Humanism* and William Gerhardi's *Futility*. The eleventh category focuses on Wharton's favorite writers and artists, such as Johann Wolfgang von Goethe, Walt Whitman, George Sand, Homer, Tiepolo and Joseph Mallord William Turner. A number of people are included here who were close to Wharton and who also published but whose principal occupation was something other than writing. Examples of the latter are the jurist Judge Robert Grant of Boston, a novelist and short story writer whose work she praised, and Anna Bahlmann, Wharton's early governess, then secretary, who translated Gottfried Keller's novella *A Village Romeo and Juliet*. Theodore Roosevelt, who wrote a number of books, was a distant cousin and personal friend, and Nicky Mariano, companion and assistant to Bernard Berenson, later wrote a well-received memoir, *Forty Years with Berenson*. The historian and statesman Henry Adams was an esteemed friend; he wrote *Mont-Saint-Michel and Chartres*. She also knew F. Scott Fitzgerald and Sinclair Lewis.

Finally, there is a section on the honors, awards and prizes given to Wharton. The Pulitzer Prize (1921) was her best-known honor, but she was also given an honorary doctorate by Yale University (1923) and was made a chevalier of the Legion of Honor by the French government during World War I.

I have given particular attention to the illustrations for the book. Some of the New York churches associated with Edith Wharton's life are reproduced. Scott Marshall of the Edith Wharton Restoration has provided photographs of Irene Dunne and John Boles in the film *The Age of Innocence*, of Bette Davis in *The Old Maid*, and of Judith Anderson in *The Old Maid*. He has also permitted me to reproduce a receipt for World War I war work signed by Edith Wharton. I have sought photographs of many people close to Edith Wharton who have seldom been pictured, such as Paul Bourget. I have tried also to show the varied ways in which many of her works, both fiction and nonfiction, were illustrated. There is an account of her dealings with publishers in this matter (*see* ILLUSTRATIONS). Examples in the text range from one of Maxfield Parrish's watercolors for *Italian Villas and Their Gardens* (1904) to a Scribner's illustration for "The Last Asset" (1904) and drawings for short stories published in the *Saturday Evening Post*, including "Pomegranate Seed" (1931) and "A Glimpse" (1932). I have obtained a photograph of the steam yacht *Vanadis* on which the Whartons made a Mediterranean cruise in 1888 and have also found an Edith Wharton stamp (1980), which is reproduced. The book includes a photograph of the French Legion of Honor citation (1916). I was able to obtain, from the Bibliothèque Historique de la Ville de Paris, a seldom-published photograph of Edith Wharton by Thérèse Bonney, along with a scene on Armistice Day, 1918. In addition there are photographs of Edith and Teddy Wharton at various times and pictures of her Massachusetts and French homes.

This project has been one of the most rewarding I have ever undertaken, leading me into libraries in search of Edith Wharton's own writings and the large body of criticism now published about them. I have retraced some of her Italian and French footsteps and look forward to following more of the diverse byways of her travels. Cosmopolitan yet domestic, highly social yet addicted to time alone for writing, bred in an elite society with rigid mores of behavior yet departing radically from convention in her life, Edith Wharton remains an enigma, but one made, I hope, more accessible by the present volume.

ABBREVIATIONS

To simplify citation, the following abbreviations have been used at times for primary and secondary sources. For complete publication information, see the full bibliography at the back of this volume.

IV	*Italian Villas and Their Gardens*
MFF	*A Motor-Flight Through France*
SF	*A Son at the Front*
VD	*The Valley of Decision*

I. PRIMARY WORKS

AI	*The Age of Innocence*
BG	*A Backward Glance*
CC	*The Custom of the Country*
CV	*The Cruise of the Vanadis*
CSS	*Collected Short Stories*
DH	*The Decoration of Houses*
EF	*Ethan Frome*
FD	*False Dawn*
FFDB	*Fighting France, from Dunkerque to Belfort*
FWM	*French Ways and Their Meaning*
GM	*The Glimpses of the Moon*
GA	*The Gods Arrive*
HM	*The House of Mirth*
IB	*Italian Backgrounds*
IM	*In Morocco*

II. SELECTED SECONDARY TEXTS

CR	James W. Tuttleton, Kistin O. Lauer and Margaret P. Murray, *Edith Wharton: The Contemporary Reviews*
EW	R. W. B. Lewis, *Edith Wharton: A Biography*
FWDB	Stephen Garrison, ed., *Edith Wharton: A Descriptive Bibliography*
Letters	R. W. B. Lewis and Nancy Lewis, eds., *The Letters of Edith Wharton*
NGC	Shari Benstock, *No Gifts from Chance*
SSF	Barbara White, *Edith Wharton: A Study of the Short Fiction*
UCW	Frederick Wegener, ed., *Edith Wharton: The Uncollected Critical Writings*

Académie française Important constituent of the Institut de France, founded by Cardinal Richelieu in 1635. The academy, which has forty elected members at any one time (sometimes called the "Forty Immortals"), has great influence on French grammar, rhetoric, spelling and literary matters. New members are elected by the current membership when a death has created a vacancy. Traditionally members are conservative literary figures, but they have also come from the church and the military. Paul BOURGET, a close friend of Wharton, was a member, and his prestige helped bring about her acceptance into French literary and social circles during the early years of her expatriation in France. In FRENCH WAYS AND THEIR MEANING she praises Richelieu for creating, at a time of political and religious instability, an "ark in which thought and taste and 'civility' could take shelter" (*FWM* 47).

Academy, French   *See* ACADÉMIE FRANÇAISE.

Academy of Arts and Letters   *See* AMERICAN ACADEMY OF ARTS AND LETTERS.

Academy, The   London periodical in which Edith Wharton's early books were frequently reviewed. The editors were sensitive to the women's movement, which was getting under way in the early years of the 20th century. The reviewer of *The House of Mirth* praised Wharton's "sympathetic delineation of her heroine's character, her acute analysis of a woman's mind."

Adams, Henry (Brooks)   American historian and man of letters (1838–1918). A member of the distinguished Adams family of Massachusetts, Henry Adams was the son of Charles Francis Adams, Lincoln's ambassador to Britain during the Civil War, and the grandson and great-grandson, respectively, of Presidents John Quincy Adams and John Adams. Although he was heir to the Adams traditions of public service and literature, he was better suited to the study of history than to the practice of politics. He was editor of the *North American Review* and assistant professor of history at Harvard, where he taught medieval, European and American history. His first important work was *The History of the United States of America during the Administrations of Thomas Jefferson and James Madison* (nine volumes,

1889–91), which argued that men cannot alter the course of history. Adams married Marian Hooper in 1872; she committed suicide in 1885, after which he traveled to Asia and developed an interest in technology as the source of historical change.

His best-known works are the historical idyll *Mont-Saint-Michel and Chartres* (privately printed 1904, published 1913) and the autobiographical work *The Education of Henry Adams* (privately printed 1906, published 1918). They reflect his quest for order and unity in the modern world, which he considered to be disintegrating. The American architect Ralph Adams Cram described *Mont-Saint-Michel* as "one of the most distinguished contributions to literature and one of the most valuable adjuncts to the study of medievalism America thus far has produced" (Briggs, Introduction.)

Adams had known Edith Wharton for a number of years through such mutual friends as Margaret ("Daisy") Terry CHANLER, George Cabot ("Bay") LODGE and Walter BERRY. He became a regular visitor to her "salon" (or, as he called it, her "saloon") at 58, rue de Varenne in PARIS. In 1908 he remarked, "Our little American family-group here is more closely intimate and more agreeably intelligent, than any now left me in America . . . [and] Edith Wharton is almost the center of it" (*EW* 214). Lewis remarks that she rejoiced in his "piercing destructive wit and the sheer range of his knowledge" (*EW* 226).

Adams found late 19th-century America to be unparalleled in its concentration of material power, yet he saw the capitalist government as corrupt and fin-de-siècle democracy as fragmented. The new scientific discoveries had, in his view, eroded religious faith; the world as he knew it was chaotic and disintegrating. He considered history a sequence of forces, and wished to order that sequence, using the unifying principle of energy. At the Chicago Exposition of 1893, he perceived the dynamo as the embodiment of the force of power, opposed to the force of the spirit represented by the Virgin at Chartres. He developed this metaphor in *The Education of Henry Adams.*

Adams wrote a biography of his and Wharton's friend George Cabot LODGE, who died young in 1909. *See also* Wharton's "GEORGE CABOT LODGE."

Bernard BERENSON once remarked to a French colleague that "the four most authentic" Americans in his generation were Edith Wharton, Henry James, Henry Adams and himself, meaning that they did not attempt to camouflage themselves with European habits of speech or try to take on a quasi-European identity (*EW* 206).

aesthetic views, of Edith Wharton   *See* CONNOISSEURSHIP

"After Holbein"   Short story published in the *Saturday Evening Post* in May 1928 and collected in CERTAIN PEOPLE (Appleton, 1930). This is considered one of Wharton's finest short stories. It concerns the imaginary conversations of an aging and senile hostess, Evelina Jaspar, with guests of past years. The lead character may have been based on Caroline Schermerhorn ASTOR, a cousin of Wharton's father.

The tale opens with an elderly man-about-town, Anson Warley, a "relic of the old regime," as one reviewer termed him. He has suffered increasing spells of dizziness and confusion during the past few days but now, on a snowy night, is dressing for dinner at Mrs. Jaspar's, against his devoted valet's advice. In his past social life, he had often declined Mrs. Jaspar's invitations, fearing boredom. As he sets out, temporarily forgetting his destination, he senses the fragility of life: "that very morning he had arrived at the turn in the path from which mountains look as transient as flowers . . . one after another they would all arrive there, too."

He comes to Mrs. Jaspar's brilliantly illuminated house; she has been dressed by her elderly maid, Lavinia, in finery and jewels to receive her nonexistent guests. Her guest list is always the same as it had been the night before her stroke. Warley and Mrs. Jaspar advance to the long dining room table, ornamented with candelabra and bunched-up pieces of newspaper serving as flowers. She seats herself in the center of one side, telling Anson to seat himself "on my right." There may be a suggestion that Death sits on the left. The "ghastly banquet of two old mummies," as one reviewer termed it (*CR* 483), proceeds. They dine slowly on mashed potatoes, thinking them oysters, and spinach. The meal is solemnly served by the footman, who repeatedly passes a bottle of Apollinaris water, announcing different vintages. After dinner, Mrs. Jaspar slowly ascends the stairs with her night nurse and Lavinia. Anson Warley leaves convinced he has had a brilliant evening, only to step off into oblivion.

Dorothy Foster Gilman, a reviewer for the *New York Herald Tribune*, called the story "indescribably tragic and magnificently written" (*CR* 479).

For further reading: McDowell, "Edith Wharton's 'After Holbein': A Paradigm of the Human Condition."

"Afterward"   Short story first published in *The CENTURY MAGAZINE* in January 1910, reprinted in *TALES OF MEN AND GHOSTS* (Scribner's, 1910). It is a ghost story set in an English Tudor-style manor house rented by a wealthy young American couple, Mary and Edward (Ned) Boyne. They insist that, to be authentic, the house must be uncomfortably deficient in heating and water supply, and also have a resident ghost. Their English friend Alida Stair assures them the house has one, but they will "never know it" until "long long afterward." They enjoy their country retreat until, one day, Mary calls Edward's attention to the wraith of a young man approaching the house from a distance. Edward rushes to meet him and vanishes, but then returns to the house. Later, he disappears a second time. The servants explain to Mary that he has had a caller in the library, and that the two gentlemen have gone out together. Boyne is not seen again.

The truth gradually emerges when a lawyer calls on Mary to ask her to assist the widow of a young man, Robert Elwell, who had been associated with her husband in the development of the Blue Star Mine in America. Boyne had taken advantage of Elwell's naivete and ruined him. Elwell has committed suicide, forcing his widow to appeal for public aid. The specter of Elwell has crossed the Atlantic to seek justice by finding Boyne in England. Mary realizes that the day Elwell first appeared was the day of his death; he had not been "dead enough" then to have the power of claiming her husband. Looking at a photograph of Elwell, Mary perceives the ghost through the eyes of her husband and slowly comes to comprehend that Elwell has succeeded in taking him. She faints, hearing the voice of Alida Stair declaring that the house does have a ghost, but she will not realize it until after its manifestation: " 'You won't know till long, long afterward.' "

For further reading: Heller, "Ghosts and Marital Estrangement: An Analysis of 'Afterward.' "

Afterward **(teleplay, 1983)**   *See* Appendix II.

Age of Innocence, The   This novel, published in 1920 by Appleton and winner of the 1921 PULITZER PRIZE for literature, is generally considered one of Wharton's finest works. It is a novel of manners, in which the real story is played out beneath a surface of cordial but obligatory calls, elaborate dinner parties, carriage rides and opera performances in the old Academy. This world of old (by New York standards) money was small and still attempting to keep out the "new people"—that is, the new rich who derived their fortunes from railroads, heavy industry and large-scale financial speculation—beginning to invade New York society in the 1870s, the early GILDED AGE. As a satiric portrayal of the closed circle of interrelated families within which Wharton was brought up, it is virtually unequaled.

The plot revolves about Newland Archer and Ellen Olenska, Ellen being a member of a prominent New York family who is separated from her husband, a Polish count. The two reveal their love for each other

Scene from the 1928 Broadway production of The Age of Innocence, *dramatized by Margaret Ayer Barnes* (see *Appendix II*). *Left to right: Rollo Peters (Newland Archer), Katharine Cornell (Ellen Olenska) and Eden Gray (May van der Luyden [May Welland in the original]).* (Courtesy Vandamm Collection, Billy Rose Theater Collection, New York Public Library, Library for the Performing Arts, Lincoln Center)

only after Newland's engagement to Ellen's cousin, May Welland, has been announced. After the wedding, their relationship develops when Archer, an attorney, is asked to handle Ellen's divorce action and begins, under cover of kinship, to call on her and lend emotional support. Ellen evokes for Newland the unconventional intellectual and artistic world she had known in Europe. She attends, for example, a festive dinner escorted by Julius Beaufort, who is not only married but Jewish. He has mysterious antecedents, suspicious financial dealings, and "passes" for an Englishman, although he is technically a member of "society" through his wife, Regina Dallas, a Manson cousin (his character was based on the financier August Belmont). Ultimately, however, the unlicensed love between Newland and Ellen is thwarted. They find themselves subject to tribal rituals of exclusion and inclusion pre-

vailing within the extended family circle, a hierarchy of families strictly ranked by dynastic alliances and social eminence, and ruled by formidable dowagers such as Mrs. Manson Mingott (grandmother of Ellen and May). In a chilling dinner party scene toward the end of the novel, Newland realizes their separation is a fait accompli. He perceives the "harmless-looking people engaged upon May's canvas-backs" as a "band of dumb conspirators, and himself and the pale woman on his right as the centre of their conspiracy." Ellen has already been, in the eyes of the family, dispatched to Europe and has only to depart in person. Newland has no choice in the matter. Ellen returns to PARIS, and Newland settles down to a dull and placid marriage. In a brilliant final scene 26 years later, Archer, now a widower, goes to Paris with his son Dallas, who, having heard the story of the failed relationship from his mo-

Scene from the 1934 RKO film The Age of Innocence, *with screenplay by Sarah Y. Mason and Victor Heerman, based on Wharton's novel and the stage adaptation by Margaret Ayer Barnes* (see *Appendix II*). *Shown are Irene Dunne (Ellen Olenska) and John Boles (Newland Archer).* (Collection of Scott Marshall)

ther, urges him to call on Ellen. He refuses, sending his son instead to convey his greetings, reluctant to disturb his memories and, perhaps, to reawaken "the composite vision of all he had missed."

Wharton's sense of place was as extraordinary as that of Henry JAMES. The principal settings of *The Age of Innocence* are NEW YORK and NEWPORT, Rhode Island, where Wharton's family had had a summer home, and where she and her husband also owned a home, LAND'S END, where they summered before building The MOUNT. In "The Sense of Newport" (1870), James remarked that the gaieties and vanities of Newport life were, as a spectacle, extremely amusing and worth observing, "if only to conclude against them." The juxtaposition of natural grandeur, idleness and frivolity were of interest, he said, because "a society that does nothing is decidedly more pictorial, more interesting to the eye of contemplation, than a society which is hard at work." This "pictorial" aspect of Newport, with its large summer houses, flower-bordered terraces, tennis casino

and ocean views, is much in evidence in *The Age of Innocence.* The Mingotts and Wellands, however, would have abhorred, as did Wharton on their behalf, the grandiose mansions built in the Gilded Age by later millionaires such as the Vanderbilts. Men of such families as the Mingott and Van der Luyden clans do not "go to business" or have an occupation, but live in gentlemanly style on the income of inherited mercantile fortunes, often invested in New York real estate, as in the case of Wharton's own family. They fail to contribute their abilities to the country at large, and even if trained in a profession such as law, consider it an ornament, an adjunct to the social calendar rather than an exacting duty.

Wharton wrote in her memoir *A BACKWARD GLANCE,* that in the 1870s New York was a world of people who "dreaded scandal more than disease, who placed decency above courage, and who considered that nothing was more ill-bred than 'scenes,' except the behavior of those who gave rise to them." At the same time, she had come to realize that such a world had a certain value. As she grew up, the society around her seemed like an "empty vessel into which no new wine would ever again be poured," with a wholehearted "dread of innovation." After what she felt was the crudeness and vulgarity of American society since the late nineteenth century and the damage sustained by civilization in World War I, however, she had come to believe that it had the virtue of "preserving a few drops of an old vintage too rare to be savoured by a youthful palate" (*BG* 5). That "vintage," the "deliberately nurtured innocence," is, however, constraining to individual growth. It is also nonproductive within a larger context, its members fit only to be onlookers at the affairs of the country. At the end of the novel, Archer recalls his failure to be re-elected to the state legislature after a single term, although he had been a benevolent spokesman for charitable enterprises. As Blake Nevius puts it, Wharton's real target is not the leisured class, but "the system which first neglected that class and then swallowed it whole" (*EW* 181). *The Age of Innocence* not only resurrects the age in which that class flourished, with all its foibles, but portrays with Olympian detachment the havoc inflicted on any member who attempted to deviate from its rigid mores.

The novel was translated into French as *Au Temps de l'innocence* by Mme. Taillandier, sister of Wharton's friend André CHEVRILLON.

For further reading: Auchincloss, "Edith Wharton and Her New Yorks"; Blackall, "The Intrusive Voice: Telegrams in *The House of Mirth* and *The Age of Innocence*"; Durczak, "America and Europe in Edith Wharton's *The Age of Innocence*"; Fracasso, "The Transparent Eyes of May Welland in Wharton's *The Age of Innocence*"; Fryer, "Purity and Power in *The Age of Innocence*"; Gibson, "Edith Wharton and the Ethnography of Old New York"; Hadley, "Ironic Structure and Untold Stories in *The Age of Innocence*"; Joslin, "*The Age of Innocence* and the Bohemian Peril"; McWilliams, "Wharton's *The Age of Innocence*"; Nevius, "On *The Age of Innocence*"; Nevius, *Edith Wharton*.

Age of Innocence, The (film, 1924)   *See* Appendix II.

Age of Innocence, The (film, 1934)   *See* Appendix II.

Age of Innocence, The (film, 1993)   *See* Appendix II.

Alfieri, Count Vittorio   *See* VALLEY OF DECISION, THE.

Algeria and Tunisia   Edith Wharton had seen the port of Tunis in 1888, during her Mediterranean cruise aboard the *VANADIS*, and had long wanted to see more of Northern Africa. On March 29, 1914, Wharton sailed aboard the S.S. *Timgad* from Marseilles to Algiers. She was accompanied by Percy LUBBOCK, the gifted young English writer, Anna BAHLMANN, her long-time secre-

tary/companion, Charles COOK, her chauffeur (who had driven their Mercedes to the ship and stowed it on board) and Elise DUVLENCK, her personal maid. Her close friend Gaillard LAPSLEY joined the party but had to turn back because of stomach flu.

She writes in *A BACKWARD GLANCE* of the journey, where they spent a day at the "exquisite oasis" of Bou-Saada and then, turning toward the mountains of Kabylia, went on to Timgad, Constantine, Tunis, Sfax, Souss, Kairouan, El Djem, Gabès and Médénine. She explains that the place names evoke "magic properties" for her. They tried in vain to visit Djerby, the Lotus-eaters' island, from Gabès, but delighted in finding vestiges of Europe, such as the Roman ruins at Timbad and Carthage. She had never written about this journey, she said, being afraid of the "perils of prolixity" and of wearying her readers in a later day, when travel in North Africa was greatly eased. It would then be of little interest to readers to learn "how Timgad looked to me under a full moon, or what song the siren sang when I tried to pick up a passage from Gabès to the Lotus-eaters." She had locked her reminiscences away and not offered them to the public, for her treasures "might turn into a pinch of dust, like that beautiful Etruscan queen too rashly dragged from her painted tomb into the daylight" (*BG* 334–35). She wrote Sara NORTON that she had looked for a world far from everything she knew. According to Lewis, this trip caused Wharton to be "infected with a passion for Africa which could never be cured" (*EW* 361).

See also MOROCCO.

"All Souls'"   Published posthumously in GHOSTS (Appleton-Century, 1937), this is Wharton's last story, sent to her agent the year she died. The story is told by a cousin of the chief character, a widow living with her servants in her large Connecticut house, Whiteside. The narrator opposes the melodramatic popular concept of ghosts, with its "headless victims" and "clanking chains," to the far more sinister sense *"that there's something wrong"* in a house.

While returning from a walk on All Souls' Eve one chilly November Saturday, Sara Clayburn overtakes an unknown middle-aged woman, who tells her she is going to see one of Sara's young servant girls. Sara continues, only to fracture her ankle on a patch of ice in front of her home. The doctor is summoned, who puts her to bed and cautions her against trying to walk. The next morning, Sunday, the servants fail to appear. She drags herself about the unheated house, discovering that the servants have all disappeared, and that the silence about her has the "cold continuity of snow." She hears a man's voice speaking in a foreign language in the kitchen, but it is coming from the radio. She makes her way back to bed, fortified with brandy and sandwiches left by her faithful maid Agnes.

She regains consciousness the next day with a young doctor bending over her and the servants back in place. Agnes denies that anything has happened. Though the mysterious thirty-six hours are still vivid to Mrs. Clayburn, she eventually declines to press Agnes and the others about them, and a year passes. The next All Souls' Eve she meets the same mysterious woman, is terrified, and flees to her cousin's New York apartment. Agnes betrays relief, confirming that Mrs. Clayburn's intuition that Agnes is part of the conspiracy against her is correct. The cousin/narrator conjectures that Agnes, being from the Isle of Skye in the Hebrides, is an "unconscious" or at least "irresponsible" channel through whom ghosts may speak or "fetch" people. The mysterious woman might have been inhabited by a witch, who may have led Agnes and the other servants to a midnight "Coven" nearby. Sara Clayburn, having escaped from Whiteside, vows never to return.

Part of the interest of the story for the modern reader is what Lewis calls the combination of "supernatural, domestic, and erotic ingredients" (*EW* 523). The orderly household, with its internal bells, precise schedule and large staff of devoted servants, shows vestiges of an earlier opulent age. This is contrasted with the primordial magnetism of the presumed coven, which "breaks down all inhibitions" and causes those who have once participated to "move heaven and earth to take part again."

Allied armies' entry into Paris   *See* ENTRY OF ALLIED ARMIES INTO PARIS.

Alps   The Swiss and Italian Alps were a favorite destination of Wharton and her husband Edward ("Teddy") WHARTON. Each year they spent several months abroad, frequently visiting the Bergamasque and Pennine Alps. In *ITALIAN BACKGROUNDS* Edith Wharton compares staying in the posting-inn below the Splügen Pass in Switzerland to "living in the landscape of a sanatorium prospectus" (*IB* 17).

She recounts their decision to leave Switzerland for Italy by diligence and their subsequent travels in what they believed were the Bergamasque Alps (Bergamasker Hochthäler). Wharton had been particularly interested in seeing this area of the mountains because of its associations with the COMMEDIA DELL'ARTE, the historic improvisatory theater which fascinated her. They later discovered they had actually been, instead, in the Pennine Alps. One chapter of *Italian Backgrounds* is devoted to the sanctuaries (monasteries and shrines) of the Pennines. Wharton delighted in the Italian mountain landscape, often seeing it in the context of paintings she knew by such artists as Claude Lorrain and Salvator Rosa.

Alsace   A region and former province of eastern France along the Rhine River border with Germany. It is crossed by the Vosges Mountains. The territory, except for Belfort, had been ceded to Germany in 1871, but was recovered by France after World War I. In early 1915, Wharton was asked by the French Red Cross to visit military hospitals at the front and report on their needs, a journey that led to several other visits. These expeditions resulted in six articles published in American magazines, calculated to alert her "rich and generous compatriots" to the desperate needs of hospitals and to bring home to her American readers "some of the dreadful realities of war" (*BG* 352).

Alsace had previously been inaccessible to civilians, but Wharton obtained a travel pass from General Headquarters as an exceptional favor. Her visit took place between August 13 and August 18, 1915. She begins her published account by describing the severe damage done by the German bombardment of the Cathedral of Rheims. The structure reminds her of "the Inferno, or some tale of Eastern magic," with the front "warmed to deep tints of umber and burnt siena . . . The Cathedral of Rheims [was] glowing and dying before us like a sunset" (*FFDB* 186–87). She and her party visited Thann, Belfort and a number of rural encampments. In one, the soldiers had built a "trapper colony" with cabins half underground and a log chapel. Compared to some of the other parts of the front, Alsace had at times a surface tranquility, although the party had a strong sense of the presence of gun emplacements throughout. At one point they sat on the side of a ridge, eating from their luncheon-basket, "swept by a great mountain breeze full of the scent of thyme and myrtle, while . . . the still and busy life of the hills went on all about us in the sunshine." It is actually in such bucolic pastures that the insanity of war is most evident; there it "lurks like a mythical monster in scenes to which the mind has always turned for rest" (*FFDB* 200). The *Chasseurs Alpins*, or mountain riders, descended on mules to distribute supplies to the front lines near a "rock-rimmed lake" surrounded by "zig-zag earthworks" (*FFDB* 199). Wharton toured the lines from Dunkerque to Belfort and came away with a memory of "the interlocked stare of innumerable pairs of eyes, stretching on, mile after mile, along the whole sleepless line from Dunkerque to Belfort" (*FFDB* 216).

SCRIBNER'S MAGAZINE published five of the articles resulting from Wharton's journeys, but she was late in sending "Alsace," which appeared in *The SATURDAY EVENING POST*. The articles were then compiled into the volume *FIGHTING FRANCE, FROM DUNKERQUE TO BELFORT*, published by *SCRIBNER'S* in 1915.

America   Edith Wharton was born into the highest level of the social hierarchy of mid-19th-century New York. She grew up in a world of luxury like that depicted in *The AGE OF INNOCENCE*, with inherited fortunes, servants, carriages and rigid social mores. Her education was private; she had a nurse and a governess/companion. When not abroad, the family spent winters in a brownstone on 23rd Street and summers in a large home in NEWPORT, Rhode Island.

As a child, Wharton, like Henry JAMES, was dipped "generously in the font of Europe" (to use the literary historian Sculley Bradley's phrase), spending eight years abroad before she was 21. Her father had suffered financial reverses in the early 1860s caused by declining real estate values in New York during the Civil War. In 1866 the Joneses went to EUROPE for six years, traveling widely in France, Germany, Italy and Spain. Wharton became fluent in Italian, German and French, acquiring a background of "beauty and old-established order"; in later years she recalled in her memoir, A BACKWARD GLANCE, "the lost Rome" of her "infancy," the "warm scent of the box hedges on the Pincian, and the texture of weather-worn sun-gilt stone" (*BG* 31).

Wharton's feelings for her native country were less comfortable and more complex. The family's return to the United States, in 1872, she later wrote, brought "bitter disappointment." Edith was only 10, but, as she put it in her unpublished memoir "LIFE AND I," she had been "fed on beauty since my babyhood"; her first thought on seeing New York was "*How ugly it is!*" She insisted she had "never since thought or felt otherwise than as an exile in America," and had often dreamed her family was returning to Europe. She would wake "in a state of exhilaration which the reality turned to deep depression." Six decades after her early disillusionment, she could still recall her abhorrence of the New York cityscape, "cursed with its universal chocolate-coloured coating of the most hideous stone ever quarried, [a] cramped horizontal gridiron of a town without towers, porticoes, fountains or perspectives, hide-bound in its deadly uniformity of mean ugliness." The houses lacked "external dignity" and were "crammed with smug and suffocating upholstery" (*BG* 54–55). Not only was the architecture poorly proportioned and inharmonious, but, as she wrote her friend SARA NORTON in 1904, the American landscape had no "accumulated beauties." (*Letters* 90). Once the Joneses returned to America, she entered the more agreeable "kingdom" of her father's library, rich with books of travel as well as philosophy, art, criticism and the classic works of Western literature, all of which contributed to her sense of being out of place. The works of John RUSKIN, for instance, "fed me with visions of the Italy for which I had never ceased to pine" (*BG* 71).

The Joneses returned to the Continent in 1880, in a futile attempt to restore George Frederic JONES's failing health. He and his daughter retraced Ruskin's "arbitrary itineraries" in Florence and Venice; when he died at Cannes in 1882, Edith Jones and her mother returned to America. This second visit, however, had confirmed Edith's adoration of Europe, where she "felt the stir of old associations." Her love for travel was life-long, and, when she married Edward (Teddy) WHARTON in 1885, he shared it; for a number of years, they spent four months abroad each year, principally in Italy. These early travels laid the groundwork for Wharton's gradual EXPATRIATION.

In 1897, Wharton wrote, with the young architect Ogden CODMAN, *The DECORATION OF HOUSES*, a learned volume laying out guidelines for applying European principles of harmony and proportion to what she saw as ungainly American architecture. Her expatriation may almost be said to begin with this book, so thoroughly oriented is she toward (classical) European architecture and design. Her increasing attachment during these years to Europe strengthened her distaste for the banality and ugliness of Victorian life in industrial America. It also confirmed her affinity for the "courtly muses" of Europe, against which Emerson had inveighed in his influential "American Scholar" address of 1837. Wharton articulated her attachment to the art and architecture of the Old World in her fiction, nonfiction and poetry; it may be said that the "courtly muses" of Europe were the bedrock of her intellectual and aesthetic conceptions. As a traveler and a connoisseur, Edith Wharton was shaped by a social milieu and literary and artistic education that most Americans (and indeed most Europeans not of the privileged classes) did not share, although they represented a cultural ideal for the rising middle class and the newly rich of the Gilded Age.

Edith Wharton was increasingly drawn to Europe in the early years of the twentieth century, despite completion of The MOUNT, the grand home she and her husband had built in Lenox, Massachusetts. Their decision to build a summer residence in Lenox was based in part on a desire to escape the "watering-place trivialities" of NEWPORT, where they had remodeled a home, LAND'S END. In *A BACKWARD GLANCE*, Wharton remarks, "If I [had moved to The Mount] sooner I daresay I should never have given a thought to the literary delights of Paris or London; for life in the country is the only state which has always completely satisfied me," but this may be doubted (*BG* 124–25).

Beginning in 1906, the Whartons spent several months of every year in Paris. At first they sublet an apartment belonging to the George VANDERBILTS at 58, rue de Varenne, in the elite Faubourg Saint-Germain. In 1908 Wharton published *A MOTOR-FLIGHT THROUGH FRANCE*, based on three automobile tours she made with her husband and other companions, including Henry James. In 1910 the Whartons moved into another apartment, also leased, at 53, rue de Varenne; Wharton kept this apartment until she bought

Kate Rogers Newell, portrait of Edith Wharton (Putnam's Monthly Magazine, *February 1908*) (Courtesy of the Library of Virginia)

the PAVILLON COLOMBE outside Paris in 1919. Teddy Wharton, however, was increasingly unhappy in France, as well as with his wife's literary and cultural interests. He also embezzled some of her trust funds and established a mistress on Beacon Hill, Boston. In 1913 the Whartons were divorced. After 1911 Edith Wharton would return to America only twice, in late 1913 for the wedding of her niece Beatrice JONES to Max FARRAND, and in 1923, to accept an honorary DOCTORATE from YALE University, the first time in Yale history a woman had been honored in this way. (For further discussion of Edith Wharton's expatriation and life in France, *see* EXPATRIATION and FRANCE.)

American Academy of Arts and Letters   An honorary group within the NATIONAL INSTITUTE OF ARTS AND LETTERS, created to honor particularly distinguished American writers and artists. Wharton was elected in 1930, after some reconsideration of the rules, which had no provision for female members.

American Hostels for Refugees   An organization established by Wharton in October 1914, in conjunction with several friends, to give relief to the many Bel-

gian refugees flooding into Paris after the battles of the Marne and Ypres. More than 10,000 people were made homeless by Ypres alone. They wandered, wrote Wharton, "dazed and slowly moving—men and women with sordid bundles on their backs, shuffling along hesitatingly in their tattered shoes, children dragging at their hands and tired-out babies pressed against their shoulders: the great army of the Refugees" (*FFDB* 33). They had no shelter or food. Many were Flemish and unable to speak French.

Some of Wharton's French friends, including Charles DU BOS and André GIDE, helped form L'Accueil Franco-Belge (later L'Accueil Franco-Américain), a clearinghouse for refugees. It was rapidly beset by too many applicants and too few funds. At their request she created her own group, the American Hostels for Refugees. Eventually they arrived at a system whereby the L'Accueil Franco-Belge would receive the refugees and classify them, then turn them over to the American Hostels, which managed to provide shelter, food and jobs.

In this project Wharton revealed a remarkable talent for organization and fund-raising. Among those assisting were Royall ("Peter") TYLER and Elisina TYLER, Geoffrey SCOTT and Percy LUBBOCK. She created a network of committees to oversee the functions of the hostels; there were nine in Paris and three in America. The latter were in New York (chaired by Wharton's sister-in-law, Mary (Minnie) Cadwalader JONES), Philadelphia and Boston (*EW* 371). She chaired the 17-member FRANCO-AMERICAN GENERAL COMMITTEE, which included Walter BERRY, her lawyer friend BOCCON-GIBOD, Matilda GAY, du Bos and Gide. She mounted appeals in American newspapers, asking for $3,000 per month to "lodge, clothe and feed 300 desolate creatures but for whom Paris would now be German, and all humane humanity in peril."

During the ensuing year the organization helped over 9,000 refugees, serving 235,000 meals, donating 48,000 garments, providing 7,700 persons with medical care and finding jobs for 3,400. Between September 1914 and December 1915 Edith Wharton raised, according to Benstock, $82,000, the equivalent today of over $1,000,000.

Eventually the American Red Cross took over the administration of the organization, along with many other American charitable efforts in France, in order to consolidate appeals in America and to run them more efficiently. (*See* WAR RELIEF.)

"L'Amérique en guerre"   Essay published in the *Revue Hebdomadaire* in March 1918.

"Angel at the Grave, The"   Short story first published in *CRUCIAL INSTANCES* (Scribner's, 1901). It centers on a fictional transcendental figure, Orestes Anson (the name recalls Orestes Augustus Brownson, an American clergyman and writer famous before the Civil War). Walter BERRY made a substantial contribution to the story. He suggested that, as a major scientific discovery she wished the hero to make, Wharton have him find the species *amphioxus*, linking the vertebrate and the invertebrate. The story of the discovery, which occurred in the distant past, is recounted in the present by his granddaughter.

Paulina Anson has been born "into a museum," her first consciousness "built on the rock of her grandfather's celebrity." She is custodian of his former residence, called simply "The House." Here "unseen caravans" bring the tribute of an "admiring world." (This had also been the case at Shady Hill, the Cambridge home of Professor CHARLES ELIOT NORTON.) She has been destined to become the interpreter of the "oracle." As a young woman, she had a brief romance with Hewlett Winsloe, but he refused to live in The House. She has spent the intervening years writing a

Life of her grandfather, completing it when she is 40. Taking it to her grandfather's Boston publishers, she realizes her loss: "All her youth, all her dreams, all her renunciations lay in that neat bundle on her knee." The publishers reject the manuscript, telling her she should have brought it 10 years earlier. "Literature's like a big railway-station now. . . . there's a train starting every minute. People are not going to hang round the waiting-room. If they can't get to a place when they want to they go somewhere else."

Despondent, Paulina returns home, believing her life has been wasted. A young man, George Corby, comes to see The House (he has been led to it because of Brook Farm, the Transcendentalist settlement). He is writing an article on Anson, and hopes to find the one remaining copy of the pamphlet on the *amphioxus* that he regards as her grandfather's most lasting contribution to science. She is mystified by his interest, but finds the pamphlet, which she has fortuitously saved when her aunts burned many of her grandfather's papers. She

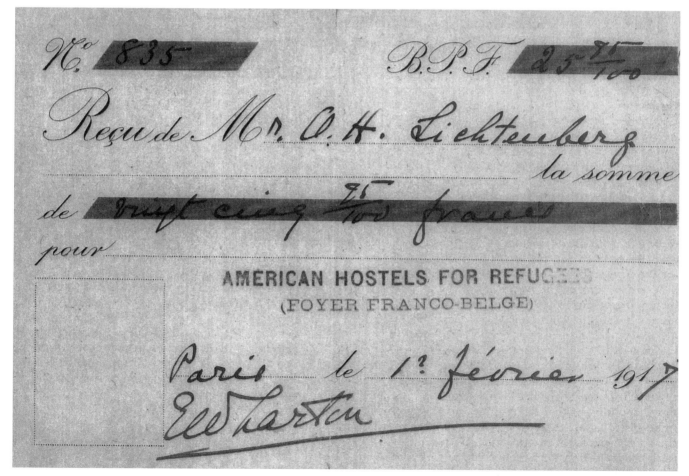

Receipt, signed "EWharton," for a contribution of approximately 25 francs from Mr. O. H. Lichtenberg to the American Hostels for Refugees in 1917. Wharton was a tireless fund-raiser for this and other war charities. (Collection of Scott Marshall)

tells Corby she once "believed" in her grandfather, but now considers that he has ruined her life: " 'I nursed his glory in my bosom and it died—and left me—left me here alone.' " He argues that her life has been worthwhile as a conservator of his discovery, which would otherwise have been irretrievably lost. She agrees to work with him in finding the letters, journals and memoranda that contributed to the original discovery.

The story recalls the life of Sara NORTON, daughter of Charles Eliot Norton, who gave up her chance for marriage to a young Englishman in order to stay near her father.

For further reading: Widdicombe, "Wharton's 'The Angel at the Grave' and the Glories of Transcendentalism: Deciduous or Evergreen?".

Amherst, Bessy Westmore   *See FRUIT OF THE TREE, THE.*

Amherst, John   *See FRUIT OF THE TREE, THE.*

Amherst, Justine Brent   *See FRUIT OF THE TREE, THE.*

Anthony, Adele   *See SON AT THE FRONT, A.*

anti-Semitism   There is mixed critical opinion as to whether Edith Wharton was prejudiced against Jews as adherents of a religious faith or as members of an ethnic group. From one point of view, it was normal for a member of her class and generation to entertain such prejudice without even perceiving it as prejudice. At the same time, Wharton did not hesitate to depict Jewish characters who were avaricious and skillful at using wealth as an entrée to society.

In *The HOUSE OF MIRTH*, for example, Simon Rosedale represents what Diana Trilling calls the "new social dispensation." He wishes to acquire a wife, such as Lily Bart, who will be a suitable ornament for his vast wealth. She observes that, although members of the old aristocratic world at first resist his entry, "they are unable to withstand the power of his money, and his urgency of personal ambition." A sense of a "secure niche" in the world, nourished by money, is fundamental before "manners" can thrive. Rosedale realizes that the prestige and power of the old families is sustained only by their fortunes.

Meredith Goldsmith, a scholar who has explored the subject, has observed, in discussions with the author, that Wharton was writing at a moment at which Jews were beginning to be defined as a separate "race" from Anglo-Saxons/Anglo-Americans. In *The House of Mirth* she uses racial language, for example, to distinguish Rosedale from Lily Bart and her circle, stating that he "had his race's accuracy in the appraisal of values" and would have gained much from being seen with her; he was "still at a stage in his social ascent when it was of importance to produce such impressions." Lily is repelled by him at first, and admits to having "snubbed and ignored him" (Ch. 2). Goldsmith points out that at times Wharton's Jewish men represent something "sexually problematic"; Rosedale has an almost effeminate concern with clothes and style and, in his last encounter with Lily, plumps up her pillows and pours her tea.

In *The AGE OF INNOCENCE*, the character of Julius Beaufort, another wealthy self-made man, was assumed by readers to be derived from August Belmont, believed by many people in NEW YORK and NEWPORT to be of Jewish descent. A millionaire, he built large homes in New York and Newport and kept a mistress in a Madison Avenue apartment (*NGC* 358). Wharton insisted, however, that Beaufort reflected her cousin George Alfred Jones, who had embezzled money to support his mistress. Beaufort has mysterious antecedents, suspicious financial dealings and "passes" for an Englishman, although he is technically a member of "society" through his wife, Regina Dallas, a Manson cousin.

Mr. Palmato, in the "BEATRICE PALMATO" fragment, is described as half-Portuguese and half-Levantine, the latter term being, according to Benstock, Wharton's code word for Jew.

While living in PARIS Wharton did not come to know Gertrude and Leo Stein, although they would have had much in common, with their mutual interest in art. In "The Salons of Wharton's Fiction," Robert A. Martin and Linda Wagner-Martin suggest that Wharton had a "given" sense that one "did not go to" the salons of Gertrude and Leo Stein.

Susan Goodman notes that Wharton's letters to her intimate friends Gaillard LAPSLEY and John HUGH SMITH sometimes expressed anti-Semitism. Even though she clearly was bigoted in some respects, Wharton also had various lifelong Jewish friends, including Minnie BOURGET and Bernard BERENSON, who was Jewish by birth although he later was baptized in the Episcopal Church. In Paris she was a devoted friend of Countess Rosa de FITZ-JAMES, whom she described as having "the easy cosmopolitanism of a rich Austrian Jewess" (*BG* 265). Her attachment to her intimate friends outweighed any preconceptions she might have had.

For further reading: Bauer, "Why Gentlewomen Prefer Blondes" [in *Edith Wharton's Brave New Politics*]; Bazin, "The Destruction of Lily Bart: Capitalism, Christianity, and Male Chauvinism"; Goldman, "The Perfect Jew and *The House of Mirth*: A Study in Point of View"; Hoeller, " 'The Impossible Rosedale': 'Race' and the Reading of Edith Wharton's *The House of Mirth*"; Martin and Wagner-Martin, "The Salons of Wharton's Fiction: Wharton and Fitzgerald, Hemingway, Faulkner and Stein"; Riegel, "Rosedale and Anti-Semitism in the *House of Mirth*"; Trilling, "*The House of Mirth* Revisited"; *see also*, for general background, Dinnerstein, *Antisemitism in America*.

Appleton and Company   Appleton and Company was Wharton's chief publisher after 1912. Her previous books had been published by SCRIBNER'S or THE CENTURY COMPANY. In 1907, Scribner's had offered a large advance for *The FRUIT OF THE TREE* (1907), based on the strength of the success of *The HOUSE OF MIRTH*. The sales figures were disappointing, however, and she was not offered as substantial an advance for *The CUSTOM OF THE COUNTRY* when she signed for that novel with Scribner's. After she became dissatisfied with Scribner's advertising budget for ETHAN FROME, she accepted a $15,000 advance from Appleton for *The REEF* (published in 1912). Charles Scribner was exceedingly disappointed. Wharton wrote her friend William Morton FULLERTON, "Mr. Scribner is mortally hurt by my infidelity" (*NGC* 250).

Two editors at Appleton with whom Edith Wharton worked closely were J. H. SEARS, the principal editor, who also acted as an agent for various authors, and Rutger Bleecker JEWETT, who came of old New York stock. The latter became one of Wharton's favorite editors and handled a number of her books in addition to acting as her agent in obtaining contracts for magazine serialization. He encouraged her to publish a collection of the articles she had written to interpret France to bewildered American soldiers, stationed there after the war, arguing that it would be "one more good blow struck for France" (Rutger B. Jewett to Edith Wharton, May 16, 1918; Beinecke Library, Yale). It was Jewett who suggested that Wharton put aside *A SON AT THE FRONT* in 1919; "War books dead in America," he cabled her (Rutger B. Jewett to Edith Wharton, July 3, 1919; Beinecke Library, Yale). He advised her to work instead on *The AGE OF INNOCENCE*, which sold well and won the PULITZER PRIZE for literature in 1921.

"April Showers"   A short story first published in *Youth's Companion* in January 1900. It did not appear in a collection. Theodora Dace is a young girl from a large, genteel family living modestly, with an invalid mother and a tired, overworked physician father. She submits her first novel, *April Showers*, to *Home Circle* magazine on the very day a manuscript with the same title arrives from a best-selling author, Kathleen Kyd. The editor mixes up the rejection and acceptance letters, accepting Theodora's novel by mistake and serializing Kathleen Kyd's.

The opening of the story, quoting the overly romantic ending of "April Showers," satirizes the type of adolescent novel Edith Wharton herself had written in FAST AND LOOSE. Lewis calls "April Showers" "trifling," but it presents a credible picture of an idealistic young would-be author, abandoning her household duties to contribute to Literature (Theodora is a surrogate mother to her younger siblings because of her mother's illness). Theodora's father is one of the more perceptive men in Wharton's short fiction. The story was turned down by Edward BURLINGAME, editor of *SCRIBNER'S MAGAZINE*, in July 1893.

Archer, May Welland   *See AGE OF INNOCENCE, THE.*

Archer, Newland   *See AGE OF INNOCENCE, THE.*

architecture   Edith Wharton's interest in architecture dates from her childhood sojourn in EUROPE from 1866 to 1872, when she was taken to visit museums, palaces and villas in FRANCE, ITALY and GERMANY. On the Joneses' return to NEW YORK she was repelled by the ugliness of the city, and never ceased to yearn for the Europe she had known. Her first published book, *The DECORATION OF HOUSES*, written with the architect Ogden CODMAN, is a treatise on vernacular architecture, with emphasis on achieving the most harmonious and pleasing rooms possible. She and Codman declared, "proportion is the good breeding of architecture" (*DH* 31), pointing the way toward the correction of many faults in American design, much of it the result of Victorian stuffiness and surfeit of ornament.

The four residences she renovated and/or built, LAND'S END in NEWPORT, R.I., The MOUNT in LENOX, Mass., the PAVILLON COLOMBE outside PARIS, and STE.-CLAIRE CHÂTEAU near HYÈRES, were all designed with the greatest care imaginable. Her gardens were planned with equal attention to proportion and harmony with their natural surroundings. She also paid careful attention to the interior decoration of PENCRAIG cottage in Newport, on the grounds of her parents' home, to the adjoining townhouses on Park Avenue, New York, where she and her husband lived, as well as to the Paris apartment at 53, rue de Varenne, Paris, which she occupied from 1910 to 1919.

Wharton's interest in the architecture of palaces, villas, churches, cathedrals, hospitals and fortresses is evident throughout her travel books: *The CRUISE OF THE VANADIS*, *ITALIAN BACKGROUNDS*, *ITALIAN VILLAS AND THEIR GARDENS*, *A MOTOR-FLIGHT THROUGH FRANCE*, *FIGHTING FRANCE, FROM DUNKERQUE TO BELFORT*, and *IN MOROCCO*. In addition, her volume of essays, *FRENCH WAYS AND THEIR MEANING*, focuses on the importance of municipal architectural planning, with examples from Paris and Boston.

Architecture is also an important component of much of Wharton's fiction. Such settings as the Trenors' home, Bellomont, in *The HOUSE OF MIRTH*, the van der Luydens' manor house, Skuytercliff, in *The AGE OF INNOCENCE*, the de Chelles family chateau, Saint Desert, in *The CUSTOM OF THE COUNTRY*, and The Willows, former home of the Lorburn family and fine example of the architectural style "Hudson River Bracketed," in the novel *HUDSON RIVER BRACKETED*, are all used as reflectors of their owners' background, taste, and values.

Few American writers have been more sensitive to the implications of architecture than Edith Wharton. She wrote that proportion in architecture produced "effects as intangible as that all-pervading essence the ancients called the soul" (*DH* 31). In her fiction she explored the symbiotic relationship between dwelling and character. In her own life, she strove to create the ideal domestic surroundings that would please her guests and put them at ease, reflect her connoisseurship and ratify her taste.

For further reading: Cohn, "The House of Fiction: Domestic Architecture in Howells and Edith Wharton"; Koprince, "Edith Wharton's Hotels"; Luria, "The Architecture of Manners: Henry James, Edith Wharton, and the Mount."

"Architecture of Humanism, The"   Edith Wharton's review of the English architect and critic Geoffrey SCOTT's notable book appeared in the *Times Literary Supplement* (London) in June 1914. As a practicing architect, she points out, Scott is able to treat the subject of architecture not only as a "purely plastic problem" but also as an "appeal to imaginative associations." He reminds his readers that one's reaction to a work of art is always "inclusive and synthetic," related to viewer's whole personality and not to his or her "specialized taste." Scott was a protégé of Bernard BERENSON. Wharton alludes to his gift for choosing images that "are always meeting him at the right point and flashing on his subject the very light it needs" (*UCW* 130–34).

Argonne   The hilly and wooded region of northeastern France, which, after four years of German occupation, was recaptured by American troops between September and November 1918. It was considered one

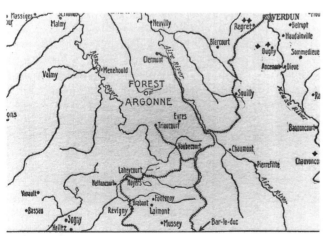

A map of the Argonne region. From Fighting France, from Dunkerque to Belfort *(1915), first edition.* (Collection of the author)

of the most brilliant tactical successes of the war and resulted in the Armistice. At the end of February 1915, Edith Wharton had visited the Argonne and written of "my first sight of War," as she put it in *FIGHTING FRANCE, FROM DUNKERQUE TO BELFORT* (*FFDB* 45). She was able to get a *laissez-passer*, or pass, with the help of Paul BOURGET and Jules Cambon, who had been the French ambassador to Berlin and was then secretary general in the Ministry of Foreign Affairs. Edith Wharton and Walter BERRY, driven in her motor car by her chauffeur, Charles COOK, made two journeys to the Argonne in late February and early March. They took clothes and medicines and, on the first trip, visited Châlons-sur-Mer, Ste.-Menehould, Clermont-en-Argonne, Blercourt and Verdun. They were not only horrified at the sight of the wounded soldiers, but were also shocked by the sight of the thousands of "éclopés," the unwounded but shattered and frost-bitten soldiers sent to rest for a short time before going back to the Front.

On the second trip they went straight to Verdun, laden with shirts, boxes of eggs and bags of oranges. Coming back, they barely found lodgings for the night in Châlons, since all available rooms were reserved for officers expected from headquarters. At last they were sent a few streets away to a house with accommodations still available. They were told the password for the night, "*Jena*," since it was after the curfew hour. Cook slept in the car. Wharton wrote Henry JAMES that, with the cavalrymen and bandaged soldiers leaning in doorways, the "boom, boom, boom, boom of the guns on the grey heights to the east," it was "Winter War to the fullest" (*Letters* 351).

Arnold, Matthew (1822–1888)   English critic and poet, the son of Thomas Arnold (headmaster of the Rugby public [private] school), Arnold was the author of *Thyrsis* (1866), an elegy written on the death of his friend Arthur Hugh Clough, *Culture and Anarchy* (1869), and *Literature and Dogma* (1873). Arnold argued for the education of the masses in England, which he felt were too oriented toward the spirit of "Hebraism," with its teachings of strict conscience, and not sufficiently toward the more spontaneous spirit of "Hellenism."

Wharton read the poetry of Arnold in the "kingdom" of her father's library, when she was a child. Later, at The MOUNT, she was delighted when Henry JAMES read his works aloud in the evening. She felt, like Arnold, that, as Singley puts it, modern life had "destroyed an important historical continuity" (Singley, *Edith Wharton: Matters of Mind and Spirit*, 21). At the same time, she embraced the aesthetic movement that had its origins in the theories of Kant, Arnold, Walter PATER and RUSKIN; her interest in art permeates not only her nonfiction, but also her fiction.

Wharton knew Matthew Arnold's daughters Eleanor (Mrs. Armine Woodhouse) and Lucy (Mrs. Frederick

Whitridge); she saw them in New York and in England (*Letters* 56n; 91n). She was also a close friend of his niece Mary Augustus Arnold Ward (Mrs. Humphry Ward), the novelist. It was her English home, Stocks, that she had arranged to let just before the outbreak of WORLD WAR I.

Wharton copied Arnold's poem "Resignation" in her Commonplace Book, about 1907. Benstock takes the title of her biography of Wharton, *No Gifts from Chance*, from this poem: "They, believe me, who await / No gifts from chance, have conquered fate. / They, winning room to see and hear, / And to men's business not too near, / Through clouds of individual strife / Draw homeward to the general life" (*NGC* 168). Wharton wished, philosophically, to take control of her own life and fate. In 1908, she quoted the first line in a letter to Morton FULLERTON asking him to "write or don't write" but to "hold me long & close in your thoughts" since "it's only there that I'm happy!" (*Letters* 149).

The year before her death, in 1936, she wrote her friend Jane (Mrs. Kenneth) CLARK, apologizing for not having given them a line of introduction to Janette and Arnold Whitbridge in America. The latter was Matthew Arnold's grandson, then the Master of Calhoun College at Yale. Wharton said they were "almost the only friends under the centenarian level that I have left in America" (*Letters* 600).

Artemis to Actæon and Other Verse   Edith Wharton's second collection of poetry, published by SCRIBNER'S in April 1909 (*see VERSES*, privately printed in 1878). The book has three sections with a total of 25 poems. Lewis calls the volume a "genuine if modest poetic accomplishment" (*EW* 236) and believes that Edith Wharton was one of the few living American novelists who excelled in fiction yet produced poetry of such quality.

The title poem, based on a tale from Ovid's *Metamorphosis*, deals with the legend of Artemis (Diana), the Greek goddess of hunting and childbirth, and her severity toward young Actæon. He happened upon Diana as she was being bathed by her nymphs, from whom she demanded chastity. She could not allow anyone who looked on her unclothed to live, and threw water on him, turning him into a stag who was chased and torn to pieces by his own hounds. Wharton's Artemis tells Actæon the gods "freeze to the marble of their images"; they are given life only by their votaries. She has divined in Actæon "the questing foot that never / Revisits the cold hearth of yesterday"; he will achieve immortality not by sitting "in dull dominion over time" but by drinking "fate's utmost at a draught." He will literally lose himself in her and "relive" in her "renewal," i.e., by becoming incarnate in her.

"Life" is a poem of thanksgiving; Benstock notes that it echoes the *LOVE DIARY* entry of May 16, 1908, "Oh Life, how I give thanks to you for this!" (*NGC* 205). The speaker is a reed growing on a shoal of forgetfulness, the Lethe bank, played on by Life as an instrument. The speaker challenges Life, "Nay, lift me to thy lips, Life, and once more / Pour the wild music through me—" She records a moment of delirious awakening, "while Life and I Clung lip to lip, and I from her wrung song / As she from me, one song, one ecstasy, / In indistinguishable union blent, / Till she became the flute and I the player." Life pipes on the reed by the sea, in "charmèd woods," cities, on Mount Olympus, in vales, and in "interstellar spaces like new worlds / Loosed from the fiery ruin of a star."

"The MORTAL LEASE," written to Morton FULLERTON, is a sequence of eight sonnets about Edith Wharton's relationship to Fullerton. Benstock observes that they form "linked dialogues" between the speaker and the lover, the speaker and Time, and that they reflect Wharton's attempt to "reconcile the sexual and the sacred, to undo oppositions and to see how the sacred—whether Attic or Christian—folds mortality into immortality" (*NGC* 207).

Astor, Caroline Schermerhorn (Mrs. William Backhouse Astor)   The first cousin of George Frederic JONES, Caroline Schermerhorn Astor was a social leader and founder of "The 400" (the social register of Old New York). This was said to be the number that could be easily fitted into her ballroom at Fifth Avenue and 34th Street and, according to the social chronicler and man-about-town Ward McAllister, also the sum total of those making up bona fide New York society (*EW* 36). According to Lewis, Mrs. Astor was the model for the senile hostess Evelina Jaspar in "AFTER HOLBEIN" (*EW* 13).

Astor, Nancy Langhorne (Mrs. William Waldorf Astor)   After her marriage to William Waldorf Astor, the brilliant and charming Nancy Langhorne Astor and her husband lived in England at Cliveden, a 300-acre estate above the Thames. In November 1908 Edith Wharton was a guest at a house party at Cliveden, along with Howard STURGIS, Lord Hugo and Lady Mary ELCHO and Lord Arthur James BALFOUR (the former prime minister). She wrote Sally NORTON that Cliveden was "exquisite" even in the "white November fog" (*Letters* 167).

In August 1912, on a visit to England, she took Henry JAMES to Cliveden and reported to Gaillard LAPSLEY that he was "captivated by Nancy Astor, & completely ravished by Cliveden itself" (*Letters* 276). He became ill, however, and she had to take him back to Rye in her motor-car; he thought it was heart trouble, but the doctor called it a "digestive upset."

In January 1915, during WORLD WAR I, she dined at the Ritz in PARIS with Nancy Astor and Lady (Adèle

Grant) ESSEX. Only four other tables were occupied, and she wrote Mary BERENSON, "I never saw anything so spectral" (*Letters* 347).

Atlantic Monthly   This magazine, founded in Boston in 1857, has published a number of America's most outstanding writers since its inception. James Russell Lowell, James T. Fields, William Dean HOWELLS, Bliss PERRY, and Ellery SEDGWICK were among the noted editors during the late 19th and early 20th centuries. Howells published five of Edith Wharton's poems anonymously in 1880. Perry edited the magazine from 1899–1909, and, in June 1900, published "An Alpine Posting-Inn," which would become the first essay in *ITALIAN BACKGROUNDS*. He also commissioned the articles resulting from Wharton's first two French "motor-flights," which were published in the magazine in 1906, 1907 and 1908 before being collected into *A MOTOR-FLIGHT THROUGH FRANCE*. Sedgwick, who succeeded Perry as editor in 1909, was a longtime friend of Wharton's, although this did not prevent his rejecting a short story called "Duration" submitted by Rutger B. JEWETT in 1933. Sedgwick found it "not cutting enough" and believed it would be damaging to her reputation, which he termed a "real American possession" (*NGC* 439).

"Atrophy"   Story published in the *Ladies' Home Journal* in November 1927 and collected in CERTAIN PEOPLE (Appleton, 1930). It deals with the conflict between duty and love experienced by a fashionable young married woman, Nora Frenway, who, as the *New York Times* critic remarked, "thought she had dared and really did not know the meaning of the word daring" (*CR* 480). She has conducted a discreet affair with Christopher Aldis beneath the eyes of her irascible, semi-invalid husband, George, and his prying sisters and dominating mother. Fearing, however, that she might lose custody of her children, she has ceased seeing her lover.

Receiving the news that Christopher is dying, she goes by train to see him, armed with the pretext that she is calling on her old governess en route. Christopher's sister, Jane Aldis, who has guessed the truth about their relationship, refuses to permit Nora to see him, pretending he is too ill. Instead, she treats Nora as George's wife, talking of the advice about tree moving he had given them on their last visit three years earlier. She then delicately dismisses Nora. The social charade in which Nora is out-maneuvered is reminiscent of the Mingott tribe's closing of ranks in *The AGE OF INNOCENCE*, which effectively ends Newland Archer's romance with Ellen Olenska. It is not, however, Jane Aldis who has defeated Nora so much as her own adherence to convention, her complicity in submitting to her hostess's pretense and her inability to be daring enough to insist on saying good-bye to her lover. V. S. Pritchett, writing

in the English *Spectator*, remarked that the story had Kipling's "sardonic realism" (*CR* 482).

Aubyn, Margaret   *See TOUCHSTONE, THE.*

Austin, Sir Alfred (1835–1913)   English poet laureate and author of 20 volumes of verse, including *Sacred and Profane Love* (1908). Edith Wharton was a friend both of Sir Alfred Austin and of his wife, the former Hester Bellair, whom she called in her memoir "my shrewd and independent old friend" (*BG* 222). In 1906 she met Sir Alfred in London and wrote Sara NORTON, "I can't take Alfred to my heart (I mean as a poet)" (*EW* 168), yet she liked the diminutive Austin very much as a person (he was about five feet tall). In the company of Henry JAMES, she paid a two-day visit to their home, Swinford Old Manor in Ashford, Kent, which she called a "pleasant old house full of books and flowers" (*BG* 248). Lewis observes that he was the "least distinguished laureate in English history" and had been an odd choice by Queen Victoria's prime minister, Lord Salisbury, to follow Tennyson in that post (*EW* 168).

"Autres Temps . . ."   First published in *The CENTURY MAGAZINE* in 1911 under the title "Other Times, Other Manners," this story was collected in XINGU AND OTHER STORIES (Scribner's, 1916). Written during the time Wharton was considering separating from her husband, it deals with the social legacy of divorce. The title derives from the French idiom *autres temps autres moeurs*, or "other days other ways." The heroine, Mrs. Lidcote, had divorced her husband many years earlier, a scandalous event, and has been attempting to live it down with a quite existence in Florence. As the story opens, she is hurriedly sailing back to New York to support her daughter Leila, who, she has discovered, is about to divorce one husband and marry another. She finds that the old mores have evaporated so far as Leila's generation is concerned, "as if an angel had gone about lifting gravestones, and the buried people walked again, and the living didn't shrink from them." Changing spouses has become the norm among Leila's set.

Mrs. Lidcote also finds, however, that she herself has not escaped the stigma of divorce. She is snubbed by the ambassador's wife, hidden by her daughter so as not to jeopardize her prospective son-in-law's possible diplomatic appointment to Rome, and shunned as an outcast by old friends. She stays in her room during the weekend party at her daughter's country house, then goes to New York for an early sailing back to Italy.

Franklin Ide, an old friend she has considered marrying, comes to the writing room at her hotel, and she tells him of her treatment by her daughter and their friends. She realizes that her "case" is not the same as Leila's. " 'I'm the woman who has been cut for nearly twenty years. The older people have half-forgotten why, and the younger ones have never really known: it's simply become a tradition to cut me.' " She feels she has paid "with the best years of her life" for the "theft of happiness her daughter's contemporaries were taking as their due." He urges her not to shrink from people, but "put them to the test" by coming out to meet them. She concedes that he may be right, and suggests that they call on a mutual friend, Margaret Wynn, who is also staying in the hotel. Ide discourages her, just as Leila has, and she realizes that at some level she is an embarrassment both to her daughter and old friend. The "veil of painted gauze" has been torn away, and she faces the reality that she will never be forgiven or "received" by society.

Lewis calls this one of Edith Wharton's "most poignant tales" (*EW* 333). It is in the light of her own decision to divorce, two years after the story was published, that "Autres Temps . . ." can best be understood. She had been living in Paris for several years. Teddy WHARTON had used part of her inheritance to keep a mistress on Beacon Hill and was increasingly unstable. She believed she had no choice, but commissioned Bernard BERENSON to sound out possible reactions on the part of proper Bostonians to her divorce. He approached Barrett WENDELL, his old professor at Harvard, as well as President Lowell of Harvard. Professor Wendell's reply has not survived, but Lewis quotes his remark to Gaillard LAPSLEY on the subject. He observed that Bostonians sympathized with Mrs.

Wharton's marital troubles and were only sorry Teddy had not been "committed, some time ago, to formal guardianship of some kind" (*EW* 334). Edith Wharton was relieved at the report and decided to proceed with her divorce. *See* DIVORCE and the novel The *MOTHER'S RECOMPENSE*, whose themes this story releases.

Auvergne   Edith Wharton, accompanied by her husband, Henry JAMES, and her brother Harry JONES, toured the old province of Auvergne on their first "motor-flight" through France, a two-week trip made in May 1906. She later described this journey in *A MOTOR-FLIGHT THROUGH FRANCE*.

Edith Wharton praised Auvergne for its individual church architecture and also for its unusual landscape with "tormented blue peaks and wide-spread forest" (*MFF* 58). Choosing Royat as the "starting-point of the perilous *circuit d'Auvergne*" (*MFF* 65), the travelers toured the valley of Mont-Dore, the baths of Saint-Nectaire-le-Bas, the lake of Chambon and several mountain towns en route to the remote village of Orcival. A cattle fair in the church square prevented their touring the noted Romanesque church, and, although they looked longingly at the Puy de Dôme mountain, they believed their touring car would not make the ascent. They left the region reluctantly, believing each "renunciation" made another visit more inevitable.

B

Babbitt *See* LEWIS, SINCLAIR.

Backward Glance, A Edith Wharton's memoir, published in 1934 by D. Appleton-Century. This volume is a highly readable self-portrait depicting Edith Wharton's life as a little girl in NEW YORK, her childhood residence abroad, the early years of her marriage and life at The MOUNT, and the pre–WORLD WAR I years in PARIS. It gives short shrift to the post–World War I years, and it has remained for her biographers to tell the whole story of her disintegrating marriage and divorce, her liaison with Morton FULLERTON and her postwar existence in her two French homes, the PAVILLON COLOMBE outside Paris at Saint-Brice-sous-Forêt, and STE.-CLAIRE CHÂTEAU on the French Riviera at HYÈRES. Louis Auchincloss, however, calls the Europe depicted in *A Backward Glance* "as elegant as a Watteau drawing" and praises the quality of her writing—as firm and crisp and lucid as in the best of her novels" (*BG* ix–x; Introd., Scribner's reprint, 1964).

"How I wish I could see again all the places that have enriched my inner eye! *Kein Genuss ist vorübergehend*, luckily," Edith Wharton wrote the American-born historian and Cambridge don Gaillard LAPSLEY in 1936 (*Letters* 593). The quotation from GOETHE's *Wilhelm Meister*, meaning "no pleasure is only transitory," is one of the two epigraphs on the title page of *A Backward Glance*. It attests to Edith Wharton's remarkable sense of place and offers a key to the satisfaction she derived from travel writing. The memoir itself, however, focuses less on the places she visited over the years than on the many relationships she established with friends in America and Europe. The volume is dedicated to "the friends who every year on All Souls' Night come and sit with me by the fire," and has been particularly praised for the portraits of Lapsley, Theodore ROOSEVELT, Henry JAMES, the English novelist and man of letters Howard STURGIS, the French writer Paul BOURGET, the critic Percy LUBBOCK, her long-time devoted friend Walter BERRY and the British writer Geoffrey SCOTT.

She presents an unforgettable glimpse of James at The Mount, in England and in Paris. At The Mount, he once was asked about his distant relations, the Emmets, and spoke of them at length, "forgetting us, forgetting the place, forgetting everything but the vision of his lost youth that the question had evoked, the long train of ghosts flung with his enchanter's wand across the wide stage of the summer night" (*BG* 193). She remembers when she and James were both visiting "Qu'Acre" ("Queen's Acre"), the home of Howard Sturgis, when James would lean against the mantel after tea and plunge into "some slowly elaborated literary disquisition, perhaps on the art of fiction or the theater, on Balzac, or Tolstoy, or, better still, on one of his own contemporaries" (*BG* 231–32). James often visited Wharton in Paris, where he was besieged by "literary ladies" who sought to translate his novels into French. One insisted she was particularly well qualified to translate *The Golden Bowl*, a complex and subtle masterpiece, because she had just dealt with a work called "The Filigree Box."

The volume contains a charming glimpse of Edith Wharton herself as hostess in Paris, at sea amidst the complexities of the French social hierarchy. Her most telling evocation of the "order" of the FAUBOURG SAINT-GERMAIN is in her account of an early dinner party, where she makes clear the viscosity of her assimilation to France. Certain democratic elements of her American nature wholly resisted alteration. She consulted a friend about the correct seating order, realizing it was important—but failing to apprehend just how critical an issue it would be. The friend, equally perplexed, decided to consult her uncle, the "Duc de D.," who was a "venerable nobleman" and former ambassador, the "final authority in the Faubourg on ceremonial questions." Wharton, "though surprised that he should be invoked in so unimportant a matter," awaited his decision. The duke supplied a plan of the table, but told his niece, " 'My dear child, Mrs. Wharton ought *never* to have invited them together'—not that they were not all good and even intimate friends, and in the habit of meeting daily, but because the shades of difference in their rank were so slight, and so difficult to adjust, that even the diplomatist Duke recoiled from the attempt" (*BG* 260).

Wharton is reticent about her writing, devoting only one chapter to it, which she calls "The Secret Garden," (published in the *Atlantic Monthly* in April 1933 as "Confessions of a Novelist"). She asserts that the act of including her work suggests it will be long-lasting, an assumption from which she shrinks. She gives an account, nevertheless, of how she would find the fictional "case," or situation, decide on names, and deal with the "spectral element" in her writing, when names would appear in her imagination without characters. This chapter may also suggest Wharton's method of reconciling her writing with her early intellectual conditioning within her parents' circle of friends, since they regarded authorship as "something between a black art and a form of manual labor" (*BG* 69). She declares that once an author has offered his or her "wares" to the public in the open market, it is best to discount the praise or blame they attract. Instead, one must "write only for that dispassionate and ironic critic who dwells within the breast" (*BG* 212).

Edith Wharton's philosophy is expressed in the opening section, "A First Word," when she states that one "*can* remain alive long past the usual date of disintegration if one is unafraid of change, insatiable in intellectual curiosity, interested in big things, and happy in small ways" (*BG* xix). She was blessed with all of these qualities, but, above all, possessed a capacity for amusement at her own foibles, as *A Backward Glance* testifies.

A Backward Glance was loosely adapted as a television film under the title *Looking Back*, in 1981. *See* Appendix II.

Baedeker The guidebooks published by Karl Baedeker (1801–59) became a metaphor for the type of journey organization Edith Wharton most disliked, when the traveler relies so totally on a guidebook he cannot perceive the byways of travel. In "The VICE OF READING," she compares the "mechanical reader" who takes "each book separately as an entity" with the "tourist who drives from one 'sight' to another without looking at anything that is not set down in Baedeker (516).

Guidebooks had become increasingly important in the latter part of the 19th century, since Europe had became more accessible to Americans owing to the proliferation of transatlantic steamships. Baedeker had published his first guidebook, on the Rhine from Mainz to Cologne, in 1828. He was quick to capitalize on the rising popularity of travel, though the era of mass tourism was still far away. The firm's first French guide was published in 1846, and their first English one in 1861. After Karl Baedeker's death, his sons carried on the business. Harper's *Handbook for Travelers in Europe and the East* was published in New York in 1862; Murray's series of handbooks for travelers dates from the 1870s.

Edith Wharton's earliest travel books were published on the eve of the era of mass tourism, but she had long deplored guidebooks because they precluded the traveler's making his own discoveries. In ITALIAN BACKGROUNDS she states that one of the "rarest and most delicate pleasures of the continental tourist" is actually to "circumvent the compiler of his guide-book . . ." The guidebook writer has already been over the ground and tested the inns; "the only refuge left from his omniscience lies in approaching the places he describes by a route which he has not taken" (*IB* 85).

In *A MOTOR-FLIGHT THROUGH FRANCE*, she recommends that her readers seek the "parentheses of travel" and trembles lest Gerhard David's painting "Virgin of the Grapes" become the "picnic-ground of the art-excursionist" and "cease to shine in its own twilight heaven when it has become a star in Baedeker" (*MFF* 23).

Bahlmann, Anna (d. 1916) Edith Wharton's early governess and lifelong companion/secretary, Anna Bahlmann entered Wharton's life when she was a child in NEWPORT, Rhode Island. She was the governess of the children of Harvard astronomist Lewis RUTHERFURD, who lived next door. Wharton continued the German studies she had begun during her family's residence on the Continent between 1866 and 1870. In *A BACKWARD GLANCE* she wrote that Anna Bahlmann had fed her fancy with "all the wealth of German literature, from the Minnesingers to Heine" (*BG* 48). When the JONES family returned to NEW YORK for the winter, Bahlmann came each day to give her language lessons. Later employed by Mary Cadwalader JONES, Edith Wharton's sister-in-law, she became a member of the Wharton household about 1904, according to Lewis (*EW* 150).

She served as secretary, literary assistant and liaison between Edith Wharton and her publishers during the early part of the century. After Edith Wharton settled in FRANCE, Anna Bahlmann came over from America and served as companion and secretary. She discovered she had cancer in the summer of 1915 and, at Wharton's urging, returned to America to be near relatives. She died in Kansas City in March 1916. Edith Wharton greatly regretted that her former governess had not been at the rue de Varenne in her final days, where she might have been "properly waited on. Poor little unquiet bewildered and tender soul! I wish I could have done more for her this last hard year," she wrote her sister-in-law, Mary (Minnie) Jones (*Letters* 374).

Balch, Annabel *See* SUMMER.

Balfour, Arthur James (1848–1930) First earl of Balfour and prime minister of Britain from 1902 to 1905, Lord Balfour was a statesman and philosopher and the author of several books, including *The Foundations of Belief* (1895). He was author of the Balfour Declaration (1917), which assured Great Britain's protection for the Jewish settlement of Palestine and formed the basis for British policy on the Mandate of Palestine for several decades.

He was a friend of Edith Wharton's; on at least one occasion, they were both houseguests at Cliveden, the estate of Nancy Langhorne ASTOR. In 1927 he supported efforts to obtain the NOBEL PRIZE for Wharton.

baroque style   A highly decorated style of architecture and decoration, richly ornamented, often extravagant in nature, which originated in ITALY in the late 16th century in order to counter classicism and flourished during the 17th and 18th centuries. Bernini's colonnades in St. Peter's Square and the interior of St. Peter's Church, ROME, epitomized the baroque, as did works by Borromini and Vignola.

One of Edith Wharton's most remarkable aesthetic achievements was to revise her readers' acceptance of the common place view held by many art historians early in the 19th century that baroque art and architecture were inferior to those of the Gothic and Renaissance periods. John RUSKIN had castigated the architects and sculptors of the baroque, a period he termed the "Grotesque Renaissance." Edith Wharton disagreed with Ruskin and the "submissive generation of art critics" he had taught to despise the style, and defended it in ITALIAN VILLAS AND THEIR GARDENS and in ITALIAN BACKGROUNDS.

Even though, by the late 19th century, baroque had been identified as an important stylistic period by art historians Cornelius Gurlitt and Heinrich Wolfflin, it was no small matter for Wharton to renounce Ruskin's dogmatic pronouncements, and to reeducate her readers about architecture, sculpture and paintings they had obediently devalued for several generations. To Ruskin the baroque was an expression of decadence, a sign of the deplorable political and moral decline of Italy, particularly VENICE, that had contaminated the successors of majestic Renaissance artists and architects. Edith Wharton, on the other hand, saw it as "a style *de parade*, the setting of the spectacular and external life which had developed from the more secluded civilization of the Renaissance as some blossom of immense size and dazzling colour may develop in the atmosphere of the forcing-house from a smaller and more delicate flower" (*IB* 185).

In using the term *style de parade*, Edith Wharton seems to defend the quality of pretentious display that Ruskin abhorred. In her detailed discussions of baroque works of art and architecture, however, she focuses on different characteristics, particularly originality and emancipation from convention, which she values over studied decorum. She sees the art of the baroque as one in which formality and ostentation are "tempered by a free play of line, as though the winds of heaven swept unhindered through the heavy draperies of a palace" (*IB* 185). Wharton's approach to a work of art is always to value the personal associa-

tions it might arouse more than the microscopic details which are the province of the "expert." In *Italian Backgrounds*, she challenged her readers who fancied they were unsympathetic to the exuberances of 17th-century art to imagine Rome without the baroque: there would be no Spanish Steps, Barberini Palace, Fountain of the Triton, Trevi Fountain, or Bridge of Sant' Angelo. They should realize that the Rome that "excites a passion of devotion such as no other city can inspire, the Rome for which travellers pine in absence, and to which they return again and again with the fresh ardour of discovery, is, externally at least, in great part the creation of the seventeenth century" (*IB* 189).

Edith Wharton's dedication to the baroque extends far beyond its representation in Venice and the physiognomy of Rome, playing a considerable role in *Italian Villas and Their Gardens*. Some of the major gardens she discusses have baroque design and ornamentation, such as grottos with statues of mythological figures, spouting Atlas fountains, and sculptured balustrades. She considered the *teatro d'acqua*, or water-theater, the pinnacle of the garden architect's art during the 16th and 17th centuries, combining natural topography and hydraulic engineering in brilliant spectacle. They were among the glories of the gardens at the Villa Pamphilij near Rome, and the palace of Mondragone, the Villa Aldobrandini and the Villa Torlonia at Frascati.

It is not only Edith Wharton's travel works that exhibit a fascination with the baroque, but also her fiction. For example, she greatly admired the fluted descending water-basins and carved entablature and statuary in the gardens at the Villa d'Este at Cernobbio on Lake COMO. Her short story "*The MUSE'S TRAGEDY*" was set in part at the hotel here. She particularly appreciated the *bosco*, or section of natural woodland climbing the cliffside, with "winding paths, summer-houses, and sylvan temples."

A devotion to the baroque period, with its "*bravura* spirit" and "exuberances" of art, leavens Edith Wharton's own style, informs her travel writing and enriches her fiction. The art, architecture, garden-magic and theater of the baroque, as she conceives them, may be discursive, irregular and even irrational, yet they are spontaneous and vibrant, rooted in a form of illusion that enlarges reality. In paying tribute to the baroque, she reshapes the preconceptions of her readers and establishes a counter-scenario refuting the *de facto* supremacy of medieval and Renaissance works.

Bart, Lily   *See* HOUSE OF MIRTH, THE.

"Beatrice Palmato"   A cover sheet, outline and brief fragment of a short story called "Beatrice Palmato" are in the Edith Wharton Collection in the Beinecke

Library, Yale University. R. W. B. Lewis believes it to have been written about 1935. Cynthia Griffin Wolff dates the fragment at sometime in 1919, however, associating it with Wharton's visit to MOROCCO in 1917 and the "precocious sexual initiations" she had observed in the harems there. She believes Mr. Palmato's "half Levantine" heritage suggests "lands beyond the Mediterranean." It is her contention that the fragment provides a link between SUMMER (1917) and *The AGE OF INNOCENCE* (1920) (*A Feast of Words*, 291). The cover sheet, apparently for a volume of short stories called *Powers of Darkness*, suggests that the story might have been intended for inclusion in a volume of ghost stories. The outline, however, is not concerned with the supernatural. It proposes, rather, a story about Beatrice Palmato, the younger daughter of a wealthy half-Levantine, half-Portuguese banker living in London and an English mother. She has a brother who is in an English boarding school and a sister who has committed suicide under mysterious circumstances after returning from a French convent. The mother has a nervous breakdown and Beatrice, then age 12, is left under the care of a governess. The governess then becomes ill also, the father cannot find a suitable replacement and Beatrice spends the winter in the company of her father. The mother seems to recover, but then goes mad, tries to kill her husband, is sent to an asylum and dies there within a few months.

Beatrice marries a stolid but kind English country squire and has two children, a boy who resembles her husband and a girl who is like her mother, "exquisite, gay, original, brilliant." Beatrice seems irrationally jealous of her husband's attachment to their daughter. When she runs to him after a business trip and he clasps her in his arms, Beatrice screams, " 'Don't kiss my child!' " Having unwittingly betrayed her terrible family secret, she runs upstairs and shoots herself. Her level-headed brother, Jack Palmato, a close friend of Beatrice's husband, comes to see his brother-in-law and they have a long talk together "about Mr. Palmato."

The fragment of the story describes, with considerable detail, an incestuous violation of Beatrice by Mr. Palmato. Wolff has speculated to Lewis that Edith Wharton might not have intended to include the fragmentary description in the narrative, but wrote it "in order to articulate fully to herself the precise nature, feeling, and history of the incestuous experience which was to lie behind and to color the actual narrative" (*EW* 544). In her psychological study of Edith Wharton's fiction, Wolff argues that the fragment represents the "suppressed horror that lay *behind* the action of the tale and made it understandable" (*FW* 299). She does not infer that the fragment is in any way a reflection of Edith Wharton's relationship with her own father, but

observes that she makes incest "irresistibly attractive." The fragment has been republished in Lewis's biography of Edith Wharton (*Edith Wharton: A Biography*) and in Wolff's *A Feast of Words: The Triumph of Edith Wharton.*

For further reading: Lauer, "Is This Indeed 'Attractive'? Another Look at the 'Beatrice Palmato' Fragment."

Beaufort, Julius   *See AGE OF INNOCENCE, THE.*

Beaufort, Regina   *See AGE OF INNOCENCE, THE.*

Beinecke Library, Yale University   In 1923 YALE University bestowed an honorary doctor of letters degree on Edith Wharton, the only academic degree she ever received. Partly out of gratitude, Edith Wharton asked her literary executor, Gaillard LAPSLEY, to donate her "literary correspondence" to Yale. The Beinecke Library now has over 50,000 items relating to Edith Wharton in many categories.

According to Lewis, the original donation consisted of letters to Edith Wharton, but, since then, many other recipients of her letters, or their heirs, have donated them, including Gaillard Lapsley, Sara NORTON, Mary Cadwalader JONES, Margaret CHANLER, John Hugh SMITH, Joseph CONRAD, Sir Kenneth CLARK, Walter BERRY, Bernard BERENSON and William Dean HOWELLS. There are also diaries, contracts, biographical sketches, holograph and typescript manuscripts (published and unpublished), photographs, house plans for STE.-CLAIRE CHÂTEAU, garden plans and lists for both French houses, information about her war charities, postcards, Christmas cards, an occasional recipe and other material.

Belchamber   A novel, published in 1904, by Howard STURGIS. Wharton was a longtime friend of this English writer and critic and often visited him at his home, QUEEN'S ACRE ("Qu'Acre"), in Windsor. She deplored the fact that his literary production was so slender; *Belchamber*, his only novel, a study of the fashionable London of the 1890s, failed to attract a large public. Wharton believed it stood "very nearly in the first rank" (*BG* 234) and tried unsuccessfully to interest William Crary BROWNELL of SCRIBNER'S in publishing it in the United States. It was published in 1905 by G. P. Putnam's Sons and, as Lewis puts it, "earned a measure of grudging admiration" (*Letters* 88).

Wharton reviewed *Belchamber* for *The Bookman* in May 1905, praising its "directness of observation," but faulting Sturgis for his inexperience in narration. The protagonist, Lord Belchamber, is the antithesis of the typical "manly hero" of British fiction; he is "lame, sickly, shy, and tormented" and is out of sympathy with the institutions he represents as peer. His personal tragedy, according to Edith Wharton, is being crushed by "vulgar" people in a "mad social race for luxury and amusement" who are actually an "engine of destruction" within society as they destroy illusions and create despair (*UCW* 109–10).

"Belgian Prisoners of War, The"   An appeal for help for the Committee for the Relief of the Belgian Prisoners in Germany, signed by Edith Wharton; the only edition was in 1916. It was a single sheet folded to make four pages. It is exceedingly rare; copies are in the Beinecke Library, Yale University, and at Alderman Library, University of Virginia (Garrison, 103).

Belknap, Troy   *See The* MARNE.

Belle Époque   The Belle Époque, a phrase Edith Wharton would probably not have thought of using, was a period of seemingly permanent equilibrium and prosperity in EUROPE as a whole. The era of the late 19th and early 20th centuries (between the Franco-Prussian War and the onset of World War I) was marked by the construction of grand hotels in European capitals and ease of transport. The arts and literature flourished, theaters and luxurious restaurants proliferated, as did horse racing, private yachts, haute couture, illustrated weeklies and artists who depicted the lives of the upper classes in an idealized way. A number of intellectual and artistic achievements marked this era: the publication of Marcel Proust's *Remembrance of Things Past*, the birth of impressionism and the art nouveau decorative style, Sarah Bernhardt's acclaimed dramatic performances and Henvide Toulouse-Lautrec's posters portraying Montmartre night life. At the same time, the age was marked by urban poverty, social injustices and the politically divisive Dreyfus affair. Wharton satirized the vulgarity of certain aspects of the age in her fiction even as she made a place for herself in the FAUBOURG, among the aristocracy and intelligentsia.

The early years of her expatriation coincided with the final years of the Belle Époque. Her assimilation to FRANCE was fulfilled during this era, her travels encouraged and expedited by the motor car, and her fiction was acclaimed in France and England as well as AMERICA. *A MOTOR-FLIGHT THROUGH FRANCE* (1908), Wharton's first French travel book, based on three automobile journeys taken in 1906 and 1907, pointed up the perfections of France during the Belle Époque: the orderly countryside, quiet historic villages un-touched by the automobile, peaceful inhabitants and traditions unchanged for centuries. Her 1913 novel *The CUSTOM OF THE COUNTRY* exposed the mercurial excesses of an aristocracy converted to capitalism by intermarriage with American heiresses,

then subject to the risk of lost fortunes. Perhaps her most poignant picture of the Belle Époque is in "The Look of Paris," the first chapter in *FIGHTING FRANCE, FROM DUNKERQUE TO BELFORT*, in which, returning to PARIS from a journey on July 30, 1914, she saw the city, "so made for peace and art and all humanest graces" (*FFDB* 6), wearing the "light of the ideal and the abstract." The opening of her war novel, *A SON AT THE FRONT*, also captured the flavor of the era, as the successful portrait painter John Campton gaily plans a trip to southern Italy and Sicily and perhaps "a push over to North Africa" with his son George, about to arrive from America. But, he reflects, "if George preferred Spain they would postpone the desert" (*SF* 7). Campton's options seem unlimited, until George, born in France, is mobilized.

WORLD WAR I brought an abrupt end to the Belle Époque. The notice for General Mobilization was posted, falling like a "monstrous landslide" across the "orderly laborious nation, disrupting its routine, annihilating its industries, rending families apart, and burying under a heap of senseless ruin the patiently and painfully wrought machinery of civilization" (*FFDB* 6–9). Lewis states that, initially, Wharton regarded World War I not as the end of the Belle Époque, but its "grandest hour" (*EW* 365). It was her belief that the Great War, which had begun by August 4, 1914, would be fought in Belgium and would be over in six weeks, though this theory was contradicted by the highest British authorities. Henry JAMES also believed that the war threatened "the crash of civilization" (*EW* 36). By November, however, Wharton had understood the full tragedy of the war and realized that France, and Europe, would never again be the same. She wrote her friend Gaillard LAPSLEY in England, "*My* sense is completely of living again in the year 1000, with the last trump imminent" (*Letters* 342). She plunged immediately into war relief work, but never ceased looking back on the era when all France, not just Paris, seemed made for "peace and art."

Bélogou, Léon   A widely traveled mining engineer, Bélogou was a favorite friend in Edith Wharton's PARIS circle. She frequently attended concerts with him and he was often a guest at her dinner parties. In 1913 he brought her a star sapphire from Ceylon (*EW* 335), and she sometimes referred to him as her "beloved Bélogou." He introduced her to a young Parisian lawyer, André BOCCON-GIBOD, who handled her divorce and also became a close friend. During the war Bélogou formed an attachment with a much younger woman of whom she disapproved. She wrote Bernard BERENSON in 1917 that Léon was "still more or less in bondage—but (as I suspect) disgusted by the milieu, & pining for good talks with his own kind" (*Letters* 391).

Bénédiction A novel by Countess Philomène de LA FOREST-DIVONNE (pseudonym, Claude Silve), which won the Prix Femina in 1935. It was published in 1936 in the United States by Appleton's with a foreword by Edith Wharton. The translator was Robert NORTON, a friend of Wharton's and coeditor of ETERNAL PASSION IN ENGLISH POETRY, an anthology of love poems published after her death.

In the foreword, Wharton praised her achievement in "acclimatizing real solid tangible people in her world of dream." She found the characters highly convincing: the old marquise, the bishop, the butler, the housekeeper-maid, the elfin children and others.

The countess was a member of "one of the leading ducal families" of France and one of the "better-known writers and journalists" in that country (*EW* 438).

Berenson, Bernard (1865–1959) The Lithuanian-born art critic, connoisseur and author was a lifelong friend of Edith Wharton. His given name was Bernhard, which friends often shortened to "B.B."; he dropped the "h" after the German invasion of France during World War I. His Jewish family emigrated to America in 1875 and Berenson entered Harvard in 1884, receiving his A.B. in 1887. In 1885 he was baptized into the Episcopal church by Phillips Brooks of Trinity Church, Boston, and began, as Samuels puts it, being "lionized as a Harvard genius" by socially prominent Boston women. He studied art history under Professor Charles Eliot NORTON at Harvard and continued his work in Italy, where he decided to devote his life to the scientific method of attribution.

After graduation, he set out to study in England and on the Continent. In 1888 he met, through mutual friends, Mary Pearsall Smith Costelloe, the daughter of wealthy Quaker-bred parents of Philadelphia and the sister of the writer Logan Pearsall SMITH. She had attended Smith College and, in fact, been a student at the Harvard Annex (later Radcliffe) while Bernard was there. She was at the time the wife of the Oxford-educated Anglo-Irish barrister Frank Costelloe and the mother of an infant daughter, Rachel Conn (called "Ray"), who had been born in June 1887. Berenson called this meeting "the determining factor in the rest of my life and career" (Samuels, 66). A second daughter, Karin, was born in 1889; she would later marry Virginia WOOLF's brother, Adrian Stephens.

Mary and Bernard began a secret love affair in 1891, Frank Costelloe apparently believing Bernard was too honorable to threaten his marriage. Mary went to the Continent to study methods for the attribution of paintings under his tutelage. Eventually the Costelloe marriage faltered and they agreed on a separation in 1892. Her children were domiciled in England, where Mary visited them. Frank Costelloe died of cancer in

1899, and Berenson and Mary decided to merge their residences. They discovered that the Villa I TATTI, near Florence, could be leased, and were married in the chapel there on December 29, 1900, after 10 years of intimacy. With its magnificent library and superb art collection, the villa has long been a magnet for art historians. Berenson bequeathed the estate to Harvard University.

Mary BERENSON played a role in launching Berenson's career. She had published on art before he did, writing, in 1894, a *Guide to the Italian Pictures at Hampton Court*, which corrected some mistaken attributions of paintings. She kept records of the paintings and drawings she and Berenson identified during their travels on the Continent, and she urged him to write. Her identity as an art scholar eventually became absorbed into his, however. In 1900, before their marriage, he wrote her from San Domenico di Fiesole in Italy, "Just now nothing touches me so close as the question whether certain drawings are or are not by Michelangelo. It would be bliss if I could decide and nothing else interests me half as much" (Kiel, ed., *The Bernard Berenson Treasury*, 103).

Berenson had met Isabella Stewart GARDNER of Boston, the wealthy and imperious "Mrs. Jack," while he was an undergraduate, probably about 1886. Norton stimulated in both a passion for Italian paintings and helped set the stage for what Samuels calls the "enlightened, if wholesale, plunder of Italian art and for the migration of European masterpieces to the New World on an undreamed-of scale" (Samuels, 35). Berenson became Mrs. Gardner's aesthetic adviser, and helped her choose the paintings for Fenway Court, the Italian-style house (later museum) she was building in Boston. The commissions from his art purchases for her and other clients helped fund his stays abroad and his studies in museums. He advised the Philadelphia millionaire Peter Widener and the Philadelphia lawyer John Graves Johnson.

Edith Wharton became a lifelong friend of the Berensons, but her earliest encounter with them was not auspicious. Her first success in the field of art history resulted in a major clash with Berenson, representative of the "culturally elite." In 1893, she and her husband journeyed to the monastery of SAN VIVALDO, ITALY, in order to see some terracotta statues of which she had heard. She believed they were the work of Della Robbia rather than Giovanni Gonnelli, a 17th-century artist to whom they were attributed. To test her theory, Edith Wharton asked the noted Florentine photographer Signor Alinari to take photographs, which she forwarded to Professor Enrico Ridolfi, at that time director of the Royal Museums at Florence. He answered that as soon as he saw the photographs he became convinced of the error of attributing them to Gonnelli. She sent Edward L. BURLINGAME of SCRIB-

NER'S MAGAZINE an account of her visit, which was published in 1895 as "A Tuscan Shrine." Bernard and Mary Berenson read the article (long before they became close friends with Wharton), went to view the terra-cottas and returned home "scoffing at Mrs. Wharton's preposterous suggestion that any of them could have been by one of the Della Robbias" (*EW* 69).

Their friendship got off to an even worse start once they were introduced to each other in 1903. A mutual friend, Henry Cannon, invited the Berensons to meet a fellow New Yorker at the Villa La Doccia. Mary and her brother Logan arrived separately. As Mary wrote, they found Bernard there, already, it was clear, "loathing her" (Samuels, 388). The Berensons found Wharton self-absorbed and haughty. Much later, Wharton explained to Berenson that she had been petrified at being in the presence of a man whose work she so much admired.

Henry ADAMS was instrumental in bringing them together again and arranged for them both to be his guests in September 1909 at a dinner at Voisin's, a famous Parisian restaurant. According to Berenson's dramatization of the evening in *Sketch for a Self-Portrait*, Adams escorted him upstairs, where Edith Wharton sat in the shadows, wearing a black lace veil. Berenson did not recognize her but was, he remembered, "soon engaged in the liveliest conversation with her," touching on art, literature and friends they had in common. Morton FULLERTON, who had a love affair with Edith Wharton, was also there. Lewis observes that Berenson had actually known Wharton was to be there, and had even seen her in Adams's apartment a few days earlier, but the meeting did launch a lifelong friendship between Wharton and the Berensons (Berenson, *EW* 269). As he reported to Mary, "I buried the hatchet and called on her yesterday" (Samuels, 389).

Edith Wharton's intimacy with the Berensons lasted until her death in 1937. She often stayed at the Villa I Tatti as she journeyed between her two French homes, and they visited her in both establishments. Edith Wharton and Bernard toured Germany together in 1913, and they corresponded frequently. Wharton also became a friend of Elisabetta ["Nicky"] MARIANO, who had joined the staff of I Tatti as librarian in 1918, coming to assist with Berenson's affairs. They are believed by many critics to have had a long-time affair. Nicky stayed with the Berensons for 40 years, and Edith Wharton came to regard her with an affection she reserved for few people. Wharton became, in addition, a longtime friend of Logan Pearsall Smith, Mary Berenson's brother, who accompanied her on her 1926 cruise aboard the chartered yacht *OSPREY*.

In *A BACKWARD GLANCE*, her 1934 memoir, Edith Wharton paid tribute to Berenson's influence when she recalled her enthusiasm for the travel books of the

Bernard Berenson (Beinecke Rare Book and Manuscript Library, Yale University)

1870s and 1880s of the "cultured dilettante" type, written by "gifted amateurs" such as Violet Paget ["Vernon LEE"], Walter PATER and John Addington SYMONDS. But then she began reading the work of Bernard Berenson, whose volumes on Italian painting combined "sternest scientific accuracy" with aesthetic sensibility. Berenson's achievement, according to Wharton, was to clear away the "sentimental undergrowth" left by the gifted amateur. Her own connoisseurship was thus engendered by her early intellectual encounter with his work, which pointed the way toward a technical approach to art history that Edith Wharton first emulated, then rejected. Bernard and Mary Berenson were among her closest lifelong friends, adding a dimension to her life it would not otherwise have had after her expatriation. In 1933, she dedicated her ninth volume of stories, HUMAN NATURE, to Berenson.

His biographer Ernest Samuels has called Berenson, who lived until 1959 and survived two world wars, "the legendary sage of I Tatti, the confidant of protégés and princes, and the serene diarist of a world transformed" (Samuels 432).

Berenson, Mary (1864–1945)   The wife of Bernard BERENSON, Mary was formerly the American-born Mary Pearsall Smith, the daughter of wealthy Quaker-bred parents of Philadelphia and the sister of the writer Logan Pearsall SMITH. She had a legal separation from her first husband, the barrister Frank Costelloe, while she led a life of intimacy with Berenson, whom she married in 1900 after Costelloe's death. She and Costelloe were the parents of two daughters, Rachel Conn (called "Ray") and Karin, who would later marry Virginia WOOLF's brother Adrian Stephens. At first Mary was not as fond of Edith Wharton as her husband, but after WORLD WAR I her "cautious admiration grew into genuine affection" (*EW* 327). For many years Edith Wharton visited them at the Villa I TATTI as she was en route between her two French homes, and they also stayed with her. Mary was the author of a *Guide to the Italian Pictures at Hampton Court* and a number of articles, including "The New and Old Art Criticism," "Sacred Pictures" and "The Woman Question in Novels," as well as articles in the *Pall Mall Gazette* and several book reviews. In 1936 she published *Across the Mediterranean*, an account of the trip she and Bernard Berenson made to Syria and Palestine in 1929; she gave Edith Wharton a copy for Christmas in 1936.

Berry, Walter (1859–1927)   Walter Van Rensselaer Berry, the second child of Nathaniel Berry and Catharine Van Rensselaer, was a distant cousin of Lucretia Rhinelander JONES. He was one of Edith Wharton's most loved lifelong friends. He grew up in Albany, NEW YORK, graduated from Harvard in 1881, traveled in EUROPE for a year and a half and then read privately for the bar. He became an international lawyer but also had a strong literary bent.

Edith Wharton first met him in 1883 at Bar Harbor, Maine. They spent several days bicycling, walking and conversing. Although they were eminently suited to each other, something kept Berry from proposing. He later stated that he felt, as a penniless lawyer, he could not offer Wharton a suitable marriage, and the moment had passed. Lewis doubts that his recollection was correct, believing that Berry was not sufficiently taken with Edith Wharton at the time to propose. From a wealthy family, Berry was far from "penniless," and in fact was drawn to women of a different type, less serious and more "frivolous and fluttery" than Edith Wharton, and was also bored by her focus on literary topics. She was ignorant of the "arts of love making" and was also

very shy (*EW* 49). It would be 14 years before their relationship was renewed, long after her marriage to Teddy WHARTON.

In 1897, Edith Wharton asked the young architect Ogden CODMAN of Boston to decorate the interior of their new home, "LAND'S END," in NEWPORT, Rhode Island. They discovered they agreed on the excesses in furnishings that were stylish at the time, and began to collaborate on a book, *The DECORATION OF HOUSES*, codifying their ideas. In its insistence on European standards of proportion and harmony, the book clarifies what Wharton found wanting in American concepts of house design. Wharton and Codman lay out guidelines for countering the unsightliness of American architecture and interior design by applying European principles of harmony and proportion. Berry visited the Whartons at Land's End as they worked on the book. In her memoir, *A BACKWARD GLANCE*, Edith Wharton states that he had been born with an "exceptionally sensitive literary instinct" as well as a fine critical sense. She asked him to look at their pages. He shouted with laughter, said "Come, let's see what can be done," and set to work making the "lump into a book" (*BG* 108). They submitted a preliminary draft, with some photographs, to SCRIBNER'S in early summer and, with the assistance of Berry, completed and revised the draft by September 1. It was published later that year.

In her memoir, Edith Wharton states that Berry had taught her all she knew "about the writing of clear concise English" (*BG* 108). He was a severe critic but respected the "artist's liberty." "He taught me," she recalled, "never to be satisfied with my own work, but never to let my inward conviction as to the rightness of anything I had done be affected by outside opinion" (*BG* 114).

After the Whartons built The MOUNT in 1902, Berry was a frequent houseguest. His career as an international lawyer led to his being one of the judges of the International Tribunal in Cairo, and they were apart for many years until ill health forced him to resign. At that time he came to live in PARIS. They seem never to have considered marriage. She wrote that, in everyone's life, there is a friend "who seems not a separate person, however dear and beloved, but an expansion, an interpretation, of one's self, the very meaning of one's soul." Their understanding endured throughout their lives; his thoughts and personality were "interwoven" with hers (*BG* 115–16). They traveled together (with servants) in Sicily, SPAIN and ITALY. In early 1915, Edith Wharton and Walter Berry made a journey to the front lines in the ARGONNE, delivering supplies. In 1917 he accompanied her on a three-week motor tour of the French colony of MOROCCO, arranged by General Hubert LYAUTEY, the governor-general. Over the years they wandered through "many lands," she recalled, and she saw with a "keenness doubled by his" (*BG* 117). Although Berry was certainly devoted to Wharton in his way, he was also something of a ladies' man and socially frivolous, causing her intermittent despair. Alfred WHITE, her butler and head of her household staff, once informed Jacques-Émile BLANCHE, her artist friend, who inquired about the possibility of marriage between them, "out of the many beautiful ladies always making up to him, Mrs. Wharton is the last one he would have sacrificed his liberty to" (*EW* 344). She eventually burned her 45-year correspondence with Berry, saving only the letters written when he advised her on literary matters (1897–1902) (*NGC* 111).

During World War I, Berry was president of the American Chamber of Commerce in Paris and acted as banker for the many expatriate Americans, including Wharton, who were having difficulty getting their funds cabled from the United States. After the war, when Wharton purchased the PAVILLON COLOMBE at St.-Brice-sous-Forêt outside Paris, he took over the lease on her apartment at 53, rue de Varenne.

Lewis states that he had been regarded as "the first American citizen in Paris" and, in 1927, took part in lengthy celebrations as the American Legion met in Paris. He died of his second paralytic stroke on October 12, 1927. His funeral on October 17 was an extremely lavish affair for a foreigner. A hearse drawn by four black horses led the procession along the Avenue George V to the American Pro-Cathedral, and representatives of the French president attended the service. Benstock gives a full account of the funeral, procession, and later problems at the Pavillon Colombe, where Wharton had established a small *chapelle ardente* with an altar (*NGC* 401–06). She planned to have a funeral mass and inter his ashes in the garden. The French police arrived to inform her that such an interment was illegal according to French law. It was not for 12 days that Berry's cousin, Harry Crosby, could arrange the final interment in the Protestant CIMETIÈRE DES GONARDS at Versailles, on the edge of the forest. Ten years later, by her expressed wish, Wharton was also buried there, near Berry's grave. Unfortunately, there was bickering later about the disposition of his possessions, described by Lewis (*EW* 476–77) and Auchincloss (*Edith Wharton: A Woman in Her Time*, 159–61).

Edith Wharton wrote Gaillard LAPSLEY that he had been "all that one being can be to another, in love, in friendship, in understanding" (*EW* 478). To John Hugh SMITH she expressed her sense of desolation during their last days together, "when he wanted me so close, & held me so fast, that all the old flame & glory came back, in the cold shadow of death & parting" (*Letters* 504). Edith Wharton wrote a memorial poem to him, "GARDEN VALEDICTORY," published in the January 1928 issue of *SCRIBNER'S MAGAZINE*.

Walter Berry, 1925 (Courtesy Lilly Library, Indiana University)

Lewis observes that, to Edith Wharton, Berry was the "*dearest*" man she had ever known, the kindest and wisest. He also points out, however, the controversy surrounding their relationship. He observes that, although Berry had penetrated more deeply than any American into "the world of French modernist art and letters" and was much liked by her French friends, he was detested by her English-speaking friends, except for Henry JAMES. Bernard BERENSON and others were shocked that her French friends had assumed he would marry her after her divorce (*EW* 478–79); there seems general critical agreement that such a marriage would not have been suitable, as Berry preferred more frivolous women than Edith Wharton. Whether he knew about Morton FULLERTON is uncertain, but Benstock believes he did not know the full extent of their relationship. For a number of years her LOVE DIARY was thought to refer to Berry.

According to Benstock, Wharton warded off two biographies of Berry, one by the French critic Gaston Riou, whose work neither had respected, and one by the young Leon EDEL, then completing a thesis on Henry James (*NGC* 405).

For further reading: James, *Letters to Walter Berry*.

"Best Man, The" Edith Wharton wrote this political short story in 1905 in the wake of a visit to the White House during Theodore ROOSEVELT's presidency. Published in *The HERMIT AND THE WILD WOMAN* (Scribner's, 1908), the story concerns a newly elected state governor who abides by his principles. He reveals a painful family secret instead of abandoning a colleague whose unsavory past may obstruct his support of an important honest policy. The governor tells himself, " 'Go ahead, and do the best you can for the country,' " hoping the public will evaluate how far a private calamity should be allowed to affect an otherwise unblemished life of public service. The critic for the English *Spectator* praised the story for its "fine picture of a really noble-minded American" (*CR* 160). Lewis, on the other hand, considers that the story shows "the author's lack of sureness in dealing with political figures" (*EW* 146).

"Bewitched"   This is a ghost story published in the collection HERE AND BEYOND (Appleton, 1926). Set in wintry NEW ENGLAND, it turns on the early sectional custom of putting to death women thought to be bewitched or to have supernatural powers. The descendants of the witch-hunting community, their stock remaining the same through various generations, include Mrs. Eliza Rutledge, a shrewd Yankee woman, self-contained, cold and solitary, drawn with as much skill as Zenobia Frome in ETHAN FROME. She has been victimized by a crime, which the perpetrator pretends to have carried out while "haunted." She calls as witnesses a church deacon and two farmers of the village, citing Scripture to show there has been a revival of witchcraft; she then uses her husband's explanation to further her own purposes.

L. P. Hartley once wrote that each of Edith Wharton's stories "makes its own private effort to win a foothold in the imagination" (*CR* 420). "Bewitched" succeeds in winning such a foothold, evoking another aspect of the New England of *Ethan Frome*, a place "far away from humanity."

For further reading: Fedorko, " 'Forbidden Things': Gothic Confrontation with the Feminine in 'The Young Gentlemen' and 'Bewitched.' "

Bewitched **(teleplay, 1983)**   *See* Appendix II.

Blanche, Jacques-Émile (1861–1942)   A distinguished portrait painter and man of letters, Blanche was among Edith Wharton's closest French friends. He spoke and wrote English fluently, and he and his wife often visited London, where they had friends in the worlds of art, society and letters. They had a half-timbered house at Auteuil near Paris, where, in Wharton's words, "pre-war Paris was first brought into familiar contact with English artists, savants and men of letters, and made aware of the riches of intellectual and artistic life in England" (*BG* 283).

Henry JAMES sat for Blanche in 1908 for a portrait commissioned by Edith Wharton. She wrote Sara NORTON that "while the result is distinctly *good* I'm not sure it was worth the price!" (*Letters* 146). In *A BACKWARD GLANCE*, however, she insists it was the only one ever done that rendered James "*as he really was*" (*BG* 175). On Sunday, Blanche, also an accomplished musician, would have friends, including George Moore,

André GIDE, the painter Walter Rickett and Diaghilev (creator of the Ballets Russes), in his studio or for tea in the garden. According to Wharton, his workroom was hidden away, but the high walls of his studio/living room held pictures by Degas, Renoir, Manet, Corot, Boudin, Manet and Whistler. He painted portraits of Igor Stravinsky, Thomas HARDY, Dégas, Debussy, George Moore and Marcel PROUST.

The Blanches' summer home was a small stone manor-house in Offranville, near Dieppe. Wharton often stayed there for a fortnight or so during the summer; Blanche noted that during her visits "our home assumed suddenly another air; there was something brighter in the atmosphere." She advised them about garden plantings, and they drove her about to call on elderly aristocratic neighbors; she would later distill her impressions of them in some of her fictional portraits (*EW* 323–24). During one of her visits, Wharton met young Jean COCTEAU, the future poet, novelist, essayist and film director. She wrote BERENSON of the encounter: "little Cocteau, whom I delight in . . . I don't know of any other spectacle in his class" (*EW* 324).

Portrait of Igor Stravinsky by Jacques-Émile Blanche. From The Book of the Homeless *(1916)* (Courtesy Picture Collection, the Library of Virginia)

One afternoon toward the end of June 1914, Edith Wharton joined the Blanches and a group of their friends for a tea party in the garden of their home at Auteuil. It was there that she first heard the news of the assassination of Archduke Francis Ferdinand of Austria-Hungary in Sarajevo by a Serbian nationalist. She recalled later that a "momentary shiver" ran through the company, but few who were present realized the implications the act might have, i.e., reprisals by the Central Powers, including Austria-Hungary, against the Allies, including England, France and Belgium (*BG* 336). War was declared just a little over a month later. When Wharton began soliciting contributions for *The BOOK OF THE HOMELESS*, Blanche responded with portraits or photographs of portraits of Thomas Hardy, George Moore and Igor Stravinsky (Price, *The End of the Age of Innocence*, 60).

After the war, a fictionalized account of the wartime flight of the Blanche family from Normandy was privately published under a pseudonym: *Les Cloches de St. Amarain*. They had made their way to a convent on the Rhone River (*NGC* 298). Wharton liked the volume and sent a copy to her friend John HUGH SMITH.

Blashfield, Edwin (1848–1936)   The noted artist and his wife, Evangeline Wilbour Blashfield (1858–1918), were within the larger perimeter of the "GENTEEL CIRCLE," the influential group of American editors and writers whose most productive years bridged the period from the end of the Civil War until about 1910. Edwin Blashfield was an artist of some note. He trained in PARIS, decorated the central dome of the Library of Congress and was represented at the World's Columbian Exposition of 1893 in Chicago. He was much in demand as a periodical illustrator. He had also exhibited at 12 Paris salons between 1874 and 1891 and painted genre pictures.

Evangeline Wilbour Blashfield, of New England Puritan stock, grew up in an intellectually rich environment Edith Wharton might have envied; it was also marked by a strong sense of cultural mission. Her mother, Charlotte Beebe Wilbour, had known Ralph Waldo EMERSON and Nathaniel Hawthorne as a child. She later worked with Susan B. Anthony for women's rights and, with Kate Field and Jane Croly, founded Sorosis when women were excluded from the New York Press Club dinner for Charles Dickens.

The Blashfields were married in July 1881 in Paris, and began traveling, studying and writing. Together they wrote a number of articles about ITALY for *Scribner's*, later compiled as *Italian Cities* (Scribner's, 1901). Separately, each also wrote learned reviews, articles and books in the fields of art and literature. Evangeline also wrote plays and learned essays. They did not become expatriated, as Wharton did, but continued to live in NEW YORK.

"A Woman's Head" (1915), Edwin Howland Blashfield. From The Book of the Homeless *(1916)* (Courtesy Picture Collection, the Library of Virginia)

Edith Wharton reviewed *Italian Cities*, complimenting them on their ability to detect some "unrecorded phase of art, some detail insignificant enough to have dropped out of the ever-growing catalogue of her treasures." She found in their book "an admirably drawn contrast between the critical standpoint of artist and amateur . . . that might be written up in every critic's laboratory, and called it the most interesting book on Italy to have appeared since John Addington Symonds's volumes." She regretted not being able to trace the "innumerable threads of suggestion branching off from every subject on which they touch" (*UCW* 63–66). Edwin Blashfield reviewed Wharton's *The DECORATION OF HOUSES* (1902), praising its contribution to American taste when the country was in an "aesthetically formative period." They read her first novel, *The VALLEY OF DECISION*, in duplicate, each with a copy, exclaiming over individual passages. In 1915 Edwin Blashfield contributed a drawing, *A Woman's Head*, to *The BOOK OF THE HOMELESS*.

Bliss, Mildred Barnes (1879–1969)   The beautiful and stylish wife of the diplomat Robert BLISS, Mildred Bliss was the daughter of Demas Barnes, U.S. congressman from Ohio; she and her husband were married in 1908. Bernard BERENSON called her "Perfect Bliss" (*EW* 372). Robert Bliss, who had served in St. Petersburg, became secretary of the American Embassy in Paris in 1912; after World War I began, Mildred Bliss and Edith Wharton worked together on various war relief efforts, especially those sponsored by the Red Cross. In 1915 Mildred accompanied Edith Wharton and Walter BERRY to VERDUN, the first of four trips to the front lines Wharton made. They went in her Mercedes, driven by her chauffeur, Charles COOK.

Mildred and Edith Wharton sometimes found it difficult to collaborate on war relief projects. Mildred, who had gone to a private school in Paris, knew the city at least as well as Edith Wharton and found her coworker to be capricious and often preoccupied with unnecessary details, while Wharton believed she had a bad effect on her friend and made her "horrid." Mildred Bliss later softened her attitude toward Edith Wharton and joined in the unsuccessful effort to obtain the Nobel Prize for her in 1927. After the Blisses toured America in 1932, Mildred wrote Edith Wharton to apprise her of the widespread economic depression, which was soon reflected in the rates she was offered for her fiction.

Bliss, Robert Woods (1875–1962)   Robert and Mildred BLISS were longtime friends of Edith Wharton's. He was a career diplomat; in 1912 he became secretary of the American Embassy in PARIS. In 1920 the Blisses purchased the Dumbarton Oaks estate in the Georgetown section of Washington, D.C. Edith Wharton's niece Beatrix FARRAND began working on the gardens there in 1921 and was involved in their creation and refinement for 30 years, until she formally retired from all projects in 1951. The estate has belonged to Harvard University since 1940 and is open to the public. It houses a museum of Byzantine art that was once supervised by William Royall TYLER, a friend of the Blisses and of Wharton, and a famous museum of pre-Columbian art.

In 1926, Robert Bliss, then the American ambassador to Sweden, led a move to obtain the 1927 NOBEL PRIZE for Edith Wharton. YALE UNIVERSITY sent a nomination to the Nobel Committee, calling her "the foremost living creative literary artist of America" (*EW* 481). It was signed by six prominent Yale professors. Others who supported the nomination were Lord BALFOUR, Paul BOURGET, and Jules Cambon, formerly the French ambassador to the United States and Britain. Wharton did not receive the prize, however. The recipients were Grazia Deledda and Henri Bergson (*EW* 481–82).

"Blond Beast, The"   "The Blond Beast" was published in the collection *TALES OF MEN AND GHOSTS* (Scribner's, 1910). The story concerns a young man, Hugh Millner,

who has been employed as the secretary of a wealthy philanthropist, Orlando G. Spence. Spence finds himself at odds with his idealistic son, Draper, who is preoccupied with the problem of the morality of goodness, whether it may be achieved by philanthropy *per se*, and the possibility of separating "conduct" from "creed." The plot turns on a scandal involving a Brazilian rubber plantation; Millner finds he must ultimately define his own scruples; previously unprincipled, he acquires, as Lewis puts it, a "moral sense" (*EW* 296).

Boccon-Gibod, André   Parisian lawyer who handled Edith Wharton's divorce; she met him through Léon BÉLOGOU. He came to admire her very much. During World War I he served as legal counsel to the AMERICAN HOSTELS FOR REFUGEES committee. In 1927 he assisted with her purchase of STE.-CLAIRE CHÂTEAU. In May 1936 she wrote a memorandum of funeral instructions stating that her French will was either in the bedroom safe at the PAVILLON COLOMBE or in the hands of Boccon-Gibod.

"Bolted Door, The"   "The Bolted Door" was the first story in the collection *TALES OF MEN AND GHOSTS* (Scribner's, 1910). The macabre plot is oddly plausible in its reliance on the powerful new specialty of psychiatry. The story concerns the plight of a failed playwright, Hubert Granice, who has suffered rejection of all his work, both comedies and tragedies, from the "light curtain-raiser" through the "bourgeois-realistic" to the "lyrical-romantic." He has even subsidized a production called *The Lee Shore* with his inheritance, only to see the week's performances draw a declining audience. He stops short of shooting himself and decides, instead, to confess that he obtained his inheritance by murdering his cousin.

His offer of atonement fails, just as his dramatic works have done. His confession is considered a revelation of insanity by both doctors and lawyers. Granice tells the story of his murder to his personal attorney, a close friend who is an editor, the District Attorney, a detective (actually an "alienist" or psychiatrist in disguise) and a young journalist, none of whom believe him—the story is too perfect, too pat. There is no flaw in his alibi. His friends conspire to cure him of his delusion; he realizes the "visible conformities" of his life disprove the possibility of one "fierce secret deviation" (*CSS* II, 31). Increasingly obsessed with proving his guilt, he approaches a young woman in Union Square with his account, is arrested, and sent to a "large quiet establishment" to reconsider his story. Peter McCarren, the reporter, finally believes Granice has told the truth, but is content to leave him in the asylum: "I couldn't hang the poor devil, could I?"

The SUPERNATURAL appealed to Edith Wharton as a subject; she defended it in *The WRITING OF FICTION* and the preface to *TALES OF MEN AND GHOSTS*.

Book of the Homeless, The   In 1915 Wharton edited a gift book, *The Book of the Homeless*, the sales of which were intended to benefit war relief efforts, including the AMERICAN HOSTELS FOR REFUGEES and the CHILDREN OF FLANDERS Rescue Committee. Alan Price has called it "the most artistically varied and beautifully made book to come out of WORLD WAR I" (Price, "The Making of Edith Wharton's *Book of the Homeless*," 20). Published by SCRIBNER'S, at Wharton's request, it was designed by the leading American printer and book designer Daniel Berkeley UPDIKE. She wrote Charles SCRIBNER that if the book were designed by Updike it would have an "international bibliophile value it could not otherwise offer" (EW to CS, July 1915, Scribner Archives, Princeton).

Edith Wharton solicited contributions from distinguished artists, writers and composers. Among the contributors were Theodore ROOSEVELT, Rupert Brooke, Sarah Bernhardt, Eleanora Duse, Auguste Rodin, Paul Claudel, Anna de NOAILLES, Max Beerbohm, Charles Dana Gibson, Jacques-Émile BLANCHE, Maurice Maeterlinck, Thomas HARDY, John Masefield, William Dean HOWELLS, John Singer SARGENT, Claude Monet, Joseph CONRAD, Henry JAMES, Edmund Gosse, and Paul BOURGET (*EW* 379–80). Maxfield PARRISH turned her down when she invited him to design the book cover, which was a great disappointment. Rudyard KIPLING, whose son later died in battle, also declined her invitation, responding that he was too busy with nonliterary work to take part.

Many of the submissions were in French and Italian; in *A BACKWARD GLANCE* Wharton remarked that she "ached with the labour of translating (in a few weeks' time) all but one of the French and Italian contributions. . . . the overwhelming needs of the hour doubled every one's strength, and the book was ready on time" (*BG* 350). Unfortunately, publication was delayed until January 1916 and the pre-Christmas sales were late; it had originally been planned as a Christmas 1915 gift book.

Scribner's only charged for the actual costs of setting and printing the book, not for advertising or editorial services. There were three editions: a trade edition for $5, a deluxe edition on special paper for $125 and a grand deluxe edition of 50 copies in large format on French handmade paper at $50, all of which were sold immediately. Sales of all three brought about $1,500. The manuscripts and drawings were later auctioned in New York, raising another sum of nearly $7,000. Edith Wharton's sister-in-law, Mary (Minnie) Cadwalader JONES, arranged to hold it in the American Art Galleries on West 23rd Street. Total sales for the book and the auction were about $9,000. Edith Wharton remarked that the "book is certain to become very valuable some day, and I have no fear of its future." Today it is a valuable collectors' item.

"Pegasus," Léon Bonnat. From The Book of the Homeless *(1916)* (Courtesy Picture Collection, the Library of Virginia)

For further reading: Price, "The Making of Edith Wharton's *The Book of the Homeless*."

"Bottle of Perrier, A"   First published as "A Bottle of Evian" in *The Saturday Evening Post* in March 1926 and collected in CERTAIN PEOPLE (Appleton, 1930), this murder mystery is one of Edith Wharton's better-known short stories and was praised by critics when it was published. Berenson erroneously believed she wrote it in a day (*EW* 522), but Benstock states it was probably written within about a week's time (*NGC* 429). It is set in the North African desert, probably a town in MOROCCO, where an American archaeologist, Medford, arrives to visit an English friend, Henry Almodham. He is told that his host is absent on some antiquarian investigations but will soon return. Medford is attended by his English cockney manservant Gosling for several days as he waits for his host and for the caravan to bring a case of Perrier water, since he doesn't drink wine and is uneasy about the local well water. Events mount to a gruesome dénouement worthy of Poe. Graham Greene called it a "superb horror story" (*CR* 537).

Edith Wharton uses her knowledge of Morocco, gained from her 1917 visit, in this story and also in "The SEED OF THE FAITH," to depict a foreign, enigmatic setting imbued with malevolent overtones.

For further reading: Singley, "Gothic Borrowings and Innovations in Edith Wharton's 'A Bottle of Perrier.' "

Bourget, Minnie David (c. 1866–1933) The wife of Paul BOURGET, Minnie Bourget was much admired by Edith Wharton. When she first met the Bourgets at NEWPORT in 1893, she was impressed by Minnie, whom she described as his "quiet and exquisite companion." She referred to her as the "Tanagra Madonna" with "remote gray eyes and sensitive mouth." With her "delicate oval of a small face crowned by heavy braids of brown hair," she seemed to combine "the gravity of a mediæval Virgin" with the "miniature elegance of a Greek figurine," as she later put it in *A BACKWARD GLANCE* (*BG* 104). Minnie seemed to feel she was her husband's shadow, but Edith Wharton eventually came to penetrate her reserve and to communicate with her on common ground, such as poetry, art and the love of "visible beauty." In her memoir, she recalled finding it impossible to describe the "Psyche-like tremor of those folded but never quiet wings of hers; and now that she is dead, and the wings are shut, there is a part of me which is dead also" (*BG* 105). Minnie was Jewish, a fact that made no difference to their friendship despite an element of what some critics have perceived as ANTI-SEMITISM in Wharton's fiction. It is not known whether Minnie knew of, or was disturbed by, Wharton's portrayals of Simon Rosedale in THE HOUSE OF MIRTH.

During the years of Edith Wharton's EXPATRIATION, the Bourgets were among here closest friends, attending her dinner parties and entertaining her in their apartment. In the late 1920s, Minnie developed senile dementia and spent the last five years of her life in a sanatorium. Her husband took a small house nearby and visited her regularly. Edith Wharton believed he had been partly responsible for her condition, as he "shut her away from life" (*NGC* 412).

Bourget, Paul (1852–1935) French novelist and critic, whose work was important to the development of the psychological novel probing inner consciousness. His best-known novels are *Cruelle énigme* (1885), *le Disciple* (1889) and *l'Étape* (1903). His critical works include *Études de portraits* (1888) and *Pages de doctrine et de critique* (1912). He also wrote works of travel, including *Sensations d'Italie* (*Impressions of Italy*, 1892) and *Outre-Mer: Impressions of America* (1895), a volume of essays about AMERICA, originally written for the *New York Herald Tribune* and first published in FRANCE.

In 1893 Bourget and his wife Minnie came to America to do research for the essays in the latter volume. They attended the World's Columbian Exposition in Chicago and, in NEWPORT, called on the Whartons, to whom they had been given a letter of introduction by a cousin of Teddy WHARTON's mother. They were among the first guests at LAND'S END. At that time Bourget was considered one of the most distinguished novelists in France and was about to be elected to the elite ACADÉMIE FRANÇAISE. A friendship developed immediately between Wharton and Bourget. Teddy was glad to show Newport to the Bourgets, and Paul and Edith Wharton, according to Lewis, exchanged views on fictional techniques (*EW* 69). He also admired her antiques and talked with her about books and writers. She later figured in one of his essays as the "intellectual tomboy" he found in Newport, "who has read everything, understood everything, not superficially, but really, with an energy of culture that could put to shame the whole Parisian fraternity of letters. . . . there is not a book of Darwin, Huxley, Spencer, Renan, Taine, which she has not studied, not a painter or sculptor of whose work she could not compile a catalogue" (*EW* 69). Bourget might have been summarizing Wharton's reading in the "kingdom" of her father's library, combined with the knowledge gleaned from her European travels.

In the summer of 1899 the Bourgets were taking the mineral baths at Pfäfers, near Ragatz, in Switzerland, where the Whartons joined them for a few days before going on to Splügen, described in the opening chapter of *ITALIAN BACKGROUNDS*. That journey through mountains they thought were the "Bergamasque Alps" (they were not, it turned out) was a magical time nevertheless and formed part of the impetus for Wharton's first novel, *The VALLEY OF DECISION*.

Bourget introduced Edith Wharton to Vernon LEE, the brilliant British expatriate who lived near Florence, and who was to prove of invaluable assistance when Wharton wrote the articles later compiled as *ITALIAN VILLAS AND THEIR GARDENS*. After *The HOUSE OF MIRTH* had been published in 1905, Bourget presented the young French critic Charles DU BOS to Edith Wharton. She asked him to choose the best translator for the novel—there had been many applicants for this task—and he selected Du Bos. After the French edition, *LA DEMEURE DE LIESSE*, was published and acclaimed in 1906, Bourget judged it "propitious," as Lewis puts it, to introduce her to French social and intellectual circles. He brought his "highborn and gifted friends" to tea at the Hotel Domenici in PARIS, where she was staying. He "put his Academician's stamp of approval upon [her] as that excellent combination, a *femme du monde* who took her creative work with the utmost seriousness." It was during these conversations over tea at the Hotel Domenici that Wharton encountered "the milieu she had long heard about, where the artistic and intellectual mingled easily with the socially distinguished" (*EW* 161).

In 1904, Edith Wharton and her husband visited the Bourgets at their villa, Les Plantiers, in Costebelle, near HYÈRES, and their friendship flourished. After her divorce, the Bourgets often dined with her in Paris and at Hyères, and she was a frequent visitor to Costebelle. After WORLD WAR I began, Bourget contributed an essay, "Après un An" ("One Year Later"), to *The BOOK OF THE HOMELESS*, the compilation of essays, sketches and other contributions Wharton edited to benefit the war effort.

The Bourgets were perpetually anxious about their health and often took rest cures. In 1914, Edith Wharton wrote Bernard BERENSON that Paul was increasingly " 'maniaque' about drugs, diseases and diets" (*NGC* 293). In later years, she felt he was overly solicitous about Minnie. She declared that it made her shudder "to think how those two played at being ill till the Furies could stand it no longer" (*NGC* 412).

Bourget was as accomplished a writer of nonfiction as of fiction. His *Impressions of Italy*, published in 1892, begins in the vein of the early 19th century, inquiring: "Reader, do you still cherish . . . a passionate admiration for Italy, and especially for the secluded spots which have longest resisted the leveling influences of cosmopolitanism?" He goes on to offer a "diary of a long excursion made in the autumn of 1890 through Tuscany, Umbria, the Marches, Otranto, and Calabria, by a novelist on a holiday who has the misfortune to be neither an archaeologist nor an art critic" (Bourget, *Impressions of Italy*, *passim*). Bourget's polite disclaimer does not mask the fact that, throughout the book, he is a thoroughly knowledgeable art critic. He discusses, for example, the works of the obscure artist Luca Signorelli in depth, mentioning the personal account of him given by Vasari (the Renaissance architect much admired by Edith Wharton and discussed in *Italian Villas and Their Gardens*), and then describing an Annunciation of Benvenuto di Giovanni. He brings to travel writing the wide-ranging background of the European connoisseur whose perspective has been enlarged by a knowledge of Plato and DANTE, and whose discrimination has been honed by years spent in museums. His modesty conceals a thoroughgoing sophistication and a knowledge of languages and of art equal to, if not excelling, that of Wharton.

Paul Bourget (l.), Edith Wharton and Joseph Conrad at La Madrague, near Giens, France, c.1921 (Courtesy Claudine Lesage)

Edith Wharton wrote a tribute to Bourget, "SOU-VENIRS DE BOURGET OUTREMER," after his death in 1935, believing it would be a corrective to articles written by younger or middle-aged " 'parties' who knew only the old stuffy Academician" (*Letters* 591). The essay contains many details about the Bourgets' travels through the western United States with John and Isabella Stewart GARDNER and about the Italian journeys the Whartons and Bourgets took together. In a cautionary note, however, Wharton complained that with age Paul became "more sedentary," refusing to make any detours to major sights from the set Paris-Costebelle itinerary they followed twice each year by automobile. Such a lack of curiosity and zest for travel was incomprehensible to Wharton, who even in her final summer was hoping to return to Venice.

For further reading: Tintner, "Edith Wharton and Paul Bourget"; Tintner, "Portrait of Edith Wharton in Bourget's 'L'Indicatrice' "; Vickers, "Women and Wealth: F. Scott Fitzgerald, Edith Wharton and Paul Bourget"; Wharton, "Souvenirs de Bourget outremer," (trans. Wegener as "Memories of Bourget Overseas").

Boylston   *See* SON AT THE FRONT, A.

Boyne, Martin   *See* CHILDREN, THE.

Brant, Anderson   *See* SON AT THE FRONT, A.

Brant, Julia   *See* SON AT THE FRONT, A.

"Bread Upon the Waters"   Short story published in William Randolph HEARST's *INTERNATIONAL–COSMOPOL-ITAN* magazine in 1934. Rutger B. JEWETT of APPLETON's acted as Wharton's agent and obtained $5,000 for it, the highest payment she had ever received for a work of its length. Jewett also sold it to the movies as "Charm Incorporated," under which title it was collected in *The WORLD OVER* (Appleton-Century, 1936). It had first been called "Kouradjine Limited," was a satire about Hollywood and oil barons, and had been rejected by Gertrude Lane, editor of *Woman's Home Companion*.

A well-to-do American bachelor, James Targatt, marries Nadeja Kouradjine, an expatriate Russian woman of aristocratic origins whose father had been chamberlain to Czar Nicholas II and owned vast landed estates. Their family has been overturned and exiled in the course of the Bolshevik Revolution. When she moves into his large flat, Nadeja dismisses Targatt's efficient German cook/housekeeper and brings along a tribe of charming, "long-lashed," needy brothers and sisters, who are musicians and artists. She insists that they all dine out each night in various ethnic restaurants. Targatt's efforts as a wage earner are increasingly diverted from business to fund-raising to support her impoverished in-laws.

The Kouradjines acquire a decided social currency as titled emigrés and succeed in marrying into NEW YORK's nouveaux riches. As soon as one of them is married off or employed, several others arrive to take his or her place. A Norwegian portrait painter, Axel Svengaart, is taken up in New York and asks to paint Nadeja, presenting complications eventually resolved by Targatt.

The story is regarded by Lewis and some present-day critics as "slight," perhaps because of its somewhat shallow characterization and its resolution. It was, however, praised for its delicate irony by one contemporary reviewer, who termed it one of Wharton's best short stories. It shows careful study of the commercial American magazine market of the 1930s, an era very different from that of the early 20th century when the literary periodicals flourished and such stories as "THE MUSE's TRAGEDY" and "THE PELICAN" were published.

One reviewer commented that it would make a "sprightly skit for some revue" (*CR* 538), and it was made into a film under the title *Strange Wives* (*see* Appendix II).

Brenta Riviera   The area surrounding the canal/river between VENICE and Padua, where the Venetian aristocracy once spent the *villeggiatura*, or vacation season (June–July and October–November). Edith Wharton and her friend Vernon LEE both wrote of life in the villas along the Brenta. *The VALLEY OF DECISION* is partly set there in an imaginary manor house owned by the Procuratore Brà, which has a trompe l'oeil purportedly by TIEPOLO. Wharton also mentions the Brenta Riviera in ITALIAN BACKGROUNDS and ITALIAN VILLAS AND THEIR GARDENS. The grand villas are also associated with the COMMEDIA DELL'ARTE, a constant source of fascination to Edith Wharton. Some of the gardens have statuary modeled on the stock characters of this kind of theater.

About 70 villas were built along the Brenta, beginning in the 15th century, by wealthy Venetians who owned fertile riverside farms and wished to supervise their cultivation while on holiday with their families. Most of them are visible from the water. Architectural styles range from the austerity of the 16th century to the fanciful baroque of the 17th century to the rational, restrained classicism of the 18th century. The Villa Pisani (or Villa Nazionale), in Strà, owned by the Italian government, is a palace rather than a villa and was once the residence of the abdicated emperor of Austria. The ballroom ceiling was painted by Tiepolo, an artist Edith Wharton greatly admired.

The Brenta Riviera was well known to Dante, who mentions it in his *Inferno* and *Paradiso*. Voltaire's Candide visited Signor Pococurante on the Brenta, and Byron composed *Childe Harold's Pilgrimage* and *Don Juan* at the Palazzo Foscarini, the villa at Mira in which he settled in 1817. George SAND walked along the Brenta, and William Dean HOWELLS described it in *Venetian Life* (1867).

Originally gilded barges transported noble families, as depicted by Canaletto and other artists. In the 18th century, a canopied and inlaid passenger vessel was built, *Il Burchiello*, providing more comfortable travel than horse-drawn carriages. GOETHE rode in this vessel from Padua to Venice in 1786 and described it in his *Italian Journey.*

Breuil de Saint-Germain, Jean du (1873–1915) French sociologist and army officer, killed February 22, 1915. In 1912 Edith Wharton had gone to SPAIN with him and another friend, Countess Rosa de FITZ-JAMES, the first time she had visited the northern part of the country. He had fallen in love with Bessy Lodge, widow of Wharton's friend Bay LODGE, who was living in PARIS with her children, but the Lodge family had disapproved of the marriage and threatened to deprive her of her children if they married (*NGC* 316).

Jean du Breuil de Saint-Germain was sympathetic toward feminism and wrote several essays about women's issues, an aberrant position for a French politician (French women could not vote until 1944). After his death, which happened as he was searching the battlefield for one of his wounded men, Wharton wrote a tribute published in the *REVUE HEBDOMADAIRE* praising the effort he devoted to the goal of "the improvement of society." She observed that, in Spain, he had been less moved by the landscape than by his worry over the imagined pain of "long generations of the dead," which he regarded with the same *"thirst for justice,* that he placed at the service of his fellow citizens" (*UCW* 199–201).

Brownell, William Crary (1851–1928) An American editor, literary critic and journalist, Brownell served on the staff of a number of publications, including the *New York World* and *The Nation*. He was a valued literary consultant to Charles SCRIBNER for over 40 years and corresponded frequently with Edith Wharton about her books published by SCRIBNER'S. He sought to promote an understanding of the culture of the past and wrote a number of learned essays. He was the author of *French Traits* (1888), *French Art* (1892), *Victorian Prose Masters* (1901), *American Prose Masters* (1909), *Criticism* (1914), *Standards* (1917), *The Genius of Style* (1924), and of *Democratic Distinction in America* (1927) and *the Spirit of Society* (1927). His wife, the former Virginia Sherbourne of NEWPORT, suffered a nervous collapse in 1897 and lived her remaining years in a house in Narragansett, R.I., with a companion. Brownell then made his home at the New York Athletic Club, refusing social invitations and concentrating on his literary labors.

In 1896 Edith Wharton submitted the manuscript she and Ogden CODMAN had prepared, *The DECORATION OF HOUSES*, to Scribner's; it was accepted on the advice of Brownell, who believed it would appeal "to the intelligent and educated rather than to the most numerous public" (*EW* 77). After several of her essays on ITALY had been published in SCRIBNER'S MAGAZINE, Wharton pleaded with Brownell for their compilation in book form, stating that she believed the book would sell well, for there was a "great rush to Italy every summer now on the Mediterranean steamers, & people so often ask me where these articles are to be found—" (*Letters* 86).

ITALIAN BACKGROUNDS was at one time planned for publication in 1904, the same year as *ITALIAN VILLAS AND THEIR GARDENS*, which she was writing for the Century Publishing Company. She asked Brownell if there would be a conflict, and his reply tells much about the polite, even courtly, state of American publishing at the time. He admitted that the "instinctive feeling" one would have on hearing another publisher was bringing out a book by the same author with a similar title would be annoyance, but little harm would actually be done: "When the houses are of the same grade each gets the benefits of the advertising of the other, while neither is put in a position of carrying the other if the other were an inferior house that had no reputation and did little if any advertising." He concluded that even if both books were published at the same time, without an interval of five months more or less, *Italian Backgrounds* would not reduce sales of *Italian Villas and Their Gardens* at all, because "the gain in widening the interest in the general subject w'd more than atone for any loss vaguely to be anticipated." (William Crary Brownell to Edith Wharton, October 5, 1903; letter in the Scribner Archives, Firestone Li-brary, Princeton University.)

Edith Wharton thought of Brownell as America's most distinguished man of letters and regretted that his reclusive lifestyle had prevented her being able to offer him hospitality in her New York town house. Their correspondence about Scribner's books spanned nearly three decades. When he died in 1928, Wharton was asked to write Brownell's obituary for *Scribner's Magazine*. She remarked that his "real self" seemed to dwell in a "recess of contemplation," and that she felt closer to him in their correspondence than in their rare personal meetings (*BG* 145). To Wharton he was the "most discerning literary critic" of her day, establishing a standard that was "classical without being academic" and that combined open-mindedness with "an unwavering perception of final values" (*UCW* 205, 209). Brownell was closely associated in her mind with Edward BURLINGAME, editor of *Scribner's Magazine* for many years. They were editors in what George SANTAYANA termed the "genteel tradition," adhering to the highest literary and ethical standards.

Bry, Mrs. Wellington   *See HOUSE OF MIRTH, THE.*

Buccaneers, The   This was Edith Wharton's final novel, begun in 1934; it had been anticipated as one of her more promising novels. After her death in 1937, when it was about three-fourths complete, it was published in 1938, with a note of appreciation by Gaillard LAPS-LEY, by APPLETON AND COMPANY. It was in print only briefly before being republished in 1993, together with the scenario Wharton left for the entire novel. Viola Winner, the editor, has characterized it as "a modern novel looking backwards" and observes that the title may have come from John Esquemeling's *The Buccaneers of America* (1678) (Winner, Introduction, xvii, xxi).

The *donneé*, or given situation, is reminiscent of that in *The CUSTOM OF THE COUNTRY*; both novels concern the capture of European titles through aristocratic matches. The form is a historical romance, taking place in Saratoga Springs, New York City and ENGLAND between 1873 and 1877. The return to the fashionable milieu of the 1870s allows not only a historical perspective, but one conducive to satire of the sort found in *The AGE OF INNOCENCE* and the OLD NEW YORK novellas. The world of *The Buccaneers* is different, however, in that Saratoga Springs is an environment somewhat more lax than the rigid NEW YORK of the Mingotts and Van der Luydens. The daughters of the parvenues help each other assail the bastions of social position in New York, or, failing that, in England. The novel concerns the fortunes of five girls who are friends: Virginia and Annabel ("Nan") St George, Lizzie and Mabel Elmsworth and Conchita Closson, who is of mysterious Brazilian ancestry. They are far more free and companionable than May Welland in *The Age of Innocence*, to whose world they aspire.

Bauer has observed that Edith Wharton's marriage plots do not "hinge on the success or failure of the individual, but on the entire class and racial heritage of the eligible suitors and women 'out' in society" (Bauer, 179). Wharton's original scenario describes the plot as based on the attempt by three American mothers, Mrs. St George, Mrs. Elmsworth and Mrs. Closson, to launch their daughters in New York, where their wealthy husbands have no social standing. The daughters are the "buccaneers" of the title. Their ordinary origins count against them, although their beauty is recognized. They are admired at Saratoga Springs, Long Branch and White Sulphur Springs, but fail at NEWPORT, where the "best people" go, and in New York. Mrs. St George's hairdresser has kept her informed of the activities of the "aristocracy," such as assemblies and operas, just as Mrs. Heeny, the masseuse, retails stories of the "best" families to Mrs. Abner Spragg and Undine in *The CUSTOM OF THE COUNTRY*. Nevertheless, the three families are still excluded.

Mrs. St George hires a governess, Laura Testvalley, for her youngest daughter, Nan, 16, who is not yet "out," to provide social rather than academic training. Miss Testvalley, of middle age, has been employed by the "best" houses in New York and is of Italian origin (the name is corrupted from "Testavaglia"). She is supposed to have been the granddaughter of a leading dissident in the 1848 revolution during the Italian Risorgimento, or period of unification, as well as a relation of the poet Dante Gabriel Rossetti. Miss Testvalley becomes very attached to Nan, and advises Mrs. St George to take the girls to England for the London season rather than attempt to "try Newport" again. Conchita Closson and the Elmsworth girls persuade their parents to let them go also. The three families, although rivals, draw strength from their solidarity. Miss Testvalley leads them "like a general," and as soon as Virginia St George finds a noble English husband, Lord Seadown, she seeks one for Nan. Nan is the "least beautiful" of the girls but the "most brilliant and seductive," and she suddenly captures the young duke of Tintagel, the "greatest match in England." Conchita Closson, daughter of a Brazilian divorcée, marries Lord Richard Marable, a connection that horrifies his mother, since her skin is "dark." Lizzie Elmsworth marries a young member of Parliament, Hector Robinson. Nevius observes that Edith Wharton is "frankly and in a thoroughly Jamesian sense delighted" with the American girls she has created, who enter the Saratoga Springs hotel dining room "like a branch hung with blossoms"; the American girl is "the world's highest achievement" (Nevius, 238; *Buccaneers*, Winner ed., 155).

Their success in marrying into the British nobility brings only disillusionment to the American heiresses, however—especially Nan, whose perception of her entrapment is the principal subject of the final third of the unfinished novel. Nan, a poetic and idealistic girl, finds that her husband is obsessed with clocks and, in Winner's phrase, an "emotional cipher." He cannot sympathize with his tenants and refuses to take steps to correct their infected milk; he is unable to empathize with Nan or to understand her dreams and ambitions, "in which a desire to better the world alternated with a longing for solitude and poetry." She miscarries her baby trying to assist his diseased tenants and thereafter fails to produce an heir to the line. She really loves Guy Thwarte, a poor officer in the Guards, who lives in a charming Gloucestershire home, Honourslove, with his widowed father, Sir Helmsley Thwarte. Sir Helmsley courts Laura Testvalley, and marriage seems imminent until he realizes that she sympathizes with Nan's unhappiness; he suspects her of plotting to help Nan leave her husband for Guy. Miss Testvalley, the "great old adventuress," for the first time seeing "deep and abiding love," helps Nan and Guy escape to South

Africa, while she herself will face a solitary, and poor, old age.

Edith Wharton was careful to use authentic settings, both in America and in England. She renamed the United States Hotel in Saratoga Springs the "Grand Union," but evoked its atmosphere of pretension, the tall columns on the portico being deliberately reminiscent of the Parthenon. In the scenario, she describes the setting as "aristocratic London in the season, and life in the great English country-houses as they were sixty years ago." Honourslove resembles Stanway, the home of Lord and Lady ELCHO in Gloucester, which she often visited. The Duke of Tintagel's name derives from a 1928 visit she made to Tintagel, the legendary castle of King Arthur on the coast of Cornwall. She wrote that she was "fulfilling an old dream in coming to this legendary headland which is as wild and haunted as its name" (*EW* 483–84).

Edith Wharton claimed she did not choose her characters' names, but that they arrived in her mind already named. This was the case with "Testvalley," which she described in *A BACKWARD GLANCE* as an "impossible patronymic." She could not change it, she explained, because it had long been attached to a "strongly outlined material form," one figuring in an "adventure I know all about and have long wanted to write." Miss Testvalley, she concluded, was too "strong-willed, and even obstinate," and turned "sulky and unmanageable" when Wharton tried to give her another name (*BG* 202–03).

Critics have disagreed about the identity of the heroine in *The Buccaneers*. Gaillard LAPSLEY argues that Miss Testvalley is the dominant character, while Geoffrey Walton believes Nan St George to be the more important. Carol Wershoven considers them opposite sides of the same person: "Nan St George is what the young Laura might have been, had she been rich; Laura, what Nan might become after a meager and disappointing life" (Wershoven, 217). Edith Wharton's concept of woman's potential had evolved, however, since *The Valley of Decision*. Fulvia Vivaldi, heroine of that novel, and Nan and Laura are willing to make considerable sacrifices rather than surrender their freedom and independence. Fulvia, however, must pay with her life, as well as her reputation. Nan gives up her place in society, as Ellen Olenska in *The Age of Innocence* was unable to do, and, according to the synopsis, would have found and dwelt in that "other country" Ellen believed to be unattainable. Laura forgoes her chance for a comfortable and happy marriage, but has the satisfaction of having helped her protégée achieve the perfect marriage Wharton never found for herself.

For further reading: Tintner, "Consuelo Vanderbilt and *The Buccaneers*"; Wershoven, "Edith Wharton's Final Vision: *The Buccaneers*"; Winner, Introduction to *The Buccaneers*.

***Buccaneers, The* (teleplay, 1995)**   *See* Appendix II.

"Bunner Sisters"   Edith Wharton wrote "Bunner Sisters" in 1892 and sent it to Edward BURLINGAME, who responded that he "liked and admired much of it quite unreservedly," but felt the "motif and the admirable detail and color" did not sustain the story for its length of 30,000 words (*EW* 66). It was not published for 24 years, when it was included in the short story collection XINGU AND OTHER STORIES (Scribner's, 1916).

The novelette concerns two unmarried sisters, Ann Eliza and Evelina Bunner, who live behind their tiny millinery shop on Stuyvesant Square. They are impoverished but genteel. Mr. Ramy, a bachelor, appears, likeable but addicted to the use of drugs. The sisters develop a bittersweet rivalry for the potential suitor. He transfers his affections from Ann Eliza, the elder, to Evelina, and marries and later deserts her, leading to the ruination of Ann Eliza and the illness and death of Evelina. The story turns on the sisters' intense relations and their transitory chance for happiness. It also reflects Edith Wharton's wish to escape from the social world of the New York in which she lived. In its sensitivity to lives marked by poverty, blighted hopes and a marginal chance of realizing change, the novella is reminiscent of "MRS. MANSTEY'S VIEW." When the collection was published, one critic praised "Bunner Sisters" for not having the "odor of condescension" about it (*CR* 236).

It is possible that the "lady in puffed sleeves" who visits the shop may contain a clue to the way Edith Wharton knew of such a world and extrapolated from it her depiction of their threadbare lives and hopeless aspirations. She may have patronized and observed just such a shabby shop, taking note of the litter outside and the artifical flowers in the window.

For further reading: Saunders, "Ironic Reversal in Edith Wharton's 'Bunner Sisters.' "

***Bunner Sisters* (play, 1948)**   *See* Appendix II.

Burlingame, Edward L. (1848–1922)   Editor of SCRIBNER'S MAGAZINE from its first issue in 1887 until 1914, when he resigned. Burlingame was the son of the diplomat Anson Burlingame and was educated in American and European universities. He was experienced in both newspaper and book publishing, and believed the magazine should offer literary as well as popular topics. When she was only 27, Edith Wharton mailed a copy of a poem, "The Last Giustiniani," to *Scribner's Magazine* and received a check for $20. "As long as I live I shall never forget my sensations when I opened the first of the three letters, and learned that I was to appear in print," she wrote in *A BACKWARD GLANCE* (109). He had not only accepted her poetry, but had asked about her other work, which encouraged her to go and see him, laying the foundation of a friendship that endured until his death.

Over 80 of her works eventually appeared in *Scribner's Magazine*, including short stories, essays, poems and serial novels. Among the books that were serialized in the magazine before they were published by Scribner's were ITALIAN BACKGROUNDS, The HOUSE OF MIRTH, The FRUIT OF THE TREE, ETHAN FROME and The CUSTOM OF THE COUNTRY.

Burlingame requested that she finish *The House of Mirth* early for serial publication, since a novel that was to have preceded hers was not ready. She later wrote, "of all the friendly turns that Mr. Burlingame ever did me, his exacting this effort was undoubtedly the most helpful." It gave her self-confidence and bent her "to the discipline of the daily task" (*BG* 208). She called him "my first and kindest critic" in the dedication to *The DESCENT OF MAN AND OTHER STORIES* (Scribner's, 1904).

To mark the centennial anniversary of the House of Scribner in 1946, Burlingame's son Roger, an editor with Scribner's, was asked to write a history of the firm and was given free rein, with access to the accumulated correspondence. In *Of Making Many Books* he presents an unforgettable portrait of his father, who, as editor of *Scribner's Magazine*, had a dual commitment to high standards of literature and to selections that would please the reader. He and William Crary BROWNELL were of one mind in attempting to give the public "education without giving it indigestion" (ix). James Barrie once wrote of Burlingame that he almost had a "frozen geniality": "He seemed to say 'you must find out how lovable I am, I want you to find it out but I can't as easily as some people show you the way'" (209).

For further reading: Bell, "Lady into Author: Edith Wharton and the House of Scribner"; Burlingame, *Of Making Many Books: A Hundred Years of Reading, Writing and Publishing*.

Byrne, Bolton   *See SPARK, THE.*

Campbell, Mrs. Patrick (1865–1940) Mrs. Campbell, the famous British actress, was born Beatrice Stella Tanner, but used her married name on the stage. In 1902 she played in *Magda*, her first appearance in AMERICA, which Edith Wharton saw in NEW YORK. In May 1902 she was persuaded by Mrs. Campbell to translate "*Es lebe das Leben*," a tragedy by Hermann SUD-ERMANN, to which she had acquired the rights. According to Wharton's account in *A BACKWARD GLANCE*, she was reluctant to undertake the translation, but eventually consented and delivered it. Mrs. Campbell refused to accept the title as ironic and rejected the translation Wharton proposed, "Long Live Life." Instead, she followed other advice and called it *The JOY OF LIVING*, a title of which Wharton strongly disapproved. The play opened under that title, which Wharton considered "comic," with Mrs. Campbell in the leading role. The play failed, but SCRIBNER's published it in 1902 under the title suggested by Mrs. Campbell. It sold steadily for over 25 years, according to Wharton's memoir. She had "none but kindly memories of the theatre-folk with whom I had to do, though in each case the doing rendered them so little service" (*BG* 168).

Cameron, Elizabeth Sherman (b. 1859) "Lizzie" Cameron, the estranged wife of U.S. Senator James Donald Cameron, was a longtime friend of Edith Wharton's. Her personal life centered on Henry ADAMS, who was about 20 years older than she but had attended her salon in Washington and become a close companion (*EW* 362). After her daughter Martha was married to Ronald Lindsay of the British Foreign Office, she divided her time between ENGLAND and PARIS. When WORLD WAR I began, Adams went to England, where he took refuge in the country house of the Lindsays near Blandford, Dorset. He saw Henry JAMES, who came over from Rye; together they deplored the war. Elizabeth Cameron went at first to Switzerland to be with her daughter, but then returned to Paris. There she assisted Wharton with a number of her relief projects. Adams spent most of the war years in America, where he died in 1918; he had not seen Mrs. Cameron again.

Campton, George *See SON AT THE FRONT, A.*

Campton, John *See SON AT THE FRONT, A.*

Cantapresto *See VALLEY OF DECISION, THE.*

Catholicism, Roman Edith Wharton was raised an Episcopalian, baptized on April 20, 1862, in fashionable Grace Church, Manhattan and married at Trinity Chapel on Wednesday, April 29, 1885. In adult life, however, she seems to have taken little interest in the Anglican Church.

She never became a Roman Catholic, but there has been speculation that she was tempted to do so much later in her life. Certainly, her reverent attitude toward Roman Catholic churches in *ITALIAN BACKGROUNDS* and *MOTOR-FLIGHT THROUGH FRANCE* suggests that she was cognizant of the rich traditions and aesthetic heritage of the Roman Catholic Church. In the former volume, she noted that "in Italy, nature, art and religion combine to enrich the humblest lives" (*IB* 52).

Benstock observes that after 1930 Wharton visited Roman Catholic churches very frequently. Daisy CHAN-LER, Matilda GAY and Elisina TYLER, three of her closest women friends, were all Roman Catholic, as was her maid, Elise DUVLENCK. Daisy Chanler had built a private chapel at her American home, Sweet Briar Farm, and her housekeeper, Catharine GROSS, was beginning instruction. Wharton read the *Office des Morts* on All Souls' Eve, 1930, in memory of Walter BERRY. (*NGC* 427). Her autobiography, *A BACKWARD GLANCE*, is dedicated to "the friends who every year on All Souls' Night come and sit with me by the fire." (Traditionally, the Roman Catholic Church observes All Souls' Eve on November 1 and All Souls' Day on November 2).

For more than 10 years after the end of WORLD WAR I, Wharton sponsored an auction in St.-Brice-sous-Forêt for the Abbé COMPTOUR, a young priest at Lutèce who was hoping to build a church to attract the impoverished residents of the *zone rouge*, the working-class suburbs nearby, to the Roman Catholic faith and away from socialist-communist thought. The bronze bell was named the Edith-Matilda in honor of Edith Wharton and Matilda Gay. (*NGC* 427).

In 1931 and 1932, Edith Wharton made two visits to ROME. In the autumn of 1931, she revisited the Rome she had known 40 years earlier, accompanied by Nicky MARIANO, longtime assistant to Bernard BERENSON. They attended a pontifical high mass in San Paolo Fuore le Mura and a requiem mass at Santa Maria sopra Minerva. In May of 1932, Wharton again came to Rome with the Berensons and Nicky. On Whitsunday they attended Mass at St. Peter's, and on Trinity Sunday went to High Mass at Santa Trinità dei Monti and vespers at Santa Agnese, in addition to a pontifical high mass at San Anselmo.

Lewis states that Wharton was quite interested in the procession through the cloister and was "beginning to interest herself strongly in the rituals and ceremonies, in the liturgical experience of the Christian religion, and in the meanings they exemplified." He is convinced that Walter BERRY's death in 1927 and Wharton's own critical illness in 1929 "while deepening her sense of physical mortality, seem to have enlarged her awareness of the life of the spirit and thence of the rituals by which that life might be exercised and enriched."

Edith Wharton's friend Gaillard LAPSLEY believed that, at the end of her life, she found a rationalist system of thought insufficient to explain "what life and reflection had taught her." Lapsley's conviction, coupled with the rich traditions of French and Italian Catholicism, led to her to reject her earlier espousal of Nietzschean philosophical ideals. Sir Kenneth CLARK, who inherited much of her library, stated that books on religion predominated. Moreover, she had, as a long-time friend in PARIS, the Abbé MUGNIER, devout yet highly rational and sophisticated. In a late commonplace book she wrote, "I don't believe in God but I do believe in His saints—and then?" (*EW* 509–10).

In her groundbreaking study *Edith Wharton: Matters of Mind and Spirit*, Carol J. Singley explores many aspects of Wharton's philosophical and religious outlook. She perceives her as antireligious during much of her life and argues that, following Vernon LEE, she developed an "aesthetic and philosophical ideal of the sort fostered by PATER and rooted in Plato" (*Singley*, 34). Singley argues that, finally, Edith Wharton adhered neither to the Protestantism of her birth nor to the rationalism of her middle years, but also failed to find Roman Catholicism fully satisfying. Her "spiritual longings sustained the search for immutable values" (*Singley*, 209).

Although Wharton did not convert to Catholicism, it is impossible to read her travel books about Italy and France without assuming that her "immutable values" rested on a profound and abiding sympathy with Christian art and artifacts. She had a lifelong devotion to the paintings of Tintoretto, Correggio and dozens of other medieval, Renaissance, and baroque artists. Just three months before she died, she wrote Bernard BERENSON that she was planning to visit Elisina Tyler in Venice to see the "Tintorets" (*Letters* 604).

At the same time, Edith Wharton's funeral plans do not indicate that she had totally abandoned the Protestantism of her birth. Her burial instructions, sent to Elisina Tyler on May 23, 1936, specified that she wished, for the sake of her French friends, a funeral or memo-

rial service to be celebrated at the American Episcopal Pro–Cathedral Church of the Holy Trinity, Paris. The service was to be choral, with three hymns: "Lead, Kindly Light," "Art thou weary?" and "O Paradise."

For further reading: Killoran, "On the Religious Reading of Edith Wharton; Singley, *Edith Wharton: Matters of Mind and Spirit*."

Century Illustrated Monthly Magazine, The One of the small group of leading intellectual periodicals that were the linchpin and showcase of American literary achievement after the end of the Civil War. The Century Company was created in 1881 when it bought *Scribner's Monthly Magazine*, which had been founded in 1870. The magazine continued under the name *The Century Illustrated Monthly Magazine*, often abbreviated to *The Century* (the name was taken from New York's Century Club). The well-known man of letters and poet Richard Watson GILDER was the editor from 1881 to 1909. There was a legal restriction for seven years against the use of the name "SCRIBNER'S MONTHLY" in a competing periodical, but in 1887 SCRIBNER'S MAGAZINE was founded, which existed until 1939. During the period of their coexistence, the two magazines competed for authors, and prices paid for fiction, articles and poetry surpassed those paid in any other country for magazine work. Two other leading literary periodicals were THE ATLANTIC MONTHLY and HARPER'S NEW MONTHLY MAGAZINE. By 1900, the heyday of literary periodicals had come to an end. *Scribner's Magazine*, which had a lower cover price, was the healthiest; the *Atlantic* was barely surviving, and the circulation of *Century Magazine* and *Harper's* had dropped to 150,000 (Quinn, 593–95). From 1909 to 1913 the magazine was known simply as *The Century*; it was then under the editorship of Robert Underwood Johnson.

Edith Wharton published fiction, nonfiction and poetry in *The Century*. Among the short stories were "The VALLEY OF CHILDISH THINGS AND OTHER EMBLEMS" (1896), "The CHOICE" (1908), "AFTERWARD" (1910), "The LETTERS" (1910), and "OTHER TIMES, OTHER MANNERS" [reprinted as "AUTRES TEMPS . . ." in XINGU (*XINGU AND OTHER STORIES* [Scribner's, 1916]). Her travel texts appeared in *The Century* as well as in *Scribner's Magazine*. The articles comprising ITALIAN VILLAS AND THEIR GARDENS, published by the Century Company in 1904, were first published in *The Century*, although Wharton and Gilder disagreed over the illustrations and she tried in vain to withdraw them. Both magazines were re-nowned for the high quality of their illustrations, which contributed greatly to the impact of their travel pieces. They were also part of corporate entities that contained book publishing divisions, a connection that played an important role in the publication of Wharton's early travel texts. The magazine also published four of her poems, including "The Sonnet" (1891), "Jade" (1895), "Moonrise Over Tyringham" (1908) and "Battle Sleep" (1915).

Certain People Short story collection published in 1930 by APPLETON AND COMPANY. It included "ATROPHY," "A BOTTLE OF PERRIER," "AFTER HOLBEIN," "DIEU D'AMOUR," "The REFUGEES" and "MR. JONES." Dorothy Gilman of the *New York Herald Tribune* praised the volume for its judicious blend of tragedy and satirical comedy. V. S. Pritchett, writing in the English *Spectator*, stated that Wharton's "caustic satire" was not written from "the tragic spleen of a divided soul" but from "some rock of belief." Florence Codman, whose review appeared in the *Nation*, praised her evocation of "a whole social order, a perfect imprint of a vanishing race," citing "After Holbein" (*CR* 479–85).

Chanler, Margaret Margaret ("Daisy") Terry, later Mrs. Winthrop Chanler, was a lifelong friend of Edith Wharton's. In 1848, when Edith Wharton's parents were staying in ROME with her two-year-old brother Freddie, her father, George Frederic JONES, had become a friend of Luther Terry, a Connecticut artist living abroad. He later married Mrs. Thomas Crawford,

the sister of Julia Ward Howe and the mother of the novelist F. Marion Crawford, and became the father of Daisy and Arthur Terry. Edith Wharton and Daisy first met in 1866, when the Joneses took Edith, age four, to Rome. She played with Daisy and Arthur on the Monte Pincio, remembering them as the most vivid of the band of children she had known (*BG* 29).

Margaret Terry married Winthrop Astor Chanler in 1886; he was related to the Schermerhorns and the Astors. They had seven surviving children. Edith Wharton attended the christening of their infant son Theodore, whose godfather was Theodore ROOSEVELT. At that time, Edith wrote Sara NORTON that Daisy was "dear & wonderful, serene & unhurried, among seven children & the turmoil of the Newport season" (*Letters* 67). In later years, the Chanlers frequently dined with Edith Wharton in PARIS and visited her at STE.-CLAIRE CHÂTEAU in HYÈRES. They knew Henry JAMES and many others in her circle.

In 1926, Daisy Chanler shared the charter of the *OSPREY* for the Aegean cruise, the subject of one chapter

Edith Wharton on the terrace at Ste.-Claire Château, her home in Hyères, France (Courtesy of the Lilly Library, Indiana University)

of *Autumn in the Valley* (1936), her volume of reminiscences. Edith Wharton asked her to find silk sleeping bags and mosquito nets, for which Daisy searched in vain in Paris. On board, according to Daisy, they read the *Odyssey*, which served as a perfect guidebook, "full of the sea wind and sea shine of those lovely shores" (*Autumn*, 212). Margaret Chanler's description of the voyage is far more complete than that of Edith Wharton, who only gives it a brief mention in *A BACKWARD GLANCE*. She kept a diary on the cruise, as Edith Wharton had on the cruise of the *VANADIS* in 1888.

Chantelle, Madame de   *See REEF, THE.*

Charities, World War I   *See WAR RELIEF, WORLD WAR I.*

"Charm Incorporated"   Short story first published as "BREAD UPON THE WATERS" in *Hearsts' International–Cos-* *mopolitan* in February 1934. It was included in the collection *THE WORLD OVER* (Appleton–Century, 1936) under the title "Charm Incorporated." *See* account under "Bread upon the Waters."

Château Ste.-Claire   Edith Wharton's winter home in Hyères, France. *See* STE.-CLAIRE CHÂTEAU.

Chelles, Raymond de   *See CUSTOM OF THE COUNTRY, THE.*

chevalier of the French Legion of Honor   On March 28, 1916, it was announced that Edith Wharton had been made a chevalier (knight) of the French Legion of Honor in recognition of her war relief work. The precise title, as shown on the certificate, was Officier de l'Ordre National de la Légion d'Honneur. This was the last award to be given a civilian and a foreigner until the war had ended, and was a signal honor. A reporter for

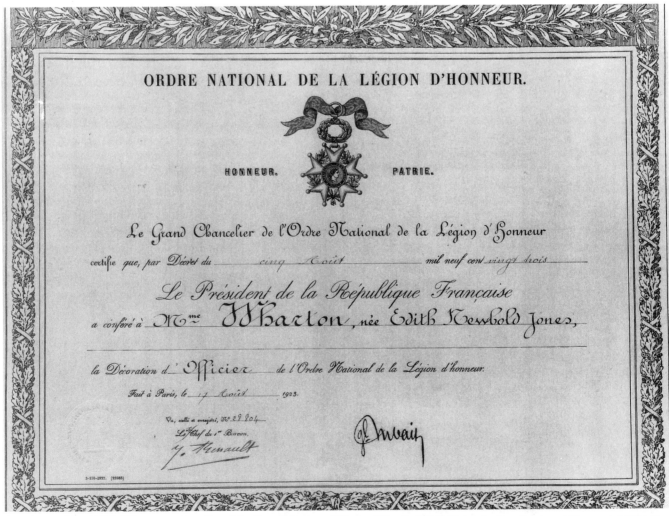

Citation making Edith Wharton a chevalier of the French Legion of Honor (March 1916) (Beinecke Rare Book and Manuscript Library, Yale University)

Le Temps wrote, when she did not attend the awards ceremony, "she does good works without seeming to notice it." Wharton received 87 letters of congratulation in a single day. Among those who sent telegrams of congratulation was Egerton WINTHROP, but by the time his message was delivered, he had died (*NGC* 324–25).

Chevrillon, André (1864–1957)   Editor of the *REVUE DE PARIS*, nephew of the historian Hippolyte-Adolphe Taine, and author of several books on English literature. He was a valued friend of Edith Wharton; it was at his home at Saint-Cloud, outside PARIS, that she met Count Robert d'HUMIÈRES, who also became an esteemed friend. According to Benstock, Edith Wharton was displeased at the French translation of her Pulitzer Prize–winning novel *The AGE OF INNOCENCE*, and withdrew it from the prestigious *REVUE DES DEUX MONDES*. She turned to Madeline St.-Renée Taillandier, sister of André Chevrillon, who, with her daughter Mariane, translated it. Titled *Au TEMPS DE L'INNOCENCE*, the book was a critical success in France (*NGC* 421).

childhood, of Edith Wharton   From all accounts, Wharton had a very happy childhood, much of which was spent in EUROPE. In her memoir, *A BACKWARD GLANCE*, she recalls being taken for a walk in NEW YORK by her father, George Frederic JONES, in an elaborate white satin and raised velvet bonnet. Soon afterwards she was given a Spitz puppy, the first of dozens of dogs she would have over her long life. From 1866 to 1872 the Joneses were abroad, living for months at a time in FRANCE, ITALY, and GERMANY; she became fluent in all three languages. Her Irish nurse, Hannah DOYLE, accompanied them. Wharton's two brothers were much older; Frederic had graduated from Columbia and Harry was at Trinity Hall College, Cambridge, but her parents saw to it that she had playmates, usually the children of Americans they knew.

She recalled a trip to SPAIN the family made, at a time when that country was almost inaccessible; she experienced "a jumble of excited impressions" (*BG* 31). In Europe she began "making up," rapidly telling stories while pacing about their various large-ceilinged apartments.

In 1872, when the Joneses returned to New York, Edith was shocked at the ugliness of the city, but found considerable compensation in the "kingdom" of her father's library and in summers at PENCRAIG, the Joneses' home in NEWPORT.

From all accounts, Edith Jones was a sensitive, intelligent child, obedient and eager to please her parents. Her mother, Lucretia Rhinelander JONES, is reputed to have been cold and insensitive, although Edith was devoted to her father. In the chapter on "The School-Room and Nurseries" in *The DECORATION OF HOUSES*, Wharton apologizes for including a section "bordering

Early portrait of Edith Wharton (Clifton Waller Barrett Library, Special Collections Department, University of Virginia)

on pedagogy." The term implies a dull approach to edification that is belied on virtually every page. The chapter is actually an anti-Victorian manifesto, presenting what might be called a modernist interpretation of aesthetic education.

By making the best of the past visible, the child's self will be opened to new levels of experience, so that he or she can fuse disparate elements into new wholes, and achieve a broadened view of life, an integrated cultural outlook. Lewis considers this volume an "indictment of the background [of Old New York] as represented by its habitual living conditions," and also suggests that the book is "paying off scores against the physical surroundings" in which Wharton had grown up, and "perhaps against her mother as their creator" (*EW* 78). It is possible that Lucretia Jones put "worthless knick-knacks" in her daughter's nursery and that the Jones home on West 23rd Street harbored cast-off "ugly furniture" in the schoolroom, left over from her brothers' tenancy. This would have been particularly repugnant to the 10-year-old Edith returning to New York from the glories of France and Italy.

As depicted in *A Backward Glance*, Wharton's childhood, up to the age of 10, was idyllic; it was only much later, when she was an adult, that she began to register complaints about her mother.

childlessness, of Wharton   It has been generally assumed that the Whartons did not have children because they ceased having sexual relations soon after they were married. They had separate rooms even when traveling. Lewis believes the marriage was not consummated for at least three weeks, and Wharton felt that Lucretia JONES' cold refusal to provide any sexual education "did more than anything else to falsify and misdirect my whole life" (*EW* 54). Benstock notes that in later years she told Elisina TYLER of her "great grief" at not having children (*NGC* 167). She was a devoted friend to William Royall TYLER, Elisina's son (born 1910), and sent him a stuffed parrot on his sixth birthday. (He later inherited her books on art, archaeology and history, but many of them were destroyed in the bombing of London.) She pronounced his son, Royall, whom she met at the age of three months the April before her death, "the nicest child I ever met" (*Letters* 604).

Lewis observes that in her fiction she is ambivalent about motherhood. If the bossy young heroine, Jane, of the short story "The Mission of Jane," is compared with Judith Wheater, surrogate mother coping gallantly with a band of six younger brothers, sisters and half-siblings, there is no clear-cut answer. Toward the end of *The HOUSE OF MIRTH*, Lily Bart holds Nettie's baby in her warm kitchen, feeling its weight increase and "penetrating her with a strange sense of weakness, as though the child entered into her and became a part of herself" (*HM* 333). In 1913, when her niece Beatrix JONES was married to Max FARRAND, Wharton wrote her a loving letter indicating her sadness at her childless marriage: "And if you have a boy or girl, to prolong the joy, so much the better . . . And times come when one would give anything in the world for a reason like that for living on" (*NGC* 290).

Wolff believes that as Wharton grew older, her concern with children was increasingly reflected in her fiction. *A SON AT THE FRONT*, *The CHILDREN*, *TWILIGHT SLEEP*, and *The MOTHER'S RECOMPENSE* are all "novels about families—about parents and children, youth and age," and it is the older generation "that commands Wharton's imaginative sympathies." She believes she was increasingly alienated from *les jeunes* as she grew older and, since she had no family, could only "infer" the feelings of parents toward their children (Woolf, *A Feast of Words*, 330–31).

Philomène de LA FOREST-DIVONNE visited Wharton one afternoon in 1935 or 1936 and was shown an album of newspaper clippings about her early writings. She noted, "It is one of my precious memories; on that afternoon I felt what Edith *could have been for the children she never had*" (*EW* 527). Although there is no clear-cut answer as to how painful it was to Wharton not to have had children, there is evidence to suggest that they would have compensated for much that was disappointing in her marriage.

For further reading: Beppu, "Wharton Questions Motherhood."

Children, The   A novel serialized in the *Pictorial Review* and published in 1928 by APPLETON AND COMPANY. The plot centers on the unsuccessful attempt of Martin Boyne, a 46-year-old American bachelor who has spent his life carrying out civil engineering projects abroad, to rescue the seven Wheater children, miscellaneous progeny of much-married parents. The Wheaters represent the affluent post–WORLD WAR I generation who, in the 1920s, are preoccupied with pleasure and novelty, changing hotels and spouses with equal alacrity.

The novel takes place on board ship in Algiers and in other settings, principally Venice and the South Tyrol, both of which Edith Wharton had visited two years earlier. Boyne is returning to Europe in order to look up an earlier attachment, Rose Sellars; he has decided his life is lonely and he can afford to marry. At Algiers he meets a tribe of six young children being led aboard his ship by their serious and maternal 15-year-old sister, Judith. They are the offspring of the various marriages of Joyce and Cliffe Wheater, who divorced, took other spouses, and eventually remarried. Boyne had known the mother in college. Accompanied by a governess and nurses, Judith is escorting the flock from Biskra to Venice to join their various parents. The other children are her full siblings, twins Terry and Blanca; her stepsister, Zinnie, whose mother is a film star; a brother, Astorre ("Bun") and his sister, Beatrice ("Beechy"), the children of their mother and an Italian nobleman; and the toddler Chipstone, another full sibling born of her parents' remarriage. The seven children have sworn on the *Cyclopædia of Nursery Remedies* never to be separated.

At Venice, on the Lido, Boyne meets the children's fathers and mothers amid feverish excitement, steam yachts, bejeweled women, restaurants and cocktails. He assists in engaging a tutor for Terry and takes an increasing interest in the children, particularly Judith. She is a charming mixture of maturity, maternal devotion and childish naivete—one of Edith Wharton's most memorable and unusual characters. Having spent her life in hotels, she has never been properly educated, yet she has a whimsical charm that engages Boyne from the outset.

Boyne leaves Venice for the Dolomites, where he becomes engaged to Rose Sellars, who has been waiting for him. He imagines, erroneously, that they might somehow become foster parents to the children, an idea Rose does not encourage. The children then come to Austria, causing him to break his engagement and propose circumspectly to Judith. " 'Well, that would be funny!' " she laughs, hardly understanding that he is proposing marriage. Boyne feels older than his years, as well as cynical. In the epilogue, he returns to Europe years later, only to learn that the children have been separated and the youngest has died. He sees Judith through a window at a dance, a vision in carnation pink, but sails without speaking to her.

The Wheaters' numerous marriages violate Edith Wharton's description of the ideal marriage in FRENCH WAYS AND THEIR MEANING. In France, she observes, marriage is "founded for the family and not for the husband and wife"; it is designed not to promote the happiness of individuals, but to "secure their permanent well-being as associates in the foundation of a home and the procreation of a family" (*FWM* 128). The Wheater children have never had an enduring home, but have been shuttled from place to place, visited only sporadically by their parents. Judith has tried to keep them all together, a plan Boyne endorses and tries unsuccessfully to implement as a sort of unofficial godfather to the group. According to Lewis, the novel reflects an "almost sociological interest in the phenomenon of children" on the part of Edith Wharton (*EW* 485).

The novel reverses the situation found frequently in Edith Wharton's fiction, when a younger man becomes attached to an older woman, as in "The MUSE'S TRAGEDY," *A SON AT THE FRONT*, and *HUDSON RIVER BRACKETED*. It also raises questions about the ultimate wisdom of altruistic self-sacrifice.

A film based on *The Children* was produced in 1929, titled *The Marriage Playground* (*see* Appendix II). The novel was translated into French by Louisette Gillet, as *Leurs Enfants*.

Children, The (film, 1990)   *See* Appendix II.

Children of Flanders Rescue Committee   One of Edith Wharton's World War I charities. In April 1915, she organized this project, caring for 750 Flemish children. The shelling of Belgium had caused many children to be left homeless, especially in the ruined city of Ypres. They were living in cellars, on abandoned farms and on the rubble-strewn streets; they were without food or clothing. The Belgian Ministry of the Interior, having heard of Edith Wharton's WAR RELIEF work, cabled to ask her to receive 60 children, mainly girls, during the summer of 1915. She located an empty school in Sèvres, outside PARIS, suitable for housing them; the Belgian Government soon asked if she could accommodate another 600.

By the end of 1915 Wharton had arranged to operate six homes for children in the environs of Paris, as well as in Normandy. Elisina TYLER assisted Edith Wharton in the project. They founded a school of lace-making to occupy the girls and offered industrial training for the boys. They also began French classes

for those who spoke only Flemish. Wharton later described the project in a brochure as "my prettiest and showiest and altogether most appealing charity." By the end of 1915, the committee had assisted more than 750 children and 150 adults.

"Choice, The"   Short story first published in *THE CENTURY* in 1908 and included in *XINGU AND OTHER STORIES* (Scribner's, 1916). It deals with a couple in an ill-suited marriage: the egotistic Cobham Stilling and his wealthy but cautious wife, Isabel. They live ostentatiously, at the husband's instigation, on an immense estate in a lakeside summer colony, with greenhouses, servants, cars and a motor launch—Cobham's latest "plaything," bought on credit. He cares about nothing except good cigars and liquor, and driving the motor launch recklessly around the lake.

Isabel had, on their marriage, imprudently made Cobham trustee of her fortune; now he has speculated and gambled it away, ruining them as well as his mother. Isabel's lover is the stable, wise lawyer and financial adviser Austin Wrayford, who is devoted to Isabel and beloved by her; her dearest hope is that her husband may die: " 'I wish it always—every day, every hour, every moment!' " (*CSS* II, 354). She is held back from divorce by the potential loss of her son and, possibly, liability in her husband's financial misdealings. Wrayford, who has tried to warn Cobham about the consequences of his recklessness, attempts to stage a drowning accident, thinks better of it, and loses his own life in rescuing the drunken Cobham.

The story was written in May 1908 aboard ship, while Edith Wharton was returning to AMERICA and in the middle of her affair with Morton FULLERTON. She wrote him from the ship that she found it difficult to go "from moments of such nearness, when the last shadow of separateness melts, back into a complete *néant* of silence." Three days later, she wrote again to Fullerton, "I am mad about you Dear Heart. . . . I am conscious of but one thing, you, and our love for each other" (*Letters* 145). Lewis notes that she wrote the story on the fifth day over. The plot mirrors not only her affair with Fullerton, but her own financial situation, since Teddy WHARTON was, like Cobham, a trustee of his wife's estate. Benstock observes that the story "dramatizes" her feelings about her own marriage: "powerlessness, rage, guilt, futility" (*NGC* 186).

Cimitière des Gonards   Cemetery in Versailles where Edith Wharton is buried near the grave of her longtime friend Walter BERRY. She died in her home, the PAVILLON COLOMBE, in ST.-BRICE-SOUS-FORÊT, just outside PARIS, on August 11, 1937. Her funeral took place on August 14. An honor guard holding French and American flags was formed in the courtyard of her

Grave of Edith Wharton in the Cimitière des Gonards, Versailles
(From Louis Auchincloss, *Edith Wharton: A Woman in Her Time;* used with permission)

home and the coffin was brought to the cemetery, where a deputation of French war veterans accompanied it to the grave. Dean Frederick W. Beekman of the American Pro-Cathedral in Paris said selected prayers. She was buried with all the honors usually given a war hero and a CHEVALIER OF THE FRENCH LEGION OF HONOR. The memorial service she had requested took place at the Pro-Cathedral in Paris on August 21 (*NGC* 455–56).

Clark, Kenneth (1903–1983)   Kenneth Clark and his wife Jane were among Edith Wharton's closest friends during her final decade of life. She met Clark at I TATTI, the home of Bernard and Mary BERENSON, near Florence, while touring in ITALY in 1930. In March 1931 he and his wife were her guests at STE.-CLAIRE CHÂTEAU.

While still young, Clark had been appointed Keeper of the Ashmolean Museum in Oxford, England; he became director of the National Gallery in London at the age of 30, in 1933. Wharton was godmother to their son, Colin David, one of twins born in April 1932 (the other was Colette, whose godmother was Nicky MARIANO). In the burial instructions Edith Wharton sent to

Elisina TYLER in 1936, she designated Kenneth Clark as one of her pallbearers, if feasible.

The Clarks were among her last visitors to the PAVILLON COLOMBE the month before Wharton died (others included Royall TYLER, John HUGH SMITH, and Robert NORTON). Kenneth Clark inherited most of Wharton's library from the Pavillon Colombe and transported it to England for safekeeping during World War II, where, unfortunately, much of it was destroyed in the bombing.

Clephane, Anne   *See MOTHER'S RECOMPENSE, THE.*

Clephane, Kate   *See MOTHER'S RECOMPENSE, THE.*

Closson, Conchita   *See BUCCANEERS, THE.*

Cocteau, Jean (1889–1963)   French poet, novelist, essayist, graphic artist and film director. Cocteau was at the forefront of many artistic movements of the first half of the 20th century, particularly cubism and surrealism. He helped promote Picasso, Stravinsky and other innovators. His most famous modern ballets are *Parade* (1916), with scenery by Picasso, and *les Mariés de la Tour Eiffel* (1921; music by Les Six). Among his more famous works are the poetic novel set in WORLD WAR I, *Thomas the Imposter*, and the film *Blood of a Poet*. The poet-angel who defies destiny and guards the divine in man is one of his principal themes.

While visiting Jacques-Émile BLANCHE and his wife at their summer home near Dieppe, Edith Wharton met Jean Cocteau. She described him as a "passionately imaginative youth to whom every great line of poetry was a sunrise" (*BG* 285).

Léon Bakst contributed an unpublished sketch of Cocteau for the BOOK OF THE HOMELESS and Cocteau contributed a poem, "La Mort des Jeunes Gens de la Divine Hellade. Fragment" ("How the Young Men died in Hellas. A Fragment").

Codman, Ogden, Jr. (1868–1951)   Born into a wealthy Boston family, the architect Ogden Codman studied in FRANCE, where he was influenced by 18th-century neoclassical architecture. He spent a year at the Massachusetts Institute of Technology while apprenticed to John Hubbard Sturgis, his uncle. He met Edith Wharton when he helped her decorate LAND'S END, her home in NEWPORT, Rhode Island. They collaborated on *The DECORATION OF HOUSES* (1897), and he was her friend for many years. Between 1896 and 1898, Ogden Codman and Beatrix FARRAND designed the garden trellis at Wakehurst, the NEWPORT, R.I., home of J. J. VAN ALEN (with whom the Whartons had chartered the VANADIS in 1888).

Codman shared Edith Wharton's revulsion against the stultifying, overly decorated interiors of the Victorian era. Their achievement in *The Decoration of Houses* was, by laying out classical principles, to correct the estrangement between house decoration and interior architecture and to reaffirm the mission of the decorator to approach the task architecturally. They insisted that "proportion is the good breeding of architecture"; it is the indefinable element "which gives repose and distinction to a room." Close attention to their principles will enable the builder to approximate the "all-pervading essence the ancients called the soul" (*DH* 31). The term "breeding" implies that they are addressing a class "to the manor born," but the passage, with typical American vigor, asserts paradoxically that breeding can be learned—that the "soul" can be shaped by "calculation"—a fine and suggestive paradox. The surprisingly warm reception of *The Decoration of Houses* signified a reaction against Victorian clutter and toward the simplicity and elegance of Italian Renaissance and French classical styles in domestic architecture.

In 1901 Edith Wharton purchased a 113-acre property in LENOX, Massachusetts, and began constructing The MOUNT. The house was designed by architect Francis Hoppin and modeled on Belton House in England. Codman had drawn preliminary sketches, but, by mutual agreement with the Whartons, withdrew from the commission. He wrote his mother the Whartons were "nearly enough to drive me crazy when they are clients." Marshall states that the break "had to do with money" and the fact that Codman "no longer needed their patronage and their advice." He hoped to secure wealthy clients elsewhere (Marshall, *The Mount: Home of Edith Wharton,* 40).

In October 1904, when he was 41, Codman married Leila Griswold Webb, widow of the railroad magnate H. Walter Webb. At the time she was six years older, with two sons. Metcalf states that she was "the ideal wife for him, both socially and financially" (*Ogden Codman and the Decoration of Houses,* 23). She died from complications after surgery in January 1910.

In 1918 Edith Wharton sent him a postcard of Jean-Marie, the estate in the village of ST.-BRICE-SOUS-FORÊT she was negotiating to buy. She wrote her sister-in-law, Mary (Minnie) Cadwalader JONES that Codman, whom she called "Coddy," was familiar with the property and had once tried to buy it; he thought "its possibilities endless—& understands it better than any of the French friends who have seen it. What a queer stick!" (*EW* 407). Throughout the years, Edith Wharton often visited Codman in France. Two months before she died, in 1937, she had a heart attack while staying at the Château de Grègy, south of PARIS, where Codman made his home in his later years. He was responsible for its expansion, interior decoration and landscape design. He is buried in the garden there.

Codman was an early preservationist and between 1895 and 1920 designed 21 houses, remodeled 10 others, and decorated 75 others. Among the buildings whose interiors he designed were the John D. Rockefeller, Jr., house in Pocantico Hills, N.Y. (1908); the Cornelius Vanderbilt II house, The Breakers, in Newport, R.I. (1894–95), the Oliver Ames House, Boston, Mass. (1899); the Oliver Ames house, Prides Crossing, Mass. (1904; exterior also), the Manhattan Country Day School, N.Y. (1912; exterior also), and La Leopolda, Villefranche-sur-Mer, France (1929–31; once owned by King Leopold I of Belgium).

For further reading: Marshall, *The Mount: Home of Edith Wharton*; Metcalf, *Ogden Codman and The Decoration of Houses*; Metcalf, "The Interiors of Ogden Codman, Jr. in Newport"; Metcalf, "Victorian Profile: Ogden Codman, Jr. A Clever Young Boston Architect."

Colefax, Lady Sybil Leading London hostess during the 1920s. At her London salon Edith met many important persons, but she was not one of her intimates. Lewis states that she was "warily fond" of her (*Letters* 568n).

"Colophon to the Mortal Lease" Written in April 1909, this 42-line poem was published in ARTEMIS TO ACTAEON AND OTHER VERSE (Scribner's, 1909). It is an unfinished sequel to "The MORTAL LEASE," the sonnet sequence written in 1908 at the height of Edith Wharton's affair with Morton FULLERTON. The "Colophon" reenacts a scene of sexual passion, building to a climax in which the body and soul appear to unite with the whole of life in a single instant. But then the woman looks into her lover's eyes and sees, as Benstock puts it, "eternity irradiated in the Moment." She perceives that he has not had the same vision and asks him to close his eyes. Wharton sent a copy of the poem to Fullerton with a dedication to "M.F." The original has disappeared, but in March 1912 he made a copy, adding, "I saw not what she saw, and that's the tragedy of it" (*NGC* 208). By then their affair had ended.

"Coming Home" Short story included in XINGU AND OTHER STORIES (Scribner's, 1916). The narrator, an American living in PARIS, has learned the story from an American relief worker back briefly from the front, H. Macy Greer. He has encountered, in a field hospital, a young French soldier, Jean de Réchamp, son of the Count of Réchamp. He is desperate for news of his parents, younger brother and sister and elderly grandmother, but has heard nothing other than a newspaper communiqué saying that the enemy had "retaken" Réchamp. Greer attempts in vain to obtain news of the village and of Jean de Réchamp's fiancée, Mlle Yvonne Malo, an orphan who had lived at Réchamp with her guardian, a marquis; she later came to Paris to study music. His conservative family had forbidden Jean to marry her, believing false rumors about her relationship with her guardian. She has gone to assist Jean's family. Greer is finally sent to the region to take supplies to front-line ambulances, and manages to have Jean assigned as his driver. He has learned that his family had survived and his fiancée, surprisingly, is still with them, nursing the wounded with his young sister.

Greer and Jean have been told of a German officer, Oberst von Scharlach, who has committed many atrocities: "Murder, outrage, torture; Scharlach's program seemed to be fairly comprehensive." When they reach the village, they find much of it in ruins, at his command. The chateau is untouched, because Mlle Malo has received the officers hospitably, with cigars, wine and coffee with whipped cream, and because she has charmed von Scharlach.

Greer and Jean leave the front and are asked to take a wounded German to the hospital. En route, Jean, who is attending the wounded German, discovers he is von Scharlach, fails to give him his hypodermic and permits him to die of his wounds. He invites Greer to join him for a *café complet*.

The story was criticized for being contrived so as to give the German officer the power of doing wrong and the French officer the maximum potential for revenge.

For further reading: Olin-Ammentorp, " 'Not Precisely War Stories': Edith Wharton's Short Fiction from the Great War."

commedia dell'arte   The "comedy of skill" was the peripatetic Italian theater of the 16th, 17th, and 18th centuries that was based in part on improvisation and incorporated famous stock characters such as Arlecchino (or Harlequin), Arlecchina, Pulcinella, Corallina, Brighella, Pantalone, Giangurgolo, and Captain Spavento. Performances were given at all social levels, from the street to the halls of villas. Actors and actresses sometimes played a single role their entire lives. The *commedia* is an enduring trope in Edith Wharton's nonfiction as well as her fiction. Her interest in it may have been stimulated by Vernon LEE's pioneering *Studies of the Eighteenth Century in Italy*, which she took with her on annual trips to ITALY.

In ITALIAN BACKGROUNDS, she spins a fanciful vision of a long-ago commedia performance in the now dusty, shabby Farnese Theater at Parma in which "Isabel and Harlequin and the Capitan Spavento . . . build on the scaffolding of some familiar intrigue the airy superstructure of their wit" (*IB* 122–23). Such theater goes beyond feigning to fictional invention, the improvisatory dialogue a catalyst for the shape-shifting of the characters. The metaphor provides the framework for Wharton's description of LAGO ISEO; she imagines the villages on the shore as a backdrop

for the performances of comedies "in the Bergamasque dialect, with Harlequin in striped cloak, and Brighella in conical hat and wide green and white trousers strutting up and down before the shuttered house in which Dr. Graziano hides his pretty ward." She imagines the lake as reflecting the "eighteenth century of Longhi, of Tiepolo and Goldoni . . . as in some magic crystal," to be discovered beneath the waves by "some later traveller. . . . if ever the boundaries between fact and fancy waver, it may well be under the spell of the Italian midsummer madness" (*IB* 34–35). The spontaneity and imaginative outreach which are the most distinctive features of the commedia dell'arte are the dramatic equivalent of the baroque flowering in architecture, sculpture, and painting which, for Wharton, eclipsed the pale formality of the Renaissance.

A recurrent theme in her Italian travel books, it is also present in *A MOTOR-FLIGHT THROUGH FRANCE*, where she describes the small theater in the home of George SAND at NOHANT. The commedia dell'arte also figures in Edith Wharton's first novel, *The VALLEY OF DECISION*.

Commonplace Book   Notebook into which Wharton jotted ideas and sometimes copied poems and other writings that interested her and that might provide future material for her poetry or fiction. In 1907 she copied Matthew ARNOLD's poem "Resignation" into her Commonplace Book. In early 1909 she copied Herbert Trench's poem "Apollo and the Seaman" into it; Benstock states that it was one source for her poem "Life" (*NGC* 205–6). She also copied lyrics and epigrams into her Commonplace Book from Anna de NOAILLES' *Les Eblouissements* ("Flowerings"). In a late Commonplace Book, she wrote, "I don't believe in God but I do believe in His saints—and then?" (*EW* 509–10).

Como, Lake   Located in the Lombardy region of ITALY, at the foot of the Italian Alps, Lake Como is the deepest in Europe (1245 ft.), with an area of about 145 square miles. The lake has a variety of settlements, from resorts to small villages to tiny ports. For centuries it has been a mecca for travelers and a retreat for the Italian aristocracy. It was a particular favorite of Wharton's friends Paul and Minnie BOURGET and Henry JAMES. There are a number of villas situated along the shore, some of which are open to the public. Edith and Teddy Wharton explored this lake as well as many others on their annual visits to Italy after their marriage in 1885, and it figures in her fiction as well as her travel writing.

The monumental 16th-century Villa d'Este, in the town of Cernobbio, was built by Cardinal Gallio. In *ITALIAN VILLAS AND THEIR GARDENS* Wharton mentions it, noting that the hotel building is not the original one, but that the old Renaissance gardens exist, plus a *bosco*, or section of natural woodland climbing the cliff-side, with "winding paths, summer-houses, and sylvan temples." In her second travel account, ITALIAN BACK-GROUNDS, she states that "visible Italy' begins with the valley of the Lira in a "wild Salvator Rosa landscape," and that, moving on toward Lake Como, her party seems to be moving through a gallery hung with Claude Lorrain's pictures (*IB* 10).

The Villa d'Este is also the setting of Wharton's short story "The MUSE'S TRAGEDY." The heroine, Mrs. Anerton, stays a month there; her suitor, Danyers, a fellow guest, sees her daily. They climb the "alleys of the hanging park."

In her 1922 novel *The GLIMPSES OF THE MOON,* Susy and Nick Lansing accept the offer of a villa on Lake Como for their honeymoon, "a lake so famed as the scene of romantic raptures that they were rather proud of not having been afraid to choose it as the setting of their own" (*GM* 5).

For further reading: Dwight, "The Influence of Italy on Edith Wharton"; Prampolini, "Edith Wharton in Italy"; St. Laurent, "Pathways to a Personal Aesthetic: Edith Wharton's Travels in Italy and France"; Wright, "Refracting the Odyssey: Edith Wharton's Travel Writing as the Cultural Capital of Her Fiction."

Comptour, Abbé The Abbé Comptour was a young priest in Lutèce, near Garges-lès-Gonesse and ST.-BRICE-SOUS-FORÊT, the primarily working-class Parisian suburb in which Edith Wharton's summer home, the PAVILLON COLOMBE, was located. Lutèce, with a population of more than 2,000, was in the *zone rouge,* built just after WORLD WAR I. These were poorly constructed villages with no water, drainage, medical care or schools. The Abbé Comptour feared that the impoverished people of the *zone rouge* might turn to socialist-communist solutions. Edith Wharton wrote the Paris *Herald* in September 1930 that he had managed to establish a thriving parish with a portable church and parish house with a dispensary; there had been 30 christenings and 12 marriages within the year. She begged the readers of the paper to contribute to the parish as they had in the past (*Letters* 531–32).

For more than 10 years Wharton sponsored an auction to benefit the church. In August 1931, her friend, the Chamoine of Garges-lès-Gonesse, christened a bronze bell named "Edith-Matilda," for Edith Wharton and her friend Matilda GAY. Funds for the bell had been raised by the impoverished parishioners of the church. Ogden CODMAN, the architect who was Edith Wharton's longtime friend and who collaborated with her on *The DECORATION OF HOUSES,* donated $4,500 to complete the belfry (*NGC* 427).

"Confession" First published as "Unconfessed Crime" in *Story-Teller* in March 1936, the story then appeared as "Confession" in HEARST'S INTERNATIONAL-COSMOPOLITAN magazine in May 1936. It was then published in the collection entitled *The WORLD OVER* (Appleton-Century, 1936). Originally the story was to have been a play, *Kate Spain,* based on the story of Lizzie Borden.

The narrator, Severance, is a NEW YORK banker who is convalescing from tuberculosis in a hotel at Mont Soleil in the fashionable Engadine region of Switzerland. A young American woman, Mrs. Kate Ingram, who appears to be wealthy, fashionably dressed, and intensely curious about her fellow residents, has arrived for the season at the same hotel, been seated at an adjacent table and catches his attention. Her companion, Miss Wilpert, takes a dislike to him and tries to keep them apart. Eventually the narrator discovers, through a newspaper reporter also staying at the hotel, that Mrs. Ingram is actually the notorious Kate Spain, who had been tried for the murder of her father and acquitted, as Lizzie Borden had been. Cassie Wilpert controls her because she was the servant girl whose testimony gave her an alibi; the consensus was that Ezra Spain had been killed by a passing homeless man.

The women flee from the hotel, but Severance tracks them down at a small pension on the Lake of Orta, rushes to propose and is accepted. Miss Wilpert threatens to tell everything, but has a stroke before she can do so. He and Kate marry, but not before she gives him an explanatory document Miss Wilpert had kept in her suitcase. After five years of happy marriage, she dies; he is alternately "blind with remembered joy" and "numb under present sorrow" (*CSS* II, 832). He then confesses he has never read the paper and is about to burn it. The *New York Times* critic Percy Hutchison stated that the story raised many "unanswerable questions" (*CR* 535).

"Confessional, The" Written in 1901, the story was published in CRUCIAL INSTANCES (Scribner's, 1901). It is a tale set in the turbulent period of Italian revolution and unification, the Risorgimento (c. 1815–70), which also figures in *The VALLEY OF DECISION.*

The narrator, a young accountant in the New England mill town of Dunstable, comes to know Don Egidio, the parish priest ministering to the largely Italian colony of mill workers. A foster child of an Italian count, Don Egidio was raised in the Val Camonica section of northern Italy, near Lago ISEO, a region Edith Wharton knew well and described in *ITALIAN BACKGROUNDS.* He is reticent about his reason for coming to America but on his deathbed reveals that it has to do with the count's elder son Roberto, his foster brother.

Roberto, who had stoutly resisted Austrian rule in Italy, had, in middle age, married a shy young girl, Faustina, whose family was sympathetic to the foreign rulers. She is reputed to have had an affair with a cousin, rumors of which had reached Roberto. On the eve of his departure to fight in the 1848 revolution against Austria, he had persuaded Don Egidio to let him hear her confession, which had satisfied him as to her innocence. She had later given birth to a daughter, and the count's younger brother and his family then occupied the palazzo, knowing the title would pass to his branch of the family.

Don Egidio had been banished to Dunstable, in America, as penance for having violated the sanctity of the confessional. He had been called to the bedside of a desperately ill professor of Italian in New York, who turned out to be Roberto. Roberto swore him to secrecy, and for eight years, until Roberto's death, they never spoke of the past. Roberto's meager earnings all went to assist exiled Italian patriots. Don Egidio has tended his grave until his own death. The story was translated into French by Jane d'Oillamson.

connoisseurship   Edith Wharton's upbringing in an elite and wealthy NEW YORK family, her wide reading and her extensive early travels endowed her with a substantial mount of what Pierre Bourdieu calls "the competence of the connoisseur" (*Distinction*, 66). This "competence" derives from long contact with cultured persons and places, and is evident in her travel accounts, fiction, poetry and criticism.

Edith Wharton's travel books are the earliest sustained manifestation of her connoisseurship and justify Blake Nevius' characterization of them as "brilliantly written and permanently interesting" (*Edith Wharton*, 37). Such works as ITALIAN VILLAS AND THEIR GARDENS, ITALIAN BACKGROUNDS, A MOTOR-FLIGHT THROUGH FRANCE, FIGHTING FRANCE, FROM DUNKERQUE TO BELFORT, FRENCH WAYS AND THEIR MEANING, and *In* MOROCCO, in addition to *The DECORATION OF HOUSES*, not only show Wharton's knowledge of art and architecture, but also her ability to juxtapose them with a complex background of theology, classical mythology, history and literature. Her cultural competence, or taste, allows her to integrate scholarly and imaginative approaches to travel, the quality most desired by her audience. This audience consisted not only of affluent Americans who went regularly to Europe, as their parents and grandparents had done, but also of literate middle-class travelers who were able, before WORLD WAR I, to travel to Europe, on a more modest level—or who, at least, could travel vicariously by purchasing Wharton's books.

Edith Wharton's connoisseurship first became clear in *The Decoration of Houses* (1897), which she wrote with the architect Ogden CODMAN. It contains an elaborate codification of European principles of harmony and design that could be employed, on a domestic scale, by wealthy Americans in their house planning. Many of its principles, such as "proportion is the good breeding of

architecture," were formulated during Wharton's early years in Europe, and, in some ways, this now constitutes an archive on which she drew in much of her travel writing. It is arguable that the book could not have been written if it had not been for Wharton's extensive European residence as a child and young adult. Taken to EUROPE in 1866, at the age of four, Wharton and her family spent six years abroad, living in ITALY, FRANCE, and Germany; she became fluent in all three languages and was constantly exposed to European art, architecture and sculpture.

Italian Villas and Their Gardens, a compilation of articles Wharton was commissioned to write for the *CENTURY Magazine*, is marked by a high level of scholarship. There are descriptions of more than 75 villas and their gardens, a bibliography of reference works in four languages, capsule biographies of 55 architects and landscape gardeners of the 15th through the 18th centuries, and a detailed index. The work is a tour de force explaining and illustrating the aesthetic principles lying behind Italian gardens.

Italian Backgrounds consists of nine essays about towns, landscapes, and cities mixed with accounts of her travels in the Italian Alps over several years. It contains learned analyses of the paintings, sculptures, frescoes, and buildings Wharton saw on her travels, but is also a narrative with both charm and insight into the lives of the inhabitants.

In *A Motor-Flight Through France* Wharton recounts three journeys by car through France in 1906 and 1907. It embodies new perspectives and new values; Wharton still seeks "by-ways," in the sense of little-known places, but her journeys are more rapid and free of the "bondage to fixed hours and the beaten track" that have characterized railway travel (*MFF* 1). She de-

Beauvais Cathedral. From A Motor-Flight Through France *(1908), first edition* (Collection of the author)

scribes both cathedrals, churches, villages and historic homes such as that of George SAND in NOHANT. Sometimes she places the art and architecture in a historical context. At other times, however, she embellishes a scene it with a "*bon mouvement* of the imagination" lending a fictional quality, as when she envisions the frenetic stonecutters of the doomed Cathedral of Beauvais crying, "We simply can't keep it up!" Their imaginary cry is a paradigm for the speed of their tours.

Fighting France, from Dunkerque to Belfort is a poignant book about WORLD WAR I based on several trips Wharton made to the Front. She mourns the threatened and destroyed treasures of France, describing, to take only two examples, the "torn traceries" of the ruined church of Clermont-en-Argonne (*FF* 61) and the shell of Rheims Cathedral, fire-bombed by the Germans.

French Ways and Their Meaning makes explicit the reasons for Wharton's profound attachment to France and her ultimate expatriation. She examines the enduring mores and philosophical outlook of the French from a post-war perspective. She discusses four salient qualities of the Gallic spirit: reverence, taste, continuity, and intellectual honesty. In the conclusion of the book, she declares, passionately, that one can answer all criticisms of French shortcomings by crying, "*Look at the results!* Read her history, study her art, follow up the current of her ideas; then look about you, and you will see that the whole world is full of her spilt glory" (*FWM* 149). It is a glory she believed would become apparent to all Americans after the Armistice.

Wharton's last travel book, *In Morocco*, resulted from an invitation to tour the country in 1917 by Louis-Hubert Lyautey, the French Resident General. Much of her discussion of the country is on its art and artifacts and the need to preserve them, further evidence of her connoisseurship.

Edith Wharton's connoisseurship is also evident in her fiction. Many of her interior settings are enriched with descriptions of paintings and furniture. The plots sometimes turn on matters of art, as in *FALSE DAWN*, which concerns the attempt of a wealthy New York businessman, Halston Raycie, to found an Heirloom Gallery of art. He sends his son to Europe to acquire 17th- and 18th-century Italian paintings for it, but Lewis Raycie meets John RUSKIN on a Swiss mountaintop, is converted to medieval art, and returns with the paintings of Piero della Francesca and Giotto di Bondone. His father is enraged and abandons the Heirloom Gallery. Lewis and his devoted wife toil the remainder of their lives soliciting visitors for their own small gallery of unappreciated primitives.

There are too many examples of her connoisseurship in Edith Wharton's fiction to enumerate in detail, but it may be said that art and artifacts play a role in the majority of her short stories and novels, from *The VALLEY OF DECISION* through *The BUCCANEERS*. Odo Valsecca's youthful odyssey in Italy in *The Valley of Decision*, which exposes him to the artistic achievements of the country, Lily Bart's portrayal of the central figure in Joshua Reynolds' Mrs. Lloyd in the *tableau vivant* in *The HOUSE OF MIRTH*. Undine Spragg's crass attempt to sell the Boucher tapestries belonging to the de Chelles family in *The CUSTOM OF THE COUNTRY*, John Campton's portrait of his son George in *A SON AT THE FRONT*, the paintings at Longlands House and Tintagel in *The Buccaneers*—these are only a few examples of the importance of art in Edith Wharton's fiction. In juxtaposing the connoisseur and the philistine, she prioritizes the subject of art and artifacts. Their aesthetic education becomes a litmus test of her characters' taste and sensitivity; conversely, their indifference to the finer attainments of civilization is an index to their lack of breeding and, sometimes, overt boorishness.

Edith Wharton's connoisseurship was also manifested in her poetry, particularly in such poems as "The Three Francescas," "Botticelli's Madonna in the Louvre" and "Chartres."

Conrad, Joseph (1857–1924)   The son of a Polish aristocrat, Conrad's original name was Teodor Józef Korzeniowski; he became a naturalized British citizen under the name Joseph Conrad. Regarded as a major 20th-century novelist, Conrad's most noted works include *Nostromo, Heart of Darkness, The Nigger of the Narcissus, The Secret Agent, The Secret Sharer, Victory* and *Under Western Eyes*. His reputation among his contemporaries was based on his sea stories, but he is now considered a masterful explorer of moral situations and the psychology of the individual's innermost urges.

Edith Wharton began reading his novella "The Secret Sharer" in 1913, just as *The CUSTOM OF THE COUNTRY* began serial publication. It concerns a ship's captain who, unknowingly, takes on board a murderer, a man physically and psychologically his "double." She exclaimed to Gaillard LAPSLEY, "What a man!" She wrote Conrad to inquire about the story's translation into French, and Conrad replied that the "appreciation of a fellow worker of such great and distinguished gifts can't but be precious to me." He did not believe it would be suitable for translation into French, however. Edith Wharton acquired all of his writings (*EW* 331).

Conrad contributed a long essay, "Poland Revisited," to *The BOOK OF THE HOMELESS*, published in 1916 to raise money for war relief (*EW* 380). Conrad termed it a "very fine vol." and the best of the wartime gift books he had seen (*Letters* V, 559). In 1917 Conrad wrote to praise Wharton for *SUMMER*, saying the book "presents itself *en beauté, toujours en beauté.*" He commented that he greatly admired her rhythms, which were "so very fine, distinct, and subtle" (*EW* 398).

Cook, Charles Edith Wharton's chauffeur from 1904 to 1923, when he had a slight stroke, gave up driving and left her employment. Cook was a native of Lee, Massachusetts and apparently was a master mechanic as well as an expert driver. Among his more trying passengers was Henry JAMES, who insisted on giving misdirections in Malvern, Windsor and other places. Cook was at the wheel when Edith Wharton made her first visit to I TATTI, the home of Bernard and Mary BERENSON near Florence. He then drove Edith Wharton and Walter BERRY on a tour of central Italy in Wharton's new 50 h.p. Mercedes, which she called a great improvement over "our old plodding Hortense" (*EW* 314).

In 1912, with remarkable skill and nerve, he drove Edith Wharton and Walter Berry up a treacherous and narrow winding road through the Apennines to the monastery of La Verna. Local peasants had to take their luggage off and bring it on carts, in addition to putting rocks behind the wheels at the steepest ascents. They did not arrive until 11:30 P.M. The next day, she wrote Bernard Berenson, the car had to be let down by ropes, with Cook "steering down the vertical descent, & twenty men hanging onto a *funa* [rope] that, thank the Lord, *didn't break*" (*Letters* 173).

It was Cook who drove when Edith Wharton went to ALGERIA and TUNISIA in March 1914. He stowed the large touring car on board the S. S. *Timgad* from Marseilles and drove through both countries. Others in the party were the young English writer Percy LUBBOCK, Edith Wharton's new maid Elise DUVLENCK and her long-time companion and secretary Anna BAHLMANN.

In 1920, Edith Wharton constructed small houses on the grounds of the PAVILLON COLOMBE at St.-Brice-sous-Forêt for Cook and his Swedish wife and for Alfred WHITE, the Englishman who had long served as her butler, but was now given the title of "general agent" (*EW* 427).

When Cook was forced to retire in the winter of 1923, Edith Wharton looked sadly back on all the days he had driven her and her guests on their "epic *randonées*" or circuits (*EW* 449) through New England and across Italy, France, Germany, North Africa and England. He and his wife retired to America on a generous pension Wharton provided.

"Copy" First published in the June 1900 SCRIBNER'S MAGAZINE, the story appeared later in *CRUCIAL INSTANCES* (Scribner's, 1901). The principal characters are a famous woman novelist and a well-known poet who conduct a love affair and later contest the ownership of their correspondence. Like *The TOUCHSTONE*, the tale raises the question of whether the sender or the recipient owns the rights to letters, particularly those of public figures.

The story takes the shape of a dramatic dialogue between the widowed Mrs. Ambrose Dale ("forty, slender, still young") sitting in her drawing room before a tea table and Paul Ventnor, married ("tall, nearly fifty, with an incipient stoutness buttoned into a masterly frock coat"), who calls on her when in town. Although they have not met for 20 years, their youthful romance is still a vivid memory to both. Ventnor brings her letters with him, claiming he always carries them, and inquires about his, which she has kept in a safe. They reminisce over the letters, but each begins to suspect the other wants to possess them to use in a memoir. Mrs. Dale refuses to let Ventnor "carry all this rubbish off," even though, as he observes, both of them are, as writers, "public property." He, similarly, declines to return hers. Since they failed, at the time, to "copyright" their remarks about the weather or keep their "epigrams in cold storage," they finally decide to burn all the letters. They are the key to their former "secret garden," which, they well know, will be explored by future "excursionists"; thus they hope to preserve their early relationship from exploitation.

"Copy" anticipates the situation Edith Wharton would face a few years later, when she requested that Morton FULLERTON return the letters she had written him and he refused to do so. They have now been made public.

Wharton chooses, for the fictive title of one of Mrs. Dale's novels, *Pomegranate Seed*, which would actually be the title of a short story she published in 1929, a demonstration of how long some of her works were inculcated and took root mentally before she began writing them.

For further reading: Margolis, "The Public Life: The Discourse of Privacy in the Age of Celebrity."

"Coward, A" First published in *The GREATER INCLINATION* (Scribner's, 1899), "A Coward" has been called by R. W. B. Lewis "an anecdote alive with comical tonalities" (*EW* 81). It concerns a young man of good family, Vibart, who has met a pretty girl, Irene Carstyle, while visiting his aunt in a New England summer colony. Mrs. Carstyle is pretentious and ambitious, complaining that, but for her husband, she would have had a New York town house, a private carriage and the advantages of a foreign education for Irene.

Vibart develops an admiration for the reticent, intellectual Mr. Carstyle, who has set up a law office but spends most of his time reading Montaigne. He learns from his aunt that Mr. Carstyle is of "the Albany Carstyles," a wealthy family. Mr. Carstyle had discovered, however, on the death of his only brother, that the brother had depleted considerable funds entrusted to the family, depriving widows and orphans of their income. For some time he has voluntarily retrenched and forced economies on his wife and daughter in order to make reparations, a quiet sacrifice Vibart regards as "heroic."

Mr. Carstyle confides to Vibart that he is continually on the lookout for a crisis in which he can act as a hero, since years before, during a world tour, he had an experience on the Greek island of Chios and discovered he was a coward. During the earthquake he had run from town into a vineyard and saved himself, but, in so doing, had abandoned Collis, the young man who was one of his traveling companions. It had been Vibart's turn to nurse his friend, who, semiparalyzed with diphtheria, was unable to escape. Mr. Carstyle has suffered for it ever since, yet fails to perceive, as Vibart does, the heroic nature of his slow, patient assumption of his brother's debt, particularly in view of Mrs. Carstyle's obtuse complaints about their economies.

The reviewer for the *Book Buyer* praised Edith Wharton's ability to suggest character in a succinct phrase, such as "Mr. Carstyle always seems to be winking at you through a slit in his professional manner" (*CR* 15). The story was accounted a failure by some reviewers, however, such as Harry Thurston Peck, who wrote in the *Bookman* it was not "consonant" with the reader's presumed expectations and lacked a "constructive coherence" (*CR* 19).

The use of Chios as a setting is authentic; Edith Wharton, her husband and James VAN ALEN had visited the island on their 1888 Aegean cruise and found it wracked by previous earthquakes. In *The CRUISE OF THE VANADIS* she mentions the earthquake of 1881, which might well be the one Mr. Carstyle experienced.

"Criticism of Fiction, The"   An essay Edith Wharton published in the *Times Literary Supplement* (London) in May 1914. She begins by referring to Henry JAMES's article "The Younger Generation," which appeared in the *Times Literary Supplement* (London) in two installments in March and April, 1914. Wegener points out that James had discussed her novel *The CUSTOM OF THE COUNTRY* in his essay. Whereas she believed he had bracketed her with John Galsworthy and Robert Hitchens, it was really Maurice HEWLETT with whom he had compared her.

Wharton distinguishes between the status of critics of fiction in English-speaking countries, where authors hold them in contempt, and in France, where they are esteemed and there is perpetual discussion of literary questions, "thus creating an atmosphere of critical sensibility into which the novelist is born." She argues that since a sense of design is inborn in humans, a certain amount of criticism of any work is inevitable. The critic must learn to dwell on and interpret the novelist's highest gift, "that divining and life-evoking faculty," which is the foundation of his art. James wrote praising the "fine strain" of her critical voice. (*UCW* 120–28).

Crucial Instances   Collection of short stories published by Scribner's in April 1901. Some critics considered the volume inferior to *The GREATER INCLINATION* and believed Edith Wharton might be recycling unpublished stories written earlier, but, according to Lewis, all the stories were written in 1900 and 1901 (*EW* 98). The volume was not acclaimed by critics. Wharton was compared somewhat unfavorably with Henry JAMES and with Honoré de Balzac. The reviewer for the *Independent* believed her genius to consist "in a delicate perception of forms and color." The *Harper's Monthly* reviewer suggested she wrote "almost too much in the manner of Mr. Henry James." The author of a long review in the *Academy* termed it a "little book of admirable tales" and professed a "sincere admiration for Mrs. Wharton's original and delicate talent," but felt she had aspired in vain to a "Balzacian" manner (*CR* 43–47).

The volume contained "*The DUCHESS AT PRAYER*," "*The ANGEL AT THE GRAVE*," "*The RECOVERY*," "COPY", "*The REMBRANDT*," "*The MOVING FINGER*" and "*The CONFESSIONAL*."

Cruises, Aegean   *See CRUISE OF THE VANADIS, THE; OSPREY.*

Cruise of the Vanadis, The   The diary of Edith and Teddy WHARTON's 1888 cruise aboard the steam yacht *VANADIS*, which they chartered with their friend James VAN ALEN for a four-month cruise. Edith Wharton was then 26. The couple had worried that they could not afford such an extravagance, but went ahead. On their return, they discovered that Edith Wharton's cousin, Joshua JONES, had left her a substantial legacy that more than covered the cost of the cruise.

In 1991, a French scholar, Claudine Lesage of the University of Amiens, discovered a detailed diary Edith Wharton had kept of the cruise. Lesage states, in her introduction, that the reasons Wharton did not publish the diary are unknown. Having discovered it, however, Lesage believed the responsibility for publication devolved upon her, and she proceeded to publish it through the University of Amiens. Lesage observes that the diary counters the widely held notion that Wharton's "beginnings as a writer were a mere accident, an occupation for an idle rich woman." Instead, she argues, it is clear that "just as a violinist diligently practises her scales before appearing in front of an audience she had been writing extensively though privately." She calls it Wharton's "maiden *Odyssey* into literature" (*CV* 10).

In a paper presented at the "Edith Wharton at Yale" conference in 1995, "1895: Edith Wharton's Silent Year," Jean Blackall proposed that the manuscript we have was not simply a journal Wharton kept during the cruise, but instead represents an edited or modified version of the original diary. (Her paper is now being prepared for publication.)

The diary contains 17 brief chapters chronicling progress from Algiers and Tunis on to Malta, Syracuse, Messina and Taormina, Palermo and Girgenti, Corfu and Zante, Milo and Santorin, Amorgos and Astypalia, Rhodes, Tenos and Patmos, Chios and Smyrna, Mitylene, Mount Athos, Athens, the Ionian Islands, Cattaro and Cettinje, and Dalmatia. At the beginning of each chapter there is a brief summary of the major sites and people discussed, a plan Edith Wharton never followed in her later works of travel.

It is unlikely Wharton ever intended the diary to be published, since in later years she denied, or failed to recall, having written it at all. She declares in *A BACK-WARD GLANCE*, "until 1918 I never kept even the briefest of diaries." (*BG* 6). Conceivably she thought of it less as a conventional diary than as a sequence of notes that she might later use in constructing a travel account. In both concept and phraseology it contains the nucleus of her later travel writing. For example, similar descriptions of the Castle of Euryalus, a fortress built by Denys the Elder during the Greek period, appear in the diary and in *ITALIAN BACKGROUNDS*.

Wharton's craving for travel is suggested by her choice of the epigraph to *The Cruise of the Vanadis*, from Goethe's *Faust* (I, 1122–25). Faust, who harbors conflicting "souls" in his breast of repose and exertion, tells the pedantic, sedentary Wagner he wishes for a magic cloak so that he might soar into *fremde Länder* or foreign lands; he would not trade such a garment for a *Königsmantel*, or king's robe. The epigraph imparts a motif of impetuous and romantic escapism, of freedom from earth-bound concerns, which confirms Wharton's later characterization of the cruise in *A Backward Glance* as having been undertaken improvidently and enthusiastically. She is a voracious intellectual wanderer, open to

all experiences and often interpreting sights she sees in the light of the extensive historic and classical reading she had undertaken in her youth. Travel not only met a deeply felt inner need on the part of Wharton, but also offered a means of escape from what had turned out to be a disappointing marriage. Clearly, re-enacting travels through writing about them was vitally important to Wharton. She called the cruise the "crowning wonder of my life" (*EW* 469).

Certain aspects of the cruise are of historic importance, particularly the visit to Mount Athos, the Greek peninsula that is home to more than 20 Byzantine monasteries, some dating from the ninth century. Women have never, since its earliest history, been allowed on Mount Athos, but the men of the party were allowed to tour the monasteries. Wharton's account of the Holy Mountain, consisting of her observations from the ship and her companions' reports, is the first known description by an American.

The cruise aboard the *Vanadis* and a second one, many years later, bracketed Wharton's travel writing chronologically. Although the chronicle of the first was not published in her lifetime, and the record of the second was an unrealized project, taken together they are evidence of Wharton's profound attachment to travel and to writing about travel. Looking back on the first cruise many years later, she termed it "the greatest step forward in my making" (*BG* 98). She valued freedom from everyday concerns: "only twice in my life have I been able to put all practical cares out of my mind for months, and each time it has been on a voyage in the Aegean" (*BG* 100).

Steam yacht Vanadis, *photo c. 1890s, probably at Dartmouth, England* (Courtesy Mystic Seaport Museum)

In 1926, Wharton again stretched her resources to share a charter for a nine-week voyage aboard the yacht *OSPREY*. She had planned to write a book about the second cruise, calling it "The Sapphire Way," which would have paid some of her expenses, but, on her return, wrote more fiction instead.

"Cup of Cold Water, A" First published in *The GREATER INCLINATION* (Scribner's, 1899), the story had been rejected by Edward G. BURLINGAME in 1894 as being "wildly improbable" (*EW* 81). Edith Wharton reworked it for this volume. It concerns a young man, Woburn, who has lost his fortune and some of his firm's funds trying to impress the girl he loves, finds himself in debt and plans to flee the country. Before he sails, he spends his last night in a cheap hotel in the room next to a young woman about to commit suicide. He spends his last few dollars rescuing her and sending her back to her husband. Afterwards, instead of fleeing, he decides to face up to his crime.

Later critics did not share Burlingame's reservations. John D. Barry, reviewing the collection for *Literary World*, praised the story for showing "insight into masculine character that is not often found in the fiction of women" (*CR* 14). Harry Thurston Peck, writing in *The Bookman*, called it a "powerful bit of emotional psychology" (*CR* 19).

Custom of the Country, The Edith Wharton considered this novel, published by Scribner's in 1913, one of her best, although critics have not, as a whole, shared her opinion. It is an international novel of manners, contrasting the limited American small-town background of the heroine, Undine Spragg, with the worlds of old NEW YORK and aristocratic FRANCE.

A native of Apex, Kansas, Undine is a ruthless social climber and fortune hunter who marries and divorces at will in order to better her lot. In the process, she hurts her parents, leads her second husband to commit suicide, deprives both sets of grandparents of their grandson, and pays little attention to her young son.

Before the novel opens, she has married and divorced a local boy, Elmer Moffatt. She then marries Ralph Marvell, scion of a conservative old New York family. After she leaves Ralph, she becomes, briefly, the mistress of Peter van Degen, a millionaire playboy. Ralph commits suicide, and Undine then marries Raymond de Chelles, son of a French count, before returning to the level of her first marriage and re-marrying Elmer Moffatt, now a millionaire. She ultimately finds that upward mobility has its penalties, and that certain social rules are inflexible for those who aspire beyond themselves. The novel presents an escalation of marriage and divorce; marriage becomes the true business of America, both a tribal ritual and a commercial

transaction. Brookner observes that Edith Wharton "knows every nuance of the world she is describing" (Brookner, "Introduction," 3).

As the novel opens, Undine Spragg is attempting to enter New York society. She is the daughter of indulgent nouveau riche parents who have moved from Apex to New York City to please her and help her recover from her first marriage. They live at first in hotel suites, where Undine attempts to learn who "counts" from her mother's masseuse, Mrs. Heeny, who has gleaned her information from the social columns of newspapers. She then begs her father for a season's subscription to an opera box, believing that such a purchase will solidify the perilous foothold she has gained in being asked to dinner by Ralph Marvell's kind sister. The opera house serves as a showcase for the "sacred semicircle" of New York society. Undine is able to recognize, if not to "name," the "fixed figure-heads of the social prow," and to formulate "one of the guiding principles of her career, 'It's better to watch than to ask questions' " (*CC* 40).

Through expert maneuvering, Undine manages to marry Ralph Marvell, of old New York lineage, a poetic and ineffectual match for Undine. He devises a sentimental Italian honeymoon, where they rest on a hillside ledge above the ilex grove of a long yellow Sienese villa. Here Ralph Marvell is at the pinnacle of happiness with Undine. Later, the memory of this scene marks the culmination of his unhappiness, after he discovers the truth about her surreptitious first marriage to Elmer Moffatt and recalls her disavowal of all prior knowledge of Elmer during their own marriage.

Undine separates from Ralph and has an affair with the wealthy playboy Peter van Degen. Ralph hopes to get custody of their young son, Paul, even if he loses his wife. He learns, however, that Elmer Moffatt's business venture, in which he has invested heavily, has failed to get a charter, and realizes he cannot afford to pay Undine the required sum in order to retain custody of their son: the "whole archaic structure of his rites and sanctions" has "tumbled down about him" (*CC* 265). He returns home and shoots himself.

Undine, meanwhile, has a loftier ambition: to become the wife of a French nobleman. She captures Raymond de Chelles, whose father is a count. They bring little Paul to France and divide their time between PARIS and their country chateau, Saint Désert. Undine is intellectually incapable of becoming the civilized "New Frenchwoman" so clearly described in *FRENCH WAYS AND THEIR MEANING*. She also fails to give Raymond an heir. When Raymond's father dies and he inherits the title, Undine expects to live in Paris with an active social life. Instead, she encounters the rigid rules of French mourning, and must stay for months at Saint Désert, the upkeep of which is a continual worry to Raymond.

Nowhere are the rubrics of French society clearer than in French attitudes toward inherited things. If such legacies are shabby and frayed, they consume the labor of the women of the family. Undine is horrified to find that she is expected to share custodianship of the de Chelles treasures. Her brother-in-law, Hubert de Chelles, refuses to carry out his duties, however. Under the influence of his American wife (appropriately named "Looty" Arlington), he violates tradition by altering the decor of their Paris *hôtel* (or town house); he and Looty have scenes of Pompeii painted on the dining room walls. There is no error more grave than to regard possessions as a liquid asset, as Undine discovers when she invites Mr. Fleischhauer, an art and antiques dealer, to Saint Désert in order to appraise the Boucher tapestries originally presented to the family by Louis XV (*CC* 298). He is accompanied by Elmer Moffatt, Undine's first husband, a collector only of things "not for sale." Moffatt is acquainted with "swells," who, when "hard-up," "generally chip off an heirloom," but is astonished to find Undine the châtelaine of Saint Désert. When Raymond de Chelles discovers the clandestine visit, he is enraged. Undine replies that she cannot live in "poverty" (i.e., she cannot be expected to sacrifice having a regular season in Paris) when " 'all you've got to do is hold out your hand and have two million francs drop into it!' " He regards her as if she were an "alien apparition," as indeed she is, and delivers a ringing indictment of the attitude of the New World to the Old. He accuses her of coming from a country she cares for "so little that before you've been a day in ours you've forgotten the very house you were born in—if it wasn't torn down before you knew it!" American hotels are as big as towns, and the towns "as flimsy as paper, where the streets haven't had time to be named, and the buildings are demolished before they're dry." Americans understand nothing of the things that make life "decent and honourable" for the French (*CC* 307).

Undine finally begins to perceive that her husband's family is profoundly inimical to evolution and change. Their heirlooms could not under normal circumstances be liquidated, but Undine does, finally, acquire the tapestries as Mrs. Elmer Moffatt, when Hubert de Chelles' American father-in-law, General Arlington, declares bankruptcy and they must be sold.

The novel questions the value of money and position. These are not intrinsically bad; in fact, they are worth possessing, but not if they are acquired in the wrong way. Moreover, they must be tempered by taste. Throughout *The Custom of the Country*, Wharton tests the standards of interior design she made explicit in *The DECORATION OF HOUSES*, which she wrote with Ogden CODMAN. The qualities of restraint and proportion she praises in that volume are also hallmarks of ideal behavior. Wealth, for Undine, becomes synonymous

with marriage; social relations and commercial value eventually become indistinguishable. The marriages of the socially prominent become public property through their dissemination in the press; Mrs. Heeny's bag of press clippings comes to symbolize the transience of social and marital fortunes. Undine herself does her own marital bargaining; daughters and young women, rather than their parents, are the sovereign agents of marriage and divorce, but wealth is dispensed by men. Lewis terms *The Custom of the Country* her "most powerful if not her most beguiling novel" (*EW* 348).

The strength of the novel lies not only in the depiction of the America of upstart millionaires as they meet the conservators of the old mercantile fortunes, but also in the delineation of the old families of Europe selling out to American wealth. The aristocracies of New York as well as Europe were, as Lewis puts it, "giving way before the two major forces of the historic moment—sexual power and financial aggressiveness" (*EW* 349).

Dupree argues that Undine Spragg, who has eluded definition as a feminist heroine because of her callous and selfish amorality, actually "mimics patriarchal discourse for the purpose of escaping its power to define her." Bentley suggests that the novel "brings to life a suspiciously commercial circulation of women, made possible by divorce and remarriage"; the American divorcée becomes a "quintessential 'alien' " (163). She observes that the publication of the novel, which ran in SCRIBNER's from January through November 1913, paralleled the ending of Wharton's marriage (her divorce was granted in Paris April 16, 1913). Between the time of her divorce and the beginning of WORLD WAR I, she began 15 months of frenetic traveling with various friends. Just as many avenues seemed open to Wharton, so, too, did many choices present themselves to Undine, made wealthy through her remarriage to Elmer Moffatt. Divorce was still, however, something of a stigma for Wharton, just as it was for Undine. At the end of the novel, she realizes that, being divorced, she can never attain the supreme status of being an ambassador's wife, "the one part she was really made for."

For further reading: Ammons, "The Business of Marriage in Edith Wharton's *The Custom of the Country*"; Bentley, "Edith Wharton and the Alienation of Divorce"; Brookner, "Introduction" *The Custom of the Country*; Dupree, "Jamming the Machinery: Mimesis in The Custom of the Country"; McDowell, "Viewing the Custom of Her Country: Edith Wharton's Feminism"; Morrow, "Games and Conflict in Edith Wharton's *The Custom of the Country*"; Voloshin, "Exchange in Wharton's *The Custom of the Country*."

Custom of the Country, The (play, 1984) *See* Appendix II.

Cutting, Bayard, Jr. (1878–1910) The son of a railroad magnate, Bayard Cutting Jr. studied under George SANTAYANA at Harvard and served as private secretary to Joseph Choate, the American ambassador in London. While there he met and married Lady Sybil Cuffe, whose father was an Irish peer. Edith Wharton had come to know the Cutting family soon after her marriage. In 1903 she befriended the young couple in Florence, taking them to call on Vernon LEE and on antique-shopping excursions. Bayard Cutting Jr. died of consumption while still young. His widow, Lady Sybil Cutting, married and divorced Geoffrey SCOTT and then married Percy LUBBOCK, both friends of Edith Wharton. Wharton came to disapprove of Lady Sybil Cutting, predicting that she would annex and marry each of her men friends in turn.

The Cuttings once spent a summer at Lenox, in the hope of improving Bayard's health. Edith Wharton wrote later that she learned in those months "of how fine and delicate a substance he was." She believed that men of his stature and capabilities had long been needed in American public life, and observed that his death "was a loss far beyond the immediate circle of his friends" (*BG* 152).

Cutting, Lady Sybil *See* LUBBOCK, LADY SYBIL

"Cycle of Reviewing, A" An article Edith Wharton wrote at the request of the London *Spectator*, it appeared in August 1928. She reviews the "zigzag course of modern reviewing" over the 29 years since she threw her "first infant to the wolves." For example, early in the century critics deplored her absence of plot, then urged her to free herself from the "incubus" of plot. The current complaint of reviewers is, she notes, that she only writes about the rich. She observes drily that PROUST's *Swann's Way* was severely criticized for dealing with fashionable people. Reviewers, she concludes, have subscribed to the fallacy of believing readers want only a specific "line of goods." The writer's principal task is not to please reviewers but to convey his "inward vision" to the reader (*UCW* 159–163).

D

Dante Alighieri (1265–1321) One of the greatest of Italian poets, Dante was the first important author to write in his native language. Born in Florence, as a young man he was involved in the wars between the Guelphs and Ghibellines. His early love was Beatrice, whom he first met at the age of nine; he next saw her when he was 18. He married Gemma Donati, by whom he had several children. He is best known for the *Commedia* or *Divine Comedy*.

In her memoir, *A BACKWARD GLANCE*, Wharton noted her early reading of Dante after her family returned from EUROPE in 1872. She also read the poet's works with her friend Emelyn WASHBURN, daughter of Dr. E. A. WASHBURN, rector of Calvary Church, NEW YORK. Lewis states that the two girls would read Dante together on the library roof outside Emelyn's window (*EW* 28). Part of Wharton's first novel, *The VALLEY OF DECISION* (1902), was set on the BRENTA RIVIERA, near VENICE, which Dante knew well. Her old friend Charles Eliot NORTON supplied her with a number of books from his library as source material. Norton was a pioneer in the establishment of Dante scholarship in America, and made the standard prose translation of the *Divine Comedy*. In 1902 she also published an essay, "The THREE FRANCESCAS," about three plays being produced, all dealing with the story of Paolo and Francesca. Their relationship is the subject of one of the most famous episodes in Dante's *Hell* (or the *Inferno*, Part I of the *Divine Comedy*).

Dante's poetry was intimately related to Wharton's deepest emotions. In 1908, during her affair with Morton FULLERTON, she cited a line from the *Purgatory* (Part II of the *Divine Comedy*) in her account of a visit they made to the town of Herblay: " '*Conosco i segni dell'antica fiamma*' " ("I recognize the tokens of the ancient flame") (*EW* 204–5). She and her friend Matilda GAY went to a Dante reading in PARIS a few evenings later. During the period of her involvement with Fullerton, Wharton also quoted various lines from Dante in her DIARY (1907, "The Life Apart").

Darrow, George *See REEF, THE.*

Dastrey, Paul *See SON AT THE FRONT, A.*

"Daunt, Diana, The" A short story published in *SCRIBNER'S MAGAZINE* in 1909 and in *TALES OF MEN AND*

GHOSTS (Scribner's, 1910). It is the story of Humphrey Neave, an American connoisseur in Rome, impoverished but with acute perceptions, something of a mystic and a poet. He works as a tutor and guide to the antiquities of Rome, occasionally finding overlooked treasures in the city and countryside such as the "amputated extremities of maimed marbles." He becomes something of an expert and is invited to London to view the "Daunt Diana," a statue of Diana in the home of Daunt, a wealthy collector. He ponders the unfair gap between taste and money; the rich collector has no discrimination; the poor connoisseur cannot afford the treasures he perceives and appreciates. Neave's taste feeds on him like a lizard, getting larger and stronger and eating away at him; his "imagination had romanticized the acquisitive instinct" (*CSS* II, 53).

Eventually Neave inherits a fortune from an uncle in the corset business and acquires the Daunt Collection. The narrator calls on him in his palazzo in Rome, only to find him apathetic. He then sells the Daunt Collection, only to buy it back piece by piece. He has missed the struggle, the "first divine moment of possession," the bonding, so to speak, with material artifacts. Acquiring works of art too easily is like a marriage of convenience, a transaction, without "wooing." He has no relationship to those of his possessions which have not begged for rescue (*CSS* II, 57).

Eventually he reacquires everything except the Daunt Diana, now owned by a wealthy, unrefined American woman and displayed under a "thousand candle power chandelier." The narrator searches for Neave again in Rome, and finds that he has managed to repossess the Diana through drastic economies. He has installed her in a tenement flat; the setting, he admits, is not worthy of the statue, but his adoration of her makes it acceptable. He has returned to the level of his early lodgings above a wineshop, but the Diana "rules there at last, she shines and hovers there above him."

Benstock believes the protagonist reflects aspects of Egerton WINTHROP (Edith Wharton's early friend in Newport, Rhode Island), Ogden CODMAN, and Bernard BERENSON (*NGC* 244).

Davies, Hylton *See MOTHER'S RECOMPENSE, THE.*

Davril, René *See SON AT THE FRONT, A.*

"Day of the Funeral, The" First published in *Woman's Home Companion* as "In A Day," the story was included in HUMAN NATURE (Appleton & Co., 1933). The opening paragraph presents a microcosm of the situation: "His wife had said: 'If you don't give her up I'll throw myself from the roof.' He had not given her up, and his wife had thrown herself from the roof." Several reviewers singled out the story as the best in the collection. It deals with the guilt experienced by Ambrose Trenham, professor at a small college in the New England town of Kingsborough on the day of his wife's funeral and his changing relationship with Barbara Wake, the woman who caused his wife's death.

The critic for the SATURDAY REVIEW OF LITERATURE praised the story as showing a glimpse "of the author's old penetration into the mysteries of personality" (*CR* 506).

"Debt, The" A short story published in SCRIBNER'S MAGAZINE in 1909 and in TALES OF MEN AND GHOSTS (Scribner's, 1910). It deals with a problem of scientific ethics, in which a young biologist, Galen Dredge, a poor student, has been befriended at college by Archie Lanfear, son of Professor Lanfear. He comes to stay for the summer in the family bungalow near Professor Lanfear's biological laboratory at Woods Hole, Massachusetts. He develops a quiet passion for Archie's mother, Mrs. Lanfear, "with her tight hair and her loose shape, her blameless brow and earnest eyeglasses, and her perpetual air of mild misapprehension" (*CSS* II, 63). Archie is something of a dilettante, trying first one profession and then another, but Galen Dredge succeeds Professor Lanfear in an endowed chair of biology at Columbia. After Lanfear's death, the family discovers that Galen has betrayed them; his great work, *The Arrival of the Fittest*, which he is presenting in public lectures, is actually a refutation of Professor Lanfear's own major opus, *Utility and Variation*. When they confront Galen, however, he points out that Professor Lanfear would have defended his duty to set forth the truth, and that it was part of the debt he owed Lanfear to "spare no advantage" in attacking him. Archie Lanfear eventually comes to agree and asks him to continue.

Decoration of Houses, The In 1897, Scribner's published Edith Wharton's first book-length prose work, *The DECORATION OF HOUSES*, written with the Boston architect Ogden CODMAN, who had advised her on the decoration of LAND'S END, the Whartons' home in NEWPORT. Walter BERRY, then a young attorney, was staying there with the Whartons at the time. He was born, according to Wharton, "with an exceptionally sensitive literary instinct" and fine critical sense, and she asked him to look at their "lumpy pages." He shouted with laughter, said " 'Come, let's see what can be done,' " and set to work making the "lump into a book" (*BG* 108). They sent the draft, with some photographs, to Scribner's and it was published that fall.

Although not a travel book in the usual sense, it contains an elaborate codification of European principles of harmony and design that could be imported by wealthy Americans into their house planning. It also clarifies what Wharton found wanting in American concepts of house design. Many of its principles, such as "proportion is the good breeding of architecture," were formulated during Edith Wharton's early years in Europe, and, in some ways, this work constitutes an archive on which she drew in much of her travel writing.

The Decoration of Houses is a manifesto of Edith Wharton's taste and evidence of her early connoisseurship. In assisting on fine distinctions as to proportion and design in furniture, ornament, walls, floors, ceilings, doors and other aspects of domestic architecture, she and Codman focus on distinctions in taste. They value, for example, proportion over decoration and propriety over ostentation. They reject unsuitable components of a given style and prize aesthetic unity, whether of a drawing room, a fountain, a sculpture or a painting. They lay out guidelines for countering the unsightliness of American architecture and interior design by applying European principles of harmony and proportion. The authors counter the prevailing theories of architects of the day who, as Wharton put it, regarded "house-decoration as a branch of dressmaking, and left the field to the upholsterers, who crammed every room with curtains, lambrequins, jardinieres of artificial plants, wobbly velvet-covered tables littered with silver gew-gaws, and festoons of lace on mantelpieces and dressing-tables" (*BG* 106–7). She wanted to elevate what had been a feminized, marginalized branch of design to a professional activity, and ennoble women's work as well.

Blake Nevius refers to *The Decoration of Houses* as a "pioneer manual of interior decoration" (*Edith Wharton*, 15), but it is far more wide-ranging than such a label suggests. As Judith Fryer notes, the book constitutes "an elaborate mapping of ideal domestic spaces," and is a handbook for the " 'American Renaissance'— a time of high Victorian splendor in architecture, sculpture and the decorative arts when models of the Italian Renaissance and classical Rome . . . represented the epitome of taste" (*Felicitous Space*, 11).

The Decoration of Houses is a necessary prelude to Edith Wharton's travel works in establishing and clarifying the taste which governs the tenor of her descriptions of other works of art, places and buildings. She had long been familiar with the finest examples of French and Italian architecture and their underlying structural and aesthetic principles. In *The Decoration of Houses*, she and Codman categorize these principles, an exercise as valuable to her in her later writings about

Europe as to American architects hoping to incorporate European principles of design into American vernacular architecture.

In building their theories, the authors rely in large part on the testimony of European architects of domestic dwellings. William A. Coles makes the point, however, that their suggestions were based on principles already beginning to be manifested in American public and private buildings. *The Decoration of Houses* did not "initiate" this taste, but "explained it, ordered and corrected it, rationalized it, and related it to the historical tradition of decoration." In this way, Wharton and Codman made it more available to "laymen of cultivated taste" (Coles, "The Genesis of a Classic," xxxiv–xxxv).

Wharton and Codman argue that a "reform in house-decoration" is badly needed. Such reform, however, can originate only "with those whose means permit any experiments which their taste may suggest. When the rich man demands good architecture his neighbors will get it too" (*DH*, Introduction). Russell Lynes observes that the "double optimism of this statement, which implies that the taste of the rich might be tempered by good judgment and filter down to exert a beneficial influence on their neighbors, is the "essence of the philosophy of the era of good taste." Instead, the reverse occurred; ordinary people began striving to imitate the rich, taking the "show" and omitting the "subtleties" (*The Tastemakers*, 165–67).

In *The Decoration of Houses*, the authors leave no doubt of the wife's responsibilities, which include surrounding children with classic prints and books (*DH* 174–75), presiding over the *salon de famille* (*DH* 124), going over accounts and interviewing servants in the morning-room (*DH* 130) and, it may be conjectured, filling library shelves with "good editions in good bindings" (*DH* 148). At the same time, it cannot be denied that a residence constructed and decorated in conformity with the principles of *The Decoration of Houses* implies a degree of affluence and style of life very close to those satirized by Thorstein Veblen in *The Theory of the Leisure Class* (1899), which T. Jackson Lears characterizes as "sybaritic waste among an overcivilized elite" (*No Place of Grace*, 28).

Walter Berry, in reviewing the book, praised it for upholding classical principles of harmony and design as opposed to "the many *Suggestions on Household Taste*, and the like, many of which have served only to aggravate the very defects which the present book is attempting to remedy" (Berry, 161).

The Decoration of Houses was republished in 1978 by Classical America as part of its series on art and architecture. That edition included two important critical essays, William Coles' "The Genesis of a Classic" in addition to John Barrington Bayley's "*The Decoration of Houses* as a Practical Handbook." In 1997 a third edition, revised and expanded, was published to coincide with the 100th anniversary of the first publication of *The Decoration of Houses*. The new edition includes 16 color plates and both essays, plus a third, "*The Decoration of Houses* as a Basic Text" by Alvin Holm, A.I.A. In his introductory note, Arthur Ross observes that the book has "stood the test of time" and that through it "we rediscover a world that heretofore we have accepted too casually, the world of our visual heritage" ("Introductory Notes" to third edition of *The Decoration of Houses*, 1997).

For further reading: Chandler, *Dwelling in the Text: Houses in American Fiction*; Jones, "Edith Wharton's 'Secret Sensitiveness,' *The Decoration of Houses* and Her Fiction"; Van Gastel, "The Location and Decoration of Houses in *The Age of Innocence*."

Delane, Hayley   *See* SPARK, THE.

Delane, Leila Gracy   *See* SPARK, THE.

Demeure de Liesse, La   Title of French translation of *The* HOUSE OF MIRTH, translated by Charles DU BOS. It ran in the *REVUE DE PARIS*, beginning in 1906. Even before it was translated, it had been read in the Faubourg. Wharton wrote Sara NORTON that, at a tea given for her by Paul and Minnie BOURGET, many of the guests had asked about the fate of "*cette pauvre Lily*" (*NGC* 152).

Descent of Man and Other Stories, The   The third collection of Edith Wharton's short stories (Scribner's, 1904). Lewis calls this the best of the various collections, showing her "full maturity as a satirist of American manners" (*EW* 133). In early 1903, Wharton offered several of the stories to William C. BROWNELL of Scribner's. Brownell asked her to write four more tales to complete the volume, observing that her imagination and energy were "equal to tasks which it is difficult to me to conceive as readily executable at all—to say nothing of the time limit" (*EW* 133).

It contains "The DESCENT OF MAN," "The MISSION OF JANE," "The OTHER TWO," "The QUICKSAND," "The DILETTANTE," "The RECKONING," "EXPIATION," "The LADY'S MAID'S BELL," and "A VENETIAN NIGHT'S ENTERTAINMENT."

"Descent of Man, The"   The title story in the collection *The* DESCENT OF MAN AND OTHER STORIES (Scribner's, 1904) is a caustic fable about the publishing industry. Professor Linyard, a renowned scientist at Hillbridge University, has a breakdown from overwork and is sent on a six-week holiday to the Maine woods to recover. He has "eloped with an idea" and occupies himself writing a skit, *The Vital Thing*, on the "popular" scientific book.

He takes it to a publisher, Ned Harviss, an old college friend who looks as though he has been "fattened on popular fiction." Harviss receives the manuscript with enthusiasm. It seems, however, he has considered it an "apologia, a confession of faith" that would appeal to the mass market rather than a satire only intelligible to a few readers. The book is launched to enthusiastic reviews. Harviss assures Linyard it will have a long life, fitting in "everywhere—science, theology, natural history—and then the all-for-the-best element which is so popular just now"; it is even on a par with the "How-to-Relax" series, selling millions of copies (*CSS* I, 357).

Linyard's son, Jack, is so impressed with his father's sudden success that he borrows money, which Linyard undertakes to repay with another fraudulent but popular project, a series of columns called "Scientific Sermons." He continues his work as an entomologist and proposes to Harviss a serious book in his field, only to find that he must keep writing popular works to sustain the sales of *The Vital Thing*. Harviss urges him to write another book: " 'write two, and we'll sell them in sets in a box: The Vital Thing Series,' " Harviss urges him. Linyard yields, postponing indefinitely his scientific treatise. The Latin coda, *Labor est etiam ipsa voluptas* ("Work is pleasing even in itself"), demonstrates his Faustian bargain.

"Diagnosis"   Rutger B. JEWETT sold this story to the *Ladies' Home Journal* in 1930 for $3,000 (*NGC* 425); it later appeared in *HUMAN NATURE* (Appleton, 1933). A satiric tragedy of modern married life, the tale concerns the sudden marriage of a successful middle-aged New York businessman, Paul Dorrance, to his mistress, a divorcée, Mrs. Welwood. An erroneous diagnosis prompts the marriage; his fluctuating medical condition sheds light on his relationship with his wife even after her death.

Diary, 1907, "The Life Apart"   Also known as the "Love Diary," this diary was begun in October 1907 and continued into the first half of 1908. It is a journal written in a hardbound notebook and lacks the first 30 pages. The remainder is written in the second person, addressed to Morton FULLERTON, and concerns the developing relationship between Morton and Fullerton. "The Life Apart" is a translation of "*L'Ame Close*," a phrase from Ronsard.

Fullerton had visited the Whartons at The MOUNT in October 1907, and she had found herself becoming more and more attached to him. She insisted on sailing with Teddy WHARTON for France in December rather than January, which they had originally planned. Teddy went to visit Walter and Matilda GAY at their chateau South of Paris, Le Bréau, while Edith Wharton stayed in Paris at her brother Harry JONES's town house; she later moved to the George VANDERBILT apartment they had leased the previous year at 58, rue de Varenne. Teddy was only intermittently in Paris during the spring. In March he returned to New York, bound for

Hot Springs, Arkansas, to take a cure for gout (his nervous condition was wrongly thought to be organic in origin). At the beginning of the year, although Fullerton called on Edith Wharton and escorted her to the theater, lunches, dinners and other engagements, he did not declare his love for her. Unknown to her, he was being blackmailed by his mistress, Mme Henrietta Mirecourt, about some indiscreet letters. Moreover, his cousin Katherine Fullerton believed she and Fullerton were engaged.

Throughout February and March, Edith Wharton saw more of Fullerton and her passion for him grew. The diary contains many entries testifying to her increasing involvement. For example, after he joined her and the BOURGETS for one act of a play called *La Femme nue*, in late February 1908, she recorded her emotions: ". . . when you came into the box . . . I felt for the first time that indescribable current of communication flowing between myself and someone else . . . and said to myself, 'This must be what happy women feel' " (*EW* 207–08). By April, according to Lewis, Edith Wharton was "deeply, helplessly in love" (*EW* 210). She addressed Fullerton in the diary on April 20: "I have no conscious existence outside the thought of you, the feeling of you" (*EW* 211).

Diary, 1908, Daily   The diary Edith Wharton began to keep in early 1908, in tandem with the more private one addressed to Morton FULLERTON, begun in October 1907 (DIARY, 1907, "THE LIFE APART"). She began it by entering two quotations about love, one about its nourishment of a shut-in soul by the French poet Ronsard, and one about isolation from a loved one by the Italian poet Giuseppe Tigri. Lewis states that such quotations were a way of "hinting to herself about her most private feelings." He believes that the two quotations, juxtaposed, show her as "gazing out through the bars of a prison at the procession of life" (*EW* 191–92).

This diary contains a record of the daily weather, along with notations about lectures and plays attended, people Edith Wharton met and other impersonal entries. However, there are allusions throughout to "M.F.," with notations in German. Lewis observes that this habit suggested she wished to set apart and "enshrine" her relationship with Fullerton.

Diary, *Vanadis*   Diary of the 1888 Aegean cruise taken by Edith and Teddy Wharton and James VAN ALEN. *See CRUISE OF THE VANADIS, THE*.

"Dieu d'Amour"   A tale of a medieval legend, as was "The HERMIT AND THE WILD WOMAN," this story first appeared in *CERTAIN PEOPLE* (Appleton, 1930). The site is the former monastery of St. Hilarion in Cyprus, which the Crusaders ruined and desecrated and

View of St. Hilarion Castle, Cyprus, subject of the short story "Dieu d'Amour" (Courtesy Swem Library, College of William and Mary)

renamed; it is now the castle of the heathen Lusignan kings. The name does not refer to the Christian God of Love, but to Eros, son of Aphrodite, "once liege lady of the island." It deals with the flight of the Princess Medea, about to be married to her uncle, into a convent through the agency of her cousin, the saintly Bridget of Sweden. The princess was beloved of the page Godfrey who, reflecting on the events years later as the Prior of a Norman Abbey, understands that it was God who had "stolen his lady from him" (*CSS* II, 569).

In the course of their 1926 cruise aboard the *OSPREY*, Edith Wharton, Daisy CHANLER, Robert NORTON and other members of the party motored and rode donkeys to the base of the castle. Chanler described it in *Autumn in the Valley* (1936). Only she and Norton managed to climb to the top, two thousand feet up, over

"precipitous broken stairs" and "rocks and ruins." She called the site a "fantastic fairy castle . . . on a high rocky peak" (230–31).

One reviewer felt the story was "out of key with Mrs. Wharton's work as a whole" (*CR* 482).

"Dilettante, The"   Published in *HARPER'S MAGAZINE* in 1903 and collected in *The DESCENT OF MAN AND OTHER STORIES* (Scribner's, 1904), the tale is based on the realization by Ruth Gaynor that her fiance, Thursdale, whom she had assumed had long been the lover of an older woman, Mrs. Vervain, had in fact been only a friend to her. Ruth perceives instantly that Thursdale uses people, as he has Mrs. Vervain; "she measured us both in a flash," Mrs. Vervain tells Thursdale. She realized Thursdale had taken "what he wanted—sifted and sorted" her as he pleased (*CSS* I, 417). Like Shylock, he had seized a pound of flesh and given little in return. Ruth, believing Thursdale "would have loved her better" if he had loved another woman first, breaks the engagement and Thursdale resolves to submit to his "punishment."

For further reading: Hoeller, "The Gains and Losses of 'Sentimental Economies' in Edith Wharton's 'The Dilettante' "; Kozikowski, "Unreliable Narration in Henry James's 'The Two Faces' and Edith Wharton's 'The Dilettante.' "

"Disintegration"   An unfinished work of fiction which later became *The MOTHER'S RECOMPENSE* (Appleton, 1925). Both holograph and typescript manuscripts exist in the BEINECKE LIBRARY, YALE UNIVERSITY.

divorce   The year 1907, when the Whartons were finally established on the rue de Varenne, marked a recurrence of the nervous instability Teddy had experienced in 1903 and the beginning of his final nervous decline, which led to divorce in 1913. The Whartons' residence in Paris emphasized Teddy's ineptitude in speaking French and conversing on a literary level with Edith Wharton's friends. He was more at home at The MOUNT, where he could indulge in hunting and other outdoor pursuits. He greatly enjoyed travelling with Edith, however, and took pleasure in catering to her "nice, to me, worldly side."

The marriage of Edith and Teddy Wharton had slowly disintegrated as Edith became more attached to France and decided to settle there permanently, and as Teddy became increasingly unstable mentally. Teddy then appeared reasonably well for several years, but he and Edith were slowly growing apart. One reason was his inability to adjust to France; a lover of animals and the relaxed outdoor life at The Mount, he was inept at speaking French. Lewis gives a poignant picture of him in early 1908, trying to succeed at French lessons, but believing that his mind was going. Wharton was not up to the intensely intellectual life of the Faubourg, which, as Lewis states, "bored, wearied, and depressed him" (*EW* 268). He had little to do except manage his wife's finances (he was dependent on her financially) and oversee the maintenance of The Mount. Wharton made a number of trips from 1907 to 1911 in the company of friends, relatives, or Alfred WHITE, Edith Wharton's butler (later, general manager), to try cures in various places, always returning miserably to the flat in Paris.

In the summer of 1909, Teddy embezzled over fifty thousand dollars of Edith Wharton's legacy, bought a building on Mountfort St., near Beacon St., in Boston, and established a mistress there. He made restitution with a legacy from his mother. In 1911 The Mount was sold. In 1912, Teddy went to England, Monte Carlo and France, traveling with White, who sent disturbing reports to Edith Wharton. Teddy wrote what Benstock calls "wildly megalomaniacal" letters to Henry JAMES in England, and bought an American automobile which he claimed he had driven at one hundred miles an hour. He visited La Bréau, home of Matilda and WALTER GAY, boasting of his conquests with variety show actresses. He showed them gold garters he was wearing to hold up his stockings; they thought his eyes appeared "insane." Back in Paris, he contacted and alarmed many of Edith Wharton's friends, although he did not attempt to see his wife (*NGC* 274).

Wharton saw no hope for her husband's recovery and proceeded early in 1913 with her divorce. She did not mention her divorce in *A BACKWARD GLANCE*, although she described Teddy's long illness. His condition, which she termed "creeping neurasthenia," had grown "steadily graver" since the early years of their marriage. She stated that some of his oldest friends helped his family realize that he would not improve and "could no longer lead a life of normal activity." She could not care for The Mount herself, as it had been Teddy's responsibility, and so it had to be sold; she "lingered" in the rue de Varenne between its sale and the years before WORLD WAR I because she did not feel like making another country home just for herself (*BG* 326).

Several factors played a role in Wharton's final realization that divorce was the only answer to her deteriorating marriage. Her expatriation and Teddy's inability to be happy in France were major reasons for the final separation. Ultimately, however, it was Teddy's deteriorating mental powers that precipitated her final decision. His father had committed suicide in McLean Hospital, outside Boston, of mental illness, and Teddy apparently inherited his condition. He had become irascible and violent, and Dr. Sturgis Bigelow of Boston had advised Wharton not to be alone with him. When he misused her legacy, she was convinced she could not live with him again.

In order to avoid publicity in New York, Wharton and her attorneys pleaded the divorce in a Paris court.

Her French lawyer was André BOCCON-GIBOD. She was also assisted by her cousin Herman Edgar and by Daisy Chanler's husband, Winthrop. When he arrived in Paris just before Easter, Teddy was served with court papers. On April 16, 1913, Wharton's degree was granted by the Tribunal de Grande Instance in Paris. She was in Sicily at the time, where she had gone with Walter BERRY, having deemed it wise not to be in Paris at the time the decree was issued. Benstock gives an interesting picture of Teddy's "martyrdom" and his family's indignant reaction as well as that of Wharton's long-time friends in America, England, and France, virtually all of whom felt her action was long overdue (*NGC* 276–80).

Edith Wharton did not remarry and only returned to the United States twice after her divorce—in December 1913 to attend the marriage of her niece Beatrix JONES to Max FARRAND and in June 1923 to accept an honorary DOCTORATE from Yale University. With the exception of the war years, her remaining life was far more satisfying than the final years with her husband had been. At the same time, it was not always easy. She remained a divorced woman within an old society in which there existed no ecclesiastical sanction for divorce, while marital infidelity was condoned or overlooked. Her readers often wrote to her as "Mrs. Edith Wharton," which irritated her a great deal. "I presume you mean Mrs. Wharton," she would instruct Anna BAHLMANN to reply.

Readers of *A Backward Glance* may be frustrated by the omission of details about her deteriorating marriage and divorce (she does not, in fact, acknowledge that she and Teddy were actually divorced). This, however, was not Wharton's purpose in writing her memoir. In the preface, she states that she does not "remember long to be angry," and attacks autobiographers who "spare no one." She insists she recalls no "sensational grievances" in her life, but has "had to make the best of unsensational material" (*BG* Preface, xix–xx).

doctorate, honorary   In 1923, Edith Wharton was awarded an honorary doctorate by Yale University and returned to America for the last time in order to receive it. At first she refused, in part because she dreaded returning to America after an absence of a decade. The president of Yale, however, pleaded with her to accept; it would be the first time the university had so honored a woman. Wharton also believed she should have a look at postwar America, since she was writing about it in her fiction. She sailed on the *Mauretania* from Cherbourg on June 9. She was met by her sister-in-law Minnie (Mrs. Cadwalader JONES), her niece Beatrix FARRAND and Beatrix's husband, Max.

After visits with the sister and daughter of her late friend Bayard CUTTING, Edith Wharton and Minnie Jones were driven to New Haven by Max Farrand. They dined in the home of Yale's president and, on June 20, she joined the procession. The graduates included F. O. Matthiessen, the teacher and critic who later wrote studies of T. S. Eliot and of Henry JAMES as well as *The American Renaissance: Art and Expression in the Age of Emerson and Whitman* (a text still studied today). The journalist Max Lerner and Gordon Haight, later the biographer of George Eliot, were also in the class.

The Yale citation read: "She holds a universally recognized place in the front ranks of the world's living novelists. She has elevated the level of American literature. We are proud that she is an American, and especially proud to enroll her among the daughters of Yale" (*EW* 452–53). It was Wharton's first and only academic degree.

Lewis states that Wharton's visit did not increase her affection for America, though she did remember, wistfully, Horton's ice cream. Yale, however, was the ultimate beneficiary of its decision to honor Edith Wharton. Before her death, she directed her literary executor, Gaillard LAPSLEY, to donate her "literary correspondence" to Yale. The Beinecke Library now has over 50,000 items relating to Edith Wharton in many categories, including letters, photographs, holograph and typed manuscript drafts, unpublished works and articles about her.

Columbia University had, several times, offered Edith Wharton an honorary doctorate. She rejected it again in 1932, writing Minnie Jones that she was "sickened" by the thought of what America had become and was glad to be ending her days among "civilized people" (*NGC* 431).

Donnée Book   A volume of notes for novels and stories in the Edith Wharton Collection at the BEINECKE LIBRARY, YALE UNIVERSITY.

Dorset, Bertha   *See HOUSE OF MIRTH, THE.*

Dorset, George   *See HOUSE OF MIRTH, THE.*

Doyle, Hannah ("Doyley")   Edith Wharton's nurse. In *A BACKWARD GLANCE*, Wharton recalled Doyley as the most enduring fixture of her childhood. She added that she pitied all children who had not had a Doyley, "a nurse who has always been there, who is as established as the sky and as warm as the sun, who understands everything, feels everything, can arrange everything, and combines all the powers of the Divinity with the compassion of a mortal heart like one's own!"

Mrs. Doyle accompanied the Jones family to Europe in 1866, when Edith was four. It was during these years, especially during a winter in Florence when she was nine, that she began "making up," when her parents were out and Doyley busy with her sewing. She would occupy herself inventing and pouring out torrents of stories about "real," rather than fanciful, people (*BG* 26, 42). Her mother, Lucretia JONES, usually thought of as unsympathetic toward her daughter, sometimes tried to write them down, but could not keep up with the speed of Edith's lively imagination.

dramatic adaptations of Wharton's work   *See* Appendix II.

Du Bos, Charles   The translator of *The HOUSE OF MIRTH*, which ran in the REVUE DE PARIS as *la* DEMEURE DE LIESSE, beginning in 1906. Wharton had left the choice of a translator up to Paul BOURGET, and he had selected Du Bos, then 25, who struck her as a "clever and agreeable young man" (*EW* 163). He found the process arduous and exacting, recalling that she "enjoyed to the utmost all the problems involved in translation" (*NGC* 420). Although he later helped revise the French translation of *ETHAN FROME*, which ran in the *Revue des deux mondes* as *Sous la Neige* (*NGC* 248), he did not translate any of her other works. He was a friend of André GIDE's and of other French intellectuals. Du Bos was bilingual, being Anglo-American on his mother's side. He later wrote a French biography of Byron and became a close friend of Edith Wharton.

During WORLD WAR I he organized the *Foyer Franco-Belge*, with a group of French and Belgian friends, including Gide. The organization grew at such a rate it had to be subdivided by functions. Du Bos helped register refugees and give out tickets for food, clothing and lodging. Eventually the committee was absorbed into the AMERICAN HOSTELS FOR REFUGEES charity founded by Edith Wharton.

"Duchess at Prayer, The"   The story was first published in SCRIBNER'S MAGAZINE in August 1900 and later appeared in CRUCIAL INSTANCES (Scribner's, 1901). Wharton wrote Sara NORTON that the story revealed a "*baissement*" (lowering) in the quality of her work (*NGC* 112). The story is told to the narrator by the old caretaker of the villa he is touring (the current duke is seldom in residence). The elderly caretaker's grandmother had been a maid attending the young duchess, wife of the cold and scholarly Duke Ercole II. He had arrived home unexpectedly after a long absence, then poisoned his first wife, Duchess Violante, believing her to be attached to his young cousin, Cavaliere Ascanio. He had brought a sculpture of her kneeling figure and placed it in the chapel. When the narrator sees the statue, he discovers it has a frozen face of horror; the caretaker insists the face changed after it was placed in the chapel. The story carries echoes of Robert Browning's dramatic monologue "My Last Duchess." As White

Illustration by Maxfield Parrish for "The Duchess at Prayer" (1900) (Courtesy Picture Collection, the Library of Virginia)

observes, this story also reflects a man's hidden corruption (*SSF* 49), a theme also found in "A CUP OF COLD WATER," "The PORTRAIT," and "The HOUSE OF THE DEAD HAND."

The setting, with detailed descriptions of the villa, its gardens, fountains, porticoes and grottoes, and the duke's Palladian palace near Vicenza, with its evocation of life on the BRENTA RIVIERA, reveals Edith Wharton's thorough knowledge of northern Italy. Her familiarity was gleaned through annual explorations she and her husband made after their marriage in 1885. She used similar settings in *The VALLEY OF DECISION* and "The

MUSE'S TRAGEDY" and discussed them in *ITALIAN BACKGROUNDS* and *ITALIAN VILLAS AND THEIR GARDENS.*

"Duration" Published in *THE WORLD OVER* (Appleton-Century, 1936), this story had been rejected in 1933 by Gertrude Lane, editor of the *Woman's Home Companion;* Edith Wharton wrote Rutger B. JEWETT she was "staggered by the insolence" of the rejection letter. She concluded she could not "write down to the level of the American picture magazines" (*SSF* 151). This is the story of Martha Little, a spinster, rebuffed for most of her life by her snobbish Boston family except when she made herself useful as a substitute governess for the young or a companion for the elderly. By sheer en-durance she reaches the age of 100 and becomes the family matriarch, outwitting her rival, Syngleton Perch, for the honor of being the family's most noted centenarian. The reviewer for the *New York Times* thought that, although its humor justified inclusion in the volume, this story was not up to Wharton's "highest standards."

For further reading: Fracasso, "Images of Imprisonment in Two Tales of Edith Wharton"; Nettels, "Texts within Texts: The Power of Letters in Edith Wharton's Fiction."

Durham, John *See MADAME DE TREYMES.*

Duvlenck, Elise Edith Wharton's pesonal maid, who joined her household in 1914 as a young woman and immediately accompanied her and Percy LUBBOCK to NORTH AFRICA. The party was driven by Charles COOK, who stowed Wharton's car aboard the *Timgad* when they sailed from Marseilles to Algiers. Elise proved herself to be extremely efficient and helpful, looking after Edith Wharton's wardrobe, labeling the luggage and sending it ahead by train during the course of their journey.

Lewis says she developed an almost "mystical reverence" for her mistress (*EW* 359). She stayed with her for 20 years, until she came down with pernicious anemia in 1934. Duvlenck died in May, followed in October by Catharine GROSS, Edith Wharton's longtime housekeeper, who had been with her 45 years and had developed senile dementia. The two were buried near each other in HYÈRES.

E

Edel, Leon (1907–1997) American critic and biographer of Henry JAMES. In 1931, as a student at the Sorbonne, writing a dissertation on James, he tried to assist a friend who wanted to obtain Edith Wharton's letters to Walter BERRY. She wrongly assumed he was embarking on a biography of Berry. Gaillard LAPSLEY vouched for his scholarship, and Edel called on Wharton, by invitation, at the PAVILLON COLOMBE. He assured her he was not thinking of writing such a biography. Lapsley and Wharton then reminisced about James; Edel used some of their recollections in his five-volume life, *Henry James*. This is still regarded by many critics as the premier American literary biography. He went to see Wharton again a few years later (*EW* 521).

Elcho, Lord Hugo and Lady Mary Lord Hugo Elcho was a member of Parliament and the son of the 10th earl of Wemyss. He and his wife lived at Stanway, in Gloucestershire. Lewis calls it "one of the most beautiful, though not the largest, of English aristocratic homes," and states that weekend house parties there glittered with Edwardian society. At the same time, there was serious conversation about literature, science, politics and art (*EW* 242–43).

It was at Stanway, probably in December 1908, that Wharton met Arthur James BALFOUR, H. G. WELLS, and Harry Cust, editor of the *Pall Mall Gazette*. She also met two young men who were to become lifelong friends, Robert NORTON and John HUGH SMITH.

In 1931 Wharton's friendship with Mary Elcho was renewed. By then her husband, Viscount Elcho, was the 11th earl of Wemyss and she was Mary, Countess of Wemyss. In 1937, the year of Wharton's death, Mary was able to visit her at STE.-CLAIRE CHÂTEAU, but died shortly thereafter in an English nursing home.

Eliot, George (1819–1880) Edith Wharton was a great admirer of the novels of George Eliot (pseudonym of Mary Ann Evans), particularly *Middlemarch*. When she was working on *The VALLEY OF DECISION*, and worrying that she was not capable of seeing it through, her friend Walter BERRY sent her a comment from George Eliot's diary, written in 1869. Eliot expressed doubts about the composition of her current novel: "I do not feel very confident that I can make anything satisfactory of Middlemarch. . . . It is worth while to record my great depression of spirits that I may remember one more resurrection from the pit of melancholy" (*NGC* 108). In the midst of her own trying marriage, Edith Wharton took some consolation in Dorothea Brooke's comment from *Middlemarch*, " 'Marriage is so unlike anything else—there is something even awful in the nearness it brings' " (*EW* 75). In 1902, Wharton reviewed Leslie Stephen's biography, *George Eliot*, for *The Bookman*. She refuted the charge that Eliot was too "scientific" and held that her studies of biology and metaphysics, along with her interest in the intellectual inquiries of Darwin and Spencer, actually freed her spirit from "the bonds of ethical pedantry" and amplified her powers as a novelist. She asked whether it might not be because Eliot was a woman that she had been "reproved" for venturing on to scientific grounds that had enriched the work of many writers, including Milton and Goethe. She also praised Eliot's dialogue and characterization, and, though she admitted that the construction of her novels was sometimes cumbersome, she attributed it to the "taste of her day."

Wharton believed that Eliot shrank "with a peculiar dread from any personal happiness acquired at the cost of the social organism," yet this attitude contradicted her personal situation, living as the "wife" of George Lewis. Like Anna de NOAILLES, Eliot lived an irregular life, but Edith Wharton was nonjudgmental about this aspect of her life, focusing only on the evolution of Eliot's fiction. The central defect she saw in the later novels was Eliot's increasing emphasis on morality and psychological depth, which Edith Wharton believed was deployed at the expense of breadth of vision ("George Eliot," *The Bookman*, May 1902).

Eliot, Thomas Stearns (1888–1965) American-born poet, critic and dramatist, who lived in England after 1914 and became a British citizen in 1927. Eliot is recognized as one of the major poets of the 20th century, principally because of his technical innovations and his revolt against the poetic conventions of the Romantic and Victorian periods.

During WORLD WAR I Edith Wharton had received a copy of Eliot's *The Love Song of J. Alfred Prufrock*, which focused on the emotional and spiritual impoverishment of the modern age. She did not find it particularly significant except as it reflected the rhythms of Walt

Whitman (an uncommon perception). Five years later, she was even less impressed with Eliot's *The Waste Land*, which appeared in the *The Criterion*. She considered it "ridden by theory rather than warmed by life," as Lewis puts it (*EW* 442). Wharton wrote her friend Gaillard LAPSLEY, "I *know* it's not because I'm getting old that I'm unresponsive" (*EW* 442). She wrote to Bernard BERENSON about both James JOYCE's *Ulysses* and Eliot's *The Waste Land*, "I shall never believe that the raw material of sensation & thought can make a work of art without the cook's intervening" (*Letters* 461).

Eliot, on the other hand, applauded her novel SUMMER (1917) and called her a "satirist's satirist" in a review for *The Egoist*. He praised her "deliberate and consistent realism" and said she had dealt a "death-blow" to the NEW ENGLAND novel "in which the wind whistles through the stunted firs and over the granite boulders into the white farmhouses where pale gaunt women sew rag carpets" (*CR* 263). (He may have had the work of Sarah Orne Jewett in mind with this remark.)

When the Spanish monarchy fell in 1931, Wharton wrote Eric Maclagan, director of the Victoria and Albert Museum in London, that she agreed with Eliot's definition of himself as "traditionalist in literature, royalist in politics, and Anglo-Catholic in religion" (*NGC* 448–49).

Elmsworth, Lizzie   *See BUCCANEERS, THE.*

Elmsworth, Mabel   *See BUCCANEERS, THE.*

Emerson, Ralph Waldo (1803–1882)   American poet, philosopher, essayist and poet, Emerson was the author of *Nature* (1835), *Essays* (first series, 1841; second series, 1944), *The Conduct of Life* (1860) and other works. He was a spokesman for Transcendentalism and noted speaker; his principal address was "The American Scholar," delivered before the Phi Beta Kappa Society at Harvard on August 31, 1837.

It was Emerson's poetry that prompted Wharton's first recognition of the achievement of American poetry and American literature as a whole; she had for many years been steeped in the European writers she had discovered in her father's library. After publication of her first collection of poems, ARTEMIS TO ACTAEON (SCRIBNER'S, 1909), she wrote William BROWNELL that Poe, Whitman and Emerson were "the best we have—in fact, the all we have" (*EW* 236).

The epigraph to *The GODS ARRIVE* (1932) was taken from Emerson's poem "Give All To Love": "When half gods go / The gods arrive," a commentary on the ambiguous extramarital relationship between Halo Tarrant and Vance Weston.

engagement, of Edith Wharton   Harry Leyden Stevens, son of Marietta and Paran Stevens, began paying attention to Edith Wharton in the summer of 1880 at

Edith Wharton in 1884 (Courtesy of the Lilly Library, Indiana University, Bloomington, Indiana)

Bar Harbor. His mother was a former grocer's daughter from Lowell, Massachusetts, and his father, who had married her after his first wife had died, had once worked in a Boston "cook house" but risen to become a successful businessman. He had managed to excel at hotel management and eventually purchased hotels in several cities. He was part owner of the Fifth Avenue Hotel and bred race horses. After his death in 1872, Mrs. Paran Stevens moved to New York and attempted to enter the closed circles of society.

Her daughter, Mary Fisk, had married Arthur Paget, son of Lord Clarence Paget, which gave her an entrée to the Court of St. James and thus to the social worlds of New York and Newport, although it horrified the British aristocracy. She must have hoped for an equally prestigious match for her son. Edith Wharton later satirized the marriages of American heiresses and British noblemen in *The BUCCANEERS*. Mrs. Stevens did not think Edith Wharton a suitable match for Harry. Nevertheless, he pursued Edith to Venice in 1881, during the Jones family's second sojourn in Europe, and accompanied them back to Cannes, staying with them throughout Frederic JONES' last illness and death in March 1882. When his widow and daughter returned to America, Harry Stevens came also. By August, he and Edith were engaged.

Although the engagement was announced in *Town Topics* in August and the marriage planned for October, Mrs. Stevens never entertained for Edith or, apparently, acknowledged it publicly. *Town Topics* announced on October 28 that the marriage had been postponed indefinitely. Lewis believes that Mrs. Stevens was reluctant to lose control over the portion of her late husband's estate that would have accrued to Harry on his marriage (*EW* 48). Harry Stevens died, apparently of a recurrence of tuberculosis, three years later, at the age of 26, six weeks after Edith and Teddy WHARTON were married.

In August 1883 Edith began seeing, at Newport, another young bachelor, Edward Robbins Wharton of Boston, who was 33 at the time, handsome and gregarious. He was a friend of her brother Harry and had graduated from Harvard in 1873. He lived with his parents and unmarried sister in Boston on an allowance from his parents. He had no job, other than helping various charitable institutions, but was popular in Boston society. He was attentive to Edith, visiting her in New York in February 1884 and escorting her to the annual Patriarchs' Ball. In March 1885 their engagement was announced in *Town Topics*; the small wedding took place at Trinity Chapel, New York, on April 29.

England   Edith Wharton's ties with England were extensive and lifelong. She began reading English literature as a child. When she was presented with the Buxton Forman editions of Keats and Shelley for her birthday one year, "the gates of the realms of gold swung wide," and she said she was never again "wholly lonely or unhappy" (*BG* 69, 70–71). She knew the works of Shakespeare and the Elizabethan dramatists, Thomas Carlyle, John Evelyn, Fanny Burney, John Milton, George Herbert, Alexander Pope, William Wordsworth, Samuel Coleridge, Lord Tennyson and other British authors.

She had always regarded England with great affection and compared it favorably with her native country. Although she first knew England in the waning Victorian era, she visited it more often and made longer-lasting British friendships during the succeeding Edwardian "garden party" age that ended in 1914. Returning to America in 1903, after several months in Europe, she wrote Sara NORTON, complaining of the "wild dishevelled backwards look of everything. . . . in England, I like it *all*—institutions, traditions, mannerisms, conversations, everything but the women's clothes and the having to go to Church every Sunday" (*EW* 120).

Edith Wharton traveled extensively in England throughout her adult life, often staying at the country estates of various friends. Soon after *The GREATER INCLI-*

NATION was published, in 1899, she and Teddy met Lady St Helier, a well-known and popular London hostess. Although her interests were different from those of Edith Wharton (she "collected" celebrities and undertook philanthropic works with equal enthusiasm), they still became close friends, and Wharton often stayed with Lady St Helier in London. It was at her table that she met the historian George Trevelyan, Thomas Hardy, and Harry Cust, editor of the *Pall Mall Gazette* and "one of the most eager and radio-active intelligences in London" (*BG* 220).

Wharton met many distinguished people through an American friend married to a British nobleman, Adèle Grant, Lady ESSEX. They included Sir Edmund Gosse, H. G. WELLS, Max Beerbohm, John Singer SARGENT and Lord BALFOUR. She also knew the poet Mrs. Wilfrid Meynell, the novelist Mrs. Humphry WARD and Mrs. Alfred Austin, wife of the poet laureate. Wharton was a frequent guest of Lord Hugo and Lady Mary ELCHO in their vast home, Stanway, in the Cotswolds in Gloustershire, where she met many luminaries in the Edwardian world.

In *A BACKWARD GLANCE*, Edith Wharton confessed that her memories of large gala luncheon parties and dinners had receded, and that, in later years, she found the frequent company of a few close friends far more rewarding. There was no companionship she enjoyed more than Henry JAMES'; he lived at LAMB HOUSE in Rye. Wharton saw a great deal of Gaillard LAPSLEY, an American who taught history at Trinity College, Cambridge; Robert NORTON, a landscape painter; John HUGH SMITH, a banker; Percy LUBBOCK, a writer and critic; and Howard STURGIS, a charming, eccentric man of letters and novelist. Edith Wharton often stayed at the home of the latter—Queen's Acre, in Windsor; her chapter on "Qu' Acre" and Lamb House is one of the most charming in *A Backward Glance*.

After her divorce in 1913, Edith Wharton considered settling in England and nearly purchased Coopersale, a 100-acre property situated 18 miles north of London, near Epping Forest. She enjoyed being in the country, and was irritated by the noise and rush of Paris. She made an offer, but then discovered that the British government levied very high taxes on foreign residents. That problem, coupled with Coopersale's proximity to London, eventually led to her decision not to live in England.

In 1906 she and Teddy, driven by Charles COOK, made a motor-car tour of southern England; Henry James joined them at Bath. They visited cathedral towns and other sights, then went to Stratford-on-Avon, Cambridge, London, Windsor and Lamb House, where they stayed a few days with Henry James. At Windsor James insisted on delivering his notoriously maze-like directions, holding up the party for some time; fortunately Cook circumvented his advice.

Edith Wharton never seems to have considered writing travel articles or books about England. Perhaps her journeys there were too sociable, or the competition too stiff. Also, unlike many of her readers, she had the advantage of knowing both French and Italian, and, on a deeper level, could interpret Renaissance and baroque art and architecture as a knowledgeable connoisseur. She did use England as a fictional setting.

Her fiction and travel texts were published in England, usually by Macmillan, Murray, Bodley Head or, in later years, by Appleton. Her work was widely reviewed and well received in England and she had a following there that was, at times, more enthusiastic and supportive than her American audience was.

entry of Allied armies into Paris   Edith Wharton witnessed the march of the Allied Armies into Paris as she stood on the balcony of a friend's apartment on the Champs-Elysées on Bastille Day, July 14, 1919. She recalled in her memoir, *A BACKWARD GLANCE*, "the significance of that incredible spectacle dazzling my heart." Although she was stunned by the glory of the sun glancing off the helmets and arms of the marching regiments, she could not help contrasting the scene with the men she had seen at the front, "dusty, dirty, mud-encrusted, blood-stained, spent and struggling on." The two visions merged into one, and, she wrote, "my heart is broken with them" (*BG* 361–62). *See also* WORLD WAR I.

eroticism   In "LIFE AND I," Edith Wharton's unpublished autobiography, she confesses to an early interest in love and marriage only equaled by her ignorance. During the Joneses' stay in Europe during her childhood, she attended dancing classes in Paris, where she was always, she recalled, in love with a little boy who was usually in love with another little girl. Later, she read Tennyson's ballad "The Lord of Burleigh," in which the noble hero, pretending to be a simple painter, wins a country maiden and takes her to his castle; she feels out of place, pines away and dies. From this poem, Wharton "drew the inference that a husband's first act after marriage was to give his wife a concert" (she misread "gentle consort" for "concert") ("Life and I," 9). She later worked out that married people had children "because God saw the clergyman marrying them through the roof of the church" ("Life and I," 34).

Before her marriage, Wharton recalled being "seized with such a dread of the whole dark mystery" that she consulted her mother and begged her to explain what "being married" was like. Lucretia Jones's expression became one of "icy disapproval" and she exclaimed, "I never heard such a ridiculous question!" Edith insisted that she wanted to know "what will happen to me." Lucretia became deeply disgusted, then

said, with an effort, "You've seen enough pictures & statues in your life. Haven't you noticed that men are made differently from women?" Edith was silent "from sheer inability to follow." Her mother exclaimed, "Then for heaven's sake don't ask me any more silly questions. You can't be stupid as you pretend!" Edith believed this conversation reflected training during her childhood and girlhood that did more than anything else "to falsify and misdirect" her entire life ("Life and I," 35). Fortunately, it only delayed her growth and did not "deflect" it.

Most scholars believe that Edith Wharton's marriage was consummated, but that physical intimacy soon ceased and the Whartons had separate bedrooms for virtually all of their married life. Lewis believes their extensive annual travels, early in their marriage, offered a means of escape from what had turned out to be a disappointing physical relationship. He suggests that Wharton's "suppressed sexual energy" was employed in planning their complex journeys, making a home, and arranging a social "ambience" (*EW* 54).

It was not for more than 20 years, until she had an affair with Morton FULLERTON, that Edith Wharton came to know physical passion, as recorded in her 1907 DIARY. Her poem "TERMINUS" records a night spent with Fullerton in the Charing Cross Hotel, London, in 1908. The worn bed has often thrilled "With the pressure of bodies ecstatic, bodies like ours,/ Seeking each other's souls in the depths of unfathomed caresses. . . . And lying there hushed in your arms, as the waves of rapture receded,/ And far down the margin of being we heard the low beat of the soul." She gave the poem to Fullerton and asked him to return it, saying, "it breaks over me like a great sweet tide." Fullerton did return it, but copied it first with notations as to when and where it was written (*EW* 259–60).

Wharton was eager to visit harems on her 1917 visit to MOROCCO, but saw little evidence of sexual ecstasy. There was much affection for the children, but the women were languid, left in their own quarters until visited by the sultan. They did not "toil" nor "spin" but left all labor to servants. Wharton concluded that in the country as a whole both sexes "live till old age in an atmosphere of sensuality without seduction" (*IM* 201).

It was more than a decade after her relationship with Fullerton had ended that Wharton wrote the outline and brief fragment of the story "BEATRICE PALMATO," about 1923. The portion of the manuscript preserved in the BEINECKE concerns an incestuous relationship between a prosperous businessman, Mr. Palmato, and his 12-year-old daughter, and describes in detail not only his seduction of Beatrice, but her ecstatic reception of his advances. Lewis observes that the story was unpublishable in any respectable magazine at the time, and expresses surprise that Edith Wharton even wrote it. He believes it may have been based on a novel roughly concerned with George Sand, whom Edith Wharton greatly admired, *Gamiani*. It was pornographic in nature and circulated privately (*EW* 544).

Edith Wharton was, according to Lewis, inconsistent with respect to homosexuality. She was tolerant of male friends known to be homosexual, such as Jean COCTEAU, André GIDE and Comte Robert d'HUMIÈRES, and called them "The Brotherhood." She was less accepting of lesbianism and was also slow to perceive it. Although she suspected her childhood friend Emelyn Washburn of "degeneracy" in that direction, she failed to recognize such an orientation in Vernon LEE. Her friend Anna de NOAILLES had affairs with both men and women, but either she did not realize it or did not care about it. Wharton did not, however, want to know the writer Natalie Barney, from Ohio, whose fortune was far greater than her own. Barney published lesbian poetry, established the Académie des Femmes and presided over a literary salon at 20, rue Jacob. She was a close friend of Bernard BERENSON and others of whom Edith Wharton was fond. Barney had unconventional afternoon entertainments, where Colette sometimes slid naked through the garden (Benstock, *Women of the Left Bank*, 270.) Lewis suspects that it was not Barney's lesbianism that offended Wharton so much as her success in maintaining a rival salon. Edith Wharton never came to know Gertrude Stein during the 1920s, although they both moved in eminent literary circles.

Essex, Countess of (née Adèle Grant)   Formerly of New York, Adèle Grant was married to the seventh earl of Essex. Edith Wharton refers to Lady Essex in her memoir as "a devoted friend and responsive companion" (*BG* 222). She was entertained by her both in her small Mayfair home and at Cassiobury, her country home with its Grinling Gibbons carvings. One Sunday after the London season the Whartons lunched at Cassiobury, finding on the lawn "the flower and pinnacle of the London world," including Henry JAMES and John Singer SARGENT. Exhausted by their social labors, they could only smile weakly, as though they were "garments hung up . . . with nobody inside" (*BG* 221–22). Lady Essex later bought a house in HYÈRES near the STE.-CLAIRE CHÂTEAU.

Eternal Passion in English Poetry   An anthology of love poems edited by Edith Wharton and Robert NORTON, with the collaboration of Gaillard LAPSLEY. The volume was published posthumously in 1939. It had been planned during evenings at the PAVILLON COLOMBE as early as 1923.

Edith Wharton wrote the preface, stating that "No antiquarian limitations, no pedantic search for the unfamiliar, no sense of the obligation to include such or such a poem because it has had the honours of previous selection, or to exclude another because it has been too often thus honoured, has been allowed to hamper" the free choice of the compilers (Preface, vi).

Shakespeare is represented by five selections from the plays, one poem ("Take, O Take those Lips Away") and 21 sonnets. The poet ranking next, numerically, is Robert Browning, with eight selections. Such major poets as Marlowe, Jonson, Marvell, Donne, Keats, Swinburne, Tennyson, Wordsworth, Shelley, Burns, Elizabeth Barrett Browning and Scott are included. Lesser poets are also present, including a few who might seem obscure today: Francis William Bourdillon, the Anglo-Marx poet Thomas Edward Brown, Harry Cust (editor of the *Pall Mall Gazette* and longtime English friend of Wharton's), the English man of letters William Ernest Henley and Captain Tobias Hume. Another poet represented is Herbert Trench; Benstock notes that Edith Wharton copied his poem "Apollo and the Seaman" (not included in the anthology) into her COMMONPLACE BOOK in early 1909 and that it was one source for her poem "Life" (*NGC* 205–206).

Ethan Frome   This novelette, published in 1911 by Scribner's, may be Edith Wharton's best-known work and is considered her most major tragic story.

Edith Wharton began the work that was eventually published as *Ethan Frome* as a writing exercise for her French tutor, probably in 1907. At the time, she was in PARIS for the winter and, although she could read and speak French easily, she felt her conversational ability was dated. She asked her friend Charles DU BOS to find a young French professor to assist her in speaking the language more idiomatically. He suggested that she prepare a writing exercise before each meeting. Drawing on her knowledge of rural NEW ENGLAND, where she and her husband had built a summer home, she began, in French, the nucleus of what would become *Ethan Frome*. The first characters were a farmer named Hart, in love with Mattie, the niece of his wife, Anna. The wife attempts to send Mattie away. Hart tries to leave with her, but Mattie refuses to let him do so, pleading that Anna has been kinder to her than any other relative. She kept the basic situation as she developed the narrative and other details.

The work became a short novel, or novella, and was published in SCRIBNER'S MAGAZINE in August, September and October of 1911; it appeared in book form in September 1911. It was her 16th books in 13 years, and was recognized by critics as a fine achievement, despite the reluctance of many readers and critics to accept the ending. The *New York Times* reviewer called it an exercise in "subtle torture" and one library critic believed it too pessimistic for the general reader. Henry JAMES praised the story, saying it contained "a beautiful art and tone and truth—a beautiful artful kept-downness" (*EW* 310).

Scene from the 1936 Broadway production of Ethan Frome, *dramatized by Owen Davis and Donald Davis (see* Appendix II*). Left to right: Pauline Lord (Zenobia Frome), Raymond Massey (Ethan Frome) and Ruth Gordon (Mattie Silver).* (Vandamm Collection, Billy Rose Theater Collection, New York Public Library, Library for the Performing Arts, Lincoln Center)

The novella did not sell well at first; just over 4,000 copies were sold in the first six weeks, but by late February 1912 sales had reached 7,000 (*EW* 311). During the decade of the 1920s sales averaged about 1,400 copies a year, and during the 1930s more than a thousand a year. It is the most translated of all of Wharton's works.

SETTING AND CHARACTERS OF *ETHAN FROME*

The reader's attention is immediately engaged by the time he has reached the second sentence:

If you know Starkfield, Massachusetts, you know the post-office. If you know the post-office you must have seen Ethan Frome drive up to it, drop the reins on his hollow-backed bay and drag himself across the brick pavement to the white colonnade: and you must have asked who he was.

In just a few words, Wharton has implied that "Starkfield," or a town very like Starkfield, is embedded in every reader's consciousness and has introduced the mysteriously afflicted Ethan; the reader is drawn quickly into the setting. It is hardly surprising that *Ethan Frome* is the principal work introducing Edith Wharton to generations of students.

In her original introduction to the tale, Wharton states that she had long believed the "outcropping granite" of New England had been overlooked in fictional depictions of the region, which focused on "sweet-fern, asters and mountain-laurel, and the conscientious reproduction of the vernacular." She wished to show the stony, tragic side of local life: farms that barely yield a living, icy weather and, above all, the rugged, stoic character of the people.

Her ties to rural New England were deep, as Wharton later wrote in *A BACKWARD GLANCE*. She became incensed when one American literary critic cited *Ethan Frome* as "an interesting example of a successful New England story written by some one who knew nothing of New England." She countered that the work had been written after she had spent 10 years in the hill region where it is set, "during which years I had come to know well the aspect, dialect, and mental and moral attitude of the hill-people" (*BG* 296). In summer 1904, Edith and Teddy Wharton had returned from a trip to the home of Charles Eliot NORTON in Ashfield, Massachusetts. She looked at a "sky of flying gleams and leaden clouds" and it seemed to her "the most beautiful, perhaps, for our austere New England landscape." Near Plainfield there was a region of "lakes and rolling fields and forest, enclosed in sombre hills, and so remote, uninhabited and tragic under the dark sky." This description was incorporated, seven years later, in Starkfield and the surrounding landscape.

In portraying the rural people of New England, Edith Wharton departs from the ironic depiction of aristocratic characters that marks many of her novels and stories. Some critics have considered her choice of setting and characters to be contrived, preoccupied as she is, in most of her fiction, with the ironic depiction of aristocratic characters. But she believed she knew the fiber of the people of New England very well, having spent part of each year in LENOX, Massachusetts, for several years.

The characters include:

ETHAN FROME: The protagonist, who is trapped by economic circumstances. He ekes out a meager living for himself and his sickly wife from a small farm and sawmill.

ZENOBIA (ZEENA) FROME (née Pierce): The wife of Ethan Frome, who once nursed his mother. Since their marriage she has become a hypochondriac.

MATTIE SILVER: A cousin of Zeena's, a pretty young girl with a sweet temper who takes a position with the Fromes as housekeeper. She recognizes Ethan's good qualities and falls in love with him.

NARRATOR: The teller of the story is an engineer who is working temporarily in Starkfield at the power-house at Corbury Junction. He frames the story, narrating the events before the story begins (prologue) and after it ends (epilogue).

HARMON GOW: A citizen of Starkfield, a former stage driver, who relates certain events to the narrator.

MRS. NED HALE (née Ruth Varnum): Another source of information for the narrator; a contemporary and close friend of Mattie Silver.

ANDREW HALE: Owner of a Starkfield construction company; Ethan asks him for a $50 advance on a load of lumber.

NED HALE: Eldest son of Andrew Hale.

MRS. ANDREW HALE: Convinces Ethan he cannot insist on the $50 advance for the lumber.

DENIS EADY: Son of a well-to-do grocer in Starkfield, he courts Mattie Silver.

JOTHAM POWELL: Works on the Frome farm as a hired helper.

WIDOW HOMAN: Storeowner in Starkfield who sells glue to Ethan.

MARTHA PIERCE: Aunt of Zeena Frome who lives in Bettsbridge; Zeena stays with her on her visit there.

DR. BUCK: Zeena consults this physician in Bettsbridge, who tells her she is not up to housework because of "complications."

PHILURA MAPLE: Zeena's aunt, who has sent her a wedding present of a red pickle dish.

DANIEL BYRNE: A Starkfield neighbor who takes Mattie's trunk to the railway station.

MRS. FROME: Mother of Ethan; he has had to leave college to care for her after his father's death.

STRUCTURE AND SYNOPSIS OF *ETHAN FROME*

In the first analysis of any of her books she had ever published, Edith Wharton provided an introduction to a special edition of *Ethan Frome* in 1922. She viewed the problem of time as central: how could she keep the reader's interest when the main events had to be told, as it were, in flashback? Some novelists might have withdrawn, fearing the story was one of the tempting "false 'good situations' " that later prove to be unworkable. But she forged ahead, believing the story was the first subject she had ever approached with "full confidence in its value." She did not believe there would be any "air of artificiality" if the "looker-on" (i.e., the author) is "sophisticated," and the people he interprets are "simple." She solved the problem of chronology by bringing in separate contemporary narrators (Harmon Gow and Mrs. Ned Hale) to tell the tale of past events. Each contributed "to the narrative *just so much as he or she is capable of understanding* of what, to them, is a complicated and mysterious case." She believed the author could convey nothing of value to his readers other than a statement as to "why he decided to attempt the work in question, and why he selected one form rather than another for embodiment" (*UCW* 259–61).

Prologue:

As in the case with much of Edith Wharton's short fiction, the story is told by a narrator who reconstructs the events with the aid of fragments of information given him by other people. He introduces Ethan Frome by giving a newcomer's first sight of him, a "ruin of a man" dragging himself into the post office. The narrator asks Harmon Gow and Mrs. Ned Hale about him, but they relate only a fragment of Ethan's background and tragic story. Harmon Gow refers to the "smash-up" that had happened 24 years earlier, and explains that he had not been able to "get away" from Starkfield as most of the "smart ones" had because he had to care for his folks: his father, mother and then wife.

The narrator, delayed from finishing his job at the power-station by a carpenters' strike, takes the "sluggish pulse" of Starkfield and learns more of Ethan from his landlady, a widow named Mrs. Ned Hale. She is reticent about Ethan; Harmon Gow explains that she cannot bear to relive the time when "it" happened. Winter weather and the illness of the horses at the local livery stable force the narrator to ask Ethan for transportation to the Corbury Flats train station. Ethan offers shelter at the farm after a particularly bad storm, and the narrator learns enough of his story to construct a "vision" of it.

Chapters 1–5:
The action is now told in a flashback to the time of Ethan's young manhood, when he is 28. It opens as he is walking toward the church hall one cold night to fetch Mattie Silver from a dance. A cousin of his wife, Zeena, who is 35, Mattie is living in Ethan's home as a house-keeper. His reactions to Starkfield are conditioned by his year at a technological college at Worcester, which had given him an interest in science. He had had to give up his studies when his father died. He reaches the hall, where Mattie is dancing the Virginia reel with Denis Eady, and recalls the year she has lived with them: "he could show her things and tell her things, and taste the bliss of feeling that all he imparted left long reverberations and echoes he could wake at will." Zeena, however, has perceived that Ethan has become fonder and fonder of Mattie, that he shaves every day and that he gets up early to assist her in the kitchen, and warns Ethan that when Mattie marries she will still need someone to "do for" her.

As Ethan escorts Mattie home, there is a foreshadowing of tragedy when she remarks that Ruth Varnum and Ned Hale nearly ran into the big elm at the bottom of the hill while sledding. He sounds Mattie out on leaving them, and is overjoyed to realize Mattie doesn't want to leave. "I guess we'll never let you go, Matt," he whispers—another prescient remark.

In the third chapter Ethan worries that Zeena will detect his love for Mattie. He comes home from work to learn that she has decided to consult her doctor in Bettsbridge, which will necessitate her staying overnight. They see Zeena off the next morning; Ethan has made the mistake of telling her he cannot drive her to the train because he needs to appeal for a cash advance for his lumber. During the day he reflects about his decision to marry her. She is Ethan's cousin, on his mother's side, and had nursed his silent mother. At the time, Zeena's "volubility was music in his ears." His mother had died in the winter, and, dreading loneliness, he had proposed to Zeena without thinking it through. She had soon become "sickly" and he had been permanently trapped. He applies to Andrew Hale for a cash advance, but is turned down, since Andrew

needs funds to fix up a house for his son Ned and his fiancée, Ruth Varnum. That evening, Mattie has used one of Zeena's prized possessions, a pickle dish, for the evening meal; the cat pushes it off the table and breaks it. He hides the pieces and plans to glue it back together.

In the fifth chapter, Mattie has cleaned up the kitchen and sits in Zeena's rocking chair. Ethan has a sudden vision of Zeena sitting there, obliterating Mattie's countenance. Although he does not even touch Mattie's hand throughout the evening, he has a vision of what their life together might be without Zeena.

Chapters 6–9:
In the sixth chapter, Ethan and Mattie breakfast with Jotham Powell before Ethan takes the lumber to the village. He searches for the proper glue for the pickle dish, but Zeena returns before he can mend it. She announces she has "complications," which is tantamount to a license for surgery or permanent invalidism. She has engaged a hired girl, believing Ethan has been paid in advance for his lumber. Ethan is infuriated when he realizes Zeena had meant to dismiss Mattie and replace her with the new girl. Zeena becomes, before his eyes, no longer "the listless creature who had lived at his side in a state of sullen self-absorption, but a mysterious alien presence." Zeena discovers the broken pickle dish, and Mattie confesses she has used it. Zeena accuses her of being a "bad girl."

Ethan retreats to his cold, dark "study" and tries to plan an escape with Mattie, but realizes he cannot afford it. The next day he plans to take her to the train station. Before the train comes, Ethan insists on taking her for a sled ride down School House Hill. They climb up again, confess their love for each other, and realize they cannot bear to live apart. Mattie asks him to take her on a suicide mission by crashing into the big elm. When they are coasting down their favorite hill one last time, he attempts to kill them both by steering the sled into a large elm. Both are injured, Mattie being severely crippled.

The sledding accident was based on an actual event in March 1904, when a group of high school students on a "double-ripper" sled crashed into a lamp post at the foot of the mile-long Courthouse Hill in Lenox (Schoolhouse Hill in the novella). One girl was killed, another lamed and another scarred.

Epilogue:
The narrator resumes; the time has shifted to his era, more than 20 years after the accident. He enters the Frome kitchen and finds two women, one a tall bony figure and one smaller and lighter, huddled in an armchair. Her hair is gray, her body immobile, her high voice complaining and demanding. Zeena is now taking care of Mattie, and Ethan has the burden of supporting both of them.

When the narrator returns to Mrs. Hale's home, she finally tells him the whole story, or her version of it. He is the only stranger to have visited the Fromes in more than 20 years. She tells him of Mattie's "sweet nature" soured, and observes that now there's little difference between "the Fromes up at the farm and the Fromes down in the graveyard; 'cept that down there they're all quiet, and the women have got to hold their tongues."

CRITICAL ANALYSIS *ETHAN FROME*

It is the moral attitude of the residents of Starkfield, combined with an actual sledding accident, that provide the nucleus of the story. Edith Wharton treats the problem of the central characters' doomed attempt to counter the barriers of social convention standing in the way of their happiness.

When Mattie then becomes a permanent member of the household, she becomes as tyrannical as Zeena, and the three live on together into isolated old age on the barren farm. The heroism of Ethan, who is kind, generous and sociable at the outset, is played off against the uselessness of his self-sacrifice. As Nevius observes, the novelette deals with the "moral order" of Ethan's world, a world characterized by "granite outcroppings": the "starved" apples, "black and brittle" trees, gray fields and Mattie's "bloodless and shrivelled" face. Such details make the starved emotional lives of all three major characters both plausible and tragic. Ethan's selflessness has prolonged their misery, not alleviated it. One of the important motifs in the book is silence. None of the characters says what he or she is really thinking and each is isolated in his own psychic world, unable to communicate honestly with the others. Mrs. Hale is reticent about the events of the past, Ethan about his true hostility toward Zeena and love for Mattie, Zeena about her perception that Ethan is growing to love Mattie, and Mattie about her love for Ethan. At the same time, each abhors silence—Ethan, particularly, had asked Zeena to marry him to escape his mother's silence.

Each character, however, entertains certain illusions, another important theme. Zeena believes in her own ill health and need for care in an impoverished but ordered world; Mattie believes her love for Ethan is undetectable; Ethan believes, at least briefly, that he and Mattie can somehow escape from Starkfield and find happiness together.

The overriding motif, however, is despair. Ethan's farm will never be successful, although, as Nevius observes, Ethan Frome has a certain "tragic dignity." But his and Mattie's youthful love cannot override Zeena's tenacious hold on her husband, and it is evident that Mattie will never make a happy marriage as her friend Ruth Varnum does. The Puritan ethic underlies the decisions of each character. Ethan cannot tread on the kindness of the Hales to acquire funds to escape with Mattie, since this would leave Zeena a helpless charity case. The consequences of each action he can imagine taking are so formidable that he is morally immobile. Lionel Trilling states that her aim was, in the end, to represent "that grim tableau . . . of pain and imprisonment, of life-in-death" ("Morality of Inertia," 142). Ethan Frome is often considered to be the "winter" half of a diptych, the other part of which is the novelette SUMMER (1917).

For further reading: Ammons, "Edith Wharton's *Ethan Frome* and the Question of Meaning"; Blackall, "The Sledding Accident in *Ethan Frome*"; Kim, "Theme and Symbol in Wharton's '*Ethan Frome*'"; Marshall, "Edith Wharton, Kate Spencer, and *Ethan Frome*"; Murad, "Edith Wharton and *Ethan Frome*"; Nettels, "Thwarted Escapes: *Ethan Frome* and Jean Stafford's 'A Country Love Story'"; Nevius, "Edith Wharton's *Ethan Frome*"; Nevius, "On *Ethan Frome*: The Story with Sources and Commentary; With introduction"; Springer, *Ethan Frome: A Nightmare of Need*; Trilling, "The Morality of Inertia"; Wolff, "Cold Ethan and 'Hot Ethan'"; Edith Wharton, "The Writing of *Ethan Frome*".

***Ethan Frome* (play, 1936)**   *See* Appendix II.

***Ethan Frome* (teleplay, 1960)**   *See* Appendix II.

***Ethan Frome* (film, 1993)**   *See* Appendix II.

Europe   Between 1866, when she was four, and 1872, when she was 10, Edith Wharton, her parents, Lucretia and Frederic JONES, along with one of her brothers, Harry (about to enter Trinity Hall College, Cambridge), lived abroad, in FRANCE, ITALY and GERMANY. This experience cast on her mind an imaginative and long-lasting overlay, giving her for the rest of her life, a longing for a European "background of beauty and old-established order," as she put it in her memoir (*BG* 44). The Jones family returned to Europe for two years in 1880, hoping in vain to restore the health of Frederic Jones, who died at Cannes in 1882.

During her childhood residence abroad, Edith Wharton not only learned Italian, French and German, but was exposed to literature, gardens, history, art and ARCHITECTURE and to European manners and modes of thought. On her family's return to AMERICA, she was repelled by the NEW YORK cityscape with its brownstones and lack of towers, fountains or perspectives. She found it a "cramped horizontal gridiron of a town . . . hide-bound in its deadly uniformity of mean ugliness" (*BG* 55). The vistas of Europe—castles, villas, winding roads, Alps, lakes and gardens were indelibly etched in Wharton's consciousness, and she never ceased yearning to return. As an adult, she traveled widely throughout Europe for more than four decades, purchased two French homes, and wrote five travel books about Italy and France.

Edith Wharton's cultural bias as she visited Europe, particularly France, was not only aesthetic but intellectual. She was convinced that, all too often, Americans only theoretically valued arts and ideas. They did not "as a people, seek or desire them," she wrote in FRENCH WAYS AND THEIR MEANING (*FWM* 69–70). Edith Wharton attributes this deficiency to the relative youth of her native country as compared with the lengthy heritage of European art and culture.

Certain American writers, such as Ralph Waldo EMERSON, manifested an allegiance to native scenes and customs, and urged Americans to discard the "courtly muses of Europe." The repudiation of Europe, however, was never one of Edith Wharton's goals. In the first chapter of The DECORATION OF HOUSES (which she wrote with the Boston architect Ogden CODMAN), entitled "The Historical Tradition," Wharton takes it for granted that, to be credible, architects must have European models, for in America they are bereft of the schools, libraries, museums and buildings of Europe. This work constitutes a paean of praise for European prototypes of vernacular architecture and a delineation of the highly civilized modes of life implicit in these structures.

Edith Wharton's distaste for AMERICA also underlies much of *French Ways and Their Meaning*. In her chapter on "Taste," she suggests that Americans are not trained to have the "seeing eye" possessed by French people, who are inherently a "race of artists." The result is the flawed cities of the United States. For example, few cities along U.S. rivers have made their quays beautiful and inviting for strolling.

Wharton also believed that Americans too often tried to acquire education by taking short cuts; brief courses in a subject were not, to her, a substitute for a lifetime of reading. The French approach learning with reverence and patience, believing there are no shortcuts to its acquisition. "As long as America believes in short-cuts to knowledge, in any possibility of buying taste in tabloids," Wharton warns, she will never come into her "real inheritance" of English culture (*FWM* 55). This paucity of cultural resources had, she was convinced, an adverse effect on the American novel. In her essay "The GREAT AMERICAN NOVEL" (1927), she points out that America has only offered "meagre material" to the artist's imagination. Price and Joslin observe that Wharton believed that "the intellect, even the soul, could expand more readily and more completely in Europe than in the United States" (*Wretched Exotic*, 5).

Gradually Wharton became more and more alienated from America. In June 1903, she wrote her good friend Sara NORTON of her unhappy return from the annual trip to Italy she and her husband had made:

. . . my first few weeks in America are always miserable, because the tastes I am cursed with are all of a kind that cannot be gratified here, & I am not enough in sympathy with our "gros public" to make up for the lack on the aesthetic side. One's friends are delightful; but *we* are none of us Americans, we don't think or feel as the Americans do, we are the wretched exotics produced in a European glass-house, the most déplacé & useless class on earth! (*Letters* 84).

Lewis observes that Edith Wharton "was of course one of the most American women of her time, and never more so than when giving vent to such utterances" (*Letters* 54).

In *The* CUSTOM OF THE COUNTRY Count Raymond de Chelles castigates Undine Spragg for trying to dispose of the Boucher tapestries that had long been family treasures. He indicts all Americans for thinking they can understand what makes European life "decent and honorable" when they come from towns "flimsy as paper" and their buildings are "demolished before they're dry" (*CC* 307).

Edith Wharton found in Europe the "things that make life decent and honourable." Although she never relinquished her American citizenship, and had many American friends until the end of her life, she believed she could not be happy living in her native country. Much of her later fiction, especially that written for magazines, was criticized as showing a lack of familiarity with American life, but Wharton considered that a small price to pay in order to continue living in a Europe, whose background of "beauty and old-established order" had first nourished her as a child. *See also* EXPATRIATION and AMERICA.

expatriation   By the time she was 21, Edith Jones had already spent eight years abroad. Her father, George Frederic JONES, had suffered financial reverses in the early 1860s caused by loss of NEW YORK real estate values during the Civil War. In 1866 the Joneses took Edith Wharton, then four, along with her older brother Harry (about to enter Trinity Hall College, Cambridge) to EUROPE for six years. The Joneses lived in FRANCE, Germany and ITALY, traveling widely in those countries and in SPAIN. Edith became fluent in Italian, German and French, reveling in the background she acquired of "beauty and old-established order."

When the Jones family returned to AMERICA in 1872, Wharton was bitterly disappointed. She later recalled in her unpublished autobiography "LIFE AND I," that, although she was only 10 years old at the time, she had been "fed on beauty" since her "babyhood" and her first thought was "*How ugly it is!*" Wharton insisted she had "never since thought or felt otherwise than as an exile in America," and had often dreamed her family was returning to EUROPE.

In 1880 the Joneses did return to the Continent in a futile attempt to restore Frederic Jones' failing health. He died at Cannes in 1882. Edith Wharton and her mother came back to New York and NEWPORT, but Edith had felt "the stir of old associations" and continued to long for Europe. After her marriage to Teddy WHARTON in 1885, the couple traveled annually to Europe, usually spending from February to May or June there every year, often in Italy. Wharton's residence abroad as a child, in addition to her adult travels, laid the groundwork for her eventual expatriation.

Edith Wharton's increasing attachment to Europe during the early part of the 20th century confirmed her affinity with the "courtly muses" of Europe against which Emerson had inveighed in his *The American Scholar* address, reflected her classicist stance and strengthened her dissociation from what she saw as the banality and ugliness of Victorian life in America. Wharton's five European travel books, together with *The DECORATION OF HOUSES*, the diary of her 1888 Mediterranean cruise, discovered in 1991 and published as *The CRUISE OF THE VANADIS*, and much of her fiction, especially *The VALLEY OF DECISION*, point the way out of the cultural solipsism in which she might otherwise have been mired. Two aspects of what Elizabeth Ammons calls Wharton's "argument with America" (Ammons, xi) go far toward explaining her final decision to settle in France: differences in visual ideals between America and Europe (especially in architecture) and disparate cultural and intellectual mores.

The Decoration of Houses, which Wharton wrote in 1897 with the young Boston architect Ogden CODMAN, presaged her expatriation. This work constitutes a paean of praise for European models of vernacular architecture and a delineation of the highly civilized modes of life implicit in these models. It also addresses the deficiencies of bourgeois American tastes and standards. Wharton constructs, from a European point of view, what she believed was missing in America. From this perspective, the work is significant in her ultimate expatriation. Even as she and Codman wrote *The Decoration of Houses*, she was quasi-professional and quasi-expatriate and spent much of her life in Europe.

Henry JAMES observed in 1902 that he "would like to get hold of the little lady [Edith Wharton] and pump the pure essence" of his "wisdom and experience into her. She *must* be tethered in native pastures, even if it reduces her to a back-yard in New York." At almost the same time, he wrote Wharton, begging her to permit him to "admonish" her "in favour of the American subject" while she was "young, free, expert." He hoped she would "profit, be warned by my awful example of exile and ignorance" (*Letters*, ed. Edel, 237). James based his advice on Wharton's first volume of short stories, *The GREATER INCLINATION*, and her historical novel set in Italy, *The Valley of Decision*, both of which had been sent him by Edith Wharton's sister-in-law, Mary (Minnie) Cadwalader JONES. R. W. B. Lewis terms James' plea "the wisest literary advice Edith Wharton ever received"

(*EW* 123). James, of course, was writing as an author who had chosen exile himself and who could perceive from her work that Edith Wharton had already been profoundly influenced by her European residence and travels. He had not met her at that time and could not have foreseen her increasing dissatisfaction with America, her difficulties with Teddy Wharton or her final expatriation and settlement in France.

In 1902, the Whartons built a large home, The MOUNT, at LENOX, Massachusetts. Lewis observes that Edith Wharton delighted in being in a home "genuinely of her own making." In *A BACKWARD GLANCE*, she comments that, had they built The Mount sooner, she would probably never have given a thought to the "literary delights of Paris or London," because she found life in the country so deeply satisfying (*BG* 124). Lewis states that Edith Wharton became, in the years between 1900 and 1905, "the first woman of American letters." Her "health and nerves were in splendid condition; and so, with some trifling exceptions, they would long remain" (*EW* 110–56). He suggests that the years following the Whartons' occupancy of The Mount saw "a gradual displacement from Newport to Lenox"; there was, simultaneously, a yearning toward Europe (*EW* 97).

Although increasingly drawn to Europe, Edith Wharton oscillated for a number of years about taking the step of expatriation. The year 1904 brought a significant shift in the Whartons' travels; they gave up their annual pilgrimage to Italy, preferring explorations in France. This change heralded Edith's later expatriation. The Whartons drove through France toward the Spanish border, visiting Pau and going through Perigueux, Limoges, Bourges and Blois back to Paris.

In 1905, during a "health" trip abroad accompanied only by her maid, Catharine GROSS, Wharton had written Sara NORTON, "I would give up all this fine civilization for a sight of my spring blossoms at Lenox" (*EW* 143). A year later, in the winter of 1906, even as she tried to overcome a case of flu and sail for Europe, Wharton wrote Sara Norton from New York: "One would feel, I am sure, if one lived in another country, the alien's inability to expatriate, to take part, help on, assert one's self for good. . . . But . . . I speak through wool, darkly" (*EW* 161). The Whartons sailed aboard the *Philadelphia* in March 1906.

Just as the Whartons' travels in 1904 brought a fundamental abandonment of Italy for France, the end of the year 1905 and the beginning of 1906 began the final period of Edith Wharton's relinquishment of America for Europe—specifically for France. The preceding two decades had led almost inexorably to her decision, though in some respects it was an enigmatic one, made just at the peak of her achievement in two literary genres: fiction and travel writing. Wharton's bi-continental lifestyle between 1885 and 1905 had, it may be argued, reinforced her concepts of both native and foreign pastures, the disadvantages of each highlighting the positive aspects of the other. Even during her annual journeys abroad, Edith seems to have exhibited a strong affinity to Homer's Odysseus, who, in the midst of his foreign travels, found "his native home deep imag'd in his soul" (*The Odyssey*, Bk. 13, 1. 38).

The years 1906–7 are regarded by both Benstock and Lewis as the decisive period of Wharton's final expatriation. Edith's physical residence in the FAU-BOURG SAINT-GERMAIN began in 1907, when she and her husband sublet the apartment of the George VAN-DERBILTS in a stately town house at 58, rue de Varenne. In January 1910, the Whartons moved into another apartment at 53, rue de Varenne. Edith was to live there until 1920, when she acquired the PAVILLON COLOMBE just outside Paris in ST.-BRICE-SOUS-FORÊT.

Teddy's nervous decline, which had begun several years earlier, intensified in France. His resistance to living permanently in Paris was abetted, according to Lewis, by his ineptitude in speaking French and conversing on a literary level with Edith's friends. He was more at home at The Mount, where he could indulge in hunting and other outdoor pursuits. Until 1902, when he was 53, he had been "robust physically and mentally alert." But he began to experience alternate episodes of mania and depression as early as 1904; by 1909, when the Whartons returned to Paris, these had intensified. In December 1908, he confessed that he had embezzled some of his wife's funds, purchased an apartment in Boston and established a mistress there; it was later revealed that he had spent at least $50,000. The funds were restored from his mother's legacy, which he had just inherited, but he was prohibited from managing Edith's financial affairs and, later, asked to resign as trustee. Lewis attributes his behavior to exaction of "financial and sexual revenge" (*EW* 265–93). Benstock emphasizes the strain of hereditary insanity in the Wharton family (*NGC* 55; 133–34). Teddy became increasingly agitated at The Mount during the summer 1911, and Edith suggested separation. She decided to move permanently to France and did so in the fall of 1911. The Mount was sold in September 1911 to Mary and Albert Shattuck of New York City for approximately $18,000. Teddy arrived back in Paris in February 1912, instigating another period of what Lewis terms "deadly marital imprisonment." By January 1913, his erratic behavior had finally convinced Edith that divorce was the only solution, despite the American social repercussions she feared. Because of Teddy's excesses and the lessening stigma of divorce, however, she actually received considerable support from friends and family.

Edith Wharton came increasingly to feel she belonged in the Faubourg, and, as Lewis puts it, "all her early aversion to the city melted away as she came to appreciate the coherence of life there, the almost effortless intermixture of the artistic and the fashion-able, the steady nourishment of "the warm dim background of a long social past" (*EW* 165). Wharton arrived in Paris, not as a displaced American, but as an exceptionally cosmopolitan one, not ready to yield her native citizenship but to refract and extend it on the basis of past travel and residence in France. In aesthetic matters, in her three French travel books, she remains very much the pro-European connoisseur of *The Decoration of Houses* and the Italian books. In some respects, however, she becomes more American, questioning some rigid European mores that seem trivial.

The early years of Edith Wharton's expatriation coincided with the final years of the BELLE ÉPOQUE. She was initially an outsider. In countering French patriarchal social authority, however, her noted professional success offset her personal "failure"; moreover, she made many intellectual friends in what Méral terms the "sacred enclave" of the Faubourg, partly as a result of Paul BOURGET's sponsorship ("Parisian Milieux before 1914," 41–64). She writes that her "girlish intimacy" with a small group belonging to the "inner circle" of the Faubourg was achieved because she had written a successful novel that had been translated into French with an introduction by Bourget. In Paris, Wharton perceived, "no one could live without literature." She believed that the fact that she was a "professional writer, instead of frightening my fashionable friends, interested them. . . . Culture in France is an eminently social quality, while in Anglo-Saxon countries it might also be called anti-social" (*BG* 261).

In contesting the implications of gender and nationality, Wharton broke culturally with her past and aligned herself permanently with the Gallic paradigm of intellectual life. She was not an observer, but a collaborator and advocate, her apartment a conduit for old friends a new acquaintances, including Geoffrey SCOTT, Theodore ROOSEVELT, Charles DU BOS and dozens of others. Her attachment to France was based on more than the cerebral satisfactions of Parisian salons, however. The country as a whole (countryside, towns, and cities) was a model for all social relations; the "muddled process of living" was lubricated by perfect good manners; the "material setting of life" had a "finish" arising from "civic dignity and comeliness" and maintained by a nation committed to intelligent living (*BG* 29).

That setting was immediately imperiled by WORLD WAR I, which caused Edith Wharton to become a passionate humanitarian, directing her energies away from social life and travel and into organizing massive war relief efforts. She launched four major charities and, in addition, used all her power as a public figure to exert pressure on America to come to the aid of France, writing letters and poems published in the *New York Times* and other newspapers and magazines. In April 1916, she was made a CHEVALIER OF THE FRENCH LEGION OF HONOR, France's highest accolade, and two years later she received the MEDAL OF QUEEN ELIZABETH from King Albert of Belgium. In 1915 she was asked by the French Red Cross to visit military hospitals at the front and report on their needs. She received permission to write magazine articles about her experiences with the hope of alerting her "rich and generous compatriots" to the desperate needs of hospitals, and of bringing "home to American readers some of the dreadful realities of war." The articles were published in SCRIBNER'S MAGAZINE and collected as FIGHTING FRANCE, FROM DUNKERQUE TO BELFORT (1915). Americans respon-ded to her appeals, and "Edith Wharton" Committees were formed in New York, Boston, and other cities (BG 350–54). In 1916, Wharton edited The BOOK OF THE HOMELESS, soliciting contributions from well-known writers and artists; it was published in early 1916. During the last two years of World War I, Wharton wrote a series of magazine articles intended to interpret France to American soldiers stationed there. They were collected as FRENCH WAYS AND THEIR MEANING, published in 1919.

After World War I, there was no question of Edith Wharton's returning to live in America. She purchased two French homes, one outside Paris at St.-Brice-sous-Forêt and one in HYÈRES. She spent the remaining 20 years of her life dividing her time between her two homes, traveling and writing. She remained, however, quintessentially American. Percy LUBBOCK once remarked that to Henry James, Edith Wharton represented "America, brilliantly flashing upon Europe . . . flashing across to meet this Europe on the highest terms, any terms she pleased" (Portrait, 5–6). James focuses on Wharton's energy and implies that she derived confidence and status from her professional recognition in France. America had become for her, as it had for James, something for her "literary and social sensibility to react on" ("Henry James," Literary History of the United States, 1041).

Although James lived in England from 1876 until his death in 1916, he did not become a British subject until 1915, when America refused to enter World War I on behalf of England, and Wharton neither forgave him for giving up his citizenship nor considered relinquishing her own. Her nationalism is a component of Wharton's connoisseurship, which cannot be properly sustained in her native country. Yet, though disaffected, she cannot sever her attachment to the country of her birth. At the same time, Wharton means to defend and justify her decision to make her home permanently in France. The country of her birth has many shortcomings but, being young, may change and cannot be wholly relinquished; the country of her maturity so nurtures her, despite its foibles, that it secures her full canonical allegiance—but not to the point of surrendering her native citizenship.

"Experience"   Poem written by Wharton in 1892, possibly influenced by the suicide of her father-in-law,

William Craig Wharton, in McLean's mental hospital outside Boston. Individuals bring the accumulated burdens and joys of their lives to the gate of death, asking if they avail nothing. Death replies, "they shall purchase sleep." As Benstock puts it, Teddy's father purchased "sleep" rather than "the mental suffering of his old age" (NGC 174).

"Expiation"   This story, a satire about authorship, appeared in Hearst's International-Cosmopolitan magazine in December 1903 and was included in The DESCENT OF MAN AND OTHER STORIES (Scribner's, 1904). Paula Feverel has written a novel called FAST AND LOOSE (a play on Edith Wharton's own early unpublished novel of the same name), and makes the mistake of trying to turn it into a best-seller. Her cousin, Mrs. Clinch, is a nonfiction nature writer whose books quietly go into many editions; she is outside the race for popular success. Their uncle, the Bishop of Ossining, is also an author, but his novel, Through a Glass Brightly, has not sold even though it has been praised by church laywomen for its morality. It is the story of a poor consumptive girl with two idiot sisters who manages to collect funds for a beautiful memorial window to their grandfather, whom they had never met. White terms the plot summary an excellent description of the "maintenance of patriarchy" (SSF 54). The Bishop reflects that his best recourse would be to have his book denounced as immoral. When Mrs. Feverel's book is damned with faint praise as a "pretty story" and "harmless," she persuades her uncle to censure her book from the pulpit by "anonymously" donating a chantry window to Ossining Cathedral (an echo of his novel). It becomes an immediate best-seller, and she begins plotting her next novel. At the unveiling of the window, however, the Bishop twists the gift around and states that his own book prompted the feminine donor's generosity. The credit for Mrs. Feverel's success thus goes, ironically, to a man.

"Eyes, The"   This story appeared in SCRIBNER'S MAGAZINE, June 1910, and was reprinted in TALES OF MEN AND GHOSTS (Scribner's, 1910). It has been praised by critics; Lewis calls it a "powerful collaboration between Wharton's unconscious and her creative genius" (EW 287). The essential story is framed by a New York dinner party attended by eight gentlemen. After most of them leave, Andrew Culwin, a dilettante who is at least latently homosexual, tells the tale of Phil Frenham, his young protégé, and to the unnamed narrator.

He has experienced two visitations of ghostly red eyes, staring at him in the darkness, after acts of cowardice and duplicity. "The orbits were sunk, and the thick red-lined lids hung over the eyeballs like blinds of which the cords are broken." They express the "vicious security" of a man who "had done a lot of harm in his life, but had always kept just inside the danger lines."

The first appearance is after he abandons his fiancée, Alice Nowell, with no explanation, and flees to Europe. The second takes place in Rome, when he takes on young Gilbert Noyes as a companion. He is a "slender and smooth and hyacinthine" youth, an ambitious writer, sent by Alice with a letter of introduction. Alice has wangled his family's permission to let him defer a desk job and try writing for a few months.

Culwin is so taken with Gilbert that he continues to praise his bad writing, ostensibly to spare his feelings, but actually in order to keep him as a companion. He even makes a private game of targeting the "wrong" thing that will inevitably strike Gilbert as "right." All his submissions are returned without comment by editors, but Gilbert keeps "battering and filing at his limp prose." Each night the eyes appear to Culwin until he tells Gilbert the truth, that his writing has no merit. Then, exhausted, he departs Rome for Frascati. Gilbert returns to America, takes a desk job and finally a clerkship in China, marries "drearily" and grows fat. In the drawing room, Phil Frenham realizes that he also has been victimized by Culwin and sees the hideous eyes as those of Culwin, who stares at his reflection in the mirror with a "glare of slowly gathering hate."

Critics have been divided as to the identity of a real-life model for Culwin. Walter BERRY, Morton FULLERTON and Henry JAMES have all been proposed. White suggests that Wharton drew on "ambivalent feelings" toward all three, but that it was actually her father, George Frederic JONES, who was the model. Her portrait of him in A BACKWARD GLANCE as "wealthy" and "dilettantish," preferring to "lead a leisurely life in Europe" rather than make use of his literary gifts, makes him a likely candidate. He also has "unrealized literary gifts" and enjoys giving dinner parties (SSF 67). Elsewhere, however, Wharton expresses profound affection for her father, which argues against such a conclusion. Nevius calls the story a "Hawthornesque study of egoism" (SSF 94), especially in the use of the mirror, and argues that it comes close to being "the pinnacle of Edith Wharton's achievement in the short story" (SSF 97).

False Dawn (The 'Forties) The first in the chronological sequence of the OLD NEW YORK series of four novellas, published in 1924 by Appleton. The plot turns on a radical revision in taste on the part of a naive young American, Lewis Raycie, sent by his father, Halston Raycie, in the 1840s on the Grand Tour of Europe for the purpose of collecting large-scale passionate religious paintings for a Raycie "Heirloom Gallery."

On a Swiss mountaintop, Lewis Raycie meets the young John RUSKIN and experiences an aesthetic epiphany. Ruskin surmises that Raycie is "one of the privileged beings to whom the seeing eye has been given" (*FD* 70). Under his influence Raycie comes to prefer the Italian primitives of Piero della Francesca and Giotto di Bondone to the work of minor painters he had been directed to acquire, such as Lo Spagnoletto of the Neapolitan School and the Florentine painter Carlo Dolce.

Raycie's eyes are thus "opened to a new world of art" and his excitement has "something of the apostle's ecstasy" (*FD* 78–79). He believes it his mission to reveal that world to others, and it is the little-known Italian primitives he proudly manages to collect rather than those his father has proposed. When the paintings are unpacked in America, the elder Mr. Raycie is enraged and abandons the Heirloom Gallery. Lewis and his

Lewis Raycie and John Ruskin at Mont Blanc. Endpaper, False Dawn (The 'Forties) *(1924), first edition* (Collection of the author)

devoted wife, Beatrice ("Treeshy"), toil the remainder of their lives soliciting visitors for their own small gallery of unappreciated primitives.

The plot of *False Dawn* re-enacts, to a certain extent, the "misguided" efforts of James Jackson Jarves, who also embarked on a pedagogical Grand Tour of Europe, bought works of art for wealthy Americans, and became a collector of previously neglected Italian paintings of her 13th through the 16th centuries, only to find them unappreciated by his fellow countrymen. He tried in vain to sell his collection to the Boston Athenaeum; 119 of the early paintings were finally sold to Yale College in 1871 for $22,000. The lamentable story of the failure of the Athenaeum to acquire the paintings was in all probability known to Edith Wharton, since her friend Charles Eliot NORTON was among the trustees of that institution who, in 1859, contributed $5,000 toward the purchase of the Jarves Gallery and urged other donors to subscribe sufficient funds, within a month, "to obtain a gallery of paintings which will be of permanent value, and which in its kind will be unrivalled in America" (Jarves, *The Art-Idea*, 13).

In writing that Ruskin attributed the trait of the "seeing eye" to Raycie as an indication of the excellence of his discrimination, Wharton recalls her characterization of the French people in FRENCH WAYS AND THEIR MEANING, where she terms the "seeing eye" the "first requisite" of taste (*FWM* 52). Edith Wharton herself came to defend the work of certain later painters who had originally been on the senior Mr. Raycie's list, but not at the expense of disregarding Giotto and della Francesca.

False Dawn is a text central to understanding Wharton's lifelong debt to Ruskin, even though she came to repudiate many of his tenets. Moreover, it is a pivotal work in its sustained exploration of the values and perils of connoisseurship, a theme playing as important a role within Wharton's fiction as her nonfiction, though not always as explicitly expressed. The elder Raycie's perception of his son's finely honed taste as flawed is also an oblique comment on the cultural abyss the upholders of the "Genteel Tradition" (including Wharton's early editors and friends, such as Charles Eliot Norton) pinpointed and tried to counter. Written after her travel texts but set in the New York of the 1870s, the era preceding their publication, *False*

Dawn brackets the years of Wharton's own developing connoisseurship, emphasizing its centrality within her fiction and travel writing.

For further reading: Tintner, "*False Dawn* and the Irony of Taste-Changes in Art."

family background *See* GENEALOGY, OF EDITH WHARTON; CHILDHOOD; *BACKWARD GLANCE, A*; EUROPE; NEWPORT; NEW YORK; Appendix IV, GENEALOGY OF EDITH NEWBOLD JONES.

Farish, Gerty *See* HOUSE OF MIRTH, THE.

Farrand, Beatrix (1872–1959) Beatrix Jones Farrand, Edith Wharton's niece, was the daughter of her brother Frederic and Mary (Minnie) Cadwalader JONES, who had married in 1870, separated in 1892, and divorced in 1896. She was married at the age of 42 to Max Farrand, 45, a professor of history at YALE UNIVERSITY and a leading authority on constitutional history; he died of cancer in 1945.

Beatrix Farrand became an internationally known landscape architect and assisted with the gardens at the Whartons' home in LENOX, Massachusetts, The MOUNT. She also designed the gardens at Dumbarton Oaks in Washington for Robert and Mildred BLISS. They had acquired it in 1920 and retired there. Farrand began working on the Dumbarton Oaks gardens in 1921, and was involved in their creation and refinement for thirty years, until she formally retired from all projects in 1951. In 1913 she designed a new garden for Mrs. Woodrow Wilson at the White House, and in 1934 she designed the courtyards of eight new residential colleges Edward Harkness had established at YALE UNIVERSITY. Farrand also designed the gardens at Glyndebourne, England; in 1936 Edith Wharton attended a performance of *Don Giovanni* there.

In the mid-1950s the town of Bar Harbor denied tax-exempt status to Reef Point Gardens, which Farrand had established on her mother's estate. She dismantled them instead of permitting them to go to weed, moving some of the trees and plants. She shipped her library and herbarium to the University of California at Berkeley and tore down the summer house, a major loss for Maine and Bar Harbor and a source of considerable heartache to her. She used some of the boards to build a small addition to her cook's farmhouse, where she lived out her life with her French maid, Clémentine. Her ashes were spread on Mount Desert Island, at her request, and no headstone was erected in her memory (*NGC* 460–61). Beatrix Jones Farrand was the last survivor of the family of George Frederic and Lucretia Jones.

Edith Wharton was extremely fond of both her niece and her sister-in-law. In 1918, she wrote Elizabeth CAMERON, "Minnie & Trix make up to me for my own wretched family, & all my thoughts & interests are with

them" (*Letters* 405). She sometimes wrote Beatrix long letters describing in detail the flowers she had seen in gardens in England and other places.

When Edith Wharton died in 1937, she had made Elisina TYLER her residuary legatee, a considerable burden since it entailed negotiating the Franco-American estate and eventually required Elisina herself to pay some of the property and inheritance taxes. Edith Wharton had designated that a substantial legacy be transmitted to William TYLER, Elisina's son and her godson, once matters were settled.

Beatrix Farrand then challenged the American will over the matter of the life trust Edith Wharton had inherited from Lucretia Jones in 1901, believing she was the lawful heir of the Rhinelander-Jones money. A full account is given by Benstock (*NGC* 457–58). Eventually the will was interpreted in favor of Beatrix Farrand. Rather than going back to court, Elisina agreed to a compromise that pleased neither of them.

Farrand, Max (1870–1945) Historian and husband of Beatrix FARRAND, Edith Wharton's niece. When they were married in 1913 he was a professor of American history at YALE UNIVERSITY and a respected constitutional scholar. By 1926 he had left Yale to become the head of a Harkness fund for postgraduate traveling fellowships. In 1935, at the time of the sudden death of Mary (Minnie) Cadwalader JONES, his mother-in-law, in London, he was director of the Huntington Library in San Marino, California (*EW* 519). He died of cancer in 1945.

Fast and Loose Edith Wharton's second attempt at writing a long narrative, this novella was begun in the fall of 1876, when she was 14 years of age, at Pencraig, NEWPORT, and finished in New York in January 1877. (Her first attempt, when she was 11, had been discouraged by her mother, Lucretia JONES.) *Fast and Loose* was not published until 1993, when Viola Hopkins Winner prepared an edition for the University Press of Virginia.

In her introduction, Winner draws a number of parallels between Edith Wharton's first long work of fiction and her final novel, *The BUCCANEERS*, published posthumously. The heroines of both novels are 16, with similar first names (Georgina ["Georgie"] Rivers and Nan St George), and both eventually endure suffocating marriages. The settings in both works include British country houses, and both depict social rites such as the coming-out of debutantes during the London season (Winner, Introduction to *Fast and Loose*, vii).

The novella has 17 chapters and is just over a hundred pages long. It was kept private; Edith Wharton notes in her memoir that it was "destined for the private enjoyment of a girl friend, and was never exposed to the garish light of print" (*BG* 75). Winner speculates that the friend was Emelyn WASHBURN, the daughter of the rector of the church the Joneses attended; she was six years older than Edith Wharton. The epigraph is from Owen Meredith's poem "Lucile": "Let Woman beware / How she plays fast and loose with human despair, / And the storm in Man's heart" (*BG* 75).

Edith Wharton used *Fast and Loose* as the fictional title of the novel Paula Feverel has written in the story "EXPIATION." In the story "APRIL SHOWERS," the young writer Theodora's first novel ends with a quotation from *Fast and Loose*.

Faubourg Saint-Germain   The residences of the old aristocracy of Paris are in the *quartier St.-Germain*, or the Faubourg, in the maze of streets near the Boulevard St.-Germain, on the Left Bank of the Seine. They are immense town houses, often with central courtyards, but the austere façades do not suggest to the visitor the quality of life within. Edith Wharton lived for 13 years in two different apartments in the rue de Varenne, at first at No. 58, in the leased apartment of the George VANDERBILTs, from 1907–09. In 1910 she and her husband leased their own apartment at 53, rue de Varenne. Wharton lived here until she moved to the PAVILLON COLOMBE in 1919.

According to Lewis, the noble families of the Faubourg conformed to "age-old patterns of domestic and social behavior." The quarter has been described as "'a piece of the ancien régime set in contemporary Paris'" (*EW* 176). Edith Wharton had several entrées to inner circles of the Faubourg. When the JONES family went abroad for the second time in 1880 and stayed at Cannes, Wharton had met some French girls who were now married and settled in Paris and welcomed her. Moreover, *The HOUSE OF MIRTH* had been serialized in France, then published in book form. Wharton believed that her "girlish intimacy" with a small group belonging to the "inner circle" of the Faubourg was achieved because she had written a successful novel that had been translated into French with an introduction by the novelist Paul BOURGET, also member of the ACADÉMIE FRANÇAISE, or French Academy. Wharton wrote that, in Paris, "no one could live without literature." She believed that the fact that she was a professional writer, instead of frightening her fashionable friends, interested them. "Culture in France is an eminently social quality, while in Anglo-Saxon countries it might also be called anti-social," she wrote in her memoir (*BG* 261).

The House of Mirth (1905) was translated into French by Charles DU BOS, who had been chosen for the task by Paul Bourget. However, even before it was translated, it had been read in the Faubourg and secured Edith Wharton's literary reputation. She wrote Sara NORTON that, at a tea given for her by Paul and Minnie Bourget, many of the guests asked about the fate of "*cette pauvre Lily*" (*NGC* 152). The novel began running in the *REVUE DE PARIS* in 1906. Wharton believed it was of interest to French readers because it depicted a society totally unknown to them.

The Faubourg, Wharton pointed out, is noted for its eclecticism, embracing noted figures from the university, both the literary and academic *milieux* and the "old and aloof society" of the quarter (*BG* 258). As a stranger and an outsider, Edith Wharton enjoyed a certain degree of freedom not experienced by those in the "old social pigeon-holes" of the quarter (*BG* 258). Such a society offers fertile ground for a novelist, as Edith Wharton and Henry JAMES both discovered. Blake Nevius argues that both writers were inspired by the "consciously developed systems of manners" of the Faubourg (*EW* 9). James sets a scene in his 1903 novel *The Ambassadors* in a garden in the Faubourg. He describes the quarter: "Far back from the streets and unsuspected by crowds, reached by a long passage and a quiet court. . . . on the other side of which . . . grave *hôtels* [town houses] stood off for privacy, spoke of survival, transmission, association, a strong, indifferent, persistent order (*The Ambassadors*, 61, 93).

In the spring of 1909 Edith Wharton's brother Harry JONES found an unfurnished apartment for her and Teddy at a cost of approximately $75 per month. It was in a prime location within the Faubourg, at 53, rue de Varenne, almost across the street form the Vanderbilt apartment, but far more spacious. It had a series of balconies overlooking the street and a large courtyard in the rear. Facing the courtyard, in a row, were a large library, drawing room with high ceilings and a good-sized dining room. There were also a kitchen, pantry, servants' sitting room, six bedrooms, several bathrooms and a guest suite with private access to the courtyard (*EW* 258). Wharton searched for furnishings in antique shops and the Paris bazaars. It was not until the end of the year that she took possession of the apartment. In January 1910 she sent Morton FULLERTON a note giving him the address and telephone number (*Letters* 195).

Edith Wharton also evokes the complex "order" of Faubourg in *A BACKWARD GLANCE*, where she makes it clear that certain democratic elements of her American nature wholly resisted alteration. She consulted the uncle of a friend, a duke, about her seating plan for her first dinner party. He sent a seating chart, but responded to his niece, "'My dear child, Mrs. Wharton ought *never* to have invited them together.'" The guests were all intimate friends; the problem was that "the shades of difference in their rank were so slight, and so difficult to adjust, that even the diplomatist Duke recoiled from the attempt" to seat them properly (*BG* 260). She admits that it took her a considerable time to acquire even the "rudiments of this 'unwritten law'" and to understand the rules of precedence—whether a duke outranked a cardinal, or a foreigner an ambassador. Wharton came to realize that "under the most exquisite surface urbanity, resentment may rankle for years in the bosom of a guest whose claims have been disregarded" (*BG* 261).

Edith Wharton spent 12 years in the rue de Varenne between 1907 and 1919, when she moved to the Pavillon Colombe and Walter BERRY took over her lease at 53, rue de Varenne. She began slowly to comprehend the cultural and social terrain of this section of Paris, continually gaining insights into the subtle mores governing relations within the Faubourg. During this time, according to Lewis, she came to feel she belonged in the Faubourg, and "all her early aversion to the city melted away as she came to appreciate the coherence of life there, the almost effortless intermixture of the artistic and the fashionable, the steady nourishment of 'the warm dim background of a long social past'" (*EW* 165). During her years there, according to Millicent Bell, Wharton actually hoped to build her own "salon" by the careful balancing of highly accomplished guests from different intellectual and social milieu (Bell, "Edith Wharton in France," 68). With her increasing literary earnings, she was able to establish a secure place within the intellectual and social circles of the Faubourg. Her principal fictional depiction of the Faubourg is in *Madame de Treymes*.

For further reading: Bell, "Edith Wharton in France."

Faust When Edith Wharton was 13 years old, her friend Emelyn WASHBURN asked her mother whether she might join her in studying German and in reading GOETHE. She was the daughter of the rector of Calvary Episcopal Church, which the Joneses attended. Lucretia JONES consented, and, as Benstock puts it, Edith Wharton discovered in the works of Goethe "a mind whose sensibilities matched her own" (*NGC* 31). Goethe's dramatic poem *Faust: A Tragedy* (1808, 1832), was a text of central importance to Edith Wharton. *Faust* was on the list she compiled in 1898 of her favorite books, along with the poetry of Walt WHITMAN and the writings of Marcus Aurelius.

A decade earlier, in 1888, Wharton had chosen the epigraph for the diary of her cruise aboard the VANADIS from *Faust*. These lines suggest her profound craving for travel. Faust, who harbors two conflicting "souls" in his breast, repose and exertion, tells the pedantic, sedentary Wagner he longs for a magic cloak so that he might soar into *fremde Länder* or foreign lands; he would not trade such a garment for a *Königsmantel*, or king's crown and robe. He appeals to the spirits of the air to enable him to escape a life of peace and quiet and convey him to a new, many-hued existence in other realms. The cruise aboard the *Vanadis* was a magical time for Edith Wharton, not to be equaled until her 1926 cruise aboard the OSPREY.

When the Whartons finally moved into The MOUNT in 1902, she wrote Sara NORTON, quoting from *Faust*— or, rather, as Lewis observes, misquoting from it—"*Zwei Seelen wohnen, ach, in meine Brust*" ("Two souls there are that live within my breast") . . . and, she added, the "Compleat Housekeeper has had the upper hand for

the last two weeks" (*EW* 111). (Here Wharton opposes the domestic and literary sides of her nature, rather than contrasting repose and exertion).

See also: GOETHE, JOHANN WOLFGANG VON; *CRUISE OF THE VANADIS*.

feminism Gender is not a clear-cut matter with Edith Wharton. On the one hand, much of her fiction deals with the plight of women who are economically and socially dependent on their husbands or fathers; on the other hand, she states in her autobiography that young women are handicapped when encouraged to take university degrees and ignore the art of "civilized living."

The increasing focus on the position of women in the past few decades, brought about by the women's movement, has caused feminist critics to turn to Wharton as a champion of women's rights. Novels such as *The HOUSE OF MIRTH* suggest that Edith Wharton deplored the fact that women were often regarded by men as no more than collectible ornaments. Feminist critics have often focused on this novel, in particular, since the tragedy of Lily Bart seems to offer a clear caveat against the tenets of the frivolous society in which she lived and the compromises she had to make, lacking wealth, to maintain her position even though, as her friend Carrie Fisher astutely observes, she "despises the very things she's trying for."

Julie Olin-Ammentorp argues that feminist critics have "shaped a Wharton that conforms to [their] expectations," and, in so doing, have "oversimplified the complexities of Wharton's personality and times . . . [and detached her genius] . . . from the woman as a whole" ("Edith Wharton's Challenge to Feminist Criticism," 243). Elaine Showalter suggests that Lily Bart's death enacts Edith Wharton's thesis that "the upper-class lady must die to make way for the modern woman who will work, love, and give birth," and that she was also "signaling her own rebirth as the artist" of her later novels ("The Death of the Lady Novelist," 88).

But a satisfactory "modern woman who will work, love, and give birth" never actually materializes in Wharton's novels. Olin-Ammentorp is closer to the mark when she comments on the "complexities" of Wharton's life and, as a corollary, on her view of women. In *A BACKWARD GLANCE*, Edith Wharton deplored the downgrading of the "ancient curriculum of housekeeping"

> . . . by the "monstrous regiment" of the emancipated: young women taught by their elders to despise the kitchen and the linen room, and to substitute the acquiring of University degrees for the more complex art of civilized living (*BG* 60).

Critics have been hard put to reconcile this defense of the domestic sphere with Wharton's avowed sympathy with women treated as artifacts, "owned" and displayed by men.

Amy Kaplan situates Wharton's writing "at the complex intersection of class and gender" (*The Social Construction of American Realism*, 66). By her own admission, Wharton felt constricted by gender as well as class. The very class that had provided the economic means for her intellectual nourishment in the form of leisure, foreign travel and richly stocked personal libraries, espoused frivolous social pursuits and denigrated public literary endeavor, specially on the part of women. Moreover, to enter the realm of professional authorship, Wharton had to "grapple with the precedent of women novelists who ventured into the market only to reinforce their place at home" (72). She thus had to distance herself from the legacy of popular and commercially successful domestic or sentimental women novelists, such as Fanny Fern, Catharine Maria Sedgwick and Harriet Beecher Stowe. In much of her fiction, Wharton depicted the societal forces limiting the professional and economic independence of women.

Some resolution may actually be found in FRENCH WAYS AND THEIR MEANING. Wharton's book was initially intended to explain France, in simple terms, to the many American servicemen who came to her adopted country's aid in World War I. In the chapter called "The New Frenchwoman," she accuses American women of not being "grown up" as French women are. Even though they may dress well and possibly cook, they are still in "kindergarten," in a "Montessori-method baby-school" (*FWM* 101). American women, although they may have more legal rights, actually enjoy only a "semblance of freedom." The middle-class Frenchwomen is always her husband's business partner, for no one else can have such a vested interest in the success of the business. She "rules French life . . . under a triple crown, as a business woman, as a mother, and, above all as an artist." France has attained the ideal of "frank and free social relations between men and women," which has been retarded in America because of the hypocritical belief in Puritan England—transmitted to America—that there was danger in such relations. The American woman in her prime, who has advanced from the freedom of girlhood to the responsibilities of marriage, motherhood and running a household, is suddenly "withdrawn from circulation." The "liberation" and "progress" of American women are but a mirage, for their economic and social security depends on marriage. In "standing by" marriage, American culture undermines freedom, because the American woman loses stature upon marriage and withers away in the company of her children and the wives of other men. The French woman is a free spirit, and her position improves after marriage. Young girls are protected and sheltered, for the woman "does not count till she is married," when she begins to enjoy "extraordinary social freedom" (*FWM* 98–121, *passim*).

In her own life, although she never relinquished her citizenship, Edith Wharton may have attained an ideal balance, despite the fact that she had been divorced in 1913. With the exception of the war years, she divided her time between work (she wrote every morning in bed, even while traveling), domestic responsibilities (both her homes had domestic staffs, but she planned the meals and arranged picnics and excursions when houseguests were present) and social life (she frequently attended and gave dinners). Since Wharton's inherited capital had dwindled over the years, it was her fiction that yielded the income necessary to live in such style. Fortunately, society at large no longer looked down on women writers, as had been the case in the elite circles of Old New York in which the writer had grown up.

Wharton does not address with the problem of how women who are not "artists" of her stature can achieve such economic independence. But she does, in France, recognize a society in which men value women for their companionship and perceives marriages in which wives are partners, rather than chattel. In France, a woman is expected to "know what's being said about things" or she cannot hold her own at mixed gatherings, as the American Madame de Trézac tells her friend, the hapless social climber Undine Spragg, who is ignored by her aristocratic French husband (*The Custom of the Country*, 305). In her vision of what women could and should achieve, Wharton was far ahead of her time. In a sense, she redefined the concept of the "all" that modern American women strive to attain: it must not stop with the rearing of cultivated children or success at the office, but also include frequently extended and reciprocated hospitality, skillfully prepared food and a domestic ambiance permitting an intellectual meeting of the minds between the sexes.

For further reading: Benert, "The Geography of Gender in *The House of Mirth*"; Foster, "The Open Cage: Freedom, Marriage and the Heroine in Early Twentieth-Century American Women's Novels"; French, "Muzzled Women"; Fryer, *Felicitous Space: The Imaginative Structures of Edith Wharton and Willa Cather*; Gilbert and Gubar, *No Man's Land: The Place of the Woman Writer in the Twentieth Century: Vol. 2, Sexchanges*; Kaplan, "Edith Wharton's Profession of Authorship"; Olin-Ammentorp, "Edith Wharton's Challenge to Feminist Criticism"; Restuccia, "The Name of the Lily: Edith Wharton's Feminism(s)"; Showalter, "The Death of the Lady (Novelist)."

Fenno, Chris *See* MOTHER'S RECOMPENSE, THE.

Fez Fez, the capital city of Fez province, in north-central Morocco, lies about 120 miles southeast of Tangier. Located on the Oued River in the northern foothills of the Middle Atlas Mountains, Fez is a sacred Islamic city and center of learning and was once the northern capital of Morocco. The main industry is tourism, and local craftspeople are known for their leather work and textiles. The city consists of an old walled section, which includes ancient mosques and the maze-like medina (native quarter), and a new section to the south.

Edith Wharton visited the city in 1917 on her tour of the French colony. Morocco at that time was untouched by tourism. Wharton's tour was organized by a friend, General Hubert LYAUTEY, resident general of French Morocco, in order that she might see one of the annual industrial exhibitions that he hoped would impress on French subjects that WORLD WAR I "in no way affected her normal activities." General Lyautey had been encouraged to invite guests from Allied and neutral countries.

Edith Wharton devoted a chapter of *In MOROCCO* to Fez, the oldest city in Morocco without a Phoenician or a Roman past. She and her companion, Walter BERRY, rode on "pink-saddled mules" to visit the palaces and government buildings of the upper town, Fez Eldjid, or the "New Fez," founded in the 14th century. Wharton felt they transcended the "Occidental" concepts of years and centuries; they were "visions of frail

A reed-roofed street in Fez. From In Morocco *(1917), first edition.* (Collection of the author)

splendor," with their many deserted passages, Venetian chandeliers, gold pendentives in tiled niches and Italian marble fountains. They seemed "overripe," about to crumble of their own weight, but also dreamlike. Wharton also saw the Medersa Attarine college and the bazaar. At night, a "misty radiance" bathes the tall houses; the moonlight "does not whiten Fez, but only turns its gray to tarnished silver" (*IM* 77–119). Her final appraisal of the beautiful old city of Fez is one of hope tempered with caution. Like all Moroccan cities, she observes, Fez "has no age, since its seemingly immutable shape is forever crumbling and being renewed on the old lines" (*IM* 88).

***Fighting France, from Dunkerque to Belfort* (Scribner's, 1915).** The onset of WORLD WAR I brought an end to Edith Wharton's travels and the harmonious balance of her prewar life in the FAUBOURG SAINT-GERMAIN, divided among social life, travel and disciplined writing. This volume offers a wrenching account of the first year of World War I, omitting all mention of her own prodigious relief efforts.

The trajectory of war cut across all French classes with its violence and horror. Wharton did not immediately perceive that the war had ended the BELLE ÉPOQUE, the era that had nurtured her work and shaped her outlook, at first considering the war to be its "grandest hour" (*EW* 365). As it continued, and she was confronted by human tragedy on every side, she became a dedicated humanitarian. At the outbreak of war, she saw that France evinced "the white glow of dedication," but she was uncertain whether the sacrifices necessary for prolonged resistance could be mustered. Then, however, she realized that "baser sentiments were silenced: greed, self-interest, pusillanimity seemed to have been purged from the race" (*FFDB* 220).

In early 1915, she was asked by the French Red Cross to visit military hospitals at the front and report on their needs; her first was at Châlons-sur-Marne. She asked permission to make other trips to the front and to write magazine articles about her experiences with the hope of alerting her "rich and generous compatriots" to the desperate needs of hospitals, and to "bring home to American readers some of the dreadful realities of war." The articles, published in *SCRIBNER'S MAGAZINE* and in the *SATURDAY EVENING POST*, were compiled into *Fighting France, From Dunkerque to Belfort*. There are six chapters, beginning with "The Look of Paris," which describes Paris on the eve of war. Four others describe the regions Wharton visited: "In Argonne," "In Lorraine and the Vosges," "In the North" and "In Alsace." The final chapter, "The Tone of France," summarizes the spirit of the country at war.

Much of the volume concerns the sights Wharton saw on her various journeys to the front. She describes attending Vespers in a small country church in the village of Blercourt in the Argonne that contained four rows of cots with gravely ill soldiers. The congregation consisted only of women and a few soldiers posted in the village; all the other men were fighting. After the Latin cadences were finished, the curé began chanting the Canticle of the Sacred Heart, composed during the Franco-Prussian War of 1870; it was taken up by the "trembling voices" of the women and able-bodied soldiers:

> *Sauvez, sauvez la France,*
> *Ne l'abandonnez pas!*

The church "looked like a quiet grave-yard in a battle-field" (*FFDB* 69–70).

The tour to the northern front brings a *cri de coeur* about the wreckage of hopes, lives, homes and towns, which had come about "not that some great military end might be gained, or the length of the war curtailed, but that, wherever the shadow of Germany falls, all things should wither at the root" (*FFDB* 157). The human cost of the war was almost unbearable. She gave an account of it not only in *Fighting France*, but also in short stories and in her 1923 novel *A Son at the Front*. *Fighting France* is also eloquent testimony to Wharton's stance as a recorder and interpreter of the national cultural heritage. Her conclusion makes clear her opinion of the glory of the French spirit: "The war has been a calamity unheard of; but France has never been afraid of the unheard of. No race has ever yet so audaciously dispensed with old precedents; as none has ever so revered their relics" (*FF* 221). Wharton notes the many "murdered houses" in whose "exposed interiors the poor little household gods shiver and blink like owls surprised in a hollow tree. . . . whiskered photographs fade on morning-glory wallpapers, [and] plaster saints pine under glass bells" (*FFDB* 153).

As the war continues, everyone shares "alike in the glory and the woe," but Edith Wharton perceives a clear danger, expressed with the dry wit that often fortifies her style and dilutes what might otherwise be sentimentality:

> But the glory was not of a kind to penetrate or dazzle. It requires more imagination to see the halo around tenacity than around dash, and the French still cling to the view that they are, so to speak, the patentees and proprietors of dash, and much less at home with his dull drudge of a partner. . . . It was possible that civilian France, while collectively seeming to remain at the same height, might individually deteriorate and diminish in its attitude toward the war (*FFDB* 222–23).

She goes on to state that individual Frenchmen and Frenchwomen never wavered about the military policy the country had adopted, and that public sentiment never changed:

Edith Wharton before a French palisade. From Fighting France, from Dunkerque to Belfort *(1915), first edition* (Collection of the author)

> In all classes the feeling is the same: every word and every act is based on the resolute ignoring of any alternative to victory. . . . the devotion, the self-denial, seem instinctive; . . . but they are really based on a reasoned knowledge of the situation and on an unflinching estimate of values. . . . real "life" consists in the things that make it worth living . . . the only death that Frenchmen fear is not death in the trenches but death by the extinction of their national ideal. It is . . . the reasoned recognition of their peril . . . which is making the most intelligent people in the world the most sublime (*FFDB* 225–38).

Edith Wharton's class exclusivity is mirrored in the phrase "in all classes," but is mitigated by the sincerity of her plea, directed at "all classes" in America in the hope that it would effect her country's entry into the conflict. Nevius's accusation that she is "too well-bred, too narrow in her social outlook" does not apply to her stance in *Fighting France*.

The Edwardian critics who considered themselves authorities on peacetime France and the ideal composition of travel books, although they may have divined that the Belle Époque had come to a tumultuous end, were incapable of conceiving the scenes described or of contravening Wharton's assessment of the nobility of the French people under siege. Critical opinion about *Fighting France* was, therefore, not divided, as it had been regarding *A MOTOR-FLIGHT THROUGH FRANCE*. Reviewers revered the text for its fidelity to the realities of war and, even more, for its portrait of the nobility of the French people. *Fighting France* delineated, with unsparing clarity, the havoc visited on the French people. The critic for the *New York Times* traced Edith Wharton's view of the evolution of the French spirit under the pressure of war from "unrealizing confidence . . . and self-restraint" to "quiet authority" to a "white glow of dedication" deepening into "exaltation." Another reviewer, Florence Finch Kelly, focused on the fortitude Wharton perceived on the part of the French. She praised *Fighting France* for its journalistic realism, calling it a narrative "of the things observed by a writer with the seeing eye in the daily life of the French people, both the civilians at home and the soldiers at the front." The reviewer for the *Springfield Republican* commented that authorial "detachment falls down before such a spectacle as time," and ranked the book with "her worthiest creations of fiction" (*CR* 221–23).

The overall context is so tragic in dimension, however, that the book can scarcely take its place as a work of travel. That it does so, even in part, is a tribute to Wharton's rare ability to present, beneath the palimpsest of destruction, a vision of the physical France travelers had once loved and would find again, even if in altered form, as well as the distilled "white hot" heroism of the besieged nation that might well elude the traveler under ordinary circumstances. It is this spirit that presages the nucleus of *FRENCH WAYS AND THEIR MEANING*. The Académie reviewer of *A Motor-Flight Through France* had called on Wharton to write a "fine, accurate, and sympathetic travel-book . . . about France." This volume could not be that work, yet it manifests in full measure "the love of that vivacious land [which] . . . is in the author's heart, betraying itself a hundred times."

films based on Wharton's works   *See* Appendix II, MEDIA ADAPTATIONS OF WHARTON'S WORK.

Firestone Library   Repository of the Scribner Archives, containing extensive correspondence between Edith Wharton and editors at SCRIBNER'S publishing firm and SCRIBNER'S MAGAZINE, including William Crary BROWNELL and Robert Underwood Johnson. The letters begin in 1891 and continue into the 1930s.

Fisher, Carry   *See HOUSE OF MIRTH, THE.*

Fiske, Minnie Maddern   Revue of Mrs. Fiske's performance in Lorimer Stoddard's dramatization of *TESS OF THE D'URBERVILLES.*

Fitzgerald, F. Scott (1896–1940)   Edith Wharton is reported to have first met the American novelist in the New York office of publisher Charles Scribner in 1923. At the time Fitzgerald was a rising young writer, selling his short stories for as much as $1,000 (she was getting the same, but had been writing for magazines for 35 years). In 1925 he sent her a copy of *The Great Gatsby* with a "friendly dedication." She wrote him praising the novel, but suggesting that he should have offered the reader more information about Gatsby's early career; Fitzgerald said it was one of only two pieces of "intelligible criticism" he had been given.

Wharton invited Fitzgerald and his wife, Zelda, to lunch at the PAVILLON COLOMBE. The other guest was Gaillard LAPSLEY. Zelda declined, but Scott came with a friend, Theodore Chanler, son of Wharton's longtime friend Daisy CHANLER. The young men had been drinking en route to lunch to fortify themselves; after the meal Scott became embroiled in an anecdote about an American couple's unwitting stay in a Parisian brothel. The story failed completely to shock Wharton and Lapsley. She actually enjoyed what Scott called "rough" stories, but protested that this one lacked "data." In her diary that night she noted, "To tea, Teddy Chanler and Scott Fitzgerald, the novelist (awful)" (*EW* 457–68).

In 1923 Fitzgerald wrote a screenplay for the film of *The GLIMPSES OF THE MOON*, but it was rejected in favor of one by Lloyd Shelton and Edfrid Bingham (*NGC* 372; *see* Appendix II).

Fitz-James, Rosa de (d. 1923)   The widowed Comtesse Robert de Fitz-James was a prominent resident of the FAUBOURG SAINT GERMAIN, the elite quarter of Paris in which Edith Wharton settled in 1907. Of Austrian Jewish descent, she had married early and spent most of her life in Paris. At Paul BOURGET's request, Wharton had been invited to attend a reception for a new Academician at the ACADÉMIE FRANÇAISE, an important constituent of the INSTITUT DE FRANCE. It was an exclusive event, invitations to which were much coveted. He asked Rosa de Fitz-James to accompany her to the Institut, and the countess invited her to lunch first—the beginning of a long friendship. Her salon looked out on the "mossy turf and trees of an eighteenth-century *hôtel* standing between court and garden in the rue de Grenelle"; a few years later it was moved to a more modern building. It was the meeting-place of many distinguished Parisians; Edith Wharton believed it had a "prestige which no Parisian hostess, since 1918, has succeeded in recovering." In her memoir, she noted that the Academicians who frequented this drawing-room were Madame de Staël's grandson and biographer the Comte d'Haussonville, the playwrights Paul Hervieu and the Marquis de Flers, the novelist Henri de Régnier and the historian Marquis de Ségur. There were also other men of letters and a number of diplomats. She was tireless in looking after her guests' comfort. The countess collected rare books, but seldom read them and made no secret of it; Edith Wharton states she was "one of the most honest women" she had ever known (*BG* 265–66).

In 1912, during the BELLE ÉPOQUE, Wharton made a trip to Spain with Rosa de Fitz-James and her young friend Jean du BREUIL DE ST.-GERMAIN; they followed Théophile Gautier's 19th-century route from Pamplona through Burgos, Avila and Salamanca to Madrid (*BG* 330).

Rosa de Fitz-James died of cancer in 1923, soon after Wharton received her honorary doctorate from Yale.

Fool Errant, The   Wharton's review of this novel by Maurice Hewlett (1861–1923), a popular English historical novelist, appeared in *The Bookman* in September 1905; the novel had been published by Macmillan earlier that year. *The Fool Errant*, unlike Hewlett's earlier medieval romances, was set in 18th-century Italy. This may be the reason Wharton was asked to review it, since she had already published *The VALLEY OF DECISION* (1902) and *ITALIAN VILLAS AND THEIR GARDENS* (1904).

Her principal criticism was that Hewlett was too heavy-handed and not attuned to the nuances of the 18th century. The carefully "reconstituted" background clashed with his characters, who were too "physiological." Wharton gave him credit, however, for trying to make his characters real people rather than marionettes, and ultimately praised the "charm and animation" of the tale (*UCW* 110–14).

Foreword to *Bénédiction*   *See* BÉNÉDICTION

Foreword to *Ethan Frome: A Dramatization of Edith Wharton's Novel*   In January 1936, Edith Wharton wrote a foreword to the dramatization of *ETHAN FROME* by Owen Davis and Donald Davis. She had recently been sent the transcript of a lecture on American letters in which the speaker asserted that everything she had written except *Ethan Frome* was destined for oblivion. Although she "took the blow meekly," it was still comforting to read the dramatization of the novella. She wished, she wrote, to record her appreciation of their "unusual achievement" and believed the dramatization would give the work a "new lease of life." She imagined few authors had had "the luck to see the characters they had imagined in fiction transported to the stage without loss or alteration of any sort, without even that grimacing enlargement of gesture and language supposed to be necessary to 'carry' over the footlights." She had lived among her characters for over a decade, "and their strained starved faces" were still near to her (*UCW* 263–64).

Fortin-Lescluze, Dr.   *See* SON AT THE FRONT, A

France   Edith Wharton was fluent in French at a very early age, having spent six years abroad from 1866 to 1872. Her father, George Frederic JONES, died at Cannes in 1882; she and her parents had gone there hoping to restore his failing health. She often visited the country as an adult, and, about 1904, she and her husband Teddy gave up their annual pilgrimages to ITALY in favor of motor trips through France. She wrote three nonfiction books about France: *A MOTOR-FLIGHT THROUGH FRANCE* (1908), *FIGHTING FRANCE, FROM DUNKERQUE TO BELFORT* (1915) and *FRENCH WAYS AND THEIR MEANING* (1919).

Despite her thorough knowledge of the country, her EXPATRIATION and final decision to settle in France require some explanation. The principal reason for her decision seems to have been her realization, soon after 1907, when she and her husband began leasing an apartment in the FAUBOURG SAINT-GERMAIN a few months each year, that the intellectual climate of France suited her far better than that of AMERICA. Sponsored by her friend Paul BOURGET, a leading French novelist and member of the ACADÉMIE FRANÇAISE, she found a ready acceptance in elite French literary circles. In her memoir, she states that in PARIS "no one could live without literature" (*BG* 261). Her status was enhanced by her achievements as a writer there, whereas in America it had meant little to her family and many of her friends. In Paris, however, she found herself making many friends who were interested in her writing and who were distinguished writers themselves. She discovered, as she put it in her memoir, "the kind of human communion I cared for" (*BG* 257). She had numerous French friends, among them the painter Jacques-Émile BLANCHE, the poet Jean COCTEAU, the novelists André GIDE, Bourget, and Claude Silve (pseudonym of Countess Philomène de LA FOREST-DIVONNE.

Bell points out that Wharton became "more intensely her native self the longer she lived abroad . . . she was one of our aboriginal 'loners' ("Edith Wharton in France," 63). This was true despite the fact that, particularly after WORLD WAR I, she became increasingly alienated from the land of her birth. Her last visit to America was in 1923 to accept an honorary doctorate given by YALE UNIVERSITY. Wharton's essential qualities of self-reliance and independence, her concept of herself as a "self-made woman," suggest that she was American to her very core; she could never have identified herself completely with French women (who, in a patriarchal society, did not achieve the vote until 1944, seven years after Wharton's death).

At the same time, she was never what might be termed a displaced American, nor would she ever have given up her United States citizenship, as Henry JAMES did when the United States, first refused to enter World War I. Her mission was not total assimilation to France.

Chateau of Maintenon. From A Motor-Flight Through France *(1908), first edition* (Collection of the author)

In her fiction dealing with the country, she sometimes exposed the legal and moral injustices of the French system as they pertained to women. She dissected the cruelty of the country's divorce laws in MADAME DE TREYMES, and, in *The REEF*, explored the implications of the country's double moral standard. Her war novels *A SON AT THE FRONT* and *The MARNE*, however, depicted the pain of the country during World War I. For her war work she was made a CHEVALIER OF THE FRENCH LEGION OF HONOR. She exhibited strong elements of Francophilia in *A Motor-Flight Through France* and grieved to her innermost depths in *Fighting France: From Dunkerque to Belfort* about the destruction of the country she had come to love. In *French Ways and Their Meaning*, she assumed the role of tutor to young American servicemen stationed in France.

As Wharton became more preoccupied in her final two decades of life with the care of her two French homes and with the writing of fiction, rather than travel texts, the connoisseurship of her nonfiction works about France gave way to novels such as *The GLIMPSES OF THE MOON, The CHILDREN, HUDSON RIVER BRACK-ETED* and *The GODS ARRIVE*. They were more concerned with the marital relationships of Americans, sometimes living in Europe, than with the aesthetic achievements she had delineated in her earlier books, when she demonstrated so clearly that she possessed the "seeing eye" she had ascribed to the French.

Wharton's professional stature was very high in France. She knew André Gide, who, with his translator Dorothy Bussy, chose Wharton to write a preface to his 1924 novel *Strait Is the Gate* (a task not undertaken, for some reason). She published a tribute to her close friend Paul Bourget and was invited to write a foreword to *Bénédiction*, the novel written by Claude Silve. *La Demeure de Liesse*, the French translation of *The HOUSE OF MIRTH* by her friend Charles DU BOS, was a critical success, as was *Au Temps de l'innocence*, the translation of *The AGE OF INNOCENCE* by Mme. Taillandier, sister of Wharton's friend André CHEVRILLON (editor of the *REVUE DE PARIS*). Had Wharton lived out her life in America, perhaps dividing her time between LENOX and NEW YORK, with regular trips abroad, it is conceivable that her work would not have had the depth, the human interest, or the international perspective conferred by her long residence abroad.

For further reading: Bell, "Edith Wharton in France"; Edel, "Summers in an Age of Innocence: In France with Edith Wharton."

Franco-American General Committee   A 17-member committee formed by Edith Wharton in PARIS during WORLD WAR I to oversee the various relief projects she had established, including AMERICAN HOSTELS FOR REFUGEES. She served as chairman; members included Walter BERRY, Charles DU BOS, André BOCCON-GIBBOD, Matilda GAY and André GIDE.

French Ways and Their Meaning **(Appleton, 1919)**   In this text Edith Wharton examines the enduring mores and philosophical outlook of FRANCE from a post–WORLD WAR I perspective. While *French Ways and Their Meaning* is not a conventional travel book, with references to places, routes and inns, it may be considered one in a general sense. The book was originally commissioned for an audience of American servicemen stationed in France after World War I, who, in Wharton's estimation, did not understand the most basic aesthetic concepts of the French. Her task was to educate them. *French Ways and Their Meaning* focuses on the ethnography of the French people, discussing their mores, kinship ties and fundamental elements of character and behavior. The book is a compendium of observations based on her intimate knowledge of the country during both war and peace. It provides a lens clarifying the underlying mores and philosophy of the French people, making it possible to account for certain patterns of behavior and attitudes. Mary Ann Caws has stated that in this text Wharton "speaks from the depths of an honorary and honorable French soul," a rare achievement for an American (Caws, "A Note and Suggestions for Further Reading," 1996).

The book extends and interprets many of the ideas contained in *FIGHTING FRANCE, FROM DUNKERQUE TO BELFORT*, focusing on the enduring spirit of the French. Wharton analyzes four salient qualities of the Gallic spirit: reverence, taste, intellectual honesty and continuity. They are deeply engrained in the lives and thoughts of every French man, woman and child, with a universal applicability to many kinds of situations.

The French have a great reverence for and interest in conserving "nearly two thousand years of history and political life." Such history continually counteracts their intellectual curiosity and desire for the "new" thing (*FWM* 35). One example is their attachment to the "republic" of precedence (the rigid laws of rank at the dinner table). Edith Wharton claims that in agonizing over the question, for instance, of whether an academician, duke, ambassador, or bishop should be seated on the hostess' right, the French are not being "snobbish" but are merely obeying the rules of *les bienséances*, or seemliness, propriety. (*FWM* 28).

In her chapter "Taste," Wharton summarizes the reasons for her profound attachment to France and her ultimate expatriation from the United States. She asserts that the French people " 'have taste' as naturally as they breathe: it is not regarded as an accomplishment, like playing the flute." Their civic designs testify to this quality: there are stone quays along rivers suitable for strolling, carefully planned prospects and, above all, "suitability," or proportion, in colonnades, cupolas and sculpture, to give three examples. Americans, she suggests, are not trained to have the "seeing eye" possessed by French people, who are inherently a "race of artists" (*FWM* 52).

The French insistence on "intellectually honesty" is complemented by an equal intellectual curiosity. Wharton praises the crowds of ordinary people who not only patronize music-halls, but also attend the Odéon or the Théâtre Français and enjoy, for instance, the plays of Racine or Victor Hugo. Throughout this work, Wharton contrasts the intellectual and aesthetic attitudes of France and AMERICA, always to the disadvantage of America. The French embrace the "culture" Americans disdain, being "persuaded that the enjoyment of beauty and the exercise of the critical intelligence are two of the things best worth living for" (*FWM* 71).

In "Continuity," Wharton insists that "French culture is the most homogeneous and uninterrupted culture the world has known" (*FWM* 80). She is not, however, oblivious of some faults of the French, such as excessive prudence about financial affairs, which she ascribes to fear of losing one's "situation in life" (*FWM* 93).

The book also contains a chapter on "The New Frenchwoman," a woman brought into prominence by the war as her husband's helper and partner in every phase of his life. It makes clear Wharton's attitude toward the economic, social and intellectual plight of American women, as opposed to their French counterparts, a subject played out in several of her novels. The final chapter, "In Conclusion," began as "The French (as Seen by an American)," which appeared in *SCRIBNER'S MAGAZINE* in December 1917.

To the delight of APPLETON's, the volume was selected by the U.S. Navy to add to ships' libraries. On October 14, 1919, the commander of the Bureau of Navigation of the U.S. Navy Department wrote Appleton's that the bureau had directed the Supply Officer of the Fleet Supply Base in south Brooklyn to "place 'French Ways,' by Edith Wharton, on the list for purchase for crews' libraries of naval vessels" (Letter from C. B. Mayo, Edith Wharton Collection, BEINECKE Rare Book and Manuscript Library, Yale University).

French Ways received mixed critical reviews. The anonymous critic for the *New Republic* accused Wharton of delivering an "apologia pro partia sua," and of being an American snob who had adopted France instead of England, forgiving France faults as "inevitably contingent on an ancient civilization" that, in America, are "coarse pioneer faults." Both societies care for money, but, in France, it is a "means of enjoying life to the full" and in America an "end in itself." He asks if it is possible "that America will survive this apologist and France this defender?" (*CR* 273). The British reviewer for the *Times Literary Supplement* was shocked that Wharton ascribed the birth of democratic institutions to France and not England; it should be "common knowledge that France derived her conceptions of liberty and justice from England, and that she has not to this day succeeded in assimilating them." The critic for the *New York Times* called her defense of the country unanswerable when she challenged critics to " 'Look about you, and you will see that the whole world is filled with her spilt glory.' " (*CR* 273–76).

"Friends"   Short story written in 1894, revised and published in *Youth's Companion* (August 1900); it was not collected. The theme is the economic dependence of women on men. The setting is Sailport, a NEW ENGLAND harbor town. Miss Penelope Bent, about 30, is returning to Sailport; she has given up her teaching career to marry, but has been jilted. She learns from the chairman of the school board, Mr. Boulton, that they have hired a close friend, Vexilla Thurber, as her replacement. She had tried to obtain a teaching position for her in the past, but had failed because the board did not consider Vexilla "smart" enough. Because Vexilla needs the post to support her poverty-stricken family, Penelope does not let the situation destroy their friendship, but plans to move her mother to the home of her aunt in NEW YORK and start a new career with private pupils.

White observes that Edith Wharton considered "Friends" a realistic depiction of New England, opposing the picture given by the regional colorists Sarah Orne Jewett and Mary Wilkins Freeman, but that the story contains little that Jewett and Freeman might not have written.

Frome, Ethan   *See ETHAN FROME.*

Frome, Zenobia (Zeena)   *See ETHAN FROME.*

Fruit of the Tree, The   This 1907 novel was Edith Wharton's one attempt at a novel of social reform. It was set in a NEW ENGLAND factory town, about which she knew little, and failed to achieve the success of her previous novel, *The HOUSE OF MIRTH*. When she first conceived the idea of the novel, Wharton thought of calling it "Justine Brent." Charles Scribner had told her jokingly that, after *The House of Mirth*, "You must give us a strong man, for I am getting tired of the comments on Selden" (*EW* 159). Wharton was grateful for Edward BURLINGAME's encouragement when it began running

as a serial in SCRIBNER'S MAGAZINE, and wrote him in March 1907, "I appreciate so much the trouble you take in writing me at various stages of the work, and giving me your impressions so fully and so sympathetically" (Bell, "Lady into Author," 300). Sales started well, but failed to mount as they had for *The House of Mirth*; it became clear that the novel had failed to capture the public's interest.

The heroine is Justine Brent, a childhood friend and nurse who cares for Bessy Westmore Amherst. Bessy's first husband, Dick Westmore, had been the wealthy owner of Westmore Mills in the manufacturing town of Hanaford, New York. On a tour of the mills after Westmore's death, Bessey had learned from the young assistant manager, John Amherst, of certain barbarous labor practices in the mills; he was sympathetic toward the mill workers, since his father was of the working class. Bessy had appeared to be deeply shocked by them, and had eventually married Amherst. She had not rehabilitated the mills, however, but spent the money on luxuries for herself. When Amherst perceived that she was selfish and shallow they had separated.

Bessy is fatally injured in a riding accident, having disregarded her estranged husband's advice; it is uncertain whether she can be kept alive until he and her father can reach her. A young surgeon considers it a "beautiful case" and prolongs her suffering in order to further his professional reputation. She pleads with Justine to release her from agony; Justine injects a lethal dose of morphine and Bessy dies. Justine forms a romantic attachment with John Amherst, and they marry. They attempt to reform employment conditions for the mill workers, but questions are raised about Bessy's death by the young doctor, who has become a morphine addict and blackmailer. Justine is nearly tried for murder.

The reviewer for the *Outlook* felt the novel lacked the power of *The House of Mirth*; however, although it was not a "bringer of joy," it was "penetrating in analysis" and did not evade the issues it raised of the morality of euthanasia, the relations between the employer and his workers, and the need for industrial reform. The critic for the *Bookman* believed the plot was too contrived and did not grow organically from the characters themselves, as it had in *The House of Mirth*; the figures were types and not individuals. The *Times* reviewer considered the novel's execution superior to its premise. Several critics commented on Edith Wharton as a follower of Henry JAMES, agreeing that the novel represented a departure from Jamesian tradition; she now matched him in "adroitness" and exceeded him in "lucidity" (*CR* 147–54).

For further reading: Carlin, "To Form a More Imperfect Union: Gender, Tradition, and the Text in Wharton's *The Fruit of the Tree*"; Prather, "The Fall of the Knowledgeable Woman: The Diminished Female Healer in Edith Wharton's *The Fruit of the Tree*"; Stein, "Wharton's Blithedale: A New Reading of *The Fruit of the Tree*."

"Full Circle"   Story published in *SCRIBNER'S MAGAZINE* in October 1909 and reprinted in *TALES OF MEN AND GHOSTS* (Scribner's, 1910). The subject is literary fame. A best-selling author, Geoffrey Betton, has been living in affluence on Fifth Avenue after years spent in lodging-houses. A former Harvard classmate, Duncan Vyse, had also aspired to write fiction, and had sent Betton a novel he had found to be excellent. Betton failed (possibly deliberately) to forward it to his publisher. Vyse has been reduced to a part-time business job, and applies to Betton for the post of secretary, handling correspondence with Betton's fans about his second book. He is hired and given carte blanche to reply to letters from readers.

Betton fabricates some readers' letters in order to impress Vyse, who quickly suspects the truth. Meanwhile, the second novel is not nearly as well received as the first, and the readers' letters dwindle. Betton is reluctant for Vyse to perceive that he doesn't like receiving critical letters. Vyse realizes it, concocts flattering letters and attempts, successfully, to launch a lengthy literary correspondence between two articulate imaginary readers and Betton. Betton discovers the deception when he tries to set up an actual meeting with one of the "writers"—a young woman—and his letter is returned by the dead letter office at the same time he receives one of the falsified missives. Betton invents many plausible excuses for Vyse's behavior, assuming that he wants to retaliate for his own shabby treatment of his book, or that he hopes to uncover the nakedness of Betton's desire for approval. He accuses Vyse of "ladling out flattery" to earn his keep. " 'I'm stone-broke, and wanted to keep my job—that's what it is,' " Vyse replies.

Fullerton, William Morton (1865–1952)   Born in Connecticut, Morton Fullerton was raised in Waltham, Massachusetts, where his father, Bradford Fullerton, was a Congregational clergyman. He attended Phillips Academy, Andover, and entered Harvard in 1882. There he studied under Charles Eliot NORTON, whose daughter Sara NORTON was one of Edith Wharton's closest friends. Fullerton became the PARIS correspondent for the London *Times* about 1892. He and Edith Wharton met in Paris, through mutual friends, and had a liaison beginning in the spring of 1908, when he was 42 and she was 45; it lasted until the summer of 1910. During this time Wharton kept an intimate diary addressed to Morton Fullerton (*see* DIARY, 1907, "THE LIFE APART").

Fullerton helped arrange for the serialization of *The HOUSE OF MIRTH* in France (*La DEMEURE DE LIESSE*). He was also an admirer and protégé of Henry JAMES. When he came back to America on a visit in the fall of 1907, he had a letter from James urging him to let Edith Wharton know he was in the country so that she might invite him to LENOX, so he would not miss "a very valu-

William Morton Fullerton (Beinecke Rare Book and Manuscript Library, Yale University)

able and charming American impression, quite a particular and (of its kind) highly characteristic." He visited the Whartons at The MOUNT in October; Edith Wharton began seeing him in Paris in the winter of 1908.

Lewis gives a full account of the progress and waning of the affair between Edith Wharton and Fullerton (*EW* 183–206, 285). Early in the process of writing his biography of her, Lewis found a letter from Fullerton to her friend Elisina TYLER urging her not to subscribe to the myth that Edith was frigid. "Edith Wharton in love . . . displayed the reckless ardor of a George Sand." On further investigation, Lewis found more than 300 letters from Edith Wharton to Fullerton that revealed their love affair and traced her erotic awakening.

In June 1908, a few months after they had begun seeing each other, Edith Wharton wrote from The Mount, "Write or don't write, as you feel the impulse— but hold me long and close in your thoughts. I shall take up so little room, & it's only there that I'm happy!" An August letter recalls their attendance at the opera *Figlia di Lorio*, when, she confesses, "I discovered in myself such possibilities of feeling on that side that I feared, if I let you love me too much, I might lose courage when the time came to go away." During that summer Fullerton had other entanglements, causing Edith to worry that he was not interested in her; she wrote that she had always understood "it would not go on for long," that she had "foreseen" and "accepted" such a "contingency."

In October 1908, when Wharton mistakenly believed her affair with Fullerton had ended, she wrote the sonnet sequence "THE MORTAL LEASE." She returned to Europe the last of the month, in advance of Teddy, who did not come until January and who was increasingly afflicted with nervous instability. She and Fullerton renewed their affair during the spring of 1909, when she wrote such poems as "COLOPHON TO THE MORTAL LEASE" and "OGRIN THE HERMIT."

In June they went together to England; Fullerton was scheduled to sail from Southampton, bound for America to visit his parents. They took Suite 92 at the Charing Cross Hotel, and, after Fullerton departed the next morning, Edith Wharton wrote one of her most remarkable poems, "TERMINUS," a frank account their night together, beginning "Wonderful was the long secret night you gave me, my Lover" and describing "the pressure of bodies ecstatic, bodies like ours, / Seeking each other's souls in the depths of unfathomed caresses" (*EW* 259). Later in the summer Wharton and Fullerton spent a month in England together. Edith, however, was already claiming to realize that their lives could not "run parallel much longer" (*Letters* 189). In November she asked him to return her letters, which he failed to do. In December she wrote again, to "Mr. Fullerton," asking him to return them by registered mail. He did not refuse directly, but never did so. Her short story "COPY," first published in the June 1900 *SCRIBNER'S MAGAZINE*, anticipates this situation.

By January 1910 Edith was settled in the new apartment she had leased and furnished at 53, rue de Varenne; Teddy was in a Swiss sanatorium for treatment, but later embarked on a world tour. The Fullerton affair was coming to an end. In the winter of 1910 Edith Wharton wrote accusing Fullerton of wishing "to take of my life the inmost & uttermost that a woman—a woman like me—can give, for an hour, now & then, when it suits you; & when the hour is over, to leave me out of your mind and out of your life as a man leaves the companion who has accorded him a transient distraction" (*Letters* 197). In mid-April she accused him of finding "cruel & capricious amusement" in demanding "passionate tenderness" one day and ignoring her the next (*Letters* 207–8). Meanwhile, Teddy Wharton was becoming more and more irascible, and wanted to be with his wife at all times. Wharton wrote Fullerton in May that his doctors said "compulsory seclusion" was impossible for Teddy (*Letters* 215). In June 1910 she assured Fullerton he was "as free as you were before we ever met" (*Letters* 218). She continued to vacillate, while Fullerton alternated between encouraging her and ignoring her. In the fall Fullerton took a long leave of absence from the London *Times*; in May 1911 Wharton wrote that she wished she had known him at the age of 25, since they

might have had some "good days together" (*Letters* 238). She continued to think of Fullerton and to write him. Her troubles with Teddy increased and, in the autumn of 1911, The Mount was sold.

Fullerton was not an entirely satisfactory lover, nor was he free of entanglements at the time they met. He had been involved for a number of years with Henrietta Mirecourt, an older woman, who, after he left her, demanded that he marry and support her. She had found compromising letters indicating that he was also having affairs with Margaret Brooke (the Ranee of Sarawak) as well as liaison with Ronald Gower. Fullerton consulted Henry James, who advised him to try to buy Mirecourt off. Fullerton underwent a secret marriage in 1903 to Victoria Camille Chabert, an opera singer; they had a daughter, Mireille. He divorced her and became engaged to his first cousin, Katherine Fullerton, who had grown up in the home of his parents, believing him to be her brother. By summer 1909 she was in despair, believing the marriage would never take place. She wrote Fullerton, "I do not believe you have ever treated another woman so ill" (*EW* 249). Apparently he was unable to make any definite wedding plans, and in June 1910 she married Gordon Gerould, a gifted young instructor of English at Princeton. Fullerton lived 15 years longer than Wharton, dying at the age of 86 in 1952. In his later years he was a frequent guest at the PAVILLON COLOMBE and she regarded him as a friend.

For further reading: Colquitt, "Unpacking Her Treasures: Edith Wharton's 'Mysterious Correspondence' with Morton Fullerton"; Erlich, "The Libertine as Liberator: Morton Fullerton and Edith Wharton"; Gribben, " 'The Heart Is Insatiable': A Selection from Edith Wharton's Letters to Morton Fullerton, 1907–1915"; Werlock, "Edith Wharton's Subtle Revenge?: Morton Fullerton and the Female Artist in *Hudson River Bracketed* and *The Gods Arrive*."

"Fullness of Life, The"   This short story was published in *SCRIBNER'S MAGAZINE* in December 1893, and reprinted in *The MUSE'S TRAGEDY AND OTHER STORIES* (New York: New American Library, 1990). It concerns a woman who has died and, in Eternity, meets the Spirit of Life, who questions her about her marriage. She reports that she has never known the "fullness of life"; her marriage has been a very "incomplete affair." Her husband, with his creaking boots and attachment to railway novels (and she had to select them for him), was unable to appreciate art or literature. He was never her soul mate. She presents an elaborate analogy between a woman's nature and a house: there is a hall, where everyone passes; a sitting room for the members of the family; and, beyond them, other rooms, "the handles of whose doors are never turned." There the woman sits, waiting for "a footstep that never comes."

The Spirit of Life introduces her to her soul mate, a man with whom she has instant telepathic communication about art and literature. " 'After a storm have you never seen—' " he asks. " 'Yes, it is curious how certain flowers suggest certain painters—the perfume of the carnation, Leonardo; that of the rose, Titian; the tuberose, Crivelli—' " " 'I never supposed that anyone else had noticed it,' " he answers. But she cannot, ultimately, abandon her husband, who had thought of her as his soul mate. She sits in Eternity, waiting for him and his creaking boots. Habit, affection and duty have won over the affinity of like minds and the possibility of profound love.

Lewis calls the story a "fairly direct transcription of [Wharton's] married life which she had no heart to tinker with further," realizing there could never be full intimacy with Teddy WHARTON. Whether Teddy read the story is unknown, but Lewis terms him "admiring and humble." He once remarked, years later, to Sara NORTON, "I am no good on Puss's high plain of thought" (*EW* 65).

Edith Wharton rejected the story when compiling *The GREATER INCLINATION*, considering it one of several that were the "excesses of youth" and "written 'at the top of my voice.' " She described it in a letter to Edward BURLINGAME as "one long shriek" (*Letters* 36). White believes it reflected her own story too closely to publish—she did not want the public to identify her as a dissatisfied wife (*SSF* 38).

funeral   *See* CIMITIÈRE DES GONARDS; CATHOLICISM, ROMAN.

Futility   Novel by William GERHARDI published in 1922. He was born in St. Petersburg of English parents. Wharton contributed a preface to the novel, stating that she reluctantly began reading it on a long railway journey, expecting only to meet the "wooden puppets" she had previously found in Russian fiction. Instead, she met "living intelligible people." She called his novel "extremely modern," but insisted it had "bulk and form, a recognizable orbit," and the promise of future work characteristic of the best novelists (*UCW* 245).

Gantier, Paul *See* MARNE, THE.

"Garden Valedictory, A" Memorial poem written to
Walter BERRY by Edith Wharton in November 1927 and
published in the January 1928 issue of *SCRIBNER'S MAGA-
ZINE*. She states, "I will not say that you are dead, but
only / Scattered like seed upon the autumn breeze, /
Renewing life where all seemed locked and lonely." She
remembers him particularly as she walks through her
"garden-close" [at the PAVILLON COLOMBE], feeling her
hand in his, hearing him in the "migrant bird /
Throating goodbye along the lime-tree aisle."

gardens and gardening Edith Wharton's love of gardens began in her childhood, in her early European
years, when her family spent six years abroad between
1866 and 1872. She remembered long afterwards the
"lost Rome of my infancy," the "warm scent of the box
hedges on the Pincian" (*BG* 31).

After her marriage, when she tired of the "watering-
place trivialities" at NEWPORT and, with her husband,
built The MOUNT in LENOX, Massachusetts, she found
gardening to be one of her most satisfying occupations.
In her autobiography she stated, "Life in the country is
the only state which has always completely satisfied me.
. . . Now I was to know the joys of six or seven months
a year among fields and woods of my own" (*BG* 124).
The Mount had a kitchen garden and a flower garden
where, for more than 10 years, Wharton gardened. She
had a variety of plants and flowers in geometrically laid-
out beds, with an overall pattern of enclosed spaces
with fountains, stone benches and ponds. The property
also had a greenhouse.

Wharton's many years of travel in Italy and France
had made her something of an expert on European gardens. In her first novel, *The VALLEY OF DECISION*, there are
careful descriptions of gardens, such as the one surrounding the duke's palace at Pianura with its
"pleached walks and parterres" and "citron-trees inge-
niously grafted with red and white carnations." There
are marble nymphs and fauns, and statues of Apollo
and the Muses. Wharton's first work of travel, *ITALIAN
VILLAS AND THEIR GARDENS*, is a notable study of Italian
garden architecture. She describes the "garden-magic"
of the baroque period: the "fern-lined grotto with a
stucco Pan or Syrinx," the water-theater with its elabo-

rate cascades, the spouting Atlas, the sculptured
balustrade. She is particularly attentive to the aesthetic
of artifice represented by their "mossy urns," mythical
sea-gods, grottoes and interplay of light, water and
shadow. Wharton praised the Boboli gardens at the Pitti
Palace for resisting the impulse to "astonish" rather
than "charm" the spectator (*IV* 29). Her observations
about gardens are enriched by mythological and literary
references. For example, she asks of the 10 terraced gardens gracing the Isola Bella in Lago Maggiore:

> Are they like any other gardens on earth? No; but nei-
> ther are the mountains and shores about them like
> earthly shores and mountains. They are Armida's gar-
> dens anchored in a lake of dreams, and they should be
> compared, not with this or that actual piece of planted
> ground, but with a page of Ariosto or Boiardo (*IV* 207).

She deplored the 18th-century horticulturists, disciples
of Capability Brown and Repton, who were bent on
transforming every garden into an English park and
eradicating old designs. Impelled by the "Britannic
craving for a lawn," English settlers in Italy effaced
Italian parterres and terraces, olive orchards and vine-
yards and introduced "specimen trees" (*IV* 21).

In the preface she cautions Americans against trying
to import Italian gardens, believing that "by placing a
marble bench here and a sun-dial there, Italian 'effects'
may be achieved. . . . a marble sarcophagus and a
dozen twisted columns will not make an Italian garden;
but a piece of ground laid out and planted on the principles of the old garden-craft will be . . . what is far
better, *a garden as well adapted to its surroundings as were
the models which inspired it*" (*IV* 12–13).

When Edith Wharton acquired her home outside
Paris, the PAVILLON COLOMBE, after WORLD WAR I she
restored the six acres of enclosed gardens there, beginning in 1919. She also acquired, on a long lease, her
Mediterranean villa, STE.-CLAIRE CHÂTEAU near HYÈRES,
which she was later able to buy. This was to be her winter
and spring home for the remainder of her life. The gardens there were even more absorbing than those in Paris,
owing to the warm climate. She wrote Bernard BERENSON
in February 1920, somewhat ruefully, of clearing the
"Paradon" gardens and planning the fall plantings:

Isola Bella, Lago Maggiore. From Italian Villas and Their Gardens *(1904), first edition* (Collection of the author)

I talk, I know, as if I were moving into Caprarola, and putting, at the same time, the finishing touches to Chatsworth; & really, I believe those two feats might have been accomplished in 1913 more easily, & at no more expense, than getting settled . . . today (*Letters*, 429–30).

Wharton found ideal climatic conditions for gardening at the Ste.-Claire Château (although the Riviera was not immune from devastating storms). In an unpublished article, "December in a French Riviera Garden," at the BEINECKE, Wharton focuses on the rewards of a garden in winter rather than early spring. She catalogs the dozens of species that may be expected if November rains have arrived in good time, among them many varieties of irises, violets, roses, *Senecio scandens, Bougainvillea sanderiana*, tulips and rich flowering shrubs. The article shows her expertise in knowing just which week each species may be expected. "The garden has yet to be found," she insists, "in which advantages are not balanced by drawbacks, and this light warm soil makes happy many moisture-

dreading plants." Her normal habit was to spend mid-December through May in Hyères, returning to Paris from June through mid-December.

Gardner, Isabella Stewart (1840–1924)   Born to David and Adelia Smith Stewart of New York, Isabella was the first of a family of four children. Her family attended Grace Church at 10th Street and Broadway, where Edith Wharton would be baptized in 1862, but the Stewarts did not belong to the JONESES' social circle. Although Stewart was a prosperous importer, his father-in-law had kept a tavern in Brooklyn. Stewart left his daughter a small fortune.

Isabella ("Belle") attended a finishing school in FRANCE, toured the arts and antiquities of ITALY with her family, and married John ("Jack") Lowell Gardner of a wealthy and socially prominent Boston family. When their only child, a son, died at the age of three in 1865, Isabella was devastated. She and her husband went abroad on an extended stay, traveling throughout Europe, Egypt and other countries. They both became interested in collecting art, an enterprise in which the young Bernard BERENSON, whom they had met in Boston, assisted. He acted as their agent for many years, negotiating not only for good prices but also for export permissions. Isabella Gardner envisioned bringing paintings and furniture back to Boston for a "wonderful little *Musée* Gardner" (Tharp, 189).

Jack Gardner died in December 1898, leaving his widow with sufficient means to expand the idea of the "little museum." She commissioned an elaborate Italianate villa, Fenway Court, to be built in Boston's Back Bay. It was opened on New Year's Eve, 1903. Wharton wrote Sally NORTON that she was hoping Mrs. Jack would invite her to her "*fête de Nouvel An*" and, if it were given by anyone else, would write and ask for an invitation (*EW* 114). The Whartons rode a private train from New York for the gala occasion. Lewis repeats a story, which he terms "probably apocryphal," that Edith whispered in French that the meal served reminded her of one that might be offered in a French provincial railway station. Mrs. Gardner reportedly said, when the Whartons departed, that she was happy she had come but that she need not worry again about being invited to eat at the station restaurant (*EW* 115).

Gardens at Ste.-Claire Château today; villa in background
(Collection of the author)

Although the Whartons and Gardners were not on intimate terms, they had many mutual friends. The Gardners knew not only Berenson but also Charles Eliot NORTON, Paul and Minnie BOURGET, and Henry JAMES.

For further reading: Shand-Tucci, Douglass, *The Art of Scandal: The Life and Times of Isabella Stewart Gardner*; Tharp, *Mrs. Jack: A Biography of Isabella Stewart Gardner*.

Gay, Matilda   The daughter of the lawyer William R. Travers, a popular member of the NEW YORK social circle into which Edith Wharton was born, and the wife of the American expatriate painter Walter GAY. She had been a childhood friend of Edith Wharton, and, after her marriage, their friendship continued. The Gays were close friends during the years of Edith Wharton's expatriate residence in France. They had a villa at Le Bréau, near Fontainebleau, where the Whartons stayed many times. Later they were frequent guests at STE.-CLAIRE CHÂTEAU in HYÈRES. In Paris, Matilda attended poetry readings and other events together with Wharton. In February 1908 Edith Wharton and Morton FULLERTON visited the Gays.

Lewis reports that their friends were devoted to Matilda, in part because of her quixotic charm. She once remarked to Edith Wharton about a new automobile, "Yes, I believe that it has the power of 40 horses, but of course I don't allow our chauffeur to make use of them all" (*EW* 197). The Gays were Roman Catholic, though Walter was said to be somewhat more willing than the devout Matilda to omit attendance at Mass. During WORLD WAR I Matilda served on Edith Wharton's FRANCO-AMERICAN GENERAL COMMITTEE, and she and Walter both assisted with the CHILDREN OF FLANDERS RESCUE COMMITTEE.

On August 4, 1937, a week before her own death, and three weeks after Walter Gay died at Le Bréau, Edith Wharton wrote Matilda Gay from St.-Brice, "I'm sending you this line by Elisina [TYLER], to tell you how sorry I am not to be able to go with her to see you this afternoon. I should have been quite willing to go, but Elisina and my maid behaved so awfully about it that I had no alternative but to go on dozing on the sofa." She was glad, she said, she had always yielded to the impulse, when passing their gate, to "stop & give a hug to dear Walter Gay" (*EW* 531).

Gay, Walter (1856–1937)   American genre and figure painter who was a native of Hingham, Massachusetts. He went to PARIS in 1876, where he studied with Bonnat and Constant. He exhibited at the Paris Salon and painted a large picture, *Le Bénédicité*, now in the museum at Amiens, France. His work is also in the Luxembourg Museum, Paris, and in the Metropolitan Museum of Art, NEW YORK.

Gay and his wife, Matilda, were longtime friends of Edith Wharton. She had known his wife since childhood,

Illustration by Walter Gay. From The Book of the Homeless
(1916) (Courtesy Picture Collection, the Library of Virginia)

and for more than 30 years in France they attended
events together and stayed at each other's homes; they
had many mutual friends. Gay died a month before
Edith Wharton, in July 1937. *See* GAY, MATILDA.

genealogy, of Edith Wharton   Edith Wharton was
related on both sides of her family to the old mercantile
families of NEW YORK who traced their ancestry to the
Netherlands and to ENGLAND. Through her mother,
Lucretia Stevens Rhinelander JONES, she was connected
to the Rhinelanders, Ledyards and Stevenses. Major
General Ebenezer Stevens of the Revolutionary War was
her great-grandfather on her mother's side and was portrayed in John Trumbull's paintings in the Capitol
rotunda in Washington, which Edith Wharton saw at
the age of 15. Her father, George Frederic JONES, was
the youngest of three surviving children of Edward Renshaw and Elizabeth Schermerhorn Jones. Through him,
she was also related to the Schermerhorns and Pendle-
tons. Edith Wharton's parents were distantly related
through the Gallatins. According to Benstock, the
father of Lucretia, Frederick William Rhinelander, was
bored by account books, preferring literature, and,
when he died young, left his widow and children in
reduced circumstances. His brother treated them
unfairly and enriched himself. Lewis points out, however, that "poverty" is a relative term when used to

describe the Rhinelanders. Hell Gate, their estate north
of New York, was large, with numerous servants. Each
child had his or her horse and riding habit, and they
had English governesses and tutors; they learned the
principal European languages. There was "old money"
on both sides of Edith Wharton's family, derived from
the early fortunes made in real estate in Manhattan.
Few of the men worked.

Two rumors persisted about Edith Wharton's paternity. One was that she was the daughter of her
brothers' English tutor. The father of Matilda GAY,
William R. Travers, stated that, as a child, Edith
Wharton was the "image" of the tutor and that George
Frederic Jones had known of her parentage yet agreed
to consider the child his own and provide for her. Her
friend Margaret Terry CHANLER said that Edith did
believe her father was the tutor and that she tried to
trace him, but found he had died (*NGC* 11). The other
rumor was that she was the child of a Scots nobleman,
Henry Peter Brougham, first baron of Brougham and
Vaux, chancellor of Edinburgh University, who possibly
had an affair with Lucretia Jones at Cannes in spring
1861. At the time he lived most of the year in the Villa
Eléanore at Cannes, which, according to Benstock, he
had transformed from a small fishing village into a
"society capital." Edith's red hair, similarly shaped nose,
and certain gestures lend credence to this speculation
(*NGC* 9–10), but, at the time, he would have been 82
years old, which makes it unlikely.

"Genteel Circle"   A distinguished group of American
editors and writers whose most productive years began
in the 1850s and continued through the 1870s. They
exerted a strong influence in American letters during
the GILDED AGE, and their influence was felt into the
20th century to some degree. Custodians of the belle-
tristic tradition first practiced by Washington IRVING and
Nathaniel Hawthorne, among others, members of the
"Genteel Circle" were great admirers of the Romantic
poets and were devoted to "beauty" wherever it could be
found. They gave precedence to culture over theology.
Toward the turn of the century, as John Tomsich puts it,
their attachment to 19th-century romanticism "led logi-
cally to the languid and sophisticated aestheticism that
was later called the fin de siècle" (Tomsich, 193).

Although the more materialistic forces of modernity
in time effaced the aestheticism of the "Genteel Era," it
greatly influenced the development of Wharton's connoisseurship, embodied as it was in the work of such figures as Walter PATER, John Addington SYMONDS, and
Vernon LEE. Among the members of the "Genteel
Circle" were Richard Watson GILDER, the youngest, poet
and editor of *Scribner's Monthly* and *The CENTURY ILLUS-
TRATED MONTHLY MAGAZINE*; Bayard TAYLOR, poet, novelist,
playwright, and world-traveler; Richard Henry Stoddard,
poet; Thomas Bailey Aldrich, editor of the *Saturday Press*

and *The ATLANTIC MONTHLY*, as well as poet, novelist and short-story writer; George Henry Boker, poet and playwright; George William Curtis, editor of *Harper's Weekly* and *HARPER'S MAGAZINE*; Charles Eliot NORTON, specialist in late medieval literature and architecture; and Edmund Clarence Stedman, critic. Of these, Norton was an early friend of Edith Wharton and Gilder assigned the articles on Italian villas that were compiled as *ITALIAN VILLAS AND THEIR GARDENS*, Wharton's first travel book.

For further reading: Cary, *The Genteel Circle: Bayard Taylor and His New York Friends*; Tomsich, *A Genteel Endeavor: American Culture and Politics in the Gilded Age.*

"George Cabot Lodge" Essay Edith Wharton wrote as a tribute to George Cabot ("Bay") LODGE (1873–1909), published in *SCRIBNER'S MAGAZINE* in February 1910. He was an aspiring poet, but, at the time they met in 1898, when he was 25, he was secretary to his father, Senator Henry Cabot Lodge. Edith Wharton called him "one of the most brilliant and versatile youths I have ever known" (*BG* 149). He died at the age of 36 of a heart attack brought on by food poisoning, leaving his wife, Elizabeth Frelinghuysen Davis Lodge ("Bessy"), and three children, Henry Cabot, eight; John Davis, seven, and Helena, five.

His father, Senator Lodge, told Edith Wharton he hoped she would write something about his son: "I need not tell you how much he loved you—how grateful he was to you for all your sympathy and kindness. . . . You I know loved him. You are the one person of all others that I would have write about him." In the essay Wharton described their first meeting, Lodge's exuberant spirit and his capacity to give of himself, though she was guarded about the merits of his poetry. She had told his widow of her sense of his "luminous presence" (*EW* 280).

George Eliot **(review of biography by Leslie Stephens)**
See ELIOT, GEORGE.

Gerhardi, William Alexander (1895–1977) English novelist, born in St. Petersburg of English parents, who became a friend of Edith Wharton after she praised his novel *FUTILITY* (1922). She was responsible for its publication of in America and contributed a preface to it, praising his ability "to focus the two so utterly alien races to which he belongs almost equally by birth and bringing-up—the English and Russian; to sympathise with both, and to depict them for us *as they see each other*" (*Letters* 457). In January 1924 Gerhardi visited her at the STE.-CLAIRE CHÂTEAU, bringing large chunks of buttered bread, as he had been under the impression, according to legend, that Mrs. Wharton was an impoverished elderly woman. According to Lewis, she revelled in the "unpremeditated quality of his talk" (*EW* 462). His *Anton Chekov* (1923) was the first study of Chekov in English; he also wrote *The Romanoffs: An Historical Biography* (1940) and other books.

Germany As a child, Edith Wharton spent six years abroad with her parents, from 1866–72. They spent extensive periods of time in Germany, FRANCE and ITALY, and she became fluent in all three languages. At the outbreak of the Franco-Prussian war of 1870 they were at Bad Wildbad in the Black Forest, a health resort where Lucretia JONES had been sent for a cure. Edith Wharton recalled in her autobiography taking "happy rambles in the pine-forests" with her young nursery-governess, who taught her such "Gretchenish arts" as knitting and making wild-flower garlands. She also taught her how to read German from the New Testament. Edith contracted typhoid fever, but nearly all of the local physicians had been called up for military service. A Russian physician had, by chance, come to the resort to tend an ailing prince, and he was persuaded to treat Edith. He recommended the now standard treatment of plunging her into ice-cold water, but Lucretia could not bring herself to follow his advice. She did, though, wrap her daughter in cold wet sheets and she recovered. By the time the Jones family went on to Florence for the winter Edith was already fluent in German (*BG* 40–41).

In her youth, Edith Wharton developed a lifelong passion for German literature, especially the works of GOETHE, in which she was well versed. Much of her fiction and nonfiction contains quotations from Goethe's *Faust*, *Wilhelm Meister* and the *Italienische Reise*. She also translated Hermann SUDERMAN's play *Es Lebe das Leben* (*The JOY OF LIVING*) into English from the German for Mrs. Patrick CAMPBELL, the actress.

Before WORLD WAR I Edith Wharton took pleasure in traveling to Germany for the purpose of visiting museums. While living in Paris, in 1908, she and Anna BAHLMANN went to Munich for a week at a time when Teddy WHARTON was increasingly unstable; he had departed with his sister to Pau. During the summer of 1913 Wharton and Bernard BERENSON met in Luxembourg and embarked on a four-week tour; he was surprised to see that she was accompanied by her chauffeur, Charles COOK, her footman and general factotum, Alfred WHITE, a new maid to replace Catharine GROSS, who was ill, and her small dog Nicette. She had been exhausted by work on *The CUSTOM OF THE COUNTRY* and by her divorce, and nearly collapsed in Cologne. Berenson refused her offer of the car to continue alone, and they went on to a small resort, Oberhof, then to Dresden and Berlin for 10 days. Most of their time was spent in museums and at concerts. Although Berenson had found Wharton difficult and demanding, he missed her when she went to Baden-Baden to rest before returning to Paris (*EW* 351–55). Lewis points out that the strain of the events in Wharton's life during 1913 prevented her from perceiving the growing militancy in Germany.

Having enjoyed a childhood sojourn in Germany as well as other rewarding visits to the country's museums, gardens and opera-houses, Wharton was at first oblivious of the serious implications of the assassination of the Archduke Francis Ferdinand at Sarajevo, the desire of Austria and Germany to retaliate and the inevitability of war. On July 10, 1914, Wharton and Walter BERRY embarked on a motor trip to SPAIN with her staff. By July 26, she had begun to perceive that hostilities were building between Germany and France, and wrote Bernard Berenson that the international news in the paper was "pretty black." On July 30, en route home, they had reached Poitiers, France. She later remembered it as a time when she was, as Lewis puts it, attuned "to everything that was enduring, strong, and beautiful in France." On July 31, however, when they reached Paris, there was an unmistakable aura of peril (*EW* 362–63). She wrote Berenson that the city had "never looked so appealingly humanly beautiful as now—poor Andromeda!—with the monster careering up to her" (*Letters* 334).

It was Wharton's belief that the Great War, which had fully begun by August 4, 1914, would be short, though this theory was contradicted by the highest British authorities. Lewis observes that the British foreign secretary, Lord Grey, looked down from his Whitehall window and stated, "The lamps are going out all over Europe; we shall not see them lit again in our lifetime." Lord Kitchener, war minister, believed the war would last at least three years. Walter Berry, however, assumed optimistically that the German people would revolt and allow a temporary government to make peace (*EW* 365). Edith Wharton's sense of the monstrosity of the war had deepened considerably by early September, when she wrote Sara NORTON (from England):

> The "atrocities" one hears of *are true*. I know of many, alas, too well authenticated. Spread it abroad as much as you can. It should be known that it is to America's interest to help stem this hideous flood of savagery by opinion if it may not be by action. No civilized race can remain neutral in feeling now (*Letters* 335).

This letter demonstrates an appreciation of the power of America and of the desperate need of France for her moral support. At this stage, Wharton's appeal is on the general ground of a civilized society attacked by a savage one. She does not plead specifically for money or technological assistance (though later she will do so); her appeal is on humanitarian grounds. She was, within a year, to use all her power as a public figure to exert pressure on America to come to the aid of France. She soon came to concur with Henry JAMES that the war represented "the crash of civilization."

The war had a powerful effect on Edith Wharton's writing, making the social satire of her most recent novels irrelevant and acting as a catalyst to reshape her creative direction and ally it with her relief work. In early 1915, she was asked by the French Red Cross to visit military hospitals at the Front and to report on their needs, a journey that led to several other visits. These expeditions resulted in six magazine articles calculated to alert her "rich and generous compatriots" to the desperate needs of hospitals and to bring home to her American readers "some of the dreadful realities of war." She went to the rear of the fighting lines from Dunkerque to Belfort; hence, the title of the book in which the articles were collected, *FIGHTING FRANCE, FROM DUNKERQUE TO BELFORT* (1915), a compilation of articles about her journeys to the Front. She later wrote *FRENCH WAYS AND THEIR MEANING* (1919), a study of French mores and character as shaped not only by long-standing traditions but also by the war. She also edited *The BOOK OF THE HOMELESS*, published in 1916, soliciting contributions from well-known writers and artists to aid victims of war. This work produced profits for war relief not only from the sale of copies, but also from the auction of the original manuscripts and sketches it contained. Americans responded to her appeals, and "Edith Wharton" Committees were formed in New York, Boston and other cities (*BG* 350–54).

After her return from the Front, Wharton was possessed by an "intense longing to write" even as her mind was "burdened with practical responsibilities" and her "soul wrung with the anguish of the war." *Fighting France* has many moving images, such as Wharton's description of the burnished ruin of the facade of the cathedral at Rheims, shelled while already enveloped in scaffolding for repair work ("one must search the Inferno, or some tale of Eastern magic, for words to picture the luminous unearthly vision" [*FFD* 185]). The full sense of her horror of Germany and the war is evident throughout the book, as well as in her war novels *The MARNE* and *A SON AT THE FRONT*. Her story "COMING HOME" deals with a deed of revenge enacted by a French woman against a German soldier.

Alan Price concludes his study of Edith Wharton and World War I by stating that the coming of the war was in reality the end of the "age of innocence" for Wharton (*The End of the Age of Innocence: Edith Wharton and the First World War*, 181). Wolff suggests that, for Wharton, the most heartbreaking aspect of the war was the German ruthlessness that destroyed "the simple piety of many pasts, the penates of countless hearths" (*A Feast of Words: The Triumph of Edith Wharton*, 254). She did not again travel to Germany.

Gerould, Katherine Fullerton First cousin and fiancée of Morton FULLERTON, who had grown up in the home of his parents, believing him to be her brother. She was a poet, essayist and novelist and taught literature at Bryn Mawr College. In June 1910, giving up the idea of marrying Fullerton, she married Gordon Gerould, an instructor of English at Princeton. She gave birth to a son in April 1911. Edith Wharton admired her poetry and in 1908 had invited her to stay as a houseguest in her Paris apartment without realizing that she was Fullerton's cousin, not his sister, and that they had been engaged (*NGC* 211–12).

In 1922 Katherine Gerould reviewed Edith Wharton's novel *The GLIMPSES OF THE MOON* for the *New York Times*, praising her "superb gift of narrative" and "well-nigh faultless building of a plot." She considered it superior to *The AGE OF INNOCENCE* and insisted no recent American novel could compare with it.

ghosts   In her unpublished autobiography "LIFE AND I," Edith Wharton asserts that until she was 27 or 28 she could not sleep in a room containing a book with a ghost story. She dates her fear to the reading of a "robber-story" when she was recuperating from typhoid fever in Germany at the age of four. It was "perilous reading" coupled with her "intense Celtic sense of the supernatural," and brought on a serious relapse. She had to have a light in her bedroom in addition to a nurse-maid in order to sleep, and she could feel "it" behind her on the doorstep when returning from walks, leading to a "choking agony of terror." She was frightened of waiting on doorsteps for the next eight years, a fear which apparently elicited only sympathy and understanding from her parents. Her superstitions lingered well into adulthood ("LIFE AND I," 17–19).

Her unusual sensitivity to the supernatural led to many of Wharton's best short stories, including "A BOTTLE OF PERRIER," "AFTERWARD," "MR. JONES," "The TRIUMPH OF NIGHT," "POMEGRANATE SEED," "ALL SOULS'," "The LADY'S MAID'S BELL," and "The EYES." In the preface to her final collection of short stories, *GHOSTS*, published posthumously, Wharton insists that there is "internal proof" of validity within good ghost stories. She recommends that, to secure authenticity, the author of a ghost story be "well frightened in the telling" (*UCW* 273).

In *Gender and the Gothic*, Kathy Fedorko observes that certain critics, including R. W. B. Lewis, have seen, in Edith Wharton's fondness for writing ghost stories, a "vehicle for exploring otherwise taboo feelings and experiences." She links her interest in Gothic architecture, with its overtones of fear and the warding-off of evil, to her absorption in ghost stories and to other fiction as well, including *SUMMER*. In the latter, Lawyer Royall poses an incest threat to his ward Charity, who feels an "amorphous apprehensiveness . . . [and] sense of pervading danger" (74.)

Smith points out that in the ghost story Edith Wharton is able to "penetrate into the realm of the *unseen*, that is, into the area that her society preferred to be unable to see, or to construe defensively as super (i.e., not) natural" ("Edith Wharton and the Ghost Story," 89). Some of her stories are grounded in the

rational, such as "BEWITCHED" and "MISS MARY PASK," while others are "predicated on the marvelous," such as "The TRIUMPH OF NIGHT" and "Pomegranate Seed." Still others, such as "The Eyes," belong to the realm of the grotesque. At times, the horror of the natural exceeds that of the supernatural.

Further reading: Banta, "The Ghostly Gothic of Wharton's Everyday World"; Elbert, "The Transcendental Economy of Wharton's Gothic Mansions"; Elbert, "T. S. Eliot and Wharton's Modernist Gothic"; Fedorko, " 'Forbidden Things': Gothic Confrontation with the Feminine in 'The Young Gentleman' and 'Bewitched' "; Fedorko, *Gender and the Gothic*; Heller, "Ghosts and Marital Estrangement: An Analysis of 'Afterward' "; Kaye, " 'Unearthly Visitants': Wharton Ghost Tales, Gothic Form and the Literature of Homosexual Panic"; McDowell, "Edith Wharton's Ghost Stories"; McDowell, "Edith Wharton's Ghost Tales Reconsidered"; Smith, "Edith Wharton and the Ghost Story"; Zilversmit, "Edith Wharton's Last Ghosts."

Ghosts   Short story collection published posthumously, in October 1937, by D. Appleton-Century. It contains a preface by Edith Wharton about the writing of ghost stories, along with 11 stories. Among them were included "POMEGRANATE SEED," "ALL SOULS," "A BOTTLE OF PERRIER," "The EYES," and "The LADY'S MAID'S BELL."

In the preface, Edith Wharton distinguishes between the rare "*ghost-seer*" and the "*ghost-feeler*," who is sensible of "invisible currents of being" at certain times and in certain places. Good ghost stories, she asserts, bring with them their own "internal proof" of validity. She fears for their survival because the "ghost instinct" in the modern generation has been atrophied by the wireless and the cinema, both enemies of the imagination. She praises the ghost stories of Robert Louis Stevenson, Sheridan Le Fanu, Fitz James O'Brien and F. Marion Crawford. The volume is dedicated to Walter de la Mare, the English poet, novelist and anthologist who was interested in dreams and the uncanny. Wharton calls him "the only modern ghost-evoker whom I place in the first rank" (*UCW* 273).

Gide, André (1869–1951)   French novelist, critic, translator, playwright and editor. In 1947, he was awarded the Nobel Prize for his many contributions to literature. He was an influential editor of the *Nouvelle Revue française* and the author of many works, including the satires *Preludes* (1895), *Marshlands* and *Prometheus Misbound* (1953), the plays *Philoctète* (1899), *Saül* (1903) and *Œdipe* (1931), the satiric farce *Lafcadio's Adventures* (1914) and *The Pastoral Symphony* (1931). He was also author of *The Fruits of the Earth* (*les Nourritures terrestres*, 1897), a hymn in prose and poetry exhorting youth to cast off the conventional and receive the joy of life in all its varieties of experience. It was espoused by restless young people during the 1920s as justifying the unconventional and the experimental. A homosexual, in 1902 he wrote *The Immoralist* (*l'Immoraliste*) a tale of a young Frenchman who takes his bride to North Africa, develops tuberculosis and finds himself attracted to young Arab boys.

Edith Wharton met Gide at the home of Jacques-Émile BLANCHE in Autueil, outside PARIS, and became a friend of his, although their correspondence was on a somewhat formal basis; she wrote him in her fluent French. In 1917 she thanked him for sending a copy of *l'Immoraliste* and promised him a copy of her new novel SUMMER, begging that he "read it with indulgence, for it was done in fits and starts because of the refugees" (*Letters* 397). Dorothy Bussy, sister of Lytton Strachey and wife of the artist Simon Bussy, translated many of Gide's works into English. For many years she was in love with Gide; the Bussys gave him shelter during World War II. After Gide's novel *Strait Is the Gate* (*la Porte étroite*) was published in 1909, Edith Wharton was the choice of both Dorothy Bussy and Gide to write a preface for it, but she never did so.

In 1915 Gide was working with the Foyer Franco-Belge, a clearinghouse for refugees Wharton helped create, then run by Charles DU BOS. She appointed him to the general committee of the AMERICAN HOSTELS FOR REFUGEES. In November of that year she visited Paul BOURGET and his wife at Les Plantiers on the French Riviera, a brief respite before she received the devastating news that Henry JAMES had suffered a stroke in December; he died in February 1916. Gide wrote her several letters of sympathy after his death, knowing of her deep affection for him. She particularly liked Gide's *Prétextes*, and they spent many evenings discussing writers and literature.

She once wrote her friend Gaillard LAPSLEY that Gide was a "mass of quivering 'susceptibilities,'" & invents grievances when he can't find them ready made. Luckily he is so charming that one ends by not minding" (*Letters* 410).

Gift from the Grave, A Title of the English edition of the novella *The* TOUCHSTONE, published by Scribner's in America in 1900 and by John Murray in England the same year.

Gilded Age When, in 1867, the novelist John de Forest called for a "great American novel," Mark Twain and Charles Dudley Warner collaborated on *The Gilded Age: A Tale of To-Day* (published in 1873). The title, which became synonymous with the entire cultural era, was taken from Shakespeare's *King John*: "To gild refined gold, to paint the lily, / . . . Is wasteful and ridiculous excess."

The phrase has been adopted by critics and writers to describe the hectic post–Civil War period in America, a time of anxiety and uncertain values, but also an expansive era, one of unprecedented affluence, gilded with money and material objects. The nouveaux riches, whose fortunes were made in steel, railroads, lumber and manufacturing, were forging industrial America. T. Jackson Lears, in *No Place of Grace*, has written of the "Promethean optimism of the official culture" of the late 19th century, and states that the tendency to equate material and moral progress was a hallmark of the Victorian era.

The three decades between 1880 and 1910 were an unparalleled era of opulence. Many fortunes had been made in railroads and Civil War profiteering. Nineteenth-century entrepreneurs, a new vector of society who found the old NEW YORK society impenetrable, sought to capitalize on the increasing capacity for leisure manifested within the American economy. It was a time when the "robber barons" accumulated vast fortunes and built large mansions in Philadelphia, NEWPORT and other places. Newport was one of the more stylish summer retreats. Soon 75 large Victorian mansions had been built on Bellevue Ave. It was already graced by the Belmonts, who were gilded with the fortunes of the Rothschilds.

The new millionaires also summered at Hot Springs, Saratoga and also Long Branch, N.J., less well known today, which was a watering place for financiers such as Jay Gould and the "summer capital" during the presidencies of Ulysses S. Grant, James Garfield and Chester Arthur. It was here that Jim Fiske would arrive on his 345-foot steamer, the *Plymouth Rock*, broadcasting his ownership by having his face painted in color on either side of the ship's boiler. Long Branch declined after gambling clubs were built, another outgrowth of the Gilded Age.

In New York the new millionaires attempted to enter "society" but were at first rejected by the "old guard," which included members of Edith Wharton's extended family: the Joneses, Stevenses and Rhinelanders, who had avoided publicity and ostentation. In 1877, an editorial in the magazine *Town Topics* asked, "Where were the Vanderbilts, socially, even five years ago? the Astors had just fifteen years the social start" (*EW* 41). The Metropolitan Opera House was founded because the newcomers could not buy into the old Academy of Music; boxes there could not be had for any price.

A number of American writers treated the Gilded Age in fiction: Theodore Dreiser (*An American Tragedy*), F. Scott FITZGERALD (*The Great Gatsby*), William Dean HOWELLS (*The Rise of Silas Lapham*) and Edith Wharton. During the Gilded Age great fortunes produced a substantial degree of "guilt," both social and sexual. In many Gilded Age novels, the financiers were compelled to assume a philanthropic mask in order to make their gains palatable to themselves and to others. Behind nearly every self-made millionaire was a commodity, a wife or "helpmeet" whose task was to empower him to make his way in society. His daughters must find husbands, take up philanthropy as spinsters, become social facilitators or descend beyond the perimeter of society into depravity. Society as a "guild" is both class-bound and convention-ridden; entry could only be gained by a long apprenticeship. Money, essentially a sin, could be converted into a virtue by sufficient guilt and redemptive action in the form of good works (social reform). Assimilation into the "guild" of elite social class could, at least theoretically, follow.

Edith Wharton treated the Gilded Age in a number of works, including the *The CUSTOM OF THE COUNTRY*, the *OLD NEW YORK* series of novellas, *The AGE OF INNOCENCE*, and her final posthumously published novel *The BUCCANEERS*. The latter opens at Saratoga, where the St George family is established at the Grand Union Hotel. The St George daughters are languidly waiting on the terrace for the gentlemen to return from racing. Their mother realizes, however, that Newport has eclipsed the other watering places and that no amount of wealth displayed at Saratoga will substitute for Newport or secure an entree to New York society. She eventually secures an English governess, Laura Testvalley, who launches the girls in London and aids them in making titled marriages, thus circumventing the social hierarchy of New York.

Thorstein Veblen's *Theory of the Leisure Class*, published in 1899, could almost be taken as a textbook explanation of the excesses in consumption which marked social life in Newport during the latter part of the 19th century; he may, in fact, have founded his observations on Newport. Consumption and leisure are, to Veblen, in a symbiotic relationship; leisure becomes its own form of consumption. Veblen argues that leisure is as effective evidence of wealth as consumption, and traces the "work" of leisure that falls on the millionaires of the Gilded Age. They must engage in performance of conspicuous leisure, in the way of calls, drives, clubs, sewing-circles, sports, charity organizations, and other like social functions. . . . the apparatus of living has grown so elaborate and cumbrous, in the way of dwellings, furniture, bric-a-brac, wardrobe and meals that the consumers of these things cannot make way with them in the required manner without help" (Veblen, *Theory of the Leisure Class*, 59 ff.). In *A BACKWARD GLANCE*, published in 1934, Wharton recalls the formidable social rituals of the old Newport, with afternoon calls and drives, archery parties and evening dinners.

Wharton witnessed the initial clash and gradual blending of those with "old money" and those with "new" as she documented the excesses of the Gilded Age in many of her works. Although her expatriation effectively ended her actual participation in the Gilded Age in America, the subject fascinated her, and she continued to write about it as late as 1920, when she published *The Age of Innocence*. In *A Backward Glance* she confessed that in her youth she had viewed the society of Old New York as "an empty vessel into which no new wine would ever again be poured." In her matu-

rity, however, she perceived it differently, as a vessel preserving "a few drops of an old vintage too rare to be savoured by a youthful palate" (*BG* 5). She could not, she admitted ruefully, have guessed that New York

. . . would fifty years later be as much a vanished city as Atlantis or the lowest layer of Schliemann's Troy, or that the social organization which that prosaic setting had slowly secreted would have been swept to oblivion with the rest (*BG* 55).

For further reading: Brinker, "The Gilded Void: Edith Wharton, Abraham Cahan, and the Turn-of-the-Century American Culture."

Gilder, Richard Watson (1844–1909)   A member of the "GENTEEL CIRCLE" of editors, writers and poets who flourished in the GILDED AGE after the Civil War and into the early years of the 20th century. He was a poet, newspaper writer and editor of one of the most prestigious literary periodicals of the day, *Scribner's Monthly* (which he edited from 1870–81); it later became *The CENTURY ILLUSTRATED MONTHLY MAGAZINE* and was under his editorship from 1881 until his death in 1909. (*Scribner's Magazine* was a different publication, succeeding *Scribner's Monthly* and competing with *The Century*). Among Gilder's volumes of poetry are *The New Day* (1876) and *Five Books of Songs* (1900).

In 1902, after *The VALLEY OF DECISION* was published, Gilder wrote a congratulatory note to Edith Wharton. Later that year he invited her to contribute the text to *The Century* for a series of articles about Italian villas that Maxfield PARRISH had been commissioned to illustrate. In early 1903 Edith and Teddy sailed for ITALY and began touring villas. Wharton had agreed on a fee of $1,500 for the articles, but, as they traveled, seeing the villas became more and more expensive. She wrote Gilder, stating, "You know, of course, that I do not 'live by my pen' and did not expect these articles to pay for the expenses of our Italian trip," but asked that the advance be increased to $2,000; Gilder agreed (*EW* 117).

The articles were published in the magazine and were then collected in Wharton's first published travel book, *ITALIAN VILLAS AND THEIR GARDENS*, considered one of the most thorough and scholarly of her works. She pleaded in vain for the inclusion of architectural drawings and garden plans, but Gilder was adamant in his refusal to authorize them. At one point Wharton wanted to withdraw the articles entirely from the magazine, but he refused. As Wharton astutely realized, Gilder wanted to offer the public a romantic subject treated by a popular artist, not a technical treatise. The book was published with only one plan, the Botanic Garden at Padua, although there were 52 illustrations, including 15 watercolors by Parrish. More than 30 years later, Wharton was still fretting over the outcome. In *A BACKWARD GLANCE* she wrote that the Parrish watercolors had been wrong for the text and, as she put it, "should have been used to illustrate some fanciful tale of Lamotte-Fouqué, or Andersen's 'Improvisatore' " (*BG* 139).

Edith Wharton did not let her misunderstanding with Gilder prevent her from publishing short fiction in *The Century*, including "The CHOICE" (1908). The stories "AFTERWARD" and "The LETTERS" (1910) and "AUTRE TEMPS" (1911) were published after Gilder's death. Wharton did not again, however, undertake works of travel for the *Century Magazine* or for the Century Company; they were published by Scribner's and Appleton.

Glennard, Stephen   *See TOUCHSTONE, THE.*

"Glimpse, A"   Short story published in *The SATURDAY EVENING POST* in November 1932 and included in *HUMAN NATURE* (Appleton, 1933). The hero is John Kilvert, a prosperous American bachelor traveling in Italy, summoned by an old friend, Sara Roseneath, to help her choose a costume for a fancy-dress ball in Venice.

On the boat from Fusina to Venice he observes a middle-aged couple in the midst of what he takes to be a lovers' quarrel; she leaves the boat in haste and Kilvert makes enquiries about their identities. They turn out to be Julian Brand, a famous cellist, and the pianist Margaret Aslar, who accompanies him. Sara Roseneath has booked them to play in her home, but they send word they must cancel. Kilvert calls on Margaret Aslar and learns that the couple were having a professional, not a personal, quarrel over the billing for the program. They ultimately realize they have a symbiotic professional relationship; each needs the other and both serve the higher cause of music. As the story ends, they begin mending their fences and agree to play at the party.

"Tea? How Can I Take Tea? Take it Away! . . . It's a Catastrophe," Mrs. Roseneath Lamented, Sinking Back Discouraged Among Her Pillows

Illustration by John Lagatta for "A Glimpse" (The Saturday Evening Post, *1932*) (Courtesy Alderman Library, University of Virginia, Charlottesville, Virginia. ©The Curtis Publishing Company)

"Lovers' Quarrel? Between Us? Do You Take Us for Children? Lovers' Quarrels are Pastry Eclairs. Brand and I are Artists"

Illustration by John Lagatta for "A Glimpse" (The Saturday Evening Post, *1932)* (Courtesy Alderman Library, University of Virginia, Charlottesville, Virginia. ©The Curtis Publishing Company)

Glimpses of the Moon, The   A novel published in 1922 by D. Appleton, which received mixed critical reviews. It was acclaimed by Katherine Fullerton GEROULD in the *New York Times* and sold well in both England and America. The story, set in the 1920s, deals with a young pair, Nick Lansing and Susy Branch, each of whom is poor. They agree to marry and spend a year's honeymoon as parasitical guests of various wealthy people, paying for their stay by charm. As Susy puts it, "We both know the ropes so well; what one of us didn't see the other might—in the way of opportunities, I mean. And then we should be a novelty as married people. We're both rather unusually popular—why not be frank?—and it's such a blessing for dinner-givers to be able to count on a couple of whom neither one is a blank" (*GM* 19). Each is free to dissolve the marriage if a more promising partner appears. The novel unfolds as a comedy of man-

ners, depicting the foibles of the immoral and frivolous life of the international "set" of wealthy Americans during the 1920s, the same era in which Wharton's novel *The CHILDREN* is set. In 1921 Wharton wrote Bernard BERENSON about it, saying it "tries to picture the adventures of a young couple who believe themselves to be completely affranchis & up-to-date, but are continually tripped up by obsolete sensibilities, & discarded ideals.—A difficult subject, which of course seemed the easiest in the world when I began it" (*Letters* 446).

Not all reviewers agreed with Katherine Gerould. Burton Rascoe, writing in the New York *Tribune*, found the novel repetitious despite the intimate picture it gave of life "as lived among the leisured and sophisticated class of cosmopolitans." His most serious complaints were that Wharton's emotions were "not at all engaged by Nick and Susy Lansing," and that her human beings seldom seemed "more than slugs and parasites, moths and butterflies." The *New Republic* stated that the author had done "less" than she had earlier, but believed the book had merit in presenting certain "wholesome" aspects of American life. Rebecca West, writing in the *New Statesman*, found it "competent" with flashes of insight, but, surprisingly, accused the author of wanting to imitate Henry JAMES and falling short. The critic for the *Bookman* dismissed it as a "puppet show" (*CR* 307–21). Lewis terms it a "light-fingered work at best" (*Letters* 418), and there is evidence that Edith Wharton did not take it as seriously as *The AGE OF INNOCENCE*, which preceded it in 1920, or as *A SON AT THE FRONT*, which followed it in 1923. She wrote Berenson to thank him for saying he had liked the novel, but insisted that it was a "very slight thing, of course" (*Letters* 453). Today the novel is not considered by the majority of critics as one of Wharton's more enduring works.

For further reading: Killoran, "An Unnoticed Source for *The Great Gatsby*: The Influence of Edith Wharton's *The Glimpses of the Moon*."

Gods Arrive, The Published by D. Appleton in 1932, this novel and its predecessor, HUDSON RIVER BRACKETED, explore the subject of creativity and the artist. The first novel brought Vance Weston from the Midwest to the Atlantic seaboard, where he realized his ambition to become a writer, and depicted the "artistic" NEW YORK and Greenwich Village Wharton despised. *The Gods Arrive* takes him among the left-wing writers' colony in PARIS, which Wharton depicts as specious and frivolous. Vita-Finzi notes that, while *Hudson River Bracketed* focuses on the writer's learning to use his imagination and inspiration, *The Gods Arrive* is concerned with his ability "to keep his internal world in balance with his external experiences" (*Edith Wharton and the Art of Fiction*, 53).

As the novel opens, Weston is aboard a steamship bound for Europe with Halo Spear Tarrant, who has left her husband, Lewis, the scion of one of New York's old genteel families, who has refused to divorce her. They call themselves Mr. and Mrs. Weston. The title of the novel comes from Ralph Waldo EMERSON's poem "Give All To Love": "When half-gods go, / The gods arrive," and deflects the reader's attention away from the individual characters to the more abstract problem of the working-out of the extramarital relationship. "Marriage is a frame," one of the characters remarks, and Halo and Vance at first find that the frame is lacking in their ambiguous lives. They snatch happiness from "half-gods," but it cannot be from "whole" gods, given their situation. Before they can arrive, much else must happen.

Weston eventually deserts Halo, who sits "alone among the ruins." He returns to her, as does Tarrant, who begs her to return to him. Pregnant by Weston, she refuses. She finds herself through her child, just as

Vance does through his failure as a writer. She returns to her old home on the Hudson to prepare for the birth of her illegitimate child. There is a "happy" ending, however, which provoked one critic to remark that Halo faces "a long life of boredom . . . in her ministering to Vance's vanity" (*CR* 496). He has not fulfilled the artistic promise he possessed in *Hudson River Bracketed*, but both come to realize that marriage is an essential bond.

The epigraph, "The gods approve / The depth and not the tumult of the soul," is from Wordsworth's *Laodamia*, about the wife of Protesilaus, slain by Hector before Troy; she followed the specter of her dead husband to the shades. In order to bring the talents lying deep within himself to full fruition, Vance must transcend the agitations and "tumult" of daily life. He must reach deep within himself and make use of the primordial roots he had once tried to discard. In *Hudson River Bracketed* Vance reads GOETHE's *FAUST* and encounters the mysterious Mothers, the origins of creativity, the eternal and infinite resources available to all men. In *The Gods Arrive*, he also reflects on the Mothers. He returns to his home town, Euphoria, to read *Colossus*, his latest novel, and realizes its people and values have not only contributed to his own makeup but have their own validity; they must be accepted as part of the universal Mothers. Artistic inspiration comes only partly from perception of the exterior world; it must necessarily arise also from the inner depths of the soul.

For further reading: Olin-Ammentorp, "Wharton through a Kristevan Lens: The Maternality of *The Gods Arrive*"; Vita-Finzi, *Edith Wharton and the Art of Fiction*; Werlock, "Edith Wharton's Subtle Revenge?: Morton Fullerton and the Female Artist in *Hudson River Bracketed* and *The Gods Arrive*."

Glimpses of the Moon, The (film, 1923)   *See* Appendix II.

Goethe, Johann Wolfgang von (1749–1832) Considered the greatest of German poets, Goethe was a native of Frankfurt-on-Main. Educated by his patrician father and various tutors, he grew up in a large house in Frankfurt. Under the French occupation of Frankfurt during the Seven Years War, he had free access to French theater, which kindled his imagination. He went on to the university at Leipzig, where he began writing poetry and plays and taking lessons in art. After recuperating from a serious illness at home, he continued his studies in Strasbourg, where he became more oriented toward romanticism than classicism. While training as a lawyer, he wrote his first important drama, *Götz von Berlichingen* (1773), which initiated the *Sturm und Drang* literary movement. This movement concerned itself with the clash between the energetic, self-reliant Promethean individual and the rationalistic, neoclassical enlightenment; he wrote the well-known poem *Prometheus* (c. 1774) during this period. His later works included the epistolary novel *The Sorrows of Young Werther* (1774), the *Roman Elegies* (1788), the drama *Egmont* (1788), the domestic epic *Hermann und Dorothea* (1797), the novel *Wilhelm Meisters Lehrjahre* (1796) and FAUST (first part published in 1808), which has been called Germany's most national drama. Although Goethe has been regarded as a "poet for all time," he was actually multifaceted, writing plays, art criticism and novels.

Goethe's philosophy and writings had a profound influence on Edith Wharton. In *A BACKWARD GLANCE* she recalls the long hours on the floor of her father's library reading his major works. A quotation from *Wilhelm Meister*, "Kein Genuss ist vorübergehend" ["No pleasure is only transitory]," serves as one of the epigraphs to her memoirs. In 1898 she wrote a list of "my favorite books," and Goethe's *Faust* was among the first six. His influence pervades both her fiction and her travel writing. On the day she moved into The MOUNT she wrote Sally NORTON, "*Zwei Seelen wohnen, ach, in meine Brust,*" a quotation from *Faust* meaning "Two souls there are that live within my breast," adding that "the Compleat Housekeeper has had the upper hand for the last two weeks" (*EW* 111; Lewis points out that she misquoted Goethe slightly).

Wharton's profound craving for travel is suggested by her choice of the epigraph to *The CRUISE OF THE VANADIS*, the diary of her 1888 MEDITERRANEAN cruise, from Goethe's *Faust* (I, 1,122–25). Faust, who harbors the conflicting "souls" in his breast, repose and exertion, tells the pedantic, sedentary Wagner he wishes for a magic cloak so that he might soar into *fremde Länder* or foreign lands; he would not trade such a garment for a *Königsmantel,* or king's crown and robe. Faust appeals to the spirits of the air to enable him to escape a life of peace and quiet and convey him to a new many-hued existence in other realms. The *Vanadis* diary and its epigraph suggest that travel not only met a deeply-felt inner need on the part of Wharton, but also offered a means of escape from what had turned out to be a disappointing marriage.

The Whartons spent several months in ITALY each year after their marriage in 1885, continuing this practice until about 1904. Wharton had read Goethe's *Italienische Reise* (*Italian Journey*) and was familiar with the BRENTA RIVIERA, the canal/river between VENICE and Padua, where the aristocracy had villas and spent the *villeggiatura,* or vacation season (mid-June/July and October-mid-November). In 1786 Goethe had traveled along the Brenta on *Il Burchiello,* a canopied and inlaid passenger vessel that was modeled after the original gilded barges that once transported noble families along the Brenta. In his *Italian Journey* he records going down the Brenta in a "public boat and in well-behaved company"; he found the banks "studded with

gardens and summer houses." As the boat progresssed through the chain of locks, Goethe would step ashore and purchase fruit, then resume gliding "through a fresh and animated world." In her first novel, *The VALLEY OF DECISION* (1902), Wharton describes an imaginary villa on the Brenta with a ceiling by TIEPOLO depicting "Olympian revels" and as well as the COMMEDIA DELL'ARTE figures in some of the villa gardens.

In *A MOTOR-FLIGHT THROUGH FRANCE* (1908), Wharton recounted visiting George SAND's home at NOHANT. She was particularly fascinated by the small theater, which includes two stages, one with life-size scenery for actors and actresses, and the other a marionette theater recalling the COMMEDIA DELL'ARTE as it was incorporated by Goethe in his fiction: "just such a "*Puppen-theatre* as Wilhelm Meister described to Marianne."

Goethe was still in Wharton's thoughts two decades later. In her 1929 novel *HUDSON RIVER BRACKETED* Vance Weston reads Goethe's *Faust* and encounters the mysterious Mothers, the origins of creativity, the eternal and infinite resources available to all men. In *The GODS ARRIVE* (1932), the sequel, Vance again reflects on the Mothers, who dwell in the primal depths of the soul, the genesis of artistic inspiration, which comes only partly from perception of the exterior world.

Perhaps the most poignant reference to Goethe occurs in Wharton's 1915 travel book about WORLD WAR I, *FIGHTING FRANCE, FROM DUNKERQUE TO BELFORT*. In her final chapter, "The Tone of France," she notes, "Goethe was never wiser than when he wrote: "A god gave me the voice to speak my pain." It is ironic that the German poet for whose work she had a lifelong passion should provide the perfect, bitter epitaph for the destruction and desecration of the country she loved at least as much as that of her birth.

For further reading: Lawson, *Edith Wharton and German Literature*; Wagner, "A Note on Wharton's Use of Faust."

Goldoni, Carlo (1707–1793) Italian playwright, born in Venice, noted for his comedies. In the beginning of *ITALIAN BACKGROUNDS*, Wharton evokes an imaginary scene in the Splügen town square, just before the arrival of the diligence for Chiavenna, with generic village types such as the Innkeeper or the Postmistress enacting "some comedy of Goldoni's, perhaps" (*IB* 11). She describes, later in the book, the Lake of Iseo, imagining the villages on the shore as a backdrop for the performances of the COMMEDIA DELL'ARTE, a distinctive trope in much of Wharton's travel writing and her fiction. She visualizes actors speaking "in the Bergamasque dialect, with Harlequin in striped cloak, and Brighella in conical hat and wide green and white trousers strutting up and down before the shuttered house in which Dr. Graziano hides his pretty ward." She conceives of the lake as reflecting the "eighteenth century of Longhi, of Tiepolo and Goldoni . . . as in some magic crystal," to be discovered beneath the waves by "some later traveller. . . . if ever the boundaries between fact and fancy waver, it may well be under the spell of the Italian midsummer madness" (*IB* 35). Goldoni also figures in Wharton's first novel, *The VALLEY OF DECISION* (1902), set in 18th-century Italy.

It is possible that Wharton first became interested in Goldoni when she met the expatriate English writer Vernon LEE [Violet Paget], who lived in a villa, Il Palmerino, in Maiano, near Florence; Wharton met her in 1894. Lee wrote extensively about 18th-century Italy and the commedia dell'arte. Wharton was much influenced by Lee's *Studies of the Eighteenth Century in Italy*.

Gracy, Bill   *See SPARK, THE.*

Grant, Judge Robert (1852–1940)   Boston novelist, short story writer and jurist who was a close friend of Wharton. He had been a boyhood friend and college classmate of Teddy WHARTON and was a trustee of Harvard and a judge of the probate court in Boston (*EW* 148). Lewis believes that Wharton's novel *The CUSTOM OF THE COUNTRY* owed "more than a little" to his naturalistic novel *Unleavened Bread* (1900), which also anticipated the work of Theodore Dreiser and Sinclair Lewis. On publication, Wharton wrote Grant a letter stating that it seemed to her one of the best American novels she had read in years and praising him for his use of the "objective method" (*Letters* 41n). In 1907 he sent her a long critique of *The FRUIT OF THE TREE*; she agreed that some of her characters were "mere building blocks" (*Letters* 7).

He was sympathetic to Wharton about the necessity of her divorce from Teddy, and, in Boston, argued against the Wharton family's suggestions that he was a "suffering martyr" (*EW* 335). He contributed a poem to *The BOOK OF THE HOMELESS* when Wharton appealed to him. After Teddy's death, she wrote Grant that she was thankful he was at peace; he had been the "kindest of companions till that dreadful blighting illness came upon him" (*Letters* 515).

"Great American Novel, The"   Essay, first published in the *Yale Review* in July 1927, in which Edith Wharton complained that American life offered only "meagre" "material to the imagination." Nevius observes that her appreciation of American literature is limited at best; she classes Melville with Dumas and Stevenson as a writer of adventure stories and fails to appreciate Hawthorne or Twain.

Much of the essay deals with the work of Sinclair LEWIS, who had been a friend for several years. She terms his novel *Main Street* "epoch-making," but reminds her readers that Robert GRANT's *Unleavened Bread* (1900) was also situated in Main Street. She concludes that, although publication of the "great American novel" is announced each year, the country has produced only about 10 in that category. She discounts those of Melville and Hawthrone, but includes *McTeague* (by Frank Norris) and *Susan Lenox: Her Fall and Rise* (by David Graham Phillips). She believes no American novel ranks with those of Jane Austen and Honoré de Balzac, rooted deep in the soil of their respective countries.

"Great Blue Tent, The"   A poem written in the first year of WORLD WAR I, which Edith Wharton cabled to the *New York Times*; it was published August 25, 1915. The American flag conceives of itself as a peaceful "great blue tent," giving shelter and sustenance to all who enter but unstirred at the "wind of wars." Its self-satisfaction is suddenly challenged by the cries of the flags of freedom from Valley Forge, Lexington and Concord that bid it "come up to the stormy sky / Where our fierce folds rattle and hum." The Flag awakes, and pleads to be off on "the old fierce chase / Of the foe we have always fought." It proclaims that it is still "the shot-riddled rag, / That shrieks to be free, to be free," and begs that its "silken ties" be cut loose from the "roof of the palace of peace," its stars "given back to the skies," and its stripes "to the storm-striped sea." The final stanza, which echoes John McRae's "In Flanders Fields," has the ring of heraldry as well:

> Or else, if you bid me yield,
> Then down with my crimson bars,
> And o'er all my azure field
> Sow poppies instead of stars.

The third stanza of McRae's poem is:

> Take up our quarrel with the foe:
> To you from failing hands we throw
> The torch; be yours to hold it high.
> If ye break faith with us who die
> We shall not sleep, though poppies grow
>   In Flanders fields.

If America "breaks faith" with its heroic heritage, the flag may as well grow poppies (emblematic of the fallen victims of the war buried in Flanders fields) instead of the stars of freedom and opportunity. Wharton here assumes the stance of a patriot that counters the image of her depicted by some critics. An editorial ran the day after the poem was published, praising Edith Wharton's stance and opposing it to a speech by Mrs. P. V. Pennypacker, who, speaking for the Federation of Women's Clubs of America, had argued that the "United States had no reason or excuse to enter the present conflict." The editor asserted that nine out of ten of its women correspondents (many of whom had also sent poems) are "about as far as possible from being for peace at any price and consider war, dreadful as it is, preferable to peace at the cost of the national honor and dignity" (*New York Times* August 26, 1915).

Greater Inclination, The   First volume of short stories published by Scribner's (1899). In *A BACKWARD GLANCE* Edith Wharton writes that after it was published, she "felt like some homeless waif who, after trying for years to take out naturalization papers, and being rejected by every country, has finally acquired a nationality. The Land of Letters was henceforth to be my country, and I gloried in my new citizenship" (*BG* 119). The reception was highly favorable. The *Book Buyer* called this a "remarkable first book," and the English *Athenaeum* found it equally remarkable as the first book of an American: "Miss Wharton has the further merit that, though presumably an American herself and writing of American men and women, she yet has a command of good English, and her nationality merely serves to add an alertness to her style which is usually lacking in this particular form of literature." Several reviewers, including John D. Barry of *Literary World*, compared Wharton with Henry JAMES, but Harry Thurston Peck, writing in *The Bookman*, declared that James had nothing to teach her: "There is a finish, an assurance, and a tenacity of grasp about her work that show her to be already an accomplished literary artist" (*CR* 13–25).

The volume contained "The MUSE'S TRAGEDY," "A JOURNEY," "The PELICAN," "SOULS BELATED," "A COWARD," "The TWILIGHT OF THE GOD," "A CUP OF COLD WATER," and "The PORTRAIT."

The volume was one of the two sent by her sister-in-law, Minnie (Mary Cadwalader) JONES, to Henry James.

Gross, Catharine   Edith Wharton's longtime Alsatian housekeeper. She began working for the Jones family as Edith's attendant in 1884, the year before Edith married Teddy WHARTON. At the time, according to Lewis, she was still in her early thirties. Her husband had apparently deserted her, and she had a teenage son who lived in Europe (*EW* 54).

After the Whartons' marriage, she traveled with them abroad for several months each year. After they built The MOUNT, she and Alfred WHITE, the Whartons' butler, headed the corps of domestic servants, which also included Edith's personal maid, housemaids, footmen, a cook, several gardeners, kitchen boys and Charles COOK, their chauffeur.

In 1907, when the Whartons leased the George Vanderbilt apartment at 58, rue de Varenne in PARIS, Catharine Gross came along and lived in the flat. In the apartment the Whartons leased beginning in 1910, at 53, rue de Varenne, she and Edith's personal maid shared a sitting room.

After WORLD WAR I, when Edith Wharton purchased the PAVILLON COLOMBE outside Paris and the STE.-CLAIRE CHÂTEAU in HYÈRES, on the French RIVIERA, Gross moved between them seasonally with the other members of the household; they spent summer at the former and winter at Ste.-Claire. Gross died in October 1933 at the age of 80, after two years of failing health. She had been attended by local nuns at the Ste.-Claire Château, but was suddenly, one afternoon, seized by "senile dementia and suicidal mania." She could not be handled at home and was sent to the convent. She was buried in Hyères beside Elise DUVLENCK, who had served Edith Wharton as personal maid for many years.

Gryce, Percy   *See HOUSE OF MIRTH, THE.*

Hale, Andrew   See *ETHAN FROME*.

Hale, Ned   See *ETHAN FROME*.

Hale, Ruth Varnum   See *ETHAN FROME*.

Hardy, Thomas (1840–1928) English novelist and poet, a native of Dorsetshire. Originally an architect, he wrote poetry for a number of years, but failed to find a publisher. His career as a novelist began in 1873 with *A Pair of Blue Eyes,* which was followed by 10 other novels over the succeeding 24 years. His work is marked by a tragic intensity, his characters defeated by their own flaws and inability to counteract the strictures of society. Among his best-known novels are *Return of the Native* (1878), *Tess of the d'Urbervilles* (1891) and *Jude the Obscure* (1896; serialized under a different title in 1895).

Soon after her first volume of short stories (*The GREATER INCLINATION*) was published in 1899, Edith Wharton and her husband met the popular London hostess Lady St. Helier. They became friends, and she invited the Whartons several times to dinner parties at which Hardy was present. Wharton recalls in *A BACKWARD GLANCE* that he was "as remote and uncommunicative as our most unsocial American men of letters" (*BG* 215–16), but attributed this attitude to his inborn shyness. In 1902 *Tess of the d'Urbervilles* was dramatized by Lorimer Stoddard and she reviewed the performance of Mrs. [Minnie Maddern] Fiske (*see TESS OF THE D'URBERVILLES* (A PLAY). During WORLD WAR I Hardy contributed a poem, "Cry of the Homeless," to *The BOOK OF THE HOMELESS.* In the chapter on telling a short story in *The WRITING OF FICTION* (1925), Wharton singles out Hardy for praise, along with Henry JAMES and Joseph CONRAD.

harems   See *IN MOROCCO*.

Harney, Lucius   See *SUMMER*.

Harper's Magazine   Literary magazine begun in 1850, primarily as an "eclectic" publication. From 1869 to 1919, Henry Mills Alden was editor. Beginning in 1886, William Dean HOWELLS held an editorial post with the magazine, taking charge of the influential "Editor's Easy Chair" department. Later, he began writing the "Easy Chair" columns.

In 1889 Wharton sent a poem to *Harper's Magazine,* accompanied by her visiting card, at the same time that she submitted poems to SCRIBNER'S MAGAZINE and *The CENTURY.* All three were accepted; of these, "The LAST GIUSTINIANI," which appeared in *Scribner's Magazine,* was the most significant (*EW* 6). In 1901 Wharton published a poem about St. Margaret of Cortona in *Harper's Magazine.* She also published another poem, "The Bread of Angels," in the magazine in 1902. Seven of her short stories appeared in *Harper's Magazine:* "The MOVING FINGER" and "The RECOVERY" (1901), "The MISSION OF JANE," "The RECKONING" and "The QUICKSAND" (1902), "The DILETTANTE" (1903) and "The LETTER" (1904). In 1938, the magazine published, posthumously, an autobiographical article, "A Little Girl's New York."

Hatchard, Miss   See *SUMMER*.

Hazeldean, Charles   See *NEW YEAR'S DAY*.

Hazeldean, Lizzie   See *NEW YEAR'S DAY*.

Hearst, William Randolph (1863–1951) American newspaper and magazine publisher who acquired a vast empire after beginning his career on the San Francisco *Daily Examiner* in 1887. He is regarded as the father of sensational "yellow journalism" aimed at selling copies with little regard for accuracy, style or substance and with a cavalier disregard for facts. Edith Wharton detested the mass-market magazines owned by Hearst, but in her eagerness to maximize the income from her novels and nonfiction works, she occasionally permitted her work to appear in his publications. Several of her early stories were published in *Hearst's International-Cosmopolitan,* including "The REMBRANDT" (1900) and "EXPIATION" (1903).

In 1916, Wharton solicited the help of Morton FULLERTON and Walter BERRY in attempting to stop negotiations with *Cosmopolitan* for the serialization of *SUMMER,* hoping it would be published by *McClure's,* as it was. She wrote Fullerton, "I don't care a fig if people know that the Cosmopolitan belongs to Hearst—& I agree with you that few *do.* What I hate is taking money from such a hound, & helping 'boom' his magazine— as I suppose my novel would; or else, why give me such a price? . . . The only thing I want to know—if this change of magazine can be managed—is whether McClure is solvent—at least presumably. I want the money! I am sorry to have given you so much trouble" (unpublished correspondence, BEINECKE LIBRARY, YALE UNIVERSITY).

It is unlikely that Wharton would have termed Hearst a "hound" or expressed her interest in making money so candidly to anyone but a close friend. Nevertheless, such an admission of her financial goals is indicative of the erosion WORLD WAR I had made in her literary income. During the war, most of her energies were devoted to her war relief efforts rather than to her writing, though she continued to produce some fiction.

In 1933 Rutger B. Jewett, of Appleton's, sold Wharton's story "BREAD UPON THE WATERS" to *Hearst's International-Cosmopolitan* for $5,000 (it was later reprinted as "CHARM INCORPORATED" in *The WORLD OVER*). When she began her final novel, *The BUCCANEERS*, which she had thought would be serialized for $50,000 in the *PICTORIAL REVIEW* until the editor left, Jewett approached *Cosmopolitan*. The editor asked for an outline and offered a $1,000 option on the novel. Edith Wharton was indignant and wrote Jewett, "I have never before been treated like a beginner, and do not like it . . . I have never before been treated so casually" (*EW* 507–08). The magazine was still a lucrative market for short stories, however. In 1933 the magazine published "The LOOKING GLASS" and in 1936 "CONFESSION."

Heeny, Mrs.   *See CUSTOM OF THE COUNTRY, THE.*

"Henry James in His Letters"   Essay published in the *Quarterly Review* in July 1920 after publication of Percy LUBBOCK's two-volume edition of *The Letters of Henry James*. In a rather Jamesian phrase, Wharton states that it "is a matter of rejoicing to the friends of Henry James that his letters should so largely show the least familiar side of his manifold nature." In his correspondence JAMES was able to put himself in the presence of the recipient by using vivid allusions or by referring to recent meetings. His letters, nevertheless, fail to match his actual conversation, which Wharton describes as being marked by "images so vivid and appreciations so penetrating, the whole so sunned over by irony, sympathy, and wide-flashing fun" that it could be said of James, as he had said of Paul BOURGET, "he was the first, easily, of all the talkers I ever encountered."

She includes anecdotes from her journeys with James in England, America and France and points out that even in his later years, when his writing was more formalized and disciplined, his greatest interest was in the work of contemporaries, such as H. G. Wells and the French novelist Pierre Loti. Even if all James's books perished, she concludes, he would survive in the hearts of the friends who had known him (*UCW* 137–49).

"Her Son"   Short story, of novella length, published in HUMAN NATURE (D. Appleton, 1933). The theme is one of flawed parent/child relationships. An elderly widowed gentlewoman, Mrs. Catherine Glenn, has lost her son Philip in World War I and now searches Europe for Stephen, the son she and her husband had before their marriage and gave up to foster parents to avoid scandal. She has not seen him since infancy; he would now be approximately 27. She is naive and taken in by an unscrupulous expatriate couple she meets by accident in a hotel lounge, a Mr. and Mrs. Boydon Brown, who pretend they are the foster parents and can't give up Stephen. "Stephen," an artist, is produced and introduced to his new "mother." She settles an allowance on the three and supports them in their European travels. Catherine Glenn has been so willing to believe that she would find her son that she asks little in the way of proof.

"Stephen" dies of tuberculosis, having confessed to Mr. Norcutt, the narrator, an old family friend of Mrs. Glenn, that he is not her son. Mr. and Mrs. Brown continue mourning for "Stephen" and preying on Mrs. Glenn until the final scene, when Mr. Norcutt arrives just in time to prevent her from signing over all her assets to Mrs. Brown, who turns out to have been "Stephen's" lover. She had invented the story in order to get treatment for "Stephen," who was already ill. Mrs. Brown tells the truth to Catherine Glenn, who responds, "My dear—your hat's crooked," a final "shaft" launched at her enemy. Mrs. Glenn fades into confusion, her mind mercifully clouded "at the exact moment when to see clearly would have been the final anguish."

The story was criticized for its lack of suspense by one critic, but praised in the *New York Times Book Review* as an "ameliorating and comforting document" (*CR* 503–07).

Here and Beyond   Short story collection published by D. Appleton in 1926. It contains the stories "BEWITCHED," "MISS MARY PASK," "The YOUNG GENTLEMEN," "The SEED OF THE FAITH, "The TEMPERATE ZONE," and "VELVET EAR PADS." The settings are varied, including Brittany, NEW ENGLAND and MOROCCO. The collection was criticized by John T. Rodgers in the *North American Review* as not up to Wharton's earlier standard and containing too much "padding" of "gay repartee." Although Rodgers praised her gift for "character-sketching," he recommended that she reread the stories of O. Henry before writing more short stories. L. P. Hartley, writing for the British *Saturday Review*, said the volume had an architectural quality; the stories "do not come up as flowers but as buildings." Louise Maunsell Field praised it in the *Literary Digest* as thoroughly worth while, showing her "artistry at its best," and Frances Newman of the *New York Evening Post Literary*

Review suggested that she ought to win the PULITZER PRIZE every year (*CR* 415–25). Lewis argues that it is the only one of Wharton's short story collections with little to commend it (*EW* 522).

Hermit and the Wild Woman and Other Stories, The Short story collection published by Scribner's in 1908. It includes "The HERMIT AND THE WILD WOMAN," "The LAST ASSET," "IN TRUST," "The PRETEXT," "The VERDICT," "The POTBOILER" and "The BEST MAN." The critic for the British *Spectator* believed the first story, which gives its title to the volume and takes the form of a medieval Italian legend (echoing "DIEU D'AMOUR," based on a medieval French fable), was out of place among the other "ultra-modern" ones and that there was an insufficient element of surprise. The reviewer for the British *Athenæum,* however, thought Wharton had reached her highest level in the title story. The critic for the *New York Times Saturday Review* praised Wharton's ability to rise to the level of her subject and to find suitable situations involving "extreme moral delicacy and a controlling emotion" (*CR* 157–60). Several stories, including "The Pretext," "The Last Asset" and "In Trust," share a theme of male dominance, female social climbing and manipulation, and estrangement within marriage.

"Hermit and the Wild Woman, The" Short story published in *Scribner's Magazine,* 1906, and collected in *The HERMIT AND THE WILD WOMAN AND OTHER STORIES* (Scribner's, 1908). It takes the form of a medieval allegory set in Italy, incorporating much of the Italian history, literature, art and faith Wharton had discussed in *ITALIAN BACKGROUNDS*. The critic for *The Nation* seemed to expect, based on Edith Wharton's previous urbane fiction, that the "hermit" might be living in a Washington Square studio, tempted by a "wild woman," and seemed surprised to find that the central figure was actually a hermit living in a wilderness. Had the reviewer read *The VALLEY OF DECISION* or the essays making up *Italian Backgrounds,* however, the subject would not have seemed out of the ordinary.

The central figure is a quiet, scholarly knight's son who has reveled in the frescoes of angels done by a visiting painter in his family's chapel. His parents and sister are murdered by a marauding band, after which he flees to a cave on a hillside, takes solace in Christianity and lives a godly life. He composes lauds in honor of Christ, sometimes written down by a priest from the town, who pays occasional visits. He sets out to visit a solitary called "The Saint of the Rock" on the other side of the mountains. The solitary receives him angrily, since he has violated his sanctuary and privacy, so the hermit returns home.

He finds that his gardens have not perished but grown green and tall. A young woman with amulets about her neck is sleeping nearby. The hermit fears she is the devil, come in a tempting guise, but she insists she is also a refugee from armed companies and marauding bands. She is also of noble birth and has escaped during a Saracen attack from a filthy, harsh convent, where she was forbidden to bathe or look outside on green hills. She has also been disillusioned by bands of wandering, idle monks. She heals a goatherd who has suffered a seizure and fallen, and prepares to depart, so that the village folk, who will hear about her good deed, will not discover the hermit and ruin his life, or drag her back to the cloister.

He persuades her not to leave and they live a pious life for two years, dwelling apart in separate caves but praying together. Her reputation for healing grows; she cures plague victims but grows weak. Just as the villagers and church dignitaries come to praise the pair, she takes off her gown and sandals and slips into a pool of water. Although the hermit curses her for immodesty, the villagers perceive her as a dying saint and revile him for his misjudgment. Anguished, he proclaims his sins and prepares to die; he is granted absolution. As he dies, he hears his lauds chanted by the throng and by a peal of voices seeming to come from the heavens.

Hewlett, Maurice (1861–1923) Author of erudite historical romances, including *Richard Yea-and-Nay* (1900), *The Queen's Quair* (1904) and *The FOOL ERRANT* (1905). He was praised for his fictional portraits of Richard Coeur de Lion and Mary Queen of Scots. Wharton reviewed *The Fool Errant* for the *Bookman* in 1905.

Wharton was sometimes linked by critics with Hewlett because of her historical novel *The VALLEY OF DECISION* and the essays making up *ITALIAN BACKGROUNDS*. One reviewer of the latter volume criticized her for attempting, as an amateur, to "till" the soil of Italy in an academic way, and remarked that she belonged to the "cult of Symons, Hewlett & Co. [Arthur Symons, Maurice Hewlett, and Edward Hutton]."

See SYMONS, ARTHUR.

"His Father's Son" Short story published in *SCRIBNER'S MAGAZINE* in 1909 and later reprinted in *TALES OF MEN AND GHOSTS* (Scribner's, 1910). Like "Her Son," this story focuses on a gentle, self-effacing parent who makes sacrifices for a thoughtless child. Ronald Grew, the son of Mason Grew, a businessman in Brooklyn and a widower. Mr. Grew goes into the city "to feel under his feet the same pavement that Ronald trod," but is obsessed with not being a burden. His principal aim in life is to work hard and provide well for Ronald.

Ronald suddenly becomes engaged to a society girl, Daisy Bankshire, who, Mr. Grew believes, must have all the charm and beauty his wife, the former Addy Wicks, had lacked. His economies have enabled him to offer Ronald a good annual income, but Ronald insists he can't take it, since he is the child of the famed European pianist Fortuné Dolbrowski. He has come to this conclusion after reading the fond letters his mother received from Dolbrowski. He assumes his love of music and art must have derived from this romantic and accomplished father.

Mason Grew assures him he is wrong—"you're your father's son, every inch of you!" He explains that he was, as a gawky youth, an outsider, the one "that had to eat the drumsticks and dance with the leftovers," but he was starved for the arts. He confesses that, after he and Addy once attended a concert given by Dolbrowski, he wrote him, on Addy's behalf, a flattering letter, which she copied. When the musician answered, Mr. Grew kept inventing letters for the inarticulate Addy to copy and send. Addy never heard him play again, although Mr. Grew attended several of his concerts without introducing himself. After a few months the correspondence ceased. It had, however, fed Mr. Grew's appetite for music, ideas and good talk, whereas Ronald has only had to "put out his hand" and grasp such things. Ronald is deflated, but his father understands that, too, and assures Ronald he had felt the same kind of "fool nonsense" at his age, thus proving his paternity.

Edith Wharton addressed the theme of illegitimacy in several other stories, possibly stemming in part from the rumors of her own extra-marital paternity, of which she was well aware (*see* GENEALOGY, OF EDITH WHARTON).

Homer   Edith Wharton read the works of Homer when she was quite young, and developed a lifelong admiration and affection for the poet. She first encountered the *Iliad* and the *Odyssey* in her father's library and, in her memoir, recalled reading Schliemann's "Ilias" and "Troja" (*BG* 67). The Butcher and Lang translation of the *Odyssey* was aboard the steam yacht VANADIS for the Whartons' 1888 cruise. Wharton wrote Sally NORTON that it was their "constant companion" in their "wanderings through the Aegean" (*Letters* 100). At their ports of call, she eagerly visited every accessible Greek archaeological site.

In 1902 Wharton reviewed ULYSSES: A DRAMA, by the English poet and playwright Stephen Phillips, for the *Bookman.*

In 1905, when she and Teddy were at Biltmore House in Asheville, home of George VANDERBILT and his wife, she was delighted when Sally sent her *Some Aspects of Greek Genius,* by Butcher. She wrote that she was in the "mood for the Hellenic," as she had just been reading *Plato and Platonism,* a volume of Walter PATER'S lectures.

In 1926, the *Odyssey* was in the ship's library of the OSPREY. She wrote Gaillard LAPSLEY that in the evening they either read from it or from Anita Loos's "Gentlemen Prefer Blondes," which she considered quite a good novel (*Letters* 491).

See ULYSSES: A DRAMA.

"House of the Dead Hand"   Short story written in 1898 and published in the ATLANTIC MONTHLY in 1904 but not collected. It is the story of a connoisseur, Wyant, who is carrying out some historical research in Siena. He is asked by an English art collector to look up old Dr. Lombardi, an English dilettante reputed to have a famous Leonardo. He calls on the eccentric doctor at his house, which takes its name from the antique marble hand above the doorway. He meets his pale, resigned wife, who still resides mentally in England, perhaps as a form of escape from his sarcasm, and his slim, apathetic daughter, Sybilla.

Accompanied by Sybilla, Dr. Lombardi displays the remarkable painting, filled with symbolism and juxtaposed figures and landscapes, but forbids Wyant to photograph or sketch it. Sybilla, he learns, is the actual owner; she purchased it with her grandmother's legacy. Wyant has asked directions to the house from a young man who turns out to be a count in love with Sybilla. The couple cannot marry until she has a proper dowry. To raise the money for one, she must sell the painting. She proposes a way Wyant can help her slip away, but he refuses to assist her. Eventually Dr. Lombardi dies, but Sybilla still fails to sell the painting because of Lombardi's fierce intimidation—he is almost Dickensian in his malicious treatment of his wife and daughter. White calls this a melodrama with "Gothic trappings" (39); Lewis labels it "inept" (*EW* 81). As a first ghost story, and as evidence of Edith Wharton's developing connoisseurship, however, the story has merit.

For further reading: Carpenter, "Deadly Letters, Sexual Politics, and the Dilemma of the Woman Writer: Edith Wharton's 'The House of the Dead Hand.'"

House of Mirth, The   Edith Wharton's first best-selling novel (serialized in *Scribner's Magazine* January–November, 1905, and published in 1905 by Scribner's). Sales far surpassed those of any other works of Wharton's and those of other best-sellers at the time. It came at a time when the role of women in marriage was being examined by other writers, such as Tolstoy in *Anna Karenina,* George ELIOT in *Middlemarch,* Gustave Flaubert in *Madame Bovary* and Thomas HARDY in TESS OF THE D'URBERVILLES.

In this novel Wharton established herself as a unparalleled social satirist, exposing the weaknesses of NEW YORK society and denouncing the power of wealth to distort character. She saw the society she depicted as basically immoral, organized as a quest for pleasure and "mirth." The title is from Ecclesiastes 7:4: "The heart of the wise is in the house of mourning; but the heart of fools is in the house of mirth." At the time of the novel, the 1890s, Old New York was being confronted by nouveaux riches "invaders," resulting in a society in which the wealthy man must have the ideal wife to get ahead; she was not a luxury but a necessity. The patriarchal control of all wealth by men was a given in marriage, but it was balanced to some degree by the power of the proper wife to advance her husband socially. This motif is evident in many of Wharton's works, including *The CUSTOM OF THE COUNTRY* and her final unfinished novel, *The BUCCANEERS.* At the beginning of the latter, it is clear that the parvenu millionaire Colonel St George can only negotiate with the even wealthier financier Closson if Mrs. Elmsworth welcomes his "women-folk" as social equals (he secures her cooperation with an expensive brooch).

The House of Mirth concerns the fate of Lily Bart, an orphan dependent on the charity of her austere Aunt Peniston. Lily has beauty and charm and is well-connected, but, at 29, is still unmarried. Ambitious for wealth and position, she tries to secure a prosperous husband. She rejects Lawrence Selden, whom she loves, since he has no fortune. She dreads the prospect of living like his self-sufficient cousin Gerty Farish in a "horrid little place" with "no maid, and such queer things to eat." It is Gerty, however, who later takes her in and comforts her. Lily is still decorative and desirable, however, and receives many invitations to country house parties. Increasingly they are given by newly rich women rather than members of old society, and she is often able to repay their hospitality by doing small favors for her hostess and assisting with social lists and correspondence.

Lily is cosmopolitan and perceptive. When she does not have complete knowledge of a field, she has the ability to simulate it, as in her partial apprehension of early Americana in order to interest the wealthy Percy Gryce, a fellow guest at a weekend party early in the novel. Lily's discrimination and ability to imitate the role of the connoisseur are prized by hostesses and have value for certain men. Through a curious inertia, however, she misses a chance to marry Percy and he becomes engaged to Evelyn Van Osburgh, daughter of another old New York family.

Lily's social stock steadily declines throughout the novel; she begins as a decorative and highly "collectible" artifact, but misses one chance after another. She attracts a wealthy financier, Simon Rosedale, but first rejects him as a suitor; when she later tries to change her mind, his pride is hurt and he refuses. She allows a friend's husband, Gus Trenor, to parlay her small assets into what she believes is a legitimate investment that will enhance her fortunes; actually the "profits" he delivers to her are from his own funds. He then demands that she repay him by satisfying his passion. Lily purchases incriminating letters from Bertha Dorset, an aspiring and wealthy social climber, to Lawrence Selden from a needy and unscrupulous cleaning woman in order to protect him; the letters were found by the charwoman in Selden's apartment, which is in a building owned by Rosedale, who knew about them. Colquitt observes that the letters "function symbolically on an economic and metaphorical level: the letters not only signify the means by which Lily can achieve her material and social redemption. . . . they also represent an individually crafted emotional value, the 'secret' of which the 'negative' heroine longs to know" ("Succumbing to the 'Literary Style': Arrested Desire in *The House of Mirth*," 159–60). She never discovers how to use the letters to reenter society, and finally burns them in Selden's apartment, a gesture he scarcely notices. Lily is largely disinherited by Mrs. Peniston in favor of her cousin, Grace Stepney.

Lily flees from her worsening plight and is taken on a Mediterranean cruise as a social mentor to the Dorsets, becoming a pawn to Bertha. Having failed to capture Selden, Bertha uses Lily to conceal her affair with Ned Silverton and then charges her with having designs on her husband. Dismissed from their yacht, she is taken on by Wellington and Louisa Bry, and later, sinking lower, by Sam and Mattie Gormer, who live in a "social out-skirt." Ultimately she fails as an "ornament of the privileged class," as Maureen Howard observes (1).

The set within which Lily moves is continually fluctuating; people whose social currency declines in value give way to others on the way up. The self-made man may grumble about costs, but leaves the acquisition of subtle nuances to his wife. To gain power, she must learn how to develop her own style and assert her taste. For example, Wharton sets several scenes at Monte Carlo, on the French RIVIERA, where groups of guests from the Dorsets' yacht mingle with titled British aristocrats. Lily realizes, for example, as Bertha and Louisa do not, that the truly cosmopolitan woman must not only know the "best" restaurants but must then have the confidence to reject them on virtually any pretext. Lily is well able to tutor the Dorsets, Brys and Gormers but is defeated by her own ambivalence about the compromises she must make. Carry Fisher characterizes her as an uncontrolled and erratic gardener: "she works like a slave preparing the ground and sowing her seed; but the day she ought to be reaping the harvest she over-sleeps herself or goes off on a picnic." She pinpoints, astutely, the real reason for Lily's failure: "Sometimes . . . I think it's just flightiness—and sometimes I think it's because, at heart, she despises the things she's trying for."

As Lily sinks on the social scale and is finally cast out, she attempts to become a milliner, but lacks skill. She eventually dies of an overdose of sleeping medicine just before Selden is seemingly poised to ask her to marry him. Before her suicide, Lily puts aside her Aunt Peniston's entire bequest to repay Gus Trenor for his loan.

Few of Wharton's works have received more critical attention than *The House of Mirth*. In *A BACKWARD GLANCE* Edith Wharton asserted that the "frivolous society" depicted in *The House of Mirth* acquired dramatic significance only in its "power of debasing people and ideals" (*BG* 207). In a Marxist reading of the novel, "Debasing Exchange: Edith Wharton's *The House of Mirth*," Wai-chee Dimock emphasizes the importance of the marketplace: "the realm of human relations is fully contained within an all-encompassing business ethic" (783). Money is only one form of currency; social gestures are another. Prices, she observes, "will remain arbitrary as long as the exchange rests on a negotiated parity between the exchange items" (784). Lily has been "purchased" for the Dorsets' Mediterranean cruise in order to deflect George Dorset's attention from his wife's dalliance.

Judith Fryer suggests that the narrative follows "the downward path of the protagonist through a series of actual houses," but that it is also about "symbolic houses." She identifies Lily Bart with the decorative motif of the Art Nouveau movement, which reached its pinnacle in the Paris Exposition of 1900 and was symbolized by Loïe Fuller. That exposition was attended by Henry ADAMS, who first sensed the power of the 20th-century dynamo in the Gallery of Machines. Adams believed that, before 1900, there was no distinction between "force and taste, between physical and spiritual power"; a chasm, however, developed during the period of the American Renaissance that saw the building of gilded mansions for newly made millionaires. The central conflict, Fryer argues, is between "classical purity" and "sensuous decadence," or the displacement of Adams's Virgin from her powerful axis. This deviation is indicated, in the novel, by a series of "illuminating moments," including the TABLEAU VIVANT. Lily Bart, she states, is an "argument from design," a "devotee of taste rather than a source of power" [as the medieval Virgin would have been]. She is reflected in the tableau (as Joshua Reynolds's *Mrs. Lloyd*) and in the minds of the other characters (*Felicitous Space: The Imaginative Structures of Edith Wharton and Willa Cather*, 75–77).

Diana Trilling pronounces *The House of Mirth* "one of the most telling indictments of the whole of American society, of a whole social system based on the chance distribution of wealth, that has ever been put to paper" ("*The House of Mirth* Revisited," 127). Julie Olin-Ammentorp, Annette Benert and Frances Restuccia have examined feminist implications of the novel, while Susan Koprince has discussed the symbolism of physical sites in the novel. Irene Goldman, Hildegard Hoeller and Christian Riegel have analyzed Simon Rosedale in the light of Wharton's ANTI-SEMITISM.

Linda Wagner-Martin has pointed out that Lily's death raises as many questions as it answers; the reader seeks "vindication" for her death, yet Wharton leaves it open as to whether society ever pays for its "brutal and meaningless vengeance" on Lily. In its failure to provide a pat answer or interpretation of the problem, *The House of Mirth* is in the modernist tradition. Wagner-Martin believes she influenced later writers in this tradition, such as F. Scott Fitzgerald (*The House of Mirth: A Novel of Admonition*, 5–7).

In 1936, *The House of Mirth* was republished by the Oxford University Press in its World's Classics series. Wharton contributed an introduction in which she reflected on her astonishment when the novel, which she had conceived as a "simple and fairly moving domestic tragedy," was criticized by those who made up the society of the time. She recalled that "this supposed picture of their little circle, secure behind its high stockade of convention, alarmed and disturbed the rules of Old New York." Lily had gambled, smoked, had tea in a bachelor's flat and run up debts. Wharton observed that if the novel had been presented 20 years later, i.e., during the early 1930s, to the same audience, "they would have smiled instead of shuddering, and have wondered why I had chosen the tame and blameless Lily Bart as a victim of avenging moral forces." She wondered if contemporary novelists might not envy her, however, when she could evoke far-reaching scandal "from the mere appearance of lapsing from conventional rules of conduct." Present-day writers were forced to find "new horrors in the domestic circle" and new forms of perversity in medical encyclopedias and theological manuals (*UCW* 267–69).

For further reading: Benert, "The Geography of Gender in *The House of Mirth*"; Cain, "Wharton's Art of Presence: The Case of Gerty Farish in *The House of Mirth*"; Colquitt, "Succumbing to the 'Literary Style': Arrested Desire in *The House of Mirth*"; Dimock, "Debasing Exchange: Edith Wharton's *The House of Mirth*"; Dixon, Roslyn, "Reflecting Vision in *The House of Mirth*"; Goldman, "The Perfect Jew and *The House of Mirth*: A Study in Point of View"; Hoeller, " 'The Impossible Rosedale': 'Race' and the Reading of Edith Wharton's *The House of Mirth*"; Howard, "On *The House of Mirth*"; Koprince, "The Meaning of Bellomont in *The House of Mirth*"; Miller, " 'Natural Magic': Irony as Unifying Strategy in *The House of Mirth*"; Olin-Ammentorp, "Edith Wharton's Challenge to Feminist Criticism"; Quoyeser, "The Antimodernist Unconscious: Genre and Ideology in *The House of Mirth*"; Restuccia, "The Name of the Lily: Edith Wharton's Feminism(s)"; Riegel, "Rosedale and Anti-Semitism in *The House of Mirth*"; Showalter, "The Death of the Lady (Novelist): Wharton's *House of Mirth*"; Shulman, "Divided Selves and the Market Society: Politics and Psychology in *The House of Mirth*"; Trilling, "*The House of Mirth* Revisited"; Wagner-Martin, The House of Mirth: *A Novel of Admonition;* Wershoven, "The Awakening and *The House of Mirth*: Studies of Arrested Development."

House of Mirth, The (play, 1906)   *See* Appendix II.

House of Mirth, The (film, 1918)   *See* Appendix II.

House of Mirth, The (play, 1977)   *See* Appendix II.

House of Mirth, The (teleplay, 1981)   *See* Appendix II.

Howells, William Dean (1837–1920)   American novelist, editor, critic and poet. He became editor of the ATLANTIC MONTHLY in 1871, a post he retained until 1881. In 1885, after various freelance endeavors, he assumed an editorial position with HARPER'S MAGAZINE. Henry Mills Alden had become editor in chief in 1869, a post he retained until 1919. Howells took charge of the "Editor's Study" department, writing a monthly essay from January 1886 to March 1892. In 1900 he began writing the "Editor's Easy Chair" columns.

He was also a prolific writer of fiction; *Their Wedding Journey, A Modern Instance* and *The Rise of Silas Lapham* were among his best-known novels. Before his death, he was considered the dean of American letters; he was president of the American Academy of Arts and Letters, and had substantial influence on the course of American literature during the GILDED AGE. He was a close friend of Mark Twain.

In 1880, Howells published five of Edith Wharton's poems anonymously in the *Atlantic Monthly*. They had been sent to him by Henry Wadsworth Longfellow, to whom they had been recommended by Allen Thorndike Rice (later owner and editor of the *North American Review*) (*NGC* 38). In 1902 Wharton wrote him at *Harper's Magazine* proposing an article on the "three Francescas now before the public" (three plays based on the legend of Paolo and Francesca). "*The THREE FRANCESCAS*" was not accepted by Howells, but was published in the *North American Review* (*EW* 61–62).

Howells admired Wharton's work very much. In 1900, he wrote her that more than once since she had begun to do the "fine things" in prose (she had, he asserted, done the "fine things in poetry long ago!"), he had wanted to write of the pleasure he had taken in them, but, ". . . with years come misgivings; we are not sure that our praise is wanted; in your case I knew that mine was not needed; and I should not now perhaps be offering your charming talent my recognition if I had not Business to back me and support me with a practical motive."

He went on to state that he had a formed a "close literary relation" with the firm of Harper & Brothers and wanted to appeal to her for a book of some sort, particularly a "story of contemporary American life, with no hint of history in it" (unpublished letter, the BEINECKE LIBRARY, YALE UNIVERSITY). She seems to have felt obligated to SCRIBNER'S, and apparently did not

submit such a book to Howells. She did publish a poem about St. Margaret of Cortona in *Harper's Magazine* as well as a number of short stories.

There was a considerable difference in age between Edith Wharton and Howells, but she states that she "was in a way accredited to him" by her friendships with Charles Eliot NORTON and Henry JAMES. As a favor Howells accompanied the Whartons to the New York opening of the dramatization of *The HOUSE OF MIRTH* by Clyde Fitch, starring Fay Davis, at the Savoy Theater in October 1906 (*see* Appendix II). Although it had succeeded in Detroit, she sensed that it was doomed to failure because she refused to let Lily Bart survive; it was, in fact, panned by critics. As they left the theater Howells summed up the reason for the play's failure in a "lapidary phrase" she recorded in her autobiography: " 'Yes—what the American public always wants is a tragedy with a happy ending' " (*BG* 146–47).

Both Howells and Edith Wharton wrote books of travel about ITALY and, for this reason, have often been linked critically. Howells was consul in VENICE from 1860 to 1865; his *Venetian Life* (1866) and *Italian Journeys* (1887) were widely read. Edith Wharton's invitation from *The CENTURY* in 1902 to write the text accompanying Maxfield PARRISH's illustrations of Italian villas is reminiscent of the invitation Howells himself received from the same periodical in the 1880s to write a series of articles on Tuscan cities. A comparison of their work reveals major dissimilarities in their style, sensibility and interests. In writing of travel, Howells is closer to James, in taking notice of people. For example, his accounts of Venice are crowded with the people he has known there—the housekeeper, the gondolier, etc. He is not averse to cataloging the discomforts of travel. Unlike Wharton, he seldom describes a work of art in detail and discounts the usefulness of prolonged contemplation of sites. Wharton, on the other hand, describes works of art at length but seldom mentions hotels, meals or the minutiae of travel.

In March 1913 Howells and Wharton cosigned an ill-through-out appeal to raise $5,000 for Henry James's 70th birthday that was sent to 40 people (James learned of the project and became exceedingly angry; Wharton was mortified at her part in the affair).

In 1915, when Wharton was compiling *The BOOK OF THE HOMELESS* (published in early 1916), Howells contributed a poem, "The Little Children." The illustrated book was sold to aid the relief efforts during WORLD WAR I.

Wharton states in her autobiography that she admired Howells's novels *A Modern Instance* and *The Rise of Silas Lapham* and would have liked to talk with him about "the art in which he stood so nearly among the first," but believed her "timidity" and his "aloofness" kept them apart. They seldom met; she regretted that he eventually became an "irreducible recluse" because of his wife's illness.

Hudson River Bracketed   Novel published by D. Appleton in 1929. In this work Edith Wharton explores the development of the artistic consciousness in an individual. The hero, Vance Weston, makes the transition from his midwestern hometown of Euphoria to the Atlantic seaboard, where he realizes his ambition to become a writer. When the novel opens, he has attended the College of Euphoria in Illinois, toyed with a new religion in Chicago and tried his hand at launching an avant-garde literary magazine.

While convalescing from typhoid fever, he is sent to visit his mother's cousin, the widowed Lucilla Tracy, and her children, Laura Lou and Upton, at Paul's Landing on the Hudson River. He and Laura Lou visit, as caretakers, The Willows, former home of the late Miss Elinor Lorburn, a distant relative. It is a fine example of the architectural style "Hudson River Bracketed," a pseudo-Italian style named by the horticulturist and landscape architect Andrew Jackson Downing, which gives the novel its name. It is here that he meets Héloïse ("Halo") Spear, a distant relation of his cousin, who introduces him to a world of letters he had not known; she stands, like the house, for wisdom and for an ordered inheritance from the past. Vance discovers Coleridge, Marlowe and "the mighty shock of English prose" in the library (critics were quick to point out that he might well have been exposed to them even in his midwestern college). He reads GOETHE's *FAUST* and encounters the mysterious Mothers, the sources of creativity, the eternal and infinite resources available to all men.

Vance suppresses his artistic side and becomes the protective male, marrying his frail, warmhearted cousin Laura Lou. Partly for economic reasons, Halo marries Lewis Tarrant; he can restore the family fortunes to her and to her aging parents. Vance is introduced to influential editors and launches a career as a novelist. He writes a well-received novel and obtains a job with an unscrupulous review that has forbidden him, in a contract, to write for other publications for several years, thus limiting his ability to provide for Laura Lou, who is mortally ill. He meets Halo again and confesses his love. After Laura Lou's death, Halo, unaware of it, finds Vance again; she has separated from her husband. The working out of their relationship is deferred and taken up again in *The GODS ARRIVE*, the sequel to the novel.

When she was composing *Hudson River Bracketed* in 1928, Edith Wharton had been living in FRANCE for two decades. The novel deals with a milieu she knew to a certain extent, that of authors, publishers and the "artistic" New York and Greenwich Village she despised. But it could be said that in some respects Wharton was by then out of touch with American literary and critical movements. Lewis points out that she was hurt at being considered out of date in this regard. She sought a "meaningful connection with the youthful heralds of the future" (*EW* 485).

Critics felt the novel lacked Wharton's usual irony, but that her portrait of Laura Lou, the "girl-wife," was a moving one; one critic felt she was the only real person in the book. Percy Hutchison, writing in the *New York Times*, believed Edith Wharton had risen above what might have been a hackneyed theme—the "genius from the prairies conquering with his literary power the Philistines of the great city" by focusing on Vance himself and not his career (*CR* 468). L. P. Hartley, writing in the British *Saturday Review*, believed the novel gave an invaluable portrait of what America was like then, and added, "though there are moments when we could wish the canvas smaller, we never wish that it was being painted by another hand." Wharton's European perspective enables her to separate men's occupations and their essential selves, and the book, he concludes, is a "contribution to our knowledge of America" (*CR* 475–76).

For further reading: Werlock, "Edith Wharton's Subtle Revenge?: Morton Fullerton and the Female Artist in *Hudson River Bracketed* and *The Gods Arrive.*"

Hugh Smith, John   Long-time friend of Edith Wharton whom she met at Stanway, the home of a British couple, Lord Hugo and Lady Mary (later Lady Wemyss) ELCHO. In December 1908, when Edith Wharton met the young banker, he was 27. He and Percy LUBBOCK had been at Cambridge together. They, Robert NORTON, Gaillard LAPSLEY and Howard STURGIS formed an intimate circle of Wharton's friends for many years.

Hugh Smith considered Edith Wharton a "mistress of the civilised life" and became a close friend. Henry JAMES wrote him, after they met, "Ah, my dear young man . . . you have made friends with Edith Wharton. I congratulate you: you may find her difficult, but you will never find her stupid, and you will never find her mean" (*EW* 246).

In July 1911, Lapsley, James and Hugh Smith, who was visiting the United States for the first time, stayed at The MOUNT with Edith Wharton. Goodman states that Hugh Smith was rabidly anti-Semitic and that, after Wharton's death, he wrote Lubbock that the "American middle class was poisoned by a plague of Jews" (letter in the BEINECKE LIBRARY, quoted in Goodman, 131, n. 33). Through the years of her life in FRANCE, Edith Wharton stayed in close touch with Hugh Smith; they often exchanged books and she valued his literary opinion. She dedicated her novel *HUDSON RIVER BRACKETED* to "A.J.H.S.," writing Elisina TYLER that he was "an excellent critic, & was so patient in reading the early part in type, that I wanted to thank him by my dedication" (*Letters* 525).

Wharton had asked that Hugh Smith be one of her pallbearers, but he was unable to attend (*NGC* 456).

For further reading: Goodman, *Edith Wharton's Inner Circle.*

Human Nature   Collection of short stories published by D. Appleton in 1933. The book was dedicated to Bernard BERENSON. It contains "HER SON," "The DAY OF THE FUNERAL," "A GLIMPSE," "JOY IN THE HOUSE," and "DIAGNOSIS." The collection received mixed reviews. The *New York Herald Tribune Books* critic, Florence Britten, praised Wharton's technique of modulating persons and incidents while maintaining a high level of suspense. Within 6,000 to 8,000 words there is "amplitude of event, and under and through all is a steadily marching plot." The reviewer for the *New York Times* observed that the stories exhibit a bitter irony, but sometimes lack a "humanizing pity." Raymond Mortimer, writing in the *New Statesman and Nation,* applauded Wharton's "uncanny knowledge of the human heart." Graham Greene, writing in the British *Spectator,* observed that the author wrote "in the tradition of Henry James" and had borrowed some "tricks" from him, including the use of alliteration and "the habit of introducing her minor characters in an ironic vignette" (*CR* 503–09).

Benstock states that the weakest story, "Diagnosis," had been rejected by 14 British magazines before Edith Wharton withdrew it. Rutger B. JEWETT sold it to the *Ladies' Home Journal* for $3,000 in 1930 (*NGC* 435).

Humières, Count Robert d'   French translator of the works of Rudyard KIPLING and a friend of Edith Wharton. In her autobiography, Wharton called him "one of the most versatile" of the group of cultivated people she met in the home of André CHEVRILLON at Saint Cloud, in the suburbs of PARIS. He was the author of books on the English in India and on contemporary ENGLAND. He began a translation of her novel *The CUSTOM OF THE COUNTRY* in 1914, but he was killed at the front in WORLD WAR I before he could complete it.

Hunter, Mary   One of Edith Wharton's most intimate English friends. During the years when Wharton divided her time between America and Europe, she often visited the Hunters' home, Hill Hall, in Essex, for a few weeks before she left France for America or after she returned from The MOUNT in the autumn. The large house, built around a quadrangle, was the site of house parties every weekend; the Hunters' married daughters and granddaughters and other relatives came and went. Mary Hunter was a friend of Henry JAMES, who had long wanted them to meet, although Wharton was reluctant, believing Mary Hunter to be only a frivolous society hostess. Yet when they did meet the women became close friends. Though not a brilliant conversationalist herself, Mary Hunter had a talent for bringing together congenial people with similar literary and artistic tastes. Her house parties often included James, Percy LUBBOCK, and Howard STURGIS, all devoted friends of Edith Wharton. In *A BACKWARD GLANCE,* she states that at Mary Hunter's death in 1933, "almost the whole fabric [of the English world] went with her" (*BG* 297).

Mary Hunter's fortune came from forebears in the coal industry; she was quite vague about money, but was extremely generous to others. She later lost most of her fortune and was materially aided by Edith Wharton.

Hyères   Edith Wharton had long known this town on the French RIVIERA. It was not far from Costebelle, where the Paul BOURGETs had a villa. Wharton, Léon BÉLOGU and André GIDE spent several days in Hyères and neighboring Toulon in the late fall of 1915 (they had met in the course of war work in PARIS). In 1919 Wharton stayed at the Hôtel du Parc in Hyères for four months, much of it in the company of Robert NORTON, in an attempt to escape the peace conference taking place in Paris. Bernard BERENSON joined them for two weeks. It was at this time that Wharton became interested in a ruined convent within the walls of a former château on a hillside in Hyères. She and Norton inspected it several times, and she decided to try to obtain it on a long lease. She was able to buy it later, although it needed much repair and landscaping.

See STE.-CLAIRE CHÂTEAU.

illegitimacy, of Edith Wharton *See* GENEALOGY, OF EDITH WHARTON.

illustrations In 1900, Wharton wrote William Crary BROWNELL, her SCRIBNER'S editor, who had considered asking Maxfield PARRISH to illustrate *The VALLEY OF DECISION,* "I don't care for illustrated books" (Dwight, *EWEL* 296). Against her better judgment, she permitted the 1903 novel SANCTUARY to be published with illustrations by Walter Appleton Clark. In 1905, she consented to publication of *The HOUSE OF MIRTH* with drawings by A. B. Wenzell, and wrote Brownell again: "Even when I sank to the depth of letting the illustrations be put in the book—& oh, I wish I hadn't now!—I never contemplated a text on the title-page." It may be argued that such illustrations fused, in the reader's imagination, the artist's conception of character and setting and those of the author. They thus altered one of her favorite tenets, that there is what she called, in both *The House of Mirth* and *ITALIAN BACKGROUNDS,* a "boundary world between fact and the imagination" that cannot be altogether defined; this world is invaded and destroyed by literal depiction. In specifically "clothing," as it were, her characters, the artist actually renders them less distinct. Some of her later works of fiction published by Scribner's were illustrated, such as *MADAME DE TREYMES* (1907) and *The FRUIT OF THE TREE* (1907). A few of her works of fiction published by Appleton were illustrated also. The four novellas making up *OLD NEW YORK* had endpaper line decorations by E. W. Caswell, who provided decorations for the short story collection HERE AND BEYOND.

Critics have assumed that, since Wharton disapproved of the illustrations for *The House of Mirth* and, apparently, ruled them out for much of her other fiction, she deplored all book illustrations on principle and only agreed to them under editorial duress. Further investigation suggests, however, that this was far from the case with her nonfiction works. *The DECORATION OF HOUSES* (1897) had been copiously illustrated with photographs of European interiors and examples of furniture, most of which Wharton had obtained herself, since her architect/collaborator, Ogden CODMAN, failed to do so.

In 1902, having published several articles about Italy for *SCRIBNER'S MAGAZINE,* she was invited by Richard Watson GILDER, editor of *The CENTURY MAGAZINE,* to contribute the text of a series of articles about Italian villas which Maxfield PARRISH had already been commissioned to illustrate with watercolors and paintings. Wharton accepted with alacrity, considering the offer an honor, but discovered that her concept of a technical architectural treatise, with architectural drawings of villa facades and plans of the gardens, was at variance with that of Gilder. The series of articles as well as the book compilation, ITALIAN VILLAS AND THEIR GARDENS (1904), were published with photographs and color illustrations by Parrish but with only one garden plan. In *A BACKWARD GLANCE,* written 30 years after publication, Wharton was still regretful. The Parrish watercolors, she felt, "should have been used to illustrate some fanciful tale of Lamotte Fouqué, or Andersen's 'Improvisatore' " (*BG* 139).

Copious illustrations, nevertheless, were the rule in the literary periodicals in which Wharton's earliest stories and articles appeared. In his monumental *History of American Magazines,* Frank Luther Mott states that it was because of their "leisurely, stylized, well-illustrated articles" that HARPER'S MAGAZINE, *Scribner's Monthly* (later *The Century*), and SCRIBNER'S MAGAZINE "were able to win an international reputation as the best general magazines in the world" (III, 190). (This reputation was achieved without the endorsement of Henry JAMES, who referred to them as the "New York picture books.") Clearly Wharton fully understood the importance of having a visual complement to a travel text, and preferred that her articles and books in this genre have illustrations, as long as the artist's vision did not compete with her own.

The five chapters of *Italian Backgrounds* published serially in *Scribner's Magazine* contained a total of 42 illustrations (5 halftones and 37 line drawings), most of them by the American artist Ernest PEIXOTTO, in the vein of the picturesque, with Alps, rivers, lakes, rushing streams and rock formations. In the book compilation the 42 illustrations had been reduced to 10, plus a frontispiece. They show a clear preference for the architectonic over what might be termed the "scenic," with municipal buildings and churches favored.

Wharton clearly expected *Italian Backgrounds* to be illustrated, as she did her later travel books. Peixotto, however, would not have been the artist of choice. On receiving the proof of the frontispiece for *Italian Backgrounds,* a sepia halftone of one of the SAN VIVALDO terra-cotta groups, she wrote Brownell, "How charming the frontispiece is! So much more real than those speckly Peixottos." But she had to reckon further with "speckly Peixottos." A misunderstanding at Scribner's, arising from Charles SCRIBNER's absence in Europe, led to Peixotto's being commissioned to illustrate *A MOTOR-FLIGHT THROUGH FRANCE,* published in 1908, three years after *Italian Backgrounds.* She wrote Brownell in May 1907 that she was dazed by Peixotto's request for postcards of Bourges Cathedral and several other monuments, so that he could "do his sketches in West 59th St.!" It seemed to her, she wrote, that "good photographs would have been better as illustrations than sketches done 'de chic' [without a model] from post cards" (unpublished correspondence between Edith Wharton and William Crary Brownell in the Scribner Archives, Firestone Library, Princeton University). Scribner made haste to drop Peixotto as illustrator, and the book appeared with photographs. *FIGHTING FRANCE, FROM DUNKERQUE TO BELFORT* (1915) and *IN MOROCCO* (1920) were also illlustrated by photographs. The former had a map of one of the war fronts, and there were maps in the latter also. *The BOOK OF THE HOMELESS* (1916) contained 15 contributions by artists, including sketches, drawings and portraits.

It could be argued that the use of photographs in Wharton's last three works of travel, rather than sketches or watercolors, place her work firmly in the 20th century rather than the 19th. There remains, however, a paradox central to the matter of illustrations for Wharton's travel works: how may we explain her preference for literal photographs over the interpretations of artists, when her texts are saturated with her devotion to the paintings of Turner, Longhi, Rosa, Tiepolo, Correggio and dozens of other artists? It is possible that no contemporary artist could have offered an interpretation conforming to her ideals, grounded in the baroque. Perhaps, moreover, she believed illustrations were best, as she said of reproductions in *The Decoration of Houses,* when they did not veer toward "artistic interpretation," but were "literal and mechanical" in rendering the original (*DH* 192). Artistic interpretations of sites by commissioned artists conceivably undercut her aesthetic commentary and become an unwelcome substitute for the mental images she hoped to conjure.

In any case, it is clear that Wharton did not repudiate the illustrated book entirely when it was a travel text. Instead, she sought images that would reinforce her connoisseurship, not compete with it. She had transcended the sentimental, picturesque views of lakes, waterfalls and mountains that pervaded what she called, in a letter to Brownell, "our grandfathers' Italy." She had no wish to encumber her sharp observations and sure analysis with unsuitable or poorly executed

sketches and paintings. For the publishers, it was a question of sales. Gilder, as Wharton astutely realized, wanted to offer the public a romantic subject treated by a popular artist, not a technical treatise. Scribner, once the problem with Peixotto was forcefully expressed, was amenable to whatever Wharton, his new best-selling novelist, wanted for *A Motor-Flight Through France,* which she herself termed a "series of desultory essays." Both Gilder and Scribner ultimately privileged the marketplace over aesthetic concerns. The photographs Wharton chose made better marriages with the texts, demonstrated her increasing influence over her publishers and finally produced the "harmony between text and pictures" she had long hoped would be the hallmark of her travel books.

In Morocco   Published by Scribner's in 1920, the book is an account of Edith Wharton's visit to the French colony in 1917, perhaps the worst of the war years. It was the result of an invitation from a French friend, General Hubert LYAUTEY, resident general of French MOROCCO. He invited her to tour one of the annual industrial exhibitions that he had been organizing in

In Morocco *(1920). Cover, first edition* (Collection of the author)

the French colony since 1914 in order to impress on French subjects that WORLD WAR I "in no way affected her normal activities." General Lyautey had been encouraged to invite guests from Allied and neutral countries. Morocco at that time was "untouched by foreign travel," and Lyautey organized for Wharton and her companion, Walter BERRY, a three-week motor tour of the colony. Upon her return to FRANCE, her war efforts demanded all Wharton's energy, and she did not write about the trip until 1920.

In Morocco is imbued with Wharton's appreciation of French contributions to that country. Her journey confirms the value of French expertise, brought benevolently to bear in promoting the country's traditional crafts and in conserving the country's aesthetic treasures. It is evident, from the acknowledgments, that she spoke and read French throughout the journey, and relied on more French than English sources to round out and substantiate her facts. Throughout the book, Wharton never ceases to remember that her status in Morocco is that of guest of the resident general, not that of a professional writer. Wharton insists that she is not addressing those who wish "authoritative utterances," which are principally available in French, but the "happy wanderers" who may be planning to visit Morocco. She supplies what she terms a "slight sketch of the history and art of the country," asserting that its chief merit is "absence of originality"; she makes a point of thanking various "cultivated and cordial French officials," such as the director of the French school of fine arts in Morocco (*IM* xii).

Such disclaimers cannot mask the achievement of *In Morocco*, which is one of the most finely wrought of Wharton's travel books. She records the sounds and sights (many of them forbidden to women before that time) of a little-known "*country without a guidebook*." Even visiting such a country, Wharton declares, is "a sensation to rouse the hunger of the repletest sightseer" (*IM* 3). In the preface to the first edition, Wharton acknowledges that some readers might have expected her to remedy this deficiency and supply a complete guide. She has been unable to do so, however, because the approach of the rainy season limited her time, and the conditions under which she traveled were "not suited to leisurely study of the places visited" (*IM* vii). With this admission, Wharton might seem to have done an about-face with respect to guidebooks, which she had previously scorned in ITALIAN BACK-GROUNDS. In that volume, she declared that one of the rarest pleasures of the traveler is to "circumvent the compiler of his guide-book" (*IB* 85). A country without one, uninscribed as it were, should be ripe for her own imprint. She could plausibly be an authoritative guide, initiating readers to the unknown Morocco. What she actually does, however, suggests that she had never taken the idea of writing a guidebook seriously. She

Roman ruins at Volubilis. From In Morocco *(1920), first edition* (Collection of the author)

presents a book that contains few dates and facts and little systematic description, yet which captures the essence of the country in a timeless way. She remains a connoisseur, freeing herself from all necessity for historical particulars and focusing on imaginative description and interpretation. This approach allows her to state, for example, that the "fallen columns and architraves" of the ruins at Volubilis "strew the path of Rome across the world," yet imposes no obligation to depict the ruins in a realistic way or give the precise history of the settlement. The preface points the reader toward useful works about Morocco in French, and a separate chapter summarizes Moroccan history as a whole.

By 1927, 10 years after her visit, surprisingly few of Wharton's earlier dire predictions had come true. She writes in a preface to the second edition that an "admirable" *Blue Guide* has been published. Wharton had originally worried that archaeological excavations and the advent of the "circular ticket" would eradicate ways of life that had existed since the time of the Crusaders. In 1912, before the French and Spanish protectorates were established, the country had had no wheeled vehicles and allowed few foreign visitors. In the first edition of *In Morocco* Wharton's aim had been

Marketplace in Moulay-Idriss, Morocco, before the ritual dance of the Hamadchas. From In Morocco *(1920), first edition* (Collection of the author)

to transcribe as much of it as possible before it disappeared, when "even the mysterious autocthones of the Atlas will have folded their tents and silently stolen away" (*IM* x). In the second preface, she praises, with relief, the skillfully built roads and other conveniences that have not been allowed by the French protectorate to "mar the ancient wonder."

The principal places Wharton visits are Rabat, Salé, Volubilis, Moulay Idriss, Meknez, Fez and Marrakech. She also visits harems in several of these towns—a particular privilege, since few foreign women had ever been admitted to the women's quarters of the various sheiks. Despite her own position as an official guest, Wharton writes frankly, though tactfully, about her two major concerns—the denigration of women within the Moroccan social system and the country's indifference to the conservation of its architecture and art.

Wharton criticizes the deleterious effects on women of lives spent within harems and the "shadowy evils of the social system that hangs like a millstone about the neck of Islam" (*IM* 201). In the harem at Marrakech, she finds a stifling atmosphere in which the young female inhabitants are idle and without curiosity. In *Edith Wharton's Argument with America*, Elizabeth Ammons states that in Morocco Wharton sees for herself

"patriarchal sex pushed to its logical, primitive—and very depressing—extreme. . . . [and concludes] that the free expression of female sexuality represents a profound threat to patriarchal power" (49). Seated in the harem before tea, trying to make conversation with the other women, Wharton concedes that there are

> . . . few points of contact between the open-air occidental mind and beings imprisoned in a conception of sexual and domestic life based on slave-service and incessant espionage. These languid women on their muslim cushions toil not, neither do they spin. The Moroccan lady knows little of cooking, needlework or any household arts (*IM* 193).

She finds that in Morocco both sexes "live till old age in an atmosphere of sensuality without seduction." The status of women in Morocco is clearly worse than that of their American or French counterparts.

Wharton is extremely concerned about the vanishing aesthetic heritage of Morocco. In Fez, for example, she notes the "indifference to the completed object . . . like a kind of collective exaggeration of the artist's indifference to his completed work" (*IM* 86). As a result, the furniture and works of art she

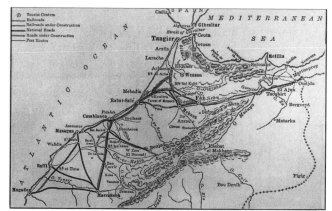

A map of Wharton's travels in Morocco. From In Morocco *(1920), first edition* (Collection of the author)

believes must once have filled the buildings of the Merinid period have fallen to ruin. It sometimes seems that Wharton is driven by aesthetic concerns more than distress at the blighted development of Moroccan women. In what may be an oblique indictment of Islamic priorities, she comes to feel that little is deliberately conserved in Morocco except mosques and shrines of saints. She mourns, on behalf of Morocco, the loss of the material artifacts that would have testified to the rich cultural capital of the country.

In Morocco was Wharton's final travel book. She did not supply the guidebook she knew the country lacked at the time, but instead depicted the Morocco that had been for her (as she said in the preface to the second edition) like a "Persian illuminated manuscript all embroidered with bright shapes and subtle lines" (*IM,* Century edition, 16).

"In Trust"   Story published in *Booklover's* in 1906 and reprinted in *The HERMIT AND THE WILD WOMAN* (Scribner's, 1908). Paul Ambrose, one of three young men who are close friends, lives in his inherited house in an ugly "setting of black walnut and pier glasses." He becomes attuned to these surroundings, saving his money to endow traveling scholarships for students and to found a grandiose Academy of Arts. The narrator and a friend, Ned Halidon, attempt to persuade Paul to replace some of the furniture, but he becomes more and more miserly, conserving money for his philanthropic projects.

Despite his economies, Paul never quite follows through on his schemes. Ned has long been an enthusiastic advocate of Paul's ideas and encourages him to draw up plans. Paul had even thought of leaving his money in trust for Ned, who would "put the job through" for him. Paul goes abroad without doing so, marries and then dies. His American-born widow marries Ned, who vows to use his wife's fortune to carry out Paul's plans, but keeps procrastinating year after year. His wife has two children and adds a wing to their New

York townhouse; meanwhile, they travel abroad in luxury. The vision of the Academy of Arts gradually recedes until Halidon, grown stout and inactive, tells the narrator, "Paul's work won't come in *my* day, of course," but he is sure that when his three-year-old son grows up, "*he'll put it through.*"

Institut de France (Institute of France)   National French society founded in 1795 to replace five royal academies that had been suppressed in 1793. It contains five Academies: the ACADÉMIE FRANÇAISE, the Académie des inscriptions et belles-lettres, the Académie des Sciences, the Académie des beaux arts and the Académie des sciences morales et politiques. Edith Wharton's friend Paul BOURGET was a member of the prestigious Académie française, which has only 40 members.

"Intense Love's Utterance"   A poem written in 1881, but not published. That year Edith Wharton and her parents were staying in VENICE, where her friend Harry STEVENS (later her first fiancé) came to visit them. He was an earnest suitor and she, at 19, was very interested in him. George Frederick JONES was in poor health, and his doctors had hoped he would benefit from the climate in Italy and France. The poem was influenced by the presence of Stevens and by the discourses on beauty given by John RUSKIN in *The Stones of Venice* and Walter PATER in *The Renaissance: Studies in Art and Poetry.* Wharton's father had given her both works.

Lewis terms the poem an "elegant hoax," in which the male lover, who has professed yearning for his "heart's lady," advises her to return to her "dadoes and friezes" (*EW* 43). He admits he does not have the means to give her the art treasures which could, according to Pater, make the "fleeting pulsations" of life precious. The speaker gives art a higher priority than love, which is transitory.

interior design   Edith Wharton considered interior design to be an important matter. *The DECORATION OF HOUSES,* which she wrote with Ogden CODMAN, is a manifesto of taste and a testament to her early connoisseurship. The authors address deficiencies in bourgeois American standards of house design and ornamentation and construct, from a European point of view, what Wharton believed was missing in AMERICA. Her early travels, as well as Codman's education abroad, both contributed to their knowledge of classical French and Italian principles of design. The authors explain how Americans can follow European models of vernacular architecture and offer examples of good proportion and restrained styles of furniture. The volume covers ornament, walls, floors, ceilings, doors and other aspects of domestic architecture. In her three homes, The MOUNT, the PAVILLON COLOMBE, and STE.-CLAIRE CHÂTEAU, Edith Wharton followed her own advice, avoiding ostentation and emphasizing furnishings suitable for the functions of the various rooms.

In Edith Wharton's fiction, interior design also plays an important part. Often decorative details are used as metonymies connoting certain root traits and social modes of her characters. In *The HOUSE OF MIRTH*, for example, Lily Bart begins by being highly collectible herself; by the end of the novel, she has declined in value as an artifact. Simon Rosedale, finding her in a boardinghouse, surveys in disgust the "peacock blue parlour, . . . bunches of dried pampas grass, and discoloured steel engravings of sentimental episodes." He lays his hat "distrustfully on the dusty console adorned with a Rogers statuette" (*HM* 313). The statuette is an emblem of cheap sentimentality, part of what Wharton terms, in *The Decoration of Houses,* the "debasement of bibelots" caused by "the substitution of machine for hand-work" (*DH* 191).

In *The AGE OF INNOCENCE,* to take another example, furnishings reflect the New World propensity for remaking oneself. Newland Archer hopes to validate his own taste after marriage by rejecting the "purple satin and yellow tuftings" favored by his prospective in-laws, the Wellands, and installing in his study stylish " 'sincere' Eastlake furniture, and the plain new bookcases without glass doors" (*AI* 71). In *The Decoration of Houses* (*DH* 150), built-in bookcases are preferred over movable ones with glass doors.

In *A SON AT THE FRONT,* John Campton's studio is shabby; he is relatively indifferent to comfort and appearance, though he has a fleeting moment of wanting to assemble a few good things and provide a small home for his son, George, in the fashionable FAUBOURG ST.-GERMAIN. His studio has "tattered tapestries" with "huge heroes and kings," "blotched walls hung with pictures," "canvases stacked against the stair-legs" and a "long littered table at which he wrote and ate and mixed his colors" (*SF* 127). This could be a sketch for a painting of his actual studio. Similarly, the home of Dr. Fortin-Lescluze has what is called a "studio," where he receives celebrities, but it seems to be more of a masculine salon. It is "a lofty room with Chinese hangings, Renaissance choir-stalls, organ, grand piano, and post-impressionist paintings." Instead of this affluent setting, Campton is received in an "honest *bourgeois* dining-room" out of keeping with the rest of the house.

Throughout Wharton's short stories, which are of necessity tightly woven, furniture and decorative accessories provide vital information about the characters. The narrator of "The CONFESSIONAL," for example, establishes his impeccable taste by receiving the impoverished priest, Don Egidio, in his lodgings, where a wood fire gives "a factitious luster" to his bookshelves . . . "bringing out the values of the one or two old prints and Chinese porcelains that accounted for the perennial shabbiness" of his wardrobe (*CSS* I, 316). In

"IN TRUST," Paul Ambrose lives in his inherited house in a "setting of black walnut and pier glasses," hoping to launch various philanthropic projects. Edith Wharton's focus on furnishings, art and artifacts does not merely round out her characters and interior settings, it underlies her very conception of them.

"Introducers, The" Short story published in *Ainslee's* in December 1905 and January 1906. Set in NEWPORT, it is a light satire about the new millionaires who have established themselves in grand palaces overlooking the sea, but who have not managed to break into "society." Frederick Tilney and Miss Grantham are "introducers," social mentors in adjoining villas, well-connected but poor, who arrange for invitations for their respective employers, Mr. Magraw and the Bixby family, who wish their daughter to marry advantageously. "Les METTEURS EN SCÈNE," "The Producers" (1908), is a French version of the story, the only one Wharton wrote in French. White states that both stories make a "mockery of marriage," as the characters try to disguise their view of the institution as a business partnership (77). In *The HOUSE OF MIRTH,* Wharton indicts the entire "frivolous society" she described in *A BACKWARD GLANCE* as having dramatic significance only in its "power of debasing people and ideals" (*BG* 207); on a smaller scale, "The Introducers" reflects that society with equal discernment.

Introductions *See* ETHAN FROME; HOUSE OF MIRTH, THE, *and* VILLAGE ROMEO AND JULIET, A.

Irving, Washington (1783–1859) American essayist, historian and biographer. Born in New York City, Irving was the youngest member of a prosperous merchant family. He traveled through Europe, and was received into the bar in 1806. He came to prefer writing to the law and was allowed by his family to lead the life of a man of letters. Beginning in 1807, he wrote a number of books, many under pseudonyms. His earliest work, the *Salamagundi* papers, was written in collaboration with his brothers. He then wrote, under the pseudonym of a Dutchman, Dietrick Knickerbocker, *A History of New York from the Beginnings of the World to the End of the Dutch Dynasty.* His fiancée died, after which he spent 17 years in Europe. It was here that he wrote *The Sketch Book of Geoffrey Crayon, Gent.,* his best-known work, as well as *Bracebridge Hall and Tales of a Traveller.* He was influenced by the work of Sir Walter Scott, Oliver Goldsmith and Joseph Addison. Irving's style, with its delicate irony and precision, attracted readers not only in America but also in England and other countries, where people had been skeptical about the appeal of an American author.

Irving lived for a time in the Alhambra, the storied castle in Granada, and evoked its romantic past in *The*

Legends of the Alhambra (1832). He returned to America, traveled widely in the West, and spent four years as U.S. minister to Spain (1842–46).

Irving had a profound appeal for Edith Wharton, particularly in her youth, perhaps because he was one of the authors the Joneses most revered. She recalls that, though her parents and their group ". . . held literature in great esteem, [they] stood in nervous dread of those who produced it. Washington Irving, Fritz-Greene Halleck and William Dana were the only representatives of the disquieting art who were deemed uncontaminated by it" (*BG* 68).

In *A BACKWARD GLANCE,* Wharton recalls her family's arduous journey by diligence to Spain during the second year of their European residence; from this trip she brought back an incurable passion for the road." The family had taken along a copy of the *Alhambra,* which she later called the "Pierian fount" of her inspiration. When they returned to Paris, she walked the floor, sometimes holding the book upside down but absorbed in its thick black type, "swept off full sail on the sea of dreams." Learning to read converted her delight in "making up" into a "frenzy" (*BG* 31–43). She made a number of trips to Spain after this early journey and may have considered writing a travel book about it (*see* "MOTOR-FLIGHT TO SPAIN, A").

Irving had a subtle influence on her imagination throughout her life. Many decades after the trip, she regretted that she could not recall enough of it to write a work of travel about it; otherwise, she "might conceivably produce a tale as captivating as Théophile Gautier's or Washington Irving's" (*BG* 334). In the novella *SUMMER,* Honorius Hatchard, founder of the Hatchard Memorial Library, is said to have prided himself on his acquaintance with Irving.

Iseo, Lake   Situated in the Lombardy region of ITALY, Lake Iseo is less well known than Lake COMO or Lake MAGGIORE, but it has a dramatic beauty that appealed to Edith Wharton. Surrounded by a high mountain fringe, its banks are sometimes steep, dotted with peaceful villages. The island of Monte Isola is located near the eastern shore.

After their marriage in 1885, Edith Wharton and her husband Teddy traveled to Italy annually for several months, often staying in the Lake District. In *ITALIAN BACKGROUNDS,* Lago Iseo serves as the starting point for several of Wharton's imaginative tropes. She observes that Lady Mary Wortley Montagu, noted English traveler and letter writer, had immortalized the town of Lovere, where she had a villa and garden. Critics believed her description inaccurate, since they could not pinpoint the exact spot of which she wrote, but Wharton insists that "every lover of Italy will understand the mental process by which she unconsciously created an imaginary Lovere." Though dull on the surface, the town, taken with its surroundings, "might well form the substructure of one of those Turnersque visions which, in Italy, are perpetually intruding between the most conscientious traveller and his actual surroundings. It is indeed almost impossible to see Italy steadily and see it whole" (*IB* 33).

She also visualizes the lake as an ideal setting for the COMMEDIA DELL'ARTE. Villages along the shore might serve as a backdrop for the performances of comedies "in the Bergamasque dialect, with Harlequin in striped cloak, and Brighella in conical hat and wide green and white trousers strutting up and down before the shuttered house in which Dr. Graziano hides his pretty ward." She imagines the lake as reflecting the "eighteenth century of Longhi, of Tiepolo and Goldoni . . . as in some magic crystal," to be discovered beneath the waves by "some later traveller. . . . if ever the boundaries between fact and fancy waver, it may well be under the spell of the Italian midsummer madness" (*IB* 35).

For further reading: Dwight, "The Influence of Italy on Edith Wharton"; Prampolini, "Edith Wharton in Italy."

Italian Backgrounds   Published by Scribner's in 1905, this volume is a compilation of essays about ITALY. Five had appeared in SCRIBNER'S MAGAZINE, including "A Tuscan Shrine" (January 1895), "Sub Umbra Liliorum: An Impression of Parma" (January 1902), "Sanctuaries of the Pennine Alps" (March 1902), "A Midsummer Week's Dream: August in Italy" (August 1902) and "Picturesque Milan" (February 1903). They were lavishly illustrated, in keeping with the style of the magazine, which was renowned for the quality of its wood engravings. After several articles had appeared, Edward C. BURLINGAME, the editor, "wondered whether there might not be a volume of these things, including Mrs. Wharton's pieces on SAN VIVALDO, the coaching inn at Splügen, and the Bergamasque" (*EW* 107). "An Alpine Posting Inn," which had appeared in the ATLANTIC MONTHLY, was added, along with three others written for the book: "What the Hermits Saw," "March in Italy" and "Italian Backgrounds."

Both *Italian Backgrounds* and *ITALIAN VILLAS AND THEIR GARDENS,* along with *The DECORATION OF HOUSES,* represent a synthesis of Wharton's travels in Italy, which spanned two decades. *The Decoration of Houses* focuses on interior design, much of it drawn from Italian vernacular architecture, emphasizing the best placement of paintings, tapestries and artifacts within a domestic setting; *Italian Villas and their Gardens* formulates, with considerable detective work on the part of Wharton, the historic designs of selected Italian gardens and the tripartite relationship connecting garden, villa and contiguous landscape. *Italian Backgrounds* examines landscape in a broader context and also contains descriptions of towns

Italian Backgrounds *(1905). Cover, first edition* (Collection of the author)

and cities mixed with analyses of paintings, sculptures, frescoes, courtyards and architecture. Wharton discusses PARMA, MILAN, the northern Italian lakes, VENICE, Sicily and the Pennine Alps (Apennines), among other places.

The "abroad" that Wharton evokes in her first two published works of travel, *Italian Villas and Their Gardens* and *Italian Backgrounds,* largely predates the automotive era, and partakes far more of the 19th century than of the 20th. She and her party traverse little-known Italian routes at a leisurely pace, by horse-drawn carriage and stagecoach, lingering in the aura of such earlier travelers as Goethe, Hester Piozzi, Lady Mary Montague and Stendhal. Wharton traveled in the last days of the elite stately Grand Tour before the onset of mass tourism. Between *Italian Backgrounds* (1905) and *A MOTOR-FLIGHT THROUGH FRANCE* (1908), she crosses a Rubicon; henceforth, leisurely exploration gives way to rapid visitation, and Italy succumbs to FRANCE. Her travel writing becomes less a compilation of heuristic essays than a chronicle of sites and routes.

Edith Wharton's travel writing both derived from and transcended the genteel literary tradition. During the

GILDED AGE, Wharton tried to impart a cosmopolitan knowledge of little known byways and "parentheses" of Europe to her fellow Americans. To that extent, her aspirations were congruent with those of the proponents of the Genteel Tradition (see GENTEEL CIRCLE). She did not consciously address any class, but implicitly directed her writing toward anyone who could join her in responding to beauty. She often went beyond these aims, however, according a new importance to aesthetic expertise that set her travel narratives apart from those of her contemporaries. She was schooled in the work of John RUSKIN, Vernon LEE, Walter PATER and Paul BOURGET, who were disciplined to assess architecture and painting with a critical eye, and was greatly influenced by Bernard BERENSON's scientific approach to the attribution of paintings. Wharton thus developed a scholarly approach and tightly focused connoisseurship that conformed to the new standards of professionalism and functioned to elevate her travel writing beyond an appreciation of mere "beauty." One of the most notable chapters in *Italian Backgrounds* is "Sanctuaries of the Pennine Alps," in which she describes her major contribution to art history, the reattribution of the terra-cotta sculpture groups at the Monastery of SAN VIVALDO to Giovanni della Robbia.

According to unpublished correspondence at the BEINECKE LIBRARY, YALE UNIVERSITY, and the FIRESTONE LIBRARY, Princeton, Edith Wharton objected to the illustrations of the American artist Ernest PEIXOTTO for *Italian Backgrounds.* Peixotto was a native of San Francisco, a few years younger than Wharton and an established illustrator whose work the editors at *Scribner's Magazine* knew well. He provided 42 line drawings for the five chapters of the book that appeared in the magazine before the book's compilation. The periodical articles were far more lavishly illustrated than they were when compiled in the book, which contained only 12 illustrations, plus a frontispiece. In the periodical articles, the vein of the "picturesque" predominated over architectural views. There were Alps in the background, mountain passes with rushing streams, steep valleys, rocky islands in the middle of lakes and a canal in Milan bordered by flower boxes. Such views were typical of the fare often offered readers of literary periodicals, and quiet similar to those in *Picturesque Europe,* the imposing three-volume set of signed sketches and anonymous essays edited by Bayard Taylor, a noted member of "the Genteel Circle." There were also photographs of sculptural groups (the Sacred Mounts, or Stations of the Cross) at the monasteries of Varallo and San Vivaldo.

When *Italian Backgrounds* was published, architectonic views predominated, giving a certain visual exactitude to the text. Most of the pastoral views are omitted, along with all of the religious scenes except that shown in the frontispiece. Instead, there are municipal buildings, courtyards, quadrangles, churches and an occasional townscape with buildings in the background. The periodical editors of the Gilded Age clearly believed that a strong scenic component increased circulation and improved the presentation of all articles. It is arguable that Edith Wharton, by her choice of architectural views for the book, was distancing her work from the tradition of the quaint or the picturesque.

Some reviewers of *Italian Backgrounds* thought it too pedantic and not "feminine." G. R. Carpenter, writing in the *Bookman,* complained that the author had "denationalised, defeminised herself." Her writing was not that of an "American of today, not even of a woman, but merely of the art-antiquarian" (*CR* 101–02). For the most part, the book was well received. The reviewer for the *Independent* declared Wharton "wonderfully successful at wandering in new by-paths and in discovering new shrines for the adoration of the artistic traveler." He approved of her incorporation in *Italian Backgrounds* of streets, landscapes and pictures "such as these she has already drawn in her novels."

Like Wharton's other travel books, this volume manifests not only a thorough knowledge of art and architecture, but also an ability to juxtapose them against a complex background of theology, classical mythology, history and literature. Such cultural competence allows her to integrate the scholarly and imaginative approaches to travel, qualities most desired by her audience. This ability is what distinguishes her travel books from many contemporary accounts and justifies Blake Nevius's characterization of them as "brilliantly written and permanently interesting" (37).

For further reading: Bailey, "Aesthetics and Ideology in *Italian Backgrounds*"; Dwight, *Edith Wharton: An Extraordinary Life;* Goodwyn, *Edith Wharton: Traveller in the*

Land of Letters; Joslin and Price, eds., *Wretched Exotic: Essays on Edith Wharton in Europe,* St. Laurent, "Pathways to a Personal Aesthetic: Edith Wharton's Travels in Italy and France"; Schriber, "Edith Wharton and the Dog-Eared Travel Book"; Wright, *Edith Wharton Abroad: Selected Travel Writings, 1888–1920;* Wright, *Edith Wharton's Travel Writing: The Making of a Connoisseur.*

Italian Cities A two-volume work on the historical art and architecture of ITALY by Edwin H. and Evangeline W. BLASHFIELD, published by SCRIBNER'S in 1901. Wharton reviewed it in the *Bookman* in August 1901. She complimented the Blashfields on their ability to detect some "unrecorded phase of art, some detail insignificant enough to have dropped out of the ever-growing catalogue of [Italy's] treasures." She called this the most interesting book on Italy to have appeared since Arthur SYMONS'S volumes and regretted not being able to trace the "innumerable threads of suggestion branching off from every subject on which they touch" (*UCW* 63–66). She suggested that Edwin Blashfield's technical competence as an artist had enabled him to analyze rather than "rhapsodise" over works of art.

Blashfield was an artist of some note, having decorated the central dome of the Library of Congress. He and his wife collaborated on travel books and articles; separately, each also wrote learned reviews, articles and books in the fields of art and literature. The Blashfields were within the larger perimeter of the GENTEEL CIRCLE, the influential group of American editors and writers who were custodians of the belletrist tradition.

Italian Villas and Their Gardens Usually considered Edith Wharton's first published travel book (The Century Company, 1904), this work is marked by a high level of scholarship. It comprises a compilation of a series of articles commissioned by Richard GILDER, editor of *The* CENTURY MAGAZINE, to accompany the watercolors of Maxfield PARRISH for which the magazine had contracted. It includes color illustrations of gardens and villas, in addition to drawings from photographs and black and white line drawings. Other artists who contributed were C. A. Vanderhoof, Malcolm Fraser and Ella Denison.

Italian Villas is a learned survey of garden architecture and ornamentation rather than a study of villas. We may imagine Edith Wharton visiting the gardens in 1903 with a scholar's eye, detecting, beneath the palimpsest of 18th-century horticulturists bent on transforming every garden into an English park, the original garden outlines and plantings. She sketches the history of more than 75 villas and their gardens, most of which were built during the Renaissance and baroque periods. The volume contains a bibliography of reference works in four languages, capsule biographies of 55 architects and landscape gardeners of the

Publisher's advertisement for Italian Backgrounds *(1905)*
(Courtesy Scribner, a division of Simon & Schuster)

Italian Villas and Their Gardens *(1904). Cover, first edition*
(Collection of the author)

atmosphere" to a site (*MFF* 151). In other words, she goes beyond mere surface description, positing quasi-fictional or dramatic vignettes based on history, mythology or literature to bring a lake, villa, theater, church, village or painting to life. In *Italian Villas* Edith Wharton not only documents the noblemen and cardinals who caused the original villas and their gardens to be built, as well as the architects, landscape architects and horticulturists who designed them, she also conjectures what contemporary life in some of the villas might have been like. For example, she describes the fortified villa of Caprarola, near Rome, built by Cardinal Alexander Farnese and designed by the renowned 16th-century architect Vignola:

> To pass from the threatening façade to the wide-spread beauty of pleached walks, fountains and grottoes, brings vividly before one the curious contrasts of Italian country life in the transition period of the sixteenth century. Outside, one pictures the cardinal's soldiers and *bravi* lounging on the great platform above the village; while within, one has a vision of noble ladies and their cavaliers sitting under rose-arbours or strolling between espaliered lemon-trees, discussing a Greek manuscript or a Roman bronze, or listening to the last sonnet of the cardinal's court poet (*IV,* 128).

Wharton thus peoples the military domain without and the leisurely company within, suggesting their intellectual pursuits and way of life.

The reenactment of travel through writing about it was vitally important to Wharton; in this volume she is a voracious intellectual wanderer, open to all experiences, often interpreting the sights she sees in the light of the extensive historic, literary and classical reading she had first undertaken in her youth. Her erudite background, her zest for detecting the original lineaments of gardens obliterated by later "improvements," her mastery of Italian and the Italian friendships that gained her entry to closed villas and gardens came together in this masterful volume.

For further reading: Dwight, *Edith Wharton: An Extraordinary Life;* Foster, "Making It Her Own: Edith Wharton's Europe"; Joslin and Price, eds., *Wretched Exotic: Essays on Edith Wharton in Europe;* Schriber, "Edith Wharton and the Dog-Eared Travel Book"; Wright, *Edith Wharton Abroad: Selected Travel Writings, 1888–1920;* Wright, *Edith Wharton's Travel Writing: The Making of a Connoisseur.*

15th through the 18th centuries and a detailed index. As was the case with most of Edith Wharton's travel books, serial publication preceded compilation of the book. Wharton was disappointed that Gilder refused to include detailed plans of each garden, a defect noted by early reviewers, which would have undoubtedly clarified much of the text (*see* ILLUSTRATIONS).

The author's mission is to evoke, for the reader, the original tripartite relationship connecting villa, garden and surrounding landscape. She is careful to point out that *villa,* in Italian, connotes both house and pleasuregrounds rather than the house alone. Throughout the book, Wharton's emphasis is on the gardens. She deplores the attempts of affluent Americans to fashion "Italian" gardens by importing bits of statuary and laying out English-style lawns without understanding the principles behind Italian "garden-magic." The book is a tour de force explaining and illustrating the aesthetic principles underlying Italian gardens.

A hallmark of Edith Wharton's travel writing is what she called in *A MOTOR-FLIGHT THROUGH FRANCE* the "*bon mouvement* of the imagination" in order to "restore an

Italy   Edith Wharton developed a passion for Italy in her childhood, when the JONES family spent six years abroad, living for long periods of time in ROME and Florence. As an adult Wharton recalled "the lost Rome" of her "infancy," the "warm scent of the box hedges on the Pincian, and the texture of weather-worn sun-gilt stone" (*BG* 31). In her unpublished autobiography,

"LIFE AND I," she recalled her shock at returning to the ugliness of NEW YORK after she had been "fed on beauty since my babyhood." Fluent in Italian, she never ceased longing to return to Italy. As an adolescent she read books on Italian art and architecture in her father's library. During the second European stay of the Jones family, in 1881, when Wharton was 19, she and her father, with *The Stones of Venice* and *Mornings in Florence* in hand, followed John RUSKIN's "arbitrary itineraries" in VENICE and Florence (*BG* 87).

After their marriage in 1885, Edith and Teddy Wharton went annually to Italy, spending two or three months exploring the country by diligence and rail. It was not until 1904 that their interest shifted to France; by that time she had published the articles that would be compiled into her two Italian books of travel, *ITALIAN BACKGROUNDS* and *ITALIAN VILLAS AND THEIR GARDENS*. There had been, of course, a long history of Americans traveling to Italy, and many descriptive books about the country, such as Hawthorne's *The Marble Faun* and *Italian*

Villa Campi, Florence, by Maxfield Parrish. From Italian Villas and Their Gardens *(1904), first edition* (Collection of the author)

Notebooks, Bayard Taylor's *Views A-Foot: or Europe Seen with Knapsack and Staff,* and Mark Twain's *The Innocents Abroad.* In 1903, while working on the essays for SCRIBNER'S MAGAZINE that were later to be published as *Italian Backgrounds,* she urged the compilation in a letter to William Crary BROWNELL: "I believe the book would sell well, for there is such a great rush to Italy every summer now on the Mediterranean steamers, & people so often ask me where these articles are to be found—" (*Letters* 86).

In *Italian Backgrounds* Wharton wrote that, in the landscape of Italy, "the face of nature seems moulded by the passions and imaginings of man" (*IB* 3). In the second chapter, she and her party, staying high in the Swiss Alps at Splügen one August, observed the arrival each evening of the diligences from Thusis (Switzerland) and Chiavenna (Italy). Was it better, she pondered, "to be cool and look at a waterfall, or to be hot and look at Saint Mark's? Was it better to walk on gentians or on mosaic, to smell fir-needles or incense?" (*IB* 19). They boarded the diligence to Chiavenna. In Italy, Wharton held that the "onset of impressions and memories" was so overwhelming that "observation" was lost in "mere sensation" as their explorations unfolded, but her statement was belied by her remarkable descriptions of landscapes, sites and works of art "unmeasured by the guide-book" (*IB* 33, 86). Wharton described the journey she and her party made through what they believed to be the Bergamasque Alps with their connotations of the COMMEDIA DELL'ARTE, the improvisatory strolling theater that began during the 16th century in Italy—though it later developed that they had missed that section of the Alps and had to defer it until another journey. They visited LAGO DI MAGGIORE, LAGO D'ISEO, LAGO DI COMO, PARMA, Lago d'Orta, SAN VIVALDO, MILAN, Syracuse, Tuscany, Rome, Volterra, Venice and other sites. Many of Wharton's favorite places in Italy figure in her short stories and novels, including Rome, Venice, Lago di Como, Lago di Maggiore and Lago d'Orta.

After her separation from Teddy and her resettlement in PARIS, Wharton frequently traveled to Italy and often stayed with the BERENSONS at I TATTI. In 1911 she and Walter BERRY made a memorable journey through central Italy. In 1912 they made another journey, which she called an "unlucky giro" (*Letters* 272). Chauffeured by Charles COOK, they attempted to visit the monastery at La Verna, the 13th-century monastery at which St. Francis of Assisi received the stigmata. It could only be reached over high precipices in the Apennines. Peasants had to push the car up in stages, placing rocks beneath the tires. The next morning they let it down precariously by ropes.

Edith Wharton never lost her attachment to the country and, the summer she died, was still hoping to return to Venice to see her favorite Tintoretto paintings. The BEINECKE LIBRARY, YALE UNIVERSITY, contains an unpublished holograph manuscript titled "Italy Again."

For further reading: Joslin and Price, eds., *Wretched Exotic: Essays on Edith Wharton in Europe;* Dwight, "The Influence of Italy on Edith Wharton"; Prampolini, "Edith Wharton in Italy."

I Tatti, Villa   Home of Bernard and Mary BERENSON, at Settignano, near Florence, ITALY. The Berensons were married in the chapel there on December 29, 1900, after 10 years of intimacy. I Tatti was a rural villa three stories high, dating from the 16th century, with thick walls of Tuscan stone. There were stone outbuildings and tributary farms; more fields and olive groves were added until the estate eventually reached about 70 acres.

At the time the Berensons first came to know it, the property was owned by a wealthy, eccentric Englishman, John Temple Leader, who had many holdings in the area, including the Castle of Vincigliata, and who had devoted much of his fortune to the archaeology of Tuscany. The villa lacked modern conveniences, which the Berensons added. They collected antique furnishings for the villa throughout Italy. The central panels of a Sassetta altarpiece were among Berenson's most important acquisitions for I Tatti.

Edith Wharton frequently stayed with the Berensons at I Tatti. Her first visit was in 1911 (*EW* 314) and she went almost annually thereafter. She wrote in her autobiography that she had never before stayed in a house where she could replicate her own life, as devoting her mornings to work and browsing at will in the library. Wharton called the library a "book-worm's heaven . . . not a dusty mausoleum of dead authors but a glorious assemblage of eternally living ones" (*BG* 327). It had been added to the villa by the firm, established in Florence at the time, of her friend Geoffrey SCOTT, an architect and the author of *The Architecture of Humanism.*

Elizabeth (Nicky) MARIANO, of Baltic and Neapolitan origins, joined the staff of I Tatti in 1918 as librarian and, in time, handled many of Berenson's affairs; she stayed there for 40 years and was his lover. With its magnificent library and superb art collection, the villa has long been a magnet for art historians and scholars interested in the Wharton/Berenson correspondence of more than 600 letters. Berenson bequeathed the estate to Harvard University, which administers it as the Harvard University Center for Italian Renaissance Studies.

Jackson, Sillerton   *See AGE OF INNOCENCE, THE;* and *NEW YEAR'S DAY.*

James, Henry   (1843–1916) This American novelist, short-story writer and man of letters was a close friend of Edith Wharton for a number of years. He came from a distinguished and wealthy family. His grandfather had been a millionaire, but the family fortune had dwindled in time and James had only a modest income. He, like Edith Wharton, had been "dipp[ed] . . . generously in the font of Europe" (Spiller, 1041). Having spent his childhood on the Continent with his parents, three brothers and sister, his French was indistinguishable from that of a native. James entered Harvard Law School

Portrait of Henry James *(1913), John Singer Sargent. From* The Book of the Homeless *(1916)* (Courtesy Picture Collection, the Library of Virginia)

in 1862 but withdrew to write, publishing fiction and book reviews in the *North American Review,* the *Atlantic Monthly* and other periodicals. He made two trips to EUROPE as an adult and, in 1875, decided to make his home abroad. He first settled in PARIS and in 1876 decided on ENGLAND. He spent the rest of his life there, living in LAMB HOUSE, Rye, Sussex and in London.

Among the works for which James is best known are *The American* (1877), *The Wings of the Dove* (1902), *The Ambassadors* (1903) and *The Golden Bowl* (1904). His craftsmanship and impeccable technique in the art of fiction, as well as some of his themes—the confrontation between American and European civilization, the dilemma of the artist in an unsympathetic society and the development of moral perception—caused Wharton to be unjustly compared with him and even to be considered his imitator. James believed the novelist should be "one on whom nothing is lost." Edith Wharton was devoted to him and reveled in his sense of humor. She had reservations about his major late novels, however, and in 1902 wrote William Crary BROWNELL of SCRIBNER's, "Don't ask me what I think of the Wings of the Dove" (*Letters* 71). She wrote Gaillard LAPSLEY, after James's death, that his friendship had been "the pride and honour of my life." They had met at a dinner in the late 1880s, possibly at the home of Boston friends, Mr. and Mrs. Edward Boit, but Wharton had made no impression on him, as she had wrongly believed that a new dress from Doucet would be the best way to engage James's attention. A year or so later, other mutual friends invited them to dinner in VENICE. Again, James failed to notice Wharton—she had then decided a new hat would impress him. When they met a third time and finally had a real conversation, neither could recall the year or the date, but she thought they suddenly felt as if they had always been friends. She attributed this to a similar sense of humor and of irony, so that they looked at any subject "like interarching search-lights" (*BG* 173).

In 1902, Edith Wharton's sister-in-law, Minnie CADWALADER JONES, sent James two volumes of Wharton's short stories, which he thought inferior to *The VALLEY OF DECISION,* her historical novel set in Italy. He wrote Mrs. Jones that he "would like to get hold of the little lady and pump the pure essence" of his "wisdom and experience into her. She *must* be tethered in native pastures, even if it reduces her to a back-yard in New York." At almost the same time, he wrote Edith Wharton, begging her to permit him to "admonish" her "in favour of the American subject. Don't pass it by—the immediate, the real, the only, the yours, the novelist's that it waits for . . . *Do New York!* The 1st-hand account is precious" (*Letters* 71). James hoped Wharton would "profit, be warned by my awful example of exile and ignorance" (Edel, IV, 23). Lewis terms James's plea "the wisest literary advice she received" (*EW* 127).

Edith Wharton's zest for travel sometimes alarmed James. In December 1908, he wrote Margaret White, his niece: "We have been having here lately the great and glorious pendulum in person, Mrs. Wharton, on her return oscillation." As Lewis observes, however, he was "disturbed by the rush and movement" of her life and characterized her visit in "mock-heroic" terms: "General eagle-pounces and eagle-flights of her deranging and desolating, ravaging, burning and destroying energy . . . the Angel of Devastation was the mildest name we knew her by." James said of Wharton's passion for travel that she

> . . . rode the whirlwind, she played with the storm, she laid waste whatever of the land the other raging elements had spared, she consumed in 15 days what would serve to support an ordinary Christian community (I mean to regulate and occupy and excite them) for about 10 years. Her powers of devastation are ineffable, her repudiation of repose absolutely tragic and she was never more brilliant and able and interesting [EW 247, 323].

He wrote to Mrs. Humphry WARD of Wharton's "dazzling, her incessant, braveries of far excursionism."

Both James and Wharton had an intense yearning for travel. In May 1904, according to Lewis, Edith and Teddy WHARTON appeared before Lamb House in a "shiny and resplendent new motorcar," a Panhard-Levassor purchased in Paris with, she told James, the proceeds from *The VALLEY OF DECISION.* They took a drive, and, gazing from the window, James responded that, with the proceeds of his last novel, *The Wings of the Dove,* he had purchased "a small go-cart, or hand-barrow" on which his guests' luggage was transported from the station. It needed painting, he continued, which he planned to do with the proceeds of his next novel (*EW* 130–31).

Wharton's portrait of James in *A BACKWARD GLANCE* is considered one of the finest ever written of him. She describes their early meeting, their travels and his sense that he had failed by only being able to depict older societies in his fiction and not the contemporary American scene. His talk with his intimates was like a "cobweb bridge flung from his mind to theirs, an invisible passage over which one knew that silver-footed ironies, veiled jokes, tiptoe malices, were stealing to explode a huge laugh at one's feet." She delighted in

his retelling of good jokes, upon which he would raise "an intricate superstructure of kindred nonsense." She recalls his visit to The MOUNT, when he would evoke his Emmet cousins, "the long train of ghosts flung with his enchanter's wand across the wide stage of the summer night . . . they glimmered at us through a series of disconnected ejaculations, epithets, allusions, parenthetical rectifications and restatements" until suddenly they would appear "sharp as an Ingres, dense as a Rembrandt" (*BG* 193–94). He took great pleasure in automobile outings over the New England countryside. His days at The Mount, especially in the company of what Wharton called their "inner group," Walter BERRY, Bay LODGE, Gaillard LAPSLEY, Robert NORTON and John HUGH SMITH, were the most cherished of her memories as she reconstructed the period in her autobiography. Henry James delighted in life at The Mount; he was surrounded, as he put it, "by every loveliness of nature, and every luxury of art, and treated with a benevolence that brings tears to my eyes" (*EW* 140).

In March 1907 Edith and Teddy Wharton made a "motor-flight" with James from Paris to Poitiers, Pau,

Charcoal sketch of Henry James (1912), John Singer Sargent. Wharton commissioned this drawing for herself, but disliked it and presented it to the subject (Courtesy Clifton Waller Barrett Library, Special Collections Department, University of Virginia)

Lourdes, through sections of the Pyrenees and Provence, and back through Lyons to Paris. The journey is the basis for the second section of Edith Wharton's 1908 travel book *A MOTOR-FLIGHT THROUGH FRANCE*. James then stayed with the Whartons for a month, writing Charles Eliot NORTON that "living in singularly well-appointed privacy in this fine old Rive Gauche quarter" was one of the "most agreeable times" he had ever had in Paris (*Letters* 115).

In 1911 Edith Wharton launched an effort to secure the NOBEL PRIZE for James. The time seemed propitious: the NEW YORK edition of his novels had been published, and he was at the peak of his achievement in fiction. The idea was supported by the British critic Edmond Gosse, a member of the English nominating committee, by Rudyard KIPLING, and by William Dean HOWELLS in America. Unfortunately, the 1911 prize went to a Belgian playwright, Maurice Maeterlinck, author of *The Bluebird*.

Edith Wharton also launched an ill-fated effort to raise the sum of $5,000 for James on the occasion of his 70th birthday in March 1913. Edmund Gosse had instigated an appeal in England for a portrait of James to be given to the National Portrait Gallery. When Edith Wharton learned of it, she realized Americans could not be asked to subscribe to a portrait for an English gallery, but believed it imperative to launch a similar appeal in America. She and Howells then cosigned an appeal; the money was to be given to James for a gift of his choice, such as the purchase of a piece of old furniture or other possession. The letter was sent to 40 people, including George VANDERBILT, Charles SCRIBNER, Minnie Cadwalader JONES, Robert GRANT, George Abbot James and others. It was through his friend George Abbot James that James's American nephews, Harry and Billy, learned of the scheme. Billy cabled the news to his uncle, who was exceedingly hurt and angry. He wrote a letter to Edith Wharton that "completely poisoned" a journey she was then making to Italy. The appeal was canceled. She was mortified at her part in the affair and deeply hurt at James's reaction. Lewis gives a full account of the unfortunate affair (*EW* 339–41).

Although he made his home in England from 1876 until his death in 1916, James did not become a British subject until 1915, when America refused to enter WORLD WAR I. To him the war signified the "plunge of civilization into this abyss of blood and darkness" (*NGC* 302). Although Wharton was also ashamed of her country, her protest took the form of public appeals for war relief and efforts to educate her fellow countrymen, by deed and word, about the tragic progress of the war in France and Belgium. She never considered relinquishing her own citizenship, but still tried to be understanding about his decision.

James suffered a stroke in December 1915 and died on February 28, 1916. Edith Wharton wrote Gaillard Lapsley that his close circle of friends must "keep together all the closer now, we few who had him at his best."

Jean du Breuil de Saint-Germain *See* BREUIL DE SAINT-GERMAIN, JEAN DU.

Jewett, Rutger Bleecker (1867–1935) One of Edith Wharton's favorite editors once APPLETON AND COMPANY became her principal publishers following their release of *THE REEF* (1912). Born in Ohio, Jewett was a son of Bishop Edward Hurt Jewett and Sophia Seymour Bleecker Miller. His mother came of old New York Dutch lineage; one of his great-uncles, Horatio Seymour, had been governor of New York, and another, Roscoe Conklin, a U.S. senator. He attended Hobart College and had been professor of Greek and Latin at the New York Military Academy before going into publishing. In 1911 he joined Appleton & Co. as vice president and editor in chief.

Jewett began working with Wharton in 1917, when J. H. Sears, the principal editor, became ill. He was not only astute about publishing trends in America but witty and sympathetic toward Wharton. He acted as her agent in negotiating for pre-publication serial rights of many of her novels that his firm published. The first project Jewett handled was *FRENCH WAYS AND THEIR MEANING*, two chapters of which had been serialized. He wrote Wharton that he hoped it might be possible to publish the volume of French articles in the autumn; it would be "one more good blow struck for France."

Jewett had an excellent understanding of the American market. Edith Wharton's 1915 account of her journeys to the front during World War I, *FIGHTING FRANCE, FROM DUNKERQUE TO BELFORT*, published by SCRIBNER'S, was regarded by many reviewers as a moving journalistic account of the triumph of the French spirit rather than a call to arms. The essays, focusing on the enduring spirit of the French and the massive atrocities France suffered, had induced a certain degree of critical amnesty. But when Wharton offered Jewett her war novel, *A SON AT THE FRONT*, in July 1919, he cabled, "War books dead in America," and advised delaying the novel five years, by which time conditions might be receptive. At present, he assured her, "the retail bookseller is gun shy and runs like a rabbit if you mention a war book to him or try to sell him anything that even suggests war in its title or subject matter." Edith Wharton resisted Jewett's advice, having been absorbed in the novel for a long time, but finally realized he was right. She put aside *A Son at the Front*. It was serialized in *SCRIBNER'S MAGAZINE* from December 1922 through September 1923 and then published by Scribner's (unpublished correspondence is in the BEINECKE LIBRARY, YALE UNIVERSITY). Jewett generously wrote her that it was "the best novel written by you or anyone else for years" (*EW* 456). Appleton's became her principal publisher, and Jewett her most enthusiastic promoter. He negotiated pre-publication serial, film, and dramatic rights for her novels and had a hand in publicizing them.

In December 1918, Sears wrote Edith Wharton that Jewett would be sailing to France on the *Adriatic* and would try to see her in Paris. He made a point of telling her that Jewett had attended to the placing of all her manuscripts serially, and that it was he who saw her books through the press. He became a personal friend, and over the years they often met in France. In 1928 and in 1930 he visited her at STE.-CLAIRE CHÂTEAU; Benstock notes that the latter was their sixth meeting in 11 years (*NGC* 422).

Appleton's published *The Marne* in 1918, which Jewett called "the most poignant story of the war which I have read" (*EW* 422). In early 1920 she was finishing *The* AGE OF INNOCENCE at a busy time, when she was preoccupied with furnishing two houses, leaving her apartment at 53 rue de Varenne, and leasing another temporary home in HYÈRES, as well as many other domestic matters. When she notified Jewett she had finished the novel, he wrote her, "You are a wonder. Do you marvel that I bow low before such energy?" (*EW* 428).

By 1932, when *The* GODS ARRIVE was published, Edith Wharton had become, in the words of Lewis, "something of an institution." However, the years of the Depression had led to a taste for what she called "bland nonsense" on the part of magazine editors, stories that would distract readers from the bitter realities surrounding them. She produced inferior, frothy stories. In time, her prestige declined and she became less of an "institution," having to engage in acrimonious bargaining (through Jewett) with magazine editors (*EW* 506–08). Her fiction failed to command high rates, however, and she complained rather unjustly that Appleton's was not advertising her work sufficiently. This was the same complaint she had made to Scribner's as early as 1899, on publication of her first volume of short stories, *The* GREATER INCLINATION.

In 1934, when the HEARST magazine *Cosmopolitan* asked for an outline of her proposed novel *The* BUCCANEERS, she was indignant and began searching for another agent, hurting the feelings of Jewett and of D. W. Hilman, chairman of Appleton's board, who noted how much she had earned from the publishing firm. During the two decades between 1914 and 1934, Appleton's had paid her about $580,000 in royalties, plus subsidiary rights. Including *The Buccaneers* and the collection GHOSTS, both published posthumously, the firm had brought out 16 novels, two works of nonfiction and five collections of short stories. The same year Jewett had a nervous breakdown from overwork (*EW* 508). He died in late January 1935; the cause was given in the *New York Times* as arteriosclerosis.

For further reading: Levine, "Discretion and Self Censorship in Wharton's Fiction: 'The Old Maid' and the Politics of Publishing."

Jones, Beatrix   Edith Wharton's niece; *see* FARRAND, BEATRIX JONES.

Jones, Frederic Rhinelander ("Freddy") (1846–1918) The eldest brother of Edith Wharton, Freddy graduated from Columbia College in 1865 with a "gentleman's degree" in fine arts. He later completed a master of arts degree and by 1872 was established in New York as a bookbinder (*NGC* 18, 30).

In 1870 he married Mary Cadwalader Rawle ("Minnie"—*see* JONES) of Philadelphia and, in 1872, became the father of Beatrix Jones, later FARRAND. As early as 1887, she had realized he was an adulterer, but they did not separate until 1892; they divorced in 1896 (*NGC* 81). After his father's death in 1882, his mother, Lucretia JONES, purchased a house on West 25th Street in New York. Lucretia took his side in the divorce and resented Minnie; Wharton sided with Minnie and became her affectionate, lifelong ally. Harry (*see* JONES, Henry Edward) legally adopted Beatrix at the time of the divorce in order to make sure she received her rightful portion of the Jones fortune. Lucretia then revised her will (*see* JONES, Lucretia Stevens Rhinelander). Frederic and Mary Jones lived in New York on East 18th St.; he visited his widowed mother daily. Their daughter, Beatrix, was devoted to her grandmother (*NGC* 44).

After his divorce, Frederic married his longtime lover, Elsie D. West. According to Benstock, during their travels in France together before they were married, he was known as "Mr. West" (*NGC* 82). She died in Paris in 1905. Frederic died there also, in 1918 at the age of 72.

Jones, George Frederic (1821–82)   Edith Wharton's father, the youngest of three surviving children of Edward Renshaw and Elizabeth Schermerhorn Jones. He graduated from Columbia College, where, according to Lewis, he followed a program titled "The Literature and Scientific Course." When he was 17, he and his father made a Grand Tour of EUROPE. It was his parents' house, along with the Raycie supper table, along Long Island Sound that Edith Wharton evoked in her novella FALSE DAWN; the house had a lawn sloping to the Sound. Jones's parents objected to his courtship of Lucretia Stevens RHINELANDER, youngest of four sisters; their father had died, and their uncle had mismanaged their property, leaving their mother and children poorer than they should have been. He persevered, however, in courting Lucretia, sailing to her home, Hell Gate Farm, across Long Island Sound in a rowboat with a mast rigged of oars and sails made of a quilt.

They were married October 17, 1844; Lucretia was 19 and George Frederic was 22 (*EW* 11–12). Their first child, Frederic Rhinelander Jones, was born in 1846; their second, Henry Edward (Harry—see JONES) in 1850 and their last, Edith Newbold, in 1862.

It is clear from *A* BACKWARD GLANCE that George Frederic was a loving and devoted father to Edith when she was a child. One of her earliest memories is of a walk up Fifth Avenue with him, her hand held in "the large safe

George Frederic Jones, Edith Wharton's father (date unknown)
(Courtesy Clifton Waller Barrett Library, Special Collections Department, University of Virginia)

hollow" of his, his head so far "aloft" she could not see his face. At that time, there were still plots of ground where cows grazed. In 1866, her father, who had suffered reverses in the New York real estate market, took his family to Europe for six years (*see* entries on EXPATRIATION and AMERICA). Upon the family's return to America, Edith Wharton entered the "kingdom" of her father's "gentleman's" library and read widely in history, literature, philosophy, poetry and travel. Her father was partial to arctic explorations (*BG* 64–76). In her memoir, Wharton stated that she believed he had a "rudimentary" love of poetry that would have developed further if he had anyone with whom to share it. "But my mother's matter-of-factness must have shrivelled any such buds of fancy." He encouraged her, however, to memorize Tennyson's *The Idylls of the King* (*EW* 5–6).

Between the ages of 10 and 18, Edith Wharton longed to return to Europe. In 1880, George Frederic's health was failing, and doctors believed he would benefit physically from a change of climate. In "LIFE AND I," Edith Wharton wrote of the close companionship she and her father enjoyed during the second trip,

My father, who had a vague enjoyment in "sight-seeing," unaccompanied by any artistic or intellectual curiosity, or any sense of the relations of things to each other, was delighted to take me about, & with our Ruskin in hand we explored each corner of Florence & Venice.

Wharton's father died at Cannes in 1882. She recalled in her autobiography his being paralyzed, and, years later, she was still haunted by "the look in his dear blue eyes, which had followed me so tenderly for nineteen years, and now tried to convey the goodbye messages he could not speak." She wrote that twice in her life she had been at the death-bed of someone she "dearly loved, who has vainly tried to say a last word to me; and I doubt if life holds a subtler anguish" (*BG* 88). The death of Walter BERRY was probably the other occasion.

There has been some question regarding the paternity of Edith Wharton, with rumors persisting that she was actually the daughter of her brothers' English tutor or the child of a Scottish nobleman. At least one of Wharton's close friends, Margaret ("Daisy") Terry CHANDLER, stated that she believed the rumors. A friend of Daisy's father, William R. Travers, father of Matilda GAY, believed Wharton's father was the tutor and insisted to his daughter that George Frederic Jones had known of her parentage yet agreed to consider the child his own and provide for her (*see* GENEALOGY, OF EDITH WHARTON). Benstock states that, in her old age, Beatrix FARRAND confirmed that Wharton had known the story but had "realized the entire unlikelihood of a happening of that sort." Benstock points out, however, that, in the light of her father's infidelities, Farrand had good reason to dismiss the rumours about her aunt (*NGC* 377).

Jones, Henry Stevens ("Harry") (1850–1922) Although 12 years older than his sister Edith, Harry Jones was close to her for most of his life. When the JONES family went to EUROPE for six years in 1866, he accompanied them in order to enter Trinity Hall College, Cambridge University, England, from which he received a bachelor of arts degree in 1872. He became engaged to Caroline Hunter, who was drowned in 1873 when the *Ville de Havre* sank. Edith Jones met Teddy WHARTON through Harry, who had been one of his Harvard friends and often visited PENCRAIG in NEWPORT. In 1888, when the Whartons shared the charter of the *VANADIS* for a Mediterranean cruise, both Harry and Frederic JONES, as co-executors of Edith's trust fund, advised them against going, but Teddy Wharton decided they should undertake the cruise. In September 1904 Harry, then living in Paris, came to America and stayed with the Whartons at The MOUNT. In 1906 he accompanied the Whartons on a motor trip through France. In 1907 the Whartons, who had been occupying the Paris apartment of Edith and George VANDERBILT, spent a fortnight in Harry's townhouse at 3, Place des États-Unis, on the Right Bank, before sailing back to America.

In 1911 he began living with a Russian-born countess, Anna Julia Tekla, and in 1913 he began making plans to marry her. He suddenly accused Wharton, who had only vaguely been aware of his liaison with the Countess Tekla, of being unkind to his prospective sister-in-law. According to Lewis, they resented what they thought was Edith's "stiff moral disapproval" of the relationship. The countess refused to allow Harry to see his sister for 10 years before his death. Harry's action coincided with Wharton's divorce plans; she was deeply wounded, as she had long relied on her attachment to Harry, since she was already estranged from their brother Frederic. Writing Bernard BERENSON of Harry's death, she said "he was the dearest of brothers to all my youth . . . my feeling is one of sadness at the years of lost affection & companionship, & all the reawakened memories of youth" (*Letters* 453). Harry and the countess were married in 1920. At his death two years later he bequeathed to her, according to Benstock, money that should have gone to Edith and to his niece Beatrix FARRAND, whom he had legally adopted (*NGC* 458).

Jones, Joshua A cousin of Edith Wharton's grandfather Edward Renshaw, Joshua Jones was an eccentric relative who left a substantial legacy to his nephews, nieces and cousins at his death in March 1888. Edith Wharton's portion was approximately $120,000, which was providential news, coming just as she and her husband Teddy had returned from a cruise aboard the chartered yacht *VANADIS*, which they had not really been able to afford (*EW* 59). In *A BACKWARD GLANCE* Wharton remarked that Joshua Jones had been a "miser and he nearly turned me into a spendthrift!" She reflected that, with all his economies, living in one room for many years in the New York Hotel, he would surely have disapproved of the form her gratitude took. She had learned, nevertheless, never to turn down a chance to do "something difficult and wonderful," but cautioned that the "risk should not be run for anything not really worth it" (*BG* 100–01).

Jones, Lucretia Stevens Rhinelander (1825–1901) The eldest of four daughters of Mary Stevens and William Frederic Rhinelander, Lucretia grew up at Hell Gate Farm on Long Island after her uncle mishandled her father's estate.

She and George FREDERIC JONES were married October 17, 1844, when she was 19 and he was 22 (*EW* 11–12). Their first child, Frederic Rhinelander, was born in 1846; their second, Henry Stevens (*see* JONES) in 1850 and their last, Edith Newbold, in 1862.

Edith Wharton credits her mother's English forebears for her insistence on speaking impeccable English at home. Lucretia was not altogether receptive, however, to her daughter's first attempt at fiction. Wharton tried her hand at a novel when she was only

Lucretia Stevens Rhinelander Jones, Edith Wharton's mother (date unknown) (Courtesy Clifton Waller Barrett Library, Special Collections Department, University of Virginia)

11. It began: " 'Oh, how do you do, Mrs. Brown?' said Mrs. Tompkins. 'If only I had known you were going to call I should have tidied up the drawing-room.' " When Edith Wharton showed it to her mother, Lucretia Jones responded, " 'Drawing-rooms are always tidy' " (*BG* 73). This icy response was so discouraging that Edith gave up fiction and turned to poetry. In 1878, when she was 16, her mother arranged for the private publication of a volume of poetry, *VERSES*.

Edith Wharton remembered her mother as a cold, haughty person, preoccupied with appearances and social rituals such as the custom of paying calls. She sent out wedding invitations omitting her daughter's name and was sarcastic when Edith, on the eve of marriage, questioned her about what would "happen" to her. She spent her last years in Paris, and, although she was in touch with her sons, her daughter rarely saw her.

Lucretia Jones died in Paris on June 1, 1901, having been in a coma for nearly a year. Edith Wharton was in LENOX at the time. According to Benstock, Lucretia left cash bequests to her two sons and ordered that her estate be divided equally among her three children. Unfortunately, women could not inherit legacies outright, which protected them against unscrupulous husbands, but worked against Edith Wharton, since her portion was held in a life trust that would have gone to Frederic on her death. Harry and Edith forced Frederic to resign as trustee; he was replaced by Teddy WHARTON. Edith never received the full monies due her (*NGC* 120). After her death, her niece, Beatrix FARRAND, contested Wharton's American will; Benstock gives a full account of the dispute (*NGC* 456–61).

Jones, Mary Cadwalader Rawle ("Minnie") (1850–1935)
A member of the distinguished Rawle and Cadwalader families of Philadelphia, she married Edith Wharton's brother Frederic in 1870; her daughter, Beatrix Jones FARRAND, was born in 1872. Frederic was unfaithful to her, which she realized as early as 1887. They did not actually separate, however, until 1892; they divorced in 1896 (*NGC* 81). She then took the name "Mrs. Cadwalader Jones." Benstock theorizes that she remained formally married because of societal taboos against divorce and because of their daughter.

The close attachment between Mary (called "Minnie") and Edith Wharton continued throughout their lives. After her divorce Minnie lived on East 11th Street in New York; her home was a meeting place for Henry JAMES and many others. She and her daughter also had a summer home at Bar Harbor, Reef Point (*see* entry on Beatrix Farrand). They lived together until the marriage of Beatrix to Max Farrand. In 1911, Minnie stayed with her cousin, a Mr. Cadwalader, in Scotland, as hostess; one of their guests was Henry James.

Minnie was an excellent proofreader and often acted as New York agent for Edith Wharton, handling negotiations for both articles and books. As she lived in New York, she could easily talk with editors and read proofs with no loss of delivery time.

During WORLD WAR I she chaired the New York committee formed to oversee the functions of the AMERICAN HOSTELS FOR REFUGEES Edith Wharton had founded to provide relief to the many Belgian refugees flooding into Paris after the Battle of the Marne and the devastating battle at Ypres (*EW* 371). It was one of three such committees in the United States; others were established in Paris.

Lewis states that although Edith Wharton was devoted to Minnie, her tone in her letters was sometimes impatient, "as to one whose thought processes were never as rapid or as lucid as they might be" (*Letters* 21). It could be said, however, that sometimes Edith's letters to Minnie about her travels are cast like an archive for Wharton's later travel accounts. For example, in 1917 she wrote from MOROCCO of the "fairy world" of Rabat, reached after a "wild flight across the desolate bled," and of touring the exhibition organized by General LYAUTEY, when the sultan galloped away with his guard "in scarlet tunics & green & white turbans, all on white horses."

In 1918, Edith Wharton wrote her friend Elizabeth CAMERON that "Minnie and Trix [Beatrix] make up to

me for my own wretched family, & all my thoughts & interests are with them. I never saw Minnie younger, braver, more gallant & altogether admirable than during the month of really hard work that she spent here with me." Despite the "bad knocks" Minnie had suffered, each one seemed to make her "more resolute to play her part to the full & to the end" (*Letters* 405). Her visits to Wharton continued after the war was over. In 1924, they spent some time at I TATTI with Bernard and Mary BERENSON, returning to the PAVILLON COLOMBE.

Wharton sometimes confided her discouragement about her own writing to Minnie. After *The MOTHER'S RECOMPENSE* was published to mixed reviews in 1925, she wrote Minnie, "As my work reaches its close, I feel so sure that it is either nothing, or far more than they know. And I wonder, a little desolately, which?" (*EW* 465).

For many years Wharton supplemented Minnie's income, providing a motorcar and chauffeur from the proceeds of her earnings. The 1929 stock market crash reduced the value of her New York real estate holdings, and she cut back on her two staffs of gardeners in PARIS and HYÈRES. Wharton wrote Gaillard LAPSLEY in 1933 that she had to keep on writing because, it she did not, "Minnie will have no motor—nor I either, much longer." She was also committed to continuing generous assistance to other friends in impoverished circumstances (*EW* 506–08).

Portrait of Mary Cadwalader Rawle c. 1865 by William Oliver Stone (Courtesy The Metropolitan Museum of Art. Gift of Mrs. Max Farrand and Mrs. Cadwalader Jones, 1953)

In 1935 Minnie, then in her early eighties, came to stay with Edith Wharton at the Pavillon Colombe, when she seemed well. She then went to ENGLAND and died suddenly in a London hotel. Beatrix Farrand was ill at the time in New York, and Max FARRAND was at the Huntington Library in California. Wharton handled all the arrangements and disposition of Minnie's effects. She was buried beside Mrs. Humphry WARD (*EW* 510–20).

Minnie Jones wrote part of a volume of reminiscences, *Lantern Slides,* which was published posthumously in 1937. It was privately printed by Berkeley UPDIKE, founder of the Merrymount Press. The dedication reads: "This book really belongs to my daughter and son-in-law, Beatrix and Max Farrand, for they pleased and teased me into writing it." The Farrands wrote an introduction explaining that Minnie had planned to take her story to the end of World War I, but that only five chapters had been completed at the time of her death. They remark that Wharton had encouraged her to undertake the volume, although during the writing of *A BACKWARD GLANCE* she herself had found "what difficulties bristled in making a book or reminiscences into a literary work."

The Farrands state that Wharton had offered to contribute an introduction, but, at the time of her own death, had only a few pencilled sentences. She had intended to say that Minnie "seems to lay her ear to each sentence sounding it to catch its beat. She would not consider this a merit or the reverse; it is simply her way of working. She has such a love of our English speech, such a sense of its rhythmic beauty, that she is forever trying to keep step with it as she goes on; and the attempt is not a labour, but an enchantment."

The completed chapters are about Minnie's childhood in Philadelphia, the Civil War, the family's journey to Savannah and Charleston in 1865 and return via Cuba, and a trip to Europe with her father, after her mother's death. She apparently met Frederic Rhinelander Jones aboard the Cunard liner *Scotia* in June 1869; he was traveling with some Newbold cousins who were already known to the Rawleses. He came to see them in Switzerland. In the spring of 1870 Minnie and Fred were married in a quiet ceremony at her Philadelphia home.

In the final chapter Minnie recalls her new sister-in-law: "a clever child with a mane of red-gold hair, always scribbling stories on any paper that came handy . . . to me she became closer than a sister of my own blood" (*Lantern Slides,* 121). Minnie also describes her walking tours in Switzerland and GERMANY with her husband.

Journal For Edith Wharton's journal of her 1888 Mediterranean cruise, *see* CRUISE OF THE VANADIS, THE. For her journal of her affair with Morton FULLERTON, *see* DIARY, 1907, "THE *LIFE APART.*"

"Journey, A" Short story published in *The GREATER INCLINATION* (Scribner's, 1899). It is a morbid tale in which a young couple are returning by rail to NEW YORK from Colorado, where the once charming, robust husband has been sent because of failing health. He dies along the way, but his wife conceals his demise, fearing they will be put off at a remote station. To one contemporary critic it was a "study in nervous tension" (*CR* 19). Lewis terms it a "macabre story" that may express Wharton's desires and fears about "ditching poor Teddy" (*EW* 85).

"Joy in the House" Short story published in *Nash's Pall Mall Magazine* (December 1932) and collected in *HUMAN NATURE* (D. Appleton, 1933). The ghost story concerns a wife, Christine Ansley, who has left Devons Ansley, her benevolent, paternalistic husband, for a lover, Jeffrey Lithgow, but who then returns home. Devons, his mother and her son tolerantly welcome her with flowers, proclaiming that there is now "joy in the house." Her husband believes the past can be denied and/or buried. Christine then learns from her lover's rejected wife, Mrs. Lithgow, that her lover committed suicide after her departure. She realizes she can never escape being tormented by his avenging spirit. White states that the story has a more "social orientation" than Wharton's ghost stories, representing "the web of lies as a social attitude" (103).

Joy of Living, The Translation of *Es lebe das Leben,* a tragic drama by Hermann SUDERMANN, which Edith Wharton reluctantly undertook in 1902 as a favor to Mrs. Patrick CAMPBELL, the actress, who had the rights to it. Mrs. Campbell failed to understand that the title was ironic and rejected the translation Edith Wharton proposed, "Long Live Life," calling it instead "The Joy of Living." The play opened under that title, which Edith Wharton though "comic," with Mrs. Campbell in the leading role. It failed on the stage, but when it was brought out by Scribner's in 1902, under the title *The Joy of Living,* it sold for many years.

Joyce, James (1882–1941) Irish novelist, poet and short-story writer. One of the great literary figures of the 20th century. Joyce was responsible for many innovations in the novel. He introduced the stream of consciousness technique, in which a character's thoughts and emotional reactions to the exterior world are represented in detail. His early short stories were published in *Dubliners* (1914). His major novels were the autobiographical *A Portrait of the Artist as a Young Man* (1916), *Ulysses* (1922), and *Finnegans Wake* (1922–1939). He wrote two collections of poetry, *Chamber Music* (1907) and *Pomes Penyeach* (1927), and a play, *Exiles* (1918).

Although both lived in Paris for many years, and consulted the same ophthalmologist, there is no evidence that Edith Wharton and Joyce ever met. There are several intersections between her literary world and that of Joyce, however. Grant Richards, first husband of her close friend Elisina TYLER, published his play *Exiles,* and his first volume of poetry, *Chamber Music,* was published because of a recommendation by Arthur SYMONS. Wharton did not, however, approve of the interior monologue as a fictional technique. In her 1934 essay "PERMANENT VALUES IN FICTION," she attacked Virginia WOOLF and Joyce for lack of form. Benstock observes that Wharton disliked "the cult of the self" she found in the fiction of Joyce and D. H. Lawrence (*NGC* 282), and abhorred the work of Joyce more than any other modern writer. The reason was not "prudishness," but fundamental disagreement with his concept of fiction (*NGC* 419).

Wharton read *Ulysses* in 1922, but wrote Bernard BERENSON in early 1923 that she found it a "welter of pornography (the rudest school-boy kind), and unformed and unimportant drivel" (*Letters* 461). Lewis argues that Wharton "struggled for years against what she regarded as the exaggerated claims" made for the book and was particularly skeptical "about the psychological authenticity of Molly Bloom's long concluding erotic monologue" (*EW* 8). Lewis suggests that the unpublished erotic "BEATRICE PALMATO" fragment may be the result of Wharton's conviction that she could surpass Joyce in depicting sensuality (*EW* 525).

For further reading: Fargnoli and Gillespie, *James Joyce A to Z: The Essential Reference to the Life and Work.*

Kate Spain An unfinished drama based on the story of Lizzie Borden, accused of two murders in 1892 and then acquitted. It became a short story, first appearing in *Story-Teller* as "Unconfessed Crime" in March 1936, and then as "CONFESSION," in *Hearst's International-Cosmopolitan* magazine in May 1936. It was then published in the collection entitled *The World Over* (Appleton's) in 1936.

"Kerfol" Short story published in SCRIBNER'S MAGAZINE in March 1916 and reprinted in XINGU AND OTHER STORIES (SCRIBNER'S, 1916). The story offers another instance of what White terms Edith Wharton's "protective" ghosts (69). The narrator, visiting a friend in Brittany, goes to see the house Kerfol, in the village of the same name, with the thought of buying it. It is considered the "most romantic house in Brittany." With its thick walls and narrow stairway, it suggests to him "a perspective of stern and cruel memories stretching away, like its own gray avenues, into a blur of darkness" (*CSS* II, 283). On trying to enter, he sees a strange little dog of a Chinese breed; later he sees several more, but they merely gaze at him passively as he circles the outside. He tells his hosts, the Lanrivains, he has seen no caretaker, only the dogs. Mme Lanrivain informs him they are the ghosts of Kerfol; there are no dogs at the house now. He learns from M. Lanrivain of the shocking events that took place at Kerfol in the early 17th century, recorded in *A History of the Assizes of the Duchy of Brittany, Quimper, 1702*.

The tale concerns the murder trial of a young wife, Anne de Cornault. She tells the judges she was married by her father, as a young woman, to Yves de Cornault, 60 years old, the lord of Kerfol. Although she was not allowed to leave home, her husband brought her many presents, including a necklace of emeralds, pearls and rubies strung on a gold chain, and a valuable small brown dog from China. She later discovered the body of Yves de Cornault, covered in blood. An ancestor of M. Lanrivain was arrested for the crime. Further investigation reveals that Yves had kept his young wife a virtual prisoner. Yves's aunt had invited her to go on a pilgrimage with her; in the course of it she had met young Hervé Lanrivain and appealed to him to take her away. She gave him her necklace, which Yves then used to strangle her little dog, causing her to fear for her life. She had acquired several other dogs, and Yves had strangled each one.

One night she tried to slip out to meet Hervé; her husband heard the latch, screamed and fell. She found his body, covered in blood, with dog bites, murdered by the ghosts of the dogs he had killed. Hervé, standing outside, was accused of the murder but exonerated. The patriarchal judges refused to believe Anne, insisting her story proved nothing except that, although she knew her husband disliked dogs, she "ignored this dislike." She was handed over to her husband's family, who kept her locked up at Kerfol until she died many years later, a "harmless madwoman." Lanrivain was set free, went to Paris and joined the austere Jansenists, an intellectual Roman Catholic order that was eventually banished from France but defended by Blaise Pascal.

The *New York Times* reviewer praised the "innumerable, skillful little touches which make person, situation or scene real and vivid to the reader" and recommended the tale for "careful study on the part of those interested in the art of short-story writing" (*CR* 227–28).

For further reading: Killoran, "Pascal, Bronte, and 'Kerfol': The Horrors of a Foolish Quartet."

Kinnicutt, Dr. Francis Parker A leading NEW YORK physician, he had married the daughter of a banker and lived in a grand style, summering at LENOX in Deepdene Cottage. A general practitioner, he had been Teddy WHARTON's personal family physician as of about 1899. In June 1909, when Teddy complained of many aches and pains, Dr. Kinnicutt suggested that his trouble was of mental, not organic, origin. During the summer Teddy's behavior became "exalted," or manic, as long as he was functioning as Edith Wharton's estate trustee or planning future projects at The MOUNT. He also speculated with his wife's money, converting her holdings into cash and purchasing an apartment in Boston, where he had established a young woman as his mistress. Edith Wharton knew nothing of these activities until several months later. Dr. Kinnicutt, however, having talked with Teddy in Lenox during the summer, rightly worried that a return to PARIS, where he felt ill at ease, would bring on a bout of depression—which happened in November 1909. Teddy began making restitution, and Wharton reported the whole business to Dr. Kinnicutt. In early 1910 Teddy entered a Swiss sanatorium for treatment and recovered enough to leave, in October, for a world tour with the Whartons' family friend Johnson Morton, which Edith Wharton offered to underwrite. As Dr. Kinnicutt had anticipated, however, Teddy continued to decline mentally, and the Whartons were divorced in 1913.

On the publication of *ETHAN FROME* in September 1913, Dr. Kinnicutt wrote Edith Wharton that it was a "classic" that would be "read and re-read with pleasure and instruction" (*EW* 94, 267–93, *passim*).

Kipling, Rudyard (1865–1936) English novelist, poet and short-story writer. He was born in India of English parents, who took him to England when he was six. He returned to India when he was 17. His most popular works include *Barrack-Room Ballads* (1892), *The Light That Failed* (1890), *The Jungle Book* (1894), and *Just So Stories* (1902). He glorified British imperialism, which antagonized many critics, and interpreted India and army life. In 1892 he married an American girl, Carrie Balestier, in London; Henry JAMES escorted Carrie, whose father was deceased. Kipling and his family settled in Brattleboro, Vermont, and lived there for the next five years, then returning to England. In 1899, while he and his family were on a visit to New York, his daughter Josephine, 7, died of pneumonia, and Kipling was gravely ill with it. He regarded America with bitterness after that, though he was more popular than any other writer in the United States, with the exception of Mark Twain. In 1907 he became England's first Noble Prize winner for literature.

In 1915, when Edith Wharton was writing the articles for *SCRIBNER'S MAGAZINE* that would later be pub-

lished as *FIGHTING FRANCE, FROM DUNKERQUE TO BELFORT*, she suggested "France at War" as a title. The editor, Edward BURLINGAME, replied that Kipling had chosen that title and asked her for a new one, explaining, "He has an undoubted priority" (letter September 17, 1915, from Burlingame to Wharton, Scribner Archive, Princeton). *France at War*, a slender volume, was published in 1915, consisting of six articles from the London *Daily Telegraph* and the *New York Post*.

In 1915 Wharton asked Kipling for a contribution to *The BOOK OF THE HOMELESS*. He declined, saying he was unable to write during the war, a response she resented very much (*EW* 380). His son, John, was wounded in the Battle of Loos in September 1915; his death was not confirmed for two years. Kipling paid a British gardener to sound the Last Post at the Menin Gate every night in remembrance, a rite that continued until 1940 and the German occupation of France.

In 1924 Wilbur Cross wrote an essay pairing Kipling and Wharton for the *Bookman* as leading contemporary novelists. She pronounced his essay "very kindly meant but not nearly as good as Mrs. Gerould's" (*EW* 459–60) (*See* GEROULD, Katherine.)

In 1927, Wharton mentioned a recent address by Kipling in her essay "*The GREAT AMERICAN NOVEL*." He had discussed certain classic works that had undergone a metamorphosis in public memory, such as *Gulliver's Travels*, a biting satire that later became "one of the favorites of the nursery" (*UCW* 152).

A friend of Wharton's, Count Robert d'HUMIÈRES, was Kipling's French translator.

Ladies' Home Journal, The Women's magazine founded in 1883 by C. H. K. Curtis, E. W. Bok was the editor from 1889 until 1920; he encouraged articles about social reform and aesthetic improvements in urban life and obtained famous contributors. Edith Wharton's article "Is There a New Frenchwoman?" was published in the magazine in April 1917; a revised version, "The New Frenchwoman," appeared in FRENCH WAYS AND THEIR MEANING (1919). The article made clear Wharton's attitude toward the economic, social and intellectual plight of American women as opposed to their French counterparts.

In 1923 Rutger B. JEWETT placed the novella FALSE DAWN with the magazine, getting $5,500 for it (*EW* 444). It ran in November. In May 1924 another novella in the group, *The* SPARK, was published. The editor turned down The OLD MAID, a companion novella, saying it was a "bit too vigorous for us" (*EW* 435).

Three of Wharton's short stories appeared in the magazine: "ATROPHY" in November 1927, followed by "Mr. JONES" in 1928. In 1930 JEWETT sold "DIAGNOSIS" to the magazine for $3,000. According to Benstock, this was the highest price Wharton ever received for short fiction. *The* SATURDAY EVENING POST paid the same price for "POMEGRANATE SEED" in 1931 (*NGC* 425).

Wharton's autobiography, *A* BACKWARD GLANCE, was also published in the magazine in 1933 and 1934. She had contracted several years earlier for a fee of $25,000. Loring Schuyler, the editor, later tried to reduce the amount because the magazine was having difficulties during the depression. When Jewett reported the news to Wharton, she was indignant, and wrote that she would "neither take back the manuscript nor accept a lower price for it." The magazine, she continued, might be "hard up, but so am I, and I imagine that they have larger funds to draw upon than I have." She threatened to sue, and Schuyler yielded (*EW* 507).

"Lady's Maid's Bell, The" Edith Wharton's first published ghost story, it appeared in SCRIBNER'S MAGAZINE in November 1902 and was collected in *The* DESCENT OF MAN AND OTHER STORIES (Scribner's, 1904). In some respects the story is a puzzling one. It is told by a working woman, Hartley, who has recovered from typhoid fever and been recommended for a position as a lady's maid with a young semi-invalid, Mrs. Brympton, who lives year-round at her country estate on the Hudson River.

Her husband is said to be seldom at home; their children have died. On arrival, Hartley sees a thin, pale woman with a dark gown and apron down a hallway in the servants' quarters. Her presence is never explained, but Hartley deduces that she must be the ghost of Emma Saxon, Mrs. Brympton's former maid, who had died a year earlier. In the interim there have been four other maids, none of whom could bear to stay. The bell for the lady's maid only rings in the middle of the night; otherwise, Mrs. Brympton sends the housemaid, Agnes, to fetch Hartley.

Mr. Brympton's rare visits disrupt the household staff, who are clearly terrified of him and devoted to his wife. When he is away, a neighbor, Mr. Ranford, frequently calls on Mrs. Brympton. During one of her husband's absences, Hartley is summoned by what she takes to be the phantom of Emma Saxon to follow her through the woods on a mysterious and unexplained errand to the home of Mr. Ranford. She faints at his house and is driven back home.

That night Hartley hears the faint noise of a door opening and closing down below. In the middle of the night she thinks her mistress has rung for her and rushes to her room, hearing, en route, a latchkey stealthily turning in the front door of the house. Mrs. Brympton insists she has not rung, but at the news that Hartley believes Mr. Brympton has entered the house, she faints. He marches in from the snow, muttering that he is going to meet "a friend" in the dressing room. Hartley and Mr. Brympton hear a noise from within the dressing room and he flings her door open only to find the ghost of Emma Saxon stating at them, the rest of the room being dark. Mrs. Brympton then dies. Mr. Ranford attends the funeral, pale and distraught, and Mr. Brympton drives away, leaving the house to the servants.

Although the reviewer for the *Critic* called it an "admirable" ghost story, the critic for the *Bookman* did not find the story convincing and the reviewer for the *Athenæum* found it "fantastic" and puzzling.

For further reading: Fedorko, "Edith Wharton's Haunted Fiction: 'The Lady's Maid's Bell' and *The House of Mirth*"; Killoran, "Sexuality and Abnormal Psychology in Edith Wharton's 'The Lady's Maid's Bell' "; Stengel, "Edith Wharton Rings 'The Lady's Maid's Bell' "; Wilson-Jordan, "Telling the Story That Can't Be Told: Hartley's Role as Dis-eased Narrator in 'The Lady's Maid's Bell.' "

"Lady's Maid's Bell, The" (teleplay, 1983) *See* Appendix II.

La Forest-Divonne, Philomène de (1887–?) Countess Philomène de La Forest-Divonne was a member of one of the principal ducal families of France and a well-known writer. Under the pseudonym Claude Silve she wrote a novel called *BÉNÉDICTION*, which won a noted French literary prize, the *Prix Fémina*, in 1935. Edith Wharton urged APPLETON to publish the English translation of it by Robert NORTON, which they did. It appeared in 1936 with a foreword by Edith Wharton.

Philomène was one of Wharton's closest friends in her last years. She visited her one rainy afternoon in the autumn of 1936 at the PAVILLON COLOMBE, and Wharton brought out a scrapbook of press clippings prepared by Anna BAHLMANN. Philomène wrote that she cherished that hour when her "pale hand . . . turned the leaves of the album. . . . Her work, her art, her fame, were the gold in it, and as the story grew the gleam absorbed it all. Sitting by her side . . . I felt the presence of a power at rest, controlled by a lonely and generous spirit. It was a spirit that could take nothing from another, but it gave and gave to the end." Benstock calls her evocation of Wharton that afternoon "the most eloquent ever written" (*NGC* 454).

Philomène dedicated her 1948 novel *Eastward in Eden* to Wharton: "To the dear and great memory of *EDITH WHARTON* to whom this book owes its inspiration." In a prefatory note she also expressed "grateful acknowledgements" to Bernard BERENSON, "who, by introducing her to the real Sablomine, provided the setting for this story."

For further reading: Lubbock, *Portrait of Edith Wharton,* 208–09; 212–15.

Lamb House The home of Henry JAMES in Rye, Sussex, England. The Whartons—or at times Edith alone—often visited James there. As she described it in her autobiography, her arrival would bring a sense of "joyous liberation." James would come to the car, "uttering cries of mock amazement and mock humility at the undeserved honour" of the visit, pause for a "hug and the two solemn kisses executed in the middle of the hall rug," and then escort her through the house. Lamb House, "the best of its sober and stately sort in the town," was a small Georgian house with books, old prints in the white-paneled hall, an oak-paneled morning-room, enclosed garden with mulberry tree, and "garden-room" with a high ceiling and windows overlooking two streets, where the housemaid would serve tea (*BG* 244–47).

Lamb House, Rye, 1937, garden view. The garden room is to the right (Courtesy Clifton Waller Barrett Library, Special Collections Department, University of Virginia)

James was looked after by two or three long-time servants. He enjoyed having one or two guests for meals, but, as Edith Wharton recalled in *A BACKWARD GLANCE*, they were marked by "anxious frugality"; he was haunted by the "spectre of impoverishment," serving pies and puddings that had been partially consumed at the previous meal, worrying that he might be thought "rich, worldly or luxurious," and apologizing for his food.

Nevertheless, she wrote, her "richest hours" were spent under his roof. When she stayed at Lamb House, both she and James would work privately in the morning; at one o'clock they would stroll down the main street before luncheon, and, after luncheon, motor through the countryside to visit such places as Bodiam Castle. He did not keep a car, and excursions in his guests' vehicles were a source of great pleasure (*BG* 243–49).

After his death in 1916, Robert NORTON, a mutual friend of both James and Edith Wharton, lived in the house. Later, it was inhabited by E. F. Benson, brother of Arthur Benson, also a friend of both. E. F. Benson immortalized the house and the town of Rye in his series of "Lucia" novels. During World War II the garden room was destroyed, but the house itself still stands and may be visited.

"Lamp of Psyche, The"   Short story published in *SCRIBNER'S MAGAZINE* in October 1895 but not collected. The title comes from the myth of Cupid and Psyche. Psyche is married to Cupid, the god of love, whom she has never seen, since he only visits her at night. They dwell in a magnificent palace in a beautiful garden. One night, at her sister's urging, she hides a lamp and shines it on him, revealing his true self. At once the palace and gardens vanish and Cupid flies away, observing that love cannot dwell with suspicion.

Delia Benson Corbett, who has been bored with her first husband, had long loved an older bachelor, Laurence Corbett, kindly, cosmopolitan and well-traveled. She conceals her emotions until after her first husband's death. She and Corbett marry and live in perfect bliss and mutual devotion, dwelling in his PARIS townhouse, which is "framed for noble leisure."

She takes her husband back across the Atlantic to Boston to meet her aunt, Mrs. Mary Mason Hayne, a brisk, wealthy philanthropist in an austere townhouse on Mount Vernon Street, Beacon Hill. One day Aunt Mary illuminates Corbett's past by means of a "lamp" of inquiry directed at Delia, asking whether Laurence had seen any active service in the Civil War. She tells her aunt coldly she doesn't know and had never asked him, but the question eats at her until she confronts Laurence. He has brought her an antique miniature, under cracked crystal, of a Union officer, which he has come across in a shop. This provokes her to ask about his service. Had he, perhaps, been in poor health and unable to serve? No, he had enjoyed robust health

since having the measles at the age of twelve. He admits he stayed at home, but insists he doesn't know why, though no doubt he had "excellent reasons" at the time. She accuses him of being a coward, since he was neither "lame, deaf, blind, nor ill."

Her love for him cannot endure this illumination but has "undergone a modification which the years were not to efface." Her ideal of him has been "shivered like the crystal above the miniature of the warrior of Chancellorsville." She has the crystal in the miniature replaced by glass, which "cost less and looked equally well," and, for the passion once felt for her husband, substitutes "a tolerant affection which possessed precisely the same advantages" (*CSS* I, 57).

Although Edward BURLINGAME wanted to include the story in the 1899 collection *The GREATER INCLINATION*, Edith Wharton refused, saying it had been written "at the top of my voice" (*EW* 86).

Lewis points out that she "playfully" incorporated the name of a Jones relative, Mary Mason (Mrs. Isaac) Jones, in the story. Mrs. Manson MINGOTT in *The AGE OF INNOCENCE* was also modeled on Aunt Mary, "shrewd, overwhelming, profoundly benevolent." She had shocked Old New York by building a Parisian-style mansion on Fifth Avenue between 57th and 58th Streets (*EW* 13).

Landers, Fred   *See MOTHER'S RECOMPENSE, THE.*

Land's End   In 1893, Edith Wharton used part of her legacy from her cousin Joshua JONES to purchase Land's End, a wooden house on Ledge Road, NEWPORT, on a half-acre of rocky cliff at the easternmost tip of Rhode Island, for $80,000. According to Lewis, she was attempting to distance herself from her mother, who lived at PENCRAIG. She and her husband laid out a circular court surrounded by hedges and trellises to lend dignity to the exterior.

The purchase of Land's End led indirectly to Edith Wharton's first book of nonfiction. She recalled in her autobiography that she and her husband invited Ogden CODMAN, then a "clever young Boston architect" from a wealthy family, to assist in altering and redecorating the house. This was considered somewhat eccentric, since "architects of that day looked down on house-decoration as a branch of dress-making" (*BG* 107). Codman had been educated in Europe and shared with Edith Wharton a distance for Victorian velvet-covered tables displaying trinkets and overstuffed upholstery. He believed, as she did, that interior decoration of private homes should be "simple and architectural . . . the interior of a house is as much a part of its organic structure as the outside; . . . its treatment ought to be based on the right proportion, balance of door and window spacing and simple, unconfused lines" (*BG* 106–07).

Even Wharton is unclear how they began working on a book together; she writes, "finding that we had the same views we drifted, I hardly know how, toward the notion of putting them into a book." They worked out their argument, and sat down to begin, "only to discover that neither of us knew how to write!" She found this deficiency excusable in an architect but discouraging to a "young woman who had in her desk a large collection of blank verse dramas and manuscripts fiction." A young lawyer, who was both friend and distant cousin—Walter BERRY—came to their rescue; Wharton describes him as possessing an "exceptionally sensitive literary instinct." He laughed at her "lumpy pages," said, "Come, let's see what can be done," and began to "try to model the lump into a book." She states that through the process of his editing "I had been taught whatever I know about the writing of clear concise English." (*BG* 106–11).

Paul and Minnie BOURGET were among the first and most distinguished guests at Land's End. In the autumn of 1893 Paul, a prominent French novelist, was working on *Outre-Mer: Impressions of America* (1895), a volume of essays about America originally written for the New York *Herald* and first published in France. After attending the World's Columbian Exposition in Chicago, he and his wife came to Newport to write, as Edith Wharton put it, his "fashionable watering-place" article. They were immediately invited to lunch by the Whartons, to whom they had been given a letter of introduction by a cousin of Teddy WHARTON's mother.

Although Edith Wharton loved the house, she found the climate depressing, and she became increasingly tired of what her friend "Bay" LODGE called "the philistine-plutocrat atmosphere" of Newport (*EW* 68–81). In 1899, she and her husband began searching for property in the fashionable summer resort of LENOX, Massachusetts, where his mother had a home, Pine Acre. They purchased a 113-acre farm there and built The MOUNT, finished by 1902. Her "first real home," it was named for Wharton's great-grandfather's estate. Land's End was sold in 1903 to Eleanor Beeckman, wife of Robert Livingston Beeckman, for $122,500.

Lansing, Nick *See GLIMPSES OF THE MOON, THE*

Lansing, Susy Branch *See GLIMPSES OF THE MOON, THE*

Lapsley, Gaillard (1871–1949) A don at Trinity College, Cambridge, Gaillard (pronounced "Gillyard") Lapsley was originally from NEW ENGLAND. He graduated from Harvard, then went to Cambridge University to do graduate study in medieval English history, and stayed on to teach in that field. He and Edith Wharton met in 1904; Lewis states that by then he was solidly established as a historian. Their friendship continued throughout her life, and she invited him to be her literary executor.

He often visited at The MOUNT, as did the other men in her inner circle: the novelist Henry JAMES, Robert NORTON, a landscape painter; John HUGH SMITH, a banker; Percy LUBBOCK, a writer and critic; and Howard STURGIS, a charming, eccentric man of letters and novelist. Wharton saw a great deal of Lapsley, both in ENGLAND and in FRANCE, when she began staying in the FAUBOURG ST.-GERMAIN in PARIS during the winter and early spring months. In April 1907, she, Henry James and Lapsley made an excursion from Paris to NOHANT, home of George SAND. The previous month, Edith and Teddy Wharton and Henry James had made a more extensive motor tour of France, a journey on which the second part of *A MOTOR-FLIGHT THROUGH FRANCE* is based. In April 1914 she, Percy Lubbock and Lapsley embarked on a trip to NORTH AFRICA, driven in her motorcar, but Lapsley became ill and had to return to England.

WORLD WAR I began that summer, and Lapsley, in Cambridge, shared her horror of it. In November 1915, she wrote him from France, "*My* sense is completely of living again in the year 1000, with the last trump imminent" (*Letters,* 342). She urged him to come to Paris for a visit while he could, saying people who were fond of each other should be together when they could: "Do come, my dear, and let us warm both hands a little at the good fire of our old affection for each other" (*EW* 370).

During the 1920s and 1930s, Edith Wharton usually had winter house parties at HYÈRES, at STE.-CLAIRE CHÂTEAU; Lapsley, Norton, and Hugh Smith were regular guests.

As early as 1923, during evenings at Edith Wharton's home near Paris, the PAVILLON COLOMBE, she and Lapsley had discussed editing an anthology of love poems. Together with Norton, they edited *ETERNAL PASSION IN ENGLISH POETRY*, which was published posthumously in 1939. Lapsley also wrote the introduction to *The BUCCANEERS*, Edith Wharton's unfinished last novel, published posthumously in 1938. In addition, he wrote several books, including *The America of Today* (1919), *The County Palatine of Durham; A Study in Constitutional History* (1924) and *An Essay on the Origins of the House of Commons* (1925).

Partly out of gratitude to YALE UNIVERSITY, which in 1923 bestowed on her an honorary doctor of letters degree, Wharton asked Lapsley to donate her "literary correspondence" to Yale. The BEINECKE LIBRARY now has more than 50,000 items related to Edith Wharton in many categories. Lapsley invited Percy Lubbock to write a memoir of Wharton, a decision which has puzzled some biographers because of a rift in Wharton's friendship with Lubbock (*see* entry on LUBBOCK, Percy).

It was Edith Wharton's wish that John Hugh Smith, Robert Norton and Gaillard Lapsley be among her pallbearers.

For further reading: Goodman, *Edith Wharton's Inner Circle.*

Gaillard Lapsley, at Trinity College, Cambridge. (Florence, Berenson Archive, reproduced by permission of the President and Fellows of Harvard College)

"Last Asset, The" Short story published in *SCRIBNER'S MAGAZINE* in August 1904 and collected in *TALES OF MEN AND GHOSTS*. Set in PARIS, the story is based on a situation that is a reversal of the arranged marriage. It is told by a narrator or "reflector," the newspaper correspondent Paul Garnett, who has, for two years, exchanged pleasantries with a shabby old gentleman who takes his meals in the same café.

Mrs. Newell, an American-born international society woman he knows, suddenly summons him to a meeting at the Ritz, at which she reveals her daughter Hermione's engagement to a young French count; she has managed it by shamelessly using her friends to further her daughter's prospects. A legacy from a mysterious "aunt" has provided the dowry, but Garnett suspects Mrs. Newell's unsavory friend, Baron Schenkelderff, has actually underwritten it.

The only obstacle is that Hermione's estranged father, Mr. Newell, who is living alone in Paris in poverty, must be produced; his parents won't allow the marriage unless her parents make an appearance together at the wedding as evidence of her father's formal consent and the fact that they are not divorced. Garnett discovers that the old gentleman from the café is Mr. Samuel Newell, Hermione's "last asset," and that the match depends on his being able to persuade him to appear. Mr. Newell deplores the wedding scene and "his own share in it," but finally realizes that Hermione's marriage may be sanctified despite her mother's "base connivances" and that it draws "fragrance from corruption."

Benstock believes the story sheds light on the strange omission of Wharton's own maiden name from the wedding invitation her mother sent in 1885: "Mrs. George Frederic Jones requests the honour of your presence at the marriage of her daughter to Mr. Edward R. Wharton, at Trinity Chapel . . ." Hermione and Edith Jones were both age 23 in 1885, somewhat old for the marriage market. She suggests that Hermione's invitation, in which her mother's name is omitted but her father's included, is an oblique com-

Drawn by Raymond M. Crosby.

As Hermione entered the vestibule, he advanced quietly to meet her.—Page 187.

Illustration by Raymond Crosby for the short story "The Last Asset" (1904) (Courtesy Scribner, a division of Simon & Schuster)

ment on Edith's wish that her father could have been present at her own wedding (*NGC* 56). He might then have been the dominant parent and protected her.

White calls the story "the most Jamesian of Wharton's first-rate tales" in its focus on the international scene, the transformation of Hermione into a financial investment, and the unpalatable baron, who regards Mrs. Newell as his own social "last asset" (*Edith Wharton: A Study of the Short Fiction,* 78).

"Last Giustiniani, The"   The first poem published by Edith Wharton, when she was 27. It was accepted by Edward BURLINGAME for *SCRIBNER'S MAGAZINE* and published in October 1889. She received a check for $20.

The poem is based on a Venetian legend in which the last surviving male of a noble family is released from his vows as a monk to marry. He addresses his bride, saying that previously all women for him had been embodied in the figure of the Virgin, and he is uncertain about earthly love. He entreats her to "invest your slim young form with majesty / As when, in those calm bridal clothes arrayed,' You stood before me, and I was afraid." Lewis terms it a "slender portion of historical romance" (*EW* 60).

Leath, Anna   *See REEF, THE*

Leath, Effie   *See REEF, THE*

Leath, Owen   *See REEF, THE*

Lebel, Mme.   *See SON AT THE FRONT, A*

Lee, Vernon (1856–1935)   Vernon Lee was the pseudonym of Violet Paget, a British writer living in ITALY, whose *Studies of the Eighteenth Century in Italy* (London: Unwin, 1887) Edith Wharton had known and admired before she first met her in Lee's villa, Il Palmerino, in

Maiano, near Florence, in 1894. Wharton had been given a letter of introduction to her by the French novelist Paul BOURGET. Eugene Lee-Hamilton, Lee's invalid half-brother, lived with her. He had served as a secretary in the British Embassy in Paris during the Franco-Prussian War but was now incapacitated by a nervous condition and spent his days in bed or on a stretcher. He later recovered and visited the Whartons at LAND'S END in NEWPORT. He had read one of Edith Wharton's poem in *SCRIBNER'S MAGAZINE* and persuaded his sister to invite her to call on them.

Vernon Lee served as a mentor to Edith Wharton. She reviewed *The VALLEY OF DECISION* (in Italian) in *La Cultura,* which brought the following warm response from Edith Wharton:

> To tell you what pleasure your article on my book has given me I should have to go back to the days "quand j'avais vingt ans et le coeur me battait"—when your *Euphorion* and the *Eighteenth Century Studies* [sic] were letting me into that wonder world of Italy which I had loved since my childhood without having the key to it [Christine Richards, letter to the *Times Literary Supplement,* Sept. 10, 1993].

In her memoir *A BACKWARD GLANCE,* Edith Wharton describes her friendship with Lee and states that her works on Italy were among her "best-loved companions of the road" (*BG* 130).

She referred to Lee as one of the three great women talkers she had ever known, the others being the Neapolitan journalist and novelist Matilde Serao and the French poet Comtesse Anna de NOAILLES (*BG* 130–32). Wharton dedicated *ITALIAN VILLAS AND THEIR GARDENS* to Lee: "To Vernon Lee, who, better than any one else, has understood and interpreted the garden-magic of Italy." Lee had taken a great interest in the book and gained admission for Wharton to many private villas near Florence she otherwise would not have been able to visit. Lewis states that Lee was mannish in appearance and had lesbian inclinations of which Edith Wharton seemed unaware (*EW* 72).

Lee published travel articles in *Macmillan's Magazine, HARPER'S MAGAZINE* and other literary periodicals. In some ways she was more attuned to her fellow travelers' tastes than Edith Wharton. She argued that tourists should not be looked down upon merely because they are tourists, but only if they have arrived in a country without having visited it in "fancy" first: "Honor the tourist; he walks in a halo of romance." She does not mean that he has simply read about a place in a guidebook, but that he has thoroughly internalized it from paintings and literary references, even to the point of making a mental collage. If "the town of our building" does not tally with reality, it will slowly dissolve, "leaving sometimes airy splendors of itself hanging to the solid structures of its prosaic rival" (Lee, "On Modern Travelling," *Littell's Living Age*, March 10, 1894, 634–639). Lee possessed an almost encyclopedic knowledge of Italian life and history.

Lee-Hamilton, Eugene   *See* SONNETS OF THE WINGLESS HOURS, THE.

"Legend, The"   Short story first published in *SCRIBNER'S MAGAZINE* in March 1910 and reprinted in *TALES OF MEN AND GHOSTS* (SCRIBNER'S, 1910). It is a satire on literary cults. As it opens, the narrator, Arthur Bernald, learns from a physician friend, Bob Wade, that he has treated a gentleman who has collapsed of heat prostration in Central Park. He calls himself "John Winterman" but seems tentative about his identity. Winterman is living in a small bungalow owned by the doctor but built originally for his brother Howland, a plodding but persistent writer. Doctor Wade wants Howland to evaluate Winterman's manuscript. Howland has been working on a tedious study of John Pellerin, a prominent intellectual who had disappeared 25 years earlier; Bernald has also been writing on Pellerin and has a better grasp of his theories. He thinks of Howland sarcastically as "The Interpreter." When he meets Winterman, Bernald begins to wonder, based on his conversation and ideas, whether he might not, in fact, be John Pellerin. Winterman's conversation is, to Bernald, "as good as Pellerin"; in fact, it "*is* Pellerin." Winterman admits his true identity.

John Pellerin had disappeared and then returned as Winterman to see what the world had "made of him." Howland, meanwhile, has read Winterman's manuscript and identified the ideas in it as those of Pellerin, but decides Winterman has plagiarized them. As "Winterman," Pellerin is lionized by the ladies in a literary society but not identified; he finally disappears again. The story has echoes of "XINGU," which also mocks the willingness of pseudo-literary followers to espouse a vague movement or philosophical cult of which they actually know nothing.

Legion of Honor   Edith Wharton was made a CHEVALIER OF THE FRENCH LEGION OF HONOR on March 28, 1916. She received so many letters of congratulations she fled to HYÈRES, asking her friend Elizabeth ("Lizzie") CAMERON to open her mail and summarize the important personal and business correspondence (*see* Price, *The End of the Age of Innocence: Edith Wharton and the First World War*).

Lenox (Massachusetts)   Fashionable town in the Berkshires where Teddy WHARTON's mother had a country home, Pine Acre. It was here that wealthy families began to create large country estates, particularly in the later 19th century. Nathaniel Hawthorne had completed *The House of the Seven Gables* in Lenox, and Herman Melville's Arrowhead farm was in nearby Pittsfield, giving the Berkshires a strong literary heritage. By the turn of the century, Lenox was known as the "inland NEWPORT."

As early as 1899 the Whartons considered selling their Newport home, LAND'S END, and building a country home in Lenox. They looked at property for some time, and in 1901 they acquired Laurel Lake Farm and began building The MOUNT, completed by 1902.

The Whartons spent part of almost every year at The Mount until 1911. Walter BERRY, Henry JAMES, Gaillard LAPSLEY, Robert NORTON and John HUGH SMITH were frequent houseguests. Edith participated in a number of community affairs and was particularly interested in the Lenox Library. She was on the Village Improvement Committee and the Flower Show Committee and took a number of horticultural prizes (Marshall, *The Mount: Home of Edith Wharton*).

Lenox was an ideal central base from which the Whartons could tour the region with their houseguests. Driven by Charles COOK, the new chauffeur of the Pope-Hartford motorcar, they made automobile trips throughout much of Massachusetts, and sometimes went as far afield as the Hudson River (*see* NEW ENGLAND). A favorite destination was Ashfield, Massachusetts, where the Whartons' close friend Charles Eliot NORTON lived during the summer with his daughters Sara and Lily (Elizabeth).

By 1911, Teddy Wharton's mental state had declined, and Wharton seriously considered separating from him and living permanently in PARIS. She gave him authority to put the property on the market. The Mount was sold in September 1911 to Mary and Albert R. Shattuck of New York City for approximately $180,000. The final transactions were not completed, however, until early 1912.

Once The Mount was sold, Wharton considered herself severed from Lenox and her native country; she wrote in her autobiography that she had been too happy at The Mount to "revisit it as a stranger" (*BG* 125). Wharton only returned to America for two brief visits, in 1913 when her niece Beatrix Jones FARRAND was married, and in 1923 when she was given an honorary doctorate from YALE UNIVERSITY. She did not visit Lenox during those journeys.

For further reading: Marshall, *The Mount: Home of Edith Wharton*.

"Letter, The"   Short story published in *HARPER'S MAGAZINE* in April 1904 and in the English edition of *The DESCENT OF MAN*, but not in the American one. This story, which is altogether different from "The LETTERS," has been called Edith Wharton's "worst effort" (White, 78). Like "The HOUSE OF THE DEAD HAND," it concerns a scholarly, but eccentric, expatriate Englishman living in Italy. The narrator had called on Colonel Alingdon, a specialist in Tuscan art, before his death. Their conversation had turned to the nature of courage, and the colonel began telling him of the bravest woman he had ever known. His first love was a widow, Donna Candida Falco, whose husband had been unkind. Her only brother, Emilio Verna, had been executed by an Italian duke pandering to the Austrians during the Austrian-Italian struggle. Her mother believed her son must have sent her a last letter from the scaffold, as other young men did; Italian patriots treasured the letters and regarded them as an incentive to further bravery. No letter had appeared, however.

When Colonel Alingdon met Donna Candida, she was in love with Fernando Briga, a leading Italian liberal. He knew of the hope she and her mother held that Emilio had sent a letter. The colonel had discovered such a letter in the ducal archives in Modena; it had, puzzlingly, been presented by Briga, then only 15, to the warder of the prison. The colonel gives the letter to Donna Candida, who manages to put it in a good light, insisting that the young Briga put Italy ahead of friendship. She does not show the letter to her mother, lest she refuse to forgive Briga, but burns the letter, for Italy.

The structure of "The Letter" is typical of many of Edith Wharton's stories, with an embedded narrator and successive flashbacks.

"Letters, The" Short story first published in *The CENTURY MAGAZINE* in three installments in 1910 and reprinted in *TALES OF MEN AND GHOSTS* (Scribner's, 1910). The story concerns Lizzie West, a young American in FRANCE who turns to tutoring Juliet, the young daughter of an American artist, Vincent Deering, to support herself. Mrs. Deering is an invalid, taking little part in the household at Saint-Cloud, outside PARIS. Lizzie and Vincent Deering fall in love and meet surreptitiously in various museums until after the early death of Mrs. Deering. Deering then places Juliet with friends and returns to AMERICA to settle his wife's estate. He writes a few ardent letters, but never answers those Lizzie writes.

She takes up her bleak life of tutoring again, confiding her despair to a fellow boarder at her pension, Andora Macy. Andora comforts her as best she can, although she has seemingly never had an emotional attachment and, in Lizzie's view, cannot really share her feelings.

After Lizzie receives a substantial inheritance she encounters Deering again. He has returned to Europe after his career stalled in America and is barely eking out a living. They marry and have a son; Lizzie establishes the family in a charming house with a garden at Neuilly. Andora Macy visits for long periods, helping with the little boy. Lizzie is ecstatically happy taking care of her husband and encouraging him.

One day she and Andora are sorting through Vincent's worn luggage forwarded from New York and find a beaded bag. Lizzie refuses to take part in Andora's speculations as to whether it might have belonged to a woman in America. Her son opens it, and her letters to Deering, all unopened, tumble out. Andora is shocked and Lizzie is disillusioned. She briefly considers leaving him, understanding that he has probably married her for her money. She decides to stay with him, however, realizing that, although he has not been "the hero for her dreams," he is still the man she loves and who loves her. She justifies her decision, reasoning that, "as a comedy marble may be made out of worthless scraps of mortar, glass, and pebbles, so out of mean mixed substances may be fashioned a love that will bear the stress of life" (*CSS* II, 206). Andora volunteers to challenge Deering with the letters, but Lizzie refuses. "Oh, poor Andora, you don't know anything—you don't know anything at all!" she cries.

The story may well reflect Edith Wharton's affair with Morton FULLERTON and her sense of the euphoria even a flawed relationship may bring. The reviewer for the *Nation* asserted that the story was in the style of Paul BOURGET with an "Anglo-Gallic manner, with its nuances, its compunctions, its hiatuses," but was glad it did not "go further by reminding us of Henry James" (*CR* 175).

For further reading: Stein, *After the Vows Were Spoken: Marriage in American Literary Realism.*

Lewis, Sinclair (1885–1951) American novelist. A native of Minnesota, Lewis graduated from Yale University in 1908 and spent several years in newspaper work before turning to fiction. His novels are tinged with satire. His *Main Street* (1920), portraying the provincialism and bigotry of small-town America, created a sensation. He failed, however, to receive the 1921 Pulitzer Prize, which went to Edith Wharton for *The AGE OF INNOCENCE*. In 1930 he was awarded the Nobel Prize for literature, the first American to be so honored.

The Pulitzer committee had actually chosen *Main Street* to receive the prize, but the Columbia University trustees vetoed their choice on the grounds that it had offended some people in the Middle West. Lewis knew this, but, in what R. W. B. Lewis calls a "sportsmanlike gesture," wrote a note congratulating Edith Wharton. She replied that it was the first sign she had ever had that " '*les jeunes*' at home had ever read a word of me. . . . Your book and *Susan Lenox* (expurgated) [by Graham Phillips] have been the only things out of America that have made me cease to despair of the republic—of letters, so you can imagine what a pleasure it is to know that you have read *me*, and cared, and understood." She had assumed she was regarded as "the Mrs. Humphry Ward of the Western Hemisphere" (*Letters* 445). (Mrs. WARD was a popular English novelist who wrote religious polemical works.)

She invited him to visit her at the PAVILLON COLOMBE in St.-Brice-sous-Forêt. Lewis and his wife, Grace Hegger

Lewis, did come to see her two months later, and over the ensuing years met at intervals for luncheon or tea.

Lewis dedicated *Babbitt,* published in 1922, to Wharton, and she wrote him a long letter of thoughtful criticism, saying that it had "life and glow and abundance" and that she warmly admired and applauded it, but advised his using less slang in his dialogue lest it become outdated (*Letters* 454–55).

There were further visits, and in the summer of 1923 Edith went to the country home near Fontainebleau they had leased; she brought along Gaillard LAPSLEY and John HUGH SMITH. Lewis thought them "delightful." The same summer she went to lunch at Pontigny in the company of the Lewises, Walter BERRY, Charles DU BOS, André MAUROIS, Gustave SCHLUMBERGER and Lytton STRACHEY. (*EW* 455–56). (The *décades,* or ten-day meetings at the Abbaye de Pontigny, in the Yonne, were one of the foremost occasions for eminent scholars and writers from other countries to meet French specialists or generalists and to hold long discussions. Strachey attended a *décade* August 16–27, 1923).

In "The GREAT AMERICAN NOVEL" (1927), she called *Main Street* a "pioneering work which with a swing of the pen hacked away the sentimental vegetation from the American small town and revealed Main Street as it is, with all its bareness in the midst of plenty" (*UCW* 152).

A few years later, in her essay "TENDENCIES IN MODERN FICTION" (1934), she remarked that Lewis's success was probably due more to his ability to draw people "with recognizable faces" and to tell their stories "with a vigorous simplicity" than to the public's recognition of his "rare gift of tragic irony" (*UCW* 178–79).

Sinclair Lewis wrote to tell her of their divorce in 1929, and some months later she wrote Grace Hegger Lewis to tell her how saddened she was since she had had a pleasant memory of seeing them together. She was glad, she said, to hear that Grace and their son (Wells, then about 12) had been traveling together, and invited her to come and see her when she was next abroad.

For further reading: Coard, "Edith Wharton's Influence on Sinclair Lewis."

"Life and I" Unpublished holograph autobiography by Edith Wharton, now at the BEINECKE LIBRARY, YALE UNIVERSITY. The early chapters of *A BACKWARD GLANCE* are an expansion of the manuscript. It consists of 52 pages, beginning with Wharton's early memory of walking down Fifth Avenue with her father, and ending with her recollection of a flirtation she had at Wild Bad, Germany, during the Joneses' second European trip, in 1881 or 1882. She had met a young man unofficially engaged to a Miss Livington, whose family was from New York.

Lilly Library The Lilly Library at the University of Indiana, Bloomington, is the repository of a large collection of correspondence and writings of Edith Wharton.

There are letters, diaries and typescripts, including those for *The AGE OF INNOCENCE, A BACKWARD GLANCE,* and *The GODS ARRIVE.* In addition, there are photographs and biographical material held by Elisina TYLER for a biography of Edith Wharton she once planned. The collection contains approximately 850 items.

"Line of Least Resistance, The" Short story published in *Lippincott's* in October 1900, but not collected. Set in the NEWPORT of the GILDED AGE, the tale concerns Mr. Mindon, owner of a large villa on the cliffs and father of two little girls who are learning all the arts and artifice of their mother, Millicent. Mindon discovers his wife's infidelity and repairs to a musty hotel room, which contrasts unfavorably with his home. He meditates on how best to journey to New York and begin divorce proceedings. His wife alerts his uncle and senior partner, as well as their New York rector and family physician. They converge on him at the hotel and manage to persuade him to take the "line of least resistance" and return home. Mindon feels the "drowning clutch" on his arm of courage and resolve, but stammers, "It's for the children."

Edith Wharton omitted the story from the collection *CRUCIAL INSTANCES* because Henry JAMES found it flawed. Although he praised the "admirable sharpness and neatness, and infinite wit and point," he observed that the story was too large to be treated in a short story. He applauded Wharton for evoking the "human life that surrounds you" and called it an "untouched field." Nevertheless, he found the story "a little *hard,* a little purely derisive. But that's because you're so young, and with it so clever" (*EW* 125).

"Literature" Unfinished projected novel by Edith Wharton. The theme was to be similar to that of *HUDSON RIVER BRACKETED*—the effect of American life on the writer. She made her first notation about it in 1913, in Dresden, when she was touring GERMANY with Bernard BERENSON. WORLD WAR I prevented Wharton from working on it, and in 1916 she wrote Charles SCRIBNER that, although she hoped to finish it some day, she could make little progress until after the end of the war. The Beinecke Library, Yale, has a notebook and notes for the novel, in addition to a holograph manuscript and several typescript drafts of Book I.

As Lewis observes, it contains many elements of Edith Wharton's childhood. Dicky Thaxter, the hero, has a devoted nurse (as Doyley was to Edith) and shouts poetry into his grandmother's ear trumpet, as Edith Wharton did, in Paris, when her mother's mother stayed with them during the Joneses' first European journey. The scenario outlines a book that would have followed Dicky as he attended college, conducted various affairs, married, traveled in Europe and published a major trilogy (*EW* 394–95, 490–91).

"Little Girl's New York, A"   An essay written in 1934. Wharton termed it a "post-script" to A BACKWARD GLANCE (*NGC* 451). It was published posthumously in HARPER'S MAGAZINE (March 1938).

Lodge, George Cabot ("Bay") (1873–1909)   Scion of two patrician NEW ENGLAND families and the son of Senator Henry Cabot Lodge, he and Wharton were introduced by Walter BERRY when the Whartons spent several months in Washington in 1899. She called him "one of the most brilliant and versatile youths I have ever known." He published several volumes of poetry, but Wharton believed his family inhibited his development by considering him a "young genius." In his youth he was surrounded by such prominent figures as Henry ADAMS, Sir Cecil Spring-Rice, J. J. Jusserand and John Hay. These circumstances produced, Wharton believed, a "slightly rarefied atmosphere of mutual admiration, and disdain of the rest of the world," which produced in Bay a certain "brilliant immaturity." He wrote poetry marked by a "grave and rhetorical beauty." She admired his intelligence, sensitivity and scholarly mind, but blamed the Lodge family for "smoothing the way" and keeping him "out of the struggle of life." She believed the atmosphere at The MOUNT, where he often visited, benefited him intellectually; he made contact with "minds as active as his own, but more unprejudiced" (*BG* 149–51).

Bay Lodge died at the age of 36 of a heart attack brought on by food poisoning, leaving his widow, Elizabeth Frelinghuysen Davis Lodge ("Bessy"), and three children, one of whom was Henry Cabot, the future U.S. senator. Bessy Lodge later moved to PARIS and fell in love with JEAN DU BREUIL DE ST. GERMAIN, a French sociologist and army officer, but the Lodge family disapproved of the marriage and threatened to deprive her of her children if they married (*NGC* 316). He was killed in WORLD WAR I. *See* "GEORGE CABOT LODGE," Wharton's tribute to him.

London   Edith Wharton had first visited London when the Jones family spent six years in EUROPE between 1866 and 1872. In 1880 they returned to Europe via London, spending most of their time in ITALY and on the French RIVIERA; George Frederic JONES died at Cannes in 1882. In A BACKWARD GLANCE she recalled their stay in London: "A happier pilgrim has never set foot in the November fogs of London; for what I had dimly loved as a child I was now to look on again with grown-up eyes (as I thought them!)." She went with her governess to the National Gallery, where she first saw the works of Pinturicchio and other artists (*BG* 85–86).

Wharton never wrote a travel article about London, or about ENGLAND, but visited the city throughout her life, seeing old friends and making new ones. She and Teddy frequented the city often during the Edwardian era, and some of her oldest English friendships date from that time. Many of her English friends had townhouses in London, including Mary Augusta (Mrs. Humphry) WARD. Her American friend Lady ESSEX, married to an Englishman, entertained Wharton both in London and at her country estate, Cassiobury. Often she met people at London dinners who later invited her to their country homes; this was the case with Alfred AUSTIN and his wife.

In 1909 Wharton spent a night with Morton FULLERTON at the Charing Cross Hotel that she commemorated in a poem, "TERMINUS." In 1911 Edith Wharton called on the painter John Singer SARGENT at his London studio on Tite Street to commission a charcoal drawing of Henry JAMES (*NGC* 260). James kept a flat in London on Cheyne Walk, and Wharton sometimes dined with him in the city, although most of her time with him in England was spent touring or at LAMB HOUSE.

After her DIVORCE in 1913, Wharton frequently spent a fortnight in London during the summer. She liked to stay at the Cavendish Hotel on Jermyn Street, which Lewis calls "somewhat racy" (*EW* 346). In July that year she invited James, Bernard BERENSON and Gaillard LAPSLEY to dine with her at the hotel.

In July 1929 Wharton took the Golden Arrow train from Paris to Calais and Dover, where she and Geoffrey SCOTT wandered through the National Gallery (*EW* 489). Scott died of pneumonia the next month in New York. Wharton also visited the city in September 1934, where Kenneth CLARK gave her a tour of the National Gallery (he had become the director in 1933). The Clarks gave a luncheon in their London home on Portland Place honoring William Royal ("Bill") TYLER and his new bride; they had married in August (*EW* 518).

When Wharton's sister-in-law, Mary Cadwalader JONES, died suddenly in 1935 in a London hotel, she came immediately to England and saw to the burial and the disposition of her effects (*EW* 519–20).

"Long Run, The"   Short story published in the *Atlantic Monthly* in February 1912 and collected in XINGU AND OTHER STORIES (Scribner's, 1916). The narrator, after a 12-year absence from New York, meets an old Harvard classmate, Halston Merrick, at a dinner party. Merrick had been promising as a student and has studied at Oxford. After a failed attempt to enter state politics, and the death of his father, he has taken over the family iron foundry. Though he had literary aspirations, he has now grown "conventional and dull." The narrator perceives that he is attentively watching one of the other guests, Paulina Reardon.

During the narrator's subsequent stay at his country cottage, Merrick gives him his unpublished essays to read and tries to explain why he rejected Paulina, whom he loved and who tried to leave her first husband and live with him without divorce and remarriage. He refused at the time, thinking her impulsive and illogical. When her husband is killed in an accident, he fails to ask her to marry him, since he had declined her initial offer to live with him. She has summarized their case by saying, "one way of finding out whether a risk is worth taking is *not* to take it, and then to see what one becomes in the long run." Their lives have turned out unhappily, Merrick living alone and Paulina marrying a second husband, a bluff, insensitive man she does not love. " 'The worst of it,' " he tells the narrator, " 'is that now she and I meet as friends' " (*CSS* II, 324).

Lewis points out that Merrick and Paulina linger on through life "like Ethan [Frome] and Mattie [Silver], psychically if not physically mutilated." Edith Wharton's message is that no matter how wretched life is within marriage, extramarital love "is likely to be miserable and impoverished" (*EW* 318).

Looking Back   A 1981 television film based loosely on Wharton's memoir *A BACKWARD GLANCE. See* Appendix II.

"Looking Glass, The"   Short story published in *Hearst's International-Cosmopolitan* in December 1933 and collected in *The WORLD OVER* (Appleton-Century, 1936). The story concerns an elderly Irish masseuse, Mrs. Cora Attlee, now quite infirm. She is reluctantly attended by her widowed daughter-in-law, Moyra Attlee, her granddaughter, and one or two servants, including a kitchen-girl. She reminisces to her granddaughter about the "wrong" she has done long ago to one of her clients, a Mrs. Clingsland. Moyra knows her grandmother has only been able to buy her little house in Montclair with the aid of Mrs. Clingsland's investment advice. Mrs. Attlee recalls Mrs. Clingsland's obsession with losing her beauty. She has surrounded herself with looking glasses, but has failed to ward off the ravages of age, which have made her bitter.

Mrs. Attlee believes she has inherited powers of clairvoyance from her Irish ancestors. During World War I she has related encouraging messages she has dreamed to some of her clients worried about their sons in the army. Mrs. Clingsland confides she once loved a young man, Harry, drowned on the *Titanic* but has now met a foreign "count"; she is sure, however, she can see through his motives and resist his attentions. On her next professional visit, Mrs. Attlee meets a well-known "tout," an unscrupulous medium, leaving Mrs. Clingsland's home. She is sure the tout will prey on Mrs. Clingsland, either giving purported news of Harry or pretending the count was taken with her beauty. One way or another she will "bleed her white, and then leave her without help or comfort" (*CSS* II, 852).

With the aid of a poetic young tutor dying of alcoholism, whom she has visited on behalf of another client, Mrs. Attlee invents letters of love from Harry, describing how he had been struck dumb by her beauty and had wanted to propose, but that an "evil influence" had intervened. Mrs. Clingsland has consulted the "tout" but feels Mrs. Attlee's messages from Harry are more genuine. The young tutor dies, and Mrs. Clingsland is mortally ill. Mrs. Attlee delivers the final letter from Harry for which she has asked, one he wrote but didn't mail. Mrs. Clingsland's faith in her is restored and she eagerly gives Mrs. Attlee a hundred dollars to say masses for the young man. The masseuse keeps part of the money and gives the priest a portion. The story belongs to the category of what White calls "servant stories," having a common theme of the power of servants over their masters (*Edith Wharton: A Study of the Short Fiction*, 97).

For further reading: Inness, "An Economy of Beauty: The Beauty System in 'The Looking Glass' and 'Permanent Wave' "; Sweeney, "Mirror, Mirror, on the Wall: Gazing in Edith Wharton's 'Looking Glass.' "

Lorburn, Elinor   *See HUDSON RIVER BRACKETED.*

love affair   *See* "COLOPHON TO THE MORTAL LEASE"; FULLERTON, Morton; "LOVE DIARY"; "MORTAL LEASE, THE"; "OGRIN THE HERMIT"; "SENLIS, MAY 16"; "TERMINUS."

"Love Diary"   *See* DIARY, 1907, "THE LIFE APART." This is a diary Edith Wharton began in October 1907 after Morton FULLERTON visited The MOUNT.

Lovell, Charlotte   *See OLD MAID, THE.*

Lubbock, Percy (1879–1965)   English literary critic, best known for *The Craft of Fiction* (1921). He was a disciple of Henry JAMES, a Cambridge classmate of John HUGH SMITH, and a friend of Howard STURGIS, all of whom came to be close friends of Edith Wharton. She first met Lubbock in 1906 at QUEEN'S ACRE ("Qu'Acre"), the home of Sturgis, when he was 27. Their friendship endured for many years. He visited the Whartons at The MOUNT and in the FAUBOURG ST.-GERMAIN; later, he was Edith Wharton's frequent houseguest at the PAVILLON COLOMBE and STE.-CLAIRE CHÂTEAU.

Edith Wharton had long wanted to see North Africa and asked Gaillard LAPSLEY and Percy Lubbock to accompany her on a trip there in 1914. According to Lewis, she knew that Lubbock could not afford such a trip but delicately offered her hospitality on the journey as she had at her home. He accepted with alacrity. Lapsley was reluctant to go, having other commitments, but finally agreed; however, he had to turn back because he became ill with dysentery. They set out on March 29 aboard the S.S. *Timgad* from Marseilles to

Algeria. In addition to Lubbock, the party consisted of Anna BAHLMANN, Edith Wharton's longtime secretary/companion; Charles COOK, her chauffeur (who had driven their Mercedes to the ship and stowed it on board); and Elise DUVLENCK, her personal maid. (*See* entry on ALGERIA for their itinerary.) During WORLD WAR I Lubbock was a "faithful volunteer" in her work on behalf of refugees (*BG* 347).

Edith Wharton and Lubbock had a falling out when he married Lady Sybil CUTTING, whose first husband had been her friend Bayard CUTTING. After Cutting died in 1910 of consumption, a disease he had contracted as a young man, Lady Sybil married Edith Wharton's friend Geoffrey SCOTT in 1918 and, after their divorce, Percy Lubbock in 1926. Edith Wharton was indignant, finding Lady Sybil aggressive and manipulative rather than harmless, as she had when first meeting her.

Lubbock was chosen by Gaillard Lapsley, Edith Wharton's literary executor, to write a memoir of her. It has puzzled some biographers, particularly Lewis, why Lapsley invited Lubbock to undertake this task, since she had never forgiven him for marrying Lady Sybil. Lubbock's *Portrait of Edith Wharton* appeared in 1947 (Appleton-Century-Crofts). Lewis detects, beneath the author's "stylistic grace," much malice toward his subject and a "muted downgrading" of her as a writer. On publication, some of his friends pointed out the concealed tone of hatred, which, according to Lewis, was a considerable surprise to Lubbock. He replied, " 'But I *adored* her!' " (*EW* 516).

Much of the study illuminates Wharton's personality and the reasons for her expatriation as no other study has done. For example, Lubbock remarks that she came to France "not as a seeker, not as a votary, not as a strayed exile," but

> to enjoy what had long been hers at home, only she had not had enough of it—the best society within view, the best talk within earshot. . . . She never became, she had no call to become, any more of a European than she had been from the first; but with Europe around her she had room, liberty, encouragement, to be what she was (49).

Lubbock describes her as a traveler, "blithe and purposeful," at the onset of "one of her buccaneering raids, with her cargo of books, her well-plotted itinerary, and a partner who shared her zeal without questioning her course." He states that she had "possessed herself of wide lands and riddled their recesses" before she even began, and was not to be hindered in her progress. If her requests were denied, she was prepared to pay (but not to squander money); she "rustled unhesitatingly into the locked church, the gallery that happened to be closed that day, the palace that wasn't shown to visitors" (109–10).

His Edith Wharton thus took the initiative in preparing the practical ground for the aesthetic interpretations of sights that were the core of her travel works. His portrait of her seems more consonant with the energetic organizer who was to oversee four war relief charities simultaneously during WORLD WAR I than with the detached visionary who imagined a performance of the *commedia dell'arte* at Lake ISEO. It is also hard to reconcile Lubbock's portrayal of a highly organized "buccaneer" with the authorial presence of *A BACKWARD GLANCE*, who, while reveling in travel and in congenial gatherings, is also shy in the presence of noted figures and frequently agitated about her household, her friends and her publishers.

For further reading: Goodman, *Edith Wharton's Inner Circle;* Hecht, "The Poisoned Well: Percy Lubbock and Edith Wharton"; Joslin, "What Lubbock Didn't Say."

Lubbock, Lady Sybil Born Lady Sybil Cuffe, the daughter of an Irish peer, she was the young wife of Bayard CUTTING, Jr., son of one of Wharton's oldest New York friends, Bayard Cutting. Wharton invited her to tea in 1901, an invitation Lady Sybil eagerly accepted. She remembered later feeling that Edith Wharton had been "the person I most wished to meet in New York." Her hostess, however, was disappointed in her, finding her frivolous, preoccupied with balls and dinners, and unable to converse with her about London's intelligentsia. In 1903, when the Whartons were in ITALY so that Edith Wharton might conduct research for her articles on Italian villas, the Whartons and the Cuttings drove from Florence to the villa of Vernon LEE. They later went shopping for antiques, and Lady Sybil wrote a vivid description of Edith Wharton's rapacious eye, "hooded and hawklike," and her skillful bargaining (*NGC* 137–38).

After Bayard Cutting died in 1910 of consumption, a disease he had contracted as a young man, Lady Sybil married two friends of Wharton's, Geoffrey SCOTT in 1918 and, after their divorce, Percy LUBBOCK in 1926. Edith Wharton thoroughly disliked Lady Sybil by this time, and told Gaillard LAPSLEY she feared he might go next, followed by Bernard BERENSON and Walter BERRY, "kicking and screaming!" (*EW* 474). In 1933, Lady Sybil and the Lubbocks were both attending the Salzburg music festival, staying in the same hotel. Edith Wharton saw Percy Lubbock in the lobby and asked if she might call on Lady Sybil. She received word that "tomorrow" would be the earliest time, since she was indisposed. Later she was seen driving about Salzburg. Although Lubbock tried to make amends, Edith Wharton never forgot this slight.

Lyautey, Louis-Hubert Gonzalve (1854–1934) Marshal of France and French resident general in MOROCCO (1912–16, 1917–25). He was an able colonial administrator and may be said to have created modern Morocco. He wished to show French subjects that WORLD WAR I "in no way affected her normal activities," and in 1914 began organizing annual industrial exhibitions in Morocco. He had been encouraged to invite guests from allied and neutral countries. Morocco at that time was largely untouched by foreign travel. He invited Edith Wharton on a three-week motor tour of the colony; she was accompanied by Walter BERRY. Lyautey's wife often invited Wharton for tea and accompanied her on expeditions to bazaars and to harems not previously accessible to Western women.

The final chapter of Wharton's IN MOROCCO (1920), "General Lyautey's Work in Morocco," gives a full account of the tangled political situation he encountered with the European nations desiring to colonize Morocco and the various dissident tribes. Under his administration of the French protectorate, the economy improved, ports and medical centers were established, courts were created to protect French nationals, and reforms in education and art conservation were carried out.

Wharton's book about wartime France, FIGHTING FRANCE, FROM DUNKERQUE TO BELFORT (1915), contains a photograph of the shell of General Lyautey's house, which was destroyed by the Germans. The Germans considered Lyautey their worst enemy in Africa. Wharton states that when the first German soldiers reached the village of Crévic, "the officer in command asked for General Lyautey's house, went straight to it, had all the papers, portraits, furniture and family relics piled in a bonfire in the court, and then burnt down the house" (FFD 116), the only one damaged in the village. Wharton interviewed the gardener to corroborate the story.

Germany and Spain had had imperialist ambitions in Morocco because of its strategic and economic importance. In 1906 the Algeciras Conference protected German investments there while allowing France and Spain to police the country. In 1911 Germany "traded" Morocco to France in exchange for French territory in Africa, but the establishment of the French protectorate did not ultimately resolve the problem of Moroccan autonomy. Moroccan sovereignty was not recognized by France until 1956, when it became a member of the United Nations, but there remained further disputes with Spain.

Wharton gratefully dedicated *In Morocco* to "General Lyautey, Resident General of France in Morocco and to Madame Lyautey, thanks to whose kindness the journey I had so long dreamed of surpassed what I had dreamed."

MacCarthy, Desmond (1877–1952) English essayist, drama critic and journalist. His periodical writings have been collected into several volumes, including *Portraits* (1931), *Criticism* (1932), *Experience* (1935), *Memories* (1953), *Humanities* (1953), *Drama* (1940) and *The Court Theatre 1904–1907* (reptd. 1966). MacCarthy was literary editor of the *New Statesman* and, after 1929, literary critic of the *Sunday Times*. Many of his essays were never collected, nor were his major book projects, such as studies of Byron and Tolstoy, completed. At the age of 54 he dedicated a collection of his essays and reviews to the young Desmond MacCarthy, acknowledging that his younger self was undoubtedly disappointed with what he had accomplished, reading and writing criticism instead of projecting what he thought about the world "into a work of art—a play, a novel, a biography" (*Desmond MacCarthy: The Man and His Writings*, 37). In 1952, just before his death, Cambridge University conferred on him an honorary doctorate.

He has been associated with the Bloomsbury Group of writers and artists and, at Cambridge, was a member of the Apostles, an exclusive intellectual society. In 1912 he assisted Roger Fry in producing the first exhibition of postimpressionist paintings; he knew Virginia Woolf, Vanessa Bell, Duncan Grant, E. M. Forster and other Bloomsbury figures. It has been said that the artist in him manifested itself more clearly in his talk than in his writing. He had many literary friends, including Henry JAMES, Max Beerbohm and Logan Pearsall SMITH. Edith Wharton had admired an early essay he wrote praising John Donne. In August 1928 he accompanied Smith to the PAVILLON COLOMBE to meet Wharton; she thought him delightful. He later described her as displaying an "admirably furnished, clear strong mind" (*EW* 485–86). At the time MacCarthy was editor of the British journal *Life and Letters*. In October of the same year he wrote a letter thanking Wharton for the "delightful afternoon" he and Smith had enjoyed and soliciting an "article on the novel," of which they apparently had spoken. "A contribution from you would be a feather in my cap as an Editor, and a great help to the Review," he added. Wharton promptly replied that she had written Mary BERENSON their visit had provided the "best book-talk of the summer." She explained that the article she mentioned, "VISIBILITY IN FICTION," had been promised to the *Yale Review*, but that he could bring it out at the same time. She also mentioned wanting to write an article called "Deep Sea Sounding" on the "stream-of-conscious theory which is deflecting so much real narrative talent out of its proper course." MacCarthy's reaction to her proposal of what would have been, presumably, an attack on the novels of James JOYCE and his friend Virginia WOOLF is unknown; that article was not published. Possibly, however, the subject had been discussed during the afternoon at the Pavillon Colombe and Wharton believed MacCarthy would be receptive.

On Thursday, March 26, 1933, MacCarthy wrote Wharton from the Villa I TATTI near Florence, home of Bernard and Mary Berenson, that he and his wife, Molly, were delighted to accept her invitation to stay at STE.-CLAIRE CHÂTEAU. He proposed to arrive by train the following Thursday, April 2. The same year he read the manuscript of *A BACKWARD GLANCE* and was, Edith Wharton reported to Rutger B. JEWETT, enthusiastic about it (unpublished correspondence, BEINECKE LIBRARY, YALE UNIVERSITY).

McLellan, George Philadelphia physician who treated Edith Wharton in November and December, 1898. The grandson of the founder of Jefferson Medical College, Philadelphia, he was on the staff of the Orthopaedic Hospital and Infirmary for Nervous Diseases and a colleague of Silas Weir MITCHELL. It had been assumed that Wharton suffered a nervous breakdown in 1898 and was treated by Mitchell; Benstock believes she did not have such an illness and that Mitchell did not see her.

Maclew, Horace *See MOTHER'S RECOMPENSE, THE.*

Madame de Treymes Novella first published in *SCRIBNER'S MAGAZINE* (August 1906) and then published in book form by Scribner's in 1907. The subject is the clash between new American and old European culture. The subject has been treated by many writers, particularly Henry JAMES, in *Daisy Miller* (1878), *The American* (1877), and *The Golden Bowl* (1904). In *The Ambassadors* (1903), James depicts the setting of the novella, the elite FAUBOURG ST.-GERMAIN, a quarter where "grave *hotels* [townhouses] stood off for privacy, spoke of survival, transmission, association, a strong, indifferent, persistent order" (*The Ambassadors*, Bk. 5,

Ch. 1). When she began to consider settling in FRANCE, about 1906, Edith Wharton was gradually initiated into the force and implications of that order. The Faubourg has been described as " 'a piece of the *ancien regime* set in contemporary Paris' " (*EW* 176). Lewis cautions that, although Edith Wharton perceived the "iron authority" exercised by the matrons of the Faubourg, she also felt it valued the "assertion of one's individuality," as the social hierarchy of New York had not.

In the novel, the American-born Madame de Malrive, formerly Fanny Frisbee, has escaped the stifling society of New York only to find that she is entrapped far more miserably by her European marriage. Lewis believes there is much of Edith Wharton herself in her portrait of Fanny (*EW* 164). She is separated from her faithless husband and is raising her son alone, a situation countenanced by his family. However, if she divorces him and remarries, she risks losing her child. An amiable and wealthy American, John Durham, an old American friend, wishes to extricate Fanny from her situation so that they may marry; he tries to exact a promise of marriage contingent on a legal separation from her husband. A divorce is within her right, but she refuses to take such a step unless she can be assured her in-laws will neither permit the scandal of publicity nor oppose her in any way, lest her son blame her later.

Fanny's sister-in-law, Madame de Treymes, is sympathetic to her plight to a certain degree. She invites Durham to tea at the home of Fanny's august mother-in-law, the old Marquise de Malrive. Here he begins to perceive the complexity of the problem and the strength and rigidity of the Faubourg. He finds himself surrounded by

> . . . amiably chatting visitors, who mostly bore the stamp of personal insignificance on their mildly sloping or aristocratically beaked faces, hung together in a visible closeness of tradition, dress, attitude, and manner, as different as possible from the loose aggregation of a roomful of his own countrymen. Durham felt, as he observed them, that he had never before known what "society" meant; nor understood that, in an organized and inherited system, it exists full-fledged where two or three of its members are assembled [Chapter 5].

Madame de Treymes has squandered her husband's and brother's money to pay the gambling debts of her lover, a nobleman. She makes it known, in a very subtle fashion, that she will use her influence in persuading the family not to contest a divorce if Durham will pay the gambling debts. He refuses and renounces all hope, disliking subterfuge and fearing his happiness would be contaminated if effected in this way.

One critic called the novel "an absolutely flawless and satisfying piece of workmanship"; another praised Edith Wharton for achieving a "miracle of condensation," forgoing a long novel for a shorter work containing the essence of the situation (*CR* 142–43).

Maggiore, Lake   The largest and most famous of the Italian lakes, Maggiore is fed by the Ticino River, which originates in Switzerland; its waters are pale green in the north and change to a deep blue in the south. Its shores are lined with beautiful villas, inns and small villages. The resort town of Stresa attracts many artists and writers, and is the principal point of departure for the Isola Bella, one of the Borromean Islands. These islands have belonged since the 12th century to the princely Borromeo family. In the 17th century they built a handsome palace on Isola Bella, with striking terraced gardens.

Lake Maggiore and the Isola Bella figure in many of Wharton's works, principally in ITALIAN BACKGROUNDS and ITALIAN VILLAS AND THEIR GARDENS. In the former she describes the lake at length, with "Isola Bella moored like a fantastic pleasure-craft upon its waters" (*IB* 62). In *Italian Villas and their Gardens* she praises the 10 terraced gardens gracing Isola Bella:

> Are they like any other gardens on earth? No; but neither are the mountains and shores about them like earthly shores and mountains. They are Armida's gardens anchored in a lake of dreams, and they should be compared, not with this or that actual piece of planted ground, but with a page of Ariosto or Boiardo [*IV* 207].

The gardens echo Tasso's enchantress Armida, whose garden of hedonistic delights symbolizes the power of the senses over human reason, as well as the romantic poems and epics of Matteo Boiardo and Lodovico Ariosto (*see* page 96).

The gardens at Isola Bella are a prime example of the use of the water theater, one of the components of Baroque garden architecture that most appealed to Wharton. In *Italian Villas and Their Gardens* Wharton frequently discusses such structures, which were often used when the garden prospect culminated in a hillside. Cascades of water would flow down from the top, providing a theatrical backdrop for the large and splendid companies gathering in the garden. The inlaid shell water-theater on the Isola Bella was built between 1632 and 1671; the arcades and niches imitate the galleries of a theater. The shell motif is repeated in a grotto within the adjacent palace and is also suggested in the plasterwork of the entryway at The MOUNT, Wharton's home in LENOX, Massachusetts.

For further reading: Dwight, "The Influence of Italy on Edith Wharton"; St. Laurent, "Pathways to a Personal Aesthetic: Edith Wharton's Travels in Italy and France"; Prampolini, "Edith Wharton in Italy."

Mahatma   *See TWILIGHT SLEEP.*

Maisons Américaines de Convalescence A WORLD WAR I relief project begun by Edith Wharton in the summer of 1916, in PARIS. Many soldiers had contracted tuberculosis in the trenches, as had civilians living in unsanitary conditions. Benstock reports that by September 1916 as many as 100,000 men had been invalided out of service by the disease; they received no pensions, salaries or medical care. If they returned home they passed the infection to their families. The civilian fear of tuberculosis was so great that physicians were forbidden to put the diagnosis on death certificates and they often termed it "chronic bronchitis." There were seven convalescent homes, two at Groslay, two at Arromanches, one at Taverny, one in Paris and a halfway house offering counseling to patients who had been released. During the winter of 1917 there was so much ice on the Seine River that trucks did not have enough gasoline to deliver food and fuel to the convalescent homes; this period was, for many, including Wharton, the darkest of the war (*NGC* 330–31). That spring her efforts were undercut by the fund-raising activities of the American Red Cross, which diverted potential contributions to her charities. Wharton continued to raise money for the Maisons de Convalescence, however, until after the Armistice in 1918. In 1921 the Maisons were turned over to the Department of Public Hygiene of the Seine-et-Oise region (*NGC* 347).

Malrive, Fanny de *See MADAME DE TREYMES.*

Malrive, Marquise de *See MADAME DE TREYMES.*

Manford, Dexter *See TWILIGHT SLEEP.*

Manford, Nona *See TWILIGHT SLEEP.*

Manford, Pauline *See TWILIGHT SLEEP.*

manners, novel of Written in the tradition made popular by Jane Austen, this type of novel focuses on the customs, habits and structure of society. As one critic remarked, "so long as there are old families or new millionaires, debutantes or dowagers, transatlantic liners and international marriages, boarding-house parlors and summer hotels—so long as there are social contrasts and social crises—the comedy of manners is sure to survive (Kronenberger, *The Thread of Laughter,* 289). The novel of manners frequently deals with the conflict between an individual and the rigidly held principles of his class.

Edith Wharton is strongly associated with this tradition, as are Henry JAMES, William Dean HOWELLS, Ellen Glasgow and, in a later generation, Louis Auchincloss and John P. Marquand. Her novels and short stories are not merely in the vein of drawing-room comedy but raise serious questions of moral values. She is perhaps best known for her treatment of the old NEW YORK society in which she was raised: her work demonstrates its fate and its collective power over the nonconformist. Wharton also examined the multilayered and complex world of the elite FAUBOURG SAINT-GERMAIN in PARIS and, in later novels, the "artistic" and bohemian Greenwich Village and Paris of the 1920s, which she despised for espousing novelty at the expense of substance. She sought in her novels to expose sham and pretense, particularly disliking the arrivistes, the nouveaux riches who lack taste and assume that social position can be purchased. In *The AGE OF INNOCENCE* (1920), dealing with the New York of the 1870s, Mrs. Archer annually remarks that New York is very much changed, with "strange weeds pushing up between the ordered rows of social vegetables" (*AI* 256). The novel also treats the narrow attitude of old New York toward divorce. *The HOUSE OF MIRTH* (1905) and *The CUSTOM OF THE COUNTRY* (1913) are set in the beau monde of New York in the 1890s and turn of the century, respectively. In these novels Wharton treats the effect of the unconventional mores of a new group of people, catapulted to prominence by wealth and seeking acceptance within the old mercantile class of New York aristocracy. In *The Custom of the Country* she exposes the hypocrisy of upper-class French families toward marital infidelity. Although she disapproved of moral corruption within the aristocracy, in *A MOTOR-FLIGHT THROUGH FRANCE* she praised the general French "passion for form and fitness" and its long practice of manners [that] has so veiled its keenness with refinement as to produce a blending of vivacity and good temper nowhere else to be matched" (97, 76).

In "Our Literary Aristocrat," Vernon Parrington observes that, in her fiction, Edith Wharton suggests the idolatry of big business only indirectly; she "loathes the world of [the self-made millionaire] Jim Fiske too much to understand it." Fortunes might be made, lost and regained; however, it is the invisible yet rigid customs and cast of mind that constitute the true battleground between the newly arrived and the custodians of "old New York." In part, this may be because Wharton often focuses on the world of women, which—if at times cataclysmically changed by the "steal"—is still distinct from the passions that make it move. The reader's view is circumscribed by the European or neo-European settings in which the "old tradition of European culture" is domiciled (or approximated in the New World): the opera box, the watering place, the drawing room, the private yacht, the dining room, the library, the country estate with its grounds and gardens, the urban townhouse. These privileged settings suggest the physical boundaries of the worlds Edith Wharton explored, but not the depths of morals and manners she plumbed and exposed.

For further reading: Ammons *Edith Wharton's Argument with America;* Maxwell, *American Fiction: The Intellectual Background;* Milne, *The Sense of Society: A History of* the America Novel of Manners; Parrington, "Our Literary Aristocrat"; Tuttleton, *The Novel of Manners in America.*

Maple, Philura   See ETHAN FROME.

Marable, Richard   See BUCCANEERS, THE.

March, Jacqueline   See BUCCANEERS, THE.

Mariano, Elizabeth ("Nicky")   Of aristocratic Baltic and Neapolitan origins, Nicky Mariano joined the staff at the Villa I TATTI, the home of Bernard and Mary BERENSON, near Florence, ITALY, in 1918. She began as librarian and became a valued assistant in dealing with Berenson's affairs. She stayed with the Berensons for 40 years, writing of her experience at I Tatti in *Forty Years with Berenson* (1966). According to Benstock, she became Berenson's lover as well as companion (*NGC* 340). She also compiled the voluminous *Berenson Archive: An Inventory of Correspondence*, listing more than 1,200 correspondents from all over the world, published in Florence after his death.

Wharton came to regard Nicky Mariano with the affection she reserved for few people. When they first met in 1923, however, Nicky had a very negative impression of Wharton. She and the Berensons were in London, and invited her to lunch; she was accompanied by the charming painter and ex-diplomat Robert NORTON. Wharton did not address a personal word to Nicky then, although on a later visit to I Tatti she did ask her to accompany her to some Florentine shops. In 1926, the OSPREY came into the port of Naples while the Berensons and Nicky were in the city. Wharton invited them to inspect the ship. Nicky immediately inquired how Wharton's maid, Elise DUVLENCK, had fared during the cruise. She had come to know Elise well during several of Wharton's visits to I Tatti. At once Nicky became aware of a "complete change" in Wharton's manner toward her. "There was a warmth, a tone of intimacy that I had never heard before. A gesture that was natural to me had let down the drawbridge leading into the fortress of her small intimate circle." She saw Wharton again that autumn, during her last trip with Walter BERRY, to the Italian lakes. Nicky and Berenson had been visiting Piedmontese sights and the four met in Aosta. She took a message from Berenson to Wharton one morning, finding her propped in bed in an "elegant wrapper" surrounded by books and writing things, her dogs asleep at her feet. Berry sat nearby. She was in "excellent spirits" and "as happy as a young girl to have him all to herself and to let herself be teased by him." Nicky had previously only seen Berry in Paris, "surrounded by his super-chic lady friends and a slave to their values and tastes" (Nicky Mariano, *Forty Years with Berenson*, 172–73). Berry had a stroke in the spring and died the following autumn.

Nicky and the Berensons spent Christmas of 1929 at STE.-CLAIRE CHÂTEAU. However, as Nicky remarked in the memoir she contributed to Percy LUBBOCK's *Portrait of Edith Wharton*, when Wharton invited her to accompany her on a week's visit to Rome in autumn 1931 she hesitated. As she explained, Edith Wharton often gave her the impression that she was not coming up to her expectations, that she had been "weighed in the balance and found wanting" (Mariano, 178). Berenson insisted on going, however, and they set off with Elise and two dogs. They revisited the churches and other places she had known before the turn of the century, and Nicky revised her opinion, describing Wharton, on visiting St. Peter's, as "someone quite close to me, carried away with me and like me into another sphere, with no stiffness or impatience left in her, no thought of the passing hour or of other plans" (Mariano, 179). Six months later, she, Nicky, and Berenson spent the Whitsunday holiday in Rome and attended services at several churches and at St. Peter's.

Nicky called Wharton's relationship to Berenson "like that of a somewhat older, loving and pedagogical sister" (Mariano, 185). When Wharton died, she wrote Berenson that her heart was "full of the sad news," and "to know for certain that she is no more, that these two houses have shut their doors for ever, that we shall never again be able to grumble over her whims and caprices only to enjoy her good and delightful moods even more, is difficult to realize" (Mariano, 189).

Marne, The   This novella appeared in the *Saturday Evening Post* (October 26, 1918) before being published by Appleton in 1918. It deals with the battle experience of Troy Belknap, a young American who had, as a child, come to know France through his French tutor, Paul Gantier. Trapped in Paris, with his mother, during the early part of the war, Troy discovers Gantier's grave and is determined to avenge his death. He and his mother return to America, but, as soon as he is 18, he goes to France as an ambulance driver and is wounded and rescued at the 1918 battle of the Marne. Edith Wharton wrote her editor at Appleton, Rutger B. JEWETT, that the details abut the Front were taken from eyewitness descriptions. He thought it "the most poignant story of the war" he had read. She asked Jewett to consider publishing it in the same volume with another novella called "The REFUGEES," suggesting that, because the name had "such magic about it," Appleton's consider titling the volume *The Marne.* The Appleton's editors, Jewett and J. H. Sears, did not include the second novella in the volume with *The Marne.* However, they negotiated with the *Saturday Evening Post,* which purchased both works (unpublished correspondence between Wharton and Appleton's, BEINECKE LIBRARY, YALE UNIVERSITY). *The Marne* is dedicated to Wharton's young friend Ronald

SIMMONS, killed in battle, as was her other war novel, *A SON AT THE FRONT* (1923).

The two battles of the Marne were critical in the defeat of Germany during World War I. During the first battle, September 6–9, 1914, General Joseph-Simon Galliéni dispatched a "taxicab army" of 5,000 soldiers to the front from Paris to halt the German advance. The last major German offensive was repulsed in the course of the second Battle of the Marne, in July 1918. Edith Wharton was in Britain during the first battle, and wrote Sara NORTON she felt like a "deserter" (*Letters* 335).

Contemporary critics have denounced the novella as sentimental and slight; Lewis believes it has "little staying power" (*EW* 422). It was, however, praised on publication. Frederic Taber Cooper, writing in *Publisher's Weekly,* called it "one of the very few clear-cut, pure-water, almost flawless gems of war fiction . . . simple in its art and single-purposed in its theme." One achievement of the novella, he suggested, was to highlight the monstrous superiority of American war workers attempting to "teach French mothers to love children, to teach French sons to honor their mothers, to teach the French nation how to live clean lives!" This is harder for Troy to bear than the neutrality that prevailed earlier in the war. Americans, however, learned their lesson "when brought face to face with the great leveling forces of actuality." The reviewer for the *Times Literary Supplement* believed Edith Wharton had managed, with an "acute social sense," to chronicle the changing attitude of America toward France in the course of the war and to reveal that the American eagerness to teach "poor France the civic and domestic virtues" was confounded by the reality of France (*CR* 268–70).

Marriage Playground, The (film based on *THE CHILDREN*, 1929).   *See* Appendix II.

Marsh, Verena   *See* SUMMER.

Marvell, Paul   *See CUSTOM OF THE COUNTRY, THE.*

Marvell, Ralph   *See CUSTOM OF THE COUNTRY, THE.*

"Matthew Arnold"   Review of a biography of Matthew Arnold by Herbert W. Paul, an essayist, historian and Liberal member of Parliament (London: Macmillan, 1902). Titled "Mr. Paul on the Poetry of Matthew Arnold," it was published in the *Lamp*, February 1903. Wharton was a lifelong admirer of Matthew ARNOLD, having read his poetry as a child. Later, Henry JAMES read his works aloud at The MOUNT.

Wharton attacks the choice of Paul as a biographer and considers him devoid of sufficient critical gifts to undertake such a task. She dislikes his "axiomatic flippancies" about Arnold's prose and the "consoling density" of his remarks about his poetry. She disagrees with his evaluation of the poems she regards as Arnold's best, such as "The Scholar Gypsy," and condemns his capacity for judging poetry. Wharton makes a good case for Paul's scholarly shortcomings, but the chief interest of the review is its revelation of her incisive critical ability and wide knowledge of English poetry.

Maurois, André (1885–1967)   Pen name of Émile Herzog, French biographer, novelist and essayist. He wrote biographies of Shelley, Byron, Disraeli, Victor Hugo, George SAND and other prominent literary and political figures. Edith Wharton was inclined to dismiss him, according to Lewis, until he wrote an excellent biography of her friend General Hubert-Louis LYAUTEY. In the summer of 1923, on a journey to NOHANT with Walter BERRY, she went to lunch at Pontigny in the company of Maurois, along with Sinclair LEWIS and his wife, Charles DU BOS, Gustave SCHLUMBERGER and Lytton STRACHEY. They discussed the problem of translation (*EW* 456).

Maynard, Eunice Ives   A longtime friend of Edith Wharton in LENOX, where she spent summers with her parents, Eunice married Walter MAYNARD in 1903. In December 1913 Wharton returned to AMERICA to attend the wedding of her niece, Beatrix JONES, to Max FARRAND. She was a week late sailing because of illness and missed the wedding. The Maynards were among those who postponed their intended celebrations and "petted and feasted" her (*Letters* 313).

During WORLD WAR I, Eunice, whose husband was president of the Edith Wharton War Charities of America, assisted with Wharton's war relief charities. She later wrote Percy LUBBOCK that "Every face—adults and children alike—lit with pleasure when she entered the wards" (*NGC* 324). When Wharton returned to America in 1923 to receive her honorary DOCTORATE from Yale University, she also visited the Maynards.

Maynard, Walter (1871–1925)   Walter Maynard inherited a school book publishing firm and made his home in NEW YORK; he was also a realtor and financier, and helped plan the construction of the Fifth Avenue Building, which replaced the Fifth Avenue Hotel. In 1903 he married Eunice Ives, a friend of Edith Wharton from LENOX; Wharton remained close friends with the Maynards throughout her life. She states in her memoir that Maynard was one of the "few men of exceptional intelligence" she had known, along with Egerton WINTHROP, Ogden CODMAN, Bayard CUTTING and the architect Stanford White. They had "at last stirred the stagnant air of old New York" with "the dust of new ideas" (*BG* 149).

During WORLD WAR I Maynard was president of the Edith Wharton War Charities of America. For his services he was decorated by the French government and made a knight of the Legion of Honor, a distinction Wharton also was awarded. He was the only lay member of the Beaux Arts Institute in New York.

Medal of Queen Elisabeth (Médaille Reine Elisabeth)
In 1918 Edith Wharton received the Medal of Queen Elisabeth from King Albert of Belgium for her war relief efforts. The decoration was a minor one compared with that of the French government, which had made her a CHEVALIER OF THE LEGION OF HONOR in 1916. In 1919 King Albert also named her Chevalier of the Order of Leopold, the equivalent of the French Legion of Honor (*NGC* 343–44). Price observes that Wharton was always ambivalent about receiving medals for her war charities, believing there were numerous unrecognized volunteers who had contributed more than she (*The End of the Age of Innocence: Edith Wharton and World War I*, 139).

Mediterranean cruises   In 1888, Edith, then 26, and Edward WHARTON shared with their close friend James VAN ALEN in the charter of the steam yacht *VANADIS* for a four-month Mediterranean cruise. The Whartons had realized that such a venture was actually beyond their means, but they went ahead anyway, alarming both the Jones and Wharton families. Fortuitously, while they were away, Edith received a substantial legacy of $120,000 from Joshua JONES, a distant cousin, which provided amply for their travels on the *VANADIS*. They visited a number of Mediterranean ports of call in ITALY, NORTH AFRICA, Greece, Malta and Turkey, including Valetta, Syracuse, Messina, Taormina, Corfu, Athens and Mount Athos. The men of the party, but not Wharton, were allowed to tour the Byzantine monasteries of Mount Athos, which has been closed to women since the ninth century. Wharton's account of the holy mountain and its monasteries, consisting of her observations from the ship and her companions' reports, is the first known description by an American.

Until 1991, it had been supposed that Edith Wharton's first travel writings were her articles for *ITALIAN BACKGROUNDS*. That year a French scholar, Claudine Lesage of the University of Amiens, discovered a detailed diary Wharton had kept of the cruise in the HYÈRES Public Library, near Wharton's winter home, STE.-CLAIRE CHÂTEAU; she published it in 1992. She calls the diary Wharton's "maiden *Odyssey* into literature." Looking back on the first cruise many years later, she termed it "the greatest step forward in my making. . . . a taste of heaven."

In 1926, Wharton again stretched her resources to share a charter for a nine-week voyage aboard the yacht *OSPREY*, leaving from the Old Port of Hyères on March 31, 1926. Among the places visited were Delphi, Alexandria, Mistra, Cyprus and Crete, as well as some ports of call they had visited in 1888. In her memoir Wharton recalled being one of ". . . a congenial party, with lots of books, a full set of Admiralty charts, a stock of good provisions and *vins du pays* in the hold, and happiness in our hearts." The party included her long-

time friends Margaret ("Daisy") Terry CHANLER, Robert NORTON and Logan Pearsall SMITH. In addition there was Harry Lawrence, an Englishman, who was director of the Medici Society in London. Wharton planned to write a travel book about the cruise, *The SAPPHIRE WAY*, that would have been, she thought, "charming," and would have offset some of the expenses of the cruise, but when she returned home she turned again to fiction. *See* CRUISE OF THE VANADIS, THE.

"Memories of Bourget Overseas"   Memorial essay about the French novelist Paul BOURGET, published as "Souvenirs de Bourget d'outre-mer" in the *REVUE HEBDOMADAIRE* June 21, 1936. The translation used for the present discussion is by Frederick Wegener; *see also* the translation by Adeline Tintner, "Memories of Bourget from Across the Sea." According to Wegener, the essay was originally commissioned by the *REVUE DES DEUX MONDES* but the editor suggested unacceptable cuts and changes, causing her to withdraw it.

Paul Bourget had died in 1935. In her tribute, Edith Wharton opposes her own recollections to the "official" obituary essays that had represented him as the "intransigent moralist, the unsmiling pedagogue." Writing not of the "writer" but of the "friend," she evokes her 1893 meeting with Bourget and his wife Minnie in NEWPORT and recalls his reaction to their Newport home, unexpectedly full of books. Having come for a few days, they stayed for a month. Like many Europeans, Bourget mistakenly assumed that North America was the "land of dollars." Wharton points out that Wall Street was never mentioned by members of her family's social circle, and if members were "very rich," it was because of urban land they had inherited. She blames the breakdown of the old New York society in which she had grown up on the development of western railroads that introduced a "harsh desire for profit."

Much of the essay is devoted to memories of the early journeys the Whartons and Bourgets made in Italy, before the advent of the automobile. One highlight was Bourget's discovery that the elderly son of the duchess of Langeais was staying in their hotel; Edith Wharton rarely saw him "as moved, as delighted, as he was at the idea of conversing with the son of a woman Balzac had immortalized" (in *La Duchesse de Langeais*). She also recalls the Bourgets in later years, after her divorce and after WORLD WAR I, when they lived at Costebelle, near HYÈRES, where she stayed each winter and spring; they often exchanged visits. Wharton felt Bourget had become far too sedentary in later life, refusing to explore new places; he would only do the "*already done.*"

In her conclusion, Edith Wharton makes the surprising admission that she never liked Bourget's novels as much as his critical essays, although she enjoyed discussing fictional techniques with him. She considered his characters pawns in a scheme contrived beforehand that obviated the element of surprise. Yet his "heart was filled to the bottom with good-will," and he was always willing to help young writers. In addition, he had a "fundamentally generous nature" and "magnificent professional integrity."

For further reading: Wharton, "Souvenirs de Bourget d'outre-mer," trans. as "Memories of Bourget Overseas" by Wegener, *The Uncollected Critical Writings of Edith Wharton;* Tintner, "Edith Wharton and Paul Bourget"; Tintner, "Memories of Bourget from across the Sea (Souvenirs de Bourget outremer)."

Meredith, George (1828–1909)   English novelist, poet and critic; his earliest work of distinction was *The Ordeal of Richard Feverel* (1859). His later novels, such as *The Egoist* (1879) and *Diana of the Crossways* (1885), were flawed by opaque style and dialogue. His novels were notable for their psychological insight and emphasis on the relations between the individual and social events. Edith Wharton read *The Adventures of Harry Richmond,* a picaresque romance (1870), in her youth and included it in 1898 on a list of her favorite books; she also admired *The Egoist.*

Just after publication of *A MOTOR-FLIGHT THROUGH FRANCE,* Edith Wharton (then 46) was taken by Henry James to Box Hill, the cottage of the aged novelist, then 80 and very deaf, to make an unannounced call. " 'My dear child, I've read every word you've written, and I've always wanted to see you! I'm flying through France in your motor at this moment,' " said Meredith, and held up *A Motor-Flight Through France.* Wharton was stunned to discover that he had been reading it, not knowing she was to be brought to see him. He was, she recalled, "all amenity, all kindliness, as if the voice were poured in a healing tide over the misery of my shyness." " 'Well, my dear,' " James asked her when they departed, " 'wasn't I right?' " She had to admit he was (*BG* 252–54).

In *The WRITING OF FICTION* (1925), Wharton praised Meredith's ability to make his "art as landscape painter contribute to the interpretation of his tale," describing the farmhouse in *Harry Richmond* and the sunrise in his 1866 novel *Vittoria* so that they are "seen as the people *to whom they happened* would have seen them" (*WF* 85).

"Metteurs en Scène, Les" ("The Producers")   Short story published in French in the *Revue des Deux Mondes* in October 1908. The plot is another version of the one used in "The INTRODUCERS," dealing with ambitious young people, socially *au courant,* who advance themselves by arranging for their wealthy employers to meet and marry in a quasi-business partnership.

Edith Wharton wrote it in French because she was tired of the "arid work of translating." She was then

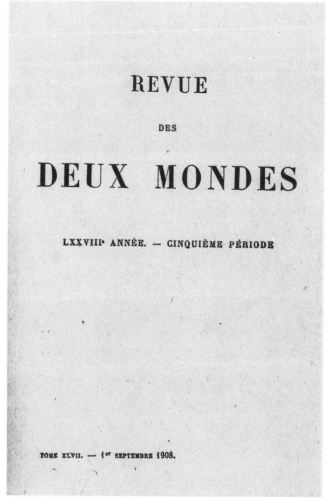

Cover of Revue des Deux Mondes, *September 1908, containing "Les Metteurs en Scène," the only short story Wharton published in French* (Courtesy Alderman Library, University of Virginia)

embarrassed when Henry JAMES read it; he drily congratulated her on "the way in which you've picked up every old worn-out literary phrase that's been lying about the streets of Paris for the last twenty years, and managed to pack them all into these few pages." He told a mutual friend that it was a "creditable episode in her career. *But she must never do it again*" (*EW* 234).

Milan   In the heart of alpine northern ITALY, Milan is the capital of Lombardy; it is now a huge industrial city and design center. One of the more prominent sights is the cathedral, in the city center, a magnificent building that has taken more than five centuries to complete. With its 135 spires and gilt statue of the Madonna, it is the traditional symbol of Milan. The city is also home to the Pinacoteca di Brera (the Brera Picture Gallery) and the renowned opera house La Scala; in addition, Leonardo da Vinci's *Last Supper* is in the

LES
METTEURS EN SCÈNE

I

C'était l'heure du thé à l'hôtel Nouveau-Luxe.

Depuis quelques instans Jean Le Fanois se tenait à l'entrée d'un des petits salons à boiseries Louis XV qui donnent sur le vaste hall central. De taille moyenne, svelte et bien pris dans sa redingote de coupe irréprochable, il avait l'allure narquoise et légèrement impertinente du Parisien de bonne famille qui s'est frotté trop longtemps au monde exotique et bruyant des hôtels élégans et des cabarets ultra-chics. De temps à autre, cependant, sa figure pâle et nerveuse était assombrie par une expression d'inquiétude, qui se dissimulait mal sous le sourire insouciant avec lequel il saluait les personnes de sa connaissance.

Plusieurs fois il jeta un coup d'œil impatient sur sa montre; puis son visage se rasséréna, et il s'avança d'un pas rapide à la rencontre d'une jeune fille qui venait de franchir le seuil du hall. Fine et élancée, dans son costume de ville d'une élégance sobre, elle avait, sur un cou long et gracile, une jolie tête d'éphèbe, aux lèvres d'un rose très pâle, aux grands yeux clairs et transparens, sous un front intelligent qu'ombrageaient des cheveux d'un blond doux et indécis. Cherchant le jeune homme du regard, elle traversait seule la salle encombrée, avec la mine

First page of "Les Metteurs en Scène." From Revue des Deux Mondes, *September 1908* (Courtesy Alderman Library, University of Virginia)

former monastery refectory in the Church of St. Mary of Grace, outside the city.

Edith and Teddy WHARTON knew the city best before the turn of the century. Milan and PARMA were the two northern Italian cities Wharton chose for detailed discussion in *ITALIAN BACKGROUNDS* (1905). The chapter on Milan provides a prime example of Wharton's habit, in travel writing, of focusing not on the principal tourist sites but on the "uncatalogued riches" of a particular place. The sights listed above do not figure in the chapter on Milan. Instead she describes the Sforza Castle, the Palazzo Borromeo, the Ospedale Maggiore with its splendid loggia, the Portinari Chapel and the gardens overhanging the Naviglio, the canal that "intersects Milan with a layer of Venice" (*IB* 162). She observes that the city abounds in "suggestive juxtapositions of different centuries and styles" (*IB* 158). She also recommends the nearby pilgrimage church of the Madonna of Saronno. She advises the reader to focus on the "parentheses of travel," gathering intimate glimpses of sites not in guidebooks. The traveler will thus be able to "compose the image of each city" and "preserve its personality" in his or her own mind.

Miles, Mr.   *See* SUMMER.

Mingott, Mrs. Manson   *See* AGE OF INNOCENCE, THE.

Mirandolina of Chioggia   *See* VALLEY OF DECISION, THE.

"Miss Mary Pask"   Published in the *Pictorial Review* in April 1925, the story then appeared in *HERE AND BEYOND* (Appleton, 1926). This story concerns an elderly spinster, Miss Mary Pask, who disguises herself as a ghost and brings on the narrator's nervous collapse. The narrator, an expatriate painter, decides to look up Miss Pask, the sister of Grace Bridgeworth, wife of an old friend, at her house in Brittany. He assumes Miss Pask is like "hundreds of other dowdy old maids, cheerful derelicts content with their innumerable little substitutes for living," but discovers he is wrong.

After a frightening journey by horse and cart in thick fog, the narrator reaches the house, only to realize that he has suffered a terrible memory lapse—Miss Pask had died the previous year and is buried in the garden of the house. He recalls her sister wearing crepe and showing him the cable with news of her death. Suddenly, the apparition of Miss Pask comes to the door, welcoming him in a tremulous voice: "I've had so few visitors since my death, you see," she murmurs. She wants to know how Grace took the news of her death, and refuses to let him leave, begging him to " 'stay with me . . . just tonight . . . It's so sweet and quiet here. . . ' " The narrator finally breaks free and stumbles away.

He recovers from his breakdown and, in New York, visits the Bridgeworths to make sure they have provided for a marked grave. Grace is bewildered by his query, not realizing she had never informed him that Mary had not died but was in a cataleptic trance that confounded the doctors. " 'Surely she must have told you that she wasn't dead?' " she asks, near hysteria. " 'No . . . she didn't tell me that,' " he responds (*CSS* II, 379–84).

White suggests that after WORLD WAR I Wharton broadened her scope and included characters who were female, lower-class, elderly, and/or dispossessed, the "old maid" Miss Mary Pask being an example. It could be argued, however, that she had been aware of such bleak lives early in her career. A story called "BUNNER SISTERS," about two spinster sisters, proprietors of a millinery shop, was written in 1892, though it was rejected by Edward BURLINGAME because of its length; it was not published until 1916.

For further reading: Thomas, "Spook or Spinster? Edith Wharton's 'Miss Mary Pask.' "

"Mission of Jane, The"   A short story published in HARPER'S MAGAZINE in December 1902 and collected in THE DESCENT OF MAN AND OTHER STORIES (Scribner's, 1904), this story is a wry commentary on the power of a child to bring both dissension and unity to a dull marriage in which husband and wife lead relatively separate lives. Mrs. Lethbury has, according to her husband, "heirloom" ideas and a "stout set of everyday prejudices," whereas Mr. Lethbury believes he never uses an opinion twice if he can help it. Nevertheless, it is Mrs. Lethbury who, after many years of childlessness, discovers an orphaned baby in the course of her volunteer work and coaxes her husband into adopting her. As Jane grows up, her mother expands and becomes assertive; Mr. Lethbury is also transformed into the father of Jane rather than the husband of Mrs. Lethbury and lets down "barrier after barrier."

At first Jane seems a failure as a debutante, but she attracts an earnest young man, Mr. Budd. After a tumultuous courtship causing her parents to fear Jane's fiancé will call it off, the wedding takes place, followed by a celebratory breakfast at the home of her parents. The young couple drives off in a brougham for their wedding trip. Mr. Lethbury invites his wife out to a "jolly little dinner at a restaurant": Jane has "drawn them together at last."

The reviewer for the *Critic* termed the story a "sardonic little comedy, one of the best Mrs. Wharton ever wrote." He considered it a satire of the hackneyed popular short story built on the theme of the "well-worn home-and-fireside motive of an estranged husband and wife brought together through the agency of a child" (*CR* 84–85).

Mitchell, S[ilas] Weir (1829–1914)   A Philadelphia writer of historical romances and psychological studies, Mitchell was also a well-known neurologist. He developed his theory of the rest cure during the early 1870s. Mitchell's therapy, which emphasized concentrated rest, massage, electrical stimulation and massive overfeeding, epitomized, in the words of critic Daniel Rodgers, "passivity and ingestion." The cure spread widely, appealing to the middle and upper classes. In Charlotte Perkins Gilman's short story "The Yellow Wallpaper," the heroine, descending into madness, is threatened with referral to Dr. Mitchell. As late as 1904, a neurologist who criticized "neurasthenia" as a vague diagnosis "felt impelled to apologize for questioning one of the country's 'most distinctive and precious pathological possessions' " (Rodgers, *The Work Ethic in Industrial America 1850–1920*, 104–12).

It has been widely reported that Mitchell treated Wharton during her 1894–95 breakdown, but Benstock questions whether Wharton actually had a breakdown or a severe depression in 1895. Although she had attacks of flu, bronchitis and sinus infections, she

believes Wharton was "in good health most of the time and radiated *bien-être*" (*NGC* 78).

Lewis states that Wharton also consulted Mitchell in 1898, when she was suffering from extreme fatigue, inability to work, loss of weight, depression, headaches and nausea. Her chief physician in Philadelphia was Dr. George McClellan. Freed of household cares and given massages and electric treatment, she revived and was able to work on her fiction and galley proofs.

There is doubt, however, as to whether Wharton was ever treated by Mitchell. Benstock believes that she never underwent a rest cure of the type Mitchell advocated and that it has become an unsubstantiated and erroneous "fact" of her medical and personal history. She states that Wharton was not admitted to the Orthopaedic Hospital in Philadelphia but stayed at the Stenton Hotel, where Teddy was often with her. Walter BERRY frequently wrote her there. According to Benstock, Mitchell's newly cataloged records show no mention of Wharton. He was, moreover, grief-stricken over the death of his 22-year-old daughter and he and his wife were away on an extended voyage from October 1898 to January 1899.

Nor was Wharton treated by his deputies. Benstock's research shows that McClellan was a faculty colleague of Mitchell's, but was not on the staff at the Orthopaedic Hospital and not experienced in the Mitchell cure. She believes critics have extrapolated data from other documented examples of the Mitchell cure and erroneously deduced that Wharton had similar symptoms and treatment.

In any case, Wharton did not return to 884 Park Avenue in New York, but, with Teddy, took a rental house in Washington for several months after her Philadelphia stay. She continued, according to Benstock, to have cycles of flu and bronchitis for four years that improved when they built The MOUNT and began spending several months each year in the Berkshire mountains (*NGC* 94–98).

For further reading: Poirier, "The Weir Mitchell Rest Cure: Doctor and Patients."

Moffatt, Elmer   *See* CUSTOM OF THE COUNTRY, THE.

Moffatt, Undine   *See* CUSTOM OF THE COUNTRY, THE.

Morocco   A country in northwest Africa bordered by the Spanish Sahara and Algeria. European encroachments began as early as the 15th century. In the 19th century the strategic and economic importance of the country became apparent, and FRANCE, GERMANY and SPAIN all became rivals for control of it. In 1911 Germany agreed to a French protectorate in exchange for other French territory in Africa. In 1912 General (later Marshal) Hubert-Louis LYAUTEY rescued the Sultan of Morocco from a Berber uprising and was instrumental in establishing the French protectorate; the Spanish protectorate was established the same year. In 1956 France recognized Moroccan sovereignty, Spain turned over control of the Spanish zone and the country joined the United Nations.

Morocco was a country Edith Wharton found extraordinarily fascinating. It was the subject of her final travel book, *IN MOROCCO* (Scribner's, 1920). During one of the worst years of WORLD WAR I, 1917, General Lyautey, who had become resident general of French Morocco, invited her to visit Morocco as his guest. Several times in PARIS she had met the "soldier-statesman," to use Lewis's term, and considered him a "genuine modern hero," a view later historians have confirmed (*EW* 404). His purpose was to show her one of the annual industrial exhibitions that he had been organizing in the French colony since 1914 in order to impress on French subjects that World War I had not affected its normal activities. He had been encouraged to invite guests from Allied and neutral countries, and he arranged for Wharton, accompanied by Walter BERRY, to take a three-week motor tour of the colony. Few foreign travelers had visited Morocco at that time, and as late as a decade before Edith Wharton's visit, the country had no wheeled vehicles. Even as General Lyautey focused on modernization, he was careful to protect the heritage of the old Arab cities and to respect Muslim customs and traditions.

Edith Wharton's party made a circuit of the major cities, including Rabat and Salê, Moulay Idriss, Fez and Marrakech. She was privileged not only to ride through desert and town but to stroll in bazaars, to witness rare ceremonies and dances, to visit harems and to tour mosques and colleges seldom opened to foreigners, particularly women.

Two major concerns preoccupied Wharton: the country's indifference to conservation and the plight of the concubines brought from the countryside and mountain villages to lead an indolent life within the harem. The French administration had insisted both on saving and restoring native art and buildings. General Lyautey and the Moroccan director of fine arts had worked, for example, to repair the tombs of the Saadian Sultans at Marrakech (*IM* 149–50). Wharton observes that, were it not for French intervention, the "charming colonnades and cedar chambers" of the college of the Oudayas in Rabat would be "a heap of undistinguished rubbish—for plaster and rubble do not 'die in beauty' like the firm stones of Rome" (*IM* 22). Morocco, Wharton decided, was a "land of perpetual contradictions," projecting a mixture of "democratic familiarity and abject servility" (*IM* 90–91). She mourned the absence of even the most basic preservation, objecting that "the passion for building seems allied, in this country of inconsequences, to the supine indifference that lets existing constructions crumble back to clay. 'Dust to dust' should have been the motto of the Moroccan palace-builders" (*IM* 86).

With a discerning eye honed by previous travel writing, a hallmark also of her fiction, Wharton describes plump, slippered merchants riding abroad behind footmen, and dignitaries of the sultan's government traveling with their servants, along with water-carriers, sorcerers, Jews, university students, Islamic beggars and veiled women. She also brings to life famous traditional ceremonies, such as the Sacrifice of the Sheep. At the latter event, the contrast between the serene, plump sultan, a "hieratic" figure on a gray horse, and the "wild factious precipitate hordes" typifies "the strange soul of Islam, with its impetuosity forever culminating in impassiveness" (*IM* 166–70). It is as though Morocco, unlike France, is not "grown-up" (a term she also uses to describe American women compared with their French counterparts in *French Ways and Their Meaning*), but is dominated by talented adolescents who have an attitude of *carpe diem*.

Wharton and Berry were accompanied on part of their tour by the marquis de Segonzac and his wife. Their presence is not apparent from the text but is stated in a letter to her sister-in-law, Mary ("Minnie") JONES, where she describes the marquis as an authority on the tribes of the Atlas and an "intimate friend of all the great Caïds of the south." He is cited in her bibliography as the author of *Voyages au Maroc* and *Au Coeur de l'Atlas*, and his presence undoubtedly paved the way for visits to other places ordinarily inaccessible. En route back to Paris, Wharton was detained in Biarritz by a missed train; she wrote Minnie from the Hôtel du Palais how glad she was to have taken the chance, which would never come again, of "seeing that land of fairy-tale in fairy-tale fashion," and describes Marrakech as like "a sort of dream-Timbucktoo, all palms and red walls and fairy palaces against the sun-covered background of the Atlas" (unpublished letter to Mary Cadwalader Jones, Oct. 5, 1917; Edith Wharton Collection, BEINECKE LIBRARY, YALE UNIVERSITY).

She records the sounds and sights of a little-known "*country without a guide-book.*" Even visiting such a country, she declares, is "a sensation to rouse the hunger of the repletest sight-seer" (*IM* 3). When she dedicated *In Morocco* to "General Lyautey, Resident General of France in Morocco and to Madame Lyautey, thanks to whose kindness the journey I had so long dreamed of surpassed what I had dreamed," she anticipated one of the strongest motifs in the critical reception of the book: Morocco was a closed, exotic land few foreigners had visited. That an American woman had not only done so, but that she had been privileged to attend ceremonies and see sites prohibited to Western women in the past caused more than one writer to invest *In Morocco* with the aura of the *Arabian Nights.* The writer for the *Times Literary Supplement* was pleased that Mrs. Wharton had been "vouchsafed a Pisgah sight of a forbidden land," and had "grasped the broad masses of its colouring and the main outline of its form." Irita Van Doren, writing in the *Nation,* declared that "all the properties of an Arabian Nights tale are here—camels and donkeys, white-draped riders, palmetto deserts, camel's hair tents, and veiled women." It is a country "where dreams and realities are inextricably intermingled by the all-pervading spirit of languor." Morocco had been impenetrable, observed Dorothy Lawrence Mann in the *Boston Evening Transcript:* travelers might journey as far as Tangier, "but beyond Tangier lies mystery" (*CR* 299–303).

Compared with her earlier travel works, Wharton's last book maintains a balance between objectivity and involvement. Her authorial voice is actually far more personal here than in *ITALIAN BACKGROUNDS* or *ITALIAN VILLAS AND THEIR GARDENS.* She mentions her traveling companions by name and gives an exact description of some of the hazards of their journey—from the reviewers' point of view, welcome information about a country long perceived as an exotic enigma. The writer for the *Independent* stated that, ordinarily, "the average mortal is bound to feel a certain gnawing envy of the writer [of a book of travel]." Wharton, however, so captures the atmosphere "with all its blinding light, desert heat and vivid colors," that the reader can absorb for himself the sensations and emotions of having been in Morocco. The external realities of the journey have been converted, by the writer's imagination, into literary realities. As the critic for the British *Saturday Review* put it, "Nothing seen by her sensitive, unsparing eye is omitted, and her nervous style never fails to convey the effect at which she aims." The word "nervous" suggests a slight note of dismissal; Wharton has presented a convincing portrait of Morocco, but not without self-conscious effort.

Critical opinion was divided as to whether General Lyautey was rightly praised by Wharton for having "saved" what was not ruined of Morocco before his arrival or whether he was an agent of unjustified European imperialism. Van Doren believed Wharton's pro-French political orientation compromised her depiction of Morocco. She observes that Wharton considered the French occupation a "benevolent institution" and accepted without question the general theory of imperialism. She challenged Wharton's premise that the country originally had a "demoralised" condition that made European interference "inevitable" (*CR* 301). The reviewer for the *Dial* wrote that Wharton had "caught Morocco in a mood which its after-the-war exploitation will efface for ever," and Mann, foresaw an "influx of tourists" that would banish "that atmosphere of strangeness which is so binding today." Paradoxically, Wharton had written the book in part for the postwar tourists she felt sure would visit Morocco. Her

motivation may have been mixed: by validating and explaining the work of General Lyautey, she justifies his hospitality in arranging her journey.

Though the book is polemical to some extent in its praise of France's colonial policy, its prevailing perspective is that of the connoisseur. Critics may well have preferred this angle in dealing with the "sticky" imperialist problem that they themselves had conceivably not resolved.

For further reading: Funston, "*In Morocco:* Edith Wharton's Heart of Darkness."

"Mortal Lease, The"   Poem written in 1908 and published in *ARTEMIS TO ACTAEON AND OTHER VERSE* (Scribner's, 1909). This poem was written in October 1908, when Edith Wharton mistakenly believed her affair with Morton FULLERTON had ended. She then returned to a favorite genre, poetry, writing William Crary BROWNELL in October 1908, "I have perversely and inexcusably taken to warbling again" (*EW* 234). Lewis observes that her liaison with Fullerton inspired at least 10 poems in 1908 and 1909. Of these, "The Mortal Lease" is considered by many critics to be the most successful.

It is a sequence of eight sonnets; the title suggests the boundaries of mortality. It retraces the stages of the DIARY of 1907 (the "Love Diary") she had kept of her developing relationship with Fullerton. Having stood apart from life, she is astonished to find herself drawn into the maelstrom of sexual passion; she has been like a "nun entranced" who has held her "Bridegroom in her soul." She will live amid his kisses "as in some island of a storm-blown sea." The storm has receded, but the speaker has reached a state of detached resignation, finding solace in a life of hard work. Lewis observes that in actuality the affair was far from finished. She saw Fullerton again in Paris during the spring of 1909 and in April wrote an unfinished sequel to the poem, "COLOPHON TO THE MORTAL LEASE."

Both Lewis and Benstock provide extensive analyses of the poem and its sequel.

Mother's Recompense, The   Novel serialized in the *PICTORIAL REVIEW* and published in 1925 by APPLETON, it first took shape as an unpublished story, "Disintegration," of which a 74-page typescript exists in the Edith Wharton Collection in the BEINECKE LIBRARY, YALE UNIVERSITY. It deals with the relationship between an unhappy expatriate woman, Kate Clephane, who has spent 18 shabby years in EUROPE, and her daughter, Anne, whom Kate deserted when she was only three in order to escape her husband's grim house. Kate lived at first as the mistress of Hylton Davies, "the agent of her release," but later fell violently in love with Chris Fenno, a man about 14 years younger than she. Anne, who has grown up in luxury in America, is now, as Percy

A. Hutchison put it in a review for the *New York Times,* "by law and by temperament the mistress of her own destinies" (*CR* 397). She is in love with Fenno. Kate does not confess their past. She herself is also still in love with him, even though she perceives him as a fortune hunter and dilettante, but, more than that, she fears to jeopardize her daughter's happiness. Anne proposes that they should all live together after their marriage. Rather than explain her real reasons for refusal, Kate states that she is getting married again herself to a former beau, Fred Landers. Fred, however, becomes jealous of Kate's past, one of many reasons she eventually decides against the marriage.

The novel had a very long gestation in Wharton's imagination. Cynthia Griffin Wolff believes she reflected on the novel for 25 years, since she discussed its metamorphosis in the various DONNÉE BOOKS between 1900 and 1925, and also in the 1918–23 notebook; both the final title and an alternative one, "DISINTEGRATION," were considered. She believes the novel represents the desire of Kate to reestablish her maternal bond with Anne, but not in a healthy way. Kate is actually an actress, in Wolff's view, refashioning herself for her role of mother, yet preying on Anne in a cannibalistic way: "she can continue to *be,* so long as she participates in Anne's reality." Kate, however, pulls back from the precipice of sacrificing Anne by "attempting to engross all of the girl's affections into herself" (Wolff, *A Feast of Words,* 350–51). She ultimately chooses, despite the "old horrors and the new loneliness . . . shutting away in a little space of peace and light the best thing that had ever happened to her" (*The Mother's Recompense,* 342).

Katherine Joslin calls the novel "an unconventional retelling of the incest story," a theme of great interest to Wharton because it represents "the powerful pull of the initial community, parents and family, on the individual" (Joslin, *Edith Wharton,* 110–11). She links it to ETHAN FROME, the BEATRICE PALMATO fragment and SUMMER. In the view of Dale Bauer, one of the most horrifying revelations for Kate Clephane is that Anne's submission to Chris Fenno "reproduces her father's authority"; he represents for Kate "the patriarchal authority she flees and which Anne embraces" (*Edith Wharton's Brave New Politics,* 78).

The novel was well received by the public, vying for a time with F. Scott FITZGERALD's *The Great Gatsby* for the top position on the best-seller list. Kate, in the opinion of some reviewers, was so sharply etched as to rival Lily Bart, in *The HOUSE OF MIRTH,* as Wharton's most lasting feminine creation. Some reviewers objected, however, that Chris Fenno was a shadowy character, and others complained that the novel should have had a happy ending. "Never did a novel scream so loudly for a sentimental ending," Hutchison remarked, but praised the author's restraint in not providing one. Edith Wharton

retorted that the epigraph, from Shelley, "Desolation is a delicate thing," explained her decision. Louis Auchincloss, however, suggests a different explanation, that she was attempting to focus on Kate's "belated stand against the tolerances of post–World War I American society which . . . had reached a pitch of blandness that threatened to destroy all the old standards of taste and morality" (Introduction, xii). Wharton had treated the theme of the stigma of divorce in the short story "AUTRES TEMPS . . ." (1916). In that story, Leila Lidcote, who has also deserted a husband and daughter, finds on returning to America that, as Auchincloss puts it, "society does not revise its judgments for those already condemned" (Introduction to Scribner's 1986 reprint of the novel, viii). Leila's daughter, on the other hand, receives full social dispensation for having left her husband and married her lover. Kate Clephane, however, suffers less from the stigma of divorce than from the fact that she still loves Chris Fenno despite his flaws.

Financially, the novel did well. The serial rights alone, purchased by Arthur Vance for the *Pictorial Review,* brought in about $32,000.

For further reading: Auchincloss, Introduction to reprint of *The Mother's Recompense;* Bauer, *Edith Wharton's Brave New Politics;* Joslin, *Edith Wharton;* Raphael, "Shame in Edith Wharton's *The Mother's Recompense";* Tonkovich, "An Excess of Recompense: The Feminine Economy of *The Mother's Recompense";* Walker, "Mothers and Lovers: Edith Wharton's *The Reef* and *The Mother's Recompense";* Wolff, *A Feast of Words: The Triumph of Edith Wharton.*

Motor-Flight Through France, A Travel book about FRANCE published by Scribner's in 1908. The essays comprising this volume, Edith Wharton's first book describing automobile travel and her first about France, had been published serially in the ATLANTIC MONTHLY: one installment in 1906, two in 1907 and three in 1908. *Motor-Flight* points up the perfections of France during the BELLE ÉPOQUE. It is based on three automobile journeys the Whartons took in 1906 and 1907.

In May 1906, Teddy and Edith, accompanied by her brother Henry Edward JONES, made what she described as a "giro" around portions of France. Picking up their car at Boulogne, they went via Arras to Amiens, on to Beauvais and Rouen, down the Seine to Les Andelys, Nantes, Versailles, Fontainebleau, Orleans, Tours and into the Auvergne, visiting George SAND's home at NOHANT. They continued on to Vichy, Royat, Bourges and Chartres.

In March 1907, the Whartons made a second motor tour, accompanied by Henry JAMES, who had greatly envied Edith Wharton her earlier visit to Nohant. Teddy had closed in the Panhard-Levassor and added an electric light, along with "every known accessorie and comfort," as he wrote Sara NORTON. He took pleasure in catering to his wife's "nice, to me, worldly side," even though he was admittedly "no good on Puss's high plain of thought" (*EW* 177). Benstock observes that "Teddy proved a resilient and good-humored companion" whose "spirits seemed to soar at the prospect of motor-flights" (*NGC* 170). The Whartons' second "flight" took them on an itinerary of more than 2,000 miles, from PARIS to Poitiers, the Pyrenees and Provence. The final "flight" was a tour of the northeast section of France. Ironically, some of the towns described, such as Meaux, would later figure in *FIGHTING FRANCE, FROM DUNKERQUE TO BELFORT* as examples of the devastation caused by the war.

Wharton begins the book by extolling the way in which "the motor-car has restored the romance of travel." Her journeys are more rapid and free of the "bondage to fixed hours and the beaten track" that have characterized railway travel (*MFF* 1). The number of towns visited and described suggests that the motorcar could, and did, cover far more territory than the carriages and diligences of the author's Italian journeys. She cautions the traveler, however, that rapid travel entails the sacrifice of many charming byways and little-known places that are well worth seeing. Although Wharton sees the car as an improvement over the uncertainties of travel once experienced by her "posting grandparents," the slow tours and pilgrimages of IRVING, Hawthorne, Cooper and Emerson had their value in thorough observation and assimilation of sights. Mobility has eroded leisure by opening more and more possibilities; her habituated responses are adapting to the changes in travel. The freedom of the motorcar almost undergoes a metamorphosis into tyranny. The unexplored towns of France fly by as the motorcar rushes through the various provinces; it is impossible to see every town in the time allotted. The new mode of transport suggests that Wharton is abandoning the scholarly stance that had been the hallmark of *ITALIAN BACKGROUNDS;* her arguments are directed less at refuting art critics and more at guiding her fellow travelers.

Wharton's French travels also served to justify her expatriation. Schriber suggests that America is actually a strong component of *Motor-Flight,* arguing that Wharton's French motor trips "offer us a journey back into early 20th-century America. The hum and buzz of American culture, the issues of the era, the insecurity of America in the face of the cultural superiority of Europe are the intertexts of Wharton's text (Introduction to rpt., *A Motor-Flight Through France,* xli–xlii). This may imply that Wharton was attempting to reinforce her decision to live in France permanently. In a rather oblique way, she also indicts NEWPORT and American materialism when she praises Vichy, a resort that is ". . . to the American observer . . . most instructive just because it is not the millionaire's wand which has worked the spell; because the town owes its gaiety and its

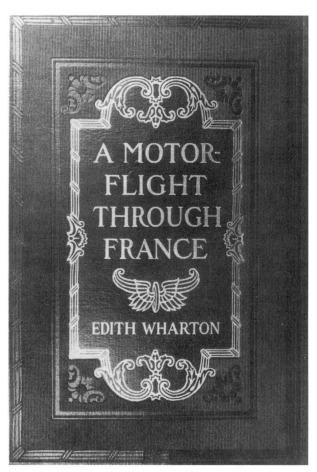

A Motor-Flight Through France *(1908). Cover, first edition* (Collection of the author)

elegance, not to the private villa, the rich man's 'show-place,' but to wise public expenditure of the money which the bathers annually pour into its exchequer" (*MFF* 52). Here Wharton discloses her objections to the insular American culture evident at Newport.

Motor-Flight is the first of Edith Wharton's travel books to provide itineraries that could be reenacted by travelers today. Almost every chapter offers a precise description of the route the party followed. *Italian Backgrounds,* in contrast, represents a conflation of the Whartons' many perambulations, which took place over several years. *ITALIAN VILLAS AND THEIR GARDENS,* similarly, is not based on a linear itinerary. The Whartons often stayed in a central city, such as Florence, Genoa or Rome, and made excursions out to villas.

Lewis calls this volume "perhaps the best of Edith Wharton's always superior and original travel books" (*EW* 168). Contemporary critics, however, received the book version with the same "confused atavistic enjoyment" Wharton recommended for travelers to France.

One critic regretted that she was not the novelist of *The Valley of Decision,* nor the Henry James of *English*

Hours, nor the fine book designer who produced *Italian Backgrounds.* Another wished to shrink the book, and a third believed the book should have been delayed and much expanded. The writer for the *Nation* wished the author had concentrated upon one region and "given us a picture of a French province as complete and unforgettable as that of Northern Italy in her *The Valley of Decision.*" The reviewer for the British journal *The Academy* felt the title suggested hurry, and wished she had waited until she could write "that fine, accurate, and sympathetic travel-book that we are sure she will at length compose . . . [probably] about France, for the love of that vivacious land is in the author's heart, betraying itself a hundred times." She did not compose such a volume, but showed her love of her adopted country seven years later, during World War I, in *Fighting France, from Dunkerque to Belfort.*

Wharton was delighted when Henry James took her to call on George MEREDITH in 1908 and learned that he was "flying through France" in her motor at that very moment.

For further reading: Foster, "Making It Her Own: Edith Wharton's Europe"; St. Laurent, "Pathways to a Personal Aesthetic: Edith Wharton's Travels in Italy and France"; Sapora, "Motor Flights through France"; Schriber, "Edith Wharton and the Dog-Eared Travel Book"; Schriber, Introduction to reprint of *A Motor-Flight Through France;* Wright, *Edith Wharton Abroad: Selected Travel Writings, 1888–1920;* Wright, *Edith Wharton's Travel Writing: The Making of a Connoisseur.*

"Motor-Flight Through Spain, A" A six-page unpublished typescript (c. 1926) in the BEINECKE LIBRARY, YALE UNIVERSITY. It consists of an untitled and unnumbered page and a half laying out a journey following "the way of the Pilgrims across the Pyrenees" and mentioning the authors whose books had whetted Edith Wharton's appetite for the undertaking. The first two pages may have been intended as a preface explaining the purpose of the journey to SPAIN. She and her party were "travellers eager to follow with our eyes what a few masterly books had so vividly put before our imagination—the way of the Pilgrims across the Pyrenees and north-west Sapin [*sic*] to the ultimate goal of Compostela."

The remaining four pages are numbered consecutively and titled "A Motor-Flight Through Spain." In Section I, "Aragon," she summarizes the ambience of Spain from the point of view of the entering motorist, its "sunlight so searching that each object stands forth with the merciless prominence of the stereopticon—Spain." Section II, beginning on page 2, is not titled, but contains a description of Jaca and its cathedral. It is possible that, had she developed the fragment into a book, she would have followed the scheme of *A MOTOR-FLIGHT THROUGH FRANCE,* partitioning the itinerary into several segments based on separate journeys.

Mount, The The home in LENOX, Massachusetts, built by Edith and Teddy Wharton, finished in 1902, and sold in 1911. By 1899, Edith Wharton was finding the frivolity of NEWPORT, as well as its damp climate, oppressive, and she and her husband began to think of selling their Newport home, LAND'S END, and building a country home in Lenox.

The Whartons had long known the area of the Berkshire mountains in Western Massachusetts, and Lenox in particular. It was a fashionable summer resort where many wealthy people from New York, Boston, Philadelphia and other cities were building country homes where they would spend a number of months each year. In 1892 Mrs. William Craig Wharton, Teddy's mother, had bought a comfortable Queen Anne–style home, Pine Acre, on one of the main streets of Lenox; it had been built in 1885 (information courtesy of Scott Marshall, Edith Wharton Restoration). During the summers of 1900, 1901 and 1902, the Whartons stayed in The Poplars, a cottage in Lenox owned by Leonard and Louisa Sands. It was across from Laurel Lake Farm, a property of 113 acres they liked very much. In February 1901 they came back to Lenox and stayed at Mrs. Curtis's lodging house; while there they made an offer to buy Laurel Lake Farm. By late April they had reached an agreement to purchase it from Miss Georgiana Sargent, a watercolorist related to John Singer SARGENT, for $40,600 (approximately $600,000 today; *NGC* 116–17). This was the same year Edith Wharton's mother, Lucretia Rhinelander JONES, died in Paris.

Wharton wrote Ogden CODMAN that she was "in love with the place—climate, scenery, life, & all—and when I have built a villa on one of the estates I have picked out, & have planted my gardens & laid out paths through my bosco, I doubt if I ever leave here—" (Dwight, 67). They began building "The Mount," named for the estate of Wharton's great-grandfather, Gen. Ebenezer Stevens, on Long Island. Many of the Whartons' friends assumed that Codman would design the house, since he had remodeled Land's End in Newport and he and Wharton had collaborated on *The DECORATION OF HOUSES.* He did submit sketches, but his initial plans were too costly. There were also other disputes.

The house was finally designed by architect Francis L. V. Hoppin. It was modeled on Belton House (1684) in Lincolnshire, England. Codman designed the interior of The Mount's principal rooms, including moldings for doors, windows and ceilings; he also designed plasterwork of fruit in the style of Grinling Gibbons and designed oak bookcases for Edith's library (*NGC* 126). The villa was a four-story structure of white stucco. When Henry JAMES saw it in 1904, he described it as "an elegant . . . wonderful abode . . . an exquisite and marvelous place, a delicate French chateau mirrored in a Massachusetts pond." (*NGC* 130). The architecture has elements of Italian and

English styles as well. The approach from what is now Plunkett Street (then Cross Road) is along a sugar maple–lined drive. The ground level entryway echoed the palace on Isola Bella, Lago MAGGIORE, Italy. The reception rooms were up one flight (a European *piano nobile* arrangement) and included a large airy drawing room and dining room, both with French doors, as well as Edith's paneled library with two French-style writing tables. All three rooms (designed *en enfilade*) opened onto a canopied terrace with a Palladian staircase leading down into formal gardens; many of the Whartons' houseguests were photographed on the terrace. On the south side of the house was an Italian-style sunken walled "secret garden." The bedroom floor had a master suite with Edith Wharton's boudoir, her bedroom and bath; Teddy's suite had a bedroom, dressing room and bath. There were several guest rooms. Luria points out that Wharton follows her own advice, given in *The Decoration of Houses,* about the importance of separating the public and private rooms; an enclosed staircase leads from the public

rooms on the second floor to the private bedrooms on the third ("The Architecture of Manners," 307). The Whartons enjoyed a view of Laurel Lake and the Tyringham Mountains. The top attic floor was given over to servants' rooms.

The house had several outbuildings as well, including a white stucco stable (also modeled after the one at Belton House), a greenhouse, a gatehouse lodge for the head gardener and his family, and several small cottages (one of these occupied by Alfred WHITE, the butler). Benstock states that construction of The Mount, including architect's and decorator's fees, was only $87,000, a fraction of the cost of building many neighboring estates (*NGC* 131). Wharton's niece, Beatrix Jones FARRAND, one of the first women landscape architects, helped plan the landscaping, including the drive and the kitchen garden.

The house was nearly finished by autumn 1902, but there were many problems remaining to be resolved before the Whartons were satisfied, including some interior details. The worst mistake, according to

East Terrace, The Mount, Lenox, Massachusetts (c. 1905) (Courtesy The Beinecke Rare Book and Manuscript Library, Yale University)

Codman, was the awkward circular forecourt; he wrote his mother it was an "utter failure, it looks like a clothes yard and is all out of proportion" (*NGC* 132).

Wharton reveled both in The Mount's physical creation and the intellectual ambiance she was able to create. For the next nine years, the Whartons spent part of every year at The Mount except for 1909 and 1910, when Teddy's mental state was precariously unbalanced. Walter BERRY, Henry James, Gaillard LAPSLEY, Robert NORTON and John Hugh SMITH were frequent houseguests, as well as Morton FULLERTON, with whom Wharton had an affair. She took part in community affairs, serving on the Lenox Library Committee, the Village Improvement Committee, and the Flower Show Committee (*EW* 136).

The Whartons sold The Mount in 1911. For an excellent account of the marital troubles leading to this decision, and for the history of The Mount since it passed out of the hands of the Whartons, *see* Scott Mar-

shall, *The Mount: Home of Edith Wharton.* Briefly, Teddy Wharton's mental state had begun declining about 1909, and had reached the point by July 1911 that Edith seriously considered separating from him and living permanently in Paris. This was a decision with which her closest friends, including James, Lapsley and Hugh Smith concurred. It was extremely difficult for Teddy, however, since managing The Mount had been his principal occupation since it was built. Wharton gave him authority to put the property on the market and it was sold in September 1911 to Mary and Albert R. Shattuck of New York City for approximately $180,000. They had rented The Mount in 1909 and 1910 while the Whartons were in Europe.

The Shattucks owned The Mount from 1912 to 1938. It was then purchased at public auction by Louise D. and Carr Van Anda and then sold in 1942 to the Foxhollow School, which used the house for junior and senior housing from 1942 to 1976. In 1978, a theatrical

Edith and Teddy Wharton, Henry James and Charles Cook in a touring car at The Mount (Courtesy Lilly Library, Indiana University)

group, Shakespeare & Company, leased the house from a developer, who had purchased it when the school went out of business, with an option to purchase it. They began presenting summer theatrical productions. In 1979, the National Trust for Historic Preservation became involved with the property. Edith Wharton Restoration was founded one year later (1980) and purchased 49 of the original acres with the house and outbuildings. The two groups were based on the property, although problems involving appropriate use and restoration priorities led to an eventual legal resolution. The result is that extensive renovation of the exterior of the house is currently under way, while restoration of the interior and the gardens is being planned.

In her autobiography, Wharton states that The Mount had been her first real home: "though it is nearly twenty years since I last saw it (for I was too happy there ever to want to revisit it as a stranger) its blessed influence still lives in me" (*BG* 125).

For further reading: Luria, "The Architecture of Manners: Henry James, Edith Wharton, and The Mount"; Marshall, *The Mount: Home of Edith Wharton.*

"Moving Finger, The" First published in *Harper's Magazine* in March 1901, the story was included in *Crucial Instances* (Scribner's, 1901). The story, termed by Lawson an "inchoate ghost story" ("Edith Wharton," *American Short-Story Writers, 1880–1910,* 312), is about Claydon, a portrait painter who has been asked by a friend, Ralph Grancy, to paint a portrait of his second wife. The finished work is much admired, not only by Grancy but also by his friends, including the narrator. After his wife's death three years later, Grancy serves as a foreign diplomat but senses his wife's continual presence, imagining her to be aging along with him. After five years, he returns to the country house they once shared, but believes the portrait of the young Mrs. Grancy mocks him. He has grown older, but she has remained young and is now a stranger. He asks Claydon to age the woman in the portrait, which he does, horrified at the result. Grancy believes Claydon has restored his wife to him, however.

The narrator sees Grancy a decade later and realizes the portrait has continued to age with him; he is ill. Moreover, the visage is of "a woman who knows that her husband is dying." On the death of Grancy, Claydon inherits the painting and restores it to its original state; her beauty, he explains to the narrator, belongs to him; he has possessed Mrs. Grancy by painting her.

"Mr. Jones" Short story published in *The Ladies' Home Journal* in April 1928; the story was collected in CERTAIN PEOPLE (Appleton, 1930). Originally called "The Parasite," the story deals with a writer, Lady Jane Lynke, who inherits Bells, an ancestral English home. "Mr. Jones" is the guardian spirit of the house; he had, in the owner's

"SHE WAS THE MOST BEAUTIFUL . . . OF EXPLANATIONS"

THE MOVING FINGER
BY EDITH WHARTON

Illustration for "The Moving Finger" (1901), artist unknown (Courtesy Alderman Library, University of Virginia)

lifetime, imprisoned his employer's deaf and dumb wife. Now dead, he protects the "secret past" of the house. White observes that the use of Edith Wharton's father's name is not accidental: "one does not have to be an analyst to wonder about these daughters with guilty secrets being preyed upon by parasitic fathers who can never be locked out" (40). A similar situation occurs in "The HOUSE OF THE DEAD HAND."

Lady Jane's chosen literary field, travel writing, echoes Edith Wharton's own interest in this genre. She describes Lady Jane as modestly independent and having written "two or three brisk business-like little books about cities usually dealt with sentimentally." Soon after she inherits the house, Lady Jane attempts to see it but is turned away by the housekeeper's niece, who states that "Mr. Jones" forbids showing the house. She and an old friend of the family, Edward Stramer, a novelist, are both guests at a country house in Kent soon afterwards, where she learns of the mysterious

"I HAD THE FEELING THAT SHE DIDN'T EVEN RECOGNIZE ME"

Illustration for "The Moving Finger" (1901), artist unknown
(Courtesy Alderman Library, University of Virginia)

reputation of Bells. Once she moves in, she invites Stramer to stay and work for a time, knowing he enjoys settling in the country where he could be "sure of not being disturbed." She also hopes that a companion will dispel the eerie atmosphere in which "Mr. Jones" governs all actions of the elderly housekeeper and her niece and, indirectly, her own. Together Lady Jane and Stramer unravel the secret of the house, relying on letters they discover in a locked desk purportedly belonging to "Mr. Jones," as well as a portrait of "Also His Wife," the unhappy, mute wife of the 15th Viscount Thudeney who died of the plague during the Regency period, at Aleppo, in 1828. White terms "Mr. Jones" the Viscount's "amanuensis" (166).

Although "AFTER HOLBEIN" and "A BOTTLE OF PERRIER" were considered more effective stories in the volume, Maxim Lièber, writing in the New York *World*, termed this a "deft little mystery story" (*CR* 483).

"Mr. Sturgis's *Belchamber*"   (Review of novel by Howard Sturgis); *see* STURGIS, Howard.

"Mrs. Manstey's View"   Published in SCRIBNER'S MAGAZINE in July 1891, this was Edith Wharton's first published work of fiction. It was not reprinted until R. W. B. Lewis published a complete edition of the short stories in 1968. White states that this early story eclipses several of those included in *The GREATER INCLINATION*, the first collection of Edith Wharton's short stories, but also observes that she liked "the idea of having some youthful excesses to repudiate" (28). The story concerns the plight of Mrs. Manstey, impoverished widow of a clerk in a wholesale house, reduced to living in a single back room of a New York boardinghouse. Her increasing infirmities prevent her from visiting her only child, a daughter in California, and her sole interest is gazing from her window at the adjacent cluttered and unkempt backyards.

For 17 years, however, the view has yielded numerous satisfactions: a magnolia here, an unfolding hyacinth there, a cook disobeying her mistress and feeding stray cats, a repainting of an exterior. These small events excel, in interest, the preoccupations of Mrs. Manstey's few visitors, such as their unknown (to her) grandchildren. She suddenly learns that a planned extension to a nearby house is about to begin that will eclipse her view and blot out her world. She offers to pay Mrs. Black, the owner of the adjacent building, not to build, but Mrs. Black considers her crazy and puts her off with deceptive promises. When building begins, Mrs. Manstey slips out at night and sets a fire that destroys the extension. In the process, however, she catches pneumonia and dies on the very day workmen resume building the extension.

The story pits the sensitive Mrs. Manstey, reveling in each blossom and small triumph of nature, against the forces of materialism and greed. Lewis calls it an "imaginative escape" toward "penury and solitude" from the life Edith Wharton was actually living at the time (*EW* 61).

Mugnier, Abbé Arthur   The vicar of the Church of Ste.-Clotilde and, later, a Canon of Nôtre Dame, the Abbé Mugnier was a well-known and much respected and loved Parisian. Edith Wharton met him about 1908, and their friendship continued for many years. As she recalled in *A BACKWARD GLANCE,* he was "the most beloved, the kindliest and one of the wittiest" of the guests who frequented Madame Rosa de FITZ-JAMES's salon. There, his "sensitive intelligence was a solvent for the conflicting ideas and opinions of the other visitors." Wharton described him as small, with eyes "always smiling behind their spectacles," a man with a "quick sense of fun and irony" lined with "tender human sympathy." He converted the famed decadent novelist Joris Karl Huysmans to Catholicism. When he was quite elderly, in the early 1930s, he gradually lost his sight, but his friends subscribed to a fund providing taxis each day so that he might go out to dine. In 1933 the fund was increased, enabling him to have eye surgery, and his sight was partially restored. Lewis believes that Edith Wharton's interest in religious questions in later life was partly due to his influence.

"Muse's Tragedy, The" Short story published in SCRIBNER'S MAGAZINE in July 1891 and collected in *The GREATER INCLINATION* (Scribner's, 1899). The story, which Lewis terms "a deft study of the contradictions of literary genius" (*EW* 81), concerns Danyers, a young poet and scholar whose work has been much influenced by the late poet Vincent Rendle. In Italy he meets Mrs. Anerton, who, with her late husband, had enjoyed a long friendship with Rendle. She has now become known in literary circles as the probable source for the Silvia of Rendle's *Sonnets to Silvia,* and has begun to edit the poet's letters for publication. They begin talking about the great man, and Danyers realizes that in a sense "Silvia had herself created the *Sonnets to Silvia.*" She confesses the significance of the asterisks punctuating the poet's letters to Mrs. A. Gradually Danyers finds he is attracted to her and cannot understand why Rendle had not married her once her husband died. He proposes to her, but, after a month together in Venice, she refuses him, believing she might wind up as a "pretty little essay with a margin." It turns out that Rendle had never loved her except in an intellectual way. From her interlude with Danyers, she realizes all that she has missed. Waid believes the story suggests Edith Wharton's "anxiety that devoting herself to art . . . may lead to a life of isolation and loneliness," as in the cases of Mrs. Ambrose Dale in "COPY" and Mrs. Amyot in "The PELICAN" (Waid, Introduction, *The Muse's Tragedy and Other Stories,* 17).

"The Muse's Tragedy" draws on many of Wharton's Italian travels and prefigures her volume on Italian villas and gardens. For instance, in *ITALIAN VILLAS AND THEIR GARDENS,* she describes the Villa d'Este at Cernobbio on Lake COMO, admiring the fluted descending water basins and carved entablature and statuary in the gardens. She detects in the gardens at the Villa d'Este "much of the Roman spirit—the breadth of design, the unforced inclusion of natural features, and that sensitiveness to the quality of the surrounding landscape that characterizes the great gardens of the Campagna" (*IV* 211). She thus invests the hillside ruins on Lake Como with the spirit of early Rome, and, moreover, links them with the ruins on the Campagna. In the story, Danyers takes a "morning ramble" among the hills and he and Mrs. Anerton converse leaning over the parapet above the lake; they later climb to the ruined temples above the villa.

Edith Wharton's editor at Scribner's, William Crary BROWNELL, wrote her that the book had been "appreciated so much in so many directions that I have heard of . . . that you can assuredly plume yourself on having joined the 'note' of universality to that of distinction" (*EW* 89). Reviewers praised the entire volume of stories; several linked Edith Wharton with Henry JAMES, which she considered a tribute at that early stage of her career. "What," asked the reviewer for the *Critic,* "is 'The Muse's Tragedy' but *The Tragic Muse* turned other end to?" (*CR* 24). (In James's novel, Nicholas Dormer, son of an English statesman, gives up fortune, position and marriage to his beautiful cousin to become a portrait painter; he is inspired by the example of his "muse," the actress Miriam Rooth). John D. Barry, of *Literary World,* found the story the finest in the volume.

N

National Institute of Arts and Letters   The parent organization, founded in 1898, of the AMERICAN ACADEMY OF ARTS AND LETTERS. The Academy was founded in 1904 to honor particularly distinguished individuals. The novelist Brand Whitlock wished to propose Edith Wharton in 1924, but could not. Only members of the National Institute of Arts and Letters were eligible for election, and that organization had no provision for female members, although it had no provision barring them either. In January 1925 Wharton was awarded the institute's Gold Medal, given for "distinguished services to art or letters in the creation of original work." She was elected to membership in the National Institute in 1926 and in the Academy in 1930. She was actually the second woman to be elected; Julia Ward Howe was the first.

New England   When *ETHAN FROME* was published, one American critic called it an "an interesting example of a successful New England story written by some one who knew nothing of New England." Edith Wharton was indignant, stating in her memoir that she had spent 10 years in the hill region where the scene is laid and "had come to know well the aspect, dialect, and mental and moral attitude of the hill-people" (*BG* 296). Although not a native, she was convinced she wrote with the authority of one. In her original introduction to the novella, Wharton states that she had long believed the "outcropping granite" of New England had been overlooked in fictional depictions of the region, which focused on "sweet-fern, asters and mountain-laurel, and the conscientious reproduction of the vernacular." She wished to show the stony, tragic side of local life: farms that barely yielded a living, icy weather and, above all, the rugged, stoic character of the people.

Donna Campbell has emphasized that Wharton repudiated the tradition of the New England local color "authoresses" very early in her career. Responding to the 1890s transition between local color and naturalism, she was impatient with what she called their "rose and lavender pages" ("Edith Wharton and the 'Authoresses': The Critique of Local Color in Wharton's Early Fiction," 169–83).

The novella *SUMMER*, which Wharton called the "hot Ethan," was set, like *Ethan Frome,* in the Berkshires near LENOX. One of its most haunting scenes is the night burial of Charity Royall's mother, Mary Hyatt, in a des-olate cabin on the "Mountain," by reputation the haunt of thieves and outlaws. Charity and the minister climb the mountain by horse and buggy, "the world dropping away below them in great mottled stretches of forest and field, and stormy dark blue distances" (*Summer,* Ch. 16). *The FRUIT OF THE TREE* was also set in New England, as well as a number of short stories, including "BEWITCHED," "THE TRIUMPH OF NIGHT," "THE ANGEL AT THE GRAVE," and "XINGU." One of Wharton's lesser known stories, "THE YOUNG GENTLEMEN," takes place on the Massachusetts coast between Salem and New-buryport. Barbara White states that about one quarter of Wharton's 85 published stories have a New England setting (*Wharton's New England,* Introd., viii).

From 1899 to 1908 Wharton spent every summer in Lenox, usually from June to December. Scott Marshall offers a detailed discussion of Wharton's life at The MOUNT and her travels through the countryside. The Whartons were chauffeured by Charles COOK in "George" (the Whartons' car, named for George SAND). He notes that they went to Worcester, Groton, Maine, New Hampshire, NEWPORT and the top of Mount Greylock, the highest peak in Massachusetts (*The Mount: Home of Edith Wharton,* 56). A favorite destination was Ashfield, where Charles Eliot NORTON and his daughters lived. Lewis points out that when Henry JAMES visited in 1904 they drove as far as New York State to see the Hudson and to the Shaker Settlement at Mt. Lebanon, New York. Wharton "regaled the fascinated James with reports that had reached her about the dark unsuspected life—the sexual violence, even the incest—that went on behind the bleak walls of the farmhouses" (*EW* 140). He had written her before the visit that he anticipated his return to "the New England beauty of forest, mountain, lake & general Arcadian ease" (Powers, *Henry James and Edith Wharton: Letters 1900–1915,* 37), so he may well have been surprised by her revelations.

White suggests that these long, slow motor trips, often fraught with breakdowns, were a particular source of inspiration for Wharton's fiction. She argues that she was disinterested in presenting "local color" but, instead, used the New England setting for "her own more Hawthornean purposes, as symbolic means of exploring favorite subjects, such as the absence of high culture in modern life, the permeation of the present by the past, and the claustrophobia of female experience" (*Wharton's New England,* Introd., xi). Lewis believes that the work of Hawthorne had an undoubted impact on *Ethan Frome* (*EW* 237). He wrote several books in Lenox in a cottage on the Tanglewood estate, now the home of the Tanglewood Music Festival.

In Lenox Wharton took a keen interest in local affairs and served on the Lenox Library Committee, the Village Improvement Committee and the Flower Show Committee (*EW* 136). Marshall states that she entered several competitions of the Lenox Horticultural Society and in 1905 received seven first prizes (*The Mount: Home of Edith Wharton,* 56).

For further reading: Campbell, "Edith Wharton and the 'Authoresses': The Critique of Local Color in Wharton's Early Fiction"; Hamblen, "Edith Wharton in New England"; Rose, " 'Such Depths of Sad Initiation': Edith Wharton and New England"; White, ed., *Wharton's New England: Seven Stories and* Ethan Frome.

New Year's Day (The 'Seventies) The last in the chronological sequence of the OLD NEW YORK series of four novellas, published in 1924 by Appleton. The others were FALSE DAWN (THE 'FORTIES), *The* OLD MAID (THE 'FIFTIES) and *The* SPARK (THE 'SIXTIES). Lewis gives a poignant evocation of Edith Wharton early on the morning of her 60th birthday, January 24, 1922, at her winter home, STE.-CLAIRE CHÂTEAU, in HYÈRES. As was her habit, she was writing in bed: "As the pages of *New Year's Day* were finished, they were allowed to drift to the floor, thence to be rescued by her secretary, Jeanne Duprat, and carried away to be typed" (*EW* 4). The success of *The* AGE OF INNOCENCE, also set in the NEW YORK of the 1870s, had convinced her that her editor at APPLETON's, Rutger B. JEWETT, was correct when he argued that the American public preferred the nostalgic evocation of the remote past to fiction about the more immediate past of WORLD WAR I.

Near the Fifth Avenue Hotel. Endpaper, New Year's Day (The 'Seventies) *(1924), first edition* (Collection of the author)

New Year's Day is set in the same time frame as *The Age of Innocence* and has a similar frame of reference, with certain identical characters. Sillerton Jackson and Mr. and Mrs. Henry van der Luyden appear as social observers and arbiters. It has been suggested that Jackson is a fictional representation of Edith Wharton's old friend Egerton WINTHROP and also that his character is derived from the "social entrepreneur" Ward McAllister, who organized the first Patriarchs' ball for "the 400" of New York society in Mrs. Astor's ballroom, which could hold 400 people comfortably (*EW* 36). As the novella opens, there is a serious fire at the old Fifth Avenue Hotel, near Twenty-third Street. (The hotel had been partly owned by Paran Stevens, father of Edith Wharton's first fiancé, Harry Leyden Stevens.) The young narrator, along with Jackson and other members of New York's elite families, watch from the Parretts' mansion windows. They see Lizzie Hazeldean, devoted to her invalid husband Charles (suffering from a recurrence of tuberculosis), emerge in the smoke and confusion with Henry Prest. Lizzie is alarmed, since "everyone in New York knew that Sillerton Jackson saw everything, and could piece together seemingly unrelated fragments of fact with the art of a skilled china-mender" (*NYD* 24). She returns home to find that her husband has gone to the fire despite his cough and has been in the Parretts' home. Later, at an evening party, Jackson talks with her about the fire, suggesting, behind his "assumed carelessness of pose, the patient fixity of a naturalist holding his breath near the crack from which some tiny animal might suddenly issue—if one watched long enough . . ." (*NYD* 63–64). She is "cut" at the party.

Her husband dies shortly afterwards, his condition aggravated by his excursion to the fire. Lizzie sails for Europe to stay with her elderly father. Eventually she returns to New York, receives Henry Prest in a friend's drawing room and rejects his proposal of marriage. She explains that she used the money he had paid her for her favors to give her husband "that last good year," when he was happy, although unsuspecting of her affair. As a widow, Lizzie is not a lady "on whom other ladies called," though, as the young narrator perceives, neither is she "a lady whom it was forbidden to mention to other ladies." She lingers on in a social limbo; well-connected men of various ages crowd her drawing room, mostly without their wives. She tries to atone for her betrayal, entertaining increasingly dull people more and more lavishly. As she grows old and ill, she turns to Roman Catholicism, a faith which absolves her and convinces her she will meet Charles again after death.

For further reading: Fishbein, "Prostitution, Morality, and Paradox: Moral Relativism in Edith Wharton's Old New York: *New Year's Day (The 'Seventies)*"; Saunders, "A New Look at the Oldest Profession in Wharton's *New Year's Day.*"

New York Birthplace of Edith Newbold Jones on January 24, 1862. She would live in New York as a small child, adolescent and young matron, but spend more than 25 years of her life in FRANCE. She was the third child and first daughter of Lucretia Rhinelander and George Frederic JONES, descendants of aristocratic old New York families whose colonial ancestry went back more than three centuries. The Joneses lived on investments from the mercantile fortunes made by their forebears, much of it in city real estate. Edith Jones was baptized in Grace Church on April 20, 1862, and grew up in a world of luxury, with servants, carriages and rigid social mores. Her education was private; she had a nurse and a governess/companion. In *The OLD MAID (THE 'FIFTIES),* one of a quartet of novellas published in 1924 under the title *OLD NEW YORK,* Edith Wharton characterized the society into which she was born: "The sturdy English and the rubicund and heavier Dutch had mingled to produce a prosperous, prudent and yet lavish society" in which a fundamental principal was to "do things handsomely." This "cautious" world was "built up on the fortunes of bankers, India merchants, ship-builders and ship-chandlers." They were "well-fed slow-moving people," living in "genteel monotony" (*OM* 3–4).

Grace Church, 10th Street and Broadway, in 1850. This was the most fashionable church in New York in the mid-19th century. Edith Newbold Jones was baptized here on April 20, 1862 (Courtesy Archives of the Episcopal Diocese of New York)

Grace Church, New York, in the 1950s (Courtesy Archives of the Episcopal Diocese of New York)

Grace Church, New York, interior, c. 1846 (Courtesy Archives of the Episcopal Diocese of New York)

The George Frederic Jones home, birthplace of Edith Wharton in 1862 (house on right, 14 West 23rd Street, New York City). The Jones family had a household staff of seven according to the 1860 census. After George Frederic Jones's death in 1882 his widow and daughter moved to a house on West 25th Street. (Copyright © Collection of The New York Historical Society)

The family spent winters in a New York brownstone on West 23rd Street and summers in a large home in NEWPORT, Rhode Island. George Frederic Jones had suffered financial reverses in the early 1860s caused by declining New York real estate values during the Civil War. In 1866 the Joneses took Edith, then four, along with her older brother, Harry, 16, to EUROPE for six years. They lived in France, GERMANY and ITALY, traveling widely in those countries and in SPAIN.

The Jones family's return to AMERICA in 1872 brought "bitter disappointment" to Edith. She was only 10, but, as she later recalled in her unpublished auto-

biography, "LIFE AND I," she had been "fed on beauty since my babyhood"; her first thought of America was " '*How ugly it is!*'" She often dreamed her family was returning to Europe and would wake "in a state of exhilaration which the reality turned to deep depression." She abhorred the New York cityscape, "cursed with its universal chocolate-coloured coating of the most hideous stone ever quarried, [a] cramped horizontal gridiron of a town without towers, porticoes, fountains or perspectives, hide-bound in its deadly uniformity of mean ugliness" (*BG* 54–55). Her principal compensation in returning to New York was her entry into the "kingdom" of her father's library. She never stopped yearning for Europe. In 1880, when she was 18, the Joneses returned to Europe for two years because of her father's bad health; he died at Cannes in 1882.

In 1885, Edith Jones married Edward ("Teddy") WHARTON of Boston; the couple lived at 882-884 Park Avenue in New York. From then until about 1900 the young couple divided their time among New York, Newport and travels abroad, usually to Italy. They then began searching for property in the Berkshires and built The MOUNT, at LENOX, Mass., completed in 1902. By 1907 the Whartons were spending winters in PARIS. Teddy Wharton's mental health declined, and Edith spent increasing periods of time in France. In 1911 The Mount was sold, and the Whartons were divorced in 1913; Wharton continued to live in France. After 1911 she would only return to America twice more. In late 1913 she planned to come for the wedding of her niece Beatrice JONES to Max FARRAND, but missed the wedding because of illness. She came a few days later in time for some of the celebratory luncheons and dinners with friends, which had been postponed (*NGC* 290). In 1923, she returned to America to accept an honorary doctor of letters from Yale University.

Few, if any, American novelists have succeeded as well as Edith Wharton in contrasting the ideals and mores of the aristocratic world into which she was born and the new industrial society of the GILDED AGE, with its fortunes made from steel, railroads and coal. In *A BACKWARD GLANCE,* Wharton states that she once viewed the New York society of the old order as "an empty vessel into which no new wine would ever again be poured." By the early 1930s, however, as she looked back, she perceived it differently, as a vessel preserving "a few drops of an old vintage too rare to be savoured by a youthful palate" (*BG* 5).

Newbold, Tom   A favorite cousin of Edith Wharton, Tom was the son of her mother's younger sister, Mary (Mrs. Thomas H.); Mrs. Newbold was also Edith Wharton's godmother. Together with Herman EDGAR and Egerton WINTHROP, Tom Newbold assisted in settling her affairs in New York after her divorce in 1913.

When it was finalized Wharton chose "Edith Newbold Wharton" as her legal name (*NGC* 279).

Newport Edith Wharton spent several months a year in Newport, Rhode Island, for over half her life, from the time she was a small child during the 1860s until The MOUNT was completed in 1902. Before her marriage to Teddy WHARTON she and her family lived at PENCRAIG, the Joneses' home; shortly after the wedding, they moved to PENCRAIG COTTAGE on the Jones property. In 1893 Wharton used a legacy from a cousin to purchase LAND'S END, at the easternmost tip of Rhode Island, for $80,000. Lewis believes she was trying to distance herself from her mother, Lucretia JONES. The Whartons improved the exterior with a circular court surrounded by hedges and trellises. She was increasingly shocked at the opulent mansions built by the "robber barons" such as the Vanderbilts and Belmonts.

Several of Wharton's lifelong friends were associated with Newport. As a child, she came to know her longtime companion and secretary Anna BAHLMANN through the family of Lewis RUTHERFURD, who lived next door to the Joneses. The family of Daisy Terry (later CHANLER) lived there also. In 1902 the Whartons were present at the christening of the Chanlers' son Theodore, who was named for Theodore ROOSEVELT, his godfather. In 1897, the same year *The DECORATION OF HOUSES* was published, the Whartons entertained the distinguished French novelist Paul BOURGET and his wife Minnie at Land's End. The Bourgets became lifelong friends of Edith Wharton. James VAN ALEN, who shared the 1888 charter of the steam yacht *VANADIS*, also had a Newport home.

In *A BACKWARD GLANCE* Wharton writes nostalgically of the Newport season during the 1870s, before the era of the ornate mansions. Although the daily social ritual of leaving calling cards was a trial to her, she remembered Bellevue Avenue many years later, when it was the scene of a "double line of glittering vehicles and showy horseflesh" parading between lawns and "scarlet geranium-borders" (*BG* 84). She also recalled the archery tournaments at the Casino and the heavy thick veils girls wore to protect their complexions against the sea air (*BG* 46).

Edith and Teddy Wharton in a carriage at Newport in the 1880s (Courtesy Clifton Waller Barrett Library, Special Collections Department, University of Virginia)

It was this era that figured in Wharton's fiction. In *The AGE OF INNOCENCE* the annual meeting of the Newport Archery Club, held in August at the Julius Beauforts' home, is the setting for an important scene. On their return from their wedding trip, Newland and May Archer attend the tournament. May, a Diana-like expert archer, wins the prize, but Newland begins to feel trapped and thinks of Ellen Olenska. She avoids him when he and May call on her grandmother, causing him to leave Newport the next day and find her in Boston. His pursuit ultimately proves hopeless when May announces her pregnancy. Wharton also set parts of her first novel, *FAST AND LOOSE,* in Newport, as well as her short story "TWILIGHT OF THE GOD."

"All that has been said of Newport you may safely set down as an understatement," said the turn-of-the-century critic James Huneker. In *The American Scene* Henry JAMES called the villas on the cliffs "White Elephants. . . . all cry and no wool, all house and no garden, which stand as a reminder of "prohibited degrees of witlessness." In *The Decoration of Houses,* Wharton and the architect Ogden CODMAN took aim at the architecture of the nouveaux riches that sprang up in Newport during the GILDED AGE. They observed that a major offense committed by American architects was design not based on function. European architects had separated family apartments and those used for entertaining. However, this distinction had been ignored in America. As a result, many large houses were currently built with ballrooms, music rooms and enormous halls but no small rooms. The family was forced to sit "under gilded ceilings and cut-glass chandeliers, in about as much comfort and privacy as are afforded by the public 'parlors' of one of our new twenty-story hotels" (*DH* 134).

Thorstein Veblen's *Theory of the Leisure Class,* published in 1899, could almost be taken as a textbook explanation of the excesses in consumption which marked social life in Newport during the latter part of the 19th century; it is possible that Veblen may have founded his observations on Newport. He considers leisure a form of necessary labor, "as effective an evidence of wealth as consumption." The calling card rituals, charity organizations, ceaseless entertaining and direction of servants were all a form of that labor.

Although Wharton loved Land's End, she found the climate depressing, and she became increasingly tired of what her friend Bay LODGE called "the philistine-plutocrat atmosphere" of Newport (*EW* 68–81). In 1899, she and her husband began searching for property in LENOX, Massachusetts, where Teddy's mother had a home. They purchased a 113-acre farm there and built The Mount, finished by 1902. Land's End was sold in 1903 to Eleanor Beeckman, wife of Robert Livingston Beeckman, for $122,500. After the Whartons' years at The Mount and their divorce, Wharton moved to FRANCE, but Newport survived vividly in her imagination throughout her life.

Nicholson, Reginald Popham ("Rex") (1874–1950) Edith Wharton had come to know Rex Nicholson, an English colonial official, during the Mediterranean cruise of 1926 aboard the *OSPREY.* In later years she visited him and his wife Molly in ENGLAND and they stayed with her at STE.-CLAIRE CHÂTEAU. Nicky MARIANO once said that Nicholson's wife resembled one of Wharton's fictional heroines (*Letters* 538).

Nicolson, Harold (1886–1961) English diplomat, historian, biographer and journalist. He was married to the novelist Victoria ("Vita") Sackville-West. Vita later had an affair with Wharton's friend Geoffrey SCOTT as well as with Virginia WOOLF. Among Nicolson's better-known works are *The Age of Reason* (1960) and *The Development of English Biography* (1928). Sir Harold was one of the group of English writers and critics with whom Edith Wharton made friends in later life. On a trip to England in July 1931 she saw him, along with Desmond MACCARTHY, H. G. WELLS and Jane and Kenneth CLARK.

Nietzsche, Friedrich (1844–1900) German poet, philosopher and classical scholar. He was born in Röcken, Saxony, to a family with a long history in the church clergy. He studied at the University of Bonn and became a close friend of Richard Wagner; they were instrumental in founding the Bayreuth theater. Nietzsche rejected rational schemes of thought, such as the systematic philosophy of Hegel, and tried to penetrate to the human level beneath. Extrapolating from Darwin's theory of evolution, he also rejected Judeo-Christian morality, believing it ran counter to the natural instincts of human nature. He advocated the maximum development and expression of animalistic instincts. In his most famous work, *Thus Spake Zarathustra* (1886), Nietzsche developed the theory of the *Übermensch,* or superman, who is an idealized person who defines his own morality. The social drive would be replaced with egoism and individualism. *Menschliches, Allzumenschliches* (*Human, All Too Human,* 1878), *Beyond Good and Evil* (1886), *Der Antichrist* (1888) and *Ecce Homo* (1888) were among Nietzsche's other well-known works.

Edith Wharton read all his books in 1907 and 1908 as part of a reading program in philosophy (*NGC* 172) and was greatly influenced by them at the time. Lewis emphasizes the role played by Nietzsche's philosophy in the antipathy to orthodox Christianity she evidenced during her adulterous affair with Morton FULLERTON (*EW* 230). Carol Singley concurs, citing her enthusiastic 1908 letter to Sara Norton about Nietzsche's *Beyond Good and Evil.* "He has no system, & not much logic, but wonderful flashes of insight, & a power of breaking through conventions that is most exhilarating, & clears the air." Singley observes, however, that Wharton's "Nietzschean energy was checked because she thought and felt through her male lover"; her joy was still subject to "cultural restrictions" (Singley, *Edith Wharton: Matters of Mind and Spirit,* 17–19). This is a theme Edith Wharton frequently explored in fiction (*see,* for example, "SOULS BELATED").

The onset of WORLD WAR I caused Wharton to revise her opinions. As Benstock puts it, she "joined the English and French in seeing the new Germans as barbarians, the destroyers of civilization." She never traveled in GERMANY again, and apparently paid little attention to German literature, although, in addition to Nietzsche, her favorite writers had once been Heine, Schiller, Kant and GOETHE (*NGC* 298).

Nijinski, Waslaw (1890–1950)   Russian ballet dancer; he won fame in *Petrouchka,* Debussy's *The Afternoon of a Faun* and other roles. In 1919 Nijinski's career was cut short by the onset of insanity. Edith Wharton attended one of his four 1913 performances of Stravinsky's *Le Sacre du printemps,* which many critics believe gave rise to modern dance. She wrote Bernard BERENSON that the performance was "extraordinary (in the good sense)" (*NGC* 280–81).

Noailles, Anna de (1876–1933)   Comtesse Anna de Noailles, wife of Comte Mathieu de Noailles, was a poet and Parisian friend of Edith Wharton. Her father was a Rumanian prince (Brancovan); her mother was Greek. They met when Paul BOURGET brought her to tea one afternoon. Wharton called her a "monologuist," given to "dazzling talk" but intolerant of interruptions (*BG* 275). Lewis states that she sometimes waved her hand for silence "while she interrupted her discourse to take a swallow of wine" (*EW* 196).

Wharton admired her poetry, of which she had published two volumes before she was 30. The poems combined "romantic evocations of natural landscapes" with erotic verse (*EW* 162). One volume had been singled out for recognition by the prestigious ACADÉMIE FRANÇAISE. De Noailles also wrote three novels about women in love. She was a friend of Marcel PROUST and Jean COCTEAU. Wharton copied lyrics and epigrams into her COMMONPLACE BOOK from her 420-page *Les Eblouissements* ("Flowerings"), which Marcel PROUST had stated ranked with Charles Baudelaire's *Fleurs du mal* (*NGC* 171–2). De Noailles was influenced by the philosophy of Friedrich NIETZSCHE, which may have precipitated Wharton's interest in him during her affair with Morton FULLERTON.

De Noailles was an "inattentive" wife to her husband, and had affairs with both men and women, according to Lewis (*EW* 444), but her private life did not diminish Edith Wharton's admiration of her. In 1908 Wharton made notes for an essay about the affinities between the poetry of Anna de Noailles and that of Walt Whitman (*EW* 193), but this was never published. Lewis states that de Noailles sometimes attended the SALON of Rosa de FITZ-JAMES (*EW* 196), but in *A BACKWARD GLANCE,* Edith Wharton says that she does not recall ever seeing her there (*BG* 275).

She contributed a poem, "Nos Morts" ("Our Dead"), to the *BOOK OF THE HOMELESS,* and, when Edith Wharton was made a chevalier of the Legion of Honor, wrote to her as "*grand écrivain et à l'admirable, à l'efficace amie de France que vous êtes*" (*EW* 386).

Nobel Prize nomination   Several of Edith Wharton's friends attempted to secure the 1927 Nobel Prize for her. The movement began as early as 1925, but no prize was given in 1926, leading Wharton's supporters to believe she had a good chance for the 1927 prize. Those responsible for the nomination were Robert BLISS, American ambassador to Sweden, and his wife Mildred, aided by William Lyon Phelps, William Howard Taft (a member of the Yale Corporation who had helped select Wharton to receive an honorary DOCTORATE from YALE UNIVERSITY in 1923), Elihu Root, Lord BALFOUR, Paul BOURGET and Jules Cambon, at one time French ambassador to America and to Britain. Lewis states that Wharton seems not to have entertained unrealistic hopes for this award, although she did have her writings sent to Stockholm. The recipients were Grazua Deledda and Henri Bergson (*EW* 481–82).

Nohant   Town that was once the home of the French novelist George SAND (pen name of Amandine Aurore Lucie Dupin, baroness Dudevant), a prolific writer Edith Wharton admired. Edith and Teddy, accompanied by Edith's brother Harry JONES, first visited the "plain-faced, fawn-coloured house, the typical *gentilhommière* of the French countryside" (*MFF* 41) in 1906, a visit that made Henry JAMES envious. They toured the garden pavilion, grounds, cottages, stable, chapel and the family graveyard. In 1907 they returned for a second visit, accompanied by James. In *A MOTOR-FLIGHT THROUGH FRANCE* Wharton described the interior of the house, particularly the dining room, salon and the two little theaters. One stage was life-size and the other held "just such a *Puppen-theatre* as Wilhelm Meister described to Marianne," with a troupe of carved commedia dell'arte marionettes dressed by Sand herself (*MFF* 79–84).

North Africa   Edith Wharton had seen the port of Tunis in 1888, during her Mediterranean cruise aboard the *VANADIS,* and had long wanted to see more of northern Africa. In early 1914 she began planning to visit regions other than western Europe, including

North Africa and the Middle East; she also spoke of wanting someday to go to Baghdad and Beirut. Lewis observes that her interest in more exotic countries reflected the influence of NIETZSCHE, who had attacked Western civilization. Her friend Walter BERRY, moreover, had recently set out for India (*EW* 357).

She invited Gaillard LAPSLEY (who joined the party but succumbed to dysentery and had to turn back) and Percy LUBBOCK as companions. Accompanied by her chauffeur, Charles COOK, secretary/companion, Anna BAHLMANN, and maid, Elise DUVLENCK, Wharton sailed from Marseilles to ALGERIA aboard the S. S. *Timgad* on March 29, 1914. Their itinerary included Orléansville, Oran, Biskra, Constantine and Tunisia. Lewis states that "every step of the way was a fascination for Edith Wharton (*EW* 359).

In 1917 she was invited to tour MOROCCO by General Louis-Hubert LYAUTEY, and spent three weeks there. The resulting book, *IN MOROCCO*, is one of the finest of her travel books. She described the journey in a letter to her sister-in-law, Mary ("Minnie") Cadwalader JONES, as "seeing that land of fairy-tale in fairy-tale fashion" (unpublished letter to Mary Cadwalader Jones, Oct. 5, 1917; Edith Wharton Collection, Beinecke Library, Yale University). Lewis, however, points out that her visit reinforced her realization of the "irreplaceable Western value of personal freedom" (*EW* 405).

Wharton also set two of her short stories in North Africa, the murder mystery "A BOTTLE OF PERRIER" and "The SEED OF THE FAITH." Both depict North African scenes, such as the desert home of an expatriate Englishman, an Arab coffeehouse, and a small, unsuccessful American Baptist mission.

Norton, Charles Eliot (1827–1908)   American man of letters and professor of aesthetics, he offered, at Harvard University, the first formal instruction in art history in America, in 1874–75, in a a course entitled "The History of Fine Arts as Connected with Literature." In 1875 Norton was appointed Harvard Professor of Fine Arts in recognition of his prominence. Bernard BERENSON, a longtime friend of Edith Wharton, studied art history under Norton at Harvard, and it was through Norton that she met his former student Morton FULLERTON, with whom she had a three-year adulterous liaison, beginning in 1908. Ironically, she recalls in *A BACKWARD GLANCE* that Norton wrote her in great alarm after *The HOUSE OF MIRTH* appeared, imploring her to remember that "no great work of the imagination has ever been based on illicit passion" (*BG* 127).

Norton was a pioneer in the establishment of DANTE scholarship in AMERICA and edited the letters of John RUSKIN, whom he knew well. He inherited Shady Hill, a large Cambridge estate near Harvard, from his father. It has been said that he represented the best of the NEW ENGLAND legacy of "piety, learning, liberal ideals, and business acumen," and that his age was that of the "first flowering of New England" (Bradley and Ousby, Introduction, *The Correspondence of John Ruskin and Charles Eliot Norton*). He participated in the rediscovery of the cultural and religious history of Europe, as shown in two of his works, *Historical Studies of Church Building in the Middle Ages* (1880) and *Notes of Travel and Study in Italy* (1881). He entertained Charles Dickens on Dickens's second visit to AMERICA (1867–68); the young Henry JAMES was among the guests.

Norton's wife died during the birth of their sixth child in 1872; he was devoted to his children and raised them with the assistance of his sister Grace. It is unclear just when Edith Wharton met him, but, according to Benstock (*NGC* 112), she had met his daughter SARA ("Sally") in New York, through mutual friends, about the time *The TOUCHSTONE* was published (1900).

When Edith Wharton was writing *The VALLEY OF DECISION*, she mentioned to Professor Norton that she was unable to find many of the books she needed for research, and he sent her a large carton of irreplaceable travel books and classics from the library at Shady Hill. Edith Wharton wrote in her memoir that to be really known Norton had to be "seen in the Shady Hill library, at Cambridge, where the ripest years of his intellectual life were lived. Against that noble background of books his frail presence, the low voice, the ascetic features so full of scholarly distinction, acquired their full meaning, and his talk was at its richest and happiest" (*BG* 154).

The Nortons spent summers in the town of Ashfield, in western Massachusetts, occupying a 1793 farmhouse called The Locusts. In *A Backward Glance* Edith Wharton recalls making frequent excursions to the "little mountain farmhouse" from The MOUNT in LENOX: "there was always a friendly welcome [and] long hours of invigorating talk" (*BG* 154). She visited the Nortons in Ashfield with James, Walter BERRY, Gaillard LAPSLEY and other friends. She stated that, although Norton was not a great talker, he was "one of the best guides to good conversation that I have ever known. Every word he spoke, every question he asked, was like a signal pointing to the next height, and his silences were of the kind which serve to carry on the talk." Norton apparently did not travel to The Mount, although Sally often stayed there. Elizabeth ("Lily") Norton, Sally's sister, recalled that Wharton never went away from Ashfield without "borrowing some book or having her intellectual horizon widened by my Father's sympathy and very real admiration for her great gifts." Edith Wharton once climbed High Pasture, a hill Norton owned, and later wrote a sonnet about it which, according to Lily's memory of the day, he "cared for." Norton was always interested in Wharton's developing literary career, though he apparently deplored the "realist" direction Wharton's fiction took. He would have liked, she felt, the "stuff of romance" (*BG* 156).

Norton, Lily (Elizabeth)   Called Lily, she was a daughter of Charles Eliot NORTON and was a friend of Edith Wharton. The two were not as close as Wharton and Sally NORTON were, but they did correspond. After Edith Wharton's death in 1937, Lily wrote a warm reminiscence about her for Percy LUBBOCK, who was preparing his *Portrait of Edith Wharton* [Sally Norton had died in 1922]. She recalled the Whartons' visits to the Nortons' summer home at Ashfield, during the years when they owned The MOUNT: "life was still the song of birds for us all" (Memory contributed by Lily (Elizabeth) Norton to Percy Lubbock, BEINECKE LIBRARY, YALE UNIVERSITY).

Norton, Robert   English watercolorist and longtime friend of Edith Wharton. His early career was in the English Foreign Office; he then served as secretary to Lord Salisbury, the Conservative Prime Minister. He made enough money in private business to retire and spend his time painting. During WORLD WAR I he served with the British Admiralty (*Letters* 363n). Edith Wharton first met him in 1908 at Stanway, home of a British couple, Lord Hugo and Lady Mary ELCHO (later Lord and Lady WEMYSS). Norton was Wharton's friend until her death, and took responsibility for carrying out her wishes regarding her funeral.

Very much a member of what Susan Goodman calls Edith Wharton's "inner circle," Norton was her companion when she first explored the area around HYÈRES in order to search for a winter home. They discovered STE.-CLAIRE CHÂTEAU, which Wharton took on a long lease. Norton, Gaillard LAPSLEY and Bernard BERENSON were regular members of the annual Christmas gathering at Ste.-Claire. Wharton sometimes visited Norton in ENGLAND at LAMB HOUSE, Rye, Sussex, former home of Henry JAMES. One such visit was in 1928, when Norton introduced her to the young Evelyn Waugh. Norton accompanied her on the cruise aboard the *OSPREY* in 1926.

Edith Wharton was very supportive of Norton's literary and artistic projects and sometimes attempted to help him place his work. In 1919, she corresponded extensively with Rutger B. JEWETT of APPLETON's about placing an article he had written about Hyères in a literary periodical. (He had written it at her suggestion, she explained, for the interest of American soldiers and officers near Hyères who knew nothing about the place.) After *SCRIBNER'S MAGAZINE* rejected it, Jewett promised "to comb the field and do my best for Mr. Norton." He was unable to place the article in any other magazine. On receiving the news, Wharton wrote Jewett, "I am quite skeptical about the judgment of the magazine editors who are deciding to publish only articles about America. . . . Until there are more definite proofs to the contrary I shall persist in thinking that the average American is more intelligent than the imaginary being for whom our magazines are edited!"

Norton had also asked Wharton to sound out Appleton's about publishing a book on Provence for which he proposed to supply his own watercolors. She queried Jewett, stating that it would be "the kind of description of the country that would be useful to sightseers." Appleton's owners proposed that the book first be published in serial form, but Jewett was unable to interest any periodical editors. He wrote Wharton, "The reports from the editors strike me as so unintelligent that I am ashamed to send them on to him. I'll enclose them in this letter and trust to your tactful handling of an embarassing [*sic*] situation. I wish it were possible to sell his articles in this country but it looks hopeless" (Wharton-Jewett correspondence, July–October 1919, BEINECKE LIBRARY, YALE UNIVERSITY).

Norton did, however, serve as coeditor with Edith Wharton of *ETERNAL PASSION IN ENGLISH POETRY*, an anthology of love poems published after her death in 1939. Gaillard Lapsley is listed as collaborator on the title page. The collection had been planned during evenings at the PAVILLON COLOMBE as early as 1923. Norton was also the English translator of *Bénédiction* by Comtesse Philomène de LA FOREST-DIVONNE [pseud. Claude Sílve], for which Edith Wharton wrote the foreword. The countess was another close friend of Edith Wharton.

Norton, Sara ("Sally") (c. 1864–1922)   Eldest daughter of Charles Eliot NORTON and a longtime friend of Edith Wharton. Called Sally, she was beautiful and gifted violinist; she had fallen in love during the 1880s with the son of the English poet Arthur Hugh Clough, who proposed marriage. She ultimately decided she could not live permanently in England and stayed at the family home in Cambridge, Shady Hill, to look after her father. When he died in 1908, she was 44. She never married, but devoted the remainder of her life to editing Norton's manuscripts and letters (*NGC* 112). Benstock suggests that Edith Wharton based her 1901 story "The ANGEL AT THE GRAVE" on the life of Sally Norton.

According to her sister Lily (Elizabeth) Norton, Sara first recognized Wharton's genius after reading some early verses published in *SCRIBNER'S MAGAZINE* or *HARPER'S MAGAZINE*. Soon afterwards, she and Wharton met through mutual friends in NEW YORK. Lily remarked that there would have seemed little chance of sympathy. Edith was "shy, outwardly worldly, and measuring life, and living, by worldly standards—and those New York standards. . . . Sally . . . was so obviously different—brought up in the sheltered cloisters of Shady Hill . . . influenced mainly by intellectual and spiritual rather than social values—but with that subtle gift of lovely looks and charm which beguiled all, and quickly won the affection and interest of the more sophisticated yet brilliant Edith." Sally wrote Wharton on publication of *The TOUCHSTONE*, praising her work, and the correspondence continued; Sally became one of Norton's closest women friends. She was the first person to realize the literary value of Edith Wharton's letters, and saved 240 of them; Lewis states that they are "some of the finest Edith Wharton wrote before the First War" (*EW* 4).

After the Whartons built The MOUNT, they often traveled the 40 miles to Ashfield, where the Nortons had a summer home, sometimes staying overnight before they acquired a motorcar, which made it feasible to go over for lunch or dinner. Lily Norton, who contributed a memoir to Percy LUBBOCK after Wharton died, preferred to remember Wharton at Ashfield, where life was informal and, fortunately, no neighbors came in for dinner parties. The Whartons, she said, "came really for endless talk." Wharton would walk with Charles Eliot NORTON to High Pasture, a hill he owned, and wrote of it later in a sonnet. Lily recalled that Edith "was at her best at such times and those who knew her at Lenox would hardly have recognized her at Ashfield, where, no longer shy, she expanded and expressed herself easily." (Lubbock, *Portrait of Edith Wharton,* 41). Lily believed it was the journeys to Ashfield, over the Berkshire Trail, which were the initial inspiration for *ETHAN FROME.* Henry JAMES, an old friend of Charles Eliot Norton, went with the Whartons on a visit to Ashfield at least once, in 1905.

It was to Sally Norton that Edith Wharton disclosed her misgivings about living permanently in France. She met Morton FULLERTON through the Nortons; he had been a student of Charles Eliot Norton. In 1907, she wrote Sally from the Vanderbilt apartment she and Teddy had leased in Paris that they frequently saw "your friend Fullerton," who was writing articles about the Rhône Valley for the *Revue de Paris;* "he is very intelligent, but slightly mysterious," Wharton observed. Her published letters to Sally at the height of her affair with Fullerton do not suggest that Wharton revealed her feelings toward him, although she may have done so during their visits. Their correspondence was intellectually wide-ranging; they exchanged views about books and writers, and Wharton advised Sally Norton on the publication of her father's letters. She also confided to her many worries about Teddy's decline and their divorce. In 1922 Sally Norton had surgery for a tumor; she died the same year.

Occult *See* SUPERNATURAL, EDITH WHARTON AND THE; *GHOSTS; TALES OF MEN AND GHOSTS*).

"Ogrin the Hermit" Long poem published in the December 1909 *ATLANTIC MONTHLY*. Based on the legend of Tristan and Iseult, in which the couple drink of a love potion, flee Iseult's husband, King Mark, and take refuge in Ogrin the Hermit's cave, the poem rationalizes their behavior, measuring it against pagan rather than Christian standards. Edith Wharton was, at this time, in the middle of her adulterous affair with Morton FULLERTON and is believed to have written this poem as justification for her conduct, inscribing the copy she gave him, "*Per Te, Sempre Per Te.*" The epigraph is taken from Joseph Bédier's retelling of the legend, "*Vous qui nous jugez, savez-vous quel boivre nous avons bu sur la mer?*" (Lewis's translation is: "You who judge us, do you know what drink we drank upon the sea?"; [*EW* 256]). Ogrin at first condemns the couple, but comes to accept their behavior as ultimately deriving from their human nature. When Iseult returns to her husband, Ogrin says, "For meet it was that a great queen should pass/Crowned and forgiven from the face of Love."

Lewis believes the poem represents Wharton's examination of the clash between her Christian upbringing and the Nietzschean principles she had embraced since reading that writer's works in 1907 and 1908. It evokes her progress from adolescent sensuality and "religiosity" on to her sexless marriage, firm self-control, "explosion of desire" with Fullerton and, finally, "intent religious questioning" (*EW* 256–57).

Old Maid (The 'Fifties), The One of the four novellas published by Appleton in 1924; the others were *FALSE DAWN (THE 'FORTIES), The SPARK (THE 'SIXTIES)* and *NEW YEAR'S DAY (THE 'SEVENTIES)*. The four stories portray the actions of various individuals in conflict with the controlling mores of a rigid society. Of the four, many readers found *The Old Maid* the most compelling. The awarding of the PULITZER PRIZE to Edith Wharton in 1921 for *The AGE OF INNOCENCE* resulted in such publicity that the novella was purchased by *REDBOOK* for $2,250. A play based on it was produced on Broadway in the 1930s and a film was also made in 1939 starring Bette Davis and Miriam Hopkins (*EW* 436).

This novella deals with an impoverished member of aristocratic old New York, Charlotte Lovell, who is about to marry into a prominent family, the Ralstons. Years before, in her youth, she had apparently been threatened with consumption and was hurried away to Georgia for a year. There she secretly gave birth to a baby girl. Since then she has busied herself running a day nursery for the poor. A little girl in the day nursery, dressed in cut-down clothes, has been brought by a "veiled lady" from the South and is treated as a pauper. Charlotte is devoted to her and to all the children, trying to conceal the fact that she is the child's mother. The Ralstons demand that Charlotte give up volunteering in the nursery after marriage because she might bring home diseases when she and her husband have their own children. Rather than do so, she breaks her engagement.

She confides her predicament to her cousin, Delia Lovell Ralston, who discovers that the father of Charlotte's daughter is Clem Spender, her own early love. She visits the child, Clementina, in the nursery and sees that she has Clem's curly hair. Charlotte coughs up blood, although her lung is supposed to be healed. Delia tells Joe about Charlotte's condition; and he needs little persuasion to understand that he cannot marry her lest she die and leave him with small children to raise. Delia plans that she and Jim will provide

Lovell Place, Hell Gate, Endpaper, The Old Maid (The 'Fifties) *(1924)* (Collection of the author)

for little Tina, who will be raised by Charlotte in their own country farmhouse.

In the second part of the book, Charlotte has grown to be a methodical, even tyrannical, "old maid." Jim Ralston has been killed in a fall from a horse and Charlotte and Delia live together with Tina and Delia's two children. Tina calls Delia "mamma" and her real mother, Charlotte, "Aunt Chatty." The two women compete for Tina's affections.

Charlotte perceives that Tina, arriving home after a grand ball with her suitor, Lanning Halsey, is on the point of making the same mistake she had made. In a

A scene from the 1935 Broadway production of The Old Maid, *dramatized by Zoë Akins (see Appendix II), as featured on the dust jacket of the book version published by D. Appleton-Century (1935). Shown are Judith Anderson (l., Delia) and Helen Menken (Charlotte). Wharton, living in France and unable to see the production, found this image "charming . . . extraordinarily pretty"* (Collection of Scott Marshall)

subtle manoeuvre, she forestalls her. The engagement between Tina and Lanning is announced and marriage plans proceed. Delia, realizing that Tina is more attached to her than to her mother, urges her to give her last kiss to Aunt Charlotte before she leaves the house for her wedding trip: " 'Don't forget—the very last.' "

For further reading: Funston, "Clocks and Mirrors, Dreams and Destinies: Edith Wharton's *The Old Maid*"; McDowell, "Edith Wharton's *The Old Maid:* Novella/ Play/Film."

Old Maid, The (play, 1935)   *See* Appendix II.

Old Maid, The (film, 1939)   *See* Appendix II.

"Old New York"   Early working title of *The AGE OF INNOCENCE* (1920), which originally dealt with two characters named Langdon Archer and Clementine Olenska. The manuscript was renamed and "Old New York" eventually evolved into *OLD NEW YORK*, the title under which four novellas were published by APPLETON in 1924: *FALSE DAWN (THE 'FORTIES), The OLD MAID (THE 'FIFTIES), THE SPARK (THE 'SIXTIES)* and *NEW YEAR'S DAY (THE 'SEVENTIES).*

Old New York   The title under which four novellas were published by APPLETON in 1924: *FALSE DAWN (THE 'FORTIES), The OLD MAID (THE 'FIFTIES), The SPARK (THE 'SIXTIES)* and *NEW YEAR'S DAY (THE 'SEVENTIES).* The stories were issued in a boxed set. Critics disagreed on their merit; Edmund Wilson called Edith Wharton "the [John Singer] Sargent of American fiction" because she was ready to deal "facilely" with her subjects. He also believed there was much of the French playwright Victorien Sardou in the four works; they had too little history to serve as social studies and insufficient drama for conventional short fiction. He considered Wharton's long residence abroad to be detrimental to her portrayal of America; the colors that had begun to pale in *SUMMER* had become even more vague and distant. Lloyd Morris, writing in the *New York Times,* observed that each story shows the danger of the least deviation from "strict conformity," although the old New York as represented in four separate decades "reveals no qualitative expansion under the flow of time, and its social organism suffers no least modification." He called *The OLD MAID* "one of the most imperishably beautiful and perfect stories in the whole range of American literature" (*CR* 357–65).

Rutger B. Jewett was able to serialize all four novellas. *The Old Maid* ran in *REDBOOK* (then titled *The Red Book Magazine*) in February, March and April 1922, and *New Year's Day* was published in the same magazine in July and August 1923. *False Dawn* ran in the *Ladies' Home Journal* in November 1923, and *The Spark* was published in the same magazine in May 1924.

Scene from the 1939 Warner Bros. film The Old Maid, *with screenplay by Casey Robinson, from the stage adaptation by Zoë Akins (see Appendix II). Wharton's 1924 novella, subtitled* The 'Fifties, *is indeed set in the 1850s; the producers moved the story, somewhat illogically, to the 1860s to take advantage of* Gone With the Wind *mania. Shown here are: Bette Davis (l., Charlotte), Miriam Hopkins (Delia) and George Brent (Clem Spender)* (Collection of Scott Marshall)

For further reading: Gibson, "Edith Wharton and the Ethnography of *Old New York*"; Richards, " 'Feminized Men' in Wharton's *Old New York*"; Shaloo, "Making Room for the Artist in Edith Wharton's *Old New York*"; Tintner, Adeline R., "The Narrative Structure of *Old New York:* Text and Pictures in Edith Wharton's Quartet of Linked Short Stories"; Tuttleton, "Leisure, Wealth and Luxury: Edith Wharton's *Old New York*."

Old New York: New Year's Day (1988, play)   *See* Appendix II.

Olenska, Ellen   *See* AGE OF INNOCENCE, THE.

"On Bayard Cutting, Jr."   Tribute to Bayard CUTTING, Jr. (1878–1910), published in a small privately printed collection of tributes, *W. Bayard Cutting Jr.: 1878–1910* (1947). He was the son of her friends Bayard Cutting, Sr. (the wealthy railroad magnate), and his wife, Olivia.

Cutting died young of tuberculosis, but might have had a distinguished diplomatic career. He had served as private secretary to Joseph Choate, the American ambassador in London.

Wharton recalls knowing Cutting as a boy, before he entered Harvard; "from the first the understanding between us was so deep and sure as to preclude . . . the least consciousness of the difference in our ages." She noted that he was already afflicted with illness when she first met him, but dismissed his "individual plight" in favor of his intellectual interests. Wharton wondered if it were his sense of doom that gave him "his rareness and his brightness, that was the undefinable essence of his soul." Wegener states that it is unknown why the book was delayed so long (*UCW* 229–31).

Origo, Iris Cutting   Daughter of Bayard CUTTING, Jr. and Sybil Cutting LUBBOCK. Edith Wharton had come to know the young Cuttings soon after her marriage.

Bayard died of consumption while still young and Sybil later married two of Wharton's friends, Geoffrey SCOTT and Percy LUBBOCK. When she came to America to receive her honorary DOCTORATE from YALE UNIVERSITY in 1923, Wharton visited Westbrook, the Cutting family's Long Island estate. The Cuttings wanted to hear about France and her new Parisian friends, but, according to Iris's account, Wharton wanted to talk only about the "milieu of her young womanhood" and hear of the people she had known before moving to Paris. For a moment Iris cutting caught a glimpse of the "other" Wharton, "elegant, formidable, as hard and dry as porcelain," but then she relaxed in the company of her old friends and became "a nice old American lady" (*EW* 452). Iris later married an Italian, Antonio Origo, and they began creating La Foce, a splendid estate in Tuscany near the home of Bernard BERENSON, which, according to Lewis, "would eventually resemble the beautifully receding landscape of a fifteenth-century Sienese painting" (*EW* 496).

Orme, Kate   *See SANCTUARY.*

ornament, interior   In *The DECORATION OF HOUSES*, Edith Wharton and Ogden CODMAN laid out certain principles of interior design and ornamentation they believed would correct America's pinched and cluttered domestic interiors, typical of the Victorian period, which were in stark contrast to the classically proportioned and decorated houses they had both known in Europe. They deplored excess ornament and bric-a-brac, as well as heavy layers of draperies.

Good decoration, they asserted, was "*only interior architecture*"; "structure conditions ornament, not ornament structure" (*DH* 10–11). Such components of rooms as walls, fireplaces and doors were essentially architectural and might themselves constitute "decoration," making further ornament unnecessary. A well-proportioned room might not need paintings, for instance, but if paintings were used, their frames would then become architectural and should harmonize with the details of the room (door and window molding, etc.). Wharton and Codman here commented obliquely on the passion for indiscriminate collecting that caused cluttered Victorian interiors. The true connoisseur, they believed, should exercise the restraint that is the subtler part of decorum.

As one example of the pitfalls of bad taste into which the nouveaux riches had fallen, the authors discussed the use of gilding. They had only contempt for those who embraced the new liquid gilding and violated the principles used in European gilding. In Europe, the art of gilding was regarded as "one of the crowning touches of magnificence in decoration, was little used except where great splendor of effect was desired, and was then applied by means of a difficult and costly process." Wharton and Codman believed it was used much too lavishly by American architects and homeowners, who suffered under the mistaken impression that gilding was a hallmark of the fashionable French style. "The result is a plague of liquid gilding. . . . In former times . . . it would never have occurred to the owner of an average-sized house to drench his walls and furniture in gilding, since the excessive use of gold in decoration was held to be quite unsuited to such a purpose" (*DH* 193). The epigraph to *The Decoration of Houses* is from Henri Mayeux's *La Composition Décorative:* "Une forme doit être belle en elle-même et on ne doit jamais compter sur le décor appliqué pour en sauver les imperfections" ["A shape should be beautiful in itself and one ought never to rely on applied ornament in order to rescue imperfections."]

The authors advised restraint and subtlety in private interiors, evincing classical simplicity and moderation, rather than the tasteless excess of overstuffed and overgilded rooms. In the conclusion of *The Decoration of Houses*, they praised the "tact of omission" that was second nature to European architects, protesting against excessive ornamentation (*DH* 198). They hoped to instill in their countrymen the ability to value the "rare vintage" of the modest effect over ostentatious display, and to teach them to understand the difference between the suitable and the pretentious.

Osprey   In 1926, Edith Wharton chartered the steam yacht *Osprey* for a second Mediterranean cruise lasting nine weeks. She paid half the charter and fuel cost (£4,000; roughly $200,000 today) and the other four members of the party shared the remainder (*NGC* 390). In addition to Wharton, there were her longtime friends Margaret ("Daisy") Terry CHANLER, Robert NORTON and Logan Pearsall SMITH. Harry Lawrence, an Englishman Wharton had not known well, was also aboard; he was director of the Medici Society in London.

The 1888 cruise aboard the *VANADIS* provided a rough itinerary. Leaving from the Old Port of HYÈRES March 31, 1926, they visited Delphi, Alexandria, Mistra, Cyprus, Delos, Patmos, Rhodes, Crete and Santorin, some of which the Whartons had visited on their 1888 cruise aboard the *Vanadis*. She planned to write a travel book about the cruise, "The SAPPHIRE WAY," that would have been, she thought, "charming" and would have offset some of the expenses of the cruise, but when she returned home she turned again to fiction.

Edith Wharton had asked Daisy to find mosquito nets and silk sleeping bags for camping out on inland expeditions; she finally located them in London but they were never used. After a long day of sightseeing, they all agreed the comforts of the ship outweighed the appeal of camping out. Daisy devoted two chapters of her memoir to the cruise (*Autumn in the Valley* [Boston: Little, Brown and Company, 1936]). She kept a detailed diary of their ports of call, including a journey from Palermo to the Greek temple at Segesta by donkey. She praised the Scots captain, who would not permit any of the crew of 16 or 18 sailors to go ashore on Sunday, but required that they listen while he read the Bible to them; it proved, she said, that he was a "man of conscience," and it gave them confidence in his seamanship.

The *Osprey*'s bookshelves were stocked with works of travel, archaeology, history, Homer, Herodotus and many classics. Daisy recalls that Robert Norton read aloud to them at night, beginning with Anita Loos's *Gentlemen Prefer Blondes* (a work Wharton did not confess reading to Gaillard LAPSLEY) and going on to Butcher and Lang's translation of the *Odyssey*.

In *A BACKWARD GLANCE,* Wharton wrote that she valued the freedom from everyday concerns: "only twice in my life have I been able to put all practical cares out of my mind for months, and each time it has been on a voyage in the Aegean" (*BG* 100). During the cruise, she lived in a state of euphoria. She had been one of

> . . . a congenial party, with lots of books, a full set of Admiralty charts, a stock of good provisions and *vins du pays* in the hold, and happiness in our hearts. . . . I lived in a state of euphoria which I suppose would seem inconceivable to most people. But I am born happy every morning, and during that magical cruise nothing ever seemed to occur during the day to diminish my beatitude, so that it went on rolling up like the interest on a millionaire's capital (*BG* 372–3).

The journey ended at Naples, where they were greeted by Mary and Bernard BERENSON and Nicky MARIANO, who took them to the recently renovated cloister of Santa Chiara. Daisy recommended such a visit to all travelers coming from Greece afflicted with "aesthetic dyspepsia," a malady preventing them from enjoying any sights dating later than 400 B.C.

"Other Times, Other Manners" (*See* "Autres Temps . . .").

"Other Two, The"   Short story published in *Collier's* (February 1904) and reprinted in *The DESCENT OF MAN AND OTHER STORIES* (Scribner's, 1904). Lewis terms this "the most nearly perfect short story" Wharton wrote, and "a model in the genre of the comedy of manners" (*EW* 134). It concerns Mr. and Mrs. Waythorn; Mr. Waythorn is Alice's third husband. He has managed to

put his predecessors out of his mind until her first husband, Mr. Haskett, comes to visit their little girl, who has been ill, and he then finds himself in business negotiations with the second husband. At first he shudders at the prospect of having Haskett in the house, but finds him to be nonthreatening, a "small, effaced-looking man . . . who might have been a piano tuner." Haskett worries about his daughter, who has become "too anxious to please." Waythorn begins to reconstruct his wife's two marriages and her social evolution, from the small-town Haskett to the successful businessman Gus Varick. Waythorn comes to perceive himself as a "member of a syndicate," holding a certain number of shares in his "wife's personality . . . his predecessors were his partners in the business." Alice becomes to him "as easy as an old shoe—a shoe that too many feet had worn." She has been pulled in different directions by each husband and, with each one, has lost some of her privacy, personality and the "inmost self where the unknown god abides."

At the conclusion of the story, Alice is about to serve tea to the three men, all gathered, for various reasons, in the Waythorn home. White makes the point that the story shows Alice and Waythorn as caught in "the contradictions of patriarchal marriage." Alice has learned from her various marriages how to please a man, teaching Lily the same art, yet Waythorn, a collector who knows the "joy of possessorship," wants her to be "fresh and unused" (*Edith Wharton: A Study of the Short Fiction,* 16). The reviewer of the collection for the *Bookman* called Edith Wharton "a marvelously clever social vivisector" (*CR* 81).

For further reading: Caws, "Framing in Two Opposite Modes: Ford and Wharton"; Inverso, "Performing Women: Semiotic Promiscuity in 'The Other Two' "; White, *Edith Wharton: A Study of the Short Fiction.*

Outre-Mer: Impressions of America   A volume of essays written by Paul BOURGET, French novelist and friend of Edith Wharton. They were originally written for the *New York Herald Tribune* and first published in France; the book was published by Charles Scribner's Sons in 1895. In 1893 Bourget and his wife Minnie came to America to do research for the essays. They called on the Whartons in NEWPORT, and later came to be their close friends.

ouvroir for seamstresses   (*See* WAR RELIEF, WORLD WAR I).

Paget, Violet   *See* LEE, VERNON.

Parrett, Mrs.   *See* NEW YEAR'S DAY.

Paris   All French roads begin from a point embedded in the stone outside the Gothic cathedral of Notre-Dame, and one famous French epigram states that "all that is not Paris is the provinces." The most central threads of Edith Wharton's life are also intertwined with the "City of Light." In Paris, she wrote, "no one could live without literature." The stature Wharton achieved as a professional author caused her to break culturally with her American past and align herself permanently with the Gallic paradigm of intellectual life. It was also in Paris that her liaison with Morton FULLERTON first flourished, and in which her DIVORCE decree was granted. For 30 years Wharton spent several months each year either in Paris or just outside the city at the PAVILLON COLOMBE in St.-Brice-sous-Forêt. Edith Wharton died at St.-Brice and her memorial service was held, as she requested, at the American Pro-Cathedral in Paris (she is buried in the CIMITIÈRE DES GONARDS in Versailles, near the grave of Walter BERRY).

Edith Wharton first came to know Paris as a small child, during the JONESES' six-year European sojourn between 1866 and 1872. From that time until her death she regarded the city as the epitome of grace, elegance, wit and civilized living. It was during one of her family's early winters in Paris that she was led into the dining room for dessert after one of her parents' intimate dinner parties while one of the guests, as she recalled in *A BACKWARD GLANCE*, "told me mythology." These tales, which became a permanent element in her writing, caused her to feel "more at home with the gods and goddesses of Olympus" than with other children. She did, however, play with other privileged children in the Champs Elysées, took dancing lessons and became fluent in French (*BG* 32–33).

As an adult, Edith Wharton continued to visit FRANCE, particularly Paris, assimilating French culture as thoroughly as she had the French language. In March 1906, she wrote Sara NORTON that she and her husband were soon sailing for Paris and ENGLAND, and that she was going "chiefly for a rest & the kind of mental refreshment that I can get only *là bas*. Oh, the curse of having been brought up there, & having it

ineradically in one's blood!" (*Letters*, 104). Her permanent transition to France took place gradually; in 1907 the Whartons spent their first winter in an apartment leased from the George VANDERBILTS in the rue de Varenne in the elite FAUBOURG SAINT-GERMAIN quarter of Paris. They took the same apartment in 1908 and 1909, and, in 1910, leased their own apartment, unfurnished, on the same street. Just as Chad Newsome, in Henry JAMES's novel *The Ambassadors*, has been "made over" by Paris, Edith Wharton was redefined by her long residence in the city. According to Lewis, by the spring of 1906 she was "beginning to feel that Paris,

53, rue de Varenne, Paris, where Wharton lived from 1910 until 1920 (Photo by Sarah Bird Wright)

and specifically the Faubourg St.-Germain, might be where she belonged . . . as she came to appreciate the coherence of life there, the almost effortless intermixture of the artistic and the fashionable, the steady nourishment of 'the warm dim background of a long social past' " (*EW* 165).

Teddy WHARTON, however, was inept at speaking French and was increasingly ill at ease and unhappy in Paris. This problem, coupled with his increasing instability and mental decline, led eventually to the Whartons' separation and DIVORCE, finalized in 1913. Meanwhile, Wharton had come to feel fully at home in Paris and did not return to AMERICA for the decade between the 1913 wedding of her niece, Beatrix JONES, to Max FARRAND, and the 1923 bestowal of her honorary degree by YALE UNIVERSITY.

The onset of WORLD WAR I brought a close to the BELLE ÉPOQUE. At the end of July 1914, Edith Wharton returned to Paris from a journey to SPAIN and found France on the verge of war. She wrote of it in "The Look of Paris," the first chapter of *FIGHTING FRANCE, FROM DUNKERQUE TO BELFORT*. There was still an ephemeral quality about the city, where ". . . the reaches of the Seine trembled with the blue-pink lustre of an early Monet. The Bois lay about us in the stillness of a holiday evening, and the lawns of Bagatelle were as fresh as June." This pastoral scene was threatened, however. "The great city, so made for peace and art and all humanist graces, seemed to lie by her river-side like a princess guarded by the watchful giant of the Eiffel Tower" (*FFD* 6).

By August 2, when Wharton looked down from the Hôtel de Crillon, the mobilized forces had departed and the city had an ominous beauty: "never had such blue-grey softness of afternoon brooded over Paris, such sunsets turned the heights of the Trocadéro into Dido's Carthage" (*FFD* 20). When the article was published in *SCRIBNER'S MAGAZINE* in July, Charles SCRIBNER wrote her, "I have had more comment on the first article 'The Look of Paris' than anything we have published in a long time." On August 22, 1915, she wrote Bernard BERENSON that Paris had "never looked so appealingly humanly beautiful as now—poor Andromeda!—with the monster careering up to her" (*Letters* 334). Much of *Fighting France, from Dunkerque to Belfort* and also of Wharton's World War I novel, *A SON AT THE FRONT*, is concerned with the transformation of Paris by the war; she saw the city as exceedingly vulnerable, and her horror of the German advance permeated both works.

In 1919, Wharton published *FRENCH WAYS AND THEIR MEANING*, a volume of essays intended to interpret France to the young American soldiers who were stationed in the country and had little understanding of it. Paris is the focus of her chapter on "Taste." As an example of French taste, she describes the home of the French Academy, on the Quai Malaquais bordering the Seine. This is a building which is "all elegance, measure and balance, from its graceful cupola to the stately stone vases surmounting the lateral colonnades." The select Academy functions as a "national conservatory of good manners and good speech." Election to the Academy, which has only 40 members, is considered one of the highest honors in the country.

The noise and congestion of postwar Paris made the city increasingly unpleasant for Wharton. She discovered the PAVILLON COLOMBE in suburban St.-Brice-sous-Forêt and purchased it in 1919. About the same time she acquired STE.-CLAIRE-CHÂTEAU near HYÈRES and until her death in 1937 divided her time between these two homes.

Parma   A city about 75 miles southeast of MILAN, on the Parma River. It was the home of Correggio, whose paintings Edith Wharton admired. She devotes a chapter, "Sub Umbra Liliorum: An Impression of Parma," of her second travel book, *ITALIAN BACKGROUNDS*, to the city. The title refers to the lilies that were emblematic of the Farnese family, who once ruled the city. Only in ITALY, Wharton comments, "could so unpromising an exterior hide such varied treasures" (*IB* 110). Among the treasures are the Farnese Palace with its ducal theater, the frescoes of the Convent of Saint Paul and the Baptistery. Wharton concluded that, for the traveler, the city would not "hang as a whole in the gallery of his mental vignettes" in the way that Siena or Vicenza might, but that "in the mosaic of detached impressions some rich and iridescent fragments will represent his after-thoughts of Parma" (*IB* 124).

Parrish, Maxfield (1870–1966)   American painter and illustrator, born in Philadelphia, the son of the painter and etcher Stephen Parrish. He studied at the Pennsylvania Academy of Fine Arts and was also taught by Howard Pyle. In 1900 he received an honorable mention in the Paris Exposition; he is also represented at the City Art Museum, St. Louis. He became a member of the National Academy in 1906. Parrish is known for his many illustrations for books, including L. Frank Baum's *Mother Goose in Prose* and *Arabian Nights*, edited by Kate Douglas Wiggin. His work appeared in many prominent magazines and periodicals, including the *LADIES' HOME JOURNAL*, *SCRIBNER'S MAGAZINE* and *The CENTURY*.

Parrish illustrated one of Edith Wharton's short stories, "THE DUCHESS AT PRAYER," for the August 1900 *Scribner's*. The imaginary gardens were formally designed, showing a circular pool in the foreground and a wide walkway, bordered with closely clipped hedges, plantings and curved walks, leading upwards around a small grotto to a distant villa, several levels above, with balustrades and ilex trees. These illustrations, according to Scott Marshall, who has pointed out

"A Characteristic Street" (Parma). Illustration by Ernest Peixotto for Italian Backgrounds *(1905), first edition* (Collection of the author)

their architectonic quality, might well have predisposed Edith Wharton to believe that Parrish understood her concept of Italy and could make it visible.

In 1902 Wharton was asked by Richard Watson GILDER, editor of *The Century,* to contribute the text of a series of articles about Italian villas that Parrish had already been commissioned to illustrate with watercolors and paintings. She accepted with alacrity, considering the offer an honor. Almost immediately, however, problems developed. Unpublished correspondence at the BEINECKE LIBRARY, YALE UNIVERSITY, reveals that from the beginning Wharton's conception

of the series—late compiled in book form as *ITALIAN VILLAS AND THEIR GARDENS*—differed rather drastically from Gilder's. Moreover, the close collaboration she had experienced with Ogden CODMAN in *The DECORATION OF HOUSES* was not to materialize, nor was she cognizant of Parrish's temperament as an artist. He preferred to visit the villas independently, although Wharton had invited him to join them in seeing a few of them. His illustrations were impressionistic rather than visually precise.

Italian Villas and Their Gardens was published in 1904 with 52 illustrations, including 15 watercolors by Parrish. In *A BACKWARD GLANCE,* written 30 years after publication, Wharton was still regretful. The Parrish watercolors, she felt, "should have been used to illustrate some fanciful tale of Lamotte Fouqué, or Andersen's 'Improvisatore.' " But, she reflected, "even had the illustrator been an architectural draughtsman, the . . . editorial scruples would not have been allayed, for what really roused them was not the lack of harmony between text and pictures but the fear their readers would be bored by the serious technical treatment of a subject associated with moonlight and nightingales" (*BG* 139).

Despite her disappointment with his illustrations, Wharton continued to consider herself a friend of Parrish. In the summer of 1905, while at The MOUNT, the

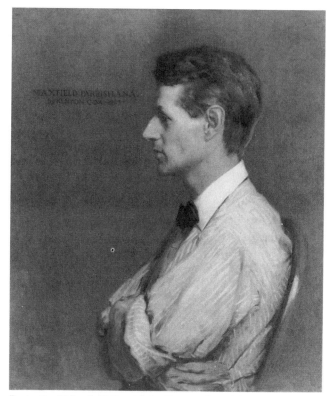

Portrait of Maxfield Parrish by Kenyon Cox, 1905 (Courtesy of the National Academy of Design, New York)

Whartons and Eunice and Walter MAYNARD went to lunch with him in Cornish, New Hampshire. Afterward, Parrish took Edith Wharton to meet the novelist Winston Churchill, whose *The Crossing* had been published in 1904 to popular acclaim. In 1915, however, she lost respect for Parrish when he declined to design the cover for *The BOOK OF THE HOMELESS*, the project she devised to raise money for war relief.

For further reading: Ludwig, *Maxfield Parrish.*

Pater, Walter (1839–94)   British essayist, critic and lifelong student of the Renaissance whose style and connoisseurship Edith Wharton greatly admired. His masterpiece is the philosophic novel *Marius the Epicurean* (1885); he also wrote *The Renaissance: Studies in Art and Poetry* (1873), *Plato and Platonism* (1893) and *Greek Studies* (1895). George Frederic JONES gave Wharton a copy of *The Renaissance,* which greatly influenced her. It includes essays on Leonardo da Vinci, Botticelli, Pico della Mirandola and Michelangelo. In this work and his other essays, Pater formulated the doctrine that art and aesthetics may constitute one of the ends of life. This was a theory Wharton found congenial; it is particularly evident in her focus on art and artists in her Italian travel books.

In *A BACKWARD GLANCE* Wharton recalled her enthusiasm for the travel books of the 1870s and 1880s of the "cultured dilettante" type, written by "gifted amateurs" such as Pater, Violet Paget ("Vernon LEE") and John Addington SYMONDS. The scientific approach to art as pioneered by Bernard BERENSON caused her to feel guilty for having read these writers with such "zest," she later remarked. Yet there still remained, in her opinion, "a field of observation wherein the mere lover of beauty can open the eyes and sharpen the hearing of the receptive traveller" in the way Pater, Lee and Symonds had done for her generation (*BG* 141).

The influence of Pater and John RUSKIN may be seen in Wharton's poem "INTENSE LOVE'S UTTERANCE," which she composed in 1881.

Pavillon Colombe   Edith Wharton's home about 10 miles north of PARIS, in the village of ST.-BRICE-SOUS-FORÊT. As early as 1917, before the end of WORLD WAR I, she began to think of acquiring a house outside the city to serve as a spring and autumn home. In *A BACKWARD GLANCE,* she described motoring north of Paris to visit her group of refugee colonies and passing through the village of St.-Brice-sous-Fôret, where wealthy Parisians had often quasi-rural retreats. Just off the main street there stood a "quiet house," called the Villa Jean-Marie, that her friend Elisina TYLER had already noticed. The latter stopped to ask the concierge if it were for sale, which it was, since, as Edith Wharton recalled, "every house in the northern suburbs of Paris was to be bought at that darkest moment of the spring

of 1918. They had all been deserted by their owners since the last German advance, for they were in the direct line of the approach to Paris, and the little house

Street sign in St.-Brice-sous-Forêt, France. This village north of Paris is the site of Pavillon Colombe, Wharton's summer and autumn home from 1919 until her death (Photo by Sarah Bird Wright)

Pavillon Colombe, view from the rue Edith Wharton (Photo by Sarah Bird Wright)

Pavillon Colombe, garden view (Courtesy Beinecke Library, Yale University)

in question was also on Bertha's trajectory" (*BG* 362). (Big Bertha was a long-range gun used by the Germans in World War I. According to Price, it was named for the inventor's wife; it had a range of 90 miles for a 240-lb. shell [Price, *The End of the Age of Innocence: Edith Wharton and the First World War,* 149]). Lewis observes that she was looking "beyond the war's end to a life of tranquillity and literary dedication" (*Letters,* 332).

Edith Wharton negotiated to acquire the house, consulting Ogden CODMAN, the coauthor of *The DECORATION OF HOUSES,* who at the time lived in a château south of Paris. On July 7, 1918, Wharton wrote her sister-in-law, Mary Cadwalader JONES, that she had had a "long letter from Coddy about Jean-Marie, of which I had sent him a p.c. He knows it, & once tried to buy it; thinks its possibilities endless—& understands it better than any of the French friends who have seen it. What a queer stick!" (*Letters,* 407). Wharton acquired the house in 1918, began renovations and in the summer of 1919 moved in, restoring its original name, the Pavillon Colombe. It had been named, according to Lewis, for two sisters, natives of Venice who had come to France with their father, an itinerant musician in the mid-18th century. They joined the Comédie Italienne as actresses

and singers, taking the stage name Colombe, and were installed in the house by their lovers (*EW* 420).

The house had extensive gardens enclosed in a high wall. In her memoir Wharton does not describe the interior renovations, except to say the "dirt and squalor" were removed. After spending the war years in the FAUBOURG SAINT-GERMAIN her greatest interest was in having a garden. Wharton describes it as "Saint Martin's summer after the long storm" (*BG* 363). She took pleasure in having "leisure for the two pursuits which never palled, writing and gardening. . . . From the day when (to the scandal of the village!) I chopped down a giant araucaria on the lawn, until this moment, I have never ceased to worry and pet and dress up and smooth down my two or three acres" (*BG* 362). In 1919, as the renovations at the Pavillon Colombe were nearing completion, Wharton obtained, on a long lease, a second estate high above the Mediterranean on the French Riviera at HYÈRES. This was a convent built within a chateau, STE.-CLAIRE CHÂTEAU, which she later purchased. From about 1922 until the end of her life, Wharton's pattern was to stay at the Pavillon Colombe from June until mid-December and at Ste.-Claire Château from mid-December through the end of May.

Commemorative plaque, Pavillon Colombe (Photo by Sarah Bird Wright)

She entertained her closest friends at the Pavillon Colombe and was within easy reach of the Parisian social life she had enjoyed.

Peixotto, Ernest (1869–1940)   An American artist and illustrator, Peixotto was a native of San Francisco. He studied with Henri Doucet in Paris and received an honorable mention at the Paris Salon in 1921. Among his books were *By Italian Seas* (New York: Scribner's, 1906), *Through Spain and Portugal* (New York: Scribner's, 1922) and *A Bacchic Pilgrimage: French Wines* (New York: Scribner's, 1922). He was the director of the Department of Mural Painting at the Beaux Arts Institute, New York. His work appeared in a number of periodicals. He was often accompanied on his travels by his wife, Mary, also an artist, illustrator and writer, who sometimes wrote articles he then illustrated.

Scribner's engaged Peixotto to illustrate the five chapters of ITALIAN BACKGROUNDS published serially in SCRIBNER'S MAGAZINE; the volume contained a total of 42 illustrations (5 halftones and 37 line drawings), most of them by Peixotto. Wharton probably had no voice in choosing the artist, but it is unlikely that Peixotto would have been her first choice. When the book was compiled and she received the proofs of the frontispiece, a sepia halftone of one of the San Vivaldo terra-cotta groups, she wrote the editor, William C. BROWNELL: "How charming the frontispiece is! So much more real than those speckly Peixottos."

A misunderstanding at Scribner's, arising from Charles Scribner's absence in Europe, led to Peixotto's also being commissioned to illustrate *A MOTOR-FLIGHT THROUGH FRANCE*, published in 1908, three years after *Italian Backgrounds*. Wharton wrote Brownell that she was dazed by the arrival of the partial proofs and by Peixotto's request for postcards of Bourges Cathedral and several other monuments so that he could "do his sketches in West 59th St.!" It seemed to her, she wrote, that "good photographs would have been better as illustrations than sketches done 'de chic' [without a model] from post cards." Moreover, the author complained that she ought to have been consulted about the illustrations, since she would have certainly protested at the "little dabby sketches" of cows and produce vendors Peixotto had produced. She then wrote directly to Scribner that she considered the small illustrations unsuitable; the book was not a "chatty" description of various adventures, but a series of essays. She preferred to restrict the illustrations to actual "portraits of places." The problem was rectified, Peixotto disengaged and photographs substituted, which Wharton helped to procure; whether Scribner's sent a photographer is uncertain.

Since Peixotto's relationship with Scribner's continued for several more decades, apparently he took no permanent offense at having been relieved of the task of illustrating Wharton's *A Motor-Flight Through France*.

"Pelican, The"   Short story published in SCRIBNER'S MAGAZINE in November 1898 and collected in *The GREATER INCLINATION* (Scribner's, 1899). The title recalls the erroneous but once prevalent theory that the pelican fed its young with its own blood. It is the story of a widow, Mrs. Amyot, descendant of several female women of intellect, including her mother, Irene Astarte Pratt, author of a poem on the Fall of Man, and an aunt who had translated Euripides. Widowed early, and with Lancelot, her young son, to support, she begins giving lectures on such subjects as Plato and Greek art. She considers art an "extension of coquetry," "flirting" with her audience.

As her son grows into young manhood, Mrs. Amyot continues lecturing, expanding her itinerary to include various fashionable resorts. On the veranda at a large southern hotel, the narrator, seated nearby, is urged by a fellow guest to purchase a ticket to the evening lecture. She presses the case: " '. . . we had six weeks of her at Bar Harbor last summer! One has to take tickets, you know, because she's a widow and does it for her son—to pay for his education. . . . we all simply ruin ourselves in tickets.' " Lancelot, married, self-supporting and a father himself, overhears the exchange and is mortified. Angry at being the object of charity, he confronts his hurt and bewildered mother.

One of Edith Wharton's better-known stories, "The Pelican" caught the attention of the *Bookman* critic, who termed it the "most amusing piece of work. . . . a perfectly delicious study of the typical 'lady lecturer,' . . . full of pure delight from the beginning to the end" (*CR* 19). White terms it one of the most Jamesian of Edith Wharton's short stories (*SSF* 36).

Pencraig The large, gabled, Tudor-style summer home in NEWPORT, Rhode Island, owned by Edith Wharton's parents, George Frederic and Lucretia JONES. The family spent several months every year there while Edith was growing up. In *A BACKWARD GLANCE* Wharton recalled that during her youthful summers every room in the house would be filled with young people; they occupied themselves playing the new game of lawn tennis, which had superseded archery. There were "jolly bathing parties from the floating boat-landing at the foot of the lawn, mackerel-fishing, and races in rival 'cat-boats.' " Sometimes there were excursions in the new white steam-yachts that were coming to be "the favourite toys of the rich" (*BG* 80). After she and Teddy WHARTON were married in March 1885, they went immediately to Pencraig, but soon moved into PENCRAIG COTTAGE, also on the Jones property.

Pencraig Cottage The NEWPORT home of Edith and Teddy WHARTON on part of the Jones property across Harrison Avenue from the principal home on the estate, PENCRAIG. Although the young couple lived at Pencraig for a few months after their 1885 wedding, they soon moved into Pencraig Cottage. They lived here from June until February each year, dividing the remainder of their time between travel abroad and New York, where they stayed with Lucretia JONES before acquiring their own house.

Pencraig Cottage was a substantial house, although much smaller than Pencraig. According to Dwight, it had four or five rooms on each of the first two floors and five or six servants' rooms on the third. The Whartons' staff included Catharine GROSS, Edith's maid, who had begun working for her in 1884; Alfred WHITE, Teddy's manservant, who joined them in 1888; a cook; several housemaids and gardeners (Dwight, 38). Catharine Gross would remain with Edith until her death at the age of 80 in 1933, and Alfred White was still in her employ, making his home in a cottage on the grounds of the PAVILLON COLOMBE, when Edith Wharton died in 1937.

Peniston, Mrs. *See HOUSE OF MIRTH, THE.*

"Permanent Values in Fiction" Essay published in the *SATURDAY REVIEW OF LITERATURE*, April 7, 1934 (rpt. *UCC* 175–79). This essay followed "TENDENCIES IN MODERN FICTION," which had appeared in the *Saturday Review* in January. The thesis is that a work of fiction ought "to tell a tale and to mirror human nature"; this mission was amply carried out by such writers as Dickens, Thackeray, Balzac and Stendhal. Edith Wharton attacks such contemporary novelists as James JOYCE and Virginia WOOLF for their lack of form. D. H. Lawrence, on the other hand, is one of a group of writers for whom a novel has become an "anthology of ideas." Too many modern writers suffer from the misconception that "new 'forms' are recurringly necessary in all the arts."

Wharton recommends, instead, that the narrative be "consecutive and significant" and that the novelist strive, in sketching his characters, to renovate "old types by new creative action." They must have such a convincing reality that the reader believes he might have known and lived with them; Tolstoy's Anna Karenina and Thackeray's Becky Sharp merit this reaction. Sinclair LEWIS is one of the few contemporary writers who has "plunged his hand into the thick of average human nature," as has Theodore Dreiser. Their works will be more enduring than the innovative ones "dressed up in a passing notoriety."

"Permanent Wave" Short story published in *REDBOOK* (then called *The Red Book Magazine*) in April 1935 as "Poor Old Vincent!"; it was then reprinted as "Permanent Wave" in *The WORLD OVER* (New York: Appleton-Century, 1936). Regarded as one of Edith Wharton's weaker late short stories, the plot concerns a married woman, Nalda Craig, who is about to leave her husband, the eminent university scholar and lecturer Vincent Craig, for another man, Phil Ingerson. Fatuous and vague, she visits her imperious hairdresser for a permanent wave on the eve of her departure, assuming it is Wednesday. The hairdresser, Gaston, declares the day is Thursday. Believing she has missed the chance to leave with Ingerson, Nalda returns home, only to discover that it is actually Wednesday and she can still abandon her husband. But he catches her as she faints and she gives up her scheme of leaving him. Perry Hutchison, in the *New York Times Book Review*, believed this ending was "touchingly human" (*CR* 535).

For further reading: Inness, "An Economy of Beauty: The Beauty System in 'The Looking Glass' and 'Permanent Wave.' "

Perry, Bliss Editor of the *ATLANTIC MONTHLY* from 1899 to 1909. In June 1900 he published "An Alpine Posting Inn," which would become the first essay in *ITALIAN BACKGROUNDS*. He also commissioned several articles resulting from Edith Wharton's first two French "motor-flights," which were published in the magazine in 1906, 1907 and 1908. They were later included in *A MOTOR-FLIGHT THROUGH FRANCE.*

Perry was a professor of English at Williams, Princeton and Harvard, editing many works on English and American literature. He also wrote biographies of Walt WHITMAN and John Greenleaf Whittier and is known for his studies *The American Mind* (1912) and *The American Spirit in Literature* (1918).

Peyton, Denis   *See* SANCTUARY.

Peyton, Dick   *See* SANCTUARY.

Pictorial Review   Slick mass market picture magazine founded in 1899 as a house organ of Albert McDowell's System of Dressmaking and Tailoring, but later acquired by William Randolph HEARST; it became a large-circulation women's magazine (Mott, III, 490). During Arthur Vance's tenure as editor, beginning in 1906, the *Pictorial Review* paid extremely well, and, after WORLD WAR I, Edith Wharton published several short stories and novels in this magazine. Rutger B. JEWETT of APPLETON & Co. frequently negotiated serialization of Wharton's novels before publication, and was always alert to the possibility of her receiving a high fee and generating publicity for a forthcoming novel.

In 1919, Vance conveyed an offer through Jewett to pay $18,000 for Wharton's next novel. She put aside *The GLIMPSES OF THE MOON,* on which she was working, as well as *A SON AT THE FRONT,* since, as Jewett astutely realized and cabled her, war books were "dead in America" (Wharton-Jewett correspondence, BEINECKE LIBRARY, YALE UNIVERSITY). She proposed that they consider a novel provisionally called *OLD NEW YORK* that was nearing completion and would be set in the New York of the 1870s. Vance was delighted to accept and the work was soon renamed *The AGE OF INNOCENCE.* Vance purchased it for $18,000 and began running it in 1920; the novel was published by Appleton's in 1920. (The four novellas making up the "Old New York" group, published in 1924, were different works, although some of the characters from *The Age of Innocence* reappear in the series.) According to Lewis, Edith Wharton had her "first taste of mass market publication" when the *Pictorial Review* editors inquired whether they might delete some installments of *The Age of Innocence* and use the space for illustrations and other purposes. She indignantly refused to have her work "treated as prose by the yard" (*EW* 428–29). *The Glimpses of the Moon* was serialized in the *Review* before being published in 1922 by Appleton as were *The MOTHER'S RECOMPENSE* (Appleton, 1925), *TWILIGHT SLEEP* (Appleton, 1927), and *The CHILDREN* (Appleton, 1928). Several of Edith Wharton's short stories were also first published in the magazine, including "The TEMPERATE ZONE" in February 1924, "MISS MARY PASK" in April 1925 and "The YOUNG GENTLEMEN" in February 1926.

picturesque tradition, in American travel literature, the   The traditional 19th-century American travel sketch often focused on elements of the picturesque, with writers recording scenery they considered majestic and sublime. Edith Wharton criticized the writers favored by the "artless travellers" before Ruskin's day, who, she states, chiefly enjoyed

> . . . scenery, ruins and historic sites; places about which some sentimental legend hung, and to which Scott, Byron, Hans Andersen, Bulwer, Washington Irving or Hawthorne gently led the timid sight-seer. . . . ruins, snow-mountains, lakes and waterfalls—especially waterfalls—were endlessly enjoyable . . . (*BG* 62–63).

Instead, Wharton's works diverge substantially from the tradition of the picturesque sketch. Art and literature frame Wharton's evocation of place. Her works of travel reflect her visual sensibility, retentive memory and imaginative powers. In reconstituting what Blake Nevius calls the "aesthetic spectra" in her travel texts, she enacts a new dialectic of tourism. As a connoisseur, she evaluates art and architecture with taste and judgment, and as a scholar and art historian, she reassesses both attribution and styles of works of art. She provides a rich aesthetic, cultural and literary context for the places, sculptures and paintings she discusses, making her travel texts of lasting interest.

poetry   Edith Wharton had a lifelong passion for poetry. Both her first published book, *VERSES* (privately printed, 1878) and her final one, of which she was co-editor, *ETERNAL PASSION IN ENGLISH POETRY* (published posthumously in 1939), were volumes of poetry. For the most part, however, her poems are not readily available except for those in the first commercially published collection, *ARTEMIS TO ACTÆON AND OTHER VERSE* (Scribner's, 1909). This volume was succeeded over two decades later by *TWELVE POEMS* (The Medici Society, London, 1920), which is extremely rare.

Wharton's poetry is, for the most part, carefully argued and learned, with references to mythological and historical figures she assumed were well known to her readers. The story of Artemis (Diana) and Actaeon, from Ovid's *Metamorphosis,* for example, is the subject of the title poem in *Artemis to Actæon and Other Verse.* This is a dramatic monologue addressed by Artemis to the youth Actaeon, who has accidentally come across her unclothed in the forest while her nymphs are bathing her. She furiously turns him into a stag and he flees, but is then killed by his hunting dogs. His fate, she tells him unpityingly, is to lose himself in her; he must find immortality in her renewal.

E. K. Brown, author of one of the few studies of Wharton's poetry (published in French in 1935), divides it into three stylistic groups: dramatic monologues, sonnets and meditative poems. He points out the influence of Matthew ARNOLD, Robert Browning, Elizabeth Barrett Browning, Alfred Lord Tennyson, Walt WHITMAN and D. H. Lawrence, but insists that Wharton has freed herself of "Victorian matters." He observes that the drama on which "The MORTAL LEASE" is based "never quite becomes tragic." He could not, of course, have known of Wharton's affair with Morton FULLERTON that occasioned the poem and its sequel, "COLOPHON TO THE 'MORTAL LEASE.'" His remark, nonetheless, pinpoints what may be the principal flaw in her verse: it is often so controlled as to be apparently devoid of emotion. He quotes a remark a critic for the *Times Literary Supplement* made about *Twelve Poems:* "'If we content ourselves with not expecting to discover great poetry here, we will not be disappointed by the particular pleasure offered by all the lovely verses'" (221). A few of Wharton's poems, however, are marked by deep personal passion, such as "TERMINUS," commemorating a night spent with Full-erton in London, and "GARDEN VALEDICTORY," ex-pressing her grief at the death of Walter BERRY.

Many of Wharton's poems were published in newspapers and literary magazines. Although they have sometimes been reprinted individually, they remain uncollected. Among them are "Only a Child" (signed "Eadgyth"; New York *World,* May 30, 1879); "The Parting Day" (unsigned; *Atlantic Monthly,* Feb. 1880); "Aeropagus" (unsigned; *Atlantic Monthly,* Mar. 1880); "A Failure" (unsigned; *Atlantic Monthly,* Apr. 1880); "Patience" (unsigned; *Atlantic Monthly,* Apr. 1880); "Wants" (unsigned; *Atlantic Monthly,* May 1880); "The Last Giustiniani" (*Scribner's Magazine,* Oct. 1889); "Euryalus" (*Atlantic Monthly,* Dec. 1889); "Happiness" (*Scribner's Magazine,* Dec. 1889); "Botticelli's Madonna in the Louvre" (*Scribner's Magazine,* Jan. 1891); "The Sonnet" (*The Century Magazine,* Nov. 1891); "Life" (*Scribner's Magazine,* June 1894); "Jade" (*The Century Magazine,* Jan. 1895); "Phaedra" (*Scribner's Magazine,* Jan. 1898); "Mould and Vase" (*Atlantic Monthly,* Sept. 1901); "The Comrade" (*Atlantic Monthly,* Dec. 1910); "Summer Afternoon (Bodiam Castle, Sussex)" (*Scribner's Magazine,* Mar. 1911); "Pomegranate Seed" (*Scribner's Magazine,* Mar. 1912); "The Hymn of the Lusitania" (*New York Herald,* May 7, 1915); "'On Active Service'; American Expeditionary Force (R.S., Aug. 12, 1918)" (*Scribner's Magazine,* Nov. 1918); "You and You" (*The Pittsburgh Chronicle Telegraph,* Jan. 24, 1919); "With the Tide" (*Saturday Evening Post,* Mar. 29, 1919); "In Provence" (*Yale Review,* Jan. 1920); "Lyrical Epigrams" (*Yale Review,* Jan. 1920); "Had I Been Only" (*Scribner's Magazine,* Aug. 1928). (Source: Stephen Garrison, *Edith Wharton: A Descriptive Bibliography,* 439–63, *passim*).

Wharton was devoted to the poetry of Johann Wolfgang von GOETHE, Percy Bysshe Shelley, John Keats, Ralph Waldo EMERSON, Matthew ARNOLD, Walt WHIT-MAN and DANTE Alighieri. When her mother gave her the Buxton Forman editions of the poetry of Keats and Shelley for her birthday one year, she recalled in her memoir that "the gates of the realms of gold swung wide" and she was never again "wholly lonely or unhappy (*BG* 70–71). She also admired the work of Anna de NOAILLES, a French contemporary poet she knew well.

Several poets contributed to *The BOOK OF THE HOMELESS* (1915), including Laurence Binyon, Rupert Brooke, Paul Claudel, Jean COCTEAU, Robert GRANT, Thomas HARDY, William Dean HOWELLS, Francis Jammes, Alice Meynell, Anna de Noailles, Lilla Cabot Perry, Henri de Régnier, Edmond Rostand, George SANTAYANA, Edith M. Thomas, Herbert Trench, Émile Verhaeren, Barrett WENDELL, Margaret L. Woods and W. B. Yeats. She included one of her own, "The Tryst."

At the PAVILLON COLOMBE there were often "poetry evenings" when guests would take down volumes of Shelley, Michel de Montaigne, Robert Browning, Thomas HARDY or A. E. Housman from the library shelves and read aloud from them (*EW* 455).

See also "The GREAT BLUE TENT; "SENLIS, MAY 16"; "OGRIN THE HERMIT"; "INTENSE LOVE'S UTTERANCE"; Review of "SONNETS OF THE WINGLESS HOURS" (Eugene Lee-Hamilton).

For further reading: Bancroft, "Lost Lands: Metaphors of Sexual Awakening in Edith Wharton's Poetry, 1908–1909"; Brown, "Edith Wharton's Poetry" (trans. Bendixen); Goodman, "Edith Wharton's 'Sketch of an Essay on Walt Whitman.'"

"Pomegranate Seed"   Story published in the SATURDAY EVENING POST in April 1931 and included in both *The WORLD OVER* (Appleton-Century, 1936) and *GHOSTS* (published posthumously; Appleton-Century, 1937). This is one of the more noted of Edith Wharton's ghost stories. It deals with the ominous experience of Charlotte Ashby, second wife of Kenneth Ashby, who discovers pale gray letters arriving regularly for her husband. The reader is left to infer that they are from his dead first wife, Elsie.

The title is taken from the Greek legend of Persephone, daughter of Demeter, goddess of fertility. Pluto abducted her and took her to Hades. Demeter persuaded Jupiter to intercede, and Persephone was able to leave Hades and revisit her mother. But Hades, her husband, had given her some pomegranate seeds to eat so that she could not remain permanently among the living but would be drawn back to the company of the dead for the winter months each year.

In a preface to the collection *Ghosts,* Edith Wharton mentioned that she had received many letters from readers asking about the meaning of the story and indicating ignorance of the legend. She impatiently lamented their lack of education: "In the dark ages of my childhood an acquaintance with classical fairy lore was as much a part of our stock of knowledge as Grimm and Andersen (Preface to *Ghosts*, 2). Readers who took the story literally, wondering how a ghost could mail a letter, were, she was sure, not of Welsh or Scottish descent.

Edith Wharton wrote Rutger B. JEWETT in 1931 that she had read this story to guests at her usual Christmas house party in HYÈRES and they all liked it and agreed that the ending was perfect. They thought it obvious from the beginning that the dead wife had written the letters and that Elsie is reclaiming Kenneth after death. One of her friends had warned Charlotte before the wedding that Kenneth had been dominated by Elsie.

One reviewer, Percy Hutchison, writing in the *New York Times Book Review,* judged the opening paragraph to be one of the most perfect Edith Wharton ever achieved, as it delineated the way in which the advent of the letters has shattered Charlotte Ashby's life. Prior to their arrival, she would pause on her doorstep before entering her home, which was a "tiny islet," a sanctuary from the glaring, noisy city, with its "congested minds" as well as traffic. Once the ambience of the interior is ruined and the happiness of her marriage destroyed by the letters, she must force herself to enter. Other reviewers, however, were bothered by Wharton's failure to make plausible the way in which the communications from the spirit world were able to enter the letter box.

In the 1900 story "COPY," which deals with a poet and a woman novelist who contest the ownership of their correspondence, Edith Wharton mentions "*Pomegranate Seed*" as the fictive title of one of Mrs. Dale's novels. The fact that the phrase was used as the title of the short story published in 1931 indicates the lengthy gestation of some of her works.

For further reading: Murray, "The Gothic Arsenal of Edith Wharton"; Singley and Sweeney, "Forbidden Reading and Ghostly Writing in Edith Wharton's 'Pomegranate Seed' "; Zilversmit, "Edith Wharton's Last Ghosts."

Illustration for "Pomegranate Seed" (artist unknown) (*The Saturday Evening Post,* April 1931. Courtesy Alderman Library, University of Virginia, © The Curtis Publishing Company)

Edith Wharton at the Pavillion Colombe, May 1931 (Bonney/BHVP. Bibliothèque Historique de la Ville de Paris)

"Portrait, The"   Short story published in *The GREATER INCLINATION* (SCRIBNER'S, 1899). The story related by an unknown narrator, opens in the midst of a Sunday afternoon gathering at the home of Mrs. Mellish. The group discusses the work of George Lillo, a portrait painter long resident in France, whose works are being exhibited in a New York gallery. The fashionable artist Little Cumberton debates with the other guests the proper intention of the artist: to portray a subject realistically, including his or her defects, as Lillo does, or to idealize and please his sitters, the specialty of Cumberton. They agree that Lillo's portrait of Alonzo Vard, notorious for his shadowy business dealings (he was involved in the "viaduct scandal"), is a failure because it doesn't portray the depth of his villainy. (Vard had committed suicide the day the pictures were first shown.)

The narrator later learns from Lillo that Vard's virtuous, but intelligent, young daughter had idolized him and persuaded him to sit for the artist while she looked on. She had made him appear at his best, but "she cheapened that best by her proximity" (*CSS* I, 180). Lillo, unable to paint Vard as he really was lest he offend Miss Vard, had resorted to a formula. Just as the sittings were coming to a close, Vard had been indicted for his crimes, then exonerated. Miss Vard had eventually come to view the portrait, of which the face was still unfinished. Lillo had realized she comprehended her father's corruption, but hoped it would not be made public. He complied with her unspoken wish, and proceeded to complete a whitewashed portrait. As a result of her realization, she died before it was exhibited, an event which, as White observes, "strains credibility" (*SSF* 38–39). Lillo, however, had sketched Miss Vard and captured her vivacity and purity.

The story received mixed reviews: John D. Barry, writing in *Literary World,* accused Wharton of "faltering treatment" of the story, and Harry Thurman Peck of *The Bookman* called it "slight" in its workmanship but "ingenious in its theme" (*CR* 12–25). Lewis terms it somewhat "confused" (*EW* 84).

postal stamp   In 1980 a U.S. postal stamp was issued honoring Edith Wharton; it had a value of 15 cents. The image used was a 1905 publicity photograph of

Edith Wharton commemorative, issued in 1980 by the U.S. Postal Service (Courtesy U.S. Postal Service and Lilly Library, Indiana University)

Wharton taken when *The HOUSE OF MIRTH* was published. Scott Marshall observes that she sent a copy of it to Henry JAMES, who wrote from LAMB HOUSE on December 18, "I must thank you very kindly, with no delay, for the so handsome photograph in which you baissez les yeux [lower the eyes] so modestly before the acclamations of the world" (Powers, *Henry James and Edith Wharton: Letters 1900–1915,* 57; personal communication with Scott Marshall).

"Potboiler, The"   Short story published in *SCRIBNER'S MAGAZINE* in December 1904 and collected in *The HERMIT AND THE WILD WOMAN AND OTHER STORIES* (Scribner's, 1908). The story is about an artist, Ned Stanwell, and an asthmatic sculptor, Caspar Arran, who have adjacent studios in a shabby New York building. Each believes himself to be true to his own concept of art. Caspar insists he would "starve in his tracks sooner than make a concession" and believes that praise is a "deadly drug," the "absinthe of the artist." Stanwell has little faith in Caspar's sculptural groups, and believes he produces "bad art in the service of the loftiest convictions." At the same time, each artist vainly hopes for popular success. Caspar receives an order to convert his sculpture group to marble, and Stanwell paints a portrait of a wealthy matron that leads to other commissions. " 'Why can't a man do two kinds of work—one to please himself and the other to boil the pot?' " asks Stanwell.

Caspar's work in marble goes slowly. He catches cold, his health declines and he receives no other commissions. Kate, his sister, agrees to marry Mungold, a well-known and popular portraitist, in order to support her brother. Stanwell, who has become romantically attached to her, refuses to paint portraits to order and returns to his earlier best work, a study of Kate. One critic called the story "a charmingly humorous exposure of the fallacy that unpopularity necessarily implies greatness" (*CR* 158). White observes that Edith Wharton "usually avoids didacticism . . . but she often has a message when it comes to art" (*SSF* 37). This story is a case in point.

prefaces   *See ETERNAL PASSION IN ENGLISH POETRY; GERHARDI, WILLIAM (FUTILITY); SPEAK TO THE EARTH: WANDERINGS AND REFLECTIONS AMONG ELEPHANTS AND MOUNTAINS.*

Prest, Henry   *See NEW YEAR'S DAY.*

"Pretext, The"   Short story published in *SCRIBNER'S MAGAZINE* in August 1908 and collected in *The HERMIT AND THE WILD WOMAN AND OTHER STORIES* (Scribner's, 1908). As the story opens, Margaret Ransom, who is "as flat as the pattern of the wallpaper," with a "flat" life as well, has been "looking after" Guy Dawnish, a young Englishman who has come to the narrow-minded NEW ENGLAND town of Wentworth.

Guy, the grandson of an earl, shows Margaret photographs of his eminent family and various homes in ENGLAND, evoking for her the "many-faceted existence in which the brightest episodes of the whole body of English fiction seemed collectively reflected" (*CSS* I, 638). Her dull, critical husband, Robert Ransom, a prominent attorney, is counsel to the University of Wentworth. He urges her to bring Guy to sit in the ladies' gallery and hear him speak after a university banquet (ladies had not been invited to dine). Margaret and Guy flee as Ransom is speaking and gesticulating far below them, and wander by the river. Margaret deflects what she believes is an imminent declaration of love on Guy's part.

After returns to England, Mrs. Ransom learns that he has broken off his engagement to a wealthy English girl, a match of which both families heartily approved, because of an attachment he formed in America. His aunt comes across the Atlantic to try to find the lady and persuade her to give Guy up. She assumes he has become interested in Mrs. Ransom's daughter-in-law, since it is not within the realm of possibility that the older, faded Mrs. Ransom could have attracted her nephew. The story ends somewhat ambiguously: was there someone else Guy loved, and was "Mrs. Ransom" a pretext for escaping from his engagement? Or had he actually loved her?

Benstock points out that the story is a reversal of the circumstances of an actual incident, known to Wharton through Henry JAMES, in which the son of an English nobleman who was a student at Harvard fell in love with the wife of a professor. He then broke off his engagement to the daughter of Holman Hunt, the Pre-Raphaelite painter (*NGC* 187).

Proust, Marcel (1871–1922)   Born in Auteuil, a suburb of Paris, Proust was the son of a French Roman Catholic physician and a Jewish mother. He was a student at the Lycée Condorcet in his youth and later studied law, philosophy and literature. He is chiefly known for the 16-volume *À la recherche du temps perdu* (*Remembrance of Things Past*), an autobiographical novel in the stream-of-consciousness form, told psychologically. In part of this novel, *The Guermantes Way,* Proust portrayed the FAUBOURG SAINT-GERMAIN, the elite literary and fashionable quarter of Paris in which Edith Wharton lived, beginning in 1906.

Edith Wharton never actually met Proust, although it is likely that they would have had much in common. She greatly admired his work, and they had a number of mutual friends, including the painter Jacques-Emile BLANCHE (who painted Proust's portrait), the art historian Bernard BERENSON, her old friend Walter BERRY and Charles DU BOS, the translator of *The HOUSE OF MIRTH*. Proust came close to finding someone to assume the task of completing the French translation of *The CUSTOM OF THE COUNTRY* after it was given up by Robert D'HUMIÈRES, according to Lewis (*EW* 400–01). Wharton's article "Marcel Proust" appeared in the *Yale Review* (January 1925) and later became the final chapter in *The WRITING OF FICTION* (Scribner's, 1925). In this chapter Wharton argues that Proust is a "renovator" rather than an "innovator." Far from being experimental, *À la recherche du temps perdu* is actually traditional; its effects are achieved through selection and design. Even though he deals with "half-conscious states of mind" and employs parenthetical constructions, Proust still achieves the novelist's primary aim, to report the "conscious, purposive conduct of his char-acters." In 1934 Wharton wrote another essay about Proust's work ("A RECONSIDERATION OF PROUST") for the *SATURDAY REVIEW OF LITERATURE*.

Pulitzer Prize   Edith Wharton won the Pulitzer Prize for fiction for *The AGE OF INNOCENCE* in May 1921; it was the first time the prize had been given to a woman and the third time an individual had been so honored. The citation was given each year for "the American novel which shall best present the wholesome atmosphere of American life and the highest standard to American manners and manhood" (*EW* 433). The committee had first chosen *Main Street* by Sinclair LEWIS, but decided parts of it might offend some people. Lewis wrote to congratulate Edith Wharton.

The prize was established by publisher Joseph Pulitzer (1847–1911), who died aboard his yacht in Charleston, S.C., on Oct. 29, 1911. In his will he left the newspapers he had owned to his three surviving sons and endowed Columbia University's journalism school; he also established a fund for annual prizes to be awarded for excellence in journalism.

Quarterly Review British periodical in which Edith Wharton published one of her essays, "HENRY JAMES IN HIS LETTERS" (July 1920). Morton FULLERTON had also published an essay on JAMES in the same periodical (April 1910).

Queen's Acre ("Qu'Acre") The home of Howard STURGIS at Windsor, England. A lifelong bachelor, Sturgis acquired the property after his mother's death. Edith Wharton often visited him there, sometimes in the company of Henry JAMES, and it was in the living room at Qu'Acre that she first met Percy LUBBOCK. Wharton described the house as "roomy and friendly." The drawing room was long and low, with watercolors, comfortable chintz-covered armchairs drawn about the hearth, a table with novels and magazines, and French windows opening to a wooden veranda with "a dancing faun poised above an incongruous 'arty' blue-tiled pool" (*BG* 225). Sturgis was looked after by a butler, cook and Scottish housemaid, in addition to an ancient coachman.

Sturgis refused to install electric lights, telephone or central heating, or to renovate the house. In *A BACK-WARD GLANCE*, Edith Wharton recalls an amusing episode when, writing in her bed one morning, as was her unvarying habit, she spilled ink on a fine monogrammed sheet. She sent Christina, the Scottish maid, with a note to Howard saying the house had had its usual stimulating effect and "this morning's chapter has come with a rush." Christina could hardly believe she was confessing to the accident instead of concealing it, but dutifully brought back a message of congratulation and a clean sheet, telling her that if she had been thinking of replacing it, they could be found at Marshall's (Edith Wharton promptly replaced the sheet at Marshall and Snelgrove). An extended account of the hospitable gatherings at Qu'Acre is given in *A Backward Glance* (230–39).

"Quicksand, The" Story published in *HARPER'S MAGAZINE* in June 1904 and reprinted in *The DESCENT OF MAN AND OTHER STORIES* (Scribner's, 1904). It concerns a difficult decision made by Mrs. Quentin, widow of a successful publisher of a newspaper scandal sheet, the *Radiator*. She must renounce her own life in persuading her prospective daughter-in-law not to make the mistake she had made earlier. Her son, Alan, who has taken over the *Radiator*, has been rejected by Hope Fenno, the girl he wishes to marry. Hope's idealism has prevented her from accepting a comfortable living from a paper that has injured many people; she also deplores Alan's lack of charitable benevolence. Mrs. Quentin at first persuades her that, as life goes on, "theories, ideas, abstract conceptions of life" weigh little against "the actual, against the particular way in which life presents itself," particularly to women (*CSS* I, 403).

She convinces Hope to marry Alan, but just as she accepts him, Mrs. Quentin reverses herself. She then

Illustration for "The Quicksand" (1904), artist unknown (Courtesy Alderman Library, University of Virginia)

insists that Hope adhere to her "beliefs, ambitions, energies," as she herself had not when she married Alan's father. Alan, like his father, had thrived on the power of the newspaper he had inherited. Mrs. Quentin had also begun idealistically, believing she could divest her husband of the newspaper, but failed. Instead, she has accommodated herself over the years to the situation. She has preserved beauty and taste in the home and tried not to think of the "monster" that has caused her to die, gradually. She urges Hope not to make the same mistake.

O. H. Dunbar, reviewing *The Descent of Man* for the *Critic,* classes the story with "The RECKONING" as a pair dealing with "the study of a reaction, mental or moral":

Edith Wharton thus begins "where most writers leave off." The critic for the *Independent* observes that the essential theme is one of moral defeat. Alan and his father suffered a vulgar "descent" in their veneration of business; had they recognized God, their descent might have been "tragic" rather than merely "vulgar" (*CR* 79–85). White comments that Mrs. Quentin's ethical standards have also declined; her real punishment is "that she has no way to educate her son in moral principles without condemning her own way of life" (*SSF* 76).

For further reading: Dittmar, "When Privilege Is No Protection: The Woman Artist in 'Quicksand' and *The House of Mirth*"; Goldsmith, "Edith Wharton's Gift to Nella Larsen: *The House of Mirth* and 'Quicksand.' "

Ralston, Delia Lovell *See* OLD MAID, THE.

Ralston, Jim *See* OLD MAID, THE.

Ralston, Tina *See* OLD MAID, THE.

Raycie, Halston *See* FALSE DAWN.

Raycie, Lewis *See* FALSE DAWN.

Raycei, Treeshy *See* FALSE DAWN.

"Reckoning, The" **Short story published in** HARPER'S MAGAZINE (August 1902) and collected in *The* DESCENT OF MAN AND OTHER STORIES (Scribner's, 1904). It is an appraisal of the "New Ethics" creed in which personal

Illustration for "The Reckoning" (1902), artist unknown
(Courtesy Alderman Library, University of Virginia)

happiness is valued above fidelity to marital vows. The dictum "*Thou shalt not be unfaithful—to thyself*" has become the "new dispensation" regulating marriage. Clement Westall, known for his "advanced" thinking, propounds it in the studio of an unsuccessful artist, Herbert Van Sideren. Van Sideren and his wife found their social existence on their studio, inviting avant garde friends for whiskey and soda instead of tea. Julia Westall and her second husband, Clement, have come to one of their "afternoons." Supposedly a free thinker, Julia is suddenly irritated by the Siderens' studio, and suspects her husband of having an interest in their daughter, Una. Her idea that marriage should be built on freedom collapses when Clement Westall leaves her for Una. She calls on her first husband to make him understand that she had not comprehended his position when she left him. The reviewer for the British periodical *Athenæum* asserted that the story had "an excellent idea well realized."

"Reconsideration of Proust, A" Essay about the novelist Marcel PROUST published in the SATURDAY REVIEW OF LITERATURE, October 27, 1934. The request from the editor, Henry S. Canby, reached Edith Wharton in the West Highlands of Scotland, where she was vacationing. She was tempted to refuse, but reconsidered: "If I *could* fish up and reconstitute Proust (*my* Proust, that is . . .) I should have applied a far severer test to his genius than if his books were under my hand, and the Parisian air in my lungs." She believed Proust was more gifted than Flaubert. His fiction, however, was flawed by "his intellectual speculations" that "hampered his genius as a story teller." Even so, Proust's claim to greatness lay in his "having called into being so immense a number of lifelike characters." He was one of a generation of novelists who tried to portray "the inward drama of life" rather than its "outward accidents." In part because Wharton believed modern readers were not interested in the "inner life," she regarded his influence as minimal. For the few readers concerned with the "inner significance" of life, however, Wharton held that "each sounding of his deep pages will continue to render up new treasures."

"Recovery, The" Short story published in HARPER'S MAGAZINE (February 1901) and collected in CRUCIAL INSTANCES

(Scribner's, 1901). The story deals with an artist, Keniston, a much venerated resident of the town of Hillbridge, whose work has been admired and promoted by the local university faculty. Claudia Day, the visiting friend of a faculty member's wife, regards Hillbridge as "Oxford" compared with her mundane home town, East Onondaigua, and is awed by the artist when they meet.

The narrative breaks at this point and resumes a decade later, with Claudia as Keniston's wife. She has worried that he is too self-satisfied with his work. When an exhibition of his paintings is arranged in Paris, she willingly accompanies him on a trip to Europe underwritten by his patroness, Mrs. Davant, to whom he has promised four large panels in return. Keniston refuses to attend his own exhibition, which hurts Mrs. Davant. Claudia visits the pictures secretly and realizes how inferior they are, only to discover her husband there, also a furtive viewer. Keniston visits the Louvre and experiences a conversion, not of shame but of hope that he can learn to paint as well as the "big fellows."

The reviewer for the *Academy* called this story "a little masterpiece" for its interpretation of the art world and the way a coterie can develop about an artist, but indicts Edith Wharton for her inability to be "direct" (*CR* 45). The writer of "The Editor's Easy Chair" for *Harper's Magazine*, on the other hand, considered that Wharton was at her best in the story, which was marked by "many precious psychological imports suggested with a constant and delicately sarcastic humor" (*CR* 47).

Redbook The magazine, which began as *The Red Book Magazine*, purchased the novella *The OLD MAID*, one of the four OLD NEW YORK novellas, in 1921 for $7,500, minus the agent fee for APPLETON's. The offer was made after Edith Wharton had been awarded the PULITZER PRIZE for *The AGE OF INNOCENCE*. Before this sale, Edith Wharton had written Bernard BERENSON that *The Old Maid* had been refused on the ground of immorality by the editors of the LADIES' HOME JOURNAL and *Metropolitan* (*Letters* 441–43). She wrote Mary BERENSON the price was "beyond my dreams, if not of Avarice." Rutger JEWETT then placed NEW YEAR'S DAY, another novella in the set, with the magazine for $6,000 (*NGC* 365–66). *The Old Maid* ran in February, March and April 1922, and *New Year's Day* in July and August 1923.

Wharton's story "Velvet Ear-Muffs" appeared in the magazine in August 1925. Retitled "VELVET EAR-PADS," it was collected in HERE AND BEYOND. In April 1935, the magazine published a story by Wharton called "Poor Old Vincent!"; it was reprinted as "PERMANENT WAVE" in *The WORLD OVER*. In April 1978 portions of Wharton's early novel FAST AND LOOSE were reprinted in the magazine, which by then had changed its name to *Redbook Magazine*.

Reef, The This 1912 novel, published by APPLETON AND COMPANY, marked a break for Edith Wharton with

SCRIBNER'S, her longtime publisher. She had found the initial sales of ETHAN FROME disappointing, and wrote Charles SCRIBNER that she hoped her next novel would receive better publicity. Because of poor sales of *The FRUIT OF THE TREE*, Scribner did not offer a good advance for what he believed would be her next novel, *The CUSTOM OF THE COUNTRY*. She proceeded instead with *The Reef*, for which Appleton's had offered a $15,000 advance. She explained to Scribner that she believed *The Reef* would reach a different audience and prepare them for *The Custom of the Country* (Scribner's, 1913; *EW* 312). He was extremely disappointed with Wharton and did not answer her for a month.

As the novel opens, George Darrow, a bachelor American diplomat, is on his way from England to France to see Anna Leath, whom he has known in New York before her marriage to an American businessman. She is the only woman he has ever wanted to marry and has proposed to her, but she has not replied. He receives a puzzling telegram putting him off for the second time and prepares to turn back to England. On the boat train platform, however, he encounters a vivacious American girl, Sophy Viner. He enjoys a dalliance with her in Paris and falls in love. A refugee from a vulgar London household where she has been employed, Sophy is eager and impulsive although inexperienced. Darrow makes arrangement for her to stay at his hotel, the Hotel Terminus near the Gare du Nord (Benstock points out that this was also where Wharton's brother Frederic JONES and his mistress stayed). Darrow assumes the role of tutor in French culture; by the end of the week he is also her lover. He returns to England without seeing Anna.

Anna Leath is now a widow, living on her late husband's French estate, Givré, with her stepson, Owen Leath, her mother-in-law, Madame de Chantelle (the widow of a French nobleman), and her nine-year-old daughter, Effie. Several months later, Darrow arrives to visit Anna and discovers that Sophy Viner has been installed as Effie's governess and is engaged to Owen Leath. Eventually the past is revealed; Owen had seen Darrow and Sophy at the theater and suspected they were lovers. Anna, who had agreed to marry Darrow, is shattered by this revelation. Darrow and Sophy leave, separately. Benstock observes that there are several "recognition" scenes: "they come enfilade, as doors opening onto a line of drawing rooms in which the mirrors of each salon provide a new perspective on the drama" (*NGC* 267). Darrow comes to Givré later, but Anna, who cannot finally overcome her conventional upbringing, is haunted by conjecture of their tryst in Paris and breaks off the engagement. Sophy goes to India with her former employer.

The plot turns on society's double moral standard for men and women. Louis Auchincloss terms this Edith Wharton's only "Jamesian novel' (Introduction to *The Reef,* Collier Books, viii). He calls Givré "the best of all the wonderful houses of her fiction, shimmering . . . like a painting by Walter Gay" (ix–x).

Henry JAMES, although ill in England, wrote Wharton the novel was "quite the finest thing you have done . . . like an 'ancient' Greek text from which [George] Eliot might have captured some 'weaker reflection' in her own writing" (*NGC* 273). He questioned, however, the validity of having all the non-French characters "localised" in France.

Reviewers were less impressed with the novel than James had been. The *Saturday Review* critic regarded the plot as too dependent on "amazing" coincidence to be convincing: had Owen not glimpsed Darrow and Sophy at the play, no harm would have been done by their brief fling. M. P. Willcock, writing in the *Bookman,* believed the "priggish hypocrisy" of Darrow was the true subject of the novel. He would not have been man enough to keep Anna's love, but in his view Wharton missed her opportunity to illuminate his character.

In early 1912, Wharton was writing the novel at a difficult time in her relationship with Teddy WHARTON. He had arrived in France and was living in her apartment at 53 rue de Varenne in Paris; she was giving up her morning writing time in an attempt to teach him French. He felt, pathetically, that his mind "was going, and the Drs don't see it." Meanwhile, the novel, as she wrote Bernard BERENSON, cried for her "every morning like an infant for the bottle" (*NGC* 262). To escape his demands, she went to SPAIN with Rosa de FITZ-JAMES and her friend Jean du BREUIL DE SAINT-GERMAIN, leaving Teddy in Paris under the care of Alfred WHITE. On her return, she sent Teddy off to New York; he never stayed in the Paris apartment again nor did they live together. Their DIVORCE became final in April 1913.

For further reading: Ammons, "Fairy-Tale Love and *The Reef*"; Faery, "Wharton's *Reef*: The Inscription of Female Sexuality"; Gooder, "Unlocking Edith Wharton: An Introduction to *The Reef*"; Jones, Jr., "Holding up the Revealing Lamp: The Myth of Psyche in Edith Wharton's *The Reef*"; Keyser, " 'The Ways in Which the Heart Speaks'; Letters in *The Reef*"; Maynard, "Moral Integrity in *The Reef:* Justice to Anna Leath"; Raphael, "Fighting the Burden of Shame: A New Reading of Edith Wharton's *The Reef*"; Walker, "Mothers and Lovers: Edith Wharton's *The Reef* and *The Mother's Recompense.*"

"Refugees, The" Short story published in *The SAT-URDAY EVENING POST* (January 18, 1918) and collected in *CERTAIN PEOPLE* (Appleton, 1930). It is a tale of British gentry determined to rescue refugees from the invasion of Belgium in September 1914. Edith Wharton had herself gone from France to England in late August 1914, having planned to lease Stocks, the country home of Mrs. Humphry WARD. After learning of the Battle of the Marne, Wharton began trying to

return to Paris but did not succeed until late September. At the time, many people in England had only reluctantly conceded that the war might not be over in six weeks but could last until November.

In "The Refugees," Professor Charles Durand, an American professor teaching at the University of Louvain, has become entangled in the throng of Belgian refugees coming to England. He resolves to spend his meager resources assisting a needy refugee among the passengers on the Folkestone platform. Suddenly he is himself "rescued" by Audrey Rushworth, the unmarried sister of an English nobleman, whom he had assumed was a refugee herself. She takes him to the luxurious small home she occupies on her brother's estate, where Durand discovers himself to be a prize catch among such refugee "raiders" as Audrey's sister-in-law and the duchess of Bolchester. He is literally, according to her niece Clio, "the first thing that's ever happened to her . . . Most [women of her time] were just put away in cottages covered with clematis and forgotten." Several years later, in April 1918, Durand has been sent to Boulogne to manage a Y.M.C.A. canteen. He encounters Clio, now under the command of her aunt Audrey, who has become a colonel, a Y.M.C.A. administrator and is about to marry the bishop of the Macaroon Islands. She doesn't recognize Durand, who has been her "great Adventure." She has never realized he was not a refugee.

Perry Hutchison, writing in the *New York Times Book Review,* found the story "negligible" compared with others in the collection and objected that Edith Wharton's attempt at humor was unsuccessful.

Olin-Ammentorp argues that Wharton's war stories ("COMING HOME," "The Refugees" and "WRITING A WAR STORY") were not typical battle stories of action and heroism, but represent her attempt to come to terms in a literary fashion with the war. She suggests that Wharton came to view writing, and the world as a whole, so differently that after the war she could be said to have "started anew."

For further reading: Olin-Ammentorp, " 'Not Precisely War Stories': Edith Wharton's Short Fiction from the Great War."

"Rembrandt, The" Short story published in the magazine founded by William Randolph HEARST, *Hearst's International-Cosmopolitan* (August 1900) and collected in *CRUCIAL INSTANCES* (Scribner's, 1901). The story is told from the viewpoint of a museum curator, who is persuaded by his cousin Eleanor Copt to evaluate a purported Rembrandt. The owner, Mrs. Fontage, is an elderly widow in greatly reduced circumstances who is forced to sell her possessions. She and her late husband had acquired the painting in Europe on their wedding trip, duped by a sophisticated courier who convinced them the painting had a sound provenance and had been owned by a Belgian countess and wealthy Scottish duke. The narrator realizes the painting is a fraud. To spare the feelings of Mrs. Frontage he purchases it with museum funds for $1,000 and stores it in the museum basement. A knowledgeable colleague on the acquisitions committee, Crozier, buys it back and presents it to the narrator. Crozier's gesture compensates the narrator for his finesse in having acquired for the museum a different and quite valuable painting at an excellent price.

The story is another with a first-person male narrator, in this case unnamed. As White observes, the male narrator is far more frequent in Edith Wharton's 85 short stories than a female one. She suggests that Wharton apparently believed the "male point of view legitimates a narrative" and argues that, to her, "men are the only legal inhabitants of the public sphere" (*SSF* 62–63).

The reviewer for the *Athenæum* called the story a "happy combination of lightness and pathos in treatment," and the critic for *Harper's Monthly Magazine* termed it a "charming sketch." The more perceptive *Academy* reviewer observed that Wharton "persistently does her best work in writing about art, artists, and the other people who make of art their chief pre-occupation," but then objected that she was thereby confining her talent to "that narrow circle of artificiality which is called art" (*CR* 44–47).

reviews   *See* ARCHITECTURE OF HUMANISM; ELIOT, GEORGE; *FOOL ERRANT, THE; ITALIAN CITIES; MATTHEW ARNOLD; SONNETS OF THE WINGLESS HOURS, THE; STURGIS, HOWARD; TESS OF THE D'URBERVILLES* (A PLAY); *ULYSSES: A DRAMA.*

Revue de Paris   Prestigious French periodical edited by André CHEVRILLON, a friend of Edith Wharton. Beginning in 1906, *The HOUSE OF MIRTH,* translated by Charles DU BOS, ran in the *Revue de Paris;* it was titled *La Demeure de Liesse.* Edith Wharton's lover Morton FULLERTON was writing for the journal when she first met him.

Frederick Wegener observes that Edith Wharton had long been familiar with the importance of the critical tradition in France and that, in her memoir, she recalled "the days when the *Revue de Paris* . . . rivalled (if it did not out-rival) the *Revue des Deux Mondes* in interest and importance" (*BG* 287; *UCW* 39). *See* REVUE DES DEUX MONDES.

Revue des Deux Mondes   A French periodical founded in 1829. In 1908 the editor of the *Revue des Deux Mondes,* Francis Charmes, asked Edith Wharton for a contribution to the magazine. Tired of coping with translation, she decided to write in French, and produced a tale that Lewis terms "bitterly ironic" (*EW* 233–34). Henry JAMES disapproved of it, saying Wharton had used too many clichés. (*See "*METTEURS EN SCÈNE, LES.*"*) In February 1912, the magazine published an unsigned translation of *ETHAN FROME* by Charles DU BOS.

Revue Hebdomadaire   Prestigious French periodical in which Edith Wharton published two essays about WORLD WAR I, "Les Français vus par une Américaine" ("The French Seen by an American"), in January 1918, and "L'Amérique en guerre" ("America in the War"), in March 1918. The *Revue* also published in 1915 Wharton's tributes to the French sociologist Jean du BREUIL DE SAINT-GERMAIN, killed near Arras in 1915, and in 1936 to her longtime friend Paul BOURGET, who had died in 1935. Translations of these tributes may be found in Frederick Wegener, *The Uncollected Critical Writings of Edith Wharton* (Princeton: Princeton University Press, 1996).

Richardson, William King   Boston patent lawyer who had been a friend of Edith Wharton since she and her husband first owned The MOUNT. In 1925 Wharton wrote Minnie Cadwalader JONES, her sister-in-law, that she numbered Richardson as one of her few "surviving intimate friends" (*Letters* 485). Lewis states that in 1906 he was one of a "stream of houseguests" at The Mount and that Wharton had "browbeaten" him into buying all the available writings of Henry James (*EW* 170). In 1913, when Wharton was in the midst of her divorce, Richardson tried valiantly to correct the impression Teddy's family gave that he was a "suffering martyr" and to "convey an adumbration of the truth" (*EW* 335).

Riviera, French   After WORLD WAR I, Edith Wharton purchased the PAVILLON COLOMBE in St. Brice-Sous-Forêt outside PARIS and began renovations before giving up her apartment on the rue de Varenne. Wharton found postwar Paris, with the peace conference and other intrusions, cold and distasteful, and she went to the Riviera town of HYÉRES for four months, accompanied by her friend Robert NORTON. They stayed in the Hôtel du Parc and toured the vicinity; Wharton wrote Bernard BERENSON that she had nearly died in Paris but had been revived "in some warm peaceful temperate heaven of the Greeks, chock-ful of asphodel and amaranth" (*EW* 420). In the course of their wanderings they came across the STE.-CLAIRE CHÂTEAU, a deserted convent within the ruins of a castle on a hillside that was available for lease. Wharton was able to lease and renovate the chateau, and for the remainder of her life spent the winter months there, writing, traveling, gardening and entertaining guests. Edith Wharton's horticultural knowledge is evident in an unpublished typescript at the BEINECKE LIBRARY, YALE UNIVERSITY, "December in a French Riviera Garden." She analyzes solutions to her problem of rocky ledges, lists plants she has grown successfully and displays a thorough knowledge of seasonal changes and challenges. If all goes well, there will be, in the "Christmas dawn, some precocious almond-bough" hanging out its "snowy garlands."

Wharton used the Riviera as settings in the short stories "THE VERDICT" and "VELVET EAR PADS" as well as in her novel *The MOTHER'S RECOMPENSE.* "

"Roman Fever" This short story, one of Edith Wharton's best known and most popular, was published in *Liberty* in November 1934 and collected in *The WORLD OVER* (Appleton-Century, 1936). The story is set in the mid-1920s ROME, where two widowed American ladies, "of ripe but well-cared for middle age," Mrs. Delphin Slade (Alida) and Mrs. Horace Ansley (Grace), are sitting after lunch on a terrace on the Janiculum overlooking the Palatine Hill. Superficially life-long friends (on the deaths of their husbands they sent each other proper wreaths and condolences), they are actually enemies. Their daughters, the effervescent Barbara Ansley and the docile, less attractive Jenny Slade, are out with young men for the afternoon.

The mothers begin reminiscing about their youth when they were both in Rome and loved the same young man, Delphin Slade. The action is entirely in the past, but it is a past that returns to haunt each of them. Alida Slade, considering herself the more brilliant of the two mothers, is domineering and condescending to her friend, although she wishes her Jenny were as vivacious and outgoing as Barbara. She tries to repress her past, including her memory of the son she lost in his boyhood and her youth in Rome. She has, as White observes, "an inkling of the awful truth" (*SSF* 9). In their youth, both mothers had been in Rome with their families. Alida had become engaged to Delphin Slade, although she knew he loved Grace. Hoping to bring about her marriage, she had written a letter purportedly from Delphin to bring Grace to the Colosseum in the dangerous evening hours. She hoped Grace might catch "Roman fever," a form of pneumonia that sometimes led to tuberculosis—which was often deadly at the time. Grace had replied to Delphin that she would be there; he let her in, and they had a moonlight tryst in the Colosseum. The meeting has been unknown to Alida Slade until now—she assumed Grace had waited alone. Grace did become "ill" (a euphemism for pregnancy), and her mother rushed her off to Florence and married her to Horace Ansley. The culmination of the story is the revelation that Delphin actually fathered Barbara. The title reflects the metaphor of disease that is essential to the plot.

Percy Hutchison, writing in the *New York Times Book Review,* called the story "as memorable a short story as Mrs. Wharton has ever done" and "as sharp-cut as a diamond, and as hard of surface." Joseph Reilly, reviewing the volume for *Catholic World,* believed the story to be one of the best she ever wrote (*CR* 533–38). Lewis calls it a "brilliant piece of short fiction" (*EW* 522) and believes it reveals "a serenity that pervades the narrative in a long atmospheric glow" (*EW* 524). John Gerlach considers the ending successful in "making the story whole" and "deepening it"; it "clarifies and binds together the beginning and the middle, revealing what in retrospect is both latent and inevitable . . . what is calm is so only as a means of concealing volcanic truth" (quoted in White, *SSF* 11–12).

For further reading: Berkove, " 'Roman Fever': A Mortal Malady"; Petry, "A Twist of Crimson Silk: Edith Wharton's 'Roman Fever' "; Sweeney, "Edith Wharton's Case of 'Roman Fever.' "

Rome Edith Wharton had lived in the city of Rome when the JONES family went to EUROPE for six years in 1866. It was one of her favorite Italian cities, and, as an adult, she recalled "the lost Rome" of her "infancy," the "warm scent of the box hedges on the Pincian, and the texture of weather-worn sun-gilt stone." She remembered playing in the ruins of the Imperial Forum, driving out to the Campagna and the Appian Way, seeing the "Piazza di Spagna throned with Thackerayan artists' models," visiting St. Peter's, which had a "mil-

Villa Medici, Rome, by Maxfield Parrish. From Italian Villas and Their Gardens *(1904), first edition* (Collection of the author)

lion-tapered blaze," and walking on the grounds of the Villa Doria-Pamphili (*BG* 29–34). Wharton actually first knew Rome as Nathaniel Hawthorne had known it; in 1857, he had gone to Europe for three years. His novel set in Rome, *The Marble Faun,* was published in 1860.

After Wharton's marriage, when she and Teddy WHARTON made annual visits to ITALY, and during her later years in France, she visited Rome regularly. She came to admire the BAROQUE architecture, sculpture and art of Rome, which was not then revered nearly as much as that of the medieval period. In *ITALIAN BACK-GROUNDS* Wharton reminded her readers who had been taught by John RUSKIN to disdain the baroque and admire the Gothic that the Rome they loved most, including the Piazza di Spagna (the Spanish Steps), Nicola Salvi's Fontana di Trevi (Trevi Fountain), and the "Angels of Passion" sculptures on the Bridge of Sant' Angelo, would disappear if all the baroque land-marks of the city were removed. One of Wharton's last visits to Rome was made over the Whitsun holiday in 1932, when she was accompanied by Bernard

BERENSON and his assistant Nicky MARIANO. They visited St. Peter's and other churches.

One of Edith Wharton's best-known short stories, "ROMAN FEVER," is set in Rome in the mid-1920s.

Roosevelt, Theodore (1858–1919)   President of the United States from 1901 to 1909, Roosevelt has been termed Edith Wharton's "model American statesman" (*EW* 6). He brought about the construction of the Panama Canal and won the Nobel Peace Prize for his intervention in the 1904–5 Russo-Japanese War; his motto was "Speak softly and carry a big stick." Like Wharton and Henry JAMES he favored U.S. participation in WORLD WAR I on the side of the Allies. He was the author of a number of books on history, hunting, wildlife and politics, including *Winning of the West* (1896–99), *The Strenuous Life: Essays and Addresses* (1900) and *The New Nationalism* (1910). Wharton had known him since her youth; his second wife, Edith Kermit Carow, was her distant cousin. Roosevelt admired *The VALLEY OF DECISION* (1902). In her memoir

Villa Borghese, Rome, by Maxfield Parrish. From Italian Villas and Their Gardens *(1904), first edition* (Collection of the author)

The Imperial Forum, Rome, with the Colosseum in the background. (Courtesy Rome Tourist Bureau)

Wharton recalled that he wanted to rearrange it "in conformity with his theory of domestic morals and the strenuous life." She convinced him that such ideals had not been characteristic of the "decadent" Italian principalities she described in the novel (*BG* 312).

In 1902 Roosevelt came to NEWPORT to attend the christening of Winthrop and Daisy CHANLER'S son Theodore, Roosevelt's godson and namesake; the Whartons were also present. After he became president, Roosevelt invited Wharton to lunch and welcomed her by a "vehement cry: 'At last I can quote "The Hunting of the Snark" '!" He explained that no one in his administration understood his references to Lewis Carroll's poem.

When Roosevelt received an honorary degree from Williams College Wharton drove from The MOUNT to attend the ceremonies. At the reception Roosevelt ignored the other guests and cornered Wharton to discuss at length a recently published history of the French Second Empire, but, as she explained, "that was the President's way, and as everybody loved him, everybody forgave him" (*BG* 313). In 1909, during his world tour, he came to dinner at the Whartons' apartment in Paris on the rue de Varenne. Unfortunately he found there a specialist who interested him and therefore failed to play the social "game" of allotting at least a few minutes to each guest (*BG* 315–16). The French were less understanding than the company in Williamstown had been.

Wharton last saw Roosevelt after his world tour of 1909–10, when she and Teddy were invited to lunch at his home, Sagamore Hill, Oyster Bay, Long Island. The house, she recalled, was "like one big library, and the whole tranquil place breathed of the love of books and of the country." As she reflected on their friendship while working on her memoir in the 1930s, she found that each of her few encounters with Roosevelt glowed "like a tiny morsel of radium" (*BG* 316–17).

Rosedale, Simon *See* HOUSE OF MIRTH, THE.

Royall, Charity *See* SUMMER.

Royall, Lawyer *See* SUMMER.

Ruskin, John (1819–1900) English writer and art critic whose wealthy father provided for his extensive travel and private drawing lessons. Ruskin's works influenced Edith Wharton, particularly *The Seven Lamps of Architecture* (1849), *The Stones of Venice* (1851–53) and *Mornings in Florence* (1875–77). In her youth, Wharton had been an ardent disciple of Ruskin's. In "LIFE AND I," she states, "And then I came upon Ruskin! His wonderful cloudy pages gave me back the image of the beautiful Europe I had lost, and woke in me the habit of precise visual observation. The ethical and aesthetic *fatras* [jumble] were easily enough got rid of later, and as an interpreter of visual impressions he did me incomparable service." Among the *fatras* Edith rejected later were Ruskin's critical views of the BAROQUE STYLE.

On the JONES's final trip to EUROPE as a family, before her father's death in 1882, Edith and her father walked, following Ruskin's itineraries. "To Florence & Venice his little volumes [*Mornings in Florence* and *Stones of Venice*] gave a meaning, a sense of organic relation, which no other books attainable by me at that time could possibly have conveyed" ("Life and I," 1085).

Wharton agreed with Ruskin's deep distrust of architectural restoration. In *The Lamp of Memory* (1903), he terms restoration "a Lie from beginning to end," arguing that it destroys "that spirit which is given only by the hand and eye of the workman." Restoring even a half-inch of lost finish can only be conjectural, and the "brute hardness" of new carving on a building effaces the "sweetness in the gentle lines which rain and sun had wrought." There can be no real fidelity to the original. Edith Wharton disliked the work of Eugène Viollet-le-Duc in restoring Carcassonne, a medieval walled city in southern France, and believed Ruskin's aversion was well-founded.

Wharton even created a fictional John Ruskin in her 1924 novella FALSE DAWN; he meets the hero as he is sketching on a Swiss mountaintop. The influence of Ruskin in shaping Wharton's aesthetic theories was profound and lifelong, as evidenced by her early journal, her 1934 memoir *A BACKWARD GLANCE*, her travel writing and her fiction. Ruskin not only taught her parents' generation to see, but gave depth and focus to her own connoisseurship.

Ruskin, John   *See FALSE DAWN.*

Rutherfurd, Lewis (1816–92)   Columbia University professor of astronomy and physicist. He set up a small observatory in New York to observe celestial bodies and was known for his photographs of the moon (*BG* 45).

The Rutherfurds had a summer home in NEWPORT, Edgerston, which adjoined PENCRAIG, the JONES property. As a child, Edith Wharton went on nature walks led by Professor Rutherfurd, played with the young Rutherfurd boys, Lewis and Winthrop, and admired the accomplishments of their older sisters, Louisa and Margaret. The family had both French and German governesses, who took Edith on as well. Anna BAHLMANN, who was German, continued to teach Edith during the Jones family's winters in New York. In 1904 she joined Wharton's household as secretary and literary assistant, remaining with her until her death in 1916.

Ste.-Claire Château Edith Wharton's winter home from 1920 until her death in 1937. After the Paris Peace Conference in 1919, which caused the capital city to be overcrowded and noisy, Wharton began searching for a possible home on the Riviera. In 1919 she stayed at the Hôtel du Parc in HYÈRES for four months, much of it in the company of Robert NORTON, who helped her look for a winter home. After Bernard BERENSON came for two weeks, they explored the area during the day and discovered Ste.-Claire du Vieux Château, now usually referred to as Ste.-Claire Château, a villa on a hillside overlooking the Mediterranean. It is known in France as Le castel Sainte-Claire. This structure was built after 1849 by Olivier Voutier (1796–1877), who discovered the Venus de Milo. It was raised within the ruins of a 17-century convent of the same name. Wharton arranged to take it on a long lease and spent her first Christmas there in 1920. Beginning about 1922, she followed a fixed year-round schedule, staying at the PAVILLON COLOMBE outside Paris from June until mid-December and at Ste.–Claire Château from mid-December through the end of May. In 1927, aided by André BOCCON-GIBBOD, the Parisian attorney who had assisted with her DIVORCE, and by Walter BERRY, Wharton arranged to purchase the property outright for roughly $40,000 (*EW* 472).

Ste.-Claire required extensive renovations. According to Robert Norton, "the house was gutted, new partitions made, roofs rebuilt, drains installed." In addition, a road was built up the hill, quarters built for Wharton's chauffeur and gardeners, and garages constructed. Once soil was added to the ledges, Wharton began the first of many seasons of enthusiastic gardening. Norton believed "the house had come alive" after a year of work (Dwight, 239). Theresa Craig depicts and describes the interior of the château after the work was finished. She observes that the rooms followed the principles given in *The DECORATION OF HOUSES*, with marble floors, classical chimney pieces, carefully proportioned furnishings and understated architectural details (*Edith Wharton: A House Full of Rooms: Architecture, Interiors, and Gardens*, 182–89).

Wharton wrote her sister-in-law Mary Cadwalader JONES about her first Christmas there: "The little house is delicious, so friendly & comfortable, & full of sun & air; but what overwhelms us all—although we thought we knew it—is the endless beauty of the view, or rather the views, for we look south, east & west, 'miles & miles,' & our quiet-coloured end of evening presents us with a full moon standing over the tower of the great Romanesque church just below the house, & a sunset silhouetting the 'Iles d'Or' in black on a sea of silver" (*Letters* 436). "We" that year were Robert Norton, Gaillard LAPSLEY and the household staff. The "Sainte Claire Christmas Club," as Wharton called it, usually included Norton, Lapsley and John HUGH SMITH (*NGC*

Ste.-Claire Château, Hyères, France. This villa on the Riviera was Wharton's home in winter and spring from 1920 until her death (Photo by Sarah Bird Wright)

219

Ste.-Claire Château. The Mediterranean Sea is in the distance
(Photo by Sarah Bird Wright)

449). The annual Christmas gatherings took place for more than a decade. After Wharton's death in 1937, Ste.-Claire Château (Le castel Sainte-Claire) was the home of Robert Mallet Stevens and other artists; the city of Hyères acquired it in 1955 and the grounds are now open to the public.

Percy LUBBOCK gives a memorable record of evening gatherings at Ste.-Claire (which he terms "*acta diurna*"). They might have included readings of poetry or prose (Shakespeare, Thackeray and Jane Austen were favorites) or, occasionally, music from a gramophone (particularly Bach, Mozart and Wagner). He remarks that Wharton never grew tired of "the number of things in the world," and Ste.-Claire was "one of the best of them . . . still more plastic under her hand than all the rest," with its gray rocks, ruins at the top of the hill, gardens and "green miles stretching away to the rim of the sea" (*Portrait*, 192).

In January, 1927, Edith Wharton wrote her sister-in-law, "I've *at last* bought Ste. Claire, 'from the centre all round to the sea.' Walter did it for me when he was at Hyères last month!" (*Letters* 498).

See also INTERIOR DESIGN; RIVIERA, FRENCH; and GARDENS AND GARDENING.

For further reading: Craig, *Edith Wharton: A House Full of Rooms: Architecture, Interiors, and Gardens;* Dwight, *Edith Wharton: An Extraordinary Life;* Fedorko, "Storming the Chateau at Hyères"; Lubbock, *Portrait of Edith Wharton,* chapter xii.

St George, Nan   *See BUCCANEERS, THE.*

St George, Virginia   *See BUCCANEERS, THE.*

salon   The salon was a social institution well known not only to Edith Wharton but also to Balzac and other French writers and intellectuals. It might include dinner, although often distinguished guests dropped in on certain evenings for gatherings in the drawing room. In her memoir, *A BACKWARD GLANCE,* Wharton explains that the salon is based on the "national taste for general conversation." In FRANCE the "two and two talks which cut up Anglo-Saxon dinners . . . would be considered not only stupid but ill-bred." French gatherings are a "perpetual exchange, a market to which every one is expected to bring his best for barter." As a rule, the evening salon took place in the drawing room; the conventional allowance for a person to speak on a subject was five minutes (*BG* 273). The most fashionable salons in PARIS were those in the FAUBOURG SAINT-GERMAIN. Among hostesses whose salons Edith Wharton frequented were Countess Rosa de FITZ-JAMES, whose guests were usually writers, diplomats, artists, politicians and members of the nobility. The French "salon," Wharton insisted, was "the best school of talk and ideas that the modern world has known" (*FWM* 117).

According to Edith Wharton, the salons were never the same after WORLD WAR I. In her memoir she cast an imaginary look back at a typical salon held by the Countess Fitz-James, where Henry JAMES stood talking with Paul BOURGET, the Abbé MUGNIER with Walter BERRY, and Bernard BERENSON with the editorial writer André Tardieu (*BG* 281–82). Wharton was completely fluent in French, as were Berry and James.

In his book about America, Edith Wharton's friend and advocate in the Faubourg, Paul Bourget, illuminated the attributes of the upper-class Parisian salon: "Extreme vicacity of thought, with its subtle variations, criticism with its startling destruction of illusion and its unexpected betrayals into enthusiasm, . . . a mad hardihood of irony . . . [and] above all, a charm, a spirit of sociability (*Outre-mer: Impressions of America,* 44).

Had Edith Wharton not found intellectual acceptance in the prewar gatherings and salons of the Faubourg and formed the close friendships she did in that milieu, it is at least debatable whether she would have chosen to spend the remainder of her life in France.

San Vivaldo   Franciscan monastery near San Gimignano, Tuscany, ITALY, where Wharton made a scholarly discovery in art history. In 1893 she and her husband Teddy went to the monastery to see some large terracotta statues of which she had heard; they were purportedly by Giovanni Gonnelli, a 17th-century sculptor. On examination she came to believe some of them were much earlier, dating from the 16th and not the 17th century. She was positive that an artist trained in an earlier tradition had executed them. They still preserved, "under the stiffening influences of convention, a touch of that individuality and directness of expression which mark the prime of Tuscan art." She recalled seeing a similar Presepio at the Bargello [in Florence], compared them, and found identical treatment of "certain details of hair and drapery" and "the recurrence of the same type of face."

Although she found it difficult to believe that the similarity between the figures at San Vivaldo and those at the Bargello could have escaped notice, she was virtually positive "that a remarkable example of late *quattro-centro* art had remained undiscovered, within a few hours' journey from Florence, for nearly 400 years" (*IB* 91–106).

Terra-cottas, San Vivaldo. Frontispiece, Italian Backgrounds *(1905), first edition* (Collection of the author)

To test her theory, Wharton asked one of the Alinari brothers of the noted Florentine photographic firm to take photographs, which she forwarded to Professor Enrico Ridolfi, then director of the Royal Museums at Florence. As soon as he saw the photographs, he became convinced of the error of attributing them to Giovanni Gonnelli. He then reattributed them to Giovanni della Robbia, although there has been some dispute about whether della Robbia executed all of the figures. Modern scholars, according to Dwight, believe three of the five groups Wharton singled out show stylistic similarities to the work of Giovanni della Robbia (*Edith Wharton: An Extraordinary Life,* 284).

Wharton's developing connoisseurship first became evident in her published account of this discovery, which appeared as "A Tuscan Shrine" in SCRIBNER'S MAGAZINE in January 1895, a decade before the essay was collected in ITALIAN BACKGROUNDS. Bernard and Mary BERENSON read the article (long before they became close friends of Wharton), went to view the series of statues and returned home "scoffing at Mrs. Wharton's preposterous suggestion that any of them could have been by one of the Della Robbias" (*EW* 269).

For further reading: Dwight, *Edith Wharton: An Extraordinary Life* (69–86).

Sanctuary Novella serialized in SCRIBNER'S MAGAZINE in 1903 and published in book form by SCRIBNER'S the same year. Lewis calls it a "relatively undistinguished piece of fiction" (*EW* 123). Composed of two sections, the first deals with Kate Orme, a young woman who discovers a character flaw in her fiancé, Denis Peyton, who has suppressed a scandal in order to preserve the family fortune. She considers not marrying him but has a vision of his marrying another woman who would be oblivious of his secret. She suddenly perceives that she is surrounded by "moral sewage"; every family has its own methods for the "disposal of family scandals" (*CR* 70). She marries him because, as one critic remarked, she is not a young woman but a "sensitised conscience" (*CR* 72).

The second section takes place long after Peyton's death and focuses on the relationship between Mrs. Peyton and her adult son, Dick, an architect. He faces a moral dilemma, which his mother succeeds in resolving by silent persuasion. He does the right thing and flies into the sanctuary of her arms.

Aline Gorren, writing in the *Critic,* stated that Edith Wharton was "of the order of those writers, indeed, with whom the saner vision is so native that it is always expected" (*CR* 75).

For further reading: Raphael, "Kate Orme's Struggles with Shame in Edith Wharton's *Sanctuary.*"

Sand, George (1804–1876) Pen name of Amandine-Aurore-Lucie Dupin, Baroness Dudevant, a French novelist. Sand's work is often divided into three periods. In the novels belonging to the first period she proclaimed the right of free love for both men and women. In her second period she was concerned with humanitarian reform movements, and in her third period, later in life, she published studies of nature and of rustic manners. The pastoral novels written during this period, such as *la Mare au diable,* are considered by many critics to be the best written in French.

She had a conventional marriage to Casimir Dude-vant, who drank to excess and had affairs with house-maids. In 1831 she left him, moved to Paris, and eventually had celebrated love affairs with Frédéric Chopin, writer Alfred de Musset and others.

George Sand was among the writers Edith Wharton most admired. In May 1906 she and Teddy, along with her brother Harry JONES, made the first of several "motor-flights" across France and visited Sand's chateau at NOHANT, near the town of Châteauroux. Henry JAMES was quite envious, since he had never visited Nohant, and exclaimed, " 'They're on their way to Nohant, d - - n them!' " (*EW* 169). He wrote Wharton, "To think that you have seen La Châtre!—& that you might move me over to Ashfield [home of Charles Eliot NORTON] again & tell me about it as we go! With these grimaces, you see, I try to pluck the javelin from my side. But it will really stick there, poisoning my blood, till you *write*—I mean till you PRINT, till you "do" the place, the whole impression for me under stress of imminent publication. For of course you *are* doing, you *have* done that. You can't *not*. I yearn & languish. Write to me that this act of piety is even already performed." (*Henry James and Edith Wharton: Letters: 1900–1915,* 65–66).

Wharton described the visit in *A MOTOR-FLIGHT THROUGH FRANCE.* She was particularly taken with the small theater, which included two stages, one with life-size scenery for actors and actresses, and the other a marionette theater recalling the COMMEDIA DELL'ARTE as it was incorporated by GOETHE in his fiction: "just such a "*Puppen-theatre* as Wilhelm Meister described to Marianne" (MFF 82). Wharton reports seeing, near the small theater, a troupe of marionettes, including stock characters from the commedia dell'arte: Harlequin, Columbine, Pantaloon and others. The house-keeper had, as a young girl, helped George Sand dress them.

Wharton's admiration of George Sand was lifelong, and affected her deepest friendships and relationships. For example, one of her gifts to Morton FULLERTON, with whom she had a love affair before her divorce, was a volume of Flaubert's letters to George Sand. Fullerton said many years later that Edith Wharton in love "had displayed the uninhibited passion of 'a George Sand' " (*EW* 343).

For further reading: Joslin, " 'Fleeing the Sewer': Edith Wharton, George Sand and Literary Innovation."

Santayana, George (1863–1952)   Spanish-born American philosopher, critic, poet and novelist, Santayana was a member of the "GENTEEL CIRCLE" of literary editors and writers who flourished in the late 19th century. He studied at Harvard and later taught philosophy there; among his better-known writings are *The Sense of Beauty* (1896), *The Genteel Tradition at Bay* (1931) and *The Last Puritan* (1935).

According to Lewis, Edith Wharton revered Santayana's philosophical writings "more than anything else in English" (*EW* 496). She did not, however, meet the philosopher until 1930, when, on a visit to the BERENSONS at I TATTI, she was introduced to him at the home of one of their neighbors.

The Last Puritan, a novel about the scrupulous, conscientious scion of an old New England family, Oliver Arden, was surprisingly successful. When sales reached 100,000 in America, Edith Wharton wrote her friend Gaillard LAPSLEY that it made her "more hopeful" about her own country (*Letters* 594).

"Sapphire Way, The"   A book Edith Wharton had, at one time, planned to write about her 1926 cruise aboard the OSPREY. She had talked with editors about writing a group of essays first and then publishing them in book form, which would have offset the considerable expenses of the charter. In her memoir, Wharton comments, "What a charming book it would have been—like so many that have never been written!" (*BG* 373). Benstock states that although Rutger B. JEWETT of APPLETON's was very interested, Wharton gave up on this idea because she did not have the necessary photographs (*NGC* 392). It seems probable, however, that other factors were involved, since either she or SCRIBNER's had obtained press photographs for IN MOROCCO (1920). They surely would have been available for many of their ports of call in Greece, Turkey and North Africa. Edith Wharton also took photographs herself, although few documented ones have survived. It is conceivable that, since she had kept a private journal of her 1888 cruise aboard the VANADIS, Wharton decided not to go over similar ground but to turn to fiction instead, which was far more lucrative. One story, "DIEU D'AMOUR," about a visit to a medieval castle in Cyprus, resulted from this cruise. (It was first published in the LADIES' HOME JOURNAL in 1928, then collected in CERTAIN PEOPLE in 1930.)

Sargent, John Singer (1856–1925)   Born in Florence of American parents, Sargent was educated in Europe as a painter. His exhibition was in 1878 in Paris. He moved to London in 1884, where he painted fashionable portraits; he is also known for his impressionistic watercolor scenes, particularly of VENICE.

In 1911 Edith Wharton called on Sargent at his London studio on Tite Street to commission a charcoal drawing of Henry JAMES (*NGC* 260). In 1913 a group of his English friends commissioned Sargent to paint James's portrait for his 70th birthday. Edith Wharton and William Dean HOWELLS, along with others, launched an unfortunate parallel drive to raise a sum of money ("not less than $5000") to be presented to James so that he might choose his own gift, but the scheme was a disaster; James learned of it and the project caused James great embarrassment and great hurt to Edith Wharton (*see* Henry JAMES). He had reluctantly agreed to the English plan for the portrait, which now hangs in the National Portrait Gallery in London. Sargent contributed a replica of it for Edith Wharton's WORLD WAR I fund-raising project, *The BOOK OF THE HOMELESS,* now a valuable collectors' item.

Saturday Evening Post, The   Philadelphia weekly magazine first published in August 1821. It was not founded by Benjamin Franklin, although its original offices were once occupied by his *Pennsylvania Gazette.* The early magazine had a distinguished list of contributors, including James Fenimore Cooper, Edgar Allan Poe and Harriet Beecher Stowe. In 1897 Cyrus H. K. Curtis purchased the *Post,* which was edited by George Horace Lorimer between 1899 and 1936. It is now published in Indianapolis.

A number of Wharton's stories first appeared in the magazine, including "AFTER HOLBEIN" (May 1928), "A Bottle of Evian" (Mar. 1926, reprinted as "A BOTTLE OF PERRIER" in *CERTAIN PEOPLE),* "A GLIMPSE" (Nov. 1932), "POMEGRANATE SEED" (April 1931) and "THE REFUGEES" (Jan. 1918). The *Post* paid $1,500 for the latter story (*EW* 422). The novella *The MARNE* was also published in the magazine in October 1918. In addition, the poem "With the Tide" appeared in the magazine (Mar. 1919) as well as "In Alsace," one of the articles making up *FIGHTING FRANCE, FROM DUNKERQUE TO BELFORT* (Nov. 1915).

The *Post* had given Wharton reason to believe they would serialize *The GODS ARRIVE,* which she completed in January 1932, but when the editors read the manuscript they wrote that "the central idea . . . puts it quite out of the question for us" (*EW* 502). They believed readers would be shocked by the prolonged affair between Halo Tarrant and Vance Weston and her out-of-wedlock pregnancy. The *Delineator* published the novel in installments between February and August 1932.

Saturday Review of Literature, The   Weekly magazine founded in 1924 by Henry Seidel Canby and several others, emphasizing book reviews and literary commentary. Wharton published three essays in the magazine, "TENDENCIES IN MODERN FICTION" (January 1934), "PERMANENT VALUES IN FICTION" (April 1934) and "A RECONSIDERATION OF PROUST" (October 1934). Canby served as editor until 1936, when Bernard de Voto assumed the post.

Schlumberger, Gustave   Historian and an early friend of Edith Wharton's in the FAUBOURG SAINT-GERMAIN. Lewis describes him as a "vastly read and entertaining man with a violent temper" (*EW* 161). Schlumberger was the author of several scholarly works, particularly on Byzantium, including *Renaud de Chatillon, prince d'Antioche, seigneur de la Terre d'Ou-tre-Jourdain* (1898) and *L'Épopée byzantine à la fin du dixième siècle* (1925).

In 1922, Wharton and Walter BERRY lunched in the French town of Pontigny with Schlumberger, Sinclair LEWIS and his wife, Charles DU BOS, André MAUROIS and Lytton STRACHEY (*EW* 456),

Scope, Miss   *See CHILDREN, THE.*

Scott, Geoffrey (1883–1929)   A British writer and longtime friend of Edith Wharton, Scott was the author of *The ARCHITECTURE OF HUMANISM* (1913), a work of cultural history thought to have been influenced by his

Geoffrey Scott at the Villa Medici, Florence. From Victoria Glendenning, Vita: The Life of Vita Sackville West (Courtesy Alfred A. Knopf)

friend Bernard BERENSON (*Letters* 303). Wharton reviewed it for the *Times Literary Supplement.*

She first met Scott in 1913, when he joined her and Walter BERRY on their return to Paris from Italy. At the end of 1917, Scott moved into Wharton's large apartment on the rue de Varenne for nearly four months to offer secretarial and administrative assistance. Lewis states that he also offered intellectual companionship, and that she would long remember the " 'flashing play' " of their conversations in the evening (*EW* 386).

In 1924, Scott, Wharton, Percy LUBBOCK, Gaillard LAPSLEY and Robert NORTON were houseguests at Hill Hall, home of Charles and Mary HUNTER in Essex, ENGLAND. Hill Hall had succeeded QU'ACRE, the home of the late Howard STURGIS, as a gathering place for the "inner circle."

Wharton was hurt when Sybil CUTTING married Scott, and was devastated when they were divorced and she married Lubbock. On the occasion of Scott's marriage, Wharton wrote Berenson that she was "overwhelmed" by the news. "I hardly ever saw Geoffrey, but some subtle link of understanding on most subjects bound us together with hooks of steel, & never again to see him except encircled by that well-meaning waste of unintelligence; oh dear—enfin, 'c'est la guerre' " (*Letters* 403).

In 1929 Scott died suddenly in NEW YORK of pneumonia. Deeply saddened, Wharton wrote Lapsley, "Oh, Gaillard, what a mockery it all is! He had got on his feet, he had pulled himself out of all the sloughs, he was happy, ambitious, hard at work, full of courage and enthusiasm. The Furies had been letting him simmer" (*EW* 489).

For further reading: Goodman, *Edith Wharton's Inner Circle.*

Scott, Lady Sybil *See* LUBBOCK, LADY SYBIL.

Scribner, Charles II (1854–1930) Charles Scribner II joined the firm founded by his father and uncles, Charles Scribner's Sons, when he graduated from Princeton in 1875. He inherited the business in 1879; in 1884 one of his brothers, Arthur Hawley Scribner, joined him. Under his guidance, Edward BURLINGAME, editor of *SCRIBNER'S MAGAZINE,* and William Crary BROWNELL, literary consultant on book manuscripts, accepted and published Wharton's earliest work in the fields of poetry, short stories, novels and nonfiction. She complained about the advertising of her first collection of short stories, *The GREATER INCLINATION,* in 1899, but continued to offer her "wares" to Scribner.

Wharton's correspondence was usually with Burlingame and Brownell, but, when *The HOUSE OF MIRTH* became a best-seller, Scribner congratulated her and informed her of the remarkable sales achieved by the novel. In November 1905 she wrote him, "it is a very beautiful thought to me that 80,000 people should

want to read "The House of Mirth," and if the number should ascend to 100,000 I fear my pleasure would exceed the bounds of decency" (*Letters* 95).

Scribner was also adept at smoothing out trouble for his best-selling author. In 1907, when she discovered that Ernest Peixotto was about to provide sketches for *A MOTOR-FLIGHT THROUGH FRANCE* done from postcards instead of from on-site visits, she was quite upset and wrote Scribner to protest. He had been traveling in Europe, but on his return hastened to let her know that the art department had mistakenly engaged Peixotto, but "we shall have the book right in the end" (unpublished correspondence, SCRIBNER ARCHIVES, Firestone Library, Princeton University). Peixotto was disengaged and the book was illustrated with photographs.

In 1907, Scribner's had offered a large advance for *The FRUIT OF THE TREE,* believing it would equal the success of *The HOUSE OF MIRTH.* It did not, and, to Wharton's dismay, the firm failed to offer a sizeable advance for *The CUSTOM OF THE COUNTRY.* She had also been dissatis-

Charles Scribner II (Princeton University Library. Archives of Charles Scribner's Sons. Manuscripts Division. Department of Rare Books and Special Collections)

fied with the advertising budget Scribner's gave to *ETHAN FROME*. She accepted a $15,000 advance offered by APPLETON's for *The REEF* (published in 1912), writing Scribner that she believed the new novel would reach a different audience and would prepare the public for *The CUSTOM OF THE COUNTRY* (*EW* 312). He was bitterly disappointed. Wharton wrote Morton FULLERTON, "Mr. Scribner is mortally hurt by my infidelity" (*NGC* 250).

Scribner continued to communicate with Wharton, however. When the first article in *FIGHTING FRANCE, FROM DUNKERQUE TO BELFORT* was published in *Scribner's Magazine* in July 1915, he wrote her, "I have had more comment on the first article 'The Look of Paris' than anything we have published in a long time." She had never hesitated to write him about publishing the work of friends, such as a translation of a book by Jacques-Émile BLANCHE or *Belchamber* by Howard STURGIS, and she continued to recommend the firm and to make such inquiries even while publishing with Appleton's.

Charles Scribner, Edward Burlingame and William Crary Brownell were the first publishers to perceive Wharton's literary potential, and, although she did succumb to Appleton's offers of higher advances and royalties, she continued to have the greatest respect for Scribner.

After Charles Scribner died in 1930, followed by Arthur Scribner in 1932, the firm carried on under other generations of the Scribner family until it was absorbed by Macmillan.

For further reading: Aronson, "Wharton and the House of Scribner: The Novelist as a Pain in the Neck"; Bell, "Lady into Author: Edith Wharton and the House of Scribner."

Scribner Archives The Scribner Archives, Firestone Library, Princeton University, house the vast archives of the publishing firm of Charles Scribner's Sons. This collection contains several thousand items, including letters written between Edith Wharton and Charles SCRIBNER II, William Crary BROWNELL and Edward BURLINGAME. The correspondence, which began in 1891, spanned more than 40 years. It also contains some of Wharton's correspondence with *CENTURY* and *Lippincott* magazines.

Scribner's (Charles Scribner's Sons) The publishing firm of Charles Scribner's Sons began in 1846, when Isaac Baker and Charles Scribner formed a partnership. Scribner was a New Yorker, then 25, who had graduated from Princeton in the class of 1840. Baker died in 1850, leaving Scribner alone. He vowed not to pirate English books, as other publishers frequently did at the time, but to publish new and current writers. In 1875 CHARLES SCRIBNER II graduated from Princeton and joined the firm; one of his brothers, John Blair Scribner, was a partner along with Edward Seymour

and Andrew Armstrong. Seymour died and Armstrong sold his shares; John Blair died in 1879, leaving Charles II to manage the business. He was joined by another brother, Arthur Hawley Scribner, in 1884. Their partnership, Charles Scribner's Sons, lasted almost 50 years. In 1894 they moved into a stately building at Fifth Avenue and 21st St., NEW YORK, with an ornate bookstore on the ground floor.

In 1870 the firm founded an illustrated monthly magazine, *Scribner's Monthly;* in 1881 it passed out of the family's hands, was sold to the Century Company and became the *CENTURY ILLUSTRATED MONTHLY MAGAZINE*. The change of ownership was occasioned by an internal business dispute. In 1887 Charles Scribner II founded *SCRIBNER'S MAGAZINE,* which was published until 1939.

Scribner's published the work of many leading authors in addition to Wharton, including Henry JAMES and George SANTAYANA. (The firm's best-selling work of all time was *The Little Shepherd of Kingdom Come* by John Fox.) The firm were Wharton's first publishers in the genres of poetry, short stories, novels and nonfiction. Her poem "THE LAST GIUSTINIANI" was accepted by Edward BURLINGAME and appeared in *Scribner's Magazine* in October 1889. In *A BACKWARD GLANCE* Wharton recalls her excitement; she could still see "the narrow hall, the letter-box . . . and the flight of stairs up and down which I ran, senselessly and incessantly, in the attempt to give my excitement some muscular outlet!" (*BG* 109). In 1890 he also accepted the short story "MRS. MANSTEY'S VIEW," Wharton's first published work of fiction. In 1895 the magazine published "A Tuscan Shrine," her first travel article. Wharton also had a close relationship with William C. BROWNELL, a valued editorial consultant on book submissions; he advised acceptance of her first book, *The DECORATION OF HOUSES,* written with Ogden CODMAN and published in 1897. Two years later, they published her first volume of short stories, *The GREATER INCLINATION,* and, in 1902, they issued her first novel, *The VALLEY OF DECISION.*

Wharton complained to Brownell that their advertising for *The Greater Inclination* was inadequate. Although the book had met with an "unusually favourable reception for a first volume by a writer virtually unknown," she wrote that she had found only one advertisement for it. This was "unjust" in an era of "energetic & emphatic advertising," and she would be reluctant, therefore, to offer her "wares" to Mr. Scribner a second time (*Letters* 38). Apparently the firm pacified her, for she continued to offer her work to Scribner's and ultimately became one of their most successful authors.

In 1905, *The HOUSE OF MIRTH* became a best-seller, to the delight of Charles Scribner. He offered a high advance for *The FRUIT OF THE TREE,* based on sales of *The House of Mirth;* but that novel sold poorly. As a result, Scribner reduced the advance for *The CUSTOM OF THE*

COUNTRY and Wharton then accepted a $15,000 advance from APPLETON for *The REEF*. From then on, Appleton's published most of her works.

Wharton did not dissociate herself entirely from the firm, however. In 1915, during WORLD WAR I, she made a series of trips to the Front and wrote the articles later published as *FIGHTING FRANCE, FROM DUNKERQUE TO BELFORT* (1915). They also published *XINGU AND OTHER STORIES* (1916), *IN MOROCCO* (1920) and *A SON AT THE FRONT* (1923). In 1919, Scribner was still hoping that the firm might publish her novel in progress, *LITERATURE*. Wharton wrote asking for a "few more weeks," but the novel was never published; a partial manuscript is in the BEINECKE LIBRARY, YALE UNIVERSITY (*Letters* 425). Scribner was extremely generous in accepting *A Son at the Front* as a substitute for a novel Wharton had promised him after *The Custom of the Country,* considering that in the intervening decade her Appleton's novels had achieved financial success and that *The AGE OF INNOCENCE* had won the PULITZER PRIZE.

Although Scribner's did publish a few of her subsequent books, Appleton became her principal publisher, particularly after World War I. During the 1920s and early 1930s Appleton was probably able to negotiate higher prices for the serialization of her fiction than Scribner's.

In 1930 Charles Scribner II died, followed by Arthur Scribner in 1932. The firm carried on under Scribner's son, Charles Scribner III, who had entered the publishing firm in 1913. In 1937, *Scribner's Magazine* ceased publication after a renowned half-century. Charles Scribner III died suddenly in 1952, and was succeeded by Charles Scribner IV, who had joined the firm after World War II. In 1994 the firm was absorbed by the Macmillan Publishing Co., although the Scribner's imprint has been retained on some books.

For further reading: Aronson, "Wharton and the House of Scribner: The Novelist as a Pain in the Neck"; Bell, "Lady into Author: Edith Wharton and the House of Scribner."

Scribner's Magazine   One of the best literary periodicals of the late 19th and early 20th centuries, the magazine was launched after Scribner & Company sold the original *Scribner's Monthly* to the Century Company in 1881. In 1887 the younger Charles Scribner founded *Scribner's Magazine,* which was published until 1939. This magazine and *The CENTURY* were the showcase of American literary achievement during the latter part of the 19th century. They were renowned for the high quality of their illustrations, which enhanced the impact of their travel pieces.

Scribner's Magazine published Edith Wharton's earliest work in the genres of poetry, fiction and travel writing. Her poem "The LAST GIUSTINIANI" was accepted by Edward BURLINGAME and appeared in *Scribner's Magazine* in October 1889. In 1890 he also

accepted the short story "MRS. MANSTEY'S VIEW," Wharton's first published work of fiction. In 1895 the magazine published "A Tuscan Shrine," Wharton's first travel article. Many of her later stories and articles appeared in the magazine before book compilation, including the majority of those making up *ITALIAN BACKGROUNDS, A MOTOR-FLIGHT THROUGH FRANCE, FIGHTING FRANCE, FROM DUNKERQUE TO BELFORT* and *IN MOROCCO.*

When Wharton turned away from the house of Scribner and began publishing her novels with APPLETON AND COMPANY, more of her stories made their first appearance in better-paying but less prestigious magazines. Rutger B. JEWETT of Appleton often acted as her agent.

Seadown, Lord   *See BUCCANEERS, THE.*

Sears, J. H.   Principal editor at APPLETON AND COMPANY when the firm became Edith Wharton's primary publisher after 1912. He and Rutger B. JEWETT also acted as agents for Wharton and other authors, often negotiating pre-publication serial rights. Wharton's relationship with Sears appears to have been more formal than that with Jewett, although she mentions him several times in correspondence with Morton FULLERTON about various works in progress.

Sedgwick, Ellery (1870–1960)   American man of letters and editor. He succeeded Bliss PERRY as editor of the *ATLANTIC MONTHLY* from 1909 to 1938. Although he was a longtime friend of Edith Wharton, in 1933 he rejected a short story called "Duration" submitted by Rutger B. JEWETT. Sedgwick found it "not cutting enough" and believed it would be damaging to her reputation, which he termed a "real American possession." This came at a time when Wharton was very anxious about marketing her work. She withdrew the story and later published it in *The WORLD OVER* (*NGC* 439).

Sedgwick wrote several books, including *Novel and Story, a Book of Modern Readings* (1939), *The Happy Profession* (1946) and *The Atlantic Monthly* (1947).

"Seed of the Faith, The"   Short story published in *SCRIBNER'S MAGAZINE* in January 1919 and collected in *HERE AND BEYOND* (D. Appleton, 1926). Written after Edith Wharton's trip to MOROCCO, the story is set in that country. It concerns a young American Baptist missionary, Willard Bent, who has spent 10 unsuccessful years in the town of Eloued attempting to convert the heathen. Harry Spink, an old friend and former lay assistant, now a rubber salesman, comes to town and finds him in an Arab coffeehouse in the bazaar.

Willard invites Harry to the American Evangelical Mission in the evening, although he fears no one will attend. His superior, Mr. Blandhorn, who has spent 25 years in Eloued, has failed to attract converts since the death of Mrs. Blandhorn. She had been a nurse and accomplished healer, and people had flocked to her dispensary. Willard actually hates Africa, although it has "awed and fascinated" him. He perceives that, although the French colonial government has had a friendly attitude toward the mission and the Pasha has tolerated its presence, the entire mission would not be missed if he and Mr. Blandhorn departed. He asks himself, "Were not they themselves equally ignorant in everything that concerned the heathen? What did they know of these people, of their antecedents, the origin of their beliefs and superstitions, the meaning of their habits and passions and precautions?"

They realize that the Negro Ayoub, who has been with the mission many years and is referred to as their "first convert," has departed to take part in the self-flagellating sect of the Hamatchas. The Jewess Myrien, who helps at the mission, has long believed he was a Hamatcha. Mr. Blandhorn admits to Willard that he believes they have failed, which raises the question of whether they or the native populace are the true heathens. The only way to convince people of their zeal would be to insult the Muslim religion and be martyred. Mr. Blandhorn spits on and tramples the Koran in a public place, crying out, " 'Trample—trample! . . . Christ! I see the heavens opened!' " and succumbs to stoning by the crowd, but Harry Spink rescues Willard.

White points out that the blinding African sun keeps Willard, the "reflector," and Blandhorn asleep. As Blandhorn erupts into his frenzy, "the boundaries between blind and sighted, heathen and civilized, black and white, are blurred" (*SSF* 91–92).

Edith Wharton incorporates many details about Morocco in the story that she developed more fully in her final travel book, IN MOROCCO. The atmosphere inside the coffeehouses, the deep spirituality, the makeup of the crowds in the bazaar, the dance of the Hamadchas (spelled with a "d" in *In Morocco*), the reed roofs, the narrow streets and the benign posture of the French government capture the ambience of much of the Morocco she saw with Walter BERRY and General Louis-Hubert LYAUTEY on their three-week tour in 1917.

For further reading: Funston, "In Morocco: Edith Wharton's Heart of Darkness."

Selden, Lawrence *See HOUSE OF MIRTH, THE.*

Sellars, Rose *See CHILDREN, THE.*

"Senlis, May 16" Poem written in 1908 to celebrate a day Edith Wharton and Morton FULLERTON spent together in Senlis, FRANCE. They returned by train, and Wharton wrote him that, during the journey home, "I knew . . . the interfusion of spirit and sense, the double nearness, the mingled communion of touch and thought . . . One such hour ought to irradiate a whole life." In the poem she reflects on the isolation they had experienced on a restaurant terrace, before dinner, as "the tides of time / Coil round our hidden leafy place . . . and leave us at the heart of space" (*EW* 223).

Silve, Claude Pseudonym of Comtesse Philomène de La Forest-Divonne. *See BÉNÉDICTION.*

Silver, Mattie *See ETHAN FROME.*

Silverton, Ned *See HOUSE OF MIRTH, THE.*

Simmons, Ronald A young American Edith Wharton came to know during WORLD WAR I. A graduate of Yale University, he had become a painter and student of art history rather than enter the family business. Wharton felt she could, as she put it, "instantly read, through his jolly fatness, all the fine things vibrating in his heart and mind" (*EW* 411). She explained in her memoir that he had been excluded from active service by a weak heart and had been appointed head of the American Intelligence service at Marseilles. In the spring of 1917 he served as secretary of the cure program she had helped establish for soldiers with tuberculosis, MAISONS AMÉRICAINES DE CONVALESCENCE.

He died, not in battle, but of an epidemic of Spanish grippe that spread to France and caused him double pneumonia, affecting his heart. Edith Wharton was grief-stricken, exclaiming, "He never had a show—and he did so want it and hope for it!" (*EW* 412). She wrote an obituary poem, " 'On Active Service'; American Expeditionary Force (R.S., Aug. 12, 1918)" which was published in *SCRIBNER'S MAGAZINE* (Nov. 1918), and dedicated her 1918 novel *The MARNE* "to the memory of Captain Ronald Simmons, A.E.F., who died for France August 12, 1918." She commissioned a new grave for Simmons at the Cimetière St. Pierre in Marseilles (*EW* 428) and sometimes visited it on excursions from HYÈRES. She also dedicated her 1923 novel *A SON AT THE FRONT* to his memory and, as another "wreath" on Simmons's grave, depicted him as young Boylston, one of the more appealing characters in the novel.

Smith, Logan Pearsall (1865–1946) An American-born essayist and critic, Logan Pearsall Smith was a longtime friend of Edith Wharton. A member of a wealthy Philadelphia Quaker family, he was the son of Robert Pearsall and Hannah Whitall Smith and the brother of Mary BERENSON. He was educated at Haverford College, Harvard and Balliol College at Oxford and became a permanent resident of England. Like Wharton, Smith was inspired by the work of Walter PATER. Among his works were *The Youth of Parnassus, and Other Stories* (1895), *Trivia* (1902), *The Life and Letters of Sir Henry Wotton* (1907) and *On Reading Shakespeare* (1933). Desmond MACCARTHY was one of his students.

Edith Wharton apparently first met Smith in 1903 at Villa La Doccia, the home of Philadelphian Henry Cannon near Florence. Smith arrived with his sister Mary. Cannon had arranged to introduce Wharton to the Berensons, who disliked her immediately, mistaking her shyness at being in Bernard BERENSON's presence for an air of condescension. She later became a lifelong friend of both the Berensons as well as of Smith. Lewis calls him "one of the witty and malicious bachelors to whom Edith was periodically drawn." He was known as an exceptionally graceful prose writer; Lewis remarks that his anthologies "displayed both his erudition and wit, and his dedication to literature" (*EW* 315–16).

In 1926 he was one of the party who shared the charter of the steam yacht *OSPREY* for a Mediterranean cruise. Wharton wrote Mildred BLISS that he had done the trip before with the Berensons and was "most helpful about knowing all the ropes" (*Letters* 491).

"Some Woman to Some Man" One of the better poems in *VERSES*, privately printed in 1878 when Edith Wharton was 16. Lewis points out that it is "based vaguely" on Browning's "Any Wife of Any Husband" (*EW* 31).

Son at the Front, A Novel serialized in *SCRIBNER'S MAGAZINE* and published by Scribner's in 1923, the last work of Edith Wharton's fiction the firm would publish. Portions of *A Son at the Front* were written during the same period as *The AGE OF INNOCENCE*, though it was not published until 1923. Rutger B. JEWETT, Wharton's editor at APPLETON's, called it "the best novel written by you or anyone else for years" (*EW* 456). Lewis observes that the depiction of Paris during WORLD WAR I is done with a "sure hand" (*EW* 457).

The plot turns on the efforts of an American portrait painter, John Campton, long resident in Paris, his ex-wife and her millionaire husband, Anderson Brant, to secure safe duty for their son George, born in France and subject to mobilization. Much of the novel is, on the surface, concerned with the subject of art. Works of art are not the much-mourned casualties of war they are in *FIGHTING FRANCE, FROM DUNKERQUE TO BELFORT*. They endure, but are warped: they have the power to fracture relationships, to generate misunderstandings and to perpetuate hate. Campton's portrait of George and his early sketch for it become commodities in the tangled web of war relief societies; they are bartered, sold and withheld for both favors and cash.

During the war Campton, unable to paint, travels to Châlons and remembers scenes of "gaunt unshorn faces of territorials at railway bridges, soldiers grouped about a provision-lorry, a mud-splashed company returning to the rear." He considers trying to interpret the war "as Raffet . . . had interpreted Napoleon's campaigns" but fails to do so, telling himself that the present world was one in which "art had lost its meaning" (*SF* 127–28). When a wounded soldier, René Davril, a promising young cubist painter, admires his work, he signs a "half-finished study" for the portrait of George and sends it to him. The study results in endless difficulty after René's death when it is returned to Campton by the family. He then offers it to a picture-broker for auction, the proceeds to be donated to "The Friends of French Art" for the Davril family's benefit. The family again rejects assistance but asks that the proceeds be used to provide employment for families of fallen artists. Campton serves on the board of the "Friends," a group eventually torn by dissension. He wonders at what an "incalculable sum of gifts and virtues" goes to make up the daily meal of that "monster," the war (*SF* 150).

Both the study and the portrait of George have ceased to be works of art. The former becomes an offering to appease the "monster," while the portrait itself is used by Campton as a weapon against Brant. By donating it to a museum, he hopes to distance George from Brant in order to establish his own claim to his son. After George is killed, Campton is inconsolable but is finally approached by George's young American friend Boylston to design a monument for him. He nearly refuses, knowing how much comfort it would give Brant to spend a large sum for it, but finally agrees to do so. He instructs Boylston, however, "not to let Brant come here and thank me—at least not for a long time!' " (*SF* 424–25). He pulls out his old sketches of George, and, as the novel ends, begins his last act of portraiture, one that is still divisive rather than restorative.

The novel has many memorable characters, including Dr. Fortin-Lescluze, who returns immediately to the Front after he learns that his only son has been killed; Adele Anthony, George's confidante; Madge Talkett, the young matron George loves; Mme. Lebel, John Campton's humble *concierge*, who suffers devastating losses; the clairvoyant, Mme. Olida and the art critic Paul Dastrey, who is determined to take part in the war, having missed the 1870 Franco-Prussian war. He exclaims bitterly, " 'Too young for 'seventy—and too old for this!' "

Boylston, who is engaged in relief work in Paris, but cannot fight because of his health, is a fictional portrait of Wharton's friend Ronald SIMMONS, to whom she was devoted and to whose memory the book is dedicated. She told her friend Elisina TYLER that the book was another wreath on his grave. Campton was based in part on Tyler's husband, Royall TYLER (*EW* 457).

Lewis comments that by 1923 the war that had threatened civilization was no longer urgent and the book "has an air of refined pugnacity over an issue long decided" (*EW* 457). He perceives the novel as embodying another theme, the wilful misuse of parental authority, shown in Campton's selfish and insensitive wish to keep George out of the war. The varieties of relationships between generations would become an enduring theme in Wharton's subsequent work.

Critical opinion was divided. Maurice Francis Egan, writing in the *New York Times,* praised the depth of emotion achieved without sentimentality and called the novel as "subtle as it is perfect in its simplicity." Many shared the surprise of Robert Morss Lovett, critic for the *New Republic,* that Wharton should attempt to revive the subject of the war. He began, "Like a soul belated comes Mrs. Wharton with her novel of the War," a reference to her short story "SOULS BELATED" (*CR* 331). In fact, Edith Wharton's correspondence with publishers shows that she did not want to delay publishing the novel, but was forced to do so. As early as July 1919, she offered *A Son at the Front* to Jewett of Appleton's, hoping he could place it first as a serial. He cabled, "War books dead in America." In the interim before publication of the novel by Scribner's, she was forced to publish other novels, such as *The AGE OF INNOCENCE* (1920) and *The GLIMPSES OF THE MOON* (1922).

For further reading: Méral, "Edith Wharton, Dorothy Canfield, John Dos Passos et la presence americaine dans le Paris de la Grande Guerre"; Price, *The End of the Age of Innocence: Edith Wharton and the First World War;* Sensibar, " 'Behind the Lines' in Edith Wharton's *A Son at the Front:* Re-Writing a Masculinist Tradition."

Songs from the Heart   Television biography of Wharton (1988) *See* Appendix II.

Sonnets of the Wingless Hours, The   A volume of poetry by Eugene Lee-Hamilton, the half-brother of Vernon LEE. Wharton reviewed it for the *Bookman* in 1907. She considered 20 of Lee's poems to be "of exceptional beauty" and four or five to rank "not far after the greatest in the language" (*UCW* 115). Lee-Hamilton was a semi-invalid as a result of the Franco-Prussian War, but later recovered enough to visit AMERICA. At the time Wharton met them, in 1903, he and his sister lived in Italy together.

"Souls Belated"   Short story first published in *The GREATER INCLINATION* (Scribner's, 1899). The story is set in Europe, to which a married American woman, Lydia Tillotson, and her lover, the novelist Ralph Gannett, have fled to be alone together. Lydia has received her divorce papers from her husband, but has not yet married Gannett; White observes that symbolically she lacks a last name, having given up "Tillotson" but not yet acquired "Gannett" (*SSF* 58). The story affords a glimpse of the "other country" to which Newland Archer, in *The AGE OF INNOCENCE*, invites the Countess Olenska, a country without rules, observers or social sanctions against unorthodox behavior.

Lydia and Ralph are accepted as the Gannetts, a settled married couple, at the Bellosguardo resort hotel, which represents "society," by everyone except an Englishwoman, Mrs. Linton. She confesses to Lydia that she is actually Mrs. Cope, a woman much publicized for running away with a young nobleman, Lord Trevenna. She fears he may be plotting to leave her and insists that Lydia help prevent it: "the first day I laid eyes on you I saw that you and I were both in the same box," she warns her. Mrs. Cope is saved by the arrival of her divorce papers and leaves with Trevenna.

Lydia realizes she cares desperately about retaining the "respectability" she thought she had left behind in America. Marriage, she concludes, serves the purpose of keeping people away from each other: "two people who love each other can be saved from madness only by the things that come between them—children, duties, visits, bores, relations—the things that protect married people from each other. We've been too close together—that has been our sin. We've seen the nakedness of each other's souls." Gannett tries to persuade her to go to Paris and marry him. She insists the solution is for her to leave him, since social acceptance hinges on their not having been divorced and remarried. She packs and goes down to the steamer, but reconsiders and returns to their room while Gannett begins looking up the trains to Paris.

The point of view switches in the course of the story from Lydia to Ralph, a technique seldom found in Wharton's later stories. White points out that this creates a "chopped-off" effect, as though the "previous center of consciousness had died—and so in a sense she has" (*SSF* 59).

The critic for the *Bookman,* Harry Thurston Peck, called the story the "longest, the strongest, and the most striking study in the book" (*CR* 20).

For further reading: Goodman, *Edith Wharton's Women: Friends and Rivals.*

"Souvenirs de Bourget d'outre-mer"   Memorial essay about the French novelist Paul BOURGET, published in the *REVUE HEBDOMADAIRE,* June 21, 1936. *See* "MEMORIES OF BOURGET OVERSEAS." Edith Wharton believed her essay would be a corrective to articles written by younger or middle-aged " 'parties' who knew only the old stuffy Academician" (*Letters* 591).

Spain   Although Edith Wharton never published a travel book about Spain, she made a number of trips there. The first was during her childhood residence abroad, about 1867, when her family made an arduous trip through the country by diligence. From this journey, as she recalled in her memoir, she "brought back an incurable passion for the road" (*BG* 31). Her family had taken along Washington IRVING's "Alhambra," which she later said was the "Pierian fount" of her inspiration. When they returned to France, she was absorbed in its thick black type. Holding it upside down, she paced the floor, making up stories, "swept off full sail on the sea of dreams." Learning to read converted her delight in "making up" into a "frenzy" (*BG* 33–43).

There is an unpublished typescript in the BEINECKE LIBRARY, YALE UNIVERSITY called "A MOTOR-FLIGHT TO SPAIN," probably dating from the late 1920s, which suggests that Wharton may have intended to write at greater length about her travels in that country. In 1912 the Whartons went to Madrid for Easter, one of the last motor trips they made together. The same year, Edith Wharton went to Spain with Rosa de FITZ-JAMES and her young friend Jean du BREUIL DE SAINT GERMAIN; they followed Théophile Gautier's 19th-century route from Pamplona through Burgos, Avila and Salamanca to Madrid (*BG* 330). In July 1914, after her DIVORCE from Teddy, Wharton and Walter BERRY, accompanied by her staff, toured Spain for three weeks. Between 1925 and 1930 she visited Spain three times—the last in 1930—when she and her longtime friend Daisy CHANLER spent five weeks there.

Spark (The 'Sixties), The

One of the four novellas published by APPLETON AND COMPANY in 1924; the others were FALSE DAWN (THE 'FORTIES), *The* OLD MAID (THE 'FIFTIES) and NEW YEAR'S DAY (THE 'SEVENTIES). This story concerns the marriage of the prosperous, stolid, philosophical Hayley Delane and Leila Gracey, whose father had been the center of a scandal and has become an alcoholic. The unnamed narrator, a recent Harvard graduate, is an onlooker at a polo match in which Leila roots for Bolton Byrne, a recent interest, against her husband. Delane thrashes Byrne for mistreating his pony, but united social opinion in their "set" forces him to apologize.

The narrator learns that Delane had run away from school to fight at the Battle of Bull Run in the Civil War.

A polo match. Endpaper, The Spark (The 'Sixties) *(1924), first edition* (Collection of the author)

He had been strongly influenced by a bearded visitor to his hospital bedside in Washington, a "queer fellow—a sort of backwoodsman." The visitor's ideas leave a profound impression on Delane, with the result that he proves to have, embedded deep within the shallow, conventional waters of his social milieu, a "granite rock thrust up," principles that he cannot ignore that impel him to conduct at variance with that of his contemporaries. The first instance is his putting a stop to Byrne's cruelty to animals. He then invites his father-in-law to live with them, despite his wife's selfish refusal; she sends the children to boarding school and leaves them alone together. Delane cares for and entertains the old man until just before Gracey's death, when Leila returns. The Washington hospital visitor turns out to be Walt WHITMAN (who was always a favorite of Edith Wharton). Delane recognizes his picture, by chance, while calling on the narrator, who happens to be reading a book of his poetry. The "spark" of Whitman's personality and philosophy have exerted a long-reaching influence on Delane, although he had not known of his verse and considers it "rubbish" when the narrator reads it to him. Lewis terms Wharton's portrait of Whitman a "quirky image" of a "wartime healer" (*EW* 373).

The Spark was considered one of the weaker novellas in the quartet by many critics. Although it purports to deal with the decade of the 1860s, the action takes place almost entirely in the latter part of the 19th century. The portrait of Whitman is not as vividly drawn as that of John RUSKIN in *False Dawn*.

Speak to the Earth: Wanderings and Reflections Among Elephants and Mountains

This volume, by the English writer and naturalist Vivienne de Watteville (her actual name was Mrs. Gerard Goschen) is a record of her second journey to Africa in 1928–29. Wharton wrote a preface extoling her "sunlit windswept pages." Although her own "mountain tent" was the "library lamp-shade" and her "wilderness" a garden, she praised de Watteville's language, evoking an "innocent Bestiary" where readers could receive the "tireless messages of Nature" (*UCW* 248–49).

After Wharton's death Mrs. Goschen contributed a memoir of her to Percy LUBBOCK. Wharton had told her she was a "born writer," which had encouraged her to publish *Speak to the Earth*. She sent the proofs to Wharton, who not only sent back a page of "dry invaluable criticism" but also went through them, penciling in incisive comments while being careful never to "destroy the cobweb texture" of her confidence. When the book appeared Wharton sent it to America and to England for reviews and gave many copies to her friends (*Portrait of Edith Wharton*, 203–205).

For further reading: Funston, Judith E., "Mackaws and Pekingese: Vivienne de Watteville and Edith Wharton."

Spender, Clem   *See* OLD MAID, THE.

Spragg, Abner   *See* CUSTOM OF THE COUNTRY, THE.

Spragg, Mrs.   *See* CUSTOM OF THE COUNTRY, THE.

Spragg, Undine (Undine Spragg Moffatt)   *See* CUSTOM OF THE COUNTRY, THE.

Stevens, Harry Leyden   *See* ENGAGEMENT.

Strachey, Lytton (1880–1932)   English biographer and historian, Strachey was the author of *Eminent Victorians* and other works. He was a close friend of Virginia WOOLF, Desmond MACCARTHY and other members of the Bloomsbury Group, an intellectual circle of writers and artists. Edith Wharton did not meet Woolf or like her novels, but she was a friend of MacCarthy's and had met Strachey several times; she liked him very much.

She first met Strachey in London in 1921. In 1922, she went to lunch at Pontigny in the company of Walter BERRY, Sinclair LEWIS and his wife, Charles DU BOS, André MAUROIS, Gustave SCHLUMBERGER and Strachey. They discussed the art of translation—a conversation Lewis wishes had been transcribed. Wharton liked the portrait of Queen Victoria in *Eminent Victorians* very much. Lewis states that she was "highly amused . . . by Strachey's flashing wit and little squeals of laughter" and felt he embodied " 'the old English culture' of men of letters" (*EW* 456).

Mary and Bernard BERENSON had long known Strachey. Mary Berenson's daughter Rachel ("Ray") Costelloe was married to Oliver Strachey, Lytton's brother. Interestingly, her other daughter, Karin, was married to Virginia Woolf's younger brother Adrian Stephen. In 1932, on learning of Strachey's death from cancer, Wharton wrote Berenson, "I am very sorry Lytton Strachey is dead. He was, with Aldous Huxley, the only light left in that particular quarter of the heavens" (*Letters* 545).

Strange Wives   A 1935 film based on the short story "BREAD UPON THE WATERS." *See* Appendix II.

Sturgis, Howard Overing (1855–1920)   The youngest son of a Boston banker, Russell Sturgis (whose career was largely spent in London), and his third wife, he was born in England and educated at Eton and Cambridge. After his mother's death, the country house in which Howard Sturgis had grown up, Givens Grove, went to his half-brother, and he settled at QUEEN'S ACRE ("Qu'Acre"), in Windsor. He was one of Edith Wharton's much-valued "inner circle" of men friends; the group also included Percy LUBBOCK, Robert NORTON, John HUGH SMITH and Gaillard LAPSLEY. She had first met Sturgis at a dinner in NEWPORT soon after

her marriage, where she was immediately drawn to his love of good talk within a small, intimate group of friends. In *A BACKWARD GLANCE* she recalled him as a stranger might find him in his living room, stretched on a lounge in the sitting room, knitting or embroidering. He was a "sturdily-built handsome man" with white hair, a black moustache, and "tender mocking eyes under the bold arch of his black brows." She visited him often at Qu'Acre, sometimes in the company of Henry JAMES, and described him as a "perfect host, matchless friend, [the] drollest, kindest and strangest of men" (*BG* 225). Her great regret was that no Boswell recorded Sturgis's conversation, with its "odd blending of the whimsical and the shrewd, of scepticism and emotion, as in his character" (*BG* 233–34).

After his visit to The MOUNT with James in 1904, Sturgis wrote Wharton from Brookline, apparently to thank her for sending a photograph: "You are indeed the veiled prophetess, the dame voilée, and I'm so glad to have that group of us all three together, & linked. Henry looks so delightfully frightened & in custody between us" (unpublished letter from Howard Sturgis to Edith Wharton, December 3, 1904; BEINECKE LIBRARY, YALE UNIVERSITY).

Sturgis's novel *Belchamber* was published in 1905 by G. P. Putnam's Sons and reviewed by Wharton for the *Bookman* in May 1905; her review is titled "Mr. Sturgis's *Belchamber*." She admitted that the work had faults of "construction and perspective, such as the hack writer would easily have avoided," but insisted that it had "freshness of sensation and perception such as he could never have achieved." The characters, she felt, followed their natures and did not act according to the author's preconceived plan; as a result, they were "all alive" and the reader could "walk all around them and see them on every side" (*UCW* 106–14). In *A Backward Glance* she calls the novel "a striking study of fashionable London in the 'nineties, lived above the level of anecdote by a touch of tragedy, and rising in certain scenes to the quiet power of great fiction" (*BG* 234). *Belchamber* had been published in England in 1904, and Wharton had tried unsuccessfully to use her influence with SCRIBNER'S to secure publication in AMERICA. She was pleased that Putnam's agreed to publish it, although it was not acclaimed by critics. The novel is now enjoying something of a critical revival, and the text is available electronically.

For further reading: Goodman, *Edith Wharton's Inner Circle*. The text of *Belchamber* may be obtained electronically from the Golden Gale Electronic Book Archive (http://eden.apana.org.au/Golden Gale/bookindex.html) or contact Robert Bamford, Internet email: rbamford@acslink.net.au; Postal: P.O. Box 894, Sandy Bay, TAS 7006, Australia.

Sudermann, Hermann (1857–1928)   German novelist and dramatist whose tragic drama "*Es Lebe das Leben*"

Edith Wharton translated; it was published in 1902. *See* *JOY OF LIVING, THE;* CAMPBELL, MRS. PATRICK.

Summer   Novella published by Appleton in 1917. Like *ETHAN FROME*, it is set in rural NEW ENGLAND. Edith Wharton termed this novella the "hot Ethan" and regarded it as one of her best works. It is the story of young girl, Charity Royall, child of a drunkard and a "half-human" woman, born into a settlement of shiftless outlaws on the sinister nearby Mountain. Her father has gone to prison, and she is adopted by Lawyer Royall, who practices in North Dormer, the small village at the base of the Mountain. When Charity grows up, Lawyer Royall wants to marry her, but she refuses, and, through his influence, is appointed librarian of the Hatchard Memorial Library, presided over by the great-niece of the founder, Miss Hatchard. Lawyer Royall hires a housekeeper, Verena Marsh.

While working in the library, Charity meets Miss Hatchard's cousin, a young architect, Lucius Harney of Springfield, who is working temporarily in the village. In the brief "summer" of her life she has an affair with him; the interlude is followed by a bitter autumn. Socially ambitious, Lucius is already engaged to Annabel Balch, a girl of good family from the neighboring town of Springfield. Charity, pregnant with his child, returns to live in the Mountain for her mother Mary's burial, over which the local minister, Mr. Miles, presides. She tries to stay on the Mountain in order to escape the censure of the village in which she has been raised. Lawyer Royall once again rescues Charity and her unborn child from the Mountain and marries her.

Lucius Harney has been termed one of Edith Wharton's "ineffectual males." Lawyer Royall, however, was praised by critics and also by Bernard BERENSON, which delighted the author, who replied, "Of course, *he's* the book." The Mountain was based on Bear Mountain, 15 miles from Lee (a town near LENOX, site of The MOUNT). The story originated in a tale told to her by the rector of the church in Lenox about a "mountain burial." The scene based on this conversation, the funeral service for Charity's mother, in a cold room illuminated by a single candle, has been called one of the best she ever wrote (*EW* 397).

Contemporary critics gave the novella mixed reviews. Edwin Francis Edgett, writing in the *Boston Evening Transcript,* believed she had imagined the entire setting and that no reader could mistake it for New England. John Macy, critic for the *Dial,* however, asserted that her New England people were "elemental, victims of circumstance," and that a woman reared on a "bleak New England farm" could not have had a better understanding of its "pitiful details and lonely aspirations." T. S. Eliott, writing in *The Egoist,* called Wharton the "satirist's satirist" and hoped *Summer* would counter New England novels saturated with "stunted firs,"

"granite boulders" and "pale gaunt women" at work on rag carpets. He believed Wharton succeeded by suppressing all evidence of European culture (*CR* 247–63). Waid calls *Summer* Wharton's "most erotic and lyrical novel" and contrasts the renewal of life depicted in the novel with the infertility and death represented by its counterpart, *Ethan Frome.* She presents a lucid analysis of the incest theme in the novel that has troubled many readers and argues that, on a wider canvas, Wharton had hoped the paternalism represented by Lawyer Royall would "counter the threat" posed by WORLD WAR I to human existence (Introduction, v–xvi).

For further reading: Blackall, "Charity at the Window: Narrative Technique in Edith Wharton's *Summer*"; Elbert, "The Politics of Maternality in *Summer*"; Pfeiffer, "*Summer* and Its Critics' Discomfort"; Waid, Introduction to Signet paperback ed., 1993; Walker, " 'Seduced and Abandoned': Convention and Reality in Edith Wharton's *Summer*"; Wershoven, "The Divided Conflict of Edith Wharton's *Summer*"; White, "Edith Wharton's *Summer* and 'Women's Fiction.' "

supernatural, Edith Wharton and the   In her autobiography "LIFE AND I" Edith Wharton asserts that until she was 27 or 28 she could not sleep in a room containing a book with a ghost story. She dates her fear to the reading of a "robber-story" in childhood when she was recuperating from typhoid fever in GERMANY. It was "perilous reading" coupled with her "intense Celtic sense of the supernatural," and brought on a serious relapse. She had to have a light in her bedroom in addition to a nurse-maid in order to sleep, and she could feel "it" behind her on the doorstep when returning from walks, leading to a "choking agony of terror." She was frightened of waiting on doorsteps for the next eight years, a fear which apparently elicited only sympathy and understanding from her parents. Her superstitions lingered well into adulthood ("Life and I" 17–19).

Her interest in the occult and her unusual sensitivity to the supernatural led to many of her best short stories. "The LADY'S MAID'S BELL" was published in *SCRIBNER'S MAGAZINE* in December 1902. Lewis states that it was the first of a series of ghost stories that would establish her as "a major practitioner in this possibly minor genre, and a sign that her own ghost-haunted days could now be drawn upon to expert literary and psychological use" (*EW* 107). Other renowned ghost stories include "A BOTTLE OF PERRIER," "AFTERWARD," "MR. JONES," "The TRIUMPH OF NIGHT," "POMEGRANATE SEED," "ALL SOULS' " and "The EYES."

Wharton compiled two collections of ghost stories: *TALES OF MEN AND GHOSTS* (1910) and *GHOSTS* (1937). In the preface to the latter, published posthumously, she remarked, ". . . when I first began to read, and then to write, ghost stories, I was conscious of a common medium between myself and my readers, of their meeting me halfway among the primeval shadows, and filling in the gaps in my narrative with sensations and divinations akin to my own." She insisted that there was "internal proof" of validity within good ghost stories and recommended that, to secure authenticity, the author of a ghost story be "well frightened in the telling" of it. In 1937, however, Edith Wharton was afraid her public had become too literal, having received letters from readers after the publication of "Pomegranate Seed" asking how a ghost could write a letter and put it in a letter-box. Today, such a reception seems all but inconceivable. With some exceptions, her ghosts are subtle creations, operating on a subconscious level and more likely to wreak psychological vengeance than physical harm.

Fedorko observes that certain critics, including Lewis, have seen in Edith Wharton's fondness for writing ghost stories a "vehicle for exploring otherwise taboo feelings and experiences." She links her interest in Gothic architecture, with its overtones of fear and the warding-off of evil, to her absorption in ghost stories and to other fiction as well, including SUMMER. In the latter, Lawyer Royall poses an incestuous threat to his ward Charity, who feels an "amorphous apprehensiveness . . . [and] sense of pervading danger" (74).

Smith points out that in the ghost story Edith Wharton is able to "penetrate into the realm of the *unseen*, that is, into the area that her society preferred to be unable to see, or to construe defensively as super (i.e., not) natural" (89). Some of Edith Wharton's ghost stories are grounded in the rational, such as "BEWITCHED" and "MISS MARY PASK," while others are "predicated on the marvelous," such as "The Triumph of Night" and "Pomegranate Seed." Still others, such as "The Eyes," belong to the realm of the grotesque. At times the horror of the natural exceeds that of the supernatural. *See also* GHOSTS, *TALES OF MEN AND GHOSTS*.

For further reading: Bendixen and Zilversmit, eds. *Edith Wharton: New Critical Essays;* Fedorko, *Gender and the Gothic in the Fiction of Edith Wharton;* Lewis, "Powers of Darkness"; Robillard, "Edith Wharton"; Smith, "Edith Wharton and the Ghost Story"; Stengel, "Edith Wharton Rings 'The Lady's Maid's Bell' "; Zilversmit, "Edith Wharton's Last Ghosts."

Symonds, John Addington (1840–1893) English historian, scholar and translator. He was perhaps best known for his *Renaissance in Italy* (1975–86), which deals with the literature and fine arts of the Renaissance, and for his translation of the *Sketches in Italy and Greece;* he also wrote critical studies of DANTE, WHITMAN and the pre-Shakespearean dramatists. He believed Walter PATER had done for the Renaissance what John RUSKIN had for the Middle Ages, and, in his writing and criticism, expanded further in some of the directions explored by Pater.

Symonds was one of Edith Wharton's European literary progenitors who embodied a greater interest in aesthetics than most American travel writers. In her memoir, *A BACKWARD GLANCE,* she classed herself with them rather than with such American predecessors as James Fenimore Cooper or Washington IRVING. In this work she recalls her enthusiasm for the travel books of the 1870s and 1880s of the "cultured dilettante" type, which had found many eager readers. "From Pater's 'Renaissance,' and Symonds's 'Sketches in Italy and Greece,' to the deliciously desultory volumes of Vernon Lee, and Bourget's delicate 'Sensations d'Italie,' . . . they all represented a high but unspecialized standard of culture; all were in a sense the work of amateurs, and based on the assumption that it is mainly to the cultured amateur that the creative artist must look for appreciation" (*BG* 140). She believed there was a place for books by such authors alongside the work of BERENSON and other scholars.

In her review of Edwin and Evangeline BLASHFIELD's *ITALIAN CITIES,* she termed their work "the most interesting book of Italian impressions that has appeared in English since Symonds's volumes" (*UCW* 64). The BEINECKE LIBRARY, YALE UNIVERSITY, contains a manuscript called "Italy Again" in which she examines, as Wegener puts it, "the impact and relative value" of Pater, Symons and Vernon LEE in the understanding of ITALY and Italian art (*UCW* 202).

Symons, Arthur (1865–1945) British poet and critic, whose critical writing, admired by Edith Wharton, covered diverse subjects. He wrote *An Introduction to the Study of Browning* (1886) and *The Symbolist Movement in Literature* (1890), a manifesto emphasizing the importance of the French symbolists. His poetry has a remoteness from contemporary society typical of the "Decadents," who were strongly influenced by Paul Verlaine and Stéphane Mallarmé, and who relied on suggestion rather than statement, as well as symbols.

During their 1888 cruise aboard the *VANADIS,* Wharton kept a diary in which she referred to Symons along with Homer, Pindar, Shelley and Alexander Kinglake.

When *ITALIAN BACKGROUNDS* was published in 1905, some critics detected the influence of Symons. Walter Littlefield of the *New York Times* attacked Wharton as being a quintessential amateur, one over-reaching herself, a convert to the "cult of Symons, Hewlett & Co. [Arthur Symons, Maurice Hewlett, and Edward Hutton]." Such a cult has long needed a "liturgy," as well as a "priestess," and has now gained both, he suggested (*CR* 103). He puts down Wharton, who is clearly an amateur, for attempting to "till" the soil of Italy as though she had an academic background (he is referring to her reattribution of the SAN VIVALDO terra-cotta statues to Giovanni della Robbia).

tableau vivant A "living picture," or a scene acted in one setting, used by Edith Wharton in *The HOUSE OF MIRTH*. Live models represented a static painting, sculpture or, sometimes, a historic personage or moment. Tableaux vivants were often presented during the 19th century as a form of religious or dramatic entertainment. They were used in the medieval period in liturgical presentations, such as the *Quem Quaeritis*, and were a feature of early French street theater. They became fashionable after GOETHE published his 1809 novel *Elective Affinities*, in which Luciana takes part in tableaux vivants to portray her charms. Wharton may be drawing on this novel in her use of the tableau vivant, since Goethe was one of her favorite writers and she had been familiar with his work since childhood.

McCullough dates the appearance of tableaux vivants in New York to 1831, when the Park Theatre presented Mrs. Barrymore illustrating famous paintings. They flourished in the 1850s, although not in the better theaters such as Brougham's (later Wallack's). Most were sensational in nature and were designed to titillate. There was an unsuccessful movement to suppress them, but they revived again after the Statue of Liberty, an ideal subject, arrived in New York (*Living Pictures on the New York Stage,* 1–17). Their heyday was the 1890s, although they were eventually eclipsed by motion pictures. Between 1860 and 1890, according to Lynes, middle-class evening parties were organized to depict tableaux vivants of John Rogers's statuette groups of sentimental scenes. Wharton looked down on the works of Rogers, using his mass-produced figures as an emblem of poor taste. For example, a Rogers statuette graces the drawing room of Lily Bart's boardinghouse.

In *The House of Mirth* Carry Fisher, social adviser to the ambitious Wellington Brys, decides that "*tableaux vivants* and expensive music were the two baits most likely to attract the desired prey," i.e., acceptance within the higher echelons of "old New York" (*HM* 138). It is not unlikely that Mrs. Bry has risen from the class partial to John Rogers's statuette groups, but Carrie persuades the fashionable portrait painter Paul Morpeth to organize a series of living pictures. Lily Bart, still beautiful and a social asset, lends her prestige to a form of entertainment otherwise slightly tainted and gracefully depicts the central figure in Joshua Reynolds's *Mrs. Lloyd,* a beautiful goddess-like woman in a simple, flowing dress nailing a letter to her lover on a tree in a forest. The tableaux vivants serve to refract Lily and to establish her, publicly, as the embodiment of taste. She is perceived by the men present as unattainable, yet highly desirable. The tableaux also present an intellectual challenge to the spectators. Wharton states that tableaux are "waxworks" only to "unfurnished minds" (to those who cannot identify the paintings or scenes represented, or attach other levels of meaning to them). If well conceived and enacted, they may give magic glimpses of the "boundary world between fact and imagination" to those who are aesthetically enlightened (*HM* 140).

For further reading: Chapman, *'Living Pictures': Women and Tableaux Vivants in Nineteenth-Century Fiction and Culture;* Hovet and Hovet, "Tableaux Vivants: Masculine Vision and Feminine Reflections in Novels by Warner, Alcott, Stowe, and Wharton"; Fryer, *Felicitous Space: The Imaginative Structures of Edith Wharton and Willa Cather;* Fryer, "Reading *Mrs. Lloyd*"; Lynes, *The Tastemakers;* McCullough, *Living Pictures on the New York Stage.*

Tales of Men and Ghosts Collection of short stories about the SUPERNATURAL published by SCRIBNER'S in 1910. It included "The BOLTED DOOR," "HIS FATHER'S SON," "The DAUNT DIANA," "The DEBT," "FULL CIRCLE," "The LEGEND," "The EYES," "The BLOND BEAST," "AFTERWARD" and "The LETTERS." The volume received mixed reviews; the critic for the *Bookman* (England) regarded it as "three parts brilliant and always readable," but complained that Wharton's characters had a "comfortable way of inheriting fortunes at convenient moments in their careers." The reviewer for the *Athenæum* (England) objected that Wharton's idea of "ghosts" as "the delicate subtle suggestion of an unseen world" does not correspond to the conception of most people. The writer for the *Nation* found the tales "ingenious and readable" but too "patent"; the style is the "alert and commonplace style of the magazine fiction of the day as turned out by an army of skillful practitioners" (*CR* 175–76). Later critics were kinder, particularly Blake Nevius, who praises "The Eyes" and calls it a "Hawthornesque study of egoism, which is worth examining if only for the special light it casts on this familiar personality" (*Edith Wharton: A Study of Her Fic-*

tion, 94). Lewis also calls it a "small masterpiece" (*EW* 296). Another collection of ghost stories, GHOSTS, was published posthumously in 1937.

Talkett, Madge   *See* SON AT THE FRONT, A.

Tarrant, Heloise ("Halo") Spear   *See* GODS ARRIVE, THE and *HUDSON RIVER BRACKETED.*

Tarrant, Lewis   *See* GODS ARRIVE, THE and *HUDSON RIVER BRACKETED.*

television adaptations of Edith Wharton's works   *See* Appendix II.

"Temperate Zone, The"   Short story published in the *PICTORIAL REVIEW* in February 1924 and collected in *HERE AND BEYOND* (Appleton, 1926). An American dilettante, Willis French, who has made "interesting failures" at both painting and poetry, has arrived in London, sent by his publisher to interview Mrs. Donald Paul, widow of an eminent painter, Horace Fingall. Formerly the American "waif" Bessy Reck, she had been sent to Paris by the people of her small town to study art under Fingall and had succeeded in marrying him. French himself had also studied under Fingall and has a sentimental attachment to him. In addition, French had submitted his poetry for evaluation to the late distinguished poet Emily Morland. Morland had influenced Fingall's art and written poetry about him, but there is no evidence of their having met, a puzzle French is determined to unravel. Morland had planned to marry Donald Paul when her divorce became final, and had bequeathed her London house to him. Fingall's widow and Morland's beloved have now married and are living in Morland's former home. French tours the house and sees a photograph of the famous Fingall portrait of Mrs. Paul; the original is in the Luxembourg Museum. He then departs for Paris to find the Pauls.

On the steamer French encounters the Gallic artist André Jolyesse, who had known Fingall years earlier. He advises French to hurry with his critical biography, since Fingall's fame may be fleeting. He also sees the Pauls on board, although he doesn't realize it until he calls on them at the Nouveau Luxe (the name Edith Wharton uses in other works to signify an ostentatious Parisian hotel). Jolyesse expresses an eager wish to paint Mrs. Paul. French discovers, on interviewing her, that Mrs. Paul has no insight into art and has understood her husband's achievement only in terms of the monetary value of his paintings. Donald Paul offers to escort him to the late painter's studio, where he finds a sketch of Emily Morland, confirming that Fingall had known her. Paul, who had not recognized Emily in the sketch, confesses that he hopes to write a life of her, since he has many of her letters, and gives French the

drawing. Bessy Paul agrees to meet with French in March for a week of interviews about Fingal; in return she insists that French assist Paul with his book and that Jolyesse do a portrait of her. French departs, having won on all fronts.

Wharton's ambivalence about women and their capacity for the visual arts is clear from the story, which focuses on the dichotomy between the artist and the Philistine. The tone of the story is, according to the *New York Times* reviewer, "richly ironic" and "completely suave." French sees his idols more clearly than their surviving lovers do; as Grace Frank, reviewing the collection for the *Saturday Review of Literature,* puts it, the dead poet and the dead painter "suffer a kind of second death at the hands of their living lovers."

"Tendencies in Modern Fiction"   Essay published in the *SATURDAY REVIEW OF LITERATURE,* January 27, 1934 (rpt. *UCC,* 170–74). This essay preceded "PERMANENT VALUES IN FICTION," which appeared in the *Saturday Review of Literature* the following April. Beginning with the premise that the novel may be defined as "a work of fiction containing a good story about well-drawn characters," Edith Wharton proceeds to attack James JOYCE and Virginia WOOLF for their lack of attention to form, Harriet Beecher Stowe and Charles Reade for their didacticism, and D. H. Lawrence for his undifferentiated characters.

Wharton praises Sinclair LEWIS for creating "live people" and believes Emily Brontë might have succeeded in doing so if she had not pictured "a houseful of madmen." In any case, novelists must contend with the unfortunate truth that "a long course of cinema obviousness and of tabloid culture has rendered the majority of readers insensible to allusiveness and to irony." They still respond, however, when they see " 'a likeness' " to "flesh-and-blood people," which Wharton considers a sound instinct. The books of Lewis and Theodore Dreiser have "more of the lasting stuff of good fiction in them" than many other works "dressed up in a passing notoriety."

"Terminus"   Poem written in 1908 recording a night Edith Wharton spent with Morton FULLERTON in the Charing Cross Hotel, London. The worn bed has often thrilled "With the pressure of bodies ecstatic, bodies like ours,/Seeking each other's souls in the depths of unfathomed caresses. . . . And lying there hushed in your arms, as the waves of rapture receded,/And far down the margin of being we heard the low beat of the soul." She gave the poem to Fullerton and asked him to return it, saying, "It breaks over me like a great sweet tide." Fullerton did return it, but copied it first with notations as to when and where it was written (*EW* 259–60).

Lewis points out that in her 1912 novel *The REEF* the room at the Gare du Nord in Paris in which George

Darrow and Sophy Viner spend several days is a replica of the room she and Fullerton occupied in the Charing Cross Hotel. Lewis compares the "bed with its soot-sodden chintz" and "the grime of the brasses" in the poem with the "featureless dullness of the room" and the "high-bolstered counterpaned bed" in the novel. Wharton, however, had visualized the scene of illicit passion as beautiful, whereas Darrow comes to hate the hotel he shares with Viner (*EW* 326–27).

***Tess of the D'Urbervilles* (a play)** A dramatization of Thomas HARDY's novel by the American playwright Lorimer Stoddard, produced at the Manhattan Theater in New York in 1902. Wharton was so moved by the performance of Minnie Maddern Fiske as Tess that she wrote an enthusiastic account of it for the *New York Commercial Advertiser.* She predicted that Mrs. Fiske might do more than "all the managers and all the dramatic critics to raise the theatrical ideals of the public and restore the dignity of the theater" (*UCW* 50). Edith and Teddy Wharton later met Thomas Hardy on several occasions in England at the home of Lady St. Helier, a well-known London hostess.

Testvalley, Laura *See* BUCCANEERS, THE.

"That Good May Come" Short story published in SCRIBNER'S MAGAZINE in May 1894 but not collected. White terms it a "slight early effort" (37). A young man, Helfenridge, is attempting to console his friend Maurice Birkton about the rejection of his poetry by magazine editors. Helfenridge quotes some of his ponderous verse and praises it, but Birkton is increasingly bitter. He lives with his mother and sister, Annette, age 15, in genteel poverty in a walkup flat. Although he has a small income from writing reviews, and his mother contributes what she can by writing out social invitations, they can barely buy necessities, let alone luxuries.

In order to buy a proper dress for the devout Annette, about to be confirmed in a high Anglican church, the Church of the Precious Blood, Birkton sells an unsigned scandalous "squib" to the tabloid publication *Social Kite.* Although he does not identify the parties, the item is about his having spotted young Mrs. Tolquitt with Dick Blason at Koster and Bial's, a music hall. At the service Birkton sees Mrs. Tolquitt, whose daughter is being confirmed with Annette. Birkton is sure "society" will have recognized her and feels guilty. The phrase in the Bible about doing evil "that good may come" is, he thinks, untrue. Helfenridge persuades him that the "good" that might come is that Birkton will not again indulge in cheap sensational journalism. Then he tells him the "anguish and humiliation" Birkton imagines Mrs. Tolquitt to have suffered are a mirage; after church he had seen her drive away with Blason, with her daughter between them.

theatrical adaptations of Edith Wharton's works *See* Appendix II.

"Three Francescas, The" Essay published in the *North American Review,* July 1902. It is an assessment of three plays being simultaneously produced, written by playwrights of different nationalities, all having to do with the subject of Francesca da Rimini. Francesca and her lover, her brother-in-law Paolo Malatesta, were put to death by her husband. Their story is one of the most famous episodes in Dante's *Inferno.*

Before beginning the essay, Wharton wrote William Dean HOWELLS about her idea, asking that he transmit her suggestion to the Boston periodical *North American Review.* "I do not know Mr. Harvey," she explained, "& am not sure if he condescends to such frivolities as a dramatic criticism by a woman" (*Letters* 62; Wharton was referring to Col. George Harvey, owner and editor from 1899 to 1921).

The productions Wharton discusses are *Paolo and Francesca* (published in 1900, performed in 1902) by the English playwright Stephen Phillips, whose play *Ulysses* she later reviewed—*see* ULYSSES: A DRAMA; the Italian novelist and poet Gabriele d'Annunzio's *Francesca da Rimini* (1902); and the American novelist F. Marion Crawford's *Francesca da Rimini* (1902).

Edith Wharton compares the playwrights' skill at plotting, their treatment of the characters' psychology, their use of scenery, history and language. Crawford's version, written for the French actress Sarah Bernhardt, had been translated into French in 1902. Of the three productions, Wharton believes Crawford's has been the most successful from "the dramatic point of view"; he has had the courage to depart from "stage conventions" and "to draw his characters as Italians of the Middle Ages."

Crawford (1854–1909), son of the sculptor Thomas Crawford, was the step-brother of Edith Wharton's lifelong friend Margaret (Daisy) Terry CHANLER. Her father, the expatriate Connecticut artist Luther Terry, had married Crawford's mother. Edith Wharton and Daisy first met in 1866, when the Joneses took Edith, age four, to ROME (*BG* 29). Since Crawford was born in Italy and educated on the Continent and in America, it is not surprising that his dramatic adaptation was the more authentic.

Thwarte, Guy *See* BUCCANEERS, THE.

Thwarte, Sir Helmsley *See* BUCCANEERS, THE.

Tiepolo, Giovanni Battista (1696–1770) The Venetian painter Tiepolo was one of Edith Wharton's favorite artists. She often refers, in her travel writing and fiction, to his religious and mythological scenes, depictions of historical events, his rococo style and the movement and spectacle of his work as a whole. In praising Tiepolo and other painters of the BAROQUE STYLE she countered the opinions of John RUSKIN and many art historians. Wharton's first novel, *The VALLEY OF DECISION*, is partly set in an imaginary villa on the BRENTA RIVIERA, which has a trompe l'oeil purportedly by Tiepolo. He also painted the ballroom ceiling at the Villa Pisani in Strà.

Tiepolo revived the grand manner of the Venetian baroque. His frescoes adorn the Doge's Palace in VENICE, and he also worked in Würzburg and Madrid. His work was not fashionable at the time Wharton wrote *ITALIAN BACKGROUNDS*, but she mentions his ceiling frescoes in the church of the Scalzi and the church of the Gesuati on the quay of the Zattere, both in Venice. In the former, unfortunately destroyed during World War I, Tiepolo, "the great painter of atmosphere," was asked to depict the transportation of the Holy House from Palestine to Loreto. "He liked to suspend his fluttering groups in great pellucid reaches of sky," Wharton explains. Accordingly, "the angels, whirling along the Virgin's house with a vehemence which makes it seem a mere feather in the rush of their flight, appear to be sweeping through measureless heights of air above an unroofed building." In three frescoes in the Gesuati, he presents the legend of Saint Dominic receiving the chaplet from the Virgin in glory. Edith Wharton observes that "the guide-books, always on the alert to warn the traveller against an undue admiration of Tiepolo," complain that the Virgin looks too much like a "Venetian lady," but that such an interpretation is indefensible, for Venetian Catholicism was a "religion of *bon ton*, which aimed to make its noble devotees as much at home in church as in the drawing room." Tiepolo, "by sheer force of technique . . . contrived to impart to his great religious pictures a glow of supernatural splendour." He was, first of all, "a great decorative artist, a master of emotion in motion" (*IB* 193–96). *See also* COMMEDIA DELL'ARTE.

Tintagel, Duke of (Ushant)   *See BUCCANEERS, THE.*

Touchstone, The   Novella serialized in *SCRIBNER'S MAGAZINE* in March and April 1900 and reprinted as a separate volume by SCRIBNER'S (1900). It was published by John Murray in England in 1900 as *A Gift from the Grave*. Edith Wharton began the story during her four-month visit to Washington with Teddy in 1899. She had been ill with digestive troubles, bronchitis and depression; Walter BERRY had urged her to come down to the capital, hoping a change of scene would effect her recovery.

Like the short story "COPY," the tale asks who owns the rights to correspondence, especially by public figures, the sender or the recipient. A young impecunious lawyer, Stephen Glennard, secretly sells a bundle of love letters from the eminent novelist Margaret Aubyn,

who has recently died, in order to marry a delightful, but impoverished, young woman. Glennard recalls Margaret as "the poor woman of genius with her long pale face and short-sighted eyes." Glennard's career and marriage prosper, but he is haunted by the posthumously published letters. Eventually he perceives Margaret Aubyn as the "one reality in a world of shadows"; the messages of the letters convince him to alter his life. He comes to appreciate her, and even to love her, through the letters. White points out that the novelist is, from her grave, both an instructor of morals and a powerful maternal presence (*SSF* 169).

Tracy, Laura Lou (Laura Lou Weston)   *See HUDSON RIVER BRACKETED.*

Tracy, Lucilla   *See HUDSON RIVER BRACKETED.*

Tracy, Upton   *See HUDSON RIVER BRACKETED.*

translations, of Edith Wharton's works   The earliest translation of one of Wharton's works may have been the 1900 French translation of "The Muse's Tragedy" by Wharton and Minnie BOURGET. It was published in the REVUE HEBDOMADAIRE with a footnote by Paul BOURGET complimenting them on the translation; Lewis states that it was "roughly done" (*EW* 97). Charles DU BOS translated *The HOUSE OF MIRTH*, which, beginning in 1906, ran in the *REVUE DE PARIS* as *La demeure de liesse* but was published in France as *Chez les heureux du monde*. In 1912 *Sous la neige*, an unsigned translation of *ETHAN FROME* by Du Bos, ran in the *REVUE DES DEUX MONDES*. In 1916, *FIGHTING FRANCE, FROM DUNKERQUE TO BELFORT* was published as *Voyages au front*. Mme. Taillandier, sister of Wharton's friend André CHEVRILLON, translated *The AGE OF INNOCENCE*, published as *Au Temps de l'innocence* in 1922. *A BACKWARD GLANCE* has been translated into French and Italian.

Wharton's fiction and nonfiction have now been translated worldwide into many languages, including French, German, Chinese, Russian, Italian and Japanese. The works most often translated are *The Age of Innocence* and *Ethan Frome*.

travels   Edith Wharton was an ardent traveler throughout her life. The epigraph to her autobiography, *A BACKWARD GLANCE*, "A backward glance o'er travell'd roads," from Walt WHITMAN's own memoir (the prose epilogue to the 1889 edition of *Leaves of Grass*), indicates her affinity for travel.

In 1866, George Frederic and Lucretia JONES, who had suffered reverses in New York real estate during the Civil War, went to EUROPE, taking their four-year-old daughter, Edith. By the time she was 21, Edith Wharton had spent eight years abroad, absorbing the landscape, art and architecture of FRANCE, ITALY and GERMANY. In

A *Backward Glance* she recalls "the lost Rome" of her "infancy," the "warm scent of the box hedges on the Pincian, and the texture of weather-worn sun-gilt stone." From an arduous trip to SPAIN during the second year of her family's European residence, she "brought back an incurable passion for the road" (*BG* 31).

It was not until 1880 that the Joneses returned to Europe, because of her father's ill health. They spent periods of time in LONDON, on the French RIVIERA, in Germany, and in Italy, where she felt the "stir of old associations." After her marriage to Edward Robbins ("Teddy") WHARTON of Boston in 1885, the young couple began a pattern of life that would endure for several years, spending June through February in NEWPORT and February through June traveling in Europe, mostly in Italy. She recalled in her memoir that she had deplored the "watering-place amenities" of Newport and welcomed the months of travel each year (*BG* 90–91). They visited Italy with Paul and Minnie BOURGET.

In 1888 the Whartons shared the charter of the steam yacht *VANADIS* for a Mediterranean cruise, visiting NORTH AFRICA and a number of Greek and Turkish islands. She replicated this experience in 1926, when she and several friends, including Daisy CHANLER, chartered the yacht *OSPREY* for another cruise in the Mediterranean.

One of Wharton's favorite traveling companions was Henry JAMES. In May 1904 the Whartons arrived at LAMB HOUSE, his residence in Rye, England, in their new Panhard-Levassor. They collected James and took him on a motor trip in England, the first of several they made together. In March 1907, when James visited the Whartons in Paris, they made a "motor-flight" with him to Pau, the Pyrenees and Provence. When he came to the MOUNT they took many automobile trips through New England. James said of Wharton's passion for travel that she

> . . . rode the whirlwind, she played with the storm, she laid waste whatever of the land the other raging elements had spared, she consumed in 15 days what would serve to support an ordinary Christian community (I mean to regulate and occupy and excite them) for about 10 years [*EW* 323].

Wharton wrote seven books of travel that were shaped not only by her childhood residence abroad and her extensive reading, but also by her proclivity for Italy, France, Greece, Turkey and Morocco. She may well have planned another book on Spain, as there is a brief typescript in the BEINECKE LIBRARY, YALE UNIVERSITY, "A MOTOR-FLIGHT THROUGH SPAIN." Her actual travels continued long after she ceased writing works of travel and focused entirely on fiction, criticism and poetry. She divided her time in France between her two homes, the PAVILLON COLOMBE outside Paris and STE.-CLAIRE CHÂTEAU in HYÈRES. She also spent several

weeks each summer in England, made a number of trips to Spain, and went to North Africa, Germany and Italy. She did not travel alone, but with a maid, secretary/companion, chauffeur, one or two dogs and at least one friend, particularly after her separation and divorce from Teddy. She made trips with Walter BERRY, Rosa de FITZ-JAMES, Jean du BREUIL DE SAINT-GERMAIN, Daisy Chanler, Bernard BERENSON, Percy LUBBOCK, Nicky MARIANO and others.

To Wharton one of the great hazards of age was a tendency to become sedentary. She had been distressed because in their later years Paul and Minnie Bourget traveled in a straight line each season between their homes in Paris and Costebelle, near Hyères, refusing to make interesting side trips. In her memoir of Bourget, she deplored his inertia about exploring new places; he would only do the "*already done.*" Wharton was not afflicted with inertia, however, but embraced the possibility of travel until the summer of her death. In April 1937, before she died in August, Wharton wrote Bernard Berenson that she was hoping to meet Elisina TYLER in VENICE and "take a look at the Tintorets" (*Letters* 664). This was a journey she was unable to make.

As a zealous traveler over six decades, by ship, horse-drawn carriage, rail and automobile, Wharton discovered little-visited places and "by-ways," the "parentheses" of travel, which she introduced to her countrymen in an era of burgeoning travel. Her travel accounts have a vigor and artistry equalled by few, if any, American travel writers of her day. Their genesis was in her zest for "travell'd roads" and conviction that they should be as numerous as they were varied. (*See also CRUISE OF THE VANADIS, THE; ITALIAN BACKGROUNDS; ITALIAN VILLAS AND THEIR GARDENS; MOTOR-FLIGHT THROUGH FRANCE, A; FIGHTING FRANCE, FROM DUNKERQUE TO BELFORT; FRENCH WAYS AND THEIR MEANING;* and *IN MOROCCO.*

Trenor, Gus *See HOUSE OF MIRTH, THE.*

Trescorre, Count *See VALLEY OF DECISION, THE.*

Treymes, Madame de *See MADAME DE TREYMES.*

tributes *See* BROWNELL, WILLIAM C.; BREUIL DE SAINT-GERMAIN, JEAN DU; "CUTTING, BAYARD, JR."; "GEORGE CABOT LODGE"; "MEMORIES OF BOURGET OVERSEAS."

"Triumph of Night, The" Short story published in *SCRIBNER'S MAGAZINE* in August 1914 and collected in *GHOSTS* (Appleton-Century, 1937). It had also been reprinted by SCRIBNER'S in a pamphlet titled *The Three Best Short Stories of a Year* (1914).

The tale turns on the corrosive power of hidden depravity to bring about a nervous collapse. It begins on a snowy night in a small train station in rural New

Hampshire. George Faxon, who has the role of "reflector" in the story (we see the action through his eyes), is a young man on his way to an interview for the post of secretary to a wealthy woman, Mrs. Culme. He is stranded when her sleigh fails to arrive. Another young man on the platform, Frank Rainer, who knows Mrs. Culme's habitual forgetfulness, offers Faxon hospitality at Overdale, the estate of his wealthy uncle, John Lavington, which Faxon accepts. Faxon speculates, glimpsing Rainer's ungloved "wasted" hand, that he is unhealthy, probably with tuberculosis (a frequent fatal disease in the young at that time). Two other guests, Mr. Grisben and Mr. Balch, arrive on the next train and share the sleigh to Overdale; they give their best wishes to Rainer, which puzzles Faxon.

At Overdale Faxon is made welcome by the expansive John Lavington. He takes the wrong staircase from his room down to the dining room and arrives instead in his host's study, where Grisben and Balch, both attorneys, are preparing Rainer's will. Faxon is called upon to witness it; he realizes it is Rainer's birthday and that he has just attained his majority. As they seal the papers, Faxon perceives a figure just like Lavington standing in the shadows behind his chair. At dinner, the figure appears again as they toast Rainer's health, regarding him with the "eyes of deadly menace." Faxon senses the ghost is trying to keep him from witnessing the will, and to warn him that Lavington will kill his nephew in order to inherit his estate. He attempts to stave off the impending horror by ordering a sleigh to leave, but the telephone and telegraph wires are down. Believing himself a "predestined victim," he departs on foot, in terror. He has guaranteed "the triumph of night," since he has failed to save Rainer by refusing to witness the will. Lavington sends Rainer to "rescue" Faxon and Rainer suffers a fatal lung hemorrhage from exposure.

Faxon has a breakdown from the guilt he feels and goes abroad. Months later in Malay Peninsula he reads old newspapers and finds that Lavington's business empire had collapsed just before Rainer signed his will. He realizes his own hands have Rainer's blood on them. Although the "powers of pity had singled him out to warn and save," he had failed to heed their call. Had he done so, he might have "broken the spell of iniquity" and the "powers of darkness might not have prevailed."

Turner, Joseph Mallord William (1775–1851)
English landscape painter and watercolorist. He had little formal education, although by the age of 14 he was a student at the Royal Academy of the Arts. He lived with his father, a barber in London, and was a virtual recluse. Early in his career he imitated the classical landscapes of Claude Lorrain and Nicholas Poussin. Later he became strikingly interested in the representation of light and produced abstract paintings such as

Snow Storm. In Turner's scenes of Venice outlines become less solid and more fluid in the intensity of natural light from sky and water.

Edith Wharton admired Turner and often referred to him in her travel writing. Her description In *ITALIAN BACKGROUNDS* of his "Road to Orvieto" illuminates her aesthetic theories. She had stopped the carriage at the point where the picture was painted and looked on the same landscape. She admires his capacity to achieve the ". . . true impressionism which consists not in the unimaginative noting of actual 'bits,' but in the reconstruction of a scene as it has flowed into the mould of memory, the merging of fragmentary facts into a homogeneous impression. This is what Turner has done to the view of Orvieto from the Bolsena road, so summing up and interpreting the spirit of the scene that the traveller pausing by the arched bridge above the valley loses sense of the boundaries between art and life, and lives for a moment in that mystical region where the two are one" (*IB* 145–46).

Wharton values the fusion of associations that may be aroused by a work of art, and that may have been combined in its inception on the part of the artist, more than the microscopic details that are the province of the "expert," and that often determine authentication. She thus rejects the methodology of art historians. To a critic such as Bernard BERENSON, Wharton's statement that the "boundaries between fact and fancy" might waver would be highly questionable, yet much of her early travel writing is concerned with the interplay between them.

It might seem that Wharton's appreciation of Turner is similar to that of John RUSKIN, who admired his "truth to nature." However, she believes that Turner's landscapes eclipse the boundaries between art and nature, which then merge in a "mystical region." Ruskin, in contrast, sees Turner's fidelity to nature as an expression of moral truth embodied in the mountains, clouds and trees of the natural world. Turner is a spiritual painter, but for Ruskin his spirituality is rooted in the moral order. His misty visions testify to that origin for Ruskin. Wharton did not subscribe to Ruskin's equation of art with morality. Such visions mask the difference between "art" and "life" for her.

Twelve Poems   A volume of poems by Edith Wharton published in 1926 by the Medici Society, London. There was only one edition of 130 copies and one printing; the dust jacket was pale blue laid paper with horizontal chain lines and the binding was gold-stamped (*EWDB* 312). Two of the poems derived from her cruise aboard the *OSPREY:* "Dieu D'Amour" and "A Castle in Cyprus." Two of the extant copies are in the collections at the BEINECKE LIBRARY, YALE UNIVERSITY and the LILLY LIBRARY, Bloomington, Indiana.

"Twilight of the God, The"   Short story published in *The GREATER INCLINATION* (Scribner's, 1899). It had been rejected by *SCRIBNER'S MAGAZINE* (*SSF* 35) and rewritten. The story is in the form of a dialogue in a NEWPORT drawing room between Isabel and Lucius Warland; the drawing room is not theirs, but that of the owner, a Mrs. Raynor. She has been called out of town to the bedside of her aunt, leaving Isabel to handle her dinner party. A former admirer of Isabel's, John Oberville, now immensely successful, is arriving from Boston for dinner, along with other guests. Lucius, who apparently has no profession and hopes for a diplomatic secretaryship, is impressed but mystified about why John and Isabel had not married a decade earlier. John arrives and tells Isabel he had been a fool to give her up. She is disillusioned by him even as she dispatches Lucius to Washington. She seems to be scheming to spend the next day with John, apparently with the idea of advancing Lucius professionally. Lewis calls the story "not altogether coherent," judging it more than "mere dialogue" but less than a "short play" (*EW* 77).

Although the reviewer for the *Book Buyer* believed the story suggested "a coming dramatist," it was largely ignored by the critics, who preferred "SOULS BELATED," "The MUSE'S TRAGEDY" and "The PELICAN."

Twilight Sleep   Novel published by D. Appleton in 1927. It was serialized in the *PICTORIAL REVIEW* from February through May. Published in June, by August it had displaced Sinclair LEWIS's *Elmer Gantry,* to become first on the best-seller list (*EW* 473). The title, which refers to the popular anesthesia then in use for childbirth, serves as a metaphor for the state of self-delusion in which most American society women lived. Lewis terms the novel "overplotted." It concerns the conflict between generations and focuses on the victimization of young people by their elders.

Pauline Manford, the central family figure, has "everything"; she divides her life into hourly compartments of fitness, good works, hospitality, social correspondence, cultural events, intellectual effort and other enterprises. She does have a "little cemetery of failures" but has planted them over with "quick-growing things" so it is scarcely visible. She has inherited a fortune from her father, which he made in the new motorcar industry. Her first husband, Arthur Wyant, has conferred upon her the social status of his old New York family; her second, Dexter Manford, is a prominent barrister. The two families, including a son by Wyant and a daughter by Manford, have achieved a remarkable state of harmony. Pauline refuses to listen to hints of trouble: the rumors connected with her favorite seer, Mahatma, and his School of Oriental Thought; her daughter Nona's love for a married man; her second husband's apathy toward her; her son Jim's marital misery; her first husband's irrational desire to seek vengeance on Jim's

behalf. These problems converge in a catastrophe she has refused to see as probable or even possible, although it is the only logical outcome. Scandal is narrowly averted and the characters scatter. Nona is the principal casualty; her illusions are shattered.

Wharton had not lived in the United States for more than 15 years when she depicted the 1920s in the novel, and was forced to do research of the kind she had undertaken for *The VALLEY OF DECISION.* Janet Goodwyn has pointed out that the speech of the younger generation is affected and less than idiomatic and that her "satirical focus" on the health and religious fads of the era is too superficial to bear the weight of the novel. The character of Pauline Manford, however, is another matter. Blake Nevius, in *Edith Wharton: A Study of Her Fiction,* sees her simply as the realization of the "Montessori infant" of *FRENCH WAYS AND THEIR MEANING,* the American woman who is not grown up. Goodwyn, however, perceives Pauline as a "self-that-might-have-been," the woman Wharton might have become had she not become a writer. She equates Arthur Wyant with Teddy Wharton and his family with the Wyants. Pauline, like Wharton, is efficient at gardening and at overseeing servants. Wharton pities her for not having a productive creative outlet; she substitutes meaningless beauty appointments and committee work that are "professionally and economically irrelevant." Mere activity becomes a virtue, whereas her husband, Dexter, expects satisfaction from his work; it is his "birthright as a man" (Goodwyn, *Edith Wharton: Traveller in the Land of Letters,* 94–97). Dale Bauer also emphasizes the ideological plight of Pauline, who wishes to forget her abjection "in a culture of masculinist and racist hegemony" (*Edith Wharton's Brave New Politics,* 102). The family cannot be healed, and the novel ends without resolution of their conflicts. Bauer argues that, nevertheless, it is an extremely rich novel.

Twilight Sleep was a best-seller when it was published, although it was not well received by most contemporary critics. Although Edmund Wilson termed it an "acute and entertaining piece of social criticism," Dorothy Gilman, writing in the Boston *Evening Transcript,* called it commonplace and, artistically, "not only painful but disastrous" (*EW* 474). Isabel Paterson, critic for the *New York Herald Tribune,* declared Edith Wharton's artistry to be "that of a first-class French modiste," and viewed the characters as "mannequins." Percy Hutchinson, writing in the *New York Times,* felt Edith Wharton would never write anything again to equal *ETHAN FROME* or *The HOUSE OF MIRTH.* He believed she had lost touch with the New York she was writing about and pointed out lapses in vocabulary that were English rather than American, such as "cinema." Charles R. Walker, writing in the *Independent,* compared Wharton unfavorably with Theodore Dreiser and Sherwood Anderson, insisting that she did not strike false notes, but that her book lacked enough "emotional immediacy" to be convincing. L. P. Hartley, critic for the English *Saturday Review of Literature*, considered the entire novel to be pervaded by the metaphor of the sickroom. William Lyon Phelps, reviewing the novel for the *Forum*, called it a "Puritan sermon preached from the text, 'For what is a man profited, if he shall gain the whole world, and lose his own soul?' " He termed the characters "horrible puppets." Mary Webb, writing in the *Bookman*, believed that to be Edith Wharton's point: she wished to expose the "absurdities" of modern American "fast life" (*CR* 429–45).

For further reading: Bauer, *Edith Wharton's Brave New Politics;* Bauer, "*Twilight Sleep:* Edith Wharton's Brave New Politics"; Goodwyn, *Edith Wharton: Traveller in the Land of Letters.*

Tyler, Elisina (Mrs. Royall) Formerly Elisina Palamadessi di Castelvecchio of Florence, daughter of Conte and Contessa di Castelvecchio, Elisina had been married to an English publisher, Grant Richards, and had three children by him. In 1909 she met the American scholar and art historian Royall TYLER ("Peter" to his friends), who was 25, nine years younger than she, who fell in love with her. In 1910, she gave birth to Tyler's son, William ("Bill") Royall TYLER. They did not marry until their son was nearly five, although she was known as "Mme Tyler." Benstock states that Edith Wharton did not object to her story, but admired her courage in starting again after having an unhappy marriage. Wharton's niece, Beatrix FARRAND, however, looked down on Elisina for her past (*NGC* 308–09). Edith Wharton had met Royall Tyler in England before World War I, but knew Elisina only slightly. They came to Paris after the war began and offered to help with her relief work; she left her older children in school in England. As Edith Wharton put it in her memoir, "never once did she fail me for an hour, never did we disagree, never did her energy flag or her discernment and promptness of action grow less through those weary years" (*BG* 349). They worked together on Edith Wharton's war charities: the AMERICAN HOSTELS FOR REFUGEES, the CHILDREN OF FLANDERS RESCUE COMMITTEE and the MAISONS AMÉRICAINES DE CONVALESCENCE, a cure program for soldiers, women and children with tuberculosis.

In 1916 Elisina's oldest son, Gerard Grant Richards, died at the age of 15 when he was smothered by sand in a beach accident. She was devastated, but threw herself into war work to escape her grief.

In July 1918 the Belgian government awarded Edith Wharton and Elisina Tyler the MEDAL OF QUEEN ELISABETH for their refugee work, but Edith Wharton was ambivalent about it, believing others had contributed more to the war effort. In 1919 she was named chevalier of the Order of Leopold, the Belgian equivalent of the French Legion of Honor, which pleased her.

After the war Edith Wharton's friendship with the Tylers continued. Benstock observes, however, that some of her men friends, including Bernard BERENSON, found Elisina abrasive and overbearing (*NGC* 309). Elisina discovered the PAVILLON COLOMBE for Wharton in 1917 (then named Villa Jean-Marie). Bill Tyler was a favorite of Wharton's as he grew up, and she lived to celebrate his marriage to Bettine Fisher-Rowe and to welcome their son, Royall, born in early 1937.

Elisina was Roman Catholic. Benstock states that Edith Wharton confided her beliefs to her and was attracted to Roman Catholicism; *see* CATHOLICISM, ROMAN. Elisina helped her a great deal when Walter BERRY died, and stood by her during many illnesses, including her final one in 1937. She was executor of her French will. Benstock gives an excellent account of the disposition of Edith Wharton's estate, which was complicated by Beatrix Farrand, who contested the American will (*NGC* 456–61).

Tyler, Royall ("Peter") Husband of Elisina TYLER and father of William ("Bill") Royall TYLER. An American scholar and art historian, he was a descendant of the first American playwright, Royall Tyler. Edith Wharton first met him before World War I at the home of a mutual friend, the archaeologist and collector Raymond Koechlin. At that time Tyler was employed by the British Record Office as an editor of state papers. He fell in love with Elisina Richards, wife of the English publisher Grant Richards, and in 1910 their son was born. They did not marry for five years (see TYLER, ELISINA).

The Tylers came to Paris after the war began and presented themselves to Edith Wharton, asking how they might help the war effort. She "took on" both husband and wife to help with her war relief charities, as she noted in her memoir (*BG* 348). Tyler helped until he joined the United States intelligence service, and Elisina continued to work with her throughout the war.

The friendship between the Tylers and Edith Wharton continued after the war until her death in 1937. She asked that he be a pallbearer at her funeral.

Tyler, William Royall ("Bill") (1910–) Son of Royall and Elisina TYLER. He was a great favorite of Edith Wharton even as a child, when she would invite him to lunch. In 1929 he was at Harrow preparing for Oxford when a spot was found on his lung. His parents sent him to the PAVILLON COLOMBE for rest, fresh air and good food; it turned out not to be serious. Edith Wharton wrote his parents that he had arrived in "very good form." His father joined them and she noted that she could hear them "shouting with laughter" as she wrote (*Letters* 524–25).

In 1933 he became engaged to a British girl, Bettine Fisher-Rowe. Wharton wrote to congratulate him, saying she was "the luckiest damsel on our planet" (*Letters* 565). She lived to meet their son, Royall Tyler, born in 1937, writing Bernard BERENSON he was "the nicest child I ever met" (*Letters* 604). He was temporarily nicknamed "Herc" or "Hercules."

Tyler presented his recollections of Edith Wharton in a paper before the Boston Club of Odd Volumes in October 1972. It was read at the May 1973 meeting of the Massachusetts Historical Society, which later published it. He had written Percy LUBBOCK, on publication of his *Portrait of Edith Wharton,* of his recollections of "Edoo," his name for her: "I knew her before the age of reason, and as my tastes and mind developed she was always there as an influence, an attraction and a force as natural and compelling as the seasons. After her death I realized that, quite literally, I could not imagine the world without her." In her earliest letter to him, in block letters, she wrote, "I thank you for your beautiful white tree: and send you a kiss as big as my writing and a brave French soldier to guard your toys when you are out walking. Your friend, Edith." He believed she was strongly drawn toward the Church of Rome, although she had never said so specifically.

Tyler inherited the portion of Edith Wharton's library at the Pavillon Colombe dealing with art, art history and archaeology, which was, unfortunately, housed in a London warehouse and destroyed in World War II. He became the owner of the Edith Wharton estate (*EW* 372).

For further reading: Tyler, "Personal Memories of Edith Wharton."

U

Ulysses: A Drama   A drama in verse by the English play-wright Stephen Phillips, published by Macmillan in 1902. Edith Wharton reviewed it in the *Bookman,* April 1902. She believed Ulysses to be a "centrifugal hero" and the saga too "episodic" to fulfill the requirements of true drama. Although she praised a few lines, calling them "detached beauties," she believed Phillips had not "crossed the line dividing rhetoric from poetry" (*UCW* 66–70). The chief interest of the review may lie in the light it sheds on Wharton's approach to the poetic process.

"Unconfessed Crime"   A story first published in *Story-Teller* in March 1936 and then as "CONFESSION" in *Hearst's International Cosmopolitan* magazine in May 1936. Based on the case of Lizzie Borden, the story was first cast as a drama, *Kate Spain,* which was never finished. It was collected as "Confession" in *The WORLD OVER* (Appleton's) in 1936.

"Unreprinted Parody: 'More Love Letters of an Englishwoman,' An "   A brief essay published in the *Bookman,* February 1901, which accompanied Frederic Taber Cooper's review of *An Englishwoman's Love-Letters,* written anonymously. Wegener calls it a "rare exercise in parodic writing" (*UCW* 289).

The narrator, a pedantic woman, addresses her beloved, "Ownest," a man who is possibly her fiancé. She tries to remedy his lack of learning, describing her experiences in Pisa in overblown language. She makes numerous references she knows he will not understand ("Don't try to make out my metaphors, Darling; at least not till you've practised a little on Meredith first!") She has called on his mother, who presumably dislikes her, since she has tried to excuse herself by pleading a headache. "I could see that she was struck by my gown—the one I copied from Elaine's, in the *Idylls of the King.* (Tennyson, dear: I mean to read him to you next summer!)"

Wharton may have met similar domineering, pseudo-learned women in England and also satirizes them in her fiction.

Updike, Daniel Berkeley (1860–1941)   Founder of the Merrymount Press in Boston in 1893 and printer of several of Edith Wharton's early books. He was one of the finest American printers of his time, which Wharton eventually came to realize. She was indignant, however, over his design for the title page of *The VALLEY OF DECISION* and wrote William Crary BROWNELL, "Words fail to express how completely I *don't* like it" (*Letters* 47). The matter was smoothed over, however, and in 1902 she invited Updike to accompany her to call on Annie Fields, widow of the publisher James T. Fields and later companion to Sarah Orne Jewett.

In 1915 he printed *The BOOK OF THE HOMELESS,* and she wrote Barrett WENDELL he had "done his part admirably" (*Letters* 373). In 1925 Wharton wrote Minnie Cadwalader JONES, her sister-in-law, that Updike numbered as one of her few "surviving intimate friends," along with Olivia CUTTING (sister of Bayard CUTTING, Jr.), Robert GRANT, Bessy Lodge, Henrietta Cram Haven, Billy RICHARDSON and Elizabeth ("Lily") NORTON.

Updike contributed a perceptive essay to Percy LUBBOCK's *Portrait of Edith Wharton,* which evoked the days at The MOUNT when he knew both Edith and Teddy WHARTON well. He recalled Edith's saying to him. " 'The XYZ's have decided, they tell me, to have books in their library.' " Lubbock remarked that such sayings "were repeated, generally inaccurately, and did not increase her popularity" (*Portrait of Edith Wharton,* 17). In 1937, two years after Minnie Jones's death, Updike printed Minnie's reminiscences, *Lantern Slides,* in a private edition.

Ushant, Duke of Tintagel   *See BUCCANEERS, THE.*

"Valley of Childish Things, and Other Emblems, The"
Short story published in The CENTURY in July 1896. The "story" is really a series of brief fables or anecdotes that expose various human foibles, such as pride, insensitivity, callousness and obtuseness. Most reflect the shortcomings of men rather than women. One concerns a couple who get along so poorly that the man seeks a divorce, but the judge says he has married himself and the union cannot be dissolved. The women in the fables are usually disillusioned about the men, such as the girl who climbs out of the valley of children, matures and meets a man who has done the same. Once they return to the valley, the man then rejects the grown-up companion in favor of a small girl; he accuses the older woman of not having cared enough for her complexion.

Valley of Decision, The Edith Wharton's first novel, published in 1902 (SCRIBNER'S). It is set in 18th-century Italy in the imaginary duchy of Pianura. Odo Valsecca, the heir presumptive, is a boy of nine when we meet him. A cousin dies and he becomes heir apparent, then finally the duke. In the meantime, he has been educated for the possibility of his inheriting the title with an odyssey through Italy. A group of freethinkers under the leadership of a philosopher, Professor Vivaldi, and his daughter Fulvia, promulgate new ideas of progress and liberty. Odo falls in love with Fulvia, but she refuses to become the regent's mistress. Later she changes her mind, comes back to him, and is killed by a bullet meant for Odo while she gives a speech. Even when she receives her doctorate and becomes Odo's mistress, Fulvia remains a rather stately, distant, wooden figure.

The plot is the least compelling aspect of the novel. Wharton's colorful evocation of the period, with details of art, dress and entertainment, does hold the reader's interest. As a young man, Odo sees Piero della Francesca's portrait of the first duke and comprehends his royal lineage. Throughout his wanderings to Turin, Genoa, MILAN, Naples, Monte Casino, ROME, Florence, VENICE and other towns, he is received in palaces owned by noblemen and bishops, introduced to their treasures and their gardens, and to architecture, sculpture and paintings. His education culminates, as Wharton's did, in the development of an appreciation of the art of TIEPOLO, imaginary examples of which Wharton weaves into the narrative.

In *A BACKWARD GLANCE,* Edith Wharton recalled her misgivings about this work. It was not, she feared, "in any sense of the term a novel at all, but only a romantic chronicle, unrolling its episodes like the frescoed legends on the palace walls which formed its background." She doubted whether she "should ever have enough constructive power to achieve anything beyond isolated character studies, or the stringing together of picturesque episodes" (*BG* 205). The taste and scholarly knowledge required, however, for the "unrolling" of episodes and the fashioning of an authentic tapestry of art, pageantry, landscape and history, lay the groundwork for her later novels, many of which were much less colorful and less wide-ranging.

Edith Wharton's early reviewers were receptive to her erudition. Frederic Taber Cooper, writing in the *Bookman,* praised her grasp of history. The shortcomings of Wharton's portrait of the Settecento itself were pointed out by Aline Gorren, reviewer for the *Critic* (*CR* 51–65). She observed that, viewed as a philosophical romance and compared with Walter PATER's *Marius the Epicurean,* which evokes the unified impetus of early Christianity, *The Valley of Decision* was a failure. The epoch itself, with its fragmented states, was without cohesion and not a particularly outstanding era in Italian history. In one way, the contradictions and discontinuities of the time make the imaginary duchy of Pianura a more convincing device, in that Wharton is free to combine elements of existing principalities and invent plausible details. With few exceptions, the characters remain largely inanimate. The ideological component of the novel remains part of what Nevius calls its "deeply-felt" background, unable in itself to give it enduring life.

The COMMEDIA DELL'ARTE also figures in the novel. Gertrude Hall termed the late 18th-century Italy Wharton depicted a "glittering, many-colored pageant," with "powdered gentlemen, rouged ladies, abbés, friars, French hair-dressers, Columbine and Scaramouch, gilt coaches, levers, vapors, pet monkeys and turbaned blackamoors to mind them" (*CR* 54). A performance in Vercelli, for example, is marked by an "inexhaustible flow of jest and repartee . . . with which the comedians caught up each other's leads, like dancers whirling without a false step through the mazes of some rapid contradance." As a boy, the hero, Odo Valsecca, first encounters his early tutor, Cantapresto, on the road with a troupe of commedia dell'arte players near his grandfather's castle. Later he keeps meeting them at Chivasso, Vercelli and at a villa on the BRENTA RIVIERA, when he becomes fascinated with the actress Mirandolina of Chioggia, who plays Columbine. Critics found Cantapresto and Mirandolina more convincing as characters than the many literary, royal and political figures who people the book, including the real-life agricultural theorist Arthur Young and the playwright Vittorio Alfieri.

For further reading: Balestra, "Italian Foregrounds and Backgrounds: *The Valley of Decision*"; Lee, "Edith Wharton's *The Valley of Decision*"; Murphy, "Edith Wharton's Italian Triptych: *The Valley of Decision*"; Vance, "Edith Wharton's Italian Mask: *The Valley of Decision*."

Valsecca, Odo   *See VALLEY OF DECISION, THE.*

Van Alen, James   A friend of Edith and Teddy Wharton from NEWPORT and NEW YORK and a member of an old New York family. Edith told him once she would give everything she owned to make a cruise through the Aegean islands, and he invited them to come as his guests on a chartered yacht. They insisted on sharing the charter of the VANADIS; Lewis reports that their share of the trip, which was to last four months, was the same as their income for the entire year (*EW* 58). Fortunately, on their return, Edith Wharton discovered that she had been left a legacy by her father's cousin Joshua JONES that amply covered their expenses.

In 1927 Van Alen put up $124,000 to assist Lt. Col. Ralph Heyward Isham, an American, in acquiring the remarkable cache of papers relating to James Boswell that had been discovered in Ireland at Malahide Castle. Boswell's *Life of Johnson* was one of Edith Wharton's favorite books. Her close friend Geoffrey SCOTT was engaged to edit the papers. It had been a YALE UNIVERSITY professor, Chauncy B. Tinker, who had first found the papers, however, and eventually the project was taken over by Yale (*EW* 475). *See also CRUISE OF THE VANADIS, THE.*

Van Degen, Clare   *See CUSTOM OF THE COUNTRY, THE.*

Van Degen, Peter   *See CUSTOM OF THE COUNTRY, THE.*

Van der Luyden, Henry   *See AGE OF INNOCENCE, THE* and *NEW YEAR'S DAY.*

Van Osburgh, Evelyn   *See HOUSE OF MIRTH, THE.*

Vanadis, The   The steam yacht chartered by Edith and Teddy Wharton and James VAN ALEN for a Mediterranean cruise in 1888. She was a ship of 333 tons, 167 feet long, with a deckhouse, saloon, three staterooms, two rooms for the maid and valet, plus a third room in which the party took their meals. The crew numbered 16, including two engineers, boatswain, five able seamen, two stewards and two cooks (*CV* 16). According to the 1887–88 *Lloyds Yacht Register,* the *Vanadis* was built in 1880 in Leith, Scotland, by Ramage and Ferguson and launched March 27, 1880; the owners in 1887–88 were J. A. Hankey and C. & H. McIver. The yacht belonged to the port of London. (Information supplied by the National Maritime Museum, Greenwich, England, the Scottish Record Office and the Mystic Seaport Museum, Mystic, Connecticut.)

The Whartons' itinerary included visits to Tunis, Malta, Sicily, Corfu, Milo, Rhodes, Mount Athos, Tenos, Mitylene, the Ionian Islands and Dalmatia, among other places. *See also CRUISE OF THE VANADIS, THE.*

Vanderbilt, George (1862–1914)   Edith and Teddy Wharton came to know George Vanderbilt, the son of William Henry Vanderbilt, and his wife Edith in NEWPORT. They went to Biltmore House, the enormous mansion built by Vanderbilt on 130,000 acres of land in North Carolina near Asheville, for Christmas 1905. Edith wrote Sally NORTON about the "divine landscape" and the fete for 350 people on the estate, "a tree 30 ft high, Punch & Judy, conjuror, presents & 'refreshments.'" She also thanked Sally for the Greek essays she had sent, and remarked that she had just been reading Walter PATER's collection of lectures on Plato (*Letters* 100). Henry JAMES had visited Biltmore earlier, and decided the enormous structure was a "waste," but Edith enjoyed the festivities (*EW* 159).

In January 1907 the Whartons rented the Vanderbilts' apartment in PARIS at 58, rue de Varenne, in the FAUBOURG SAINT-GERMAIN. Benstock states that the 1750 *hôtel particulier* (townhouse) "had the graciousness and grace of a country estate." The apartment, with a size of over 2,000 square feet, was richly furnished with art and antiques. The townhouse was across the street from the building at 53, rue de Varenne in which Edith Wharton would eventually lease her own apartment.

In 1913 she sent her ill-fated appeal for Henry James's 70th birthday fund to Vanderbilt. He contributed $250 (*EW* 340).

Varnum, Lawyer   *See ETHAN FROME.*

"Velvet Ear Pads"   Short story collected in *HERE AND BEYOND* (D. Appleton, 1926). The story is a farce, possibly intended for the American magazine market. The action is set on the French RIVIERA, a favorite destination for Americans. In the story Wharton parodies the absent-minded American academic in the protagonist, Professor Loring G. Hibbard of Purewater University, Clio, New York, who wears velvet ear pads to protect himself from "noise and promiscuous human intercourse." By chance he meets the beautiful, feckless young refugee Princesse Balalatinsky. (In this satire of impecunious European royalty she anticipates the more manipulative Marchesa di San Fedele in TWILIGHT SLEEP, published the next year.)

The reviewer for the *New York Times* called the story "negligible" but went on to qualify his estimate. He termed it "frank buffoonery, not a little in the manner of O. Henry, with his modern Baghdad. . . . It is amusing, if slight; and admirably and deftly told" (*CR* 415–17). The story had been published in REDBOOK magazine in August 1925 as "Velvet Ear-Muffs."

"Venetian Night's Entertainment, A"   Short story published in SCRIBNER'S MAGAZINE (December 1903) and collected in *The DESCENT OF MAN AND OTHER STORIES* (SCRIBNER'S, 1904). The story is framed as an after-dinner tale told by Judge Anthony Bracknell of Boston, reliving his youthful adventures, to his adult grandsons. This device lends it a degree of authenticity.

The story is set in Venice in 1760, when the gullible young Tony Bracknell flees from his sailing ship and his governor, the Rev. Ozias Mounce of Salem, to explore the city during Carnival. He is approached by young "Count Rialto," and "rescued" from various intrigues and fabricated transgressions arranged by the count. Bracknell is eventually rescued by the clearsighted Reverend Mounce, who accuses the count and his accomplices of "decoying young innocents" with "devil's bait." Some of the colorful descriptions of the city, the masques and the carnival atmosphere echo *The VALLEY OF DECISION* (1902).

Many reviewers of the collection felt the story suffered from inclusion with such masterpieces as "The OTHER TWO," "The MISSION OF JANE," and "EXPIATION." White terms it "absolutely all plot" but believes it "succeeds in being entertaining because it attempts no more" (*SSF* 6).

Venice   City of nearly half a million people built on 118 small islands within a lagoon on the Gulf of Venice, ITALY. It is known for its paintings and sculptures, splendid palaces, historic churches and hundreds of canals and bridges. As early as 697 Venice was a city-state, rising to become a major maritime power. By the Middle Ages Venice ruled the Mediterranean as "queen of the seas." Her zenith was the first half of the 15th century, when she dominated Verona, Padua, Brescia and Bergamo. The city declined when Constantinople was captured by the Turks in 1453. It was not united with Italy until 1866.

Wharton was probably first introduced to Venice as a child, when the JONES family spent six years in EUROPE between 1866 and 1872. In 1880 they returned to the Continent in a futile attempt to restore George Frederic JONES's failing health, and visited Venice in 1881. As Wharton recalled in her memoir, with John RUSKIN's " 'Stones of Venice' and 'Walks in Florence' " [i.e., *Mornings in Florence*] in hand, they followed his "arbitrary itineraries" (*BG* 87). Harry Leyden Stevens,

Illustration by Maxfield Parrish for "A Venetian Night's Entertainment" (1903) (Courtesy Picture Collection, Library of Virginia)

Wharton's first fiancé, pursued her to the city at this time and stayed with Joneses until they went to Cannes.

Venice had always been one of Wharton's most loved cities. It was known to DANTE Aligheri, Johann Wolfgang von GOETHE and Carlo GOLDONI, who were among her favorite writers, and was also associated with the COMMEDIA DELL'ARTE, a form of improvisatory theater she greatly admired. A number of contemporary writers and artists she knew, including Henry JAMES, William Dean HOWELLS and John Singer SARGENT, also embraced Venice as a subject. Howells had been the American consul in Venice and lived there for several years.

Wharton discusses the architecture of Venice in "Italian Backgrounds," a chapter in ITALIAN BACKGROUNDS, focusing particularly on the art and architecture of the 17th and 18th centuries, when Antonio Canaletto, Vecellio Titian, Giovanni Battista TIEPOLO, Pietro Longhi, Tintoretto [Jacopo Robusti] and Paolo Veronese, all major artists associated with Venice, were at work. She praises Baldassare Longhena's baroque architecture, which Ruskin had despised (although she admired him greatly, she disagreed with him on this matter).

Some of Wharton's fiction has a Venetian setting, including the novels *The VALLEY OF DECISION* and *The CHILDREN,* as well as the short stories "A GLIMPSE," "The CONFESSIONAL," and "A VENETIAN NIGHT'S ENTERTAINMENT." In the latter she evokes the atmosphere of the city in the 18th century, a "faint vision of towers and domes dissolved in golden air." The story takes place during Carnival, with masked figures; when it was "the kind of place . . . in which things elsewhere impossible might naturally happen" (*CSS* I, 475–76).

In April 1937, before she died in August, Wharton wrote Bernard BERENSON that she was hoping to meet Elisina TYLER in Venice and "take a look at the Tintorets" (*Letters* 664). This was a journey she was unable to make.

Illustration by Maxfield Parrish for "A Venetian Night's Entertainment" (1903) (Courtesy Picture Collection, Library of Virginia)

"Verdict, The"   Short story published in SCRIBNER'S MAGAZINE in June 1908 and collected in *The HERMIT AND THE WILD WOMAN AND OTHER STORIES* (SCRIBNER'S, 1908). It illustrates how art tests and deceives an artist of mediocre talent. A fashionable painter, Jack Gisburn, gives up his career, marries a wealthy widow and moves to a villa on the French Riviera. He had had devoted clients who admired his pictures, so his decision puzzles the narrator, Mr. Rickham, an old friend. On calling at his villa, Rickham perceives that Gisburn thinks of little else but art and his decision to give it up. Gisburn finally explains that he had been invited to paint a portrait of a fine artist, Stroud, the day after he died, by Stroud's widow. As he works he looks at Stroud's final painting, of a donkey, and realizes Stroud had "possessed his subject." Gisburn's own paintings, in contrast, had been "adopted"; he had not given birth to them. He knows "enough to leave off" and proposes a substitute, Grindle, to Mrs. Stroud to finish her husband's portrait. Gisburn is convinced that the better artists, the Strouds, "stand alone," but "there's no exterminating our kind of art." The story evoked little reaction from reviewers of the collection and suffered by comparison with such stories as "The LAST ASSET" and "The PRETEXT."

Verses   A volume of Edith Wharton's poetry printed when she was 16. Her mother, Lucretia JONES, arranged for it to be privately printed, anonymously, by the Newport printer C. E. Hammett, Jr. The volume was small, only 6 1/4" by 3 1/4". The binding was composed of light greenish-gray wove paper wrappers with red ornaments at the corners. The title was in ornate black capitals, below which was an epigraph in script, "Be friendly, pray, to these fancies of mine," a line by Bettine Brentano. Among the poems were "Opportunities," "Lines on Chaucer," "Bettine to Goethe," "Nothing More" and "SOME WOMAN TO SOME MAN."

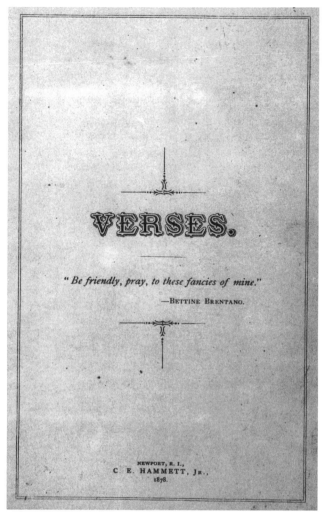

Title page of Verses, *printed privately and anonymously (by Lucretia Jones, Wharton's mother) in 1878 when Edith was 16* (Courtesy Clifton Waller Barrett Library, Special Collections Department, University of Virginia)

There was only one printing and it is very rare; copies exist in the BEINECKE LIBRARY, YALE UNIVERSITY, Alderman Library, University of Virginia and the SCRIBNER ARCHIVES, Princeton University.

"Vesalius in Zante"   Poem published in the *North American Review* in November 1902 and collected in *ARTEMIS TO ACTAEON* (SCRIBNER'S, 1909). Lewis calls the poem "occult," but notes that Edward BURLINGAME had praised it to his colleagues at Scribner's, prompting William Crary BROWNELL to ask whether she had enough poems for a volume. Edith Wharton replied that she did not think her poems worth putting in a book. Brownell then inquired whether her prose works were "so Olympian as to lose by the proximity of their comrades from Parnassus?" Wharton answered that, in her opinion, her prose was in fact better than her verse,

but that if Mr. Burlingame liked it, "there is no telling how I may rise in my own estimation" (*EW* 113). Brownell assembled her poems from various periodicals and wrote her that they were as superior to contemporary poetry as her prose was to current prose. It was, nevertheless, not for six years that she judged her poetry worth collecting.

In a long note to the poem, Wharton explains that it refers to the anatomist Vesalius, of the University of Padua, one of the first to dissect the human body, whose work was an attack on the physiology of Galen. It aroused the anger of the Roman Catholic Church, causing Vesalius to give up research and accept the position of physician at the court of Charles V in Spain. He read the work of Fallopius and came to find Spain intolerable. Legend has it that he performed an autopsy on a cataleptic girl before she had died and began a penitential pilgrimage to Jerusalem; Wharton notes that he was probably "sick of his long servitude." In any case, on his way home from Jerusalem he died at Zante, in 1564. The poem represents his agonized reflections during his final illness; he asks "to face westward as my sun goes down" (*North American Review,* November 1902, 625).

"Vice of Reading, The"   Essay published in the *North American Review* in October 1903. Wharton addresses the "born" reader, who equates reading with breathing, rather than the "mechanical" reader, who regards it as a moral obligation and sets about it conscientiously. To the latter, literature is a "cable-car that can be 'boarded' only by running." Wharton urges readers to indulge, instead, in "intellectual vagrancy" and to think of the book as the "keynote of unpremeditated harmonies, as the gateway into some *paysage choisi* of the spirit." The mechanical reader misses the by-ways and cross-cuts, the "improvised chase after a fleeting allusion, suggested sometimes by the turn of a phrase or by the mere complexion of a word." Wharton calls critics to task as well, enjoining them to analyze the subject and manner of a work and not merely to recapitulate its contents or inventory its incidents.

Village Romeo and Juliet, A   A novella (by Gottfried Keller; published by Charles SCRIBNER, 1914) taken from the Swiss novelist's *Die Leute von Seldwyla* [*Seldwyla People*] (1856). Anna BAHLMANN, Edith Wharton's early governess and longtime secretary, translated it from the German and Edith Wharton wrote the introduction; she may also have helped with the translation. She states that Nietzsche had called *Seldwyla People* one of the "four masterpieces of German prose."

Wharton's introduction is partly biographical and partly analytical. She praises the "playful simplicity" and "grace of desultory detail" in the novella, and compares the episodes to the flowers in the foreground of a primitive painting. The work is far removed from the "larger and more formalised lines of the classic tradition." Keller's real originality is his "gift of extracting from the homeliest words and the most familiar situations their hidden element of poetry" (*EWDB* 242). She even ranks certain of Keller's images with those of Shakespeare.

For further reading: Puknat and Puknat, "Edith Wharton and Gottfried Keller."

Viner, Sophy   *See REEF, THE.*

"Visibility in Fiction"   Essay published in the *Yale Review* in March 1929. Edith Wharton examines the qualities that ensure the survival of a novel, focusing on the writer's ability to create living characters. She admits that dramatic incident may be a factor, as in the case of *Moby Dick* or *Lord Jim.* Sir Walter Scott, Robert Louis Stevenson and Joseph CONRAD intertwine adventure and character-drawing, but their central characters are not animated. Dickens's characters are "close-ups before the camera" but live only within their particular story.

Wharton argues that novels live only when readers later call their characters by their first names, such as Emma (Woodhouse or Bovary), Anna Karenina, Daisy Miller or Barry Lyndon. Yet the reason characters live is elusive; it has little to do with details of physical appearance (for example, Jane Austen describes her characters sparingly, but the least of her characters is more enduring than those of George Meredith, despite his "epithets and epigrams"). Flaubert is the equal of Austen in his picture of Emma Bovary and others, as are Balzac, Thackeray and Tolstoy: "when these touched the dead bones they arose and walked." These writers not only had an "intimate sense of the reality of what they described" but also a "secret intuition that the barrier between themselves and their creatures was somehow thinner than the page of a book" (*UCW* 169).

Vivaldi, Fulvia   *See VALLEY OF DECISION, THE.*

Vivaldi, Professor   *See VALLEY OF DECISION, THE.*

Vosges   Region in eastern France, in the Lorraine. It borders on the Vosges mountain range and Alsace. In the spring of 1915 Edith Wharton and Walter BERRY obtained permission to go to Lorraine and the Vosges; the resulting article, called "In Lorraine and the Vosges," was published in *SCRIBNER'S MAGAZINE* in October 1915 and collected in *FIGHTING FRANCE, FROM DUNKERQUE TO BELFORT* (Scribner's, 1915).

war relief, World War I During WORLD WAR I Edith Wharton became a passionate humanitarian, launching major war relief efforts and seeking material assistance from her countrymen. Throughout the war, she stayed in Paris, ministering as best she could to a France "paralyzed with horror." As residents of Paris fled the city before the German advance, Belgian and French refugees swarmed in. She first established an *ouvroir*, or workroom, in Paris, with a woman manager. It employed, at its height, nearly a hundred seamstresses sewing clothes for women and children. Though successful, it did not satisfy Wharton's desire to help in the war effort.

Charles DU BOS, aided by French and Belgian friends, had helped form an emergency project, the Accueil Franco-Belge. It was rapidly beset by too many applicants and too few funds, and Wharton was asked to establish a separate committee to raise money from America, called the AMERICAN HOSTELS FOR REFUGEES to provide aid to the hundreds of civilian refugees arriving in Paris from the Battle of the Marne and other conflicts. In this and in her other war relief efforts she was ably assisted by Elisina TYLER. In April 1915 she and Elisina organized another relief project, the CHILDREN OF FLANDERS RESCUE COMMITTEE, caring for 750 Flemish children. In 1916, she began a fourth, the MAISONS AMÉRICAINES DE CONVALESCENCE, a cure program for soldiers with tuberculosis. Her fund-raising efforts in America were spearheaded by her sister-in-law, Minnie Cadwalader JONES; Walter MAYNARD was president of the Edith Wharton War Charities of America.

In 1915 Wharton edited *The BOOK OF THE HOMELESS*, with contributions from various writers and artists. The same year she wrote an article for the *New York Times* magazine section about her *ouvroir*, American hostels and Children of Flanders Rescue Committee. She explained that she was not attempting a survey of all Paris war charities but simply giving an account of the "particular patch of misery" she had tried to relieve. In April 1916, Wharton received France's highest civilian honor; she was made a CHEVALIER OF THE LEGION OF HONOR. In 1918 King Albert of Belgium awarded her the MEDAL OF QUEEN ELISABETH.

For further reading: Buitenhuis, "Edith Wharton and the First World War"; Price, *The End of the Age of Innocence: Edith Wharton and the First World War*.

Ward, Mary Augusta Arnold (Mrs. Humphry Ward, 1851–1920). English novelist and antisuffragist leader. Her husband, Thomas Humphry Ward, was an Oxford don and editor of *Men of the Reign* and other works. Mrs. Ward was a niece of Matthew ARNOLD and the granddaughter of Thomas Arnold. Her novels, which were somewhat religious and polemical, were extremely popular, particularly the spiritual romance *Robert Elsmere* (1888).

Edith Wharton knew Lucy Arnold Whitridge, wife of an American lawyer, who was the older daughter of Matthew Arnold and was Mary Augusta Arnold Ward's cousin. In 1902 Wharton wrote Sally NORTON about seeing Mrs. Whitridge at the theater (*Letters* 56). In 1904 she and Teddy lunched with the Whitridges while in London but she was disappointed not to meet Mrs. Ward, who was in Italy (*Letters* 90). By 1906 Wharton had apparently met Mrs. Ward and in 1908 she wrote Sally about Mrs. Ward's visit to America.

Her friendship with the Wards developed; she saw them again in London, possibly in the townhouse of Lady ESSEX. She was delighted to find that women writers such as Mrs. Ward and the poet Alice Meynell were honored guests in the homes of the aristocracy. In later years she often visited the Wards in their London townhouse in Grosvenor Square or at their country home near Tring (*BG* 223). Henry JAMES was a close friend of the Wards also. They introduced Wharton to George Protheroe, editor of the *Quarterly Review*, and other literary and social figures.

It was the Wards' English home, Stocks, in Buckinghamshire, that Wharton had arranged to lease just before the outbreak of World War I; she and her servants did occupy Stocks for a few weeks until she could return to France to help with the war effort.

Washburn, Edward Abiel The eighth rector of Calvary Church, New York, Dr. Washburn, whom Edith Wharton met in 1875, was an early influence on her. She was a friend of his daughter, Emelyn WASHBURN, who was six years older. Dr. Washburn allowed Wharton to use his typewriter, and together the girls spent hours in his library. Washburn published several books, including *The Two Epistles of Paul to Timothy* (1868), *The Social Law of God: Sermons on the Ten Commandments* (1875) and *Voices from a Busy Life* (1883).

Dr. Washburn was a cousin of Ralph Waldo EMERSON's first wife, Ellen Tucker, and had known the Concord Group of writers and reformers. Before the Civil War he had organized a school for slaves in Georgia and had tried to aid the Chippewa Indians. After his death Wharton wrote a poem praising him for striking out at "ignorance and crime" and helping the "maimed and bound" (*EW* 28). He is portrayed in *The AGE OF INNOCENCE* as the Reverend Dr. Ashmore.

Washburn, Emelyn The only child of Dr. E. A. WASHBURN, rector of Calvary Church, New York. She was six years older than Edith Wharton, but she was her closest friend during her early teens. In "LIFE AND I," Wharton states that they read Dante aloud together, learned Anglo-Saxon, and "ranged through four literatures" as they explored the Washburn library. She describes Emelyn as a "queer, shy, invalid girl of twenty or so, in whom I suspect there were strong traces of degeneracy [lesbianism]. This daughter became passionately, morbidly attached to me" ("Life and I," 1085).

Emelyn had eye trouble, which she attempted to cure by riding ferries, talking with deck hands and wandering all over New York City, including the Italian quarter and South Street. She had much broader interests than Wharton. She was keen on music, social reform and political conditions and wished Edith were not focused so narrowly on literature and that she knew more of the city (*EW* 28).

Welland, Mr. *See AGE OF INNOCENCE, THE.*

Welland, Mrs. *See AGE OF INNOCENCE, THE.*

Altar of Calvary Church, New York. From a painting by Edward Overton-Jones (Courtesy Archives of the Episcopal Diocese of New York)

Calvary Church, 209 East 16th Street, New York, date unknown. This was the church attended by the Jones family when they were living on West 23rd Street (Courtesy Archives of the Episcopal Diocese of New York)

Wells, H[erbert] G[eorge] (1866–1946) British novelist and journalist who is best known for his satirical novels and scientific speculation disguised as fiction. His better-known works in the latter genre include *The Time Machine* (1895), *The Invisible Man* (1897) and *The War of the Worlds* (1898). Among his comic and satirical novels are *Love and Mr. Lewisham* (1900), *Kipps* (1905) and *Tono Bungay* (1909). His *Outline of History* (1920) was extremely popular.

Edith Wharton may have met H. G. Wells in 1908 at Stanway, Cheltenham, home of Lord Hugo and Lady Mary ELCHO in England. About the same time she saw him at the home of Lady ESSEX (née Adèle Grant), a Boston friend married to an Englishman. She called Wells the "most stirring and responsive of talkers" (*BG* 220).

In her article "THE CRITICISM OF FICTION" (1914), Wharton referred to Wells's theories of fiction as expressed in "The Contemporary Novel," a chapter of his book *An Englishman Looks at the World*. She disagreed with his low estimation of the novels of Thackeray. In "HENRY JAMES IN HIS LETTERS" (1920), her review of Percy LUBBOCK's edition of *The Letters of Henry James*, she recalled JAMES remarking, " 'I do delight in Wells; everything that he does is so alive and kicking' " (*UCW* 149).

Wharton's friendship with Wells grew over the years, although she only saw him intermittently. By August 1931, she wrote Mildred BLISS that he was one of the old friends she had made a point of seeing on a recent trip to England. Lewis states that in 1934 Wells was occupying a farmhouse near Grasse, not far from the Ste.-Claire Château. Wharton might have tried to see more of him than she did, except that she considered Odette Keun, his mistress at that time, a "bad example of her kind" (*EW* 516). In 1936 she again stayed at Stanway with her longtime friend Lady Mary Elcho, quite infirm but still genial and enthusiastic. Lady Elcho was now countess of Wemyss, as her husband had succeeded to the earldom of Wemyss. The house party included Wells.

Wendell, Barrett (1855–1921) Professor of English at Harvard (1880–1917), Wendell was known for his instruction in American literature and for his *Literary History of America* (1900), as well as his biography of Cotton Mather. As a youth, Wendell had gone to Europe with Dr. E. A. WASHBURN, rector of Calvary Church, NEW YORK, who had taken an early interest in Edith Wharton's education. Henry ADAMS, Henry JAMES, Charles Eliot NORTON and his family, and Robert GRANT were also among his friends. He sent Wharton a note of congratulation on the publication of *The GREATER INCLINATION*. In March 1903 she wrote Sally NORTON asking whether she knew Wendell and, if so, whether he might be a good person to consult about a college lecture tour Vernon LEE wanted to make in order to pay for a visit to America. She decided not to write him, since Lee wanted to speak on the subject of aesthetics rather than the Italy of the 17th and 18th centuries.

When Wendell was invited to give a series of lectures at the Sorbonne in PARIS in 1904–5, Wharton arranged for him to meet Paul BOURGET. In 1911 he came to dinner in Paris with Morton FULLERTON, a former student of his, and Walter BERRY, whom he had known in college (*EW* 298–99). From France he, his wife, and daughter went on to India, where they met Teddy WHARTON, who was accompanied by another former student, Johnson Morton. In 1913 Wendell was one of the individuals who received the appeal for Henry James's 70th birthday fund (canceled when James learned of it). In 1916 Edith Wharton gave the poet Paul Claudel, who had been sent by the French government to America to give readings in French literature, a letter of introduction to Wendell.

Wendell wrote Edith Wharton a note of appreciation on publication of *The AGE OF INNOCENCE*. She remarked, according to Lewis, that "the last of the tradition we care for" would disappear with Wendell's death (*EW* 436). Barrett Wendell became ill in early 1921 and died in February.

Westmore, Dick *See FRUIT OF THE TREE, THE.*

Weston, Vance *See GOD'S ARRIVE, THE* and *HUDSON RIVER BRACKETED.*

Wharton, Edward Robbins ("Teddy") (1850–1928)
Teddy Wharton was born in Brookline, the second son of William Craig Wharton of Virginia and Nancy Spring Wharton of Boston. He graduated from Harvard in

Teddy Wharton (Courtesy Clifton Waller Barrett Library, Special Collections Department, University of Virginia)

Pine Acre, former summer home of Nancy Willing Spring Wharton, mother of Edward Robbins ("Teddy") Wharton, in Lenox, Massachusetts. Built by Mrs. M. E. Rogers of Philadelphia in 1885, the house was purchased by Mrs. Wharton in 1892. It is now The Gables Inn (Collection of the author)

Trinity Chapel, West 25th Street, New York, date unknown. Here Edith Newbold Jones married Edward Robbins Wharton on April 29, 1885 (Courtesy Archives of the Episcopal Diocese of New York)

1873, although he was not known for his intellectual interests, preferring instead fishing, riding and camping. When he met Edith Newbold Jones in the summer of 1883 at Bar Harbor, Maine, he was living on Beacon St., Boston, with his mother and unmarried sister, Nancy. His father was institutionalized at McLean Hospital near Boston with "melancholia," a condition that did not augur well for Teddy (*NGC* 55). Teddy never had a profession or a real job, but lived on a trust income of $2,000 a year. He and Edith became engaged in 1885 and were married at Trinity Chapel, New York, on April 29, 1885.

The young couple then began a pattern of life that would endure for several years, spending June through February in NEWPORT, at PENCRAIG COTTAGE, across from the Jones's home PENCRAIG, and February through June traveling in Europe, mostly in Italy. They were often accompanied by one or more family friends and at least one servant. They also stayed in the New York home of Lucretia Jones. They eventually acquired their own home in Newport, LAND'S END, in addition to a townhouse on Park Avenue in New York City. In 1888 the Whartons joined their friend James VAN ALEN in chartering the steam yacht *VANADIS* for a Mediterranean cruise, arguably the highlight of Edith Wharton's married life (*see CRUISE OF THE VANADIS, THE*). One of their most memorable journeys was the 1906 automobile trip in France with Henry JAMES. Teddy greatly enjoyed

traveling with Edith and took pleasure in catering to her "nice, to me, worldly side." He had closed in their automobile and added, as he wrote Sara NORTON, "every known accessorie [*sic*] and comfort" (*EW* 177).

In 1891, Teddy's father committed suicide at McLean. Ogden CODMAN was one of the first of the Whartons' friends to perceive that his father's breakdown might portend a similar fate for Teddy. Although it was not until after 1900 that he began to demonstrate odd behavior, Codman recognized incipient mental disease in his "childlike qualities" (*NGC* 73). By 1910 Teddy was extremely unstable mentally.

Edith Wharton summarized her husband's deterioration in her memoir, stating that since the first years of their marriage his mental condition had "become steadily graver. His sweetness of temper and boyish enjoyment of life struggled long against the creeping darkness of neurasthenia, but all the neurologists we consulted were of the opinion that there could be no real recovery; and time confirmed their verdict" (*BG* 326). In this short passage she put as favorable an interpretation as possible on a number of years of profound anxiety and even fear for her personal safety.

Trinity Chapel, New York, interior, date unknown (Courtesy Archives of the Episcopal Diocese of New York)

Lewis describes the years of Teddy's mental decline in *Edith Wharton* ("The Decline of Teddy Wharton," 265–93). Until the age of 53, when The MOUNT was completed, Wharton had been "robust physically and mentally alert." At a time when a work ethic was emerging even for members of the leisured class, his only jobs were managing Edith's trust fund and overseeing The Mount. He began to suffer from various aches and pains, which his physicians treated but attributed to a "deeper evil" of psychic origin; at times he was in an "exalted" state; at other times he was severely depressed. The first period of his illness lasted until 1904. Then, after four years of stability, he began to be less at ease with the many writers and artists who were houseguests at The Mount. Benstock terms his illness "bipolar" (*NGC* 262).

By 1908, when he and his wife returned to Paris, he was alternately depressed and manic. Although he was good-natured, he had never been wholly at ease in France. Lewis gives a poignant picture of him in early 1908, trying to succeed at French lessons but believing that his mind was going. He could not endure the intensely intellectual life of the FAUBOURG SAINT-GERMAIN, which, as Lewis states, "bored, wearied, and depressed him" (*EW* 268). He made a number of trips from 1907 to 1912 in the company of friends, relatives or Alfred WHITE, the Englishman who had begun working for the Whartons in 1888 as Teddy's manservant, to try cures in various places, always coming back miserably to the flat in Paris.

In December 1909 he confessed that he had embezzled some of Edith's funds, purchased an apartment in Boston and established a mistress there; it was later revealed that he had spent at least $50,000. The funds were restored from his mother's legacy, which he had just inherited, but Teddy was then prohibited from managing Edith's financial affairs and later asked to resign as trustee. Lewis attributes his behavior to the exaction of "financial and sexual revenge." He believes Teddy must have detected the importance of Morton FULLERTON in Wharton's life during the winters of 1908 and 1909, and may have guessed the reason for it. With a "vigorous" sexual nature, he would have been deeply hurt by it, since their marriage had long been without physical intimacy. Her affair may have sanctioned his own behavior (*EW* 278). He was referred to the American physician Dr. William Sturgis Bigelow, who was temporarily in Paris, and who expressed grave concern at Teddy's mental state, with his "imagination running riot." Teddy was admitted to a Swiss sanatorium at Kreuzlingen but did not improve; he remained extremely volatile and Edith was advised not to be alone with him unless someone else were within call. In the autumn of 1910, he was dispatched on a world tour, at Edith Wharton's expense, through the American West to Asia. He was accompanied by a family friend and caretaker, Johnnie Morton. In early 1911, in Calcutta, they met the Harvard pro-

fessor Barrett WENDELL (Morton had been his student), who was traveling in Asia with his wife and daughter. Wendell wrote Morton Fullerton that both men were in a state of "unusual nervous tension," but when they met later at Agra and visited the Taj Mahal together, Wendell was more optimistic about Teddy's condition (*EW* 299).

However, Teddy became increasingly agitated at The Mount during the summer of 1911, and Edith suggested separation. She decided to move permanently to France and did so in the fall of 1911. Henry James had written Howard STURGIS in the summer of 1911 that it was essential for Edith's peace of mind to escape from Teddy's " 'quarrelsome, abusive, perpetual scene-making.' " Though James judged him sane, he held that Teddy " 'simply and absolutely . . . will do her to death, and then where shall we be?' " (*EW* 312). The Mount was sold in November 1911. A mutual friend in LENOX, the printer Daniel Berkeley UPDIKE, contributed a perceptive essay to Percy LUBBOCK's *Portrait of Edith Wharton* recalling the days at The Mount when he knew both Edith and Teddy well. He believed that if Teddy's tendency toward "mental disturbance" had been recognized and treated earlier and the Lenox house not been sold, "the rift would not have widened and the final separation might not have come to pass (62).

In February 1912 Teddy arrived back in Paris, instigating another period of what Lewis terms "deadly marital imprisonment." By January 1913 Teddy's erratic behavior had finally convinced his wife that divorce was the only solution, despite the American social repercussions she feared. Because of Teddy's excesses and the lessening stigma of divorce, however, Edith Wharton actually received considerable support from friends and family in Boston and New York. Her divorce was granted in Paris on April 16, 1913 on the grounds of adultery.

Teddy returned to America and was well enough for some time, as Lewis puts it, to "careen about Boston and elsewhere in a high-powered automobile, delighting and alarming his female passengers." He was described by one young woman as "disturbed but not insane" (*EW* 361).

Edith Wharton heard little of Teddy in the succeeding years. He lived with his sister Nancy until her death and was then cared for by Pearl Leota Barrett, a trained nurse, to whom he left an estate of $56,685 (*EW* 481). Wharton died at the age of 79 in 1928. He is buried in the cemetery of The Church on the Hill, Lenox, Massachusetts, near the grave of his mother. Edith Wharton wrote Gaillard LAPSLEY that it was a "happy release, for the real Teddy went years ago, & these survivals of the body are ghastly beyond expression." She wrote Robert GRANT that he had been the "kindest of companions till that dreadful blighting illness came upon him" (*Letters* 514–15).

For further reading: Tintner, "Justice to Teddy Wharton: Louis Auchincloss's 'The Arbiter.' "

Grave of Edward Robbins ("Teddy") Wharton, The Church on the Hill, Lenox, Massachusetts. In the background are the graves of his mother, Nancy Willing Spring Wharton, and his sister, Nancy Craig Wharton. (Collection of the author)

Wheater, Judith   *See* CHILDREN, THE.

White, Alfred   Teddy WHARTON's English manservant, who joined the Whartons' staff in 1888. At that time he was in his late twenties. According to Lewis, he had a cockney accent, but his bearing was "benignly authoritative" (*EW* 54). From 1907 to 1912, during Teddy's years of ill health, he made a number of trips with him to try cures in various places, but they were unsuccessful. He worked for the Whartons until after their divorce in 1913, when he continued working for Edith Wharton.

It was White who seems to have offered the definitive answer as to the possibility of marriage between Edith Wharton and Walter BERRY. He told the artist Jacques-Emile BLANCHE, who asked him about it, " 'That'll never come off, sir.' " Had Berry ever intended to marry he would have done so as a younger man, he believed: "out of the many beautiful ladies always making up to him, Mrs. Wharton is the last one he would have sacrificed his liberty to" (*EW* 344).

In 1920, Edith Wharton designated White her general agent, with many responsibilities overseeing her household. She constructed small white homes on the grounds of the PAVILLON COLOMBE for him and her chauffeur, Charles COOK. White became a member of the household, more a manager of her homes and affairs than a servant, and was still in her employ, making his home in the same cottage on the grounds of the Pavillon Colombe, when Wharton died in 1937. At that time he wrote Bernard BERENSON, "I feel out of place here now and would like to vanish" (*EW* 532).

Whitman, Walt[er] (1819–1892)   American poet and journalist. The first edition of *Leaves of Grass,* his best-known work, was published in 1855. In 1862 his brother George was wounded in the Civil War and Whitman went to Washington to nurse him. Both Whitman's poetry and his hospital work play a role in Wharton's nonfiction and fiction. In 1898 she included Whitman's poetry in a list of her favorite books.

In one of her earliest travel articles, "An Alpine Posting-Inn," published in the ATLANTIC MONTHLY in June 1900, Wharton described Switzerland by Whitman's phrase about America: "one feels that it is a scene in which *nothing has ever happened;* the haunting adjective is that which Whitman applies to the American landscape—'the *large unconscious scenery* of my native land' " (*IB* 6). Another quotation from Whitman, "Something veil'd and abstracted is often a part of the manners of these beings," serves as the epigraph for Wharton's 1923 novel A SON AT THE FRONT.

In Wharton's 1924 novella *The* SPARK one of the principal characters, Hayley Delane, has been greatly influenced by the philosophy of a Civil War hospital nurse. He realizes much later, seeing a portrait of him, that the nurse was Walt Whitman. Lewis terms this depiction of Whitman a "quirky image" of a "wartime healer" (*EW* 373).

Wharton rated Whitman's lyric poetry highly, and considered him superior to Keats and Shelley. She believed his rhythms were perhaps his strongest point: "on *that* side," she commented to Bliss PERRY, who had written an essay on Whitman, "he was the great and conscious artist, and the great Originator, and most likely, therefore, to live on and be fruitful" (*EW* 237).

The title of Wharton's 1934 memoir, A BACKWARD GLANCE, came from Whitman's *A Backward Glance o'er Travel'd Roads,* the preface to *November Boughs* (1888). The phrase also served as the prose epilogue to the eighth edition of *Leaves of Grass,* published in 1889. In this memoir, written in his 70th year, Whitman sits with *Leaves of Grass,* his "*carte visite* to the coming generations of the New World." He is "gossiping in the early candle-light of old age —I and my book—casting backward glances over our travel'd road." He evokes the intellectual heritage of the Old World and the authors and works that have most influenced him, including the Old and New Testaments, Shakespeare, DANTE, HOMER, Aeschylus, Scott and Poe—a list which echoes some of the writers Wharton also loved. Whitman looks at past events in his life, "actualities," with "all their practical excitations gone. How the soul loves to float amid such reminiscences!" He concludes, as Wharton might have done, by saying he wanted to leave something "markedly *personal*" (Whitman, *Prose Works 1892*, II, 712–34, *passim*).

In *A Backward Glance* Wharton recalls that it was a joy to learn that Henry JAMES considered Whitman "the greatest of American poets." One memorable summer evening at The MOUNT he read from *Leaves of Grass*, which Wharton described in her memoir:

> . . . all that evening we sat rapt while he wandered from "The Song of Myself" to "When lilacs last in the door-year bloomed" (when he read "lovely and soothing Death" his voiced filled the hushed room like an organ adagio), and then let himself be lured on to the mysterious music of "Out of the Cradle", reading, or rather crooning it in a mood of subdued ecstasy till the fivefold invocation to Death tolled out like the knocks in the opening bars of the Fifth Symphony" [by Beethoven] (*BG* 186).

For further reading: Goodman, "Edith Wharton's 'Sketch of an Essay on Walt Whitman' "; Leach, "Edith Wharton's Interest in Walt Whitman."

Whitman, Walt   *See* SPARK, THE.

"William C. Brownell"   Essay in memory of William Crary BROWNELL, the editor at SCRIBNER's Wharton held in greatest esteem. It appeared in *SCRIBNER'S MAGAZINE* in November 1928. Brownell was a critic and for many years a "literary consultant" to Scribner's. He was the author of *French Traits; an Essay in Comparative Criticism* (1889), *French Art* (1892), *Victorian Prose Masters* (1907), *American Prose Masters* (1901), *Democratic Distinction in America* (1927) and several other works.

In *A BACKWARD GLANCE* Wharton noted that Brownell led the life of a "recluse" and that even though they both lived in New York City they communicated mainly by letter. Only rarely did he ever visit the Whartons' house. His letters, however, "brought him closer than our actual encounters." She perceived "an aloofness, an elusiveness" in his "manner and personality, something shy and crepuscular, as though his real self dwelt in a closely-guarded recess of contemplation from which it emerged more easily and freely in writing than in speech" (*BG* 144–45).

In her tribute Wharton praised Brownell's "power to comprehend and relate to each other different traditions and alien ideals," as shown in *French Traits*. She cites a few examples of his penetrating analysis of the French: " 'Temperance is the most universal rule in speech, demeanor, taste and habits. Nothing is less French than eccentricity,' " and " 'Frugality is noticeable everywhere. It is the source of the self-respect of

the poor.' " Although Brownell's book was not translated into French, it was appreciated by the well-known editor André CHEVRILLON; it probably also had at least an indirect influence on Wharton's later study, *FRENCH WAYS AND THEIR MEANING* (1919).

Wharton ends on a personal note of gratitude both to Edward BURLINGAME and Brownell. Burlingame had suggested once that she must take care not to publish too much and " 'run the risk of becoming a *magazine bore*.' " But Brownell, she pointed out, would not have "needed to say that; he made me feel it." Even as she wrote she could feel his "light hand" on her shoulder "to stimulate and restrain—surely the two chief offices of friendship. In thinking of him to-day I again give thanks for them" (*UCW* 205–10, *passim*).

Winthrop, Egerton   A friend of Edith Wharton for more than 30 years, Winthrop was a direct descendant of Governor Stuyvesant of New York and of John Winthrop, first colonial governor of Massachusetts. His family had been established in New York for several generations. He was already a widower with grown children at the time Wharton first knew him. Having lived for many years in Paris, he had returned to America and built a home in New York while his sons were attending Harvard. A bibliophile and art collector, he had enacted, in his house, many of the principles Edith Wharton and Ogden CODMAN would later expound in *The DECORATION OF HOUSES*.

In *A BACKWARD GLANCE*, Wharton wrote that never had an "intelligence so distinguished and a character so admirable been combined with interests for the most part so trivial" (*BG* 92). Though Winthrop enjoyed giving dinners and attending balls, he was also shy and at his best with a small group of serious, congenial friends. Winthrop shaped Wharton's intellect in many respects; his "ever-useful curiosities first taught my mind to analyze and my eyes to see," she remarked in her memoir (*BG* 94). They discussed books and pictures, and he directed her reading to fill in the "worst gaps" in her education. He introduced her to the works of Charles Darwin, Thomas Huxley, Herbert Spencer, Edward Westermarck and other modern scientists, social scientists and philosophers. They saw each other as often as possible and corresponded frequently.

During the difficult time of Edith Wharton's DIVORCE, Winthrop wrote that there was "no way out of the misery but the one you took," and that "no one knows better than I what the last four years have been to you in nerve waste and health waste; that there is relief in sight for you from the anguish of mind and body is a source of inexpressible joy to me" (*EW* 336).

He died two days after cabling her a message, "Congratulations with all my heart," just as she was made a CHEVALIER OF THE FRENCH LEGION OF HONOR, France's highest civilian honor (*EW* 386). He appears in *The AGE*

OF INNOCENCE and in *NEW YEAR'S DAY (THE 'SEVENTIES)*, one of the four *OLD NEW YORK* novellas, as Sillerton Jackson, the gossipy chronicler of family connections and arbiter of fashionable behavior.

At Winthrop's death Wharton wrote of him as her "dear and good and wise friend whom everyone misunderstood but the few people near him"; Lewis believed his personal advice was the most "sympathetic and understanding" she ever received (*EW* 383).

Woolf, [Adeline] Virginia (1882–1941)   English novelist, essayist and critic and member of the modernist intellectual and artistic circle called the Bloomsbury Group, Woolf's novels are poetic and symbolic. She uses the technique of the interior monologue, in the "stream of consciousness" vein of writing Edith Wharton criticizes in *The WRITING OF FICTION* (1925). Wharton suggests that this approach originated in the misuse of the "*tranche de vie*" or "slice of life" technique long employed by such writers as Guy de Maupassant and Émile ZOLA. She objects not to recording both mental and physical conditions of life, but in not being more selective. The "disengaging of crucial moments from the welter of existence" is the task of fiction, not the rendering of every moment. However, the writer must make explicit the "eternal struggle between man's contending impulses" (*WF* 14). Wharton was clearly repelled by what she saw as the abridgement of narrative and the indiscriminate magnification of emotion and incident as registered on the unconscious. Her view of Woolf may seem benighted to many critics. It can be argued that Woolf does focus on crucial—epiphanic or eternal—moments, as does James JOYCE. In "PERMANENT VALUES IN FICTION" Edith Wharton observes that her own definition of a novel, "a work of fiction containing a good story about well-drawn characters," would be anathema to Joyce and to Woolf.

The same year *The Writing of Fiction* appeared, 1925, Woolf wrote an essay, "American Fiction," for the *Saturday Review of Literature*. She declared that American readers were not interested in American writers whose works were in the European tradition but were more interested in those who were developing an American idiom. She gave "qualified praise" to Wharton and Henry JAMES, but stated that they "do not give us anything we have not got already." Instead, she commended Sherwood Anderson, Willa Cather, Fannie Hurst and Sinclair LEWIS. Wharton, according to Benstock, "let out a cry of despair—angry and frustrated, she felt dismissed" (*NGC* 385).

Wharton had several friends associated with the Bloomsbury Group, such as Harold NICOLSON, Desmond MACCARTHY, Lytton STRACHEY and Geoffrey SCOTT, who had an affair with Nicolson's wife Victoria ["Vita"] Sackville-West before Vita had one with Woolf.

Bernard BERENSON once stated that Wharton did not admire Woolf's novels but believed she had "prodi-

gious gifts in other directions." Upon hearing from Lady Aberconway that Woolf had an avid curiosity, Wharton questioned her. She had a "poetic mind" but did she have "*true* curiosity"? Lady Aberconway said later that Wharton's curiosity exceeded Woolf's, that Wharton stimulated everyone and that she herself wanted her for a friend (*EW* 483).

For further reading: Collins, "The Art of Self-Perception in Virginia Woolf's *Mrs. Dalloway* and Edith Wharton's *The Reef*"; Hussey, *Virginia Woolf A to Z*; MacMaster, "Beginning with the Same Ending: Virginia Woolf and Edith Wharton; Selected Papers from Fifth Annual Conference on Virginia Woolf."

World Over, The   Collection of short stories published by D. Appleton-Century in 1936. It contains "CHARM INCORPORATED," "POMEGRANATE SEED," "PERMANENT WAVE," "CONFESSION," "ROMAN FEVER," "The LOOKING GLASS" and "DURATION." The critic for the *Times Literary Supplement* praised Wharton for having achieved "mastery of a craft" and stated that she continues "to show to a raw world what ease, finish and lightness mean in fiction." The reviewer for the *New York Times* observed that few writers could equal Wharton in "getting under the skin of a character or in getting under the skin of a reader." Only the critic for the *Nation* took exception to the enthusiastic reception, calling the stories "slick little bits . . . exhumed from the files of the ladies' magazines." That critic selected "Charm Incorporated" as the best story in the collection, an opinion with which few contemporary critics would probably concur. Joseph Reilley, writing in *Catholic World*, considered "Charm Incorporated," "Confession" and "Roman Fever" as "among the best short stories she has ever done." Graham Greene, the *Spectator* reviewer, did not believe any of the stories was as good as "A BOTTLE OF PERRIER," but pronounced them "technically very expert" (*CR* 533–38).

World War I (1914–18)   This European conflict, the *grande guerre*, is, according to many French people, even today, more painful for the French to remember than World War II. It was precipitated by the assassination, by a Serbian, of Archduke Francis Ferdinand of Austria-Hungary at Sarajevo. Historians as a whole assign primary responsibility for the war to Germany. The hostilities terminated 43 years of peace and ended what had been during the BELLE ÉPOQUE a general state of optimism and belief in the possibility of continual economic and social progress. Germany was engaged in colonial rivalry regarding MOROCCO, and also had an aggressive military faction given to imperialistic aims.

After her divorce in 1913, Edith Wharton's stimulating, balanced life came to an abrupt halt with the onset of war. She had divided her time in the FAUBOURG SAINT-GERMAIN among her travels, social life and disciplined writing. At the end of July, 1914, she was returning from

War damage at Gerbéviller, France, 1914. From Fighting France, from Dunkerque to Belfort *(1915), first edition* (Collection of the author)

known writers and artists. It was published in early 1916, earning about $10,000 for war relief, and is now a valuable collectors' item. In April 1916 Wharton was made a CHEVALIER OF THE LEGION OF HONOR, France's highest civilian accolade. Two years later she received the MEDAL OF QUEEN ELISABETH from King Albert of Belgium (*BG* 345–57; *EW* 370–74; *Letters* 617–18). After America's entry into the war she was asked to write a series of articles making "France and things French intelligible to the American soldier" (*BG* 357). These were collected as FRENCH WAYS AND THEIR MEANING (1919). *See also:* ALSACE; ARGONNE; GERMANY; "GREAT BLUE TENT, THE"; JONES, MARY CADWALADER RAWLE ("MINNIE"); LORRAINE; MARNE, THE; PARIS; SIMMONS, RONALD; *SON AT THE FRONT, A;* TYLER, ELSINA; TYLER, ROYALL ("PETER"); VOSGES.

For further reading: Buitenhuis, "Edith Wharton and the First World War"; Price, *The End of the Age of Innocence: Edith Wharton and the First World War;* Price, "The Making of the *Book of the Homeless.*"

a journey to SPAIN, and spent the night at Poitiers. She recalled that the atmosphere had seemed "strange, ominous and unreal, like the yellow glare that precedes a storm. There were moments when I felt as if I had died, and waked up in an unknown world" (*BG* 338). Two days later, when war was declared, Wharton found she had done just that. As reflected in her letters, her attitude, at the beginning of the war, seems a curious blend of horror and fatalism. On August 22, she wrote Bernard BERENSON that PARIS "never looked so appealingly humanly beautiful as now—poor Andromeda!—with the monster careering up to her" (*Letters* 333–34). Looking back on the eve of war, Wharton extolled FRANCE and, especially, Paris, "so made for peace and art and all humanest graces" (*FFD* 6).

Wharton began at once to participate in WAR RELIEF work. She established four separate projects: an *ouvroir,* or workroom, for seamstresses; AMERICAN HOSTELS FOR REFUGEES, to assist French and Belgian refugees swarming into Paris; the CHILDREN OF FLANDERS RESCUE COMMITTEE, which cared for 750 Flemish children; and the MAISONS AMÉRICAINES DE CONVALESCENCE, a cure program for soldiers afflicted with tuberculosis. In early 1915, Wharton was asked by the French Red Cross to visit military hospitals at the front and report on their needs. Her first journey was to Châlons-sur-Marne. She asked permission to make other trips to the front and write magazine articles about her experiences with the hope of alerting her "rich and generous compatriots" to the desperate needs of hospitals, and bringing home "to American readers some of the dreadful realities of war." The articles were published in FIGHTING FRANCE, FROM DUNKERQUE TO BELFORT.

Wharton also edited *The* BOOK OF THE HOMELESS, a project for which she solicited contributions from well-

Cartoon of Edith Wharton and Walter Berry at the Front during World War I. The artist, Abel Faivre, accompanied them. The caricature was published in the humor magazine Le Rire *on May 22, 1915, with the caption* Ce n'est que ca! *("That's all there is?"). Wharton believed Faivre captured Berry's morose view of their mission very well and was pleased with the cartoon.* (Courtesy Bibliothèque Historique de la Ville de Paris)

The Place de la Concorde, Paris, November 11, 1918 (Courtesy Bibliothèque Historique de la Ville de Paris)

"Writing a War Story" Short story published in the *Woman's Home Companion,* September 1919. The story concerns an aspiring young American poet, Ivy Spang. She is assisting during World War I at the Anglo-American Hospital in Paris, and is asked to contribute a "rattling war story" to *The Man-at-Arms,* a British magazine designed for British soldiers in hospitals.

She goes to Brittany to stay with her old governess and seek inspiration. While there, she attempts to work out a technique for opening her story by reading the selections in an old copy of *Fact and Fiction,* but she is unable to shake off the memory of those she has read and produce anything original. She borrows a copy of her governess's notes about stories she has heard from soldiers during her hospital work and chooses to narrate an anecdote about a young soldier named Emile Durand. The governess helps shape and edit the story, "His Letter Home." When it is published with a flattering photograph of the young author, the soldiers pay little attention to the story but ask for extra copies of her photograph. An invalid soldier, who is also a

famous novelist, Harold Harbard, finds the story amusing but far less interesting than the photograph. Ivy is furious, especially when Harbard laughs at her, insisting that "Woman" is an "inexhaustible field."

White points out that there are obvious parallels between Ivy Spang's experience and that of Wharton. Ivy's hero, Emile Durand, is similar to Charles Durand, hero of a war story of Edith Wharton's, "Coming Home." Ivy's story is titled "His Letter Home" and Edith Wharton's tale is "Coming Home." Lewis terms it "flimsy" (*EW* 422).

"Writing of *Ethan Frome,* The" An essay published in the *Colophon* in September 1932 in which Edith Wharton describes the circumstances under which she wrote ETHAN FROME. It was actually begun in French, since she was spending the winter in Paris, and feared that her French was not idiomatic but out of date. She arranged to read and talk with a young French professor, who suggested that she prepare an "exercise" for him before each visit. She found that writing a story was easier than writing a letter, so she began it in French, although she soon abandoned the Gallic version.

She dispels the myth that she wrote *Ethan Frome* without firsthand knowledge of NEW ENGLAND, making it clear that it had been written after 10 years' residence in the hill country. Not only *Ethan Frome* but also the novella SUMMER, she points out, deals with "the same type of people involved in different tragedy of isolation." She hoped both works would serve as convincing evidence that she had known firsthand of the lives of the people she had invited her readers to enter.

Writing of Fiction, The   The five chapters making up *The WRITING OF FICTION* (New York: Scribner's, 1925) were published as periodical articles: "In General" in *SCRIBNER'S MAGAZINE* (December 1924); "Telling a Short Story" (*Scribner's Magazine,* April 1925); "Constructing a Novel" (*Scribner's Magazine,* May 1925); "Character and Situation in the Novel" (*Scribner's Magazine,* October 1925) and "Marcel Proust" (*Yale Review,* January 1925).

In the first chapter Wharton traces the evolution of fiction from its early depiction of the "street" to its later concern with the "soul." She emphasizes the role of such French writers as Abbé Prévost, Balzac and Stendhal. She discusses the "*tranche de vie*" or "slice of life" method of writing fiction, in which a situation is reproduced photographically with its sounds, smells and aspects realistically rendered, but its "suggestions of a larger whole" omitted (*WF* 10). Writers in this tradition whose reputations have survived, such as Guy de Maupassant and Émile ZOLA, explored the psychological implications of their "slices" of life. Wharton believes this technique has reappeared as the "stream of consciousness" approach to fiction, in which the characters' mental as well as physical reactions to life are recorded, but that it has been overused. In the past, novelists had wisely restricted the depiction of mental flux to moments of crisis. The "disengaging of crucial moments from the welter of existence" is the task of fiction, not the rendering of every moment. However, the writer must make explicit the "eternal struggle between man's contending impulses" (*WF* 14). The quest for novelty, Wharton asserts, has weakened the work of many modern writers. A good subject must shed light on our "moral experience" (*WF* 29).

Although Wharton insists that the modern short story has French origins, she discusses English and American writers in the chapter on "Telling a Short Story." She is partial to Thomas HARDY, Henry JAMES, Joseph CONRAD, Rudyard KIPLING and Edgar Allan Poe. Russian writers, however, also must be given credit for shaping the short story and giving it "closeness of texture with profundity of form" (*WF* 36). In the short story "every phrase must be a sign post," whereas the "least touch of irrelevance"

is a fatal weakness. In ghost stories, the horrors must not be multiplied. The theory that a good story is one that may be expanded into a novel is fallacious; the chances are that a subject seemingly adapted to both forms is "inadequate to neither" (*WF* 41).

In "Constructing a Novel," Wharton argues that the novel of psychology originated in France and the novel of manners in England. The modern novel, she suggests, sprang from their union in the mind of Balzac. In this chapter she discusses the requisite scale and form of the novel, the difficulty of the point of view and the necessity of aging characters properly (which Tolstoy was able to do brilliantly).

The chapter on "Character and Situation in the Novel" addresses the problem of whether character or plot is more essential. Wharton finds few examples of novels springing solely from situation (GOETHE's *Elective Affinities* and Tolstoy's *The Kreutzer Sonata* are examples), but many based on character, particularly the novels of Jane Austen.

Of Marcel PROUST she says he was a "great life-giver." In his "gallery of living figures" he "always knows whither his people are tending, and which of their words, gestures and thoughts are worth recording" (*WF* 160). Wharton praises Proust's passion for detail and compares his work to the marginalia on medieval manuscripts "where the roving fancy of the scribe has framed some solemn gospel or epistle in the episodes drawn from the life of towns and fields" (*WF* 166–67).

Lewis considers *The Writing of Fiction* "sane and judicious," although not highly original. He believes it may have been intended as a response or "counterargument" to Percy LUBBOCK's *The Craft of Fiction* (1921), in which Lubbock praises Flaubert and JAMES (*EW* 521). Wharton does not emphasize their work nearly as much as she does than of Proust, Tolstoy, Austen, Balzac, Stendhal, Thackeray, MEREDITH and George ELIOT. Oddly, she does not mention Theodore Dreiser, although nine years later she would single him out, along with Sinclair LEWIS, as one of the two contemporary writers whose work would endure (*see* "PERMANENT VALUES IN FICTION," 1934). The reviewer for the *Spectator* (England) considered this "a direct and thoughtful piece of communication." This was not the reaction of the critic for the *Times Literary Supplement,* however, who found *The Writing of Fiction* addressed to the novelist rather than the reader and critic of fiction, Lubbock's audience.

Wyant, Arthur   *See TWILIGHT SLEEP.*

Wyant, Jim   *See TWILIGHT SLEEP.*

Wyant, Lita   *See TWILIGHT SLEEP.*

X

"Xingu" Short story first published in SCRIBNER'S MAGAZINE in December 1911 and collected in XINGU AND OTHER STORIES (Scribner's, 1916). It is a satiric comedy about Mrs. Ballinger's Lunch Club, a small group of literary ladies in a New England town "who pursue culture in bands, as though it were dangerous to meet alone." They invite Osric Dane as a speaker. She is a distinguished but arrogant woman novelist who has just written *The Wings of Death* (a veiled reference to Henry JAMES's *The Wings of the Dove*). Fanny Roby, the prettiest and most frivolous member of the club, is castigated for not having read Dane's book, but explains that she took it on a boating party in Brazil and it fell into the river. When Osric Dane arrives, she refuses to discuss her books and asks the club difficult questions, such as how to define "objective." Mrs. Roby declares that the subject in which they are most interested is "Xingu." The others go along with her pronouncement, and Mrs. Roby asks her to explain "Xingu," since one of her last books was "saturated" with it. Dane falls into her trap, and is discomfited and confused. Mrs. Roby assures her Xingu is "really not difficult up to a certain point; though some of the branches are very little known, and it's almost impossible to get at the source." Eventually they learn that Xingu is a Brazilian river Mrs. Roby had seen on her travels.

The critic for the *Spectator* singled out the story as the only one in the collection with a "spirit of frivolity," praising the "delicate irony" with which Edith Wharton sketched the characters and the way she exposed the "snobbish sciolism which thrives in an atmosphere of mutual admiration" (*CR* 234).

For further reading: Funston, " 'Xingu': Edith Wharton's Velvet Gauntlet"; Killoran, " 'Xingu': Edith Wharton Instructs Literary Critics."

Xingu and Other Stories Short story collection published by SCRIBNER's in 1916. It contained "XINGU," "COMING HOME," "AUTRES TEMPS . . . ," "KERFOL," "The LONG RUN," "The TRIUMPH OF NIGHT," "The CHOICE" and "BUNNER SISTERS." The *New York Times* reviewer found the collection had "extraordinary variety" and showed "a deeper humanity" than the author's previous work. The critic for the *Times Literary Supplement* asserted that Edith Wharton had "never done a better thing" than "Autres Temps . . . ," in which NEW YORK "applies its new standards to new people and at the same time omits to reverse its old judgments on the old." Francis Hackett, writing in the *New Republic,* believed the volume afforded nearly complete "gratification," but observed that Wharton still dealt with people of means, "not the kind of people with whom you share cracker-jack in a day-coach." With this qualification, however, he justifies her choice of subjects. Wharton presents well-born characters not because of their "fatuous fashionableness" but because of the chance they offer for "intensive human relations" (*CR* 227–37).

Yale University   The president of Yale University wrote Edith Wharton in the winter of 1923 to say that the university wanted to bestow an honorary DOCTORATE on her in June, the first time a woman would be so honored at that university. She nearly refused but decided she should see her native country again in order to go on writing about it. The degree was granted June 20, 1923.

Wharton directed her literary executor, Gaillard LAPSLEY, to offer her "literary correspondence" to Yale. Over 50,000 items relating to her are in the BEINECKE LIBRARY.

Young, Arthur (1741–1820)   English agricultural theorist and writer who published a number of volumes of political, economic and social observation about Ireland, FRANCE and ITALY. Edith Wharton had read his *Travels in France and Italy* and mentions the real Arthur Young in *The VALLEY OF DECISION*, her historical novel about 18th-century Italy. She also creates a fictional "Arthur Young" in the novel who interacts with the other characters. She uses a similar technique in *FALSE DAWN*, the novella in which she fabricates a fictional John RUSKIN.

Young, Arthur   *See VALLEY OF DECISION, THE.*

"Young Gentlemen, The"   Short story published in the *Pictorial Review* (February 1926) and collected in *HERE AND BEYOND* (D. Appleton, 1926). The story takes place in the town of Harpledon, on the coast of New England between Salem and Newburyport, once a busy seaport and now an artists' colony. Waldo Cranch, a descendant of sea captains and a widower, is supposed by many people to be the last of his line. When a magazine article is published about the house, it emerges that he has twin dwarf sons hidden in a wing of the house. Cranch commits suicide rather than face public disclosure of their existence.

The story is narrated by an artist who is proud of the civic pride that has "taught Americans to preserve and adorn their modest monuments." (Here there is an echo of *FRENCH WAYS AND THEIR MEANING*, where Edith Wharton writes of the new American eagerness "to beautify her towns, and to preserve her few pre-Revolutionary buildings"; *FWM* 37). One of Waldo Cranch's ancestors had, in his youth, served his business apprenticeship in Malaga and brought back a Spanish bride, the great-grand-

mother of the present Waldo Cranch, whose dour portrait still hangs in the great house. The house itself was "really something to brag about," a substantial granite structure with a wing thought to have been added. Waldo Cranch has always been eccentric; the artist's aunt remembered seeing him bring home a huge black and white hobbyhorse years earlier, when he was a bachelor.

Cranch leads a quasi-civic life, willing to show his sketches, read aloud his literary articles and play his musical compositions. His longtime friend, Mrs. Durant, a widow, is the only one who can approach him, however, for such requests as lending his garden for a fund-raising fair for the local hospital. He claims to have no "rubbish" to sell, but one of the older ladies mentions the hobbyhorse. Cranch makes light of it, pretending he can't think where it would be. Mrs. Durant suggests that he is hurt because no one had asked for one of his watercolors for the sale.

Cranch is furious when he discovers a magazine article about the house by a Boston architect. It contains a drawing of the back wing, which had been concealed from all visitors for many years. The architect had been told he could neither tour the grounds nor see the back of the house, but he had managed to bribe a new and untrustworthy maid to let him into the garden.

Mrs. Durant is alarmed by a note from Cranch saying he is going on a journey. She and the narrator rush to the house to find the police there, Cranch dead upstairs, having drowned himself, and the housekeeper, Catherine, in a terrible state. Going into the wing, they see the hobbyhorse with two little boys playing nearby. They turn out to be the "young gentlemen," Waldo and Donald Cranch, retarded dwarfs about 40 years of age. Catherine and Janey Sampson, the housemaid, have cared for them secretly for many years. Catherine had warned Cranch that the new parlormaid, Hannah Oast, could not be trusted, but he didn't believe her. The mother of the children was a beautiful young English girl, who died soon after their birth, but Cranch believed their condition was a legacy from his Spanish great-grandmother. When Cranch understood their condition, he had brought them back to Harpledon. After his suicide, the children lived on in the house in the care of Catherine and Mrs. Durant, who was asked to be their guardian and moved into the house, looking in on them every day. As the story ends,

Waldo, who had been hurt the most by his father's death, is ill, and Catherine tells the narrator that Donald won't last long once Waldo dies.

Critics welcomed "The Young Gentlemen" and "BE- WITCHED," another story in the collection, as a return to the New England of ETHAN FROME, although the reviewer for the *Times Literary Supplement* believed that, at the discovery of the children, some of the "uncanny that ought to be there leaks away" (*CR* 415–25).

Z

Zola, Émile (1840–1902) French writer of the naturalist school whose best-known work is the 20-volume *Les Rougon-Macquart,* a portrait of the Rougon-Macquart family. *Germinal,* a study of the intense sufferings of French coal miners, is one of the novels in this series and exemplifies Zola's zeal for social reform.

When Edith Wharton first began writing, her friend Walter BERRY imparted his enthusiasm about Zola to her, although Zola's work did not influence her initially. In her essay "VISIBILITY IN FICTION" Wharton censured Zola's device of associating a character with certain idiosyncrasies of word or gesture, stating that Dickens excelled at this method, but that Zola used it as a "short-cut to realization." In *The WRITING OF FICTION* she was more tolerant of Zola's "slice of life" approach, explaining that he was one of a brilliant group of early French realists whose technique she had questioned. But Zola had survived and was still readable because his "slices" were "the stuff of great romantic allegories in which the forces of Nature and Industry are the huge cloudy protagonists, as in a Pilgrim's Progress of man's material activities" (*WF* 10).

Wharton sided with Zola in one of the most celebrated cases of the BELLE ÉPOQUE, the Dreyfus affair, which bitterly divided France for many years. On October 15, 1894, Alfred Dreyfus, a Jewish captain in the French army, was arrested on grounds of treason: he was thought to be selling French secrets to the German army. He was court-martialed, convicted and given a life sentence on Devil's Island. In 1899 he had another court-martial that ended in another conviction. In his defense, Zola wrote the famous letter "*J'accuse*" to President Félix Faure of France suggesting that Dreyfus had become a scapegoat for anti-Jewish sentiment. Alfred's brother Mathieu Dreyfus discovered that the letter he had supposedly written to the Germans was actually forged. This later led to Alfred's full acquittal, but not until 1906. Wharton had originally disagreed with the verdicts (*EW* 90), as had Minnie BOURGET, who was Jewish. Paul BOURGET, however, was anti-Dreyfus. The prolonged litigation and ardent public sentiment shaped the political climate of the era. It also, as Benstock puts it, crystallized hatred against Jews and "divided royalists and Catholics, artists and intellectuals" (*NGC* 103). Marcel PROUST depicted the alignment of popular opinion in *À la recherche du temps perdu.*

APPENDICES

I. Topical List of Entries

1. Acquaintances, friends, family
2. Biographical periods, topics and events
3. Fictional characters (by work)
4. Artistic, historical and literary periods, terms, events
5. Places
6. Organizations and institutions
7. Publishing (editors, publishers, periodicals, libraries)
8. Special interests and pursuits
9. Works by Wharton
10. Works by other writers
11. Writers and other artists
12. Honors, awards and prizes

II. Media Adaptations of Edith Wharton's Works

1. Edith Wharton on Film and Television: A Filmography (*by Scott Marshall*)
2. Theatrical Adaptations of Edith Wharton's Works (*by Scott Marshall and Sarah Bird Wright*)
3. Musical Adaptations of Edith Wharton's Works (*by Scott Marshall*)

III. Chronology of Wharton's Writings and Publications

IV. Family Trees

1. Edward Robbins Wharton (*compiled by Scott Marshall*)
2. Edith Newbold Jones

V. Edith Wharton: A Timeline

VI. Bibliography

1. Works by Edith Wharton
2. Selected Secondary Sources

APPENDIX I

TOPICAL LIST OF ENTRIES

1. Acquaintances, Friends, Family

Adams, Henry
Astor, Caroline Schermerhorn
Astor, Nancy Langhorne
Austin, Mrs. Alfred
Austin, Sir Alfred
Bahlmann, Anna
Balfour, Arthur James
Bélogou, Léon
Berenson, Bernard
Berenson, Mary
Berry, Walter
Blanche, Jacques-Emile
Blashfield, Edwin
Blashfield, Evangeline (*see* BLASHFIELD, EDWIN)
Bliss, Mildred Barnes
Bliss, Robert Woods
Boccon-Gibbod, André
Bourget, Minnie David
Bourget, Paul
Breuil de Saint-Germain, Jean du
Brownell, William Crary
Burlingame, Edward L.
Campbell, Mrs. Patrick
Cameron, Elizabeth Sherman
Chanler, Margaret
Chevrillon, André
Clark, Kenneth

Cocteau, Jean
Codman, Ogden, Jr.
Colefax, Lady Sybil
Comptour, Abbé
Conrad, Joseph
Cook, Charles
Cutting, Bayard, Jr.
Cutting, Olivia
Cutting, Lady Sybil (*see* LUBBOCK, LADY SYBIL)
Doyle, Hannah ("Doyley")
Du Bos, Charles
Duvlenck, Elise
Edel, Leon
Elcho Lord Hugo and Lady Mary
Essex, Countess of (née Adèle Grant)
Farrand, Beatrix Jones
Farrand, Max
Fitzgerald, F. Scott
Fitz-James, Rosa de
Fullerton, William Morton
Gardner, Isabella Stewart
Gay, Matilda
Gay, Walter
Gerhardi, William Alexander
Gerould, Katherine Fullerton

Gide, André
Gilder, Richard Watson
Grant, Judge Robert
Gross, Catharine
Hardy, Thomas
Herst, William Raudlegh
Howells, William Dean
Hugh Smith, John
Humières, Count Robert d'
Hunter, Mary
James, Henry
Jewett, Rutger B.
Jones, Beatrix (*see* FARRAND, BEATRIX JONES)
Jones, Frederic Rhinelander ("Freddy")
Jones, George Frederic
Jones, Henry Edward ("Harry")
Jones, Joshua
Jones, Lucretia Stevens Rhinelander
Jones, Mary Cadwalader Rawle ("Minnie")
Kinnicutt, Dr. Francis P.
Kipling, Rudyard
La Forest-Divonne, Philomène de

Lapsley, Gaillard
Lee, Vernon
Lewis, Sinclair
Lodge, George Cabot ("Bay")
Lubbock, Percy
Lubbock, Lady Sybil
Lyautey, General Louis-Hubert Gonzalve
MacCarthy, Desmond
Mariano, Elizabeth ("Nicky")
Maurois, André
Maynard, Eunice Ives
Maynard, Walter
Meredith, George
Mitchell, Dr. S[ilas] Weir
Mugnier, Abbé Arthur
Newbold, Tom
Nicholson, Reginald
Nicolson, Harold
Noailles, Anna de
Norton, Charles Eliot
Norton, Lily (Elizabeth)
Norton, Robert
Norton, Sara ("Sally")
Origo, Iris Cutting
Paget, Violet (*see* LEE, VERNON)
Parrish, Maxfield
Peixotto, Ernest
Perry, Bliss

273

Proust, Marcel
Richardson, William K.
Roosevelt, Theodore
Rutherfurd, Lewis
Sargent, John Singer
Schlumberger, Gustave
Scott, Geoffrey
Scott, Lady Sybil (*see*
   CUTTING, LADY SYBIL)

Scribner, Charles II
Sears, J. H.
Sedgwick, Ellery
Silve, Claude (*see* LA
   FOREST-DIVONNE,
   PHILOMÈNE DE)
Simmons, Ronald
Smith, Logan
   Pearsall

Strachey, Lytton
Sturgis, Howard
Tyler, Elisina (Mrs.
   Royall)
Tyler, Royall ("Peter")
Tyler, William Royall
   ("Bill")
Updike, Berkeley
Van Alen, James

Washburn, Edward
   Abiel
Washburn, Emelyn
Wendell, Barrett
Wharton, Edward
   Robbins ("Teddy")
White, Alfred
Winthrop, Egerton

2. Biographical Periods, Topics and Events

aesthetic views
anti-Semitism
Catholicism, Roman
charities, World War I
   (*see* WAR RELIEF,
   WORLD WAR I)
chevalier of the French
   Legion of Honor
childhood
childlessness, of Wharton
Children of Flanders
   Rescue Committee

connoisseurship
divorce
doctorate, honorary
engagement
eroticism
expatriation
feminism
films based on
   Wharton's works
forewords
gardens, and
   gardening

genealogy, of Edith
   Wharton
interior design
introductions
Maisons Américaines de
   Convalescence
musical adaptations of
   Wharton's works
National Institute of
   Arts and Letters
Nobel Prize nomination
ouvroir for seamstresses

poetry
postal stamp
prefaces
Pulitzer Prize
reviews
salon
theatrical adaptations of
   Edith Wharton's
   works
travels
tributes
war relief, World War I

3. Fictional Characters (By Work)

"After Holbein"
   Cress, Miss
   Dunn, Miss
   Filmore
   George
   Jaspar, Evelina
   Lavinia
   Munson
   Warley, Anson

"Afterward"
   Boyne, Edward
      (Ned)
   Boyne, Mary
   Elwell, Robert
      (Bob)
   Kitchenmaid
   Parvis, Mr.
   Peters
   Stair, Alida
   Trimmle

Age of Innocence, The
   Archer, Janey
   Archer, Mrs.
   Archer, Newland
   Beaufort, Julius

Beaufort, Regina
Jackson, Sillerton
Lefferts, Larry
Letterblair, Mr.
Mingott, Mrs.
   Manson
Olenska, Countess
   Ellen
Rivière, M.
Van der Luyden,
   Henry
Van der Luyden,
   Louisa
Welland, May
Welland, Augusta
   (Mrs. Welland)

"All Souls' "
   Agnes
   Clayburn, Sara
   Cook
   Doctor with x-ray
   Housemaid
   Narrator
   Price
   Selgrove, Dr.
   Woman on road

"Angel at the Grave,
   The"
   Anson, Orestes
   Anson, Paulina
   Corby, George
   Katy
   Publisher's grandson

"April Showers"
   Brill, Miss Sophy
   Dace, Dr.
   Dace, Johnny
   Dace, Kate
   Dace, Mrs.
   Dace, Theodora
   Dace, Uncle James
   Kyd, Kathleen

"Atrophy"
   Aldis, Christopher
   Aldis, Jane
   Brincker, Gladys
   Brincker, Hal
   Frenway, George
   Frenway, Nora
   Knowlton, Dr.
   Parlormaid

"Autres Temps . . ."
   Barkley, Leila
   Barkley, Wilbour
   Boulger, Mrs. Lorin
   Ide, Franklin
   Lidcote, Mrs.
   Suffern, Susy
   Wynn, Charlotte
   Wynn, Margaret

"Beatrice Palmato"
   (fragment)
   Daughter of Beatrice
      Palmato
   Husband of Beatrice
      Palmato
   Palmato, Beatrice
   Palmato, Jack
   Palmato, Mr.
   Palmato, Mrs.

"Best Man, The"
   Ashford, Mr.
   Fleetwood, George
   Gregg, Rufus
   Mornway, Ella
      (Renfield)

Mornway, Governor
    John
Nimick, Grace
Nimick, Jack
Shackwell, Hadley

"Bewitched"
    Bosworth, Loretta
    Bosworth, Orrin
    Brand, Ora
    Brand, Sylvester
    Brand, Venny
    Cheney, Aunt
        Cressidora
    Cummins, Minorca
    Hibben, Deacon
    Nash, Lefferts
    Pond, Andy
    Rutledge, Prudence
    Rutledge, Saul

"Blond Beast, The"
    Footman
    Millner, Hugh
    Spence, Draper
    Spence, Orlando G.

"Bolted Door"
    Allonby (District
        Attorney)
    Ascham, Peter
    Ashgrove, Mr.
    Ashgrove, Mrs.
    Denver, Robert
    Flint
    Granice, Hubert
    Granice, Kate
    Hewson, J. B.
    Lenman, Joseph
    McCarren, Peter
    Melrose, Rose
    Stell, Dr. John B.

"Bottle of Perrier, A"
    Almodham, Henry
    Gosling, Mr.
    Medford
    Selim

"Bread Upon the Waters"
    (later "Charm
    Incorporated")
    Bellamy, Mr.
    Guggins, Mamie
    Guggins, Mr.
    Guggins, Mrs.

Kouradjine, Boris
Kouradjine, Mamie
    (Guggins)
Kouradjine, Mouna
Kouradjine, Nick
Kouradjine, Olga
Kouradjine, Paul
Kouradjine, Prince
    Peter
Kouradjine, Serge
Leeper, Mrs.
Old Princess
Svengaart, Axel
Targatt, James
Targatt, Nadeja

Buccaneers, The
    Brightlingsea, Lady
        Blanche (later the
        Dowager)
    Brightlingsea,
        Marquess of
    Closson, Conchita
        (later Conchita
        Marable)
    Closson, Mrs.
    Dawnley, Miles
    Elmsworth, Lizzy
        (later Lizzy
        Robinson)
    Elmsworth, Mrs.
    Marable, Lord
        Richard
    March, Miss
    Parmore, Mrs.
    Robinson, Hector
    St George, Colonel
    St George, Mrs.
    St George, Annabel
        (Nan; later
        Annabel Tintagel)
    St George, Virginia
        (later Virginia
        Seadown)
    de Santos-Dios,
        Teddy
    Seadown, Lord
    Testvalley, Laura
    Thwarte, Guy
    Thwarte, Sir Helmsley
    Tintagel, Duke of
        (Ushant)

"*Bunner Sisters*" (novella)
    Bunner, Ann Eliza
    Bunner, Evelina

Geoghegan, Dalia
Hawkins, Johnny
Hawkins, Mr.
Hawkins, Mrs.
Hochmüller, Linda
Hochmüller, Mrs.
Loomis, Mrs.
Mellins, Miss
Ramy, Herman
Roman Catholic priest

"Charm Incorporated"
    (*see* "BREAD UPON
    THE WATERS,"
    original title of
    story)

Children, The
    Boyne, Martin
    Buondelmonte,
        Beechy (Astorre)
    Buondelmonte, Bun
        (Beatrice)
    Buondelmonte,
        Prince
    Dobree, Mr. Azariah
    Scope, Miss Horatia
    Sellars, Rose
    Wheater, Blanca
    Wheater, Chipstone
    Wheater, Cliffe
    Wheater, Joyce
    Wheater, Judith
    Wheater, Terry
    Wheater, Zinnia
        Lacrosse

"Choice, The"
    Emmerton, Jack
    Granger, Addison
    Granger, Agnes
    Granger, Lucy
    Stilling, Cobham
    Stilling, Isabel
    Swordsley, Mrs.
    Swordsley, the Rev.
    Wrayford, Austin

"Coming Home"
    Charlot, Captain
    de Corvenaire,
        Marquis de
    de Réchamp, Alain
    de Réchamp, Comte
    de Réchamp, Jean
    de Réchamp, Mme.

de Réchamp, Simone
Greer, H. Macy
Malo, Yvonne
Mother of Comte de
    Réchamp
Narrator
von Scharlach,
    Oberst Graf
    Benno

"Confession"
    Antoine
    Ingram, Mrs. (Kate
        Spain Severance)
    Severance, Mr.
        (narrator)
    Shreve, Jimmy
    Spain, Ezra
    Wilpert, Miss (Cassie
        Donovan)

"Confessional, The"
    Count Andrea
    Countess Gemma
    Don Egidio
    Donna Marianna
    Faustina Intelvi
        (Countess Siviano)
    Narrator (priest)
    Roberto (later Il
        Conte Siviano)
    Siviano, Il Conte
        (deceased)
    Welkenstern, Franz

"Copy"
    Dale, Mrs. Ambrose
    Hilda
    Servant
    Ventnor, Paul

"Coward, A"
    Carstyle, Andrew
    Carstyle, Irene
    Carstyle, Mrs.
    Collis
    Meriton, Charles
    Vance, Mrs.
    Vibart, Mr.

Cup of Cold Water, A"
    Gildermere, Mr.
    Gildermere, Mrs.
    Glenn, Joe
    Glenn, Mrs. (Joe's
        mother)

Glenn, Ruby (Mrs. Joe)
Maidservant
Night clerk in hotel
Talcott, Miss
Telegraph boy
Woburn, Mr.

Custom of the Country, The
de Chelles, Raymond
Estradina, the Princess
Fairford, Laura (Mrs. Henley)
Heeny, Mrs.
Lipscomb, Mabel
Marvell, Paul
Marvell, Ralph
Moffatt, Elmer
Moffatt, Undine Spragg Marvell
Popple, Claude Washington
Spragg, Abner
Spragg, Mrs.
Van Degen, Clare (Mrs. Peter)
Van Degen, Peter
Wincher, Indiana (later Madame de Trézac)

"Daunt Diana, The"
Daunt, Mr.
Finney, Ringham
Narrator
Neave, Humphrey

"Day of the Funeral, The"
Cossett, Mrs.
Jane
Lanscomb, Dr.
Trenham, Ambrose
Trenham, Milly
Wake, Barbara
Wake, Professor

"Debt, The"
Dredge, Galen
Lanfear, Archie
Lanfear, Mabel
Lanfear, Mrs.
Lanfear, Professor
Narrator

"Descent of Man, The"
Harviss, Ned
Linyard, Jack
Linyard, Millicent
Linyard, Mrs.
Linyard, Professor Samuel
Pease, Professor

"Diagnosis"
Butler
Dorrance, Eleanor (Welwood)
Dorrance, Paul
Girl in Cairo
Servant
Welwood, Horace

"Dieu d'Amour"
Abbot Hilarion
Bridget of Sweden
Circassian girl
Father Gregory
Godfrey (page, later Prior)
John of Yvetot
King of Cyprus
Pilgrim man at Famagusta
Pigram woman at Famagusta
Prince of Antioch
Princess Medea
Woman of the castle

"Dilettante, The"
Gaynor, Ruth
Thursdale, Mr.
Vervain, Mrs.

"Duchess at Prayer, The"
Cavaliere Ascanio
Duchess Violante
Duke Ercole II
Narrator
Nencia
Old custodian

"Duration"
Dressmaker
Little, Martha
Lusky, Miss
Pepperel, Grayson
Pepperel, Lyddy
Pepperel, Priscilla
Pepperel, Sara

Perch, Syngleton
Warbeck, Mrs. (Sr.)
Warbeck, Henley

Ethan Frome
Buck, Dr.
Byrne, Daniel
Eady, Denis
Frome, Ethan
Frome, Mrs. (mother of Ethan)
Frome, Zenobia ("Zeena"), née Pierce
Gow, Harmon
Hale, Andrew
Hale, Mrs. Andrew
Hale, Mrs. Ned (née Ruth Varnum)
Hale, Ned (eldest son of Andrew Hale)
Maple, Philura
Narrator
Pierce, Martha
Powell, Jotham
Silver, Mattie
Widow Homan

"Expiation"
Bishop of Ossining
Clinch, Bella
Fetherel, John
Fetherel, Paula
Gollinger, Mrs.
Hynes, Archer

"Eyes, The"
Aunt of Andrew Colwin
Colwin, Andrew
Frenham, Phil
Murchard, Fred
Narrator
Nowell, Alice
Noyes, Gilbert

False Dawn (The 'Forties)
Cosby, Netta
Dinah
Huzzard, Ambrose
Huzzard, Robert
Kent, Beatrice ("Treeshy"; later Raycie)
Kent, Donaldson

Ledgely, Commodore Jameson
Poe, Mrs. Edgar Allan
Raycie, Halston
Raycie, Lewis
Raycie, Mary Adeline
Raycie, Mrs.
Raycie, Sarah Anne (later Huzzard)
Ruskin, John
Selwyn, John
Servant to Ruskin

"Fast and Loose" (novella)
Blackstone, Miss
Breton, Lord
Egerton, Jack
French Marquise
Graham, Madeline
Graham, Mr.
Graham, Mrs.
Hastings, Guy
Matteo
Payson
Priggett
Rivers, Georgina ("Georgie")
Rivers, Julia
Rivers, Kate
Rivers, Mrs.
Sidenham
Teresina
Westmoreland, Duke of
Williamson

"Friends"
Bent, Mrs.
Bent, Penelope
Boutwell, Mr.
Dayton, Mr.
Staples, Euphemia
Thurber, Lally
Thurber, Phil
Thurber, Vexilla

Fruit of the Tree, The
Amherst, John
Amherst, Justine (Brent)
Amherst, Bessy Langhope Westmore
Amherst, Lucy Warne
Ansell, Maria (Mrs. Eustace)

Dillon, Mr.
Dillon, Mrs.
Disbrow, Dr.
Dressel, Effie (Mrs. Harry)
Dressel, Harry
Duplain, Louis
Gaines, Halford
Gaines, Juliana (Mrs. Halford)
Gaines, Westy
Garford, Dr.
Governess
Langhope, Henry
Ogan, Mrs.
Tredegar, Mr.
Truscomb, Mr.
Truscomb, Mrs.
Westmore, Cicely
Westmore, Richard
Wyant, Dr.

"Full Circle"
Betton, Geoffrey
Strett
Vyse, Duncan

"Fullness of Life, The"
Husband
Kindred Soul
Spirit of Life
Wife

"Glimpse, A"
Aslar, Margaret
Brand, Julian
Breck, Harry
Dossi, Count
Kilvert, John
Roseneath, Sara

Glimpses of the Moon, The
Altineri, Prince Nerone
Beck, Mr.
Bockheimer, Algie
Breckenridge, Eddy
Buttles, Mr.
Davenant
Fulmer, Geordie
Fulmer, Grace
Fulmer, Jack
Fulmer, Junie
Fulmer, Mrs.
Fulmer, Nat, Jr.
Fulmer, Nat, Sr.

Fulmer, Peggy
Gillow, Fred
Gillow, Ursula
Hicks, Coral
Hicks, Mortimer
Hicks, Mrs.
Lansing, Nick
Lansing, Susy (Branch)
Melrose, Violet
Senechal, Joan
Strefford, Charlie (Earl of Altringham)
Tooker, Eldoradder
Vanderlyn, Clarissa
Vanderlyn, Ellie
Vanderlyn, Nelson

Gods Arrive, The
Alders, Mr.
Alsop, Mrs. Dayton
Blemer, Gratz
Brail, Aaron
Brant, Octavius Alistair
Churley, Chris
Churley, Colonel
Churley, Mrs.
Crash, Margo
Dayes-Dawes, Lady
Delaney, Floss
Delaney, Mr.
Dorman, Mrs.
Dorman, the Rev.
Fane, Derek
Fleuret, Madame
Frenside, George
Glaisher, Mrs.
Hedstrom
Heff, Brank
Hipsley, the Hon. Ginevra
Jacob (chauffeur)
Lenz, Sady
Nevsky, Andros
Old Marquesa
Oster, Sir Felix
Pevensy, Lady
Pinson, Mimi
Plummet, Miss Pamela
Plunder, Gwen (Lady Guy)
Pulsifer, Jet
Savignac, M.

Scrimser, Grandma
Shunts, Honoré
Sidonie
Southernwood, Violet ("Jane Meggs")
Spartivento, Duke of
Spear, Lorburn (Lorry)
Spear, Mr.
Spear, Mrs.
Stram, Rebecca
Tarlton, Hon. Charles
Tarrant, Halo (Héloïse) Spear
Tarrant, Lewis
Tolby, Arthur
Tourment, Yves
Vicar of Hindhead, The
Weston, Lorin
Weston, Mae
Weston, Mrs. Lorin
Weston, Vance

"Her Son"
Brown, Boydon ("Boy")
Brown, Chrissy
Dacy, Thora
Glenn, Catherine Reamer (Mrs. Stephen)
Glenn, Stephen (son)
Norcutt, Mr.

"Hermit and the Wild Woman, The"
Hermit
Saint
Wild Woman (young woman)
Young boy

"His Father's Son"
Grew, Addie (Wicks)
Grew, Mason
Grew, Ronald
Bankshire, Daisy
Dolbrowski, Fortuné

"House of the Dead Hand, The"
Celsi, Count Ottaviano
Clyde, Professor

Lombard, Doctor
Lombard, Mrs.
Lombard, Sybilla
Maidservant
Wyant

House of Mirth, The
Barnes, Trenors' butler
Bart, Lily
Bart, Mr.
Bart, Mrs.
Beltshire, Duchess of
Bry, Mrs. Wellington
Bry, Wellington
Caretaker, Trenors' town house
Corby, Kate
Raith, Lady Cressida
Dacey, Lord Hubert
Dorset, Bertha (Mrs. George)
Dorset, George
Farish, Gerty
Fisher, Mrs. Carry
Footman, at Trenors'
Gormer, Mattie (Mrs. Sam)
Gormer, Sam
Gryce, Percy
Haffen, Mrs.
Haines, Miss
Hatch, Mrs. Norma
Housemaid, Trenors' country place
Landlady of boarding house
Melson, Mrs. Herbert
Morpeth, Paul
Peniston, Mrs. (Julia)
Pragg, Miss
Regina, Mme.
Rosedale, Simon
Selden, Lawrence
Silverton, Ned
Skiddaw, Lady
Skiddaw, Lord
Smedden, Miss
Stancy, Melville
Stepney, Jack
Stepney, Miss Grace
Steward, Dorsets' yacht
Struther, Nettie (Crane)
Trenor, Augustus

Trenor, Judy (Mrs. Gus)
Van Alstyne, Ned
Van Osburgh, Evelyn
Van Osburgh, Freddy
Van Osburgh, Gwen
Van Osburgh, Maria
Van Osburgh, Mrs. (Grace)
Weatherall, Mr.
Weatherall, Mrs.

Hudson River Bracketed
Blemer, Gratz
Delaney, Floss
Delaney, Harrison
Frenside, George
Fynes, Tristram
Hayes, Bunty
Hubbard, Mrs.
Jacob (chauffeur)
Lorburn, Ambrose
Lorburn, Miss
Lorburn, Tom
Mennenkoop, Mrs.
Lotus
O'Fallery
Pulsifer, Jet
Rauch, Eric
Scrimser, Grandma
Scrimser, Grandpa
Spear, Lorburn (Lorry)
Spear, Mr.
Spear, Mrs.
Stram, Rebecca
Tarrant, Halo (Héloïse) Spear
Tarrant, Lewis
Toler, Sadie
Tracy, Laura Lou
Tracy, Lucilla (Mrs. Lorburn)
Tracy, Upton
Weston, Lorin
Weston, Mae
Weston, Marcia
Weston, Mrs. Lorin
Weston, Pearl
Weston, Vance

"In Trust"
Ambrose, Daisy
Ambrose, Paul
Halidon, Ned
Narrator

"Introducers, The"
Bixby, Miss Sadie
Bixby, Mr.
Bixby, Mrs.
Grantham, Belle
Leicester, Aline
Magraw, Hutchins
Tilney, Frederick

"Journey, A"
Christian Scientist man
Husband
Pullman porter
Wife
Woman on train

"Joy in the House"
Ansley, Christine
Ansley, Christopher
Ansley, Devons
Bilk, Miss
Breck, Mabel
Lithgow, Jeffrey
Lithgow, Mrs.
Martha
Robbit, Mrs.
Susan (Nanny)

"Kerfol"
de Cornault, Anne
de Cornault, Yves
Judge
de Lanrivain, Hervé
de Lanrivain, M.
de Lanrivain, Mme.
Lawyer
Narrator

"Lady's Maid's Bell, The"
Agnes
Blinder, Mrs.
Brympton, Mr.
Brympton, Mrs.
Hartley, Alice
Limmel, Mr.
Railton, Mrs.
Ranford, Mr.
Saxon, Emma
Wace, Mr.
Walton, Dr.

"Lamp of Psyche, The "
Corbett, Delia (formerly Benson)
Corbett, Laurence

Hayne, Mrs. Mary Mason

"Last Asset, The"
Garnett, Paul
Hubbard, Mrs. Woolsey
Newell, Hermione
Newell, Mrs. Samuel
Newell, Samuel
Schenkelderff, Baron
du Trayas, Comte Louis

"Legend, The"
Bain, Isabella (Mrs. Beecher Bain)
Bernald, Arthur
Fosdick, Alice
Pellerin, John ("John Winterman")
Wade, Dr. Bob
Wade, Howland
Wade, Mrs. (mother of Bob and Howland)

"Letter, The"
Alingdon, Colonel
Briga, Doctor
Briga, Fernando
Duke of Modena
Falco, Donna Candida
Narrator
Verna, Countess
Verna, Emilio

"Letters, The"
Benn, Jackson
Céleste
Clopin, Madame
Deering, Juliet
Deering, Mrs.
Deering, Vincent
Macy, Andora
Mears, Harvey
Mears, Mrs. Harvey
Suzanne
West, Lizzie (later Deering)

"Line of Least Resistance, The"
Antrim, Frank
Bonifant, Reverend Doctor

Brownrigg, Ezra
Clerk, hotel
Meysy, Laurence
Mindon, Gladys
Mindon, Gwendolyn
Mindon, Millicent
Mindon, Mr.

"Long Run, The"
Cumnor, Mrs.
Cumnor, Phil
Merrick, Halston
Narrator
Reardon, Mr.
Reardon, Paulina (Trant)
Trant, Philip

"Looking Glass, The"
Attlee, Moyra
Attlee, Mrs. Cora
Clingsland, Mrs.
Divott, Father
Harry
Medium
Tutor

Madame de Treymes
d'Armillac, Madame
d'Armillac, Prince
Boykin, Bessy (Mrs. Elmer)
Boykin, Elmer
Durham, John
Durham, Katy
Durham, Mrs.
Durham, Nannie
de Malrive, Madame (Fanny Frisbee)
de Malrive, Marquis
de Malrive, Marquise
de Malrive, future Marquis (child of Fanny)
de Treymes, Madame (Christiane)

Marne, The
Belknap, Mr.
Belknap, Mrs. (Josephine)
Belknap, Troy
Gantier, M.
Gantier, Mme.
Gantier, Paul
Jacks, Hubert

Leath, Anna
Leath, Effie
Leath, Fraser
Leath, Owen
McTarvie-Birch, Mrs.
Mayne, Kitty
Murrett, Mrs.
Painter, Adelaide
Viner, Sophy

"Refugees, The"
Beausedge, Lady
Beausedge, Lord
Bolchester, Duchess
  of (Gwen)
Durand, Professor
  Charles
Rushworth, Agatha
Rushworth, Col.
  Audrey
Rushworth, Caroline
Rushworth, Clio
Rushworth, Kathleen
Trantham, Lady Ivy

"Rembrandt, The"
Copt, Eleanor
Crozier
Frontage, Mrs.
Museum Curator
  (narrator)
Rose, Jefferson

"Roman Fever"
Ansley, Grace
Ansley, Babs
Ansley, Horace
  (deceased)
Headwaiter
Slade, Alida
Slade, Delphin
  (deceased)
Slade, Jenny

Sanctuary
Darrow, Paul
Gill, Mr.
Hinton
Orme, Mr.
Peyton, Arthur
Peyton, Denis
Peyton, Dick
Peyton, Kate
  (Orme)
Peyton, Mrs.
Verney, Clemence

"Seed of the Faith, The"
Ahmed
Ayoub
Bent, Willard
Blandhorn, Mr.
Blandhorn, Mrs.
Myriem
Spink, Harry

Son at the Front, A
Anthony, Adele
Beausite, M.
Beausite, Mme.
Boylston
Brant, Anderson
Brant, Julia
Campton, George
Campton, John
Dastrey, Louis
Dastrey, Paul
Davril, Mlle
Davril, René
de Dolmetsch, Mme.
  (Daisy)
Fortin-Lescluze, Dr.
Fortin-Lescluze,
  Mme.
Isador, Ladislas
Jorgenstein, Sir Cyril
Lebel, Jules
Lebel, Mme.
Mayhew, Harvey
Olida, Mme.
Olida, Pepito
Talkett, Madge
Talkett, Ralph
de Tranlay, Marquise
de Tranlay, Mlle
  Claire
Upsher, Benny
Upsher, Madeline

"Souls Belated"
Ainger, Mrs.
Condit, Lady Susan
Gannett, Ralph
Linton, Mrs. (Mrs.
  Cope)
Pinsent, Miss
Tillotson, Lydia
Trevenna, Lord

Spark (The 'Sixties), The
Alstrop, Jack
Broad, Frederick
Byrne, Bolton

Delane, Hayley
Delane, Leila (Gracy)
Delane, Mrs.
Detrancy, Major
Gracy, Bill
Narrator
Ruscott, Colonel
Scole, General

Summer (novella)
Balch, Annabel
Cooperson, Ned
Fry, Ben
Fry, Carrick
Fry, Orma
Fry, Mrs. Tom
Harney, Lucius
Hatchard, Miss
Hatchard, Honorius
Hawes, Ally
Hawes, Julia
Hobart, Mrs.
Hyatt, Bash
Hyatt, Liff
Hyatt, Mary
Marsh, Verena
Merkle, Dr.
Miles, Mrs.
Miles, The Rev.
Royall, Charity
Royall, Lawyer
Skeff, Eudora
Sollas, Lambert
Targatt, Ida
Targatt, Mamie

"Temperate Zone, The"
Brankhurst, Lady
Fingall, Horace
French, Willis
Jolyesse, M. André
Morland, Emily
Morland, the Rev.
  Ambrose
Parlormaid
Paul, Donald
Paul, Bessy (Fingall)

"That Good May Come"
Birkton, Annette
  (sister)
Birkton, Maurice
Birkton, Mrs.
  (mother)
Blason, Dick
Buley, Baker

Helfenridge
Stapleton, Mrs.
Thurifer, Father
Tolquitt, Mrs.

Touchstone, The (novella)
Armiger, Mrs.
Aubyn, Margaret
Dinslow
Dresham, Mrs.
Flamel, Barton
Forth, Professor
Glennard, Alexa
  Trent
Glennard, Stephen
Hollingsworth
Joslin, Professor
Touchett, May
Virginia, Aunt

"Triumph of Night, The"
Balch, Mr.
Faxon, George
Grisben, Mr.
Lavington, John
Lodgekeeper
Peters
Rainer, Frank

"Twilight of the God,
  The"
Footman
Oberville, John
Warland, Isabel
Warland, Lucius

Twilight Sleep
Ardwin, Tommy
Bruss, Maisie
Bruss, Mrs.
Cardinal, The
Clapp, Orba
Greg, Parker
Heuston, Aggie
Heuston, Stanley
Klawhammer
Landish, Kitty (Mrs.
  Percy)
Lindon, Bee
Lindon, Fanny
Loft, Alvah
Mahatma, The
Maisie
Manford, Dextere
Manford, Nona
Manford, Pauline

Powder
Rivington, Mrs.
   Walter
Rivington, Walter
di San Fidele,
   Marchesa
   (Amalsuntha)
di San Fidele,
   Marchese
   (Venturino)
di San Fidele,
   Michaelangelo
Swoffer, Mrs.
Toy, Gladys (Mrs.
   Herman)
Vollard, Miss
Wyant, Arthur
Wyant, Jim
Wyant, Lita
Wyant, Old Mrs.

"Valley of Childish
   Things, and Other
   Emblems, The"
Architect
Children in valley
Death
Judgment angel
Little boy
Little girl
Maiden lady
Man and wife
Shape
Two men

Valley of Decision, The
Abbess of Venetian
   convent
Alfieri, Count Vittorio

Andreoni
Belverde, Countess
Boscofolto,
   Marchioness of
Brà, Procucuratore
Brà, Procuratessa
Bruno
Cantapresto
Castelrovinato,
   Count of
Cerveno, Marquess of
Coeur-Volant,
   Marquis de
De Crucis, Abate
Donna Laura
   (Countess Valdu)
Donna Livia
Duke of Monte
   Alloro
Duke of Pianura
   (father of Prince
   Ferrante)
Ferrante, Prince
Filomena
Gambo, Carlo
   ("Brutus")
Gervaso, Don
Giannozzo
Heiligenstern, Count
Ignazio, Father
Malmocco, Signorina
Maria Clementina,
   twice Duchess of
   Pianura
(married to two
   Dukes of Pianura)
Marquess of Donnaz
Mirandolina of
   Chioggia

Momola
Sister Mary of the
   Crucifix
Trescorre, Don Lelio
Valsecca, Odo, Duke
   of Pianura
Vanna
Vivaldi, Professor
   Orazio
Vivaldi, Fulvia
   ("Sister Veronica")
"Young, Arthur"

"Velvet Ear Pads"
Hibbert, Loring G.
Balalatinsky, Princess
   (Betsy)
Tring, Taber
Footman

"Venetian Night's
   Entertainment, A"
Bracknell, Tony
   (later Judge
   Anthony)
Cador, Donna
   Polixena
Cador, Senator
Count Rialto
Marquess Zanipolo
Mounce, the Rev.
   Ozias

"Verdict, The"
Croft, Hermia
Gisburn, Mrs.
Gisburn, Jack
Grindle, Victor
Nutley, Claude

Rickham, Mr.
   (narrator)
Stroud, Mr.
   (deceased)
Stroud, Mrs.
Thwing, Mrs. Gideon

"Writing a War Story"
Durand, Emile
Harbard, Harold
Mademoiselle
   (governess)
Spang, Miss Ivy

"Xingu"
Ballinger, Mrs.
Dane, Osric
Glyde, Laura
Leveret, Mrs.
Plinth, Mrs.
Roby, Fanny
Van Vluyck, Miss

"Young Gentlemen,
   The"
Catherine
Cook
Cranch, Waldo
Cranch, Master
   Waldo
Cranch, Master
   Donald
Cranch, Mrs. Waldo
Davids, Homer
Durant, Mrs.
Narrator
Oast, Hannah
Sampson, Janey
Selwick, Lucilla

4. Artistic, Historical and Literary Periods, Terms, Events

Académie française
aesthetic views
American Academy
   of Arts and Letters
architecture
baroque style

Belle Époque
commedia dell'arte
connoisseurship
doctorate, honorary
entry of Allied armies
   into Paris

feminism
"Genteel Circle, The"
"Gilded Age, The"
Institut de France
manners, novel
   of

National Institute of
   Arts and Letters
salon
Scribner Archives
tableau vivant
World War I

5. Places

Aegean
Algeria and Tunisia
Alps
Alsace
America
Argonne
Auvergne
Beinecke Library,
    Yale University
Brenta Riviera
Cimitière des Gonards
Como, Lake
England
Europe
Faubourg Saint-
    Germain (Paris)

Fez (Morocco)
Firestone Library,
    Princeton University
France
Germany
Hyères (France)
Iseo, Lake
I Tatti, Villa
Italy
Lamb House (Rye,
    Sussex, England)
Land's End (Newport)
Lenox, Massachusetts
Lilly Library, Indiana
    University
London

Maggiore, Lake
Mediterranean cruises
Milan
Morocco
Mount, The
Newport
New England
New York
Nohant
North Africa
Osprey (yacht)
Paris
Parma
Pavillon Colombe
Pencraig
Pencraig Cottage

Queen's Acre
    ("Qu'Acre")
    (England)
Riviera, Brenta (Italy)
Riviera, French
Rome
Ste.-Claire Château
San Vivaldo (Italy)
Scribner Archives,
    Princeton University
Spain
Vanadis (yacht)
Venice
Vosges, the

6. Organizations and Institutions

Académie française
American Academy of
    Arts and Letters
American Hostels for
    Refugees

Catholicism, Roman—
    Wharton's attitude
    toward
Children of Flanders
    Rescue Committee

Franco-American
    General Committee
Institut de France
    (Institute of France)
Legion of Honor, French

Maisons Américaines de
    Convalescence
National Institute of Arts
    and Letters

7. Publishing: Editors, Publishers, Periodicals

Academy, The
American Academy of
    Arts and Letters
Appleton and Co.
Atlantic Monthly
Beinecke Library, Yale
    University
Brownell, William Crary
Burlingame, Edward L.
*Century Illustrated
    Monthly Magazine, The*
Chevrillon, André
Edith Wharton on Film
    and Television: A
    Filmography
    (Appendix II.1)

Firestone Library
    (Princeton University)
Gilder, Richard Watson
Harper's Magazine
Hearst, William
    Randolph
illustrations, of
    Wharton's fiction and
    works of travel
Jewett, Rutger B.
Ladies' Home Journal, The
Lilly Library (Indiana
    University)
media adaptations of
    Edith Wharton's
    works (Appendix II)

musical adaptations of
    Edith Wharton's
    works (Appendix II.3)
Parrish, Maxfield
Peixotto, Ernest
Perry, Bliss
Pictorial Review
Quarterly Review
Redbook
Revue de Paris
Revue des Deux Mondes
Revue Hebdomadaire
*Saturday Evening Post,
    The*
*Saturday Review of
    Literature, The*

Scribner Archives
Scribner, Charles II
Scribner's (Charles
    Scribner's Sons)
Scribner's Magazine
Sedgwick, Ellery
theatrical adaptations of
    Edith Wharton's
    works (Appendix
    II.2)
Updike, Berkeley

8. Special Interests and Pursuits

aesthetic views
anti-Semitism
architecture
baroque style
commedia dell'arte
connoisseurship

divorce
eroticism
expatriation
feminism
gardens and gardening
ghosts

harems (*see IN MOROCCO*)
interior design, of
    rooms
occult, Wharton's
    interest in
salon

supernatural, in
    Wharton's fiction
travels
war relief, World War I

9. Works by Wharton

"After Holbein"
"Afterward"
Age of Innocence, The
"All Souls"
"Angel at the Grave, The"
"April Showers"
Architecture of Humanism (Geoffrey Scott) (review)
Artemis to Actaeon and Other Verse
"Atrophy"
"Autres Temps . . ."
Backward Glance, A
"Beatrice Palmato" (fragment)
Belchamber (Howard Sturgis) (Review)
"Belgian Prisoners of War, The"
"Best Man, The"
"Bewitched"
Blashfield, Edwin (review of *Italian Cities*)
"Blond Beast, The"
"Bolted Door"
Book of the Homeless, The
"Bottle of Perrier, A"
"Bread Upon the Waters"
Buccaneers, The
"Bunner Sisters"
Certain People
"Charm Incorporated"
Children, The
"Choice, The"
"Colophon to the Mortal Lease"
"Coming Home"
"Confession"
"Confessional, The"
"Copy"
"Coward, A"
"Criticism of Fiction, The"
Crucial Instances
Cruise of the Vanadis, The
"Cup of Cold Water, A"
Custom of the Country, The
"Cycle of Reviewing, A"
"Daunt Diana, The"
"Day of the Funeral, The"

"Debt, The"
Decoration of Houses, The
"Descent of Man, The"
Descent of Man and Other Stories, The
"Diagnosis"
Diary, 1907 ("The Life Apart") (1907)
Diary, 1908, Daily
"Dieu d'Amour"
"Dilettante, The"
"Disintegration"
Donnée Book
"Duchess at Prayer, The"
"Duration"
Eliot, George (Leslie Stephen) (review)
Eternal Passion in English Poetry
Ethan Frome
"Experience" (poem)
"Expiation"
Eyes, The
False Dawn (The 'Forties)
Fast and Loose (novella)
Fighting France, from Dunkerque to Belfort
Fool Errant (Maurice Hewlett) (review)
Foreword to *Bénédiction* (by Countess Philomène de La Forest-Divonne (pseud. Claude Silve)
Foreword to *Ethan Frome: A Dramatization of Edith Wharton's Novel*
French Ways and Their Meaning
"Friends"
Fruit of the Tree, The
"Full Circle"
"Fullness of Life, The"
Futility, by William Gerhardi (Preface)
"Garden Valedictory, A"
"George Cabot Lodge" (essay)
Ghosts
Gift from the Grave, A (English title of *The Touchstone*)
"Glimpse, A"

Glimpses of the Moon, The
Gods Arrive, The
"Great American Novel, The"
"Great Blue Tent, The"
Greater Inclination, The
"Henry James in His Letters" (review)
"Her Son"
Here and Beyond
"Hermit and the Wild Woman, The"
Hermit and the Wild Woman, The, and Other Stories
"His Father's Son"
"House of the Dead Hand, The"
House of Mirth, The
Hudson River Bracketed
Human Nature
In Morocco
"In Trust"
"Intense Love's Utterance"
"Introducers, The"
Introduction to *Ethan Frome* (1922) (in *Ethan Frome* entry)
Introduction to *The House of Mirth* (1936) (in *House of Mirth* entry)
Italian Backgrounds
Italian Villas and Their Gardens
"Jean du Breuil de Saint-Germain"
"Journey, A"
"Joy in the House"
"Joy of Living, The" (Translation of Hermann Sudermann's *Es Lebe das Leben*)
Kate Spain (see "Unconvessed Crime" and "Confession")
"Kerfol"
"Lady's Maid's Bell, The"
"Lamp of Psyche, The"
"Last Asset, The"
"Last Giustiniani, The"
"Legend, The"
"Letter, The"

"Letters, The"
"Life and I"
"Line of Least Resistance, The"
"Literature" (unfinished projected novel)
"Litte Girl's New York, A"
"Long Run, The"
"Looking Glass, The"
Madame de Treymes
Marne, The
Matthew Arnold (Herbert Paul) (review)
"Memories of Bourget Overseas"
"Metteurs en Scène, Les"
"Miss Mary Pask"
"Mission of Jane, The"
"Mortal Lease, The"
Mother's Recompense, The
Motor-Flight Through France, A
"Motor-Flight Through Spain, A"
"Moving Finger, The"
"Mr. Jones"
"Mrs. Manstey's View"
"Muse's Tragedy, The"
New Year's Day (The 'Seventies)
"Ogrin the Hermit"
Old Maid (The 'Fifties), The
Old New York
"Old New York"
"On Bayard Cutting, Jr."
"Other Two, The"
"Pelican, The"
"Permanent Values in Fiction"
"Permanent Wave"
Poetry, of Edith Wharton
"Pomegranate Seed"
"Portrait, The"
"Pot-Boiler, The"
"Pretext, The"
"Quicksand, The"
"Reckoning, The"
"Reconsideration of Proust, A"
"Recovery, The"
"Refugees, The"
"Rembrandt, The"

"Roman Fever"
Sanctuary
"Sapphire Way, The"
"Seed of the Faith, The"
"Senlis, May 16"
"Some Woman to Some Man"
Son at the Front, A
"Sonnets of *The Wingless Hours* (Eugene Lee-Hamilton) (review)
"Souls Belated"
"Souvenirs du Bourget d'Outremer"
Spark (The 'Sixties), The
Speak to the Earth: Wanderings and Reflections Among Elephants and

Mountains (Vivienne de Watteville) (preface)
Summer (novella)
Tales of Men and Ghosts
"Temperate Zone, The"
"Tendencies in Modern Fiction"
"Terminus"
Tess of the D'Urbervilles (review of performance)
"That Good May Come"
"Three Francescas, The"
"*Touchstone, The*" (novella)
"Triumph of Night, The"

Twelve Poems
"Twilight of the God, The"
Twilight Sleep
Ulysses: A Drama (Stephen Phillips) (review)
"Unreprinted Parody; 'More Love Letters of an Englishwoman, An' "
"Valley of Childish Things, and Other Emblems, The"
Valley of Decision, The
"Velvet Ear Pads"
"Venetian Night's Entertainment, A"
"Verdict, The"

Verses
"Vesalius in Zante"
"Vice of Reading, The"
Village Romeo and Juliet, A (Gottfried Keller; translated by Anna Bahlmann; introduction by Edith Wharton)
"Visibility in Fiction"
"William C. Brownell"
World Over, The
"Writing a War Story"
"Writing of *Ethan Frome,* The"
Writing of Fiction, The
"Xingu"
Xingu and Other Stories
"Young Gentlemen, The"

10. Works by Other Writers

Architecture of Humanism, The (Geoffrey Scott)
Belchamber (Howard Sturgis)
Bénédiction (Comtesse Philomène de La Forest-Divonne [pseud. Claude Silve]
Es Lebe das Leben (Sudermann, Hermann)
Faust (Johann Wolfgang von Goethe)

Fool Errant, The (Maurice Hewlett)
Futility (William Gerhardi)
George Eliot (Leslie Stephen)
"Henry James in His Letters" (review of *The Letters of Henry James*)
Italian Cities (Edwin and Evangeline Blashfield)

Matthew Arnold (Herbert W. Paul)
Outre-Mer (Bourget, Paul)
Sonnets of the Wingless Hours, The (Eugene Lee-Hamilton)
Speak to the Earth: Wanderings and Reflections Among Elephants and Mountains (Vivienne de Watteville)

Tess of the D'Urbervilles (Mrs. Minnie Maddern Fiske's performance in Lorimer Stoddard's dramatization of)
Ulysses: A Drama (Stephen Phillips)
Village Romeo and Juliet, A (Gottfried Keller)

11. Writers and Other Artists

Adams, Henry
Arnold, Matthew
Austin, Sir Alfred
Baedeker, Karl
Bahlmann, Anna (*see A Village Romeo and Juliet*)
Balfour, Arthur James
Berenson, Bernard
Berenson, Mary
Blanche, Jacques-Émile
Blashfield, Edwin
Blashfield, Evangeline
Bourget, Paul
Breuil de Saint-Germain, Jean du
Brownell, William Crary

Chanler, Margaret ("Daisy") Terry
Chevrillon, André
Clark, Kenneth
Cocteau, Jean
Codman, Ogden
Conrad, Joseph
Dante Aligheri
de Watteville, Vivienne (*see Speak to the Earth: Wanderings and Reflections among Elephants and Mountains*)
Du Bos, Charles
Edel, Leon
Eliot, George
Eliot, T.S.
Emerson, Ralph Waldo
Fitzgerald, F. Scott

Fullerton, Morton
Gay, Walter
Gerhardi, William
Gerould, Katherine
Gilder, Richard Watson
Gide, André
Goethe, Johann Wolfgang von
Goldoni, Carlo
Grant, Judge Robert
Hardy, Thomas
Hewlett, Maurice
Homer
Howells, William Dean
Irving, Washington
James, Henry
Jones, Mary Cadwalader Rawle
Joyce, James

Keller, Gottfried (*see A Village Romeo and Juliet*)
Kipling, Rudyard
La Forest-Divonne, Comtesse Philomène de (pseud. Claude Silve)
Lapsley, Gaillard
Lee, Vernon
Lee-Hamilton, Eugene
Lewis, Sinclair
Lubbock, Percy
MacCarthy, Desmond
Maurois, André
Meredith, George
Mitchell, Dr. [S]ilas Weir
Nicolson, Harold

Nietzsche, Friedrich
Nijinsky, Waslaw
Norton, Charles Eliot
Norton, Robert
Parrish, Maxfield
Pater, Walter
Paul, Herbert W. (*see Matthew Arnold,* review of)
Peixotto, Ernest
Perry, Bliss
Proust, Marcel
Roosevelt, Theodore
Ruskin, John

Sand, George
Santayana, George
Sargent, John Singer
Schlumberger, Gustave
Scott, Geoffrey
Sedgwick, Ellery
Silve, Claude (pseud. of Comtesse Philomène de La Forest-Divonne)
Smith, Logan Pearsall
Stephen, Leslie
Stoddard, Lorimer (*see* review of Mrs. Fiske's

performance in Stoddard's dramatization of *Tess of the D'Urbervilles*)
Strachey, Lytton
Sturgis, Howard
Sudermann, Hermann (*see Es Lebe das Leben,* or "The Joy of Living"; Campbell, Mrs. Patrick)
Symonds, John Addington
Symons, Arthur

Tiepolo, Giovanni Battista
Turner, William Joseph
Tyler, William Royall ("Bill")
Washburn, Edward Abiel
Wells, H. G.
Whitman, Walt
Woolf, Virginia
Young, Arthur
Zola, Émile

12. Honors, Awards and Prizes

chevalier of the French Legion of Honor
doctorate, honorary (*see* YALE UNIVERSITY)

Medal of Queen Elisabeth (of Belgium)
Pulitzer Prize
Nobel Prize nomination

Yale University, honorary doctorate

APPENDIX II
MEDIA ADAPTATIONS OF EDITH WHARTON'S WORKS

1. Edith Wharton on Film and Television: A Filmography

Scott Marshall
Deputy Director, Edith Wharton Restoration at The Mount
Lenox, Massachusetts

As Edith Wharton explained in her autobiography, *A BACKWARD GLANCE,* she was born "into a world in which telephones, motors, electric light, central heating (except by hot-air furnaces), X-rays, cinemas, radium, aeroplanes and wireless telegraphy were not only unknown but still mostly unforeseen" (6–7). She loved the motorcar, utilized the convenience of both telephone and telegraph, had electricity and central heating installed in her home, The Mount, in 1901, and saw the first airplane fly over Paris seven years later. However, one major new invention that she was never able to come to terms with aesthetically was the motion picture, or the "cinema," as she called it.

Despite her personal dislike of the medium, several of Wharton's most popular novels were filmed during her lifetime, including *The AGE OF INNOCENCE* (twice—first as a silent movie, then as a sound film), *The HOUSE OF MIRTH, The GLIMPSES OF THE MOON* and *The CHILDREN* (as "The Marriage Playground").[1] Shortly after her death one additional film was made: "The Old Maid." Following its release in 1939, no feature film of a Wharton work would appear until an unsuccessful version of "The Children" in 1990—a hiatus of more than 50 years.

After her death, most of Wharton's fiction was considered old-fashioned, and for many years her popularity waned, with the exception of *ETHAN FROME* (1911), deemed by critics to be a masterpiece. Appropriately it became the first Wharton work to be dramatized for the small screen of television, appearing in 1960. It would be almost a third of a century more before this classic story finally appeared as a major motion picture in 1993.

The publication of *Edith Wharton: A Biography* by R. W. B. Lewis (1975) and Cynthia Griffin Wolff's *A Feast of Words—The Triumph of Edith Wharton* (1977) stimulated new interest in televising both Wharton's life and her works. In 1981 the Public Broadcasting System (funded by the National Endowment for the Humanities) produced a three-part series on Wharton, consisting of one segment on her life ("Looking Back") and two dramatizations of her fiction ("The House of Mirth" and "Summer"). Two years later, three ghost stories by Wharton were filmed for the "Shades of Darkness" series by Granada Television of England: "The LADY'S MAID'S BELL," "AFTERWARD" and "BEWITCHED."

In the 1990s, Hollywood rediscovered Wharton, coinciding with and perhaps because of an increasing interest in women's issues and a resurgence in the popularity of period films. No longer considered old-fashioned, Wharton's works were recognized to be timely and dramatically compelling; her vivid evocations of a past era defined by manners and mores were also found to be commercial. Michelle Pfeiffer, Daniel Day-Lewis and Winona Ryder starred in Martin Scorsese's "The Age of Innocence," preceded by Liam Neeson in "Ethan Frome." These films were followed by BBC Television's multipart adaptation of Wharton's final novel, *The BUCCANEERS* (1938).

Wharton may have entered a movie theater only once in her lifetime; she saw a silent film on a trip to Spain in 1914 with her friend Walter BERRY. The earliest mention of film in her fiction occurred soon after in *SUMMER* (1917); the heroine's attendance at a silent movie in Nettleton on the Fourth of July represents an exhilarating expansion of her narrow world.

---

[1] To distinguish book from screen titles, film and television adaptations of Wharton's fiction appear in quotation marks.

Two of Wharton's "Jazz Age" novels, TWILIGHT SLEEP (1927) and *The Children* (1928), contain numerous references to the cinema. Wharton's portrayal of films in her fiction became quite negative; movies for her had evolved into trendy, mindless experiences to be avoided by serious, intelligent people. Wharton's final word on the medium appears in the preface to GHOSTS (1937), her last collection of stories. She scathingly denounced both the "cinema" and "wireless" radio as the "two worldwide enemies of the imagination," further lamenting that "to a generation for whom everything which used to nourish the imagination because it had to be won by an effort, and then slowly assimilated, is now served cooked, seasoned and chopped into little bits, the creative faculty . . . is rapidly withering, together with the power of sustained attention . . ." Her criticism has a contemporary sound; just substitute the concept of television today for the cinema and the radio she despised.

Despite these negative feelings, Wharton did utilize the power of film to benefit her wartime charities. According to Alan Price, she made arrangements to have films made of several of her convalescent homes for viewing in the United States in order to stimulate much-needed fund-raising (*The End of the Age of Innocence: Edith Wharton and the First World War* [New York: St. Martin's Press, 1996], 150).

Like Henry JAMES, Wharton desired successful stage adaptations of her stories and novels. In her early years, she worked on several dramatizations, and she also collaborated with the celebrated dramatist Clyde Fitch on a stage version of *The House of Mirth* (1906). She continued in her later years to evince an interest in theatrical adaptations of her novels and stories.

In her 1936 foreword to the published play version of "Ethan Frome" by Owen and Donald Davis, Wharton enthusiastically set aside her concerns regarding actors physically inhabiting the characters that she had originally conceived in fictional terms, as well as her distaste for "that grimacing enlargement of gesture and language supposed to be necessary to 'carry' over the footlights": "It has happened to me, as to most novelists, to have the odd experience, through the medium of reviews or dramatizations of their work, to see their books as they have taken shape in other minds: always a curious, and sometimes a painful, revelation." Wharton further specified her "admiration for the great skill and exquisite sensitiveness with which my interpreters have executed their task . . . [it is] an unusual achievement" (viii)—praise only accorded to an adaptation of her work for the theater.

FILMOGRAPHY

1918: *The House of Mirth* (Metro, 6 reels, silent)
Director: Albert Capellani **Screenplay:** June Mathis and Albert Capellani

Cast: Katherine Harris Barrymore (Lily Bart), with Henry Kolker, Christine Mayo, Joseph Kilgour, Edward Abeles, W. D. Fisher, Lottie Briscoe, Pauline Welsh, Maggie Western, Nellie Parker-Spaulding, Sidney Bracy, Kempton Greene, Morgan Jones
Status: lost
Notes: credits from Bodeen (81); *see also* Lewis, *Edith Wharton*, 7.

1923: *The Glimpses of the Moon* (Paramount, 7 reels, silent)
Director: Allan Dwan **Screenplay:** E. Lloyd Shelton and Edfrid A. Bingham **Presented by:** Jesse L. Lasky
Cast: Bebe Daniels (Susan), David Powell (Nick), Nita Naldi (Mrs. Vanderlyn), Maurice Costello (Mr. Vanderlyn) with Rubye De Remer, Charles Gerard, William Quirk, Pearl Sindelar, Beth Allen, Mrs. George Peggram, Delores Costello, Millie Muller, Beatrice Coburn, Fred Hadley, Robert Lee Keeling, Barton Adams, Freddie Veri
Status: lost
Notes: credits from Bodeen (81). Film rights sold for $13,500 (Lewis, *Edith Wharton*, 444) or $15,000 (Benstock, *No Gifts from Chance*, 372). Both note that F. Scott Fitzgerald wrote the film dialogue; Benstock states Fitzgerald was paid $500 for this, but "his script apparently was not used" (372). She adds that "Appleton had flooded Los Angeles and Hollywood newspapers with advertisements to create a demand for film rights to her [Wharton's] works" (371).

1924: *The Age of Innocence* (Warner Bros., 7 reels, silent)
Director: Wesley Ruggles **Screenplay:** Olga Printzlau
Cast: Beverly Bayne (Countess Olenska), Elliot Dexter (Newland Archer), with Edith Roberts, Willard Louis, Fred Huntley, Gertrude Norman, Sigrid Holmquist, Stuart Holmes
Status: lost
Notes: credits from Bodeen (81). Wharton netted $9,000 after agent's fees from the movie contract (Benstock, *No Gifts*, 361).

1929: *The Marriage Playground*, based on *The Children* (Paramount, 70 minutes, all talking)
Director: Lothar Mendes **Screenplay:** J. Walter Ruben **Adaptation and Dialogue:** Doris Anderson **Photography:** Victor Milner
Cast: Mary Brian (Judy), Fredric March (Martin), Huntley Gordon (Cliffe), Lilyan Tashman (Joyce), Kay Francis (Lady Wrench), William Austin (Lord Wrench), Phillip de Lacey (Terry), Seena Owen (Mrs. Sellars), with Anita Louise, Little Mitzi Green, Billy Seay, Ruby Parsely, Donald Smith, Jocelyn Lee, Maude Turner Gordon, David Newell, Armand Kaliz, Joan Standing, Gordon De Main

Status: exists

Notes: credits from *Variety* 5/30/90 and Bodeen (81). Wharton received $25,000 for the film rights from Paramount Famous Lasky Corporation (Lewis, *Edith Wharton,* 484, and Benstock, *No Gifts from Chance,* 407).

1934: *The Age of Innocence* (RKO Radio, 9 reels, sound, c. 80–90 minutes)

Director: Philip Moeller **Screenplay:** Sarah Y. Mason and Victor Heerman (from the novel by Wharton and the theater dramatization by Margaret Ayer Barnes) **Producer:** Pandro S. Berman **Costumes:** Walter Plunkett **Music:** Max Steiner

Cast: Irene Dunne (Countess Olenska), John Boles (Newland Archer), Julie Haydon (May Welland), Lionel Atwill (Beaufort), Laura Hope Crews (Mrs. Welland), Helen Westley (Granny Mingott), Herbert Yost (Mr. Welland), Theresa Maxwell-Conover (Mrs. Archer), Edith Van Cleve (Janey Archer), Leonard Carey (butler)

Status: exists

Notes: credits from the *New York Times* review 10/19/34 and Bodeen (81). Wharton received $15,000 for the film rights (Lewis, *Edith Wharton,* 430).

1935: *Strange Wives* (Universal, 8 reels, sound)

Director: Richard Thorpe **Screenplay:** Gladys Unger (from Wharton's short story "Bread Upon the Waters") **Additional Dialogue:** Barry Trivers and James Mulhauser

Cast: Roger Pryor, June Clayworth, Esther Ralston, Hugh O'Connell, Ralph Forbes, Cesar Romero, Francis L. Sullivan, Valerie Hobson, Leslie Fenton, Ivan Lebedeff, Doris Lloyd, Claude Gillingwater

Status: lost

Notes: Wharton to Mary Cadwalader Jones, April 10, 1934: "Thank you so much for acting as my substitute in the film contract for 'Bread Upon the Waters.' I wish the sum had more nearly approached the prices I used to get!" (Lewis and Lewis, *Letters,* 577). Benstock notes that Rutger Jewett sold the story for $5,000 to the movies (*No Gifts from Chance,* 439).

1939: *The Old Maid* (Warner Bros., 95 minutes, sound)

Director: Edmund Goulding **Screenplay:** Casey Robinson (from Wharton's novella and the theater dramatization by Zoë Akins) **Producer:** Hal B. Wallis with Henry Blanke **Photography:** Tony Gaudio **Art Direction:** Robert Haas **Music:** Max Steiner **Costumes:** Orry-Kelly **Editor:** George Amy

Cast: Bette Davis (Charlotte Lovell), Miriam Hopkins (Delia Lovell), George Brent (Clem Spender), Donald Crisp (Dr. Lanskell), Jane Bryan (Tina), Louise Fazenda (maid), James Stephenson (Jim Ralston), Jerome Cowan (Joe Ralston), William Lundigan (Lan-

ning Halsey), with Rand Brooks, Cecelia Loftus, Janet Shaw, William DeWolf Hopper, Marlene Burnett, Rod Cameron, Doris Lloyd, Frederick Burton

Status: Available for rental on videocassette, and in 16 mm or 35 mm

Notes: credits compiled from *The Films of Bette Davis* (96) and Bodeen (81). *See* Margaret B. McDowell's "Wharton's 'The Old Maid': Novella/Play/Film" for a full discussion of the various adaptations; *see also* Lewis, *Edith Wharton,* 7, 436.

1960: *Ethan Frome* (*Television*—aired February 18, 1960 as the DuPont Show of the Month)

Director: Alex Segal **Teleplay:** Jacqueline Babbin and Audrey Gellin **Producer:** David Susskind

Cast: Sterling Hayden (Ethan Frome), Julie Harris (Mattie Silver), Clarice Blackburn (Zenobia Frome), with narration by Arthur Hill.

Status: May be viewed at the Museum of Broadcasting, New York City

Notes: First Wharton adaptation on television (Marshall, 16)

1981: *Looking Back* (*Television*—biographical sketch of Wharton, 56 minutes)

Director: Kirk Browning **Teleplay:** Steve Lawson **Producers:** Sam Paul and Dorothy Cullman (A Cinelit Production) **Associate Producer:** Jackie Craig **Photography:** Francis Kenny **Art Direction:** John Kasarda **Costumes:** Jennifer Von Mayrhauser **Casting:** Bonnie Timmermann **Executive Producer:** Jack Willis

Cast: Kathleen Widdoes (Edith Wharton), John Cullum (Walter Berry), John McMartin (Teddy Wharton), Richard Woods (Henry James), Stephen Collins (Morton Fullerton)

Notes: Loosely based on *A Backward Glance* and *Edith Wharton* by R. W. B. Lewis. The Elms in Newport, Rhode Island, was used for the exteriors of The Mount. Credits transcribed from tape by Scott Marshall.

1981: *The House of Mirth* (*Television,* 95 minutes)

Director: Adrian Hall **Teleplay:** Adrian Hall and Richard Cumming **Producers:** Daniel A. Bohr and Dorothy Cullman **Executive Producer:** Jack Willis **Photography:** Paul Goldsmith and Hart Perry **Production Design:** Eugene Lee and Franne Lee **Costumes:** Karen Roston **Casting:** Bonnie Timmermann **Editor:** Charlotte Zwerin **Music:** Richard Cumming

Cast: Geraldine Chaplin (Lily Bart), William Atherton (Lawrence Selden), Barbara Blossom (Mme. Regine), Bree (Old Man), Timothy Crowe (Lord Dacey), Barbara Damashek (Nettie Struther), Virginia Donaldson (Alice Wetherall), Tim Donoghue (Ned Silverton), Elaine Eldridge (Mrs. Bart), Monique Fowler (Evie Van Osburgh), Elizabeth Franz (Grace Stepney), Peter Gerety (Jack Stepney), Bradford Gottlin (Percy

Gryce), Ed Hall (Paul Morpeth), Judith Harkness (Miss Corby), Richard Jenkins (George Dorset), David Jones (Mr. Bart), Melanie Jones (Mrs. Bry), David Kennett (butler), Richard Kneeland (Simon Rosedale), Marjorie Lee (Duchess of Beltshire), Marguerite Lenert (Mrs. Peniston), Howard London (lawyer), Mana Manente (Gerty Farish), George Martin (Gus Trenor), Barbara Meek (Mrs. Haffen), Barbara Orson (Judy Trenor), Julie Pember (Mrs. Peniston's maid), Margo Skinner (Carry Fisher), Lois Smith (Bertha Dorset), Norman Smith (Wellington Bry), William E. Smith (Mr. Wetherall), Amy Van Nostrand (Gwen Van Osburgh). With the participation of the Trinity Square Repertory Company.

Notes: Some scenes filmed in Newport, Rhode Island. Credits transcribed from tape by Scott Marshall.

1981: *Summer* (*Television,* 87 minutes)

Director: Dezso Magyar **Teleplay:** Charles Gaines **Producers:** Daniel A. Bohr and Dorothy Cullman **Executive Producer:** Jack Willis **Photography:** Michael Fash, B.S.C. **Art Direction:** Leon Munier **Costumes:** Carr Garnett **Music:** Lee Hoiby **Casting:** Bonnie Timmermann **Editor:** Janet Merwin **Sound:** Vincent Stenerson **Hair and Makeup:** Steve Atha **Associate Producer:** Walter Rearick

Cast: Diane Lane (Charity Royall), Michael Ontkean (Lucius Harney), John Cullum (Lawyer Royall), Ray Poole (Reverend Miles), Edith Meiser (Miss Hatchard), Jackie Brookes (Verena), Kevin Martin (Liff Hyatt), Kevin O'Connor (Bash Hyatt), Kathryn Dowling (Annabel Balch), Lauralee Bruce (girl in jewelry shop), Pippa Pearthree (Ally Hawes), Jarlath Conroy (gaunt man), Robin Tilghman (Charity's sister), William Preston (old man).

Notes: Filmed in Temple, New Hampshire, and Jaffrey Center, New Hampshire. Credits transcribed from tape by Scott Marshall. *Looking Back, The House of Mirth* and *Summer* were Special Presentations in the Humanities under the auspices of the National Endowment for the Humanities and the Corporation for Public Broadcasting.

1983: *The Lady's Maid's Bell* (*Television,* 53 minutes)

Series: Shades of Darkness **Production:** Granada Television of England, in association with WGBH-Boston (shown as part of the "Mystery!" series)

Director: John Glenister **Screenplay:** Ken Taylor **Producer:** June Wyndham Davies **Production Manager:** Roy Jackson **Photography:** Tony Caldwell **Designer:** Tim Farmer **Music:** Paul Reade **Sound:** Harry Brookes **Editor:** Alan Ringland **Makeup:** Julie Jackson **Costumes:** John Fraser **Casting:** Malcolm Drury **Research:** Nicky Cooney

Cast: Joanna David (Hartley), June Brown (Emma Saxon), Norma West (Mrs. Brympton), Ian Collier (Mr. Brympton), Charlotte Mitchell (Mrs. Blinder), Roger

Llewellyn (Mr. Ranford), Harry Littlewood (Mr. Wace), Diane Whitley (Agnes), Clive Duncan (Bob Burling), Malcolm Raeburn (Ted Roberts), Bernard Atha (pharmacist), Alick Hayes (Vicar)

Notes: Principal location: Arley Hall, Cheshire, England. The 1904 short story—set by Wharton on the Hudson River—works well in an English setting. Credits transcribed from tape by Scott Marshall.

1983: *Afterward* (*Television,* 53 minutes)

Series: Shades of Darkness **Production:** Granada Television of England, in association with WGBH-Boston (shown as part of the "Mystery!" series)

Director: Simon Langton **Screenplay:** Alfred Shaughnessy **Producer:** June Wyndham Davies **Executive Producer:** Michael Cox **Production Manager:** Keith Thompson **Photography:** Tony Caldwell **Designer:** Alan Price **Music:** Patrick Gowers **Sound:** Ray French **Dubbing:** John Whitworth **Editor:** Anthony Horn **Makeup:** Lois Richardson **Costumes:** Anne Salisbury **Casting:** Priscilla John **Research:** Nicky Cooney

Cast: Kate Harper (Mary Boyne), Michael J. Shannon (Edward Boyne), Penelope Lee (Alida Stair), John Grillo (Harold Parvis), Meg Ritchie (Trimmle), Rolf Saxon (Robert Elwell), William Abney (Inspector Yates), Merelinda Kendall (Agnes), Arthur Whybrow (Mr. Craig), Eric Francis (Cooper)

Notes: Credits transcribed from tape by Scott Marshall.

1983: *Bewitched* (*Television,* 48 minutes)

Series: Shades of Darkness **Production:** Granada Television of England, in association with WGBH-Boston (shown as part of the "Mystery!" series)

Director: John Gorrie **Screenplay:** Alan Plater **Producer:** June Wyndham Davies **Executive Producer:** Michael Cox **Production Manager:** Roy Jackson **Photography:** Doug Hallows **Designer:** Peter Phillips **Music:** Geoffrey Burgon **Sound:** Ray French **Dubbing:** John Whitworth **Editor:** Alan Ringland **Makeup:** Julie Jackson **Costumes:** Esther Dean **Casting:** Malcolm Drury **Research:** Nicky Cooney

Cast: Eileen Atkins (Mrs. Rutledge), Alfred Burke (Reverend Hibben), Ray Smith (Sylvester Brand), Gareth Thomas (Owen Bosworth), Alfred Lynch (Saul Rutledge), Mary Healey (Loretta Bosworth), Martyn Hesford (Andrew), MaryJo Randle (the girl)

Notes: Credits transcribed from tape by Scott Marshall.

1988: *Songs from the Heart* (*Television*—biographical sketch of Wharton, with scenes from her fiction, 56 minutes)

Director: Dennis Krausnick **Screenplay:** Mickey Friedman, from his play **Producer:** John MacGruer/

Downtown Productions **Photography:** Arnold Beckerman **Editors:** Mickey Friedman and John MacGruer **Sets:** Matthew Larkin **Costumes:** Joan DeGusto **Music:** Lawrence Wallach

Cast: Gillian Barge (Edith Wharton), with Margaret Whitton, Henry Stram, Kathleen Mahoney-Barrett, John Talbot, Caris Corfman, Peter Whittrock, Michaela Murphy

Notes: Available on videocassette. Primarily filmed at The Mount, Lenox, Massachusetts, and other Berkshire County locations. Credits compiled by Scott Marshall.

1990: *The Children* (Isolde Films, in association with Film Four International, Arbo Film & Maram GbmH and Bayerliche Landesanstalt for Aufbaufinanzierung, 115 minutes)

Director: Tony Palmer **Screenplay:** Timberlake Wertenbaker **Producer:** Andrew Montgomery **Photography:** Nic Knowland **Editor:** Tony Palmer **Sound:** John Murphy **Production Design:** Chris Bradley and Paul Templeton **Art Direction:** Renate Hofer **Costume Design:** John Hibbs **Makeup:** Penny Smith **Co-Producer:** Harold Albrecht

Cast: Ben Kingsley (Martin Boyne), Kim Novak (Rose Sellars), Siri Neal (Judith), Geraldine Chaplin (Joyce Wheater), Joe Don Baker (Cliffe Wheater), Britt Ekland (Lady Wrench), Donald Sinden (Lord Wrench), Karen Black (Sybil Lullmer), Robert Stephens (Mr. Dobree), Rupert Graves (Gerald Ormerod), Terence Rigby (Duke of Mendip), Marie Helvin (Princess Buondelmonte), Rosemary Leach (Miss Scope), Mark Asquith (Terry), Anouk Fontaine (Blanca), Ian Hawkes (Bun), Eileen Hawkes (Beechy), Hermione Eyre (Zinnie), Edward Michie (Chippo)

Notes: Filmed in Venice, Paris, Bavaria, Switzerland, Italy. Credits: *Variety* 5/30/90 and Isolde Films. Did not receive a U.S. release in theaters; the film did have a limited release on videocassette in an edited version (c. 90 minutes).

1993: *Ethan Frome* (American Playhouse Theatrical Films and Miramax Films, 99 minutes)

Director: John Madden **Screenplay:** Richard Nelson **Executive Producers:** Lindsay Law and Richard Price **Producer:** Stan Wlodkowski **Associate Producer:** Johlyn Dale **Photography:** Bobby Bukowski **Music:** Rachel Portman **Costume Design:** Carol Oditz **Production Design:** Andrew Jackness **Art Direction:** David Crank **Set Direction:** Joyce Anne Gilstrap **Editor:** Katherine Wenning **Sound:** Paul Cote **Assistant Director:** Allan Nicholls **Casting:** Billy Hopkins and Suzanne Smith

Cast: Liam Neeson (Ethan Frome), Patricia Arquette (Mattie Silver), Joan Allen (Zenobia Frome), Tate Donovan (Reverend Smith), Katharine Houghton (Mrs. Hale), Stephen Mendillo (Ned Hale), Jay Goede (Denis Eady), George Woodward (Jotham), Debbon Ayer (Young Ruth Hale), Bob Campbell (Young Ned Hale)

Notes: Available on videocassette. Final credits state: "Filmed entirely on location in the Northeast Kingdom, Vermont," including Peacham, Vermont. A Miramax Release of an American Playhouse Theatrical Films Presentation, in association with Richard Price/BBC Films. Credits transcribed from tape by Scott Marshall.

1993: *The Age of Innocence* (Columbia Pictures, 138 minutes)

Director: Martin Scorsese **Screenplay:** Jay Cocks and Martin Scorsese **Producer:** Barbara De Fina **Photography:** Michael Ballhaus, A.S.C. **Production Design:** Dante Ferretti **Editor:** Thelma Schoonmaker **Costume Design:** Gabriella Pescucci **Music:** Elmer Bernstein **Title Sequence:** Elaine and Saul Bass **Coproducer and Unit Production Manager:** Bruce S. Pustin **Associate Producer:** Joseph Reidy **Casting:** Ellen Lewis **Art Direction:** Speed Hopkins **Visual Research Consultant:** Robin Standefer **Script Supervisor:** Kathryn M. Chapin **Makeup:** Allen Weisinger **Special Effects Makeup:** Manlio Rocchetti **Michelle Pfeiffer's Makeup:** Ronnie Specter **Chief Lighting Technician:** Raymond Quinlan **Dialect Coach:** Tim Monich **19th-Century Music Consultant:** David Montgomery **Etiquette Consultant:** Lily Lodge **Dramaturg:** Michael X. Zelenak **Dance Consultant:** Elizabeth Aldrich **Table Decorations Consultant:** David McFadden **Chef for 19th-Century Meals:** Rich Ellis A Cappa/De Fina Production of a Martin Scorsese Picture

Cast: Daniel Day-Lewis (Newland Archer), Michelle Pfeiffer (Countess Olenska), Winona Ryder (May Welland), Geraldine Chaplin (Mrs. Welland), Michael Gough (Henry van der Luyden), Richard E. Grant (Larry Lefferts), Mary Beth Hurt (Regina Beaufort), Robert Sean Leonard (Ted Archer), Norman Lloyd (Mr. Letterblair), Miriam Margolyes (Mrs. Mingott), Alec McCowen (Sillerton Jackson), Sian Phillips (Mrs. Archer), Jonathan Pryce (Riviere), Alexis Smith (Louisa van der Luyden), Stuart Wilson (Julius Beaufort), Joanne Woodward (Narrator)

Notes: Stage Facilities: Kaufman-Astoria Studios, New York. Filmed in New York City; Troy, New York; Long Island, New York; and Paris. Available on videocassette. Nominated for five Academy Awards, including Best Screenplay (adapted from another medium—Cocks and Scorsese), Best Supporting Actress (Ryder), Best Art Direction, Best Costume Design, and Best Original Score. The film received one Oscar for Best Costume Design (Pescucci). The National Board of Review named it "Best Picture of the

Year," and recognized Scorsese as "Best Director" and Ryder as "Best Supporting Actress." Ryder also received the Golden Globe Award for her performance. Miriam Margolyes received the British Academy Award for "Best Supporting Actress" as Mrs. Manson Mingott. Credits transcribed from tape by Scott Marshall.

1995: *The Buccaneers* (*Television*, **BBC Productions, c. 330 minutes**)

Director/Producer: Philip Saville **Screenplay:** Maggie Wadey **Executive Producer:** Philippa Giles **Co-Producer:** Rosalind Wolfes **Associate Producer:** Nigel Taylor **Production Manager:** David Mason **Designer:** Tony Burrough **Costume Design:** Rosalind Ebbutt **Makeup Designer:** Christine Walmesley-Cotham **Casting Director:** Sarah Bird **Lighting Cameraman:** Remi Adefarasin **Sound:** John Pritchard **Editor:** Greg Miller **Art Direction:** Choi Ho Man and John Hill **Music:** Colin Towns **Choreography:** Domini Winter

Cast: Cheri Lunghi (Laura Testvalley), Carla Gugino (Nan St George), Mira Sorvino (Conchita), Alison Elliott (Virginia St George), Rya Kihlstedt (Lizzy Elmsworth), Ronan Vibert (Richard), Mark Tandy (Lord Seadown), James Frain (Julius, Duke of Trevenik), Dinsdale Landen (Lord Brightlingsea), Rosemary Leach (Lady Brightlingsea), Greg Wise (Guy Thwaite), Michael Kitchen (Sir Helmsley Thwaite), Sophie Dix (Honoria), Sienna Guillory (Felicia), Emily Hamilton (Georgina), Connie Booth (Miss March), Jenny Agutter (Idina Hatton), Gwen Humble (Mrs. St George), Peter Michael Goetz (Col. St George), E. Katherine Kerr (Mrs. Parmore), Conchata Ferrell (Mrs. Elmsworth), Elizabeth Ashley (Mrs. Closson), James Rebhorn (Mr. Closson), Sheila Hancock (Dowager Trevenick), Richard Huw (Hector Robinson), Gresby Nash (Miles Dawnley), Diana Blackburn (Gertrude Trevenick), Matt Patresi (Lord Percy), Vicky Blake (Rose), David Neilson (Blair), Richard Cubison (jeweller), Valerie Minifie (Miss French), Karen Ascoe (Mrs. Lindfry), Roger Brierley (Tory MP for Lincoln), Lloyd McGuire (Tory MP for Bath), Martin Milman (Mr. Firle), William Tapley (Thomas), Christopher Owen (Speaker, House of Commons), Stephen Reynolds (Hogwood), Alister Cameron (Longlands butler), Bev Willis (Fisher), Stephen Billington (Lieutenant James)

Notes: Credits supplied by the BBC. United Kingdom premiere: March 1995, in five segments. U.S. premiere: Masterpiece Theatre, October 8–10, 1995, in three parts (Part I: 90 minutes; Part II: 120 minutes; Part III: 120 minutes). Filmed in Newport, Rhode Island, and at various English country house locations.

2. Theatrical Adaptations of Edith Wharton's Works

Compiled by Scott Marshall and Sarah Bird Wright

Edith Wharton had long been a devotee of the theater. In *A Backward Glance* she recalled attending a dramatic class at the Paris Conservatoire given by Delaunay, a noted actor of the Théâtre Français, in which he demonstrated a love scene from the Greek drama "Phèdre" and managed to "transform himself into the guilty queen." She also wrote a play based on *Manon Lescaut* for the actress Marie Tempest and translated Hermann SUDERMANN's play "Es Lebe das Leben" for Mrs. Patrick CAMPBELL, which was produced as *The JOY OF LIVING* (*BG* 165–67). In addition, she reviewed three plays in 1902 about the legend of Francesca da Rimini (*see* "THREE FRANCESCAS, THE"). In 1902 she reviewed a New York performance by the actress Minnie Maddern Fiske (*see* *TESS OF THE D'URBERVILLES*). She welcomed the possibility of having her novels dramatized, but the first one, *The House of Mirth*, was not well received. A number of her works were dramatized for the stage; many more have been adapted for the cinema and television. The most financially successful dramatizations, according to Lewis (529), were *The Old Maid* (1935) and *Ethan Frome* (1936).

1906 *The House of Mirth* was co-dramatized by Edith Wharton and Clyde Fitch (Fitch also directed). The production, starring Fay Davis as Lily Bart, opened at the Savoy Theater in New York City in October 1906. Others in the cast included Charles Bryant (Lawrence Selden), Jane Laurel (Gerty Farish), Albert Bruening (Simon Rosedale), Lumsden Hare (Augustus Trenor), Katherine Stewart (Mrs. Trenor), Charles Lane (George Dorset), Olive Oliver (Mrs. Dorset), Frank Dekum (Ned Silverton), Grant Mitchell (Percy Gryce), Isabel Richards (Evelyn Van Osburgh), Alan Allen (Wellington Bry), Florence Earle (Mrs. Wellington Bry).

Although it had succeeded in Detroit, where it was presented at the Detroit Opera House on September 14, Wharton sensed that it was doomed to failure because she refused to let Lily Bart survive; it was, in fact, panned by critics. The dramatization was published as *The House of Mirth: The Play of the Novel*, edited, with an introduction, notes and appendices, by Glenn Loney (Fairleigh Dickinson University Press, 1981). See William Dean HOWELLS.

Major revivals: 1988 The Mint Theater Co., New York City; **1976** Long Wharf Theatre, New Haven, Conn.

1928 *The Age of Innocence* was dramatized in New York, with a script by Margaret Ayer Barnes, starring Katharine Cornell as Countess Olenska. Directed by Guthrie McClintic, the play was produced by Gilbert Miller at the Empire Theatre, New York City, November 27, 1928; it ran for 207 performances, until the end of the 1929 theatrical season, and was then taken on the road for four months to nine cities. Others in the cast included Rollo Peters (Newland Archer), Arnold Korff (Julius Beaufort), William Podmore (Sillerton Jackson), Isabel Irving (Mrs. Henry van der Luyden), Frazer Coulter (Mr. Henry van der Luyden), Katharine Stewart (Mrs. Manson Mingott), Albert Tavernier (Stephen Letterblair) and Franchot Tone (Newland Archer, Jr.).

1935 *The Old Maid,* dramatized by Zoë Akins, won the Pulitzer Prize for drama. Starring Judith Anderson (Delia Lovell, later Mrs. James Ralston) and Helen Menken (Charlotte Lovell), it opened at the Empire Theatre in New York January 7, 1935, and had 305 performances. It was produced by Harry Moses and directed by Guthrie McClintic; sets and costumes were by Stewart Chaney. Others in the cast included George Nash (Dr. Lanskell), Margaret Anderson (Tina), Warren Trent (John Halsey), Florence Williams (Delia's daughter, Dee) and John Cromwell (Lanning Halsey, Tina's fiancé).

The awarding of the Pulitzer Prize offended New York critics and led to the establishment the next season of the New York Drama Critics Circle, with its own award. It was later presented by an English touring company. The dramatization was published in 1935 by D. Appleton-Century Company.
Major revival: 1948 Chicago Women's Club Theatre.

1936 *Ethan Frome,* in a dramatization by Owen Davis and Donald Davis suggested by Lowell Barrington's earlier dramatization, was produced by Max Gordon and directed by Guthrie McClintic. The sets and costumes were by Jo Mielziner. After a Philadelphia opening in early January, where it made $10,400 at $2 per seat (*NGC* 446), it moved to the National Theatre, New York City, and ran

for 120 performances. The cast included Raymond Massey (Ethan Frome), Ruth Gordon (Mattie Silver) and Pauline Lord (Zenobia Frome). The adaptation was chosen as one of the best plays of 1935–36. It was published as *Ethan Frome: A Dramatization of Edith Wharton's Novel* by Owen Davis and Donald Davis (Charles Scribner's Sons, 1936), who dedicated it to Edith Wharton. In a foreword to the published version, Wharton remarked that she had found herself thinking, at every page, "Here at least is a new lease of life for 'Ethan.' " The discovery, she said, has "moved me more than I can say" (*UCW* 263). *See* foreword to ETHAN FROME: A DRAMATIZATION OF EDITH WHARTON'S NOVEL.
Major revival: 1982 Long Wharf Theatre, New Haven, Conn.

1948 "Bunner Sisters," billed as "The Bunner Sisters," was adapted by DeWitt Bodeen and produced at the Pasadena Community Playhouse in Southern California; Leonore Ulric and Sally O'Neil starred in the production.

1977 *The House of Mirth,* dramatized by Louis Auchincloss, November 18–30, 1977, at the HB Playwrights Foundation Theatre, New York City. Directed by Herbert Berghof.

1984 *The Custom of the Country,* dramatized by Jane Stanton Hitchcock. Opened at The Mount, Lenox, Massachusetts. Subsequently had a brief run at the Promenade Theatre, New York City. With Valerie Mahaffey as Undine Spragg.

1988 *Old New York: New Year's Day,* dramatized and directed by Donald T. Sanders for the New York Art Theatre Institute. Presented at the Joseph Papp New York Shakespeare Festival Public Theatre, and other venues in New York.

1978 to Present Adaptations of Wharton's short stories, novellas and novels have been presented at the author's home, The Mount, in Lenox, Massachusetts, by Shakespeare & Company (sometimes in conjunction with Edith Wharton Restoration).

Dramatizations have included: "AFTERWARD," "AUTRES TEMPS," "CONFESSION," "*The DESCENT OF MAN,*" *ETHAN FROME,* "EXPIATION," *The House of Mirth,* "KERFOL," "THE LEGEND," *The Old Maid,* "THE OTHER TWO," "ROMAN FEVER," "*The TEMPERATE ZONE,*" "XINGU" and others.

1994 A presentation based on Wharton's life, "Irene Worth's Portrait of Edith Wharton," starring Miss Worth, opened at the Joseph Papp Public Theatre, New York City, in January 1994 to critical acclaim. Miss Worth subsequently toured with the production to numerous towns and cities.

3. Musical Adaptations of Edith Wharton's Works

Compiled by Scott Marshall

1993 A one-act opera based on the short story "ROMAN FEVER" received its world premiere on June 9, 1993, in Durham, North Carolina; it was produced by the Triangle Opera Theater at the R. J. Reynolds Industries Theater, Duke University. **Composer:** Robert Ward **Libretto:** Roger Brunyate **Music Director:** Scott Tilley **Stage Director:** Charles St. Clair **Technical Advisor:** Charles Catotti **Scenic/Lighting Designer:** Richard Cannon **Costume Designer:** Janet Melody **Stage Manager:** Marie Merkél

Cast: Katherine Kulas (Alida Slade), Monica Reinagel (Grace Ansley), Karie Brown (Barbara Ansley), Melody Morrison (Jenny Slade), Paul Gibson (Eduardo).

In an interview with Carl J. Halperin for *Opera News* (June 1993), Robert Ward discussed the difficulties of writing the opera. "The story is subtle—no killing, no violence. But there is a kind of violence of the human spirit. The story revolves around an adulterous triangle." He focused, he said, on "the tragedy of an experience that did not turn out as one had hoped. One has to live in the aftermath of that. So, this last scene was something I had to worry about. I've known many people who had read *Roman Fever* and the first thing they always talk about is the last line, which reveals the entire plot, kind of like a mystery. This story culminates in the last words of the libretto— a sort of illumination. My job is to make sure the music for every word is appropriate to that moment. I work hard to get that."

Robert Ward received the Pulitzer Prize and the Critics' Circle Award for his 1962 opera *The Crucible,* based on the play by Arthur Miller. Roger Brunyate served as Artistic Director of the Wolf Trap Opera and Director of the Peabody Conservatory Opera Theatre.

1997 A one-act chamber opera based on the short story "XINGU" by Edith Wharton was workshopped at the Aspen Music Festival in Summer 1997. The composer expects to have the orchestration completed by Summer 1999, but a piano-percussion version is available and ready for performance. **Title:** "The Power of Xingu" **Composer:** James Legg **Libretto:** James Legg and Sharon Holland.

James Legg has been a composition fellow at Tanglewood's Berkshire Music Center. He has been commissioned by Joseph Papp of the New York Shakespeare Festival, has written six one-act operas for the stage and has composed film scores. He conceived of "The Power of Xingu" as a companion piece to "Roman Fever" for a full evening of Wharton opera.

Forthcoming: In July 1997 the Berkshire Opera Company commissioned an opera based on Edith Wharton's novella *Summer,* published in 1917. The music is by Stephen Paulus; the libretto is by Joan Vail Thorne. Both Paulus and Thorne have previously collaborated on the opera *The Woman at Otowi Crossing* (1995, Opera Theatre of St. Louis) and the 11-section work *Voices from the Gallery* (1993) for narrator and chamber orchestra. The premiere has been tentatively scheduled for summer 1999 in the Koussevitsky Arts Center, Berkshire Community College, Pittsfield, Massachusetts. *Summer* was written after Wharton had an affair with the journalist Morton Fullerton; she described it as "the hot *Ethan,*" because the action takes place in summer and because it deals with a young woman's sexual awakening. (*Ethan Frome,* a companion novella set in winter in the Berkshires, was published in 1911).

At the time the opera was commissioned, Berkshire Opera Company general director Sanford H. Fisher said it represented an effort "to move to another plateau" and to acknowledge the importance of supporting American composers.

SOURCES FOR APPENDIX II:

I. Filmography:
Benstock, *No Gifts from Chance: A Biography of Edith Wharton.* New York: Scribner's, 1994.
Bodeen, DeWitt. "Films and Edith Wharton." *Films in Review,* Feb. 1977, 73–81.

Carroll, Loren. "Edith Wharton in Profile." *New York Herald, Paris edition.* Nov. 16, 1937 ("interview" with Wharton, from the "clippings about E.W." file, Beinecke Library, Yale University).

"The Children." *Variety,* May 30, 1990, n. pag.

Larsen, William B. " 'A New Lease of Life': Cinematic Adaptations of Five Edith Wharton Novels." Diss. U. of Tennessee, Knoxville, 1995. *Dissertation Abstracts-International,* Ann Arbor, Mich. (DAI). 1996 Aug, 57:2, 682A DAI No.: DA9619626.

Lewis, R. W. B. *Edith Wharton: A Biography.* New York: Harper, 1975.

———, and Nancy Lewis (eds.). *The Letters of Edith Wharton* (New York: Scribner's, 1988).

Marshall, Scott. "Edith Wharton on Film and Television." *Edith Wharton Review,* 7:1 (Spring 1990), 15–17.

———. "Edith Wharton on Film and Television: A History and Filmography." *Edith Wharton Review* 13:2 (Spring 1996), 15–26.

McDowell, Margaret. "Edith Wharton's *The Old Maid:* Novella/Play/Film." *College Literature* 14 (Fall 1987), 246–62.

Price, Alan. *The End of the Age of Innocence: Edith Wharton and the First World War.* New York: St. Martin's Press, 1995.

Quirk, Lawrence. *The Films of Fredric March.* New York: Citadel, 1974.

Ringgold, Gene. *The Films of Bette Davis.* New York: Cadillac, 1966.

Scorsese, Martin, and Jay Cocks. *The Age of Innocence: A Portrait of the Film.* New York: Newmarket, 1993.

Sennwald, Andre. "Wax Flowers and Horse Cars: 'The Age of Innocence.' " *New York Times,* Oct. 19, 1934, 27.

Works by Edith Wharton:

A Backward Glance. New York: Appleton-Century, 1934.

"A Little Girl's New York." *Harper's,* Mar. 1938, 356–64.

The Children. New York: Appleton, 1928.

Foreword. *Ethan Frome: A Dramatization of Edith Wharton's Novel.* By Owen Davis and Donald Davis. New York: Scribner's, 1936, vii–viii.

Preface. *The Ghost Stories of Edith Wharton.* New York: Scribner's, 1973, 1–4.

The House of Mirth. New York: Scribner's, 1905.

Summer. New York: Appleton, 1917.

Twilight Sleep. New York: Appleton, 1927.

This section of the appendix is revised from a chapter originally published in *The World of Edith Wharton: New Essays on Edith Wharton,* ed. Keiko Beppu (Tokyo: Yumi Press, 1996). It appears by kind permission of Keiko Beppu. The author also wishes to acknowledge the assistance of the following in his research on this subject: Shari Benstock; the British Broadcasting Corporation; Clare Colquitt; Victor Gluck; Nathan Hasson; Isolde Films; William B. Larsen; R. W. B. Lewis; Richard P. May, Turner Entertainment Company; Alan Price; Michael Shepley Public Relations; and the Watkins-Loomis Agency.

II. Theatrical Adaptations of Edith Wharton's Works:

The Best Plays of 1899/1909–1946/1947 and the Year Book of the Drama in America [serial]. New York: Dodd, Mead and Co.

Davis, Owen and Donald Davis. *Ethan Frome: A Dramatization of Edith Wharton's Novel.* New York: Scribner's, 1936.

Guernsey, Otis L. *Directory of the American Theater 1894–1971.* New York: Dodd Mead, 1971.

Loney, Glenn, ed. *The House of Mirth: The Play of the Novel.* Madison, N.J.: Fairleigh Dickinson University Press, 1981.

Original playbills for "The House of Mirth" (1906), "The Age of Innocence" (1928), "The Old Maid" (1935), "The House of Mirth" (1977), "Old New York: New Year's Day" (1988), and others.

III. Musical Adaptations of Edith Wharton's Works:

Borak, Jeffrey. "Opera Commissioned to Tell Wharton's 'Summer' Story." *The Berkshire Eagle,* July 2, 1997.

Halperin, Carl J. "Ward Meets Wharton." *Opera News,* June 1993.

Original program for world premiere performance of "Roman Fever," Triangle Opera Theater, June 1993.

APPENDIX III
CHRONOLOGY OF WHARTON'S
WRITINGS AND PUBLICATIONS

Verses, anonymous (Newport, R.I.: C. E. Hammett, Jr., 1878);

"Mrs. Manstey's View," *Scribner's* 10 (July 1891), 117–22;

"That Good May Come," *Scribner's* 15 (May 1894), 629–42;

"The Lamp of Psyche," *Scribner's* 18 (October 1895), 418–28;

"The Valley of Childish Things," *Century* 52 (July 1896), 467–69;

The Decoration of Houses, by Wharton and Ogden Codman, Jr. (New York: Scribner's, 1897; London: Batsford, 1898); rpt. New York: W. W. Norton (Classical America and Henry Hope Reed), 1997;

The Greater Inclination (New York: Scribner's, 1899; John Lane/Bodley Head, 1899; contains "The Muse's Tragedy," "A Journey," "The Pelican," "Souls Belated," "A Coward," "The Twilight of the God," "A Cup of Cold Water," and "The Portrait");

"April Showers," *Youth's Companion* 74 (18 January 1900), 25–26;

"Friends," *Youth's Companion* 74 (23 August 1900), 405–06;

"The Line of Least Resistance," *Lippincott's* 66 (October 1900), 559–70;

The Touchstone (New York: Scribner's, 1900); republished as *A Gift from the Grave* (London: Murray, 1900);

"An Unreprinted Parody: 'More Love Letters of an Englishwoman,' " *Bookman* (Feb. 1901);

Crucial Instances (New York: Scribner's, 1901; London: Murray, 1901; contains "The Duchess at Prayer," "The Angel at the Grave," "The Recovery," "Copy," "The Rembrandt," "The Moving Finger," and "The Confessional");

"The Blashfields' *Italian Cities,*" review of *Italian Cities* (Edwin H. and Evangeline W. Blashfield), *Bookman* 13 (August 1901), 563–64;

Notes: The short stories listed separately were not published in collections edited by Edith Wharton. I am indebted to Frederick Wegener for his compilation of Edith Wharton's uncollected critical writings (*Edith Wharton: The Uncollected Critical Writings* [Princeton: Princeton University Press, 1996]).

"Stephen Phillips's *Ulysses,*" review of *Ulysses: A Drama,* by Stephen Phillips, *Bookman* 15 (April 1902), 168–70;

"George Eliot," review of *George Eliot,* by Leslie Stephen, *Bookman* 15 (May 1902), 247–51;

"The Theatres," review of Minnie Maddern Fiske's performance in Lorimer Stoddard's dramatization of Thomas Hardy's *Tess of the D'Urbervilles, New York Commercial Advertiser,* 7 May 1902, 9;

"The Three Francescas," *North American Review* 175 (July 1902), 17–30;

Translator's note to *The Joy of Living (Es Lebe das Leben),* a play in five acts, by Hermann Sudermann, trans. Edith Wharton (New York: Scribner's, 1902), v–vi;

The Valley of Decision (2 volumes, New York: Scribner's, 1902; 1 volume, London: Murray, 1902);

"Mr. Paul on the Poetry of Matthew Arnold," review of *Matthew Arnold,* by Herbert W. Paul, *Lamp* 26 (February 1903), 51–54;

"The Vice of Reading," *North American Review* 177 (October, 1903), 513–21;

Sanctuary (New York: Scribner's, 1903; London: Macmillan, 1903);

"The House of the Dead Hand," *Atlantic Monthly* 94 (August 1904), 145–60;

Italian Villas and Their Gardens (New York: Century, 1904; London: John Lane/Bodley Head, 1904);

The Descent of Man and Other Stories (New York: Scribner's, 1904); enlarged edition, London & New York: Macmillan, 1904; contains "The Descent of Man," "The Other Two," "Expiation," "The Lady's Maid's Bell," "The Mission of Jane," "The Reckoning," "The Letter," "The Dilettante," "The Quicksand," and "A Venetian Night's Entertainment");

"The Introducers," *Ainslee's* 16 (December 1905), 139–48; (January 1906), 61–67;

"Mr. Sturgis's *Belchamber,*" review of *Belchamber,* by Howard Sturgis, *Bookman* 21 (May 1905), 307–10;

"Maurice Hewlett's *The Fool Errant,*" by Maurice Hewlett, *Bookman* 22 (September 1905), 64–67;

Italian Backgrounds (New York: Scribner's, 1905; London: Macmillan, 1905);

The House of Mirth (New York: Scribner's, 1905; London: Macmillan, 1905);

"The Sonnets of Eugene Lee-Hamilton," *Bookman* 26 (November 1907), 251–53;

Madame de Treymes (New York: Scribner's, 1907; London: Macmillan, 1907);

The Fruit of the Tree (New York: Scribner's, 1907); London: Macmillan, 1907);

"Les Metteurs en Scène," *Revue des Deux Mondes* 67 (October 1908), 692–708;

The Hermit and the Wild Woman, and Other Stories (New York: Scribner's, 1908; London: Macmillan, 1908); contains "The Hermit and the Wild Woman," "The Last Asset," "In Trust," "The Pretext," "The Verdict," "The Potboiler" and "The Best Man");

A Motor-Flight through France (New York: Scribner's, 1908; London: Macmillan, 1908);

Artemis to Actæon (New York: Scribner's, 1909; London: Macmillan, 1909);

"George Cabot Lodge," *Scribner's Magazine* 47 (February 1910), 236–39;

Tales of Men and Ghosts (New York: Scribner's, 1910; London: Macmillan, 1910); contains "The Bolted Door," "His Father's Son," "The Daunt Diana," "The Debt," "Full Circle," "The Legend," "The Eyes," "The Blond Beast," "Afterward," and "The Letters");

Ethan Frome (New York: Scribner's, 1911; London: Macmillan, 1911);

The Reef (New York: Appleton, 1912; London: Macmillan, 1912);

The Custom of the Country (New York: Scribner's, 1913; London: Macmillan, 1913);

"The Criticism of Fiction," *Times Literary Supplement* (London), 14 May 1914, 229–30;

"The Architecture of Humanism," review of *The Architecture of Humanism*, by Geoffrey Scott, *Times Literary Supplement* (London), 25 June 1914, 305;

Introduction to *A Village Romeo and Juliet*, by Gottfried Keller, trans. A. C. Bahlmann (New York: Scribner's, 1914), v–xxvi;

"Jean du Breuil de Saint-Germain," *Revue Hebdomadaire* 24 (15 May 1915), 351–61;

Fighting France, from Dunkerque to Belfort (New York: Scribner's, 1915; London: Macmillan, 1915);

The Book of the Homeless, compiled by Wharton (Paris, 1915; New York: Scribner's, 1916);

"The Belgian Prisoners of War" (single sheet folded to make four pages); an appeal for help for the Committee for the Relief of the Belgian Prisoners in Germany, signed by Edith Wharton, 1916;

Xingu and Other Stories (New York: Scribner's, 1916; London: Macmillan, 1916); contains "Xingu," "Coming Home," "Autres Temps . . . ," "Kerfol,"

"The Long Run," "The Triumph of Night," and "The Choice" and "Bunner Sisters");

Summer (New York: Appleton, 1917; London: Macmillan, 1917);

The Marne (New York: Appleton, 1918; London: Macmillan, 1918);

"Writing a War Story," *Woman's Home Companion* 46 (September 1919), 17–19;

French Ways and Their Meaning (New York & London: Appleton, 1919; London: Macmillan, 1919);

"Henry James in His Letters," review of *The Letters of Henry James*, ed. Percy Lubbock, *Quarterly Review* 234 (July 1920), 188–202;

The Age of Innocence (New York & London: Appleton, 1920);

In Morocco (New York: Scribner's, 1920; London: Macmillan, 1920);

Preface to *Futility*, by William Gerhardi (New York: Duffield, 1922), 1–3;

Introduction to *Ethan Frome* (New York: Scribner's, 1922), i–v;

The Glimpses of the Moon (New York & London: Appleton, 1922; London: Macmillan, 1923);

A Son at the Front (New York: Scribner's, 1923; London: Macmillan, 1923);

Old New York: False Dawn (The 'Forties), The Old Maid (The 'Fifties), The Spark (The 'Sixties) and *New Year's Day (The 'Seventies)* (New York & London: Appleton, 1924);

The Mother's Recompense (New York & London: Appleton, 1925);

The Writing of Fiction (New York & London: Scribner's, 1925);

Here and Beyond (New York & London: Appleton, 1926; contains "Miss Mary Pask," "The Young Gentlemen," "Bewitched," "The Seed of the Faith," "The Temperate Zone," "Velvet Ear-Pads");

Twelve Poems (London: Medici Society, 1926);

"The Great American Novel," *Yale Review*, n.s. 16 (July 1927), 646–56;

Twilight Sleep (New York & London: Appleton, 1927);

"William C. Brownell," *Scribner's Magazine* 84 (November 1928), 596–602;

"A Cycle of Reviewing," *Spectator* (London), 141 (supplement, 3 November 1928), 44–45;

The Children (New York & London: Appleton, 1928); republished as *The Marriage Playground* (New York: Grosset & Dunlap, 1930);

"Visibility in Fiction," *Yale Review*, n.s. 18 (March 1929), 480–88;

Hudson River Bracketed (New York & London: Appleton, 1929);

Certain People (New York & London: Appleton, 1930; contains "Atrophy," "A Bottle of Perrier," "After Holbein," "Dieu D'Amour," "The Refugees" and "Mr. Jones");

"The Writing of *Ethan Frome*," *Colophon,* pt. 11, no. 4 (September 1932), n.p.;

The Gods Arrive (New York & London: Appleton, 1932);

Human Nature (New York & London: Appleton, 1933; contains "Her Son," "The Day of the Funeral," "A Glimpse," "Joy in the House" and "Diagnosis");

"Tendencies in Modern Fiction," *Saturday Review of Literature* 10 (7 April 1934), 603–04;

"A Reconsideration of Proust," *Saturday Review of Literature* 11 (27 October 1934), 233–34;

A Backward Glance (New York & London: Appleton-Century, 1934);

Preface to *Speak to the Earth: Wanderings and Reflections among Elephants and Mountains,* by Vivienne de Watteville (London: Methuen, 1935), vii–viii;

Introduction to *The House of Mirth* (Oxford: Oxford University Press, 1936), v–xi;

Foreword to *Benediction,* by Claude Silve (Philomène de La Forest-Divonne), trans. Robert Norton (New York: Appleton-Century, 1936), 1–6;

"Souvenirs du Bourget d'Outremer," *Revue Hebdomadaire* 45 (21 June 1936), 266–56;

The World Over (New York & London: Appleton-Century, 1936; contains "Charm Incorporated," "Pomegranate Seed," "Permanent Wave," "Confession," "Roman Fever," "The Looking Glass" and "Duration");

Preface to *Ghosts* (New York: Appleton-Century, 1937), vii–xii;

Ghosts (New York & London: Appleton-Century, 1937); published in October 1937, two months after Wharton's death; contains "All Souls'," "The Eyes," "Afterward," "The Lady's Maid's Bell," "Kerfol," "The Triumph of Night," "Miss Mary Pask," "Bewitched," "Mr. Jones," "Pomegranate Seed" and "A Bottle of Perrier");

The Buccaneers (New York & London: Appleton-Century, 1938);

"A Little Girl's New York," *Harper's Magazine* 176 (March 1938), 356–64;

Preface to *Eternal Passion in English Poetry,* selected by Edith Wharton and Robert Norton, with the collaboration of Gaillard Lapsley (New York: Appleton-Century, 1939), v–vii;

Tribute to Bayard Cutting, Jr., in *W. Bayard Cutting, Jr.: 1878–1910,* privately printed: Marshlands, 1947, 47–56;

The Collected Short Stories of Edith Wharton, 2 volumes, edited by R. W. B. Lewis (New York: Scribner's, 1968);

The Letters of Edith Wharton, ed. R. W. B. Lewis and Nancy Lewis (New York: Scribner's, 1988);

The Cruise of the Vanadis [Edith Wharton's diary of her 1888 Mediterranean cruise], ed. Claudine Lesage. Amiens: Sterne (Presses de L'UFR Clerc Université Picardie), 1992.

APPENDIX IV

Family Trees

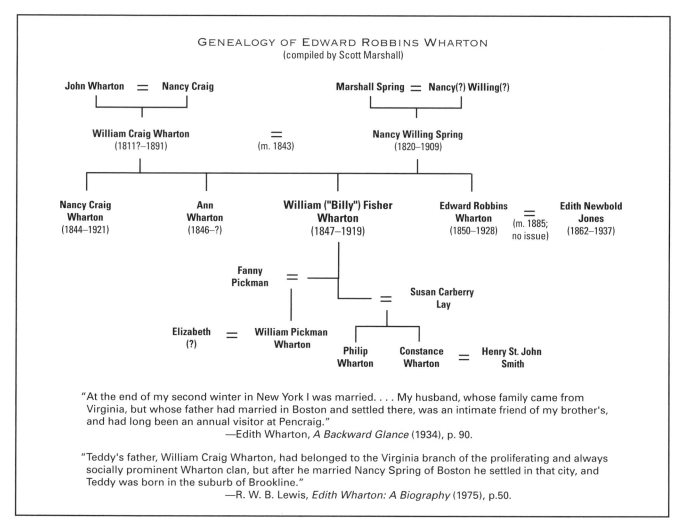

GENEALOGY OF EDWARD ROBBINS WHARTON
(compiled by Scott Marshall)

John Wharton = Nancy Craig

Marshall Spring = Nancy(?) Willing(?)

William Craig Wharton
(1811?–1891)
=
(m. 1843)
Nancy Willing Spring
(1820–1909)

Nancy Craig
Wharton
(1844–1921)

Ann
Wharton
(1846–?)

William ("Billy") Fisher
Wharton
(1847–1919)

Edward Robbins
Wharton
(1850–1928)
=
(m. 1885;
no issue)
Edith Newbold
Jones
(1862–1937)

Fanny
Pickman
=

Susan Carberry
Lay
=

Elizabeth
(?)
=
William Pickman
Wharton

Philip
Wharton

Constance
Wharton
=
Henry St. John
Smith

"At the end of my second winter in New York I was married. . . . My husband, whose family came from Virginia, but whose father had married in Boston and settled there, was an intimate friend of my brother's, and had long been an annual visitor at Pencraig."
—Edith Wharton, *A Backward Glance* (1934), p. 90.

"Teddy's father, William Craig Wharton, had belonged to the Virginia branch of the proliferating and always socially prominent Wharton clan, but after he married Nancy Spring of Boston he settled in that city, and Teddy was born in the suburb of Brookline."
—R. W. B. Lewis, *Edith Wharton: A Biography* (1975), p.50.

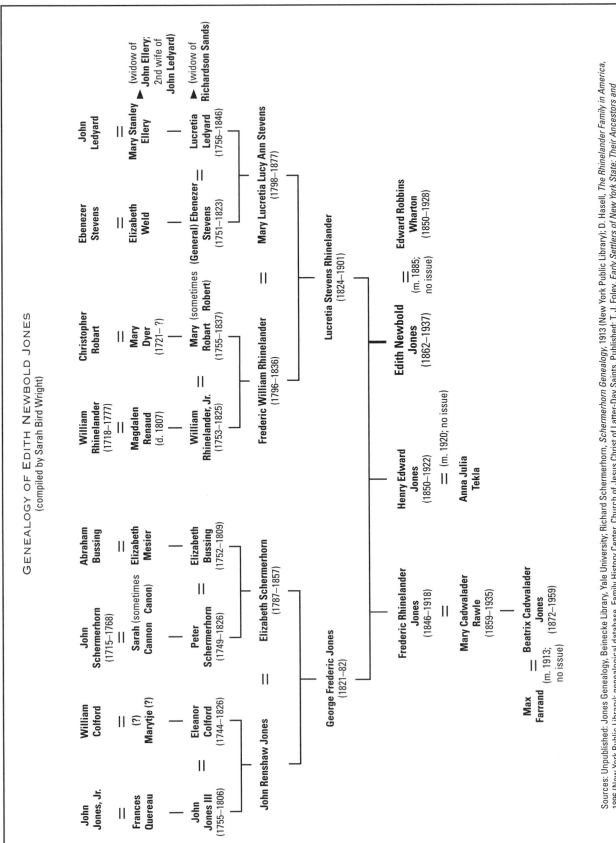

GENEALOGY OF EDITH NEWBOLD JONES
(compiled by Sarah Bird Wright)

Sources: Unpublished: Jones Genealogy, Beinecke Library, Yale University; Richard Schermerhorn, *Schermerhorn Genealogy*, 1913 (New York Public Library); D. Hasell, *The Rhinelander Family in America*, 1896 (New York Public Library); genealogical database, Family History Center, Church of Jesus Christ of Latter-Day Saints. Published: T. J. Foley, *Early Settlers of New York State: Their Ancestors and Descendants* (Indexes; 1940?); Cuyler Reynolds, *Genealogical and Family History of Southern New York and the Hudson River Valley* (New York: Lewis Historical Publishing Company, 1914); *English Origins of American Colonists. From the New York Genealogical and Biographical Record* (Baltimore: Genealogical Publishing Co., 1991); R. W. B. Lewis, *Edith Wharton: A Biography* (New York: Harper & Row, 1975); Shari Benstock, *No Gifts from Chance* (New York: Charles Scribner's Sons, 1994).

APPENDIX V
EDITH WHARTON: A TIMELINE

1862   Edith Newbold Jones born in New York January 24 to George Frederic and Lucretia Rhinelander Jones. Has two brothers, Frederic (b. 1846) and Henry ("Harry," b. 1850)

1866   Jones family in Europe until 1872, living and traveling in France, Italy, Germany, Spain; Edith learns French, German and Italian. In Rome, meets Margaret ("Daisy") and Arthur Terry, children of artist Luther Terry; Daisy becomes lifelong friend. Harry Jones enters Trinity Hall, Cambridge.

1870   Frederic Jones marries Mary ("Minnie") Cadwalader Rawle (b. 1850). Brother Harry receives bachelor of arts degree from Trinity Hall, Cambridge. Jones family in Black Forest when war breaks out. Edith contracts typhoid fever, is saved by Russian doctor. Jones family returns to New York. Lives on West 23rd Street, summers at Pencraig, Newport. Daughter Beatrix born to Frederic and Minnie Jones. Anna Bahlmann, governess of children of Harvard astronomer Lewis Rutherfurd, becomes acquainted with Jones family in Newport, gives Edith German lessons, which continue later in New York.

1875   Edith meets Emelyn Washburn, daughter of the Rev. E. A. Washburn, rector of Calvary Church, New York.

1877   Fifteen-year-old Edith finishes *Fast and Loose,* a 30,000-word novella.

1878   *Verses,* a volume of Edith's poetry, privately printed in Newport by Lucretia Jones; William Dean Howells accepts one for the *Atlantic Monthly.*

1879   Edith Jones makes her social debut in New York

1880   Jones family returns to Europe, hoping to restore George Frederic Jones's failing health.

1882   George Frederic Jones dies at Cannes. Edith's engagement to Harry Leyden Stevens announced (August) but broken off (October).

1883   Edith Jones reaches age 21, shares with brothers real estate holdings worth approximately $600,000; her portion provides annual income of about $10,000. Edith meets Walter Berry at Bar Harbor but he leaves without proposing.

1884   Edith Jones employs Catharine Gross as maid; she remains with EW as housekeeper until 1933.

1885   Edith Jones marries Edward Robbins ("Teddy") Wharton. Until 1889 they divide time between Lucretia Jones's New York house, Pencraig Cottage, Newport and travel abroad, mainly in Italy.

1888   With James Van Alen, Edith and Teddy Wharton charter steam yacht *Vanadis* for nine-week Mediterranean cruise. EW inherits estate worth $120,000 from father's cousin Joshua Jones. Whartons hire young Englishman Alfred White as Teddy's manservant. White remains in EW's employ until her death, becoming "general agent."

1889   Whartons rent house on Madison Avenue, New York. Three of EW's poems accepted for publication, including "The Last Giustiniani," in *Scribner's Magazine.*

1890   "Mrs Manstey's View" accepted by *Scribner's Magazine.*

1891   EW purchases house at 884 Park Avenue, New York; later purchases house at 882 Park Avenue for her staff. Teddy's father commits suicide at McLean Hospital.

1892   Frederic and Minnie Jones separate.

1893   EW buys Land's End at Newport for $80,000; Ogden Codman remodels and redecorates. French novelist Paul Bourget and wife Minnie visit Whartons at Land's End.

1894   Paul Bourget gives the Whartons letter of introduction to Vernon Lee, whom they meet in Italy. They visit the Monastery of San Vivaldo and see the sculpture groups. EW suffers nervous breakdown, with insomnia, nausea, fatigue, depression.

1895   EW's nervous breakdown continues. "A Tuscan Shrine," in which EW reattributes San Vivaldo terra-cottas, published in *Scribner's Magazine.*

1896   Frederic and Minnie Jones divorce. EW begins *The Decoration of Houses* with Codman.

1897   *The Decoration of Houses* published by Scribner's.

1898   Edith Wharton treated by Dr. George McLellan in Philadelphia November–December while staying at the Stenton Hotel. Critics disagree over whether she had a nervous breakdown. She and Teddy did not return to New York but took a rental house in Washington, D.C.

1899   Whartons spend four months in Washington, D.C., seeing much of Walter Berry, becoming friends with George Cabot ("Bay") Lodge; they begin search for property for summer home near Lenox, Massachusetts. Collection of short stories, *The Greater Inclination,* published by Scribner's.

1900   *The Touchstone,* a novella, serialized in *Scribner's Magazine* and published as separate volume by Scribner's.

1901   Whartons purchase Laurel Lake Farm, a 113-acre property in Lenox, Mass., and begin building The Mount. Edith's mother, Lucretia Jones, dies in Paris. EW inherits share of estate worth of $92,000 in trust. Inept lawyers and advisers prevent her receiving the full amount.

1902   Whartons move into The Mount at Lenox. EW commissioned by Richard Watson Gilder of the *Century Magazine* to write a series of articles about Italian villas. Publishes first novel, *The Valley of Decision,* with Scribner's; translates *Es Lebe das Leben,* play by Hermann Sudermann. Begins correspondence with Henry James.

1903   Whartons attend opening of Fenway Court, Isabella Stewart Gardner's home/museum in Boston. EW sells Land's End for $122,500. Whartons tour Italy for *Century* articles; EW tries in vain to communicate with Maxfield Parrish, engaged to illustrate them. Introduced to Bernard and Mary Berenson. *Sanctuary,* a novella, is published in *Scribner's Magazine* and later as book by Scribner's; *The Century* runs Italian villa articles.

1904   Whartons purchase first automobile, a Panhard-Levassor, in France; visit Henry James in England and make motor trip with him. James refers to EW as "the Angel of Devastation." *Italian Villas and Their Gardens* published by Century; collection of stories, *The Descent of Man,* published by Scribner's. Gaillard Lapsley visits The Mount (August); Henry James and Howard Sturgis also visit (October).

1905   Henry James visits Whartons in New York (January). Scribner's publishes *Italian Backgrounds* and, in October, *The House of Mirth*; sales reach 140,000 by end of year. Whartons spend Christmas at Biltmore House, the George Vanderbilts' estate in Asheville, N.C.

1906   In Paris, Paul Bourget introduces EW into French literary circles. Whartons take motor trip through France with Harry Jones. Stage version of *The House of Mirth*, dramatized by EW and Clyde Fitch, opens in New York but fails.

1907   EW rents apartment of the George Vanderbilts at 58 rue de Varenne, Paris, for winter. Whartons take motor trip through France with Henry James, March. *The Fruit of the Tree* published by Scribner's, October. *Madame de Treymes* published by Scribner's. Wharton meets Morton Fullerton.

1908   Whartons in Vanderbilt apartment for winter; at The Mount May–October. EW goes to England without Teddy, staying with Lord and Lady Elcho at Stanway. Scribner's publishes collection of stories; *The Hermit and the Wild Woman*, and *A Motor-Flight Through France*. Wharton embarks on affair with Fullerton.

1909   Whartons in Vanderbilt apartment for winter. EW enjoys Paris social life, especially salon of Rosa de Fitz-James, sees Henry Adams and Henry James; in England meets literary figures including John Hugh Smith and Robert Norton. Writes "Terminus," a poem about night spent with Morton Fullerton, published by Lewis in 1975 (*EW* 259–60). Publishes book of poetry, *Artemis to Actaeon*, in April. Teddy Wharton's mother dies.

1910   EW leases apartment at 53 rue de Varenne, Paris, moves in in January. Teddy enters Swiss sanatorium for depression; leaves in October for world tour with Johnson Morton. EW begins friendship with Bernard Berenson. Short story collection *Tales of Men and Ghosts* published by Scribner's.

1911   Teddy increasingly unstable. EW at The Mount, June. Tries unsuccessfully to obtain Nobel Prize for Henry James. Walter Berry settles in Paris, in fall he and EW tour central Italy by auto, visiting Berensons at I Tatti. *Ethan Frome* published, September; reviews good, sales disappointing. EW separates from Teddy, who has sold The Mount.

1912   EW and Berry visit Tuscan monastery. Teddy in Paris February–May; EW in England in summer, takes Henry James to Cliveden, home of the Astors. EW publishes first book with D. Appleton, *The Reef;* sales disappointing.

1913   EW and Berry tour Sicily; EW and Berenson tour Germany. EW estranged from brother Harry over Russian-born fiancée, Countess Anna Julia Tekla. Tries to raise money for 70th birthday gift for Henry James, who finds out and is deeply hurt. Meets Geoffrey Scott. EW divorces Teddy; decree finalized Apr. 16. Visits New York in December; illness prevents her from sailing in time to attend wedding of niece Beatrix Jones to Max Farrand, but sees old friends. *The Custom of the Country* published, October; sales reach 60,000.

1914   EW visits Tunis and Algeria with Percy Lubbock, March; Spain with Walter Berry, July. In England, August, visits Henry James; leases home of Mrs. Humphry Ward but returns to France at outbreak of war. In France, founds American Hostels for Refugees, *ouvroir* for seamstresses.

1915   EW founds Children of Flanders Rescue Committee. Visits front lines several times, usually with Walter Berry, and describes in articles for *Scribner's Magazine*. Publishes these in book *Fighting France, from Dunkerque to Belfort*.

1916   Henry James dies, February. EW publishes *The Book of the Homeless*, with proceeds to war relief; is made chevalier of the French Legion of Honor; establishes program for tubercular soldiers. *Xingu and Other Stories* published by Scribner's.

1917   EW tours Morocco with Walter Berry at invitation of French Gen. Louis-Hubert Lyautey. Novella *Summer* published by Appleton.

1918   Frederic Jones dies. Ronald Simmons dies. EW witnesses magnificent July 4 parade in Paris. Buys Villa Jean-Marie, north of Paris. *The Marne* published by Appleton. Silent film, *The House of Mirth*, directed by Albert Capellani (Metro).

1919   EW moves into Villa Jean-Marie, now renamed Pavillon Colombe. Leases Ste.-Claire Château, Hyères, overlooking Mediterranean near Toulon, as winter home. *French Ways and Their Meaning* published by Appleton.

1920   *The Age of Innocence* serialized in *Pictorial Review* for $18,000; published as book by Appleton to warm reception. *In Morocco* published by Scribner's. Harry Jones marries Countess Anna Julia Tekla.

1921   Begins friendship with Philomène de Levis-Mirepoix (Countess de La Forest-Divonne) in Hyères. *The Age of Innocence* wins Pulitzer Prize. Novella *The Old Maid* (*The 'Fifties*) serialized in *Redbook* for $2,250.

1922   Harry Jones dies; estate, including Jones family possessions, left to Countess Tekla. Appleton publishes *The Glimpses of the Moon*, August.

1923   Long-time chauffeur Charles Cook has slight stroke, gives up driving. EW travels to U.S. for last time; receives honorary doctorate from Yale; visits Minnie Jones and Cutting family. Film version of *The Glimpses of the Moon* (with dialogue by F. Scott Fitzgerald) opens, April. Scribner's publishes *A Son at the Front*, September; EW's friend Ronald Simmons appears as character Boylston. Silent film, *The Glimpses of the Moon*, directed by Allan Dwan (Paramount).

1924   EW awarded Gold Medal by National Institute of Arts and Letters (U.S.), first woman so honored. *Old New York*, volume of four novellas, published by Appleton, May. Silent film, *The Age of Innocence*, directed by Wesley Ruggles (Warner Bros.)

1925   EW visited at Ste.-Claire Château by William Gerhardi, January; by F. Scott Fitzgerald at Pavillon Colombe, June. Appleton publishes *The Mother's Recompense;* Scribner's publishes *The Writing of Fiction.*

1926   EW elected member of National Institute of Arts and Letters. With friends charters yacht *Osprey* for 10-week Mediterranean cruise; party includes Daisy Chanler, Robert Norton, Logan Pearsall Smith and Harry Lawrence. Travels in northern Italy with Walter Berry, September. Appleton publishes collection of short stories *Here and Beyond; Twelve Poems* printed by the Medici Society, London.

1927   Walter Berry has arranged for EW to purchase Ste.-Claire Château; suffers stroke, January; dies after second stroke, October. Appleton publishes *Twilight Sleep*, June; dis-

places Sinclair Lewis's *Elmer Gantry* on best-seller list.

1928   Teddy Wharton dies, February. Countess Tekla, Harry Jones's widow, dies. EW in England for two weeks, visits Tintagel. Appleton publishes *The Children*, September; earns $95,000 as selection of Book-of-the-Month Club. Successful stage adaptation by Margaret Ayer Barnes of *The Age of Innocence* opens, December, with Katharine Cornell.

1929   EW awarded Gold Medal for "special distinction" by American Academy of Arts and Letters, group within National Institute of Arts and Letters. Completes *Hudson River Bracketed*, October. Film with sound, *The Marriage Playground*, based on *The Children*, directed by Lothar Mendes (Paramount).

1930   EW meets Kenneth Clark, Aldous Huxley, Bronislaw Malinowski. Volume of short stories, *Certain People*, published by Appleton.

1931   EW in England for three weeks; meets H. G. Wells, Desmond MacCarthy, Harold Nicolson, others. Kenneth and Jane Clark visit EW at Ste.-Claire.

1932   EW is godmother to Clarks' son Colin. Visits Rome with Nicky Mariano, Bernard Berenson's librarian and companion. *The Gods Arrive* published by Appleton. Sales poor; world depression now at lowest point.

1933   EW attends Salzburg music festival. EW's maid Elise Duvlenck dies, May; housekeeper Catharine Gross dies, October. *Ladies' Home Journal* serializes memoir *A Backward Glance*, seeks to reduce payment but relents when EW threatens to sue. Appleton publishes volume of short stories, *Human Nature*.

1934   EW tours Netherlands and Scotland. Appleton publishes *A Backward Glance;* EW angry over poor advertising, threatens to leave firm but is placated. Film with sound, *The Age of Innocence*, directed by Philip Moeller (RKO Radio).

1935   EW has slight stroke, temporary loss of vision in right eye, April. Minnie Jones dies in London, September; EW goes to England to arrange funeral. *The Old Maid* by Zoë Akins opens in New York and wins Pulitzer Prize for drama. Film with sound, *Strange Wives,* based on short story "Bread Upon the Waters," directed by Richard Thorpe (Universal).

1936 EW visits England; attends house party at Stanway with H. G. Wells, Max Beerbohm, Cynthia Asquith, others. Appleton-Century publishes *The World Over.* Stage adaptation of *Ethan Frome* by Owen Davis and Donald Davis runs four months in New York.

1937 EW visits Ogden Codman's château near Paris; suffers stroke, June. EW dies at Pavillon Colombe, August 11; is buried in the Cimitière des Gonards in Versailles, near grave of Walter Berry. Appleton-Century publishes *Ghosts,* October.

1938 *The Buccaneers,* edited by Gaillard Lapsley, published posthumously.

APPENDIX VI
BIBLIOGRAPHY

1. Works by Edith Wharton

NONFICTION

A Backward Glance. New York: Appleton-Century, 1934. Rpt. Scribner's, 1964.

The Book of the Homeless (ed.). New York: Scribner's, 1916.

The Cruise of the Vanadis [Edith Wharton's diary of her 1888 Mediterranean cruise], ed. Claudine Lesage. Amiens: Sterne (Presses de L'UFR Clerc Université Picardie), 1992.

The Decoration of Houses (with Ogden Codman). New York: Scribner's, 1897. Rpt. New York: W. W. Norton & Company, 1978.

Fighting France, from Dunkerque to Belfort. New York: Scribner's, 1915.

French Ways and Their Meaning. New York: D. Appleton and Company, 1919. Rpt. Lenox, Mass.: Edith Wharton Restoration and Lee, Mass.: Berkshire House Publishers, 1997.

In Morocco. New York: Charles Scribner's Sons, 1920. Rpt. London: Century Publishing, 1984; New York: Hippocrene Books, 1984 (contains Preface to the 2nd edition); Hopewell, N.J.: Ecco Press, 1996.

Italian Backgrounds. New York: Charles Scribner's Sons, 1905. Rpt. New York: Ecco Press, 1989.

Italian Villas and Their Gardens. New York: The Century Co., 1904. Rpt. New York: Da Capo Press, 1976.

A Motor-Flight Through France. New York: Charles Scribner's Sons, 1908. Rpt. DeKalb, Ill: Northern Illinois University Press, 1991, ed. Mary Suzanne Schriber.

The Writing of Fiction. New York: Scribner's, 1925.

POETRY (BOOKS)

Artemis to Actaeon and Other Verse. New York: Scribner's, 1909.

Twelve Poems. London: The Medici Society, 1926.

Verses. Newport. C. E. Hammett, Jr., 1878.

PAPERS AND CORRESPONDENCE OF EDITH WHARTON

Correspondence in the Edith Wharton Collection, Beinecke Rare Book and Manuscript Library, Yale University, New Haven, Connecticut.

Correspondence in the Scribner Archives, Firestone Library, Princeton University, Princeton, New Jersey.

Correspondence in the Lilly Library, Indiana University, Bloomington, Indiana.

The Letters of Edith Wharton. Ed. R. W. B. Lewis and Nancy Lewis. New York: Scribner's, 1988.

NOVELS, NOVELLAS AND SHORT FICTION

The Age of Innocence. New York: Appleton, 1920.

The Buccaneers [unfinished; published posthumously]. New York: Appleton, 1938. Republished with *Fast and Loose,* ed. Viola Hopkins Winner. Charlottesville: University Press of Virginia, 1993. Also: *The Buccaneers,* completed by Marion Mainwaring. New York: Viking, 1993.

Certain People. New York: Appleton, 1930.

The Children. New York: Appleton, 1928.

Crucial Instances. New York: Scribner's, 1901.

The Custom of the Country. New York: Scribner's, 1913.

The Descent of Man and Other Stories. New York: Scribner's, 1904.

Ethan Frome. New York: Scribner's, 1911.

False Dawn. New York: Appleton, 1924.

The Fruit of the Tree. New York: Scribner's, 1907.

Ghosts. New York: Appleton-Century, 1937.

The Glimpses of the Moon. New York: Appleton, 1922.

The Gods Arrive. New York: Appleton, 1932.

The Greater Inclination. New York: Scribner's, 1899.

Here and Beyond. New York: Appleton, 1926.

The Hermit and the Wild Woman and Other Stories. New York: Scribner's, 1908.

The House of Mirth. New York: Scribner's, 1905.

Hudson River Bracketed. New York: Appleton, 1929.

Human Nature. New York: Appleton, 1933.

Madame de Treymes. New York: Scribner's, 1907.

The Marne. New York: Appleton, 1918.

The Mother's Recompense. New York: Appleton, 1925.

Old New York: False Dawn (The 'Forties), The Old Maid (The 'Fifties), The Spark (The 'Sixties), New Year's Day (The 'Seventies). New York: Appleton, 1924.

The Reef. New York: Appleton, 1912.

Sanctuary. New York: Scribner's, 1903.

A Son at the Front. New York: Scribner's, 1923.

Summer. New York: Appleton, 1917.

Tales of Men and Ghosts. New York: Scribner's, 1910.

The Touchstone. New York: Scribner's, 1900.

Twilight Sleep. New York: Appleton, 1927.

The Valley of Decision. 2 vols. New York: Scribner's, 1902.

The World Over. New York: Appleton-Century, 1936.

Xingu and Other Stories. New York: Scribner's, 1916.

COLLECTIONS (FICTION AND NONFICTION)

The Collected Short Fiction of Edith Wharton. Ed. R. W. B. Lewis. 2 vols. New York: Scribner's, 1968.

Edith Wharton Abroad: Selected Travel Writings, 1888–1920. Ed. Sarah Bird Wright. New York: St. Martin's, 1993.

Edith Wharton: Novellas and Other Writings. Ed. Cynthia Griffin Woolf. New York: Library of America, 1990.

The Edith Wharton Omnibus. Ed. with introduction by Gore Vidal. Garden City, N.Y.: Doubleday, 1978.

Ethan Frome and Other Short Fiction. Ed. with introduction by Mary Gordon. New York: Bantam Books, 1987.

The Ghost Stories of Edith Wharton. Illus. Laszlo Kubinyi. New York: Macmillan, 1986.

The Ghost-Feeler: Stories of Terror and the Supernatural. Selected and introduced by Peter Haining. London: P. Owen; Chester Springs, Penn.: distributed in the U.S. by Dufour Editions, Inc., 1996.

The Muse's Tragedy and Other Stories. Ed. Candace Waid. New York: New American Library, 1990.

Roman Fever and Other Stories. Ed. with introd. by Marilyn French. London: Virago, 1983.

Selected Short Stories of Edith Wharton. Ed. R. W. B. Lewis. New York: Scribner's, 1991.

The Stories of Edith Wharton. 2 vols. Selected and introduced by Anita Brookner, New York: Simon & Schuster, 1989.

Wharton's New England: Seven Stories and Ethan Frome. Ed. Barbara A. White. Hanover, N.H.: University Press of New England, 1995.

2. Selected Secondary Sources:

Ammons, Elizabeth. *Edith Wharton's Argument with America.* Athens: University of Georgia Press, 1980.

———. "The Business of Marriage in Edith Wharton's *The Custom of the Country.*" *Criticism: A Quarterly for Literature and the Arts* 16 (1974), 326–38.

———. "Edith Wharton's *Ethan Frome* and the Question of Meaning." *Studies in American Fiction,* 7 (1979), 127–40.

———. "Fairy-Tale Love and *The Reef.*" *American Literature: A Journal of Literary History, Criticism, and Bibliography,* 47 (1976), 615–28.

Aronson, Mark. "Wharton and the House of Scribner: The Novelist as a Pain in the Neck." *The New York Times Book Review,* Jan 2, 1994; Sec 7, p. 7, col. 1.

Auchincloss, Louis. *Edith Wharton.* Minneapolis: University of Minnesota Press, 1961.

———. *The Edith Wharton Reader: With Introduction.* New York: Scribner, 1965.

———. *Edith Wharton: A Woman in Her Time.* New York: Viking, 1971.

———. "Edith Wharton and Her New Yorks." *Partisan Review,* XVIII [1951], 411–19.

———. Introduction to reprint of *The Mother's Recompense.* New York: Macmillan, 1986.

———. *Pioneers and Caretakers: A Study of Nine American Women Novelists.* Boston: G. K. Hall, 1965.

———. *The Style's the Man: Reflections on Proust, Fitzgerald, Wharton, Vidal, and Others.* New York: Scribner, 1994.

Bailey, Brigitte. "Aesthetics and Ideology in *Italian Backgrounds.*" In Katherine Joslin and Alan Price, eds. *Wretched Exotic: Essays on Edith Wharton in Europe.* New York: Peter Lang, 1993.

Balestra, Gianfranca. "Italian Foregrounds and Backgrounds: *The Valley of Decision.*" *Edith Wharton Review* 9:1 (Spring 1992), 12–14, 27.

Bancroft, Catherine. "Lost Lands: Metaphors of Sexual Awakening in Edith Wharton's Poetry, 1908–1909." In Alfred Bendixen, ed. and introd.; Annette Zilversmit, ed. *Edith Wharton: New Critical Essays.* New York: Garland, 1992.

Banta, Martha. "The Ghostly Gothic of Wharton's Everyday World." *American Literary Realism* 27:1 (Fall 1994), 1–10.

Bauer, Dale. *Edith Wharton's Brave New Politics.* Madison: University of Wisconsin Press, 1994.

———. "*Twilight Sleep:* Edith Wharton's Brave New Politics." *Arizona Quarterly: A Journal of American Literature, Culture, and Theory,* 45:1 (Spring 1989), 49–71.

Bazin, Nancy Topping. "The Destruction of Lily Bart: Capitalism, Christianity, and Male Chauvinism." *Denver Quarterly,* 17:4 (Winter 1983), 97–108.

Bell, Millicent, ed. *The Cambridge Companion to Edith Wharton.* Cambridge: Cambridge Univ. Press, 1995.

———. *Edith Wharton & Henry James: The Story of Their Friendship.* New York: Braziller, 1965.

———. "Edith Wharton in France." In Katherine Joslin and Alan Price, eds. *Wretched Exotic: Essays on Edith Wharton in Europe.* New York: Peter Lang, 1993.

———. "Lady into Author: Edith Wharton and the House of Scribner." *American Quarterly* IX, No. 3 (Fall 1957), 295–315.

———. " 'Fleeing the Sewer': Edith Wharton, George Sand and Literary Innovation." In Katherine Joslin and Alan Price, eds. *Wretched Exotic: Essays on Edith Wharton in Europe.* New York: Peter Lang, 1993.

Bellringer, Alan. "Edith Wharton's Use of France." *The Yearbook of English Studies,* 15 (1985), 109–24.

Benert, Annette Larson. "The Geography of Gender in *The House of Mirth." Studies in the Novel,* 22 (Spring 1990), 26–42.

Benstock, Shari. *No Gifts from Chance: A Biography of Edith Wharton.* New York: Charles Scribner's Sons, Macmillan Publishing Co., 1994.

———. *Women of the Left Bank: Paris, 1900–1940.* Austin: University of Texas Press, 1986.

———, ed. *Edith Wharton: The House of Edith.* New York: St. Martin's, 1993.

Bentley, Nancy. "Edith Wharton and the Alienation of Divorce." In *The Ethnography of Manners: Hawthorne, James, Wharton.* New York: Cambridge University Press, 1995.

Beppu, Keiko. "Wharton Questions Motherhood." In Lyall Powers and Virginia Clare Eby, eds. *Leon Edel and Literary Art.* Ann Arbor: University of Michigan Press, 1988.

Berkove, Lawrence I. " 'Roman Fever': A Mortal Malady," *CEA Critic: An Official Journal of the College English Association,* 56:2 (Winter 1994), 56–60.

Berry, Walter. Review of *The Decoration of Houses. Bookman,* 8 (April 1898).

Blackall, Jean Frantz. "The Absent Children in Edith Wharton's Fiction." *Edith Wharton Review* 12:1 (Spring 1995), 3–6.

———. "Charity at the Window: Narrative Technique in Edith Wharton's *Summer."* In Alfred Bendixen, ed. and introd.; Annette Zilversmit, ed. *Edith Wharton: New Critical Essays.* New York: Garland, 1992.

———. "Henry and Edith: 'The Velvet Glove' as an 'In' Joke." *The Henry James Review* 7:1 (Fall 1985), 21–25.

———. "The Intrusive Voice: Telegrams in *The House of Mirth* and *The Age of Innocence." Women's Studies: An Interdisciplinary Journal,* 20:2 (1991), 163–68.

———. "The Sledding Accident in Ethan Frome." *Studies in Short Fiction,* 21:2 (Spring 1984), 145–46.

Bourdieu, Pierre. *Distinction: A Social Critique of the Judgement of Taste.* Translated Richard Nice. Cambridge: Harvard University Press, 1984.

Bourget, Paul. *Impressions of Italy* [*Sensations d'Italie*]. Translated Mary J. Serrano. New York: Cassell, 1892.

———. *Outre-Mer: Impressions of America.* New York: Charles Scribner's Sons, 1895.

Bradley, John and Ian Ousby. *The Correspondence of John Ruskin and Charles Eliot Norton.* Cambridge: Cambridge University Press, 1987.

Brinker, Ludger. "The Gilded Void: Edith Wharton, Abraham Cahan, and the Turn-of-the-Century American Culture." *Edith Wharton Review* 10:2 (1993), 3–7.

Brookner, Anita. "Introduction" to Edith Wharton, *The Custom of the Country.* New York: Viking Penguin, 1987.

Brown, E. K. "Edith Wharton's Poetry," trans. Alfred Bendixen. In Alfred Bendixen, ed. and introd.; Annette Zilversmit, ed. *Edith Wharton: New Critical Essays.* New York: Garland, 1992.

Buitenhuis, Peter. "Edith Wharton and the First World War." *American Quarterly* 18 (1966), 493–505.

Burlingame, Roger. *Of Making Many Books: A Hundred Years of Reading, Writing and Publishing.* New York: Charles Scribner's Sons, 1946.

Cain, William E. "Wharton's Art of Presence: The Case of Gerty Farish in *The House of Mirth." Edith Wharton Newsletter,* 6:2 (Fall 1989), 1–2, 7–8.

Campbell, Donna M. "Edith Wharton and the 'Authoresses': The Critique of Local Color in Wharton's Early Fiction." *Studies in American Fiction,* 22 (Autumn 1994), 169–83.

Carlin, Deborah. "To Form a More Imperfect Union: Gender, Tradition, and the Text in Wharton's *The Fruit of the Tree."* In Alfred Bendixen, ed. and introd.; Annette Zilversmit, ed. *Edith Wharton: New Critical Essays.* New York: Garland, 1992.

Carpenter, Lynette. "Deadly Letters, Sexual Politics, and the Dilemma of the Woman Writer: Edith Wharton's 'The House of the Dead Hand.' " *American Literary Realism,* 24:2 (Winter 1992), 55–69.

Cary, Richard. *The Genteel Circle: Bayard Taylor and His New York Friends.* Ithaca, N.Y.: Cornell University Press, 1952.

Caws, Mary Ann. "Framing in Two Opposite Modes: Ford and Wharton" [deals with the narrative frame of Ford's *The Good Soldier* and Wharton's "The Other Two"]; *The Comparatist: Journal of the Southern Comparative Literature Association,* 10 (May 1986, 114–20).

———. "A Note and Suggestions for Further Reading." *French Ways and Their Meaning,* Edith Wharton Restoration at the Mount, Lenox, Mass., and Berkshire House Publishers, Lee, Mass., 1997.

Cecil, David. *Desomnd MacCarthy: The Man and His Writings.* London: Constable, 1984.

Chandler, Marilyn R. *Dwelling in the Text: Houses in American Fiction.* Berkeley: University of California Press, 1991.

Chanler, Margaret Terry. *Autumn in the Valley.* Boston: Little, Brown, 1936.

Chapman, Mary (Anne) Megan. " 'Living Pictures': Women and Tableaux Vivants in Nineteenth-Century Fiction and Culture." *DAI* 53:8 (Feb. 1993), 2812A.

Coard, Robert L. "Edith Wharton's Influence on Sinclair Lewis." *Modern Fiction Studies,* 31:3 (Autumn 1985), 511–27.

Coles, William A. "The Genesis of a Classic." In reprint of *The Decoration of Houses.* New York: W. W. Norton & Company, 1978.

Collins, Alexandra. "The Art of Self-Perception in Virginia Woolf's *Mrs. Dalloway* and Edith Wharton's *The Reef.*" *Atlantis: A Women's Studies Journal Revue d'Etudes sur la Femme,* 7:2 (Spring 1982), 45–58.

Colquitt, Clare. "Contradictory Possibilities: Wharton Scholarship 1992–1994: A Bibliographic Essay." *Edith Wharton Review* 12:2 (Fall 1995), 37–44.

———. "Succumbing to the 'Literary Style': Arrested Desire in *The House of Mirth. Women's Studies: An Interdisciplinary Journal,* 20:2 (1991), 153–62.

———. "Unpacking Her Treasures: Edith Wharton's 'Mysterious Correspondence' with Morton Fullerton." *Library Chronicle of the University of Texas,* 31 (1985), 73–107.

Craig, Theresa. *Edith Wharton: A House Full of Rooms: Architecture, Interiors, and Gardens.* New York: The Monacelli Press, 1996.

Cuddy, Lois. "Triangles of Defeat and Liberation: The Quest for Power in Edith Wharton's Fiction." *Perspectives on Contemporary Literature,* 8 (1982), 18–26.

Cohn, Jan. "The House of Fiction: Domestic Architecture in Howells and Edith Wharton." *Texas Studies in Literature and Language: A Journal of the Humanities,* 15 (1973), 537–49.

Davidson, Cathy N. *Revolution and the Word: The Rise of the Novel in America.* New York: Oxford University Press, 1986.

Dimock, Wai-chee. "Debasing Exchange: Edith Wharton's The House of Mirth." *Publications of the Modern Language Association of America,* 100 (Oct. 1985), 783–92.

Dinnerstein, Leonard. *Antisemitism in America.* New York: Oxford, 1994.

Dittmar, Linda. "When Privilege Is No Protection: The Woman Artist in 'Quicksand' and *The House of Mirth.*" In Suzanne Jones, *Writing the Woman Artist: Essays on Poetics, Politics, and Portraiture.* Philadelphia: University of Pennsylvania Press, 1991.

Dixon, Roslyn. "Reflecting Vision in The House of Mirth." *Twentieth Century Literature: A Scholarly and Critical Journal,* 33 (Summer 1987), 211–22.

Dulles, Foster Rhea. *Americans Abroad: Two Centuries of European Travel.* Ann Arbor: University of Michigan Press, 1964.

Dupree, Ellen. "Jamming the Machinery: Mimesis in The Custom of the Country." *American Literary Realism,* 22 (Winter 1990), 5–16.

Durczak, Joanna. "America and Europe in Edith Wharton's *The Age of Innocence.*" In Joanna Durczak and Jerzy Durczak, eds. *Polish-American Literary Confrontations.* Lublin: Maria Curie-Sklodowska UP, 1995.

Dwight, Eleanor. *Edith Wharton: An Extraordinary Life.* New York: Harry N. Abrams, Inc., 1994.

———. *The Gilded Age: Edith Wharton and Her Contemporaries.* New York: Universe Publishing, 1996.

———. "The Influence of Italy on Edith Wharton." *Dissertation Abstracts International,* 45:2 (Aug. 1984), 520A.

Edel, Leon. "Summers in an Age of Innocence: In France with Edith Wharton." *New York Times Book Review,* June 9, 1991, 3, 44, 46.

———. "Walter Berry and the Novelists: Proust, James, and Edith Wharton." *Nineteenth Century Literature,* 38:4 (Mar. 1984), 514–28.

Elbert, Monika M. "The Politics of Maternality in *Summer.*" *Edith Wharton Review* 7 (Winter 1990), 2, 4–9, 24.

———. "The Transcendental Economy of Edith Wharton's Gothic Mansions." *American Transcendental Quarterly* 9 (Mar. 1995), 51–67.

———. "T. S. Eliot and Wharton's Modernist Gothic," *Edith Wharton Review* 11:1 (Spring 1994), 19–25.

Emerson, Ralph Waldo. "The American Scholar." In Carl Bode in collaboration with Malcolm Cowley, ed. *The Portable Emerson.* New York: Viking Penguin, 1981, 70–71.

Erlich, Gloria C. *The Sexual Education of Edith Wharton.* Berkeley: University of California Press, 1992.

———. "The Libertine as Liberator: Morton Fullerton and Edith Wharton." *Women's Studies: An Interdisciplinary Journal,* 10:2 (1991), 97–108.

Faery, Rebecca Blevins. "Wharton's *Reef:* The Inscription of Female Sexuality." In Alfred Bendixen, ed. and introd.; Annette Zilversmit, ed. *Edith Wharton: New Critical Essays.* New York: Garland, 1992.

Fargnoli, A. Nicholas and Michael P. Gillespie. *James Joyce A to Z: The Essential Reference to the Life and Work.* Facts On File, 1995.

Fedorko, Kathy A. "Edith Wharton's Haunted Fiction: 'The Lady's Maid's Bell' and *The House of Mirth.*" In Lynette Carpenter and Wendy K. Kolmar, eds. *Haunting the House of Fiction: Feminist Perspectives on Ghost Stories by American Women* (Knoxville: University of Tennessee Press, 1991).

———. "'Forbidden Things': Gothic Confrontation with the Feminine in 'The Young Gentlemen' and 'Bewitched.'" *Edith Wharton Review,* 11 (Spring 1994), 3–9.

———. *Gender and the Gothic.* Tuscaloosa: The University of Alabama Press, 1995.

———. "Storming the Chateau at Hyères," *Edith Wharton Review* 4:2 (Fall 1987), 7.

Fishbein, Leslie. "Prostitution, Morality, and Paradox: Moral Relativism in Edith Wharton's Old New York: *New Year's Day (The 'Seventies).*" *Studies in Short Fiction,* 24:4 (Fall 1987), 399–406.

Foster, Shirley. "Making It Her Own: Edith Wharton's Europe." In Katherine Joslin and Alan Price, eds. *Wretched Exotic: Essays on Edith Wharton in Europe.* New York: Peter Lang, 1993.

————. "The Open Cage: Freedom, Marriage and the Heroine in Early Twentieth-Century American Women's Novels." In Moira Monteith, ed. *Women's Writing: A Challenge to Theory.* New York: St. Martin's, 1986, 154–74.

Fracasso, Evelyn E. "Images of Imprisonment in Two Tales of Edith Wharton." *College Language Association Journal,* 36:3 (Mar. 1993), 318–26.

————. "The Transparent Eyes of May Welland in Wharton's *The Age of Innocence.*" *Modern Language Studies* 21:4 (Fall 1991), 43–48.

French, Marilyn. "Muzzled Women." *College Literature,* 14 (1987), 219–29.

Fryer, Judith. *Felicitous Space: The Imaginative Structures of Edith Wharton and Willa Cather.* Chapel Hill: University of North Carolina Press, 1986.

————. "Purity and Power in *The Age of Innocence.*" *American Literary Realism,* 17 (Autumn 1984), 153–68.

————. "Reading *Mrs. Lloyd.*" In Alfred Bendixen, ed. and introd.; Annette Zilversmit, ed. *Edith Wharton: New Critical Essays.* New York: Garland, 1992.

Funston, Judith E. "Clocks and Mirrors, Dreams and Destinies: Edith Wharton's *The Old Maid.*" In Alfred Bendixen, ed. and introd.; Annette Zilversmit, ed. *Edith Wharton: New Critical Essays.* New York: Garland, 1992.

————. "*In Morocco:* Edith Wharton's Heart of Darkness," *Edith Wharton Newsletter* 5:1 (Spring 1988), 1–3, 12.

————. "Macaws and Pekingnese: Vivienne de Watteville and Edith Wharton." *Edith Wharton Review* 7:1 (Spring 1990), 13–14.

————. " 'Xingu': Edith Wharton's Velvet Gauntlet." *Studies in American Fiction,* 12:2 (Autumn 1984), 227–34.

Gargano, James. "Tableaux of Renunciation: Wharton's Use of *The Shaughraun* in *The Age of Innocence.*" *Studies in American Fiction,* 15 (Spring 1987), 1–11.

Garrison, Stephen. *Edith Wharton; A Descriptive Bibliography.* Pittsburgh Series in Bibliography. Pittsburgh: University of Pittsburgh Press, 1990.

Gibson, Mary Ellis. "Edith Wharton and the Ethnography of Old New York." *Studies in American Fiction* 13 (Spring 1985), 57–69.

Gilbert, Sandra M. and Susan Gubar. *No Man's Land: The Place of the Woman Writer in the Twentieth Century.* Vol. 2, *Sexchanges.* New Haven, Conn.: Yale University Press, 1988.

Gimbel, Wendy. *Edith Wharton: Orphancy and Survival.* New York: Praeger, 1984.

Goldman, Irene C. "The Perfect Jew and *The House of Mirth:* A Study in Point of View." *The Modern Language Review,* 23:2 (Spring 1993), 25–36.

Goldsmith, Meredith. "Edith Wharton's Gift to Nella Larsen: *The House of Mirth* and 'Quicksand.' " *Edith Wharton Review* 11:2 (Fall 1994), 3–5, 15.

Gooder, Jean. "Unlocking Edith Wharton: An Introduction to *The Reef.*" *The Cambridge Quarterly* (Oxford, England), 15:1 (1986), 33–52.

Goodman, Susan. *Edith Wharton's Inner Circle.* Austin: University of Texas Press, 1994.

————. *Edith Wharton's Women: Friends and Rivals.* Hanover: N.H., University Press of New England, 1990.

————. "Edith Wharton's 'Sketch of an Essay on Walt Whitman.' " *Walt Whitman Quarterly Review,* 10:1 (Summer 1992), 3–9.

Goodwyn, Janet. *Edith Wharton: Traveller in the Land of Letters.* New York: St. Martin's, 1990.

Gribben, Alan. " 'The Heart Is Insatiable': A Selection from Edith Wharton's Letters to Morton Fullerton, 1907–1915." *Library Chronicle of the University of Texas,* 31 (1985), 7–18.

Hadley, Kathy Miller. "Ironic Structure and Untold Stories in *The Age of Innocence.*" *Studies in the Novel,* 23:2 (Summer 1991), 262–72.

Hamblen, Abigail Ann. "Edith Wharton in New England." *New England Quarterly: A Historical Review of New England Life and Letters,* 38 (1965), 239–44.

Hecht, Deborah. "The Poisoned Well: Percy Lubbock and Edith Wharton." *The American Scholar,* 62:2 (Spring 1993), 255–59.

Heller, Janet Ruth. "Ghosts and Marital Estrangement: An Analysis of 'Afterward,' " *Edith Wharton Review,* Brooklyn, N.Y., 10:1 (Spring 1993), 18–19.

Hoeller, Hildegard. "The Gains and Losses of 'Sentimental Economies' in Edith Wharton's 'The Dilettante.' " *American Literary Realism,* 28 (Spring 1996), 19–29.

————. " 'The Impossible Rosedale': 'Race' and the Reading of Edith Wharton's *The House of Mirth.*" *Studies in American Jewish Literature,* 13 (1994), 14–20.

Hovet, Grace Ann, and Theodore Hovet. "Tableaux Vivants: Masculine Vision and Feminine Reflections in Novels by Warner, Alcott, Stowe, and Wharton." *American Transcendental Quarterly,* 7:4 (Dec. 1993), 335–56.

Howard, Maureen. "On The House of Mirth," *Raritan: A Quarterly Review,* 15:3 (Winter 1996), 1–23.

Hussey, Mark. *Virginia Woolf A to Z: A Comprehensive Reference for Students, Teachers and Common Readers to Her Life, Work and Critical Reception.* New York: Facts On File, 1995.

Inness, Sherrie A. "An Economy of Beauty: The Beauty System in 'The Looking Glass' and 'Permanent Wave.' " *Edith Wharton Review* 10:1 (Spring 1993), 7–11.

Inverso, Mary Beth. "Performing Women: Semiotic Promiscuity in 'The Other Two.' " *Edith Wharton Review* 10:1 (Spring 1993), 3–6.

James, Henry. *The Ambassadors.* New York: New American Library, 1960. First pub. 1903.

———. *The Letters of Henry James.* Ed. Leon Edel. 4 vols. Cambridge: Belknap Press of Harvard University Press, 1974–1984.

———. *Letters to Walter Berry.* Paris: Black Sun Press, 1928.

Jarves, James Jackson. *The Art-Idea.* Ed. Benjamin Rowland, Jr. Cambridge: Harvard University Press, 1960.

Jones, Suzanne. "Edith Wharton's 'Secret Sensitiveness,' *The Decoration of Houses* and Her Fiction." *Journal of Modern Literature,* 21:2 (Winter 1997), 177–200.

———. *Writing the Woman Artist: Essays on Poetics, Politics, and Portraiture.* Philadelphia: University of Pennsylvania Press, 1991.

Jones, Wendell, Jr. "Holding up the Revealing Lamp: The Myth of Psyche in Edith Wharton's *The Reef.*" *College Literature,* 19:1 (Feb. 1992), 75–90.

Joslin, Katherine. *Edith Wharton.* New York: St. Martin's, 1996.

———. "What Lubbock Didn't Say." *Edith Wharton Newsletter,* 1 (Spring 1984), 2–4.

Joslin, Katherine and Alan Price, eds. *Wretched Exotic: Essays on Edith Wharton in Europe.* New York: Peter Lang, 1993.

Kaplan, Amy. *The Social Construction of American Realism.* Chicago: University of Chicago Press, 1988.

Kaye, Richard A. " 'Unearthly Visitants': Wharton Ghost Tales, Gothic Form and the Literature of Homosexual Panic," *Edith Wharton Review* 11:1 (Spring 1994), 10–18.

Kazin, Alfred. "Edith Wharton and Theodore Dreiser." In *On Native Grounds.* New York: Harcourt Brace Jovanovich, 1970. First pub. 1942.

Keyser, Elizabeth Lennox. " 'The Ways in Which the Heart Speaks': Letters in *The Reef.*" *Studies in American Fiction,* 19:1 (Spring 1991), 95–106.

Kiel, Hanna, ed. *The Bernard Berenson Treasury.* New York: Simon & Schuster, 1962.

Killoran, Helen. *Edith Wharton: Art and Allusion.* Tuscaloosa: University of Alabama Press, 1996.

———. "Edith Wharton's Reading in European Languages and Its Influence on Her Work." In Katherine Joslin and Alan Price, eds. *Wretched Exotic: Essays on Edith Wharton in Europe.* New York: Peter Lang, 1993.

———. "On the Religious Reading of Edith Wharton." *Resources for American Literary Study,* 19:1 (1993), 58–74.

———. "Pascal, Bronte, and 'Kerfol': The Horrors of a Foolish Quartet." *Edith Wharton Review* 10:1 (Spring 1993), 12–17.

———. "Sexuality and Abnormal Psychology in Edith Wharton's 'The Lady's Maid's Bell.' " *Critic: An Official Journal of the College English Association,* 58:3 (Spring-Summer, 1996), 41–49.

———. "An Unnoticed Source for *The Great Gatsby:* The Influence of Edith Wharton's *The Glimpses of the Moon.*" *Canadian Review of American Studies,* 21:2 (Fall 1990), 223–24.

———. " 'Xingu': Edith Wharton Instructs Literary Critics." *Studies in American Humor* NS 3:3 (1996), 1–13.

Kim, Wook-Dong. "Theme and Symbol in Wharton's *Ethan Frome.*" *The Journal of English Language and Literature,* Winter 1989, 677–94.

Koprince, Susan. "The Meaning of Bellomont in *The House of Mirth.*" *Edith Wharton Newsletter,* 2 (Spring 1986), 1, 5, 8.

Kozikowski, Stanley J. "Unreliable Narration in Henry James's 'The Two Faces' and Edith Wharton's 'The Dilettante.' " *Arizona Quarterly,* 35 (1979), 357–72.

Kronenberger, Louis. *The Thread of Laughter.* New York: Knopf, 1952.

Lauer, Kristin O. "Is this Indeed 'Attractive'? Another Look at the 'Beatrice Palmato' Fragment." *Edith Wharton Review,* 11:1 (Spring 1994), 26–29.

Lawson, Richard H. "Edith Wharton." In Bobby Ellen Kimbel, ed. *American Short-Story Writers, 1880–1910.* Detroit: Gale Research, 1989.

———. *Edith Wharton and German Literature.* Bonn: Bouvier Verlag H. Grundmann, 1974.

Leach, Nancy. "Edith Wharton's Interest in Walt Whitman." *Yale University Library Gazette,* 33 (Oct. 1958), 63–6.

Lears, T. Jackson. *No Place of Grace: Antimodernism and the Transformation of American Culture 1880–1920.* New York: Pantheon Books, 1981.

Lee, Vernon [Violet Paget]. "Edith Wharton's *Valley of Decision:* A Rediscovered Contemporary Critique." In Millicent Bell, ed. *The Cambridge Companion to Edith Wharton.* Cambridge: Cambridge Univ. Press, 1995.

———. *Studies of the Eighteenth Century in Italy.* London: Unwin, 1887.

Levine, Jessica. "Discretion and Self Censorship in Wharton's Fiction: 'The Old Maid' and the Politics of Publishing." *Edith Wharton Review* 13:1 (Fall 1996), 4–13.

Lewis, R. W. B. *Edith Wharton: A Biography.* New York: Harper & Row, Publishers, Inc., 1975.

———. "Introduction." Edith Wharton, *The Age of Innocence* (New York: Macmillan Publishing, 1958).

———. "Powers of Darkness," *Times Literary Supplement,* 13 (June 1975), 644–46.

Lewis, R. W. B. and Nancy Lewis, eds. *The Letters of Edith Wharton.* New York: Scribner's, 1988.

Lubbock, Percy. *Portrait of Edith Wharton.* New York: Appleton-Century-Crofts, Inc., 1947.

———, ed. *Letters of Henry James.* New York: Charles Scribner's Sons, 1920.

Luria, Sarah. "The Architecture of Manners: Henry James, Edith Wharton, and the Mount." *American Quarterly,* 49 (June 1997), 298–327.

Ludwig, Coy L. *Maxfield Parrish.* New York: Watson-Guptill Publications, 1973.

Lynes, Russell. *The Tastemakers.* New York: Harper & Brothers, 1954.

MacCannell, Dean. *The Tourist: A New Theory of the Leisure Class.* New York: Schocken Books, 1976.

MacMaster, Anne. "Beginning with the Same Ending: Virginia Woolf and Edith Wharton; Selected Papers from Fifth Annual Conference on Virginia Woolf." In Beth Rigel Daughterty and Eileen Barrett, eds. *Virginia Woolf: Texts and Contexts.* New York: Pace UP, 1996.

McCullough, Jack Wheelock. *Living Pictures on the New York Stage.* Ann Arbor, Mich.: UMI Research Press, 1981.

McDowell, Margaret B. "Edith Wharton's 'After Holbein': 'A Paradigm of the Human Condition,' " *Journal of Narrative Technique,* 1 (1971), 49–58.

———. "Edith Wharton's Ghost Stories." *Criticism: A Quarterly for Literature and the Arts* 12 (1970), 133–52.

———. "Edith Wharton's Ghost Tales Reconsidered." In Alfred Bendixen, ed. and introd.; Annette Zilversmit, ed. *Edith Wharton: New Critical Essays.* New York: Garland, 1992.

———. "Edith Wharton's *The Old Maid:* Novella/Play/Film." *College Literature* 14 (Fall 1987), 246–62.

———. "Viewing the Custom of Her Country: Edith Wharton's Feminism." *Contemporary Literature* 15 (1974), 521–38.

McWilliams, Jim. "Wharton's *The Age of Innocence.*" *Explicator* 48 (Summer 1990), 268–70.

Margolis, Stacey. "The Public Life: The Discourse of Privacy in the Age of Celebrity." *Arizona Quarterly: A Journal of American Literature, Culture, and Theory,* 51:2 (Summer 1995), 81–101.

Mariano, Nicky. *Forty Years with Berenson.* New York: Alfred A. Knopf, 1966.

Marshall, Scott. "Edith Wharton, Kate Spencer, and *Ethan Frome.*" *Edith Wharton Review,* 10:1 (Spring 1993), 20–21.

———. *The Mount: Home of Edith Wharton.* Lenox, Mass.: Edith Wharton Restoration, 1997.

Martin, Robert, and Linda Wagner-Martin. "The Salons of Wharton's Fiction: Wharton and Fitzgerald, Hemingway, Faulkner, and Stein." In Katherine Joslin and Alan Price, eds. *Wretched Exotic: Essays on Edith Wharton in Europe.* New York: Peter Lang, 1993.

Maxwell, D. E. S. *American Fiction: The Intellectual Background.* New York: Columbia University Press, 1965.

Maynard, Moira. "Moral Integrity in *The Reef:* Justice to Anna Leath." *College Literature,* 14:3 (Fall 1987), 285–95.

Méral, Jean. "Edith Wharton, Dorothy Canfield, John Dos Passos et la presence americaine dans le Paris de la Grande Guerre." *Caliban* 19 (1982), 73–82.

———. "Parisian Milieux before 1914." In *Paris in American Literature.* Translated Laurette Long. Chapel Hill: University of North Carolina Press, 1989.

Metcalf, Pauline, ed. *Ogden Codman and* The Decoration of Houses. Boston: D. R. Godine, 1988.

———. "The Interiors of Ogden Codman, Jr. in Newport," *Antiques,* 108 (Sept. 1980), 486–97.

———. "Ogden Codman and The Grange," *Old Time New England,* 71 (1981), 68–83.

———. "Victorian Profile: Ogden Codman, Jr. A Clever Young Boston Architect," *Nineteenth Century* 7:1 (Spring 1981), 45–47.

Miller, Carol. " 'Natural Magic': Irony as Unifying Strategy in *The House of Mirth.*" *South Central Review: The Journal of the South Central Modern Language Association,* 4:1 (Spring 1987), 82–91.

Milne, Gordon. *The Sense of Society: A History of the America Novel of Manners.* Rutherford: Fairleigh Dickinson University Press, 1977.

Mizener, Arthur. "Scott Fitzgerald and Edith Wharton." *Times Literary Supplement* (London), July 7, 1966, 595.

Morrow, Nancy. "Games and Conflict in Edith Wharton's *The Custom of the Country.*" *American Literary Realism 1870-1910* 17 (1984), 32–39.

Mott, Frank Luther. *A History of American Magazines.* 5 vols. Cambridge: Harvard University Press, 1938–68.

Murad, Orlene. "Edith Wharton and *Ethan Frome.*" *Modern Language Studies,* Summer 1983, 90–103.

Murphy, John J. "Edith Wharton's Italian Triptych: *The Valley of Decision.* Xavier Review,* 4 (1965), 85–94.

Murray, Margaret P. "The Gothic Arsenal of Edith Wharton." *Journal of Evolutionary Psychology,* 10:3–4 (Aug. 1989), 315–21.

Nettels, Elsa. *Language and Gender in American Fiction: Howells, James, Wharton and Cather.* Charlottesville: University Press of Virginia, 1997.

———. "Texts within Texts: The Power of Letters in Edith Wharton's Fiction." In Raymond Adolph Prier, ed. *Countercurrents: On the Primacy of Texts in Literary Criticism.* Albany: State University of New York Press, 1992.

———. "Thwarted Escapes: *Ethan Frome* and Jean Stafford's 'A Country Love Story.' " *Edith Wharton Review,* 11:2 (Fall 1994), 6–8, 15.

Nevius, Blake. *Edith Wharton: A Study of Her Fiction.* Berkeley: University of California Press, 1953.

———, ed. *Edith Wharton's* Ethan Frome: *The Story with Sources and Commentary; With introd.* New York: Scribner's, 1968.

———. "On *The Age of Innocence.*" In Irving Howe, ed. *Edith Wharton: A Collection of Critical Essays.* Englewood Cliffs, N.J.: Prentice-Hall, 1962.

———. "On *Ethan Frome.*" In *Edith Wharton: A Collection of Critical Essays,* ed. Irving Howe. New York: Prentice-Hall, 1962.

Olin-Ammentorp, Julie. "Edith Wharton's Challenge to Feminist Criticism." *Studies in American Fiction,* 16 (Autumn 1988), 237–44.

———. " 'Not Precisely War Stories': Edith Wharton's Short Fiction from the Great War. *Studies in American Fiction* 23 (Autumn 1995), 153–72.

———. "Wharton through a Kristevan Lens: The Maternality of *The Gods Arrive*." In Katherine Joslin and Alan Price, eds. *Wretched Exotic: Essays on Edith Wharton in Europe*. New York: Peter Lang, 1993.

Parrington, Vernon L. "Our Literary Aristocrat." In Irving Howe, ed. *Edith Wharton: A Collection of Critical Essays*. New York: Prentice-Hall, Inc., 1962.

Pater, Walter. *The Renaissance*. New York: The Modern Library, Random House, c. 1919. First pub. 1873.

Petry, Alice Hall. "A Twist of Crimson Silk: Edith Wharton's 'Roman Fever.' " *Studies in Short Fiction* 24 (Spring 1987), 163–66.

Pfeiffer, Kathleen. "Summer and Its Critics' Discomfort," *Women's Studies: An Interdisciplinary Journal*, 20 (1991), 141–52.

Poirier, Suzanne. "The Weir Mitchell Rest Cure: Doctor and Patients." *Women's Studies: An Interdisciplinary Journal*, 10 (1983), 15–40.

Powers, Lyall H., ed. *Henry James and Edith Wharton: Letters: 1900–1915*. New York: Charles Scribner's Sons, 1990.

Prampolini, Gaetano. "Edith Wharton in Italy." *Edith Wharton Review* 9:1 (Spring 1992), 24–6.

Prather, William N. "The Fall of the Knowledgeable Woman: The Diminished Female Healer in Edith Wharton's *The Fruit of the Tree*." *American Literary Realism*, 29:1 (Fall 1996), 29–53.

Price, Alan. *The End of the Age of Innocence: Edith Wharton and the First World War*. New York: St. Martin's Press, 1996.

———. "The Making of Edith Wharton's *The Book of the Homeless*." *Princeton University Library Chronicle* 47 (1985), 5–23.

Puknat, E. M. and S. B. "Edith Wharton and Gottfried Keller," *Comparative Literature* 21 (Summer 1969), 245–54.

Quinn, Arthur Hobson, ed. *The Literature of the American People: An Historical and Critical Survey*. New York: Appleton-Century-Crofts, Inc., 1951.

Quoyeser, Catherine. "The Antimodernist Unconscious: Genre and Ideology in *The House of Mirth*." *Arizona Quarterly*, 44 (Winter 1989), 55–79.

Raphael, Lev. "Fighting the Burden of Shame: A New Reading of Edith Wharton's *The Reef*." *Journal of Evolutionary Psychology*, 10:3–4 (Aug. 1989), 208–22.

———. "Kate Orme's Struggles with Shame in Edith Wharton's *Sanctuary*." *Massachusetts Studies in English*, 10:4 (Fall 1986), 229–36.

———. "Shame in Edith Wharton's *The Mother's Recompense*." *American Imago: A Psychoanalytic Journal for Culture, Science, and the Arts*, 45–2 (Summer 1988); 187–203.

Restuccia, Frances. "The Name of the Lily: Edith Wharton's Feminism(s)." *Contemporary Literature*, 28 (Summer 1987), 223–38.

Richards, Mary Margaret. " 'Feminized Men' in Wharton's *Old New York*," *Edith Wharton Newsletter*, 3:2 (Fall 1986), 2–3, 12.

Riegel, Christian. "Rosedale and Anti-Semitism in the *House of Mirth*." *Studies in American Fiction*, 20:2 (Autumn 1992), 219–24.

Robillard, Douglas. "Edith Wharton." In Everett Franklin Bleiler, ed. *Supernatural Fiction Writers: Fantasy and Horror, 2: A. E. Coppard to Roger Zelazny*. New York: Scribner's, 1985, 738–88.

Rodgers, Daniel T. *The Work Ethic in Industrial America 1850–1920*. Chicago: University of Chicago Press, 1978.

Rose, Alan Henry. " 'Such Depths of Sad Initiation': Edith Wharton and New England." *New England Quarterly: A Historical Review of New England Life and Letters*, 50 (1977), 423–39.

St. Laurent, Maureen. "Pathways to a Personal Aesthetic: Edith Wharton's Travels in Italy and France." In Katherine Joslin and Alan Price, eds. *Wretched Exotic: Essays on Edith Wharton in Europe*. New York: Peter Lang, 1993.

Samuels, Ernest. *Bernard Berenson: The Making of a Connoisseur*. Cambridge: Harvard University Press, 1979.

Sapora, Carol Baker. "Motor Flights through France." *Edith Wharton Review*, 4:2 (Fall 1987), 1–2.

Saunders, Judith P. "Ironic Reversal in Edith Wharton's 'Bunner Sisters.' " *Studies in Short Fiction*, 14 (1977), 241–45.

———. "A New Look at the Oldest Profession in Wharton's *New Year's Day*." *Studies in Short Fiction*, 17 (1980), 121–26.

Schriber, Mary Suzanne. "Edith Wharton and the Dog-Eared Travel Book." In Katherine Joslin and Alan Price, eds. *Wretched Exotic: Essays on Edith Wharton in Europe*. New York: Peter Lang, 1993.

———. "Edith Wharton and Travel Writing as Self-Discovery." *American Literature*, 59 (May 1987), 257–67.

———. *Gender and the Writer's Imagination: From Cooper to Wharton*. Lexington: University Press of Kentucky, 1987.

———. "Introduction," *A Motor-Flight Through France*. Ed. Mary Suzanne Schriber. DeKalb, Ill.: Northern Illinois University Press, 1991. First pub. 1908.

Sensibar, Judith. " 'Behind the Lines' in Edith Wharton's *A Son at the Front*: Re-Writing a Masculinist Tradition." In Katherine Joslin and Alan Price, eds. *Wretched Exotic: Essays on Edith Wharton in Europe*. New York: Peter Lang, 1993.

Shaloo, Sharon. "Making Room for the Artist in Edith Wharton's *Old New York*." In Robert A. Lee, ed. *The Modern American Novella*. New York: St. Martin's, 1989.

Shand-Tucci, Douglass. *The Art of Scandal: The Life and Times of Isabella Stewart Gardner*. New York: HarperCollins, 1997.

Sheehan, Donald. *This Was Publishing: A Chronicle of the Book Trade in the Gilded Age*. Bloomington: Indiana University Press, 1952.

Sherman, Claire Richter and Adele M. Holcomb, eds. *Women as Interpreters of the Visual Arts, 1820–1979.* Westport, Conn.: Greenwood Press, 1981.

Showalter, Elaine. "The Death of the Lady (Novelist)." In *Sister's Choice: Tradition and Change in American Women's Writing.* The Clarendon Lectures, 1989. Oxford: Clarendon Press, 1991.

Shulman, Robert. "Divided Selves and the Market Society: Politics and Psychology in *The House of Mirth,*" *Perspectives on Contemporary Literature* 11 (1985), 10–19.

Singley, Carol J. *Edith Wharton: Matters of Mind and Spirit.* Cambridge: Cambridge University Press, 1995.

———. "Gothic Borrowings and Innovations in Edith Wharton's 'A Bottle of Perrier.'" In Alfred Bendixen, ed. & introd.; Annette Zilversmit, ed. *Edith Wharton: New Critical Essays.* New York: Garland, 1992, 271–90.

Singley, Carol J. and Susan Elizabeth Sweeney. "Forbidden Reading and Ghostly Writing in Edith Wharton's 'Pomegranate Seed.'" In Carol J. Singley and Susan Elizabeth Sweeney, eds. *Anxious Power: Reading, Writing, and Ambivalence in Narrative by Women.* Albany: State University of New York Press, 1993.

Smith, Allen Gardener. "Edith Wharton and the Ghost Story." *Women and Literature,* 1 (1980), 149–59.

Spiller, Robert, ed. *Literary History of the United States,* 3rd ed. New York: The Macmillan Company, 1963–72.

Springer, Marlene. *Ethan Frome: A Nightmare of Need.* New York: Twayne, 1993.

Stein, Allen F. *After the Vows Were Spoken: Marriage in American Literary Realism.* Columbus: Ohio State University Press, 1984.

———. "Wharton's Blithedale: A New Reading of *The Fruit of the Tree.*" *American Literary Realism,* 12 (1979), 330–37.

Stengel, Ellen Powers. "Edith Wharton Rings 'The Lady's Maid's Bell.'" *Edith Wharton Review* 7 (Spring 1990), 3–9.

Sweeney, Susan Elizabeth. "Edith Wharton's Case of *Roman* Fever." In Katherine Joslin and Alan Price, eds. *Wretched Exotic: Essays on Edith Wharton in Europe.* New York: Peter Lang, 1993.

———. "Mirror, Mirror, on the Wall: Gazing in Edith Wharton's 'Looking Glass.'" *Narrative,* 3:2 (May 1995), 139–60.

Tharp, Louise Hall. *Mrs. Jack: A Biography of Isabella Stewart Gardner.* Boston: Little, Brown, 1965.

Thomas, Jennice G. "Spook or Spinster? Edith Wharton's 'Miss Mary Pask.'" In Lynette Carpenter and Wendy Kolmar, eds. *Haunting the House of Fiction: Feminist Perspectives on Ghost Stories by American Women.* Knoxville: University of Tennessee Press, 1991.

Tintner, Adeline. "Consuelo Vanderbilt and *The Buccaneers.*" *Edith Wharton Review,* 10 (Fall 1993), 15–19.

———. "Edith Wharton and Paul Bourget." *Edith Wharton Review* 8 (Spring 1991), 16–18.

———. "False Dawn and the Irony of Taste-Changes in Art." *Edith Wharton Newsletter* 1:2 (Fall 1984), 1, 3, 8.

———. "Justice to Teddy Wharton: Louis Auchincloss's 'The Arbiter,'" *Edith Wharton Review* 7:2 (Winter 1990), 17–19.

———, ed. and tr. "Memories of Bourget from across the Sea (Souvenirs de Bourget outremer)." *Edith Wharton Review* 8 (Spring 1991), 23–31.

———, "The Narrative Structure of *Old New York:* Text and Pictures in Edith Wharton's Quartet of Linked Short Stories." *Journal of Narrative Technique,* 17:1 (Winter 1987), 76–82.

———. "Portrait of Edith Wharton in Bourget's 'L'Indicatrice.'" *Edith Wharton Review* 7 (Spring 1990), 10–12.

Tomsich, John. *A Genteel Endeavor: American Culture and Politics in the Gilded Age.* Stanford: Stanford University Press, 1971.

Tonkovich, Nicole. "An Excess of Recompense: The Feminine Economy of *The Mother's Recompense.*" *American Literary Realism,* 26:3 (Spring 1994), 12–32.

Trilling, Diana. "The House of Mirth Revisited." *Harper's Bazaar,* 81 (Dec. 1947). In Irving Howe, ed. *Edith Wharton: A Collection of Critical Essays.* Englewood Cliffs, N.J.: Prentice-Hall, 1962.

Trilling, Lionel. "The Morality of Inertia," *Great Moral Dilemmas.* In Irving Howe, ed. *Edith Wharton: A Collection of Critical Essays.* Englewood Cliffs, N.J.: Prentice-Hall, Inc., 1962.

Tuttleton, James W., Kristin O. Lauer and Margaret P. Murray. *Edith Wharton: The Contemporary Reviews.* Cambridge: Cambridge University Press, 1992.

Tuttleton, James W. "Leisure, Wealth and Luxury: Edith Wharton's *Old New York.*" *Midwest Quarterly: A Journal of Contemporary Thought,* 7 (1966), 337–52.

———. *The Novel of Manners in America.* New York: Norton, 1972.

Tyler, William R. "Personal Memories of Edith Wharton." *Proceedings of the Massachusetts Historical Society* 85 (1973), 91–104.

Van Gastel, Ada. "The Location and Decoration of Houses in *The Age of Innocence.*" *Dutch Quarterly Review of Ango-American Letters,* 20 (1990), 138–53.

Vance, William L. "Edith Wharton's Italian Mask: *The Valley of Decision.*" In Millicent Bell, ed. *The Cambridge Companion to Edith Wharton.* Cambridge: Cambridge Univ. Press, 1995.

Veblen, Thorstein. *The Theory of the Leisure Class.* New York: The Macmillan Company, 1899.

Vickers, Jackie. "Women and Wealth: F. Scott Fitzgerald, Edith Wharton and Paul Bourget." *Journal of American Studies,* 26 (Aug. 1992), 261–63.

Vita-Finzi, Penelope. *Edith Wharton and the Art of Fiction.* New York: St. Martin's Press, 1990.

Voloshin, Beverly R. "Exchange in Wharton's *The Custom of the Country*." *Pacific Coast Philology*, 22 (Nov. 1987), 98–104.

Wagner, Linda W. "A Note on Wharton's Use of *Faust*." *Edith Wharton Newsletter*, 3 (Spring 1986), 1, 8.

Wagner-Martin, Linda. *The* House of Mirth: *A Novel of Admonition*. Boston: Twayne, 1990.

Waid, Candace. *Edith Wharton's Letters from the Underworld: Fictions of Women and Writing*. Chapel Hill: University of North Carolina Press, 1991.

———. "Introduction," *The Muse's Tragedy and Other Stories*. New York: New American Library, 1990.

———. "Introduction," *Summer*. New York: Signet, 1993.

Walker, Nancy. "Mothers and Lovers: Edith Wharton's *The Reef* and *The Mother's Recompense*." In Mickey Pearlman, ed. *The Anna Book: Searching for Anna in Literary History*. Westport, Conn.: Greenwood, 1992.

———. " 'Seduced and Abandoned': Convention and Reality in Edith Wharton's *Summer*." *Studies in American Fiction*, 11:1 (Spring 1983), 107—114.

Walton, Geoffrey. *Edith Wharton: A Critical Interpretation*. Rutherford, N.J.: Fairleigh Dickinson University Press, 1970.

Wegener, Frederick. *The Uncollected Critical Writings of Edith Wharton*. Princeton: Princeton University Press, 1996.

Werlock, Abby H. P. "Edith Wharton's Subtle Revenge?: Morton Fullerton and the Female Artist in *Hudson River Bracketed* and *The Gods Arrive*." In Alfred Bendixen, ed. and introd.; Annette Zilversmit, ed. *Edith Wharton: New Critical Essays*. New York: Garland, 1992.

Wershoven, Carol. " 'The Awakening' and *The House of Mirth*: Studies of Arrested Development." *American Literary Realism 1870–1910*, 19 (Spring 1987), 37–41.

———. "The Divided Conflict of Edith Wharton's *Summer*." *Colby Library Quarterly*, 21:1 (March 1985), 5–10.

———. "Edith Wharton's Final Vision: *The Buccaneers*." *American Literary Realism*, 15 (Autumn 1982), 209–20.

———. *The Female Intruder in the Novels of Edith Wharton*. Rutherford, N.J.: Fairleigh Dickinson University Press, 1982.

White, Barbara A. *Edith Wharton: A Study of the Short Fiction*. New York: Twayne, 1991.

———. "Edith Wharton's *Summer* and 'Women's Fiction.' " *Essays in Literature*, 11:2 (Fall 1984), 223–235.

White, Barbara A., ed. *Wharton's New England: Seven Stories and Ethan Frome*. Hanover, N.H.: University of New Hampshire Press, 1995.

Whitman, Walt. *Prose Works 1892*. Ed. Floyd Stovall. New York: New York University Press, 1964.

Widdicombe, Tony. "Wharton's 'The Angel at the Grave' and the Glories of Transcendentalism: Deciduous or Evergreen?" *American Transcendental Quarterly* 6:1 (Mar. 1992), 47–57.

Wilson-Jordan, Jacqueline S. "Telling the Story That Can't Be Told: Hartley's Role as Dis-eased Narrator in 'The Lady's Maid's Bell.' " *Edith Wharton Review* 14:1 (Spring 1997), 12–17, 21.

Winner, Viola Hopkins. "Introduction" to *Fast and Loose* and *Buccaneers*. In Viola Hopkins Winner, ed. *Fast and Loose* and *The Buccaneers*. Charlottesville: University Press of Virginia, 1993.

Wolff, Cynthia Griffin. *A Feast of Words: The Triumph of Edith Wharton*. New York: Oxford University Press, 1977.

———. "Cold Ethan and 'Hot Ethan.' " *College Literature*, Fall 1987, 230–45.

Wright, Lewis. "An American Views Mt. Athos—1888." *Friends of Mount Athos, Annual Report 1994*, 53–54.

Wright, Nathalia. *American Novelists in Italy: The Discoverers: Allston to James*. Philadelphia: University of Pennsylvania Press, 1965.

Wright, Sarah Bird. *Edith Wharton Abroad: Selected Travel Writings, 1888–1920*. New York: St. Martin's, 1995.

———. *Edith Wharton's Travel Writing: The Making of a Connoisseur*. New York: St. Martin's, 1997.

———. "Refracting the Odyssey: Edith Wharton's Travel Writing as the Cultural Capital of Her Fiction." *Edith Wharton Review* 13:1 (Fall 1996), 23–30.

Zilversmit, Annette. "Edith Wharton's Last Ghosts." *College Literature*, 14 (Fall 1987), 296–309.

———, ed., with Alfred Bendixen, *Edith Wharton: New Critical Essays*. New York: Garland, 1992.

INDEX

* "Film adaptations" includes television adaptations in some instances.

319